D1272022

W. H. AUDEN: THE CRITICAL HERITAGE

THE CRITICAL HERITAGE SERIES

GENERAL EDITOR: B.C. SOUTHAM, M.A., B.LITT. (OXON)
Formerly Department of English, Westfield College, University of London

For a list of books in the series see the back end paper

W.H. AUDEN

THE CRITICAL HERITAGE

Edited by
JOHN HAFFENDEN
Lecturer in English Literature
University of Sheffield

ROUTLEDGE & KEGAN PAUL
LONDON, BOSTON, MELBOURNE AND HENLEY

First published in 1983
by Routledge & Kegan Paul plc
39 Store Street, London WC1E 7DD,
9 Park Street, Boston, Mass. 02108, USA,
296 Beaconsfield Parade, Middle Park,
Melbourne, 3206, Australia, and
Broadway House, Newtown Road,
Henley-on-Thames, Oxon RG9 1EN
Printed in Great Britain by
Redwood Burn Ltd, Trowbridge, Wilts

Compilation, introduction, notes, bibliography and index
© John Haffenden 1983

Library of Congress Cataloging in Publication Data

W.H. Auden, the critical heritage.
(The Critical heritage series)
Bibliography: p.
Includes index.
1. Auden, W.H. (Wystan Hugh), 1907–1973–Criticism
and interpretation–Addresses, essays, lectures.
I. Haffenden, John. II. Series.
PR6001.U4Z893 1983   811'.52   83–3241

ISBN 0–7100–9350–0

General Editor's Preface

The reception given to a writer by his contemporaries and near-contemporaries is evidence of considerable value to the student of literature. On one side we learn a great deal about the state of criticism at large and in particular about the development of critical attitudes towards a single writer; at the same time, through private comments in letters, journals or marginalia, we gain an insight upon the tastes and literary thought of individual readers of the period. Evidence of this kind helps us to understand the writer's historical situation, the nature of his immediate reading-public, and his response to these pressures.

The separate volumes in the *Critical Heritage Series* present a record of this early criticism. Clearly, for many of the highly productive and lengthily reviewed nineteenth- and twentieth-century writers, there exists an enormous body of material; and in these cases the volume editors have made a selection of the most important views, significant for their intrinsic critical worth or for their representative quality—perhaps even registering incomprehension!

For earlier writers, notably pre-eighteenth century, the materials are much scarcer and the historical period has been extended, sometimes far beyond the writer's lifetime, in order to show the inception and growth of critical views which were initially slow to appear.

In each volume the documents are headed by an Introduction, discussing the material assembled and relating the early stages of the author's reception to what we have come to identify as the critical tradition. The volumes will make available much material which would otherwise be difficult of access and it is hoped that the modern reader will be thereby helped towards an informed understanding of the ways in which literature has been read and judged.

B.C.S

For Sue
who suffered it

Contents

Contents

Contents

Contents

Acknowledgments

While the selection and evaluations in this volume are
entirely my own responsibility, I am indebted to a number
of individuals and institutions for helping me with information. I should like to thank in particular Professor
Edward Mendelson, for his advice on the Introduction and
Contents, and for his willingness both to answer several
letters and to track down certain reviews, and Mr Brian
Southam for his constructive reading of the Introduction.
Mr Charles Monteith kindly allowed me access to the review
archives of Faber & Faber Ltd, and I am grateful to Miss
Susan Oudôt for keeping me amply supplied with files;
also to Miss Mavis Pindard, Subsidiary Rights, and to
Miss Sarah Biggs, secretary to Mr Monteith, for advice and
information. I am deeply obliged to Mr John Chapman and
Miss Judith Cooper for the many hours they spent on my
behalf in tracing references to books and articles about
Auden in the post-1970 period, and to Miss J.E. Friedman,
Senior Lecturer in the Postgraduate School of Librarianship
and Information Science, University of Sheffield, for
enabling them to do so; to Dr Michael Halls, Modern Archi-
vist, King's College Library, Cambridge, for his courtesy
and helpfulness during my examination of the Keynes
Papers; and to Mrs Frances Hickson, the Society of Authors,
and Miss Jane With, the National Book League, for helping me
to locate several copyright holders and their representatives. I must also express my gratitude to the staff of the
Inter-Library Loans Department, Sheffield University Library, and to the staff of the British Library (Newspaper
Library, Department of Printed Books, and Students' Room of
the Department of Manuscripts), for their continual helpfulness and efficiency.

I am grateful to the following individuals for answering
postal queries: Dr John B. Auden; the late Mr D.G. Bridson;
Mr Humphrey Carpenter; Professor William Coldstream;

Mr Simon Dannreuther of Curtis Brown Academic Ltd, London;
Susan Dwyer of 'Antaeus', New York; Mrs Valerie Eliot;
Mr Jason Epstein of Random House, Inc., New York; Mr Gavin
Ewart; Professor Boris Ford; Mr Anthony Hartley; Mr Desmond
Hawkins; Ms Joanne Hurst, Assistant General Manager of the
'New Statesman'; Mr A.F. Hussey; Dr Brian Inglis; Mr
Lincoln Kirstein; Mr Perry H. Knowlton of Curtis Brown Ltd,
New York; John Lancaster, Librarian of Special Collections,
Amherst College Library; the late Mrs Q.D. Leavis; Profes-
sor John Lucas; Mr A.L. Morton; Lady Diana Mosley; the
late Sir Oswald Mosley; Mr Chris Myant, Assistant Editor
of the 'Morning Star'; the late Mr Ian Parsons; Mr Hugh
Gordon Porteus; Miss Alice Prochaska; Mr Arnold Rattenbury;
Mr C.H. Rolph; Mr Michael Sayers; Mr Charles Seaton of the
'Spectator'; Mr Robert Silvers of the 'New York Review of
Books'; Miss Janet Adam Smith; Mr Stephen Spender; Mr James
Stern; Mr Julian Symons; the late Mr Philip Toynbee;
Mr Rex Warner; Mr John Whitehead; my colleague Mr Derek
Roper for his interest and encouragement; and Mr Robert
Medley, Miss Dilys Powell, and Mrs Vera Russell, for talk-
ing to me about Auden.

I would like to thank the University of Sheffield for a
sabbatical leave during which much of the work for this
book was undertaken, and the University Research Fund for
grants towards the costs of research and typing.

It has not been possible in certain cases to locate the
proprietors of copyright material. All possible care has
been taken to trace the ownership of the selections
included and to make full acknowledgment for their use.

Previously unpublished writings of W.H. Auden © 1983 by
the Estate of W.H. Auden, Edward Mendelson, Literary
Executor. Printed by permission. All rights reserved.
Extracts from the letters of Lord Keynes are published by
permission of Sir Geoffrey Keynes. The extract from a
letter by Ashley Dukes is published by permission of Mrs
Angela Ellis. Two letters by W.B. Yeats are published by
kind permission of Senator Michael Yeats.

I am grateful to the following for permission to reprint
material within their copyright or other control: Janet
Adam Smith for Nos 4, 15, 56, 63, and 81; Miriam Allott
for No. 69; George Barker for No. 71 ii; John Bayley for
No. 126; the late D.G. Bridson for No. 28; James Burnham
for No. 20; the Carcanet Press for No. 70, from 'Litera-
ture in Society: Essays and Opinions II (1931-1978)', by
Edgell Rickword (Copyright 1978 by Edgell Rickword); 'The
Christian Science Monitor' for No. 33, by Harold Hobson
(Copyright © 1935, renewed 1963, by The Christian Science
Publishing Society. All rights reserved); Collins Publishers
for No. 24, from 'Diaries and Letters', by Harold Nicolson;

Curtis Brown Ltd, London, on behalf of Christopher Isher-
wood, for No. 65 (Copyright Christopher Isherwood); Patric
Dickinson for No. 103; Valerie Eliot for No. 25; Angela
Ellis for No. 34; William Empson for Nos 1 and 83;
'Encounter' and Jeremy Robson for No. 125; the Editors of
'Essays in Criticism' and John Whitehead for No. 123; Gavin
Ewart for No. 53; Farrar, Straus and Giroux, Inc., and the
Carcanet Press for Nos 85 and 110, New Year Letter and an
excerpt from Recent Poetry, from 'Kipling, Auden & Co.:
Essays and Reviews 1935-1964' by Randall Jarrell (Copyright
© 1941, 1955 by Mrs Randall Jarrell. Copyright renewed ©
1969 by Mrs Randall Jarrell); Cornelia Fitts for No. 8;
John Fuller for No. 133; David Gascoyne for No. 71 iv;
Graham Greene for Nos 18 and 71 xi; Geoffrey Grigson for
Nos 14, 68, and 79; 'Harper's Magazine' and Jacques Barzun
for No. 100 (Copyright © 1947 by Jacques Barzun); Sir
Rupert Hart-Davis for Nos 9, 71 xii, and 78; Desmond Haw-
kins for No. 30; 'Hibernia' for No. 134; David Higham
Associates for Nos 5 and 67, by Louis MacNeice, originally
published in 'Oxford Outlook', 1931, and in 'New Verse',
1937, respectively, for No. 27, from Poetry and Satire,
by John Pudney, originally published in the 'Week-end
Review', 1933, and for No. 88, by Charles Williams, origi-
nally published in the 'Dublin Review', 1941; David Higham
Associates and the Trustees for the copyrights of the late
Dylan Thomas for No. 71 v, originally published in 'New
Verse', 1937; Lady Hopkinson for No. 93; Graham Hough for
No. 116; A.R. Humphreys for No. 50; 'International Herald
Tribune' for Nos 36, 99, and 109; 'The Kenyon Review' and
Stephen G. Valensi on behalf of Carter Lodge Productions,
Inc., for No. 98 (Copyright 1945 by Kenyon College;
copyright renewed 1972); Frank Kermode for No. 129;
King's College, Cambridge, and the Society of Authors as
the literary representative of the E.M. Forster Estate
for No. 45; Alfred A. Knopf, Inc., for No. 118, Auden
Fecit, reprinted from 'Picked-Up Pieces' by John Updike
(Copyright © 1966 by John Updike); the late Q.D. Leavis for
Nos 6, 11, 12, 26, 54, 89, 95, and 106; John Lehmann for
No. 42; Ruth Limmer, literary executor of the Estate of
Louise Bogan, for No. 97, originally published in 'The New
Yorker', 1945; Charles Madge for No. 71 viii; Naomi Mitchi-
son for No. 2; Morning Star Co-operative Society Ltd for
Nos 32, 39, 59, and 77; 'The Nation' for No. 47; 'The
Nation' and James Burnham for No. 35; 'The Nation' and
Lincoln Kirstein for No. 80; 'The New Republic' for Nos
37, 41, 57, 84, and 91; 'The New Statesman' for Nos 44, 51,
60, 61, 73, 82, 102, 105, 113, 114, 120, 122, and 124; 'The
New York Review of Books' for Nos 131 and 135, reprinted
with permission from 'The New York Review of Books' (Copy-

right © 1973, 1977 Nyrev Inc.); 'The New York Times' for
Nos 90, 96, and 108   (© 1944, 1945, 1955 by The New York
Times Company. Reprinted by permission); Diana Oakeley for
No. 17; Observer News Service for No. 132; George D. Pain-
ter for No. 104; 'Partisan Review' for No. 101 (Copyright
1947 by Partisan Review, Inc.); A.D. Peters & Co. Ltd for
Nos 29, 58, 71 vi, 74, and 76 (reprinted by permission of
A.D. Peters & Co. Ltd); 'Poetry' and Alta Fisch Sutton for
No. 7 (Copyright 1931 by The Modern Poetry Association);
'Poetry' and A.D. Peters & Co. Ltd for No. 55 (Copyright
1937 by The Modern Poetry Association); 'Poetry' and
Adam Yarmolinsky for No. 86   (Copyright 1941 by The
Modern Poetry Association);   Hugh Gordon Porteus for
No. 19;   Dilys Powell for Nos 3 and 52;   Frederic
Prokosch for No. 71 iii;   Alan Pryce-Jones for No. 10;
Michael Sayers for No. 31; 'Shenandoah' and Donald Davie
for No. 111 (Copyright 1955 by Washington and Lee Univer-
sity, reprinted from 'Shenandoah': The Washington and Lee
University Review with the permission of the Editor);
Enid Slater for No. 40; The Society of Authors as the
literary representative of the Estate of John Masefield for
No. 71 x; 'Spectator' for Nos 16, 43, 112, 119, and 127;
'Spectator' and Janet Adam Smith for No. 81; 'Spectator'
and Philip Larkin for No. 115; 'Spectator' and the late Ian
Parsons for No. 38; 'Spectator' and David Higham Associ-
ates for Nos 71 ix and 87 (Copyright the Herbert Read
Discretionary Trust); Stephen Spender for Nos 13, 23, 46,
49, 66, and 94; 'Sunday Times' for No. 92; Julian Symons
for No. 75; Helen Tate for No. 71 vii; 'Times Literary
Supplement' for Nos 6, 11, 62, 107, 121, and 130; Robert
Penn Warren for No. 22, from 'American Review' (Copyright
1934 by Robert Penn Warren); the Wyndham Lewis Memorial
Trust, John Calder (Publishers) Ltd, and University of
California Press for No. 48 (© Estate of the late Mrs
G.A. Wyndham Lewis); 'The Yale Review' for Nos 117 and 128
(Copyright Yale University).

Note on the Selection and Text

This anthology gathers together a selection of the first reviews and essays covering the volumes of poetry by Auden published between 1930 and 1976. The terminus date allows for the inclusion of selected reviews of 'Collected Poems' (1976), but not of 'The English Auden: Poems, Essays and Dramatic Writings 1927-1939' (1977). The latter collection takes Auden's career full circle, so to speak, and invaluably reprints those works which were reviewed on their first appearance in the 1930s, as rehearsed in the present anthology.

Limitations of space and expense have determined the fact that reviews of Auden's own volumes of criticism are not represented here.

Quotations from Auden's works follow the original editions, and typographical errors have been silently corrected whenever necessary.

Introduction

W.H. Auden paid little heed to reviews of his work, and evidently felt little respect for his reviewers (with exceptions including Geoffrey Grigson and Edmund Wilson whom he admired). (1) While his friend Rex Warner recalls, 'As a poet he belonged to an "irritabile genus", but enjoyed praise as much as anyone', (2) Auden's unconcern for, and indeed unconsciousness of, his critical reception is confirmed by many of his other close friends - Lincoln Kirstein, William Coldstream, Stephen Spender, Janet Adam Smith, James Stern, Jason Epstein (Editorial Director of Random House, his American publisher), and Dr. John B. Auden, his brother (3) - none of whom has any recollection of him expressing reactions to published criticisms. 'You must remember that critics write for the public, not for me,' he told interviewers late in life. 'I don't read them, and often I don't know what they say about me. You see, most critics write on the basis of reading, not from any experience of writing. I've no use for such criticism.' (4) In their contributions to 'W.H. Auden: A Tribute', edited by Stephen Spender (1975), Golo Mann, Ursula Niebuhr, with whom he loved to talk theology ('theology was his chess', as Lincoln Kirstein aptly remembers) (5), and Louis Kronenberger have likewise testified to his self-confidence and pride, (6) and to what V.S. Yanovsky has elsewhere described as 'his genuine distaste for reviews and books about him': (7)

> He was truly unhappy when forced to listen to people expressing at length an opinion about his work ('Usually they praise you for the wrong reasons'). And he did not take kindly to any criticism. What he liked, after having given us a new poem to read, was a simple 'Good, very good. It's fun!' Then he would nod, completely satisfied - or so it seemed. (During the last

1

years, the critics were often hostile to him, donkeys
kicking or trying to kick the aging lion.)... He knew his
value and did not need much support from the outside.

Auden's self-assurance began early. Even while up at
Oxford in the later 1920s, he pronounced to Christopher
Isherwood that 'Poetry must be classic, clinical and
austere'. (8) That sort of sureness prevailed throughout
his career, as Stephen Spender recalls: 'I do not think
Auden had the kind of underlying sense of insecurity about
his own work, which makes most authors, openly or secretly,
extremely sensitive to criticism.' (9) It was Spender who
first published a wee limited volume of Auden's poems
which has inevitably become the most coveted bibliographi-
cal item in his canon. (10) Auden's poetry only became
visible to the public at large, however, with the publication of 'Paid on Both Sides: A Charade' in the 'Criterion', (11) the periodical T.S. Eliot founded in the conviction that there existed an international fraternity of
men of letters. (12) Then came 'Poems' (1930), a rather
plain two-and-sixpenny paperback which at least one reviewer thought perhaps symptomatic of a general lowering
of standards consequent on trade depression. 'Poems'
brought together 'Paid on Both Sides' and thirty austerely
unnumbered poems. Christopher Isherwood had drawn Auden's
attention to the curious relatedness of their preparatory
school slang and the idiom of the Icelandic sagas that
Auden loved, with the result that 'soon after this,
[Wystan] produced a short verse play in which the two
worlds are so confused that it is almost impossible to say
whether the characters are epic heroes or members of a
school O.T.C.' (13).
The periodical publication of this play, 'Paid on Both
Sides', had not gone unobserved: it provided William
Empson with the opportunity to exercise his critical skills
in an article concluding that the charade 'has the sort of·
completeness that makes a work seem to define the attitude
of a generation' (No. 1). In turn, F.R. Leavis used
Empson's essay as a stalking-horse to subvert what he considered 'an essential uncertainty of purpose and of
self...'.

THE YOUNG PROPHET

Naomi Mitchison, who had been introduced to Auden's poetry
by his Oxford contemporary Richard Goodman, tried to give
the lead to favourable criticism by publishing her review
of 'Poems' - significantly entitled The New Generation

(No. 2) - well before others. (14) Although she also prose-
lytized for Auden among her fellow critics, she could not
help but set a pattern of ambiguous affirmation:

> Reading Auden's 'Poems' I am puzzled and excited. The
> very young, it seems, admire and imitate him. Dare I
> spot him as a winner? He is wantonly obscure sometimes.
> The 'Charade' which opens the book is curiously impres-
> sive.... But there are passages in the middle which
> seem as if they could only be understood by a psycho-
> analyst.

Auden responded to her review,

> 'Thanks awfully for your letter and the very kind
> review. Any reviewer who tells people to buy the book
> has said the right thing.
>   I don't honestly think that psycho-analytic know-
> ledge would help critics of 'Paid on Both Sides' - at
> any rate emotionally,

adding in a postscript, 'The Listener Book Chronicle says:
"As for Mr Auden we dare not even hazard a guess what his
book is all about." Am I really so obscure. Obscurity is
a bad fault.' (15) Naomi Mitchison also gave her assent to
aspects of the poems which Auden later considered wryly:
'They may be romantic, may be obscure, but they have the
curious, archaic maleness which seems to me to fit in with
three things: the fifth century before Plato came and
muddled it, the heroic age in Iceland, and the modern
youth movement in Germany.' (Auden came to mistrust and
quarrel with certain of his early works - especially his
seminal volume 'The Orators', for its dubious and possibly
fascist affiliations.) (16)
    The Cambridge periodical 'Granta' (28 November 1930)
followed Mrs Mitchison's lead by hailing Auden's poems as
a major break with forebears in an article headed The New
Gang:

> The pretty imagery of the Georgians does not hold their
> poetry together; the symbolism of Lawrence or Mr. Eliot,
> however applicable it may be to our age in general,
> remains, after all, a personal symbolism, and the sym-
> bolism of a generation now middle-aged. Part of the
> satisfaction, then, to be got from reading Mr. Auden's
> poems ... is derived from the completeness, and hence
> the realness of his picture....
>   'Death of the old gang' is very positively required
> throughout the poems; not a mere retreatism....

Both Dilys Powell (No. 3), even though she registered
excitement about 'Poems', and Dudley Fitts echoed Naomi
Mitchison's comments on obscurity. Fitts in particular
found himself baffled and irritated by verses that could
reduce themselves to 'a prosaic iteration of incoherencies' (No. 8).

In his autobiography 'World Within World' (1951),
Stephen Spender emphasizes Auden's posture of detachment
and clinicality in his early poems, and their arbitrary
qualities. (17) That feature of clinical detachment first
won most praise from Louis MacNeice in 'Oxford Outlook'
(No. 5), while Auden's putative intellectual arbitrariness
(which seems curiously at odds with intellectual clear-
sightedness) earned severe comment from F.R. Leavis
(No. 6).

Again, Spender's autobiography categorically states that
Auden 'rejected, quietly and without fuss, the moral views
of both his preceptors and his fellow undergraduates',
(18) and yet that picture of the renegade or revolutionary
youth Auden himself blandly disavowed in a late interview
published after his death: 'I accepted my parents' values
implicitly.... I don't feel misplaced. All my interests
followed from a secure root.' (19) What appears to be a
late recension on Auden's part in no way tallies, however,
with the evidence available to Michael Roberts in December
1930 - 'Mr. Auden laments virtues once purposeful, necessary to life, now revered as decorations, accomplishments, independent and meaningless Virtues...' (No. 4) -
and should perhaps be attributed to Auden's continuing
process of changing his views which so many critics in-
tolerantly remarked in the years after 1940. Even on its
own terms, however, 'Poems' does show some disconnection
between sensibility and technique, an aspect which the
'TLS' shrewdly remarked, and which F.R. Leavis later perceived in terms of Auden's 'blend of surface poise and
fundamental self-mistrust'. Leavis alerted his readers to
what he saw as Auden's 'profound inner disturbance ... a
tension of impulsive life too urgent and shifting to permit him the sense of intellectual mastery'.

In sum, while favourable critics thrilled to the new
poet's classicism, his detached clinicality of manner, and
his introduction into verse of contemporary, possibly
sinister and subversive, symbols and subjects - disintegrating industrialism, climbing, exploring, spying, plot-
ting - others saw the elements of arbitrariness in his
work as aspects of an artistic vision lacking in definition and coherence. The consensus of positive criticism
at least greeted Auden as the harbinger of a long-awaited
poetry which might surmount the unsatisfying views of T.S.

Eliot, D.H. Lawrence and the Georgians - the harbinger, indeed, of a new psychological and political mood - and awaited his development with bated interest.

Shortly after the publication of Auden's 'Poems', John Lehmann found in a fellow poet and critic, Michael Roberts, a colleague who might share his growing belief that they and their contemporaries formed 'a revolutionary movement in the arts', with the consequence that they worked to publish an anthology 'presenting all of us in some way as a *front*, so that the public, notoriously sluggish in its appreciation of individual poets, should be obliged to sit up and take notice...'. (20) Under Roberts' editorship, 'New Signatures' appeared in February 1932 from the Hogarth Press, the imprint of Leonard and Virginia Woolf.

All the contributors had already appeared either in periodicals or in their own books - Auden, John Lehmann, Cecil Day-Lewis, William Plomer, Stephen Spender; Day-Lewis's 'Transitional Poem', for example, had forerun Auden's 'Poems' by a margin which enabled the 'Poetry Review' (November-December 1930) to remark, 'Mr. Auden's work recalls that of Mr. Day-Lewis.' Michael Roberts's Preface concentrates perhaps rather wilfully on the manner in which these '"New Signatures" poets' had overtaken the obsolete language and technique of their predecessors. Indeed, the volume does not fully deserve the apocalyptic status which literary history has commonly given it, although the public response certainly matched the mood of the blurb Lehmann had first sent to Julian Bell: (21)

> These new poems and satires by W.H. Auden, Julian Bell, Cecil Day-Lewis, Stephen Spender, A.S.J. Tessimond, and others, are a challenge to the pessimism and intellectual aloofness which has marked the best poetry of recent years. These young poets rebel only against those things which they believe can and must be changed in the postwar world, and their work in consequence has a vigour and width of appeal which has long seemed lacking from English poetry.

T.S. Eliot had favoured his work, but Auden had long schooled his own contemporaries such as Spender and Day-Lewis and found himself elected the proponent, if not the leader, of a group which had willy-nilly determined to revoke and overtake the work of an older generation which included Eliot himself. 'New Signatures' served to make the public perceive the group as making common cause to a degree perhaps greater than any of its participants would have reckoned at the time, though they did have in common the fact that they wrote out of political sentiments and

social conscience. John Lehmann cautiously reviewed their
situation in an interview published in 1971: (22)

> I think it was never an entirely coherent movement.
> The various authors who were associated in the mind of
> the public did have one or two things in common. They
> had a feeling that something must happen in England to
> shake up the social order - they felt that very
> strongly. They felt that something must be done about
> unemployment; they felt that something must be done
> about the threat of war; they felt all these things
> very strongly. Apart from that - and that unites Auden
> and Day-Lewis and MacNeice and Warner all together, and
> others, including myself (we all felt that same way at
> that time) - there were elements which were strong in
> some of them and other elements strong in others....
>   Auden did this in the thirties: suddenly there was
> someone who crystallized what a lot of people were
> feeling, who created a new poetic world where what was
> inchoate entered the realm of definition in the artists'
> heightened ordering consciousness.

For his part, Stephen Spender summed up his views of 'New
Signatures' and its successor, 'New Country' (1933), in
his autobiography: (23)

> These writers wrote with a near-unanimity, surprising
> when one considers that most of them were strangers to
> one another, of a society coming to an end and of revo-
> lutionary change....
>   The writing of the 1920's had been characterized
> variously by despair, cynicism, self-conscious aesthe-
> ticism, and by the prevalence of French influences.
> Although it was perhaps symptomatic of the political
> post-war era, it was consciously anti-political....
>   Perhaps, after all, the qualities which distin-
> guished us from the writers of the previous decade lay
> not in ourselves, but in the events to which we reacted.
> These were unemployment, economic crisis, nascent
> fascism, approaching war.... The older writers were re-
> acting in the 'twenties to the exhaustion and hopeless-
> ness of a Europe in which the old regimes were falling
> to pieces. We were a 'new generation'....

Whatever his role as prophet-designate, Auden preferred
to think of himself as at most a coadjutant rather than a
commandant, the chief of peers. 'I don't like this business of lumping people together,' he told interviewers on
28 March 1972. 'People of the same age, living at the same

place, are exposed to similar influences. But to me that
would be the least interesting thing about them.   Differ-
ences are more important.' (24)

'The Orators' (1932) none the less consolidated Auden's
place in the forefront of the new poetry, as the very
voice of the age. Reading the reviews almost half a century later, it is difficult to avoid the impression that
the critics, and beyond them the public for poetry, having
been brought to salute and suffer Eliot's 'The Waste Land',
had long been hungry for a similarly substantial poem
which would succeed and even countermand the dispirited
mood of an epoch they had seen so absolutely realized in
Eliot's monumental achievement. Radical, fiercely satirical, 'The Orators' spoke for that new mood, whatever the
political colour of the reviewers. 'The Times' (10 November 1932), for example, tentatively recommended that it
'will repay study as well for its original treatment of
language as for its courageous – though often bitter and
cynical – indictment of contemporary conditions'. Apropos
the critical reception, one of the fortuitous features of
Auden's new work was that, being so provocatively obscure,
it seems to have given critics the licence to construe it
according to their own lights, and to praise its aesthetic
excitement even if they found its political implications
dubious. Only two critics, both writing two years after
its publication, effectively condemned it. Edith Sitwell,
though she allowed that Auden had 'considerable rhythmical
sense' (25) and 'at moments ... a very real and poignant
emotion', (26) nevertheless dismissed most of his poetry
as lacking in interest, and worse: (27)

> Mr. Auden does not organize his experience. It must be
> said, too, that his material is too often of a purely
> temporal interest, has no universal significance.... In
> the power of assimilating details into a whole, in the
> visual and tactile sense, Mr. Auden is, at the moment,
> almost entirely lacking. 'The Orators'...is not an
> organic whole. It may be claimed that it represents the
> disintegration of the world in its present state, but
> it shows merely lack of fusion, looseness of interest
> ....

Likewise, John Sparrow asserted that 'The Orators' had 'no
single intelligible purpose': (28)

> As it is, his work is a monument to the misguided aims
> that prevail among contemporary poets, and the fact that
> on the strength of this and similar performances he is
> hailed as 'a master' shows how criticism is helping

poetry on the downward path. (29)

In 'W.H. Auden: The Life of a Poet' (1980), Charles
Osborne has written, 'Despite the now almost celebrated
Auden obscurity, it was immediately acclaimed by its
mainly young readers, who seemed able to penetrate to its
meaning without difficulty.... It was ... certainly a work
which spoke directly and reassuringly to its audience.'
(30) The case was in fact quite otherwise: none of the reviewers presumed to comprehend 'The Orators' as a whole,
though the majority certainly found it stimulating if irritating, and hesitated to expound 'the single theme and
purpose' that the publisher's blurb had announced. (31) It
was not uncommon, in fact, for readers to register complete bafflement about the work, and even doubts about
Auden's sanity. (32) Alan Pryce-Jones, for example, failed
to figure its meaning, and concluded his review: 'It
appears to be the work of a sane imagination without a
mind - a far more complicated state than the paranoiac's -
working on fragments of knowledge and experience' (No. 10).
A good number of reviewers, however, including that for
'Poetry Review', Geoffrey Grigson, John Hayward, and Henry
Bamford Parkes, hailed it as the most significant work
since the appearance of Eliot's first poems.
    Even while making what he described as 'very difficult'
(33) headway with the work, Auden told Naomi Mitchison in
August 1931, 'In a sense the work is my memorial to [T.E.]
Lawrence; i.e. the theme is the failure of the romantic
conception of personality.' (34) Although her own review of
the book ('Week-end Review', 28 May 1932) found aesthetic
qualities to praise, she yet had to dissent from what
seemed to be its revolutionary political purport: 'It is,
I think, about what's wrong with life and what life should
be like...(though I entirely disagree with the political
implications all through the book; there is a different
way to the same goal).' Geoffrey Grigson (35) found 'The
Orators' as angry as 'Poetry Review' had found 'Poems':
'He attacks. In "The Orators" he is savage, but always
with justification; violent, but always in control of his
violence. The Enemy is individual (typical, that is) and
collective, the whole contemporary situation, the insolence of mediocrity...' (No. 14). William Plomer agreed in
viewing it as 'a brilliant attack (No. 9); and Michael
Roberts, like Plomer, found it amusing: 'even though its
admirers do not find in it the organisation which they
would like to see, it is remarkably sensitive and acute
writing, it is good fun, and incidentally it is practical
politics' (No. 15). (36) (Like other critics who preferred
to praise the book's technical ingenuity rather than to

come to terms with its possibly questionable meaning, however, Roberts cautioned earlier in his review, 'the important thing about Mr. Auden is not his message, but his
manner of writing...')

Many other critics, like John Hayward in his judici-
ously approving notice (No. 17), felt compelled to regret
the work's lack of organic unity and Auden's apparent inability to co-ordinate his lyrical and satirical gifts.
Confronted with what all reviewers acknowledged was a
masterwork of contemporary relevance whose sure drift they
could not quite catch or accommodate, the first reviews
manifestly bear out this observation by Edward Mendelson,
Auden's literary executor: (37)

> Auden's early readers missed the point when they in-
> ferred from the poem's elusive privacy the existence
> of a coterie who shared the meanings and got the jokes;
> Auden's friends were as much in the dark as everyone
> else.

(On 28 July 1932, obviously sensitive towards the accusations first levelled at 'Poems', Auden had written to
Hayward, who had indeed attributed aspects of the obscurity of 'The Orators' to the prevalence of private
jokes, 'Glad you liked the Orators. I hope as a whole
its not obscure.') (38)

Critics divided over whether 'The Orators' was more destructive than constructive in tenor. Although F.R. Leavis
later used Auden as a whipping-boy, lamenting and indeed
castigating what he saw as his failure to mature as a poet
and thinker, at least in an unsigned review in the
'Listener' of 1932 he evidently set immense store by the
poet's potential beyond the first 'groping and inconclusive' obscurity: 'The hints he drops lead one to dream of
a representative modern English poem - such as it seems
extravagant to hope for' (No. 12).

Although literary and social commentators have often
quoted Philip Henderson's 1939 discrimination that '"The
Orators" reads more like the plans for a Fascist *coup*
than a Communist revolution', (39) the antimony was in
fact first perceived by Graham Greene in an otherwise enthusiastic review in 'Oxford Magazine': 'it is hard to
tell whether the author's sympathies are Communist or
Fascist; they seem a little vaguely and sentimentally
directed towards a "strong man," a kind of super-prefect,
for the book has a slight smell of school changing-rooms,
a touch of "Stalky"' (No. 18). (40) Writing anonymously
in the 'TLS', A.C. Brock carefully elected to praise the
whole work for its aesthetic and technical expertise as

somehow absolving it of the enormity of its message
(No. 11). One critic who seemed sanguine about the political implications of the work was Stephen Spender, who at
the time took a more doctrinaire line than Auden himself
professed, and who wrote in 'The Destructive Element' that
the work of young English Communists 'is not in any sense
proletarian: it is advance-guard experimental writing with
Communist ideology'. (41) His full discussion of the
issues raised by Auden's early works (No. 13) seems to
argue the comfortable view that a dialectical relationship
existed between 'The Orators' and Auden's next production,
'The Dance of Death', and that the psychological analysis
of the first is not irreconcilable with the Marxist hypothesis of the second, (42) except for the fact that Auden
seemed to him 'sometimes irresponsible and evasive' (which
I take to mean that he found Auden too eclectic and uncommitted, since he used what may perhaps be glossed as a
pejorative phrase about Auden 'accepting more and more of
life and of ideas...').

In any event, the public was presently given to understand that 'Since writing "The Orators" Mr. Auden has become a Communist'. Among other critics who pronounced
that putative fact, Henry Bamford Parkes added a tentatively openminded caveat: 'Communism, perhaps, if it is
accepted as a technique for making the necessary changes
and not as a dogmatic religion, is the best available
method of regeneration' (No. 20).

American critical response lagged behind the British,
for the Random House edition of Auden's 'Poems' appeared
only in 1934, four years after Faber's. A number of
American periodicals had none the less given the English
editions fair attention, including 'Hound and Horn',
'Symposium' and 'Poetry' (Chicago), in which M.D. Zabel
greeted 'A Dawn in Britain' by remarking that Auden 'has
applied himself to a reconstruction of emotional values,
personal and social' (No. 7). In advance of Random House's
issue of 'Poems', James Burnham heralded Auden as the most
considerable poet of what he insisted on calling a representative 'group' of 'communists' ... wishing to work in
their own way toward, a classless society'. He served
Auden rather ill, however, by misunderstanding the drift
of Journal of an Airman ('The Orators') - at least as Auden
had privately interpreted it to Naomi Mitchison (see
above) - and declaring that 'he seems to be examining the
possibilities of the romantic attitude, summed up in the
figure of the airman, as a way out of the wasteland'
(No. 35).

American reactions were for the most part intelligent
and judicious, especially as the critics were obliged to

evaluate Auden's 'Poems' alongside Spender's 'Poems' (published in England in 1933). Louis Untermeyer ('Saturday
Review of Literature', 10 November 1934) endorsed the
English critical consensus that Spender's 'Poems' was the
most significant 'first book' of the generation (though it
was not, in fact, his first), implicitly preferring it to
Auden's for the 'vigorous and exciting ... nobility of
[its] impulse'. Malcolm Cowley agreed (No. 37), as did
David McCord ('Yale Review', December 1934), who also
shared Untermeyer's misgivings about needing to make a
choice at all: 'It seems to me unfortunate that two new
poets of obviously unequal stature and even of different
tendency should be handicapped at the outset by this implied (much more than actual) interdependence.' Babette
Deutsch ('Virginia Quarterly Review', January 1935) similarly discriminated between Auden-as-satirist and Spender-
as-romantic, and scanted the significance of Auden's
'sardonic pictures' on the grounds that he seemed insufficiently a seer. Most American critics echoed the English line on the shortcomings of Auden's obscurity, but
at least two found his satire constructive - Malcolm
Cowley, and Ruth Lechlitner (No. 36), who perceptively
predicted the reaction that would soon take place amongst
Auden's alleged allies in radicalism:

> Yet only in a transitional sense can Auden be con-
> sidered as a propagandist for advanced socialist ideas
> ....Because he can no more completely identify himself
> with the 'proletariat' than with the 'decaying aris-
> tocracy' of the middle classes, he will be condemned
> by the strictly left-wing critics.

Gifted as an eclectic technician and as a social anato-
mist or diagnostician more than as an evangelist for
communism, Auden had indeed placed himself in an anomalous
position. He found Communism opportune as an artistic
posture rather than as an article of personal belief. (43)
Left-wing critics and propagandists assuredly found reason
to cultivate their hopes in Auden when he published in
'Twentieth Century' (September 1932) the poem called 'A
Communist to Others', which reviewers took to evince
authentic communist alignment rather than sincere skill.
The Communist John Cornford, for example, who criticized
the Auden generation for essaying a 'literary fashion of
"revolution" among bourgeois intellectuals whilst denying
the possibility of the growth of a genuinely revolutionary
literature with a new class basis', pinpointed the poem as
the exception which did exemplify revolutionary 'form'.
(44) Auden even reprinted it in 'New Country' (March 1933),

an anthology which, as Julian Symons has correctly pointed
out, (45) deserves to be regarded as more of a landmark
than its vaguer predecessor 'New Signatures', since the
doyen Michael Roberts announced it in these terms: 'I
think, and the writers in this book obviously agree, that
there is only one way of life for us: to renounce the
[capitalist] system now and to live by fighting against
it.' (46) But Auden had assumed a provisional stance
rather than a long-term commitment, and it must obviously
be taken as an explicit rebuttal of Left-wing presumptions
that Geoffrey Grigson could found his enormously influential periodical 'New Verse' (January 1933) on the basis
of a belief in the artistic standards and promise of
Auden's work, not in its pure political efficacy.

Julian Symons later characterized 'New Verse' as
'humanist unpolitical'; (47) Geoffrey Grigson himself, in
the first number, stated that 'New Verse' 'favours only
its time, belonging to no literary or politico-literary
cabal', and yet his second review of 'The Orators' shows
that he was not entirely disinterested towards subject-
matter:

> In substance, 'The Orators' is a claim as forcible as
> that of 'The Waste Land' for the poet's place at the
> apex of contemporary existence. With no more of a
> system of beliefs than 'The Waste Land,' it criticises
> as much and denounces more directly the cheap evils,
> social and moral, of our time. ('Yorkshire Post', 15
> August 1932)

Grigson's stringent editorial temperament certainly
found a standard in Auden's poetry, (48) but Grigson was
by no means alone in placing faith in Auden. Whatever the
intrinsic merits of Auden's work, there is no doubting
that both the manner and the matter of his poetry set
seed. Several of his contemporaries, some of them antici-
pating that Auden had permanently nailed his colours to
the revolutionary mast, (49) proved his attitude and commanding technical individuality by emulation or mimicry -
among them Gavin Ewart, Roy Fuller, Rex Warner, Kenneth
Allott, even Randall Swingler (who joined the Communist
Party in 1934 and subsequently worked for the 'Daily
Worker' and for 'Left Review', of which he was the last
editor), and, perhaps most slavishly, C. Day-Lewis, who
invoked the new-found prophet in 'The Magnetic Mountain'
(1933; rpt Jonathan Cape, with the Hogarth Press, 1954):
'Look west, Wystan, lone flyer, my bully boy!...Gain
altitude, Auden, then let the base beware!' (50) As
Julian Symons has written, 'In truth, of the three poets

who seemed to outsiders so closely allied in the early
1930s, Day-Lewis was a natural neo-Georgian and Spender a
naive romantic, yet the example of Auden for a time
strengthened and energized their verse.' (51) Although
Symons adds that the three shared 'the belief that a poem
is first of all an event in society and only secondarily
(although simultaneously) a verbal creation', none of
Auden's contemporaries could reckon with the fact that
his natural inclinations would in time lead him to hold
opinions (52) which would surely have struck them as
treacherous to the prevalent 1930s' conception of the
primary social function of poetry:

> In some periods it has been the poet with the really
> eccentric vision who has found it hardest to dare to be
> himself. In ours it is more often to be the other way
> round – the poet whose gift is for, say, a straight-
> forward lyric nostalgia, who is frightened into trying
> to be 'apocalyptic'....
>   It seems to me that the basic impulse behind
> creativity of any kind is the desire to do something
> that is quite unnecessary; the desire that the result
> should turn out to be important, comes second.
>   ...to be indifferent to the pressure of fashion (to
> be ashamed of being fashionable is as bad as to be
> proud of it)....

There seems little reason to doubt Auden's word in the
second edition of 'Journey to a War' (1973) that 'I have
always believed that, among the many functions of the
poet, preaching is one', but it is reasonable to point
out that, at least in the 1930s, it seems to have been a
caprice of his sensibility to be as adept at preaching
against as *for*, and to agree with Symons that his work
during the period seemed more often pessimistic than
constructive.

Impish, ventriloquial, a technical virtuoso, Auden
restlessly, and not always disingenuously, assumed many
masks in the 1930s. If he struck some as fickle, others
as flexible (if sometimes too agile), it also seems fair
to infer that he found his true allegiance in indi-
vidualism and not in the Party faith other sectors expected of him. It can equally be said, however, that some
responsibility for the misapprehensions certain critics
laboured under, and the scorn that was consequently heaped
upon him from various quarters, must be laid to the charge
of his eclecticism. Versatile and perhaps irresponsibly
adaptable, he certainly disabused the hopes inspired by
his injunction, 'Harrow the house of the dead; look

shining at / New styles of architecture, a change of heart'
('Sir, no man's enemy, forgiving all', Poem XXX in 'Poems'),
when he showed himself to be even more accomplished as a
prophet of doom in 'The Dance of Death' than as the pre-
dictor of a new society.

AUDEN IN THE THEATRE: 1932-8

Although Auden had privately dabbled in play-writing with
Christopher Isherwood in 1929 (when they wrote 'The
Enemies of a Bishop'), it was not until 1932 that he chose
to put his unaided talent to the service of the Group
Theatre. Founded early that year by the ballet dancer and
choreographer Rupert Doone (who had variously worked with
Diaghilev, with Max Reinhardt in Berlin, and with Tyrone
Guthrie in Cambridge), the Group Theatre postulated an
experiment in total theatre, a co-operative exploitation
of expressionist techniques, which would integrate words,
music, and dance, and in which the audience would be
actively engaged. Rupert Doone defined his venture in
theatre style as 'realistic fantasy', (53) collaborated
directly with the painter and designer Robert Medley, and
drew at various periods on the rich talents of Michel St
Denis, Robert Speaight, Henry Moore, Benjamin Britten,
Stephen Spender, Tyrone Guthrie, and Lydia Lopokova, among
others. Christopher Isherwood, who collaborated with Auden
from 1935, later characterized Doone's 'theatre of ideas'
as 'a Revelation Suitcase, not Procrustes' bed': 'What we
aim at', he wrote in November 1937, 'is a united cultural
front...in all departments of artistic activity.' (54)
Even John Masefield and E.M. Forster lectured under the
aegis of the Group Theatre that year. Working from a large
studio rehearsal room at 9 Great Newport Street, London,
the Group gave the first performance of T.S. Eliot's first
play, 'Sweeney Agonistes', which Doone conceived as 'a
nightmare in which all the characters wore masks, except
Sweeney himself'. (55) (Eliot took an active role as con-
sultant to the Group Theatre.) Although the Group evidently drew on the theatrical theories of Edward Gordon
Craig, who had advanced his concepts in a book entitled
'On the Art of the Theatre' (first published in 1905), (56)
it was purely by coincidence that the ideas motivating
the Group Theatre and Auden's plays often appeared to
match those of Bertolt Brecht. Auden had seen 'Die Dreigroschenoper' in Berlin, but later disclaimed the influence of Brecht on his own work. (57) At any rate,
Rupert Doone and Robert Medley (58) in particular had not
heard of Brecht before he attended a performance of

'The Dance of Death' during its public run in a double
bill with 'Sweeney Agonistes' at the Westminster Theatre
late in 1934. He accordingly had no influence on their
conceptions of theatre, and probably none on Auden's. 'If
there are aspects of the plays which remind the reader of
German expressionist drama,' Auden wrote on 9 August 1965,
'this is an accident - the real influence were the English
Mystery and Miracle plays of the middle ages.' (59) His
explanation is probably borne out by the fact that when
the Group Theatre gave the first club performance of 'The
Dance of Death' on 25 February 1934, it was staged along
with Auden's own adaptation of the medieval mystery play,
'The Deluge'.

   Faber & Faber brought out 'The Dance of Death' (1933)
before it was produced on stage. The 'TLS' (15 March 1934)
called Auden 'a *gamin* jeering at a tumbril', an aphoristic
judgment which other establishment journals soon shared.
Dilys Powell (60) thought it 'crude' and 'shoddy' satire
('Sunday Times', 14 January 1934), and even Auden's old
school-friend John Pudney (61) reproved it (No. 27): both
of them turned with relief to the second edition of
Auden's 'Poems' which had appeared (with the substitution
of seven new poems) at the same time as new volumes by
Siegfried Sassoon, Herbert Read, Edith Sitwell, and D.H.
Lawrence. D.G. Bridson, who was otherwise an Auden enthusiast, had to lament that the play was no more than
'efficiently versified', badly written, lacking in directness and particularity, and not so interesting as what he
rightly called 'the Charade which put Auden on the map'
(No. 28). Gavin Ewart ('New Verse', February 1934) chose
to attribute its limpness to the demands made on Auden by
the Group Theatre; A. Desmond Hawkins, in a letter to the
'New English Weekly' (24 October 1935), to the weaknesses
of the production. The 'Socialist Review', not unexpec-
tedly delighted by Auden's Marxist partisanship - 'It is
good that Auden should be on our side' - felt sorry only
that he had chosen the indirect mode of satire.

   As Robert Medley recalls, (62) Auden's friends predicted that, because it employed devices such as doggerel,
the play would fail in the theatre, but they were proved
wrong. The fertility of Auden's work as a theatrical experiment was first announced in the 'New English Weekly'
by A. Desmond Hawkins, who attended one of the early club
performances - 'there is sufficient dynamite in Mr. Auden
to destroy the sad garbage of the contemporary theatre'
(No. 30) - and only later qualified his view. Nineteen
months later, when Anmer Hall gave the Group Theatre a
six-month season at the Westminster Theatre, the critics
turned out in force - more than twenty of them, a number

which obviously gives an index of the high expectations
aroused by the work of the Group Theatre - to the first
public performance of 'The Dance of Death' on 1 October
1935, when it shared the bill with Eliot's 'Sweeney
Agonistes'. Lilian Bayliss sat impassively in a box;
Christopher Isherwood brought along Unity Mitford, perhaps
hoping that she might provoke a row. Offended on behalf of
middle-class values, several notices - the 'Manchester
Guardian' (2 October 1935), the 'Daily Telegraph' (2 October 1935), Ivor Brown (63) in the 'Sketch' (9 October
1935), 'Punch' (9 October 1935), and Gale Pedrick, who
punned 'This play was certainly nearly the death of me' in
a review misleadingly entitled Satire with a Kick ('Star',
2 October 1935) - slated the production in almost uni-
formly facetious and condescending terms. They remarked
the irony, for example, whereby young actors could so
energetically satirize a moribund middle class. Yet it is
misleading for Charles Osborne and Brian Finney, in their
biographies of Auden and Isherwood respectively, to point
out only that the play received a generally poor press,
(64) since audiences gave it a tremendous ovation. Understandably, the 'Daily Worker', under the heading The Death
of a Class, congratulated the Group Theatre on producing
'politically, poetically, and dramatically the most effective play...in London for years' (No. 32). Yet less partisan critics also applauded the production - Harold
Hobson in the 'Christian Science Monitor' (No. 33),
Ashley Dukes, director of the Mercury Theatre and drama
critic for 'Theatre Arts Monthly', and Michael Sayers in
the 'New English Weekly' (No. 31) - not unambiguously for
its political configuration, but undoubtedly for representing the first significant advance in dramaturgy to
have appeared on the London stage in years. (65)
    The Group Theatre did accordingly succeed in one of its
primary aims, the discrediting of 'tea-cup drama'. 'It
positively opposes every tendency of to-day's theatre,'
wrote Ashley Dukes, 'from drawing-room realism to Shavian
intellectualism, and from spectacular production to
coterie symbolism. I am particularly interested in Auden's
reference to dramatic speech, for it is clear that he
thinks of the verse-play in one shape or another as the
natural dramatic medium ... the dramatic language appropriate to themes of modern life' (No. 34).
    In 'A Hope for Poetry' of 1934 (which Edith Sitwell,
who became both the antagonist and the butt of Geoffrey
Grigson's 'New Verse', called 'a thoroughly silly book'),
(66) C. Day-Lewis, who had set course to join the Communist Party within two years, pursued Dilys Powell's
shrewd view that 'The Dance of Death' 'takes on too

accurately the characteristics of what it burlesques',
(67) and expatiated soberly and incisively on the im-
balance between Auden's technical fertility and his unstable commitment of values (No. 29).

While Auden presumably took to the theatre in the first
place to clarify some of the obscurity of his earlier work
and to find an immediate audience, it is clear only with
hindsight that his shifting stance, which so vexed both
his critics and his colleagues, evinced not merely a precocious and unsettled adolescence but a certain resistance
to submitting what virtually all critics had to agree were
his rich and varied gifts to a single frame of endeavour
or a party line. Even if his conscience agreed with
Marxist sentiment, (68) he felt an equal responsibility to
the doctrine of creative independence. 'If a writer alters
his work against his own judgement', he later wrote in his
notebook, 'he cannot complain that his freedom is
violated....' (69)

Christopher Isherwood, who had a stronger sense of
structure than Auden, collaborated with him in an effort
to transform Auden's next work, 'The Chase', into a viable
play before it appeared first in print (May 1935) with
Medley's title, (70) 'The Dog Beneath the Skin'. The first
critic, Ian Parsons, condemned it as 'a shoddy ... half-
baked little satire' (No. 38). 'Did you see the wigging
"The Dog Beneath the Skin" got in the "Spectator"?' Auden
asked Geoffrey Grigson in one of his rare responses to any
published criticism. (71) Countering Parsons's opinion,
the 'TLS' (11 July 1935) thought it a 'high-spirited
satire', and applauded its 'Richness of language, a teeming range of subject-matter and types (if not characters),
and eminent diversion'.

American critics, who looked forward to a stage production in New York (which never actually came off), were
generous and moderate in their estimates of the text,
Louise Bogan's view (No. 41) that the play made a powerful
indictment being seconded by Donald Davidson, who, unper-
turbedly accepting it as Marxist propaganda, found it
masterfully relentless as satire, even though 'the
choruses jangle and break in the end' ('Southern Review',
Spring 1936). William Rose Benét ('Saturday Review of
Literature', 30 November 1935), on the other hand, considered that the choruses, 'while probably impractical
for the stage, make good reading and contain a good deal
of nobility and poetry', while Philip Blair Rice justly
and saliently remarked that 'the structure of the play resembles a club sandwich' ('Nation', 27 November 1935).

Although Mirko Jurak, in his study of the text of the
stage production (which was ineptly cut both by the censor

and by Rupert Doone, who shortened or took out some of the play's best elements, the choruses), observes that the play failed and was badly received in performance, several critics did compliment it as effective satire on the bourgeoisie and Nazism. (72) (Lady Diana Mosley attended a performance of 'The Dog Beneath the Skin' with Auden; when she asked him about the representational significance of the blackshirts in Act II, scene i, he responded only with a laugh.) (73) As one reviewer pointed out, the production won praise in almost incompatible quarters – the 'Times', the 'Daily Mirror', the 'Daily Worker' (No. 39), and even the fascist journal, 'Action' (21 February 1936) – although, despite the play's self-evident didacticism, the more Left-wing and radical periodicals regretted that Auden had not assumed a more extreme stance.

Cyril Connolly (No. 44), on the other hand, self-deprecatingly adopting what he called 'the point of view of the anarchic 1920's about the political 1930's', doubted that Auden's poetry benefited from his engagement with a popular medium, and implied that the fault lay with Doone's production, a view damningly reinforced by Auden's advocate Geoffrey Grigson, who wrote in December 1935 (before he had the chance to see the play on stage): (74)

> The Group Theatre is not good enough – let us be frank
> – for the poets it is trying to train in dramatic
> sense. Its season this year and previous activities
> have been informed by the amateurism, it seems to out-
> siders, of pretending only to be serious, of pretending
> to have a group feeling and purpose ... when it is
> socially-cum-aesthetically in the half-light, and much
> less worldly even than its chief poets; and technically
> in presentation and performance ... distressingly
> second-rate. ...we wish that Mr. Doone and his associ-
> ates would humbly discover that they have at least as
> much to learn about selecting, pruning, giving and
> acting plays as Mr. Eliot or Mr. Auden have about
> writing them. We should like less prancing and bad
> dancing, less complacence, less guidance, and more
> stiff thinking combined with spontaneity. If we don't
> have these things the Group Theatre will be just a
> laugh and a bad laugh.

Whatever Grigson's strictures, 'The Dog Beneath the Skin' succeeded with its audience of predominantly middle-class intelligentsia. Julian Symons has recalled it as 'enormously enjoyable', especially the choruses, despite his celebrated remark that 'the choruses and the action seemed to belong to different plays'. (75) Auden himself

did not later share what seems to me Isherwood's astute
judgment that 'it was really written more to be read than
to be necessarily acted'. (76) 'I have a private weakness
for "Dogskin", which I think, if properly done, is fun,'
Auden remarked, reasonably enough, though I think few
could honestly agree with his further qualification:
'except that you have to cut all the choruses. There is
some quite nice poetry in there, but dramatically it won't
do. This was something that was just selfish on my part.
Wanting to write some poetry which had nothing to do,
really, with drama'. (77) Brian Finney's observation that
'It ran for a derisorily short period' (78) neglects the
fact that the play could have run a month, and was taken
off only because of the demands of reportory. (79)

'We were truly astonished at how well it was received
at a London theatre,' Isherwood recalled, 'so we thought,
well, we must do this again'. (80) They did it again with
'The Ascent of F6', which was first published in September
1936, and performed in February 1937 at the Mercury
Theatre, where it was backed by Ashley Dukes (who also
gave it rather complaisant praise in 'Theatre Arts Monthly'
in May 1937). In Auden's absence, Doone and Isherwood de-
vised significant alterations which later provoked him to
quiz Isherwood, 'My *dear*, what have you *done* to it?' (81)

Less of a *mélange* and with more of a specific plot than
'The Dog Beneath the Skin', 'The Ascent of F6' nevertheless muddled various levels of meaning, Marx and Freud,
satire and tragedy. The authors' various skirmishes of
revision never succeeded in synthesizing the collocation
of politics and psychology, as A.R. Humphreys severely remarked at the time (No. 50). Although Isherwood explained
in a letter of 12/23 May to E.M. Forster (who was editing
T.E. Lawrence's letters, and who also suggested changes to
the play) that 'It's only about Lawrence in so far as the
problem of personal ambition versus the contemplative life
is concerned', (82) Forster's review disobligingly distilled the four levels of meaning in what he otherwise
considered 'this exciting ... tragedy' (No. 45). In any
case, Auden felt crucially ambivalent about Lawrence as a
folk hero, seemed unable to decide whether he was, to use
his own terms, a Truly Strong Man or a Truly Weak Man,
and, according to Edward Mendelson, 'had embedded an allegory of his mixed feelings into "The Ascent of F6"'....
The play traces the destruction of a mountain climber
(Auden's representative) at the moment of his greatest
triumph, as a result of conflicts inherent in a public
role his private terrors tempted him to accept'. (83)

Hugh Gordon Porteus enthusiastically highlighted the
notion that the most interesting feature of the play was

its projections of Auden's own 'complex personality' ('New
English Weekly', 11 March 1937), an opinion with which
Leavis agreed only to damn, since he found Auden's neurotic self-diagnosis immature, 'self-defensive, self-
indulgent or merely irresponsible' (No. 54). Leavis had
placed great hopes in Auden's early work, and felt betrayed by his failure to develop a vision of life in harmony with his technical virtuosity. Brian Finney has
written, 'F.R. Leavis tended to indict the entire Auden
group for protecting its members from all contact with
serious critical standards in the case of "F6". But
Spender's and Day-Lewis's outspoken public criticisms of
the play at the time show this charge to be groundless'.
(84) There is obviously a good deal of truth, however, in
Anthony Thwaite's argument that 'what Leavis found ...
repellent was not the poetry itself but the smell of conspiracy that greeted it from the beginning and that went
on greeting it'. (85) Part of the point is that, often
published and reviewed together, and (in the case, for
example, of Spender's 'Trial of a Judge', 1938) produced
by the same theatre group, the three poets became in-
delibly associated in the public mind, and Spender's and
Day-Lewis's books and many articles provided a running commentary on their common modes and *causerie*, often with the
unmistakable purpose of trying to call Auden's irregu-
larities to order.

   Believing that the play would not act well, Spender
alerted audiences to the fact that Michael Ransom, the
hero, was 'a colossal prig' (a view supported by Gavin
Ewart in No. 53), as well as a Fascist, an aspect dissected by C. Day-Lewis in two reviews (one in England, the
other in the USA), which impugned the morality of the play
as 'at best Oxford Group and at worst Fascist ... negative,
defeatist, and dangerous' (No. 55). The charge must have
been an alarming one in a year when the cause of Fascism
had swollen all over Europe and when the Spanish Civil
War appalled young Left-wing writers and intellectuals.

   E.M. Forster attended the opening night of the production, as did Auden's austere, domineering mother.
Critics divided about its merits, Julian Symons ('Twentieth Century Verse', April-May 1937), for example, much
preferring the production to the published text, while
'Left Review' (May 1937) considered that the final
appearance of the Mother as Ransom's Demon (instead of
both politician and mother, according to the printed text)
destroyed the politico-psychological balance of the play.

   W.B. Yeats, sharply and wittily preferring the political dimension, wrote this letter: (86)

My dear Doone
  I thought your production of the Auden play almost
flawless & the play itself in parts magnificent.
  My only complaint is of the final appearance of the
Mother as demon. Why not let the white garment fall to
show the mother, or demon, as Britannia. That I think
would be good theatre - a snow white Britannia.
W.B. Yeats

Despite his canny praise for 'The Ascent of F6', Yeats
did not in general approve of Auden's work, and represented it minimally in the 'Oxford Book of Modern Verse',
explaining elsewhere that Auden and his associates 'reject
drama and personal emotion; they have thought out opinions
that join them to this or that political party; they employ an intricate psychology, action in character, not as
in the ballads, character in action.... They are determined to express the factory, the metropolis, that they
may be modern'. (87) 'Yeats was suspicious of Auden's
early associations with Communism,' Richard Ellmann has
explained; 'it was for Auden's school, he said, a deus ex
machina, a Santa Claus, offering a happy ending.' (88)
After Yeats's death, Auden dubbed the 'Oxford Book' 'the
most deplorable volume ever issued' (89) under the Clarendon imprint, but he himself was protractedly indebted to
the influence of what he called Yeats's 'dishonest poems'
(90) - 'He tempted me into a rhetoric which was, for me,
oversimplified. Needless to say,' he conceded, 'the fault
was mine, not his.' (91)
  The London production of 'The Ascent of F6' enjoyed a
good box-office success, though it made little money, and
transferred from the poky Mercury Theatre in Notting Hill
Gate to the Little Theatre in the Strand.
  American critics, including Edmund Wilson (No. 57) and
Ben Belitt (No. 47), who again had no immediate prospect
of seeing a stage production, all criticized the play as
unco-ordinated and poor theatre.
  The economist John Maynard Keynes chose to back a run
of 'The Ascent of F6' at the Arts Theatre in Cambridge
(which had opened in February 1936), even though, as he
wrote to T.S. Eliot, (92) he felt less than wholehearted
warmth for it:

Taken as a whole I thought it extremely good -
obviously much the best play of the year. But I remain
exceedingly discontented with a good deal of it and
angry that being so good it should not be better, for
the gifts in it seemed to be from God and the errors
avoidable.

Although Auden and Isherwood designed their next play, 'On the Frontier', to be a West End success, for which purpose they largely eschewed expressionistic experimentation for naturalism and a greater proportion of prose, Keynes first promoted it at the Arts Theatre, Cambridge, in November 1938 (it was the first production for which the newly formed Cambridge Arts Theatre Trust took direct responsibility). In the months leading up to the opening, he chivvied and made suggestions to the authors, hoping above all that they would augment the comedy of the play, and betrayed his apprehensiveness in this unpublished letter of 30 July 1938: 'The play has been re-written and improved, I think. I have considerable confidence in it, if only the words are audible and not overwhelmed by the music. But it has serious faults (priggish and humourless)'. (93) (Benjamin Britten's music in fact won almost uniform praise.)

Keynes also felt that the Munich crisis of 1938 radically hampered the playwrights' depiction of the political confrontation of countries they called Westland and Ostnia. ('The Dance of Death' had already run foul of current affairs, as the 'Manchester Guardian' remarked at the time:

> the sting of much of Mr. Auden's fun has been plucked out by the irony of events. Now that the Communists are shouting for the British Navy (just as if they were ordinary pacifists) and now that 'The Soldiers of the King' has replaced 'The Red Flag' as the hymn of the Labour Party, it bears hardly on Left-wing dramatists who set out to mock the patriotic ditty of the old music-hall. (2 October 1935)

Keynes accordingly wrote to Isherwood (94) to suggest that they might consider emending the 'plot of the play in the light of recent events. It is a bit unlucky that the development of history is so near to the facts and yet so far from them! Do you still feel that you can go through with it in precisely its present form without feeling at all silly?' (Indeed, the concurrence of politics and the play would be harshly treated by several critics.)

In an effort to pre-empt a favourable critical reception, Keynes took a step which was possibly unprecedented in Auden's and Isherwood's experience. He proposed (95)

> a compromise by which we do not ask the London daily or Sunday press, but limit ourselves to our usual critics, the Provincial Press in the shape of the 'Manchester

Guardian' and perhaps the 'Yorkshire Post', and the
weeklies - 'New Statesman and Nation', 'Spectator' and
'Time and Tide'. I fancy that the 'New Statesman and
Nation' might give us an article which might help a
good deal and not prejudice London publicity to an extent worth bothering about.

As a director of the Statesman and Nation Publishing Company, Keynes could well anticipate a positive response
from the 'New Statesman and Nation'. His expectations were
met by no less a reviewer than his friend - the editor
himself - Kingsley Martin (writing under the name of
another great political controversialist, Tom Paine), who
gave it the best of all reviews: 'The play is precisely
topical.... Auden and Isherwood are postulating war, and
their conclusion is as honest and outspoken as it is
memorably phrased' (No. 73). Julian Symons came close to
that estimate, first after reading 'On the Frontier' -
'I think the verse will be exceedingly effective, and
dramatic, on a stage' ('Twentieth Century Verse', February
1939) - and then on reviewing it for 'Life and Letters
Today' (February 1939) when it transferred to London:
'The merits ... are considerable.... The fact that the
play is topical, a piece of *reportage* instead of a myth,
is a help...' (though he later modified his view to the
extent of writing, 'gestures towards popularity were not
enough'). (96) The 'TLS' curiously enthused over the
'complete power' of the play (No. 72), but other reviewers
were perplexed and dismissive. Kenneth Allott found it
'trite' and dull ('New Verse', February 1939); C. Day-
Lewis ('Listener', 24 November 1938) and Janet Adam Smith
('Criterion', January 1939) concurred in the view that it
was both dwarfed by the recent crisis and an unsubtle por-
trayal of the problems of power; and T.R. Barnes judged
that the authors 'continue to follow their principle of
putting Marxist pap into bourgeois bottles' ('Scrutiny'
December 1938).

T.S. Eliot, who attended the first night at Cambridge,
wrote to Keynes in praise of the last act and of the admirable way in which Lydia Lopokova (Keynes's wife), who
played the heroine, Anna, had rendered her lines, but
only Kingsley Martin unreservedly lauded the political
tenor and outcome of the action, which left other critics
divided in sympathy and interpretation. The trouble lay
partly with the way Ernest Milton played the Dictator (a
character directly modelled on Hitler) with tremendous
ironic charm and energy. The authors oddly 'revelled' (97)
in his performance, which must suggest that they failed to
conceive any set purport in their own play, but the

characterization was in any case simplistic, as Eliot
properly regretted: 'I am afraid that Hitler is not the
simpleton that the authors make him out to be'. (98)

Although American critics, including Peter Monro Jack
in the 'New York Times Book Review' (16 April 1939) and
Babette Deutsch in the 'New York Herald Tribune Books'
(26 March 1939), contrarily praised the play as much as
they had criticized 'The Ascent of F6', Auden's and
Isherwood's erstwhile patron Ashley Dukes provided perhaps
the most generous yet fair comment in this previously unpublished letter to Keynes: (99)

> As I devoted a large part of the profits of Eliot to
> the propagation of Auden and Isherwood last year, I
> know what an important thing you have done in giving
> these two undergraduates another chance to graduate.
> I do not think the play in itself is an advance upon
> 'F6', and events have made it seem trite in many places:
> but I do feel that these two at their best make all
> other young writers seem like tuppence halfpenny. Their
> instant contact with the intelligence of the audience,
> which was most marked in the first act, has something
> very valuable.

'"On the Frontier" wasn't a harrowing disaster,'
Isherwood wrote later; (100) 'it passed away painlessly.'
It was an expensive production, with a cast of fourteen
and a chorus of eight, but the authors pocketed royalties
of £12 8s 4d. each. Like its forerunners, the play enjoyed
a greater success with its popular audiences than with
professional critics, according to Keynes: (101)

> Our reception was a very great deal better from the
> public than from the critics and what you might call
> responsible opinion. All the audience were exception-
> ally enthusiastic and satisfied. Most of the pro-
> fessional critics were grumpy, doubtful or captious.
> I found myself in sympathy with both parties....

An early draft of the play had included a homosexual
relationship between Valerian and his aide Lessep which
would have given an extra depth and dimension to the
action, but the authors removed that aspect and so
weakened the play, as Isherwood admitted to Robert Medley.
(102) Like most of the critics, Doone registered a sense
of vagueness and lack of decisiveness about the ending of
the play, but when he wrote to Auden with suggestions for
emending it, the authors quarrelled and Auden unconsciously sabotaged it. In any case, Auden's association

with the Group Theatre ended with 'On the Frontier'.
Although he was always loyal to Doone, he and Isherwood
were inattentive in their approach to writing plays
(though not as much as Isherwood later made out), and not
prepared to give the task enough time and humbleness.
Auden in particular had no idea of dramatic form (he only
learnt it through his later association with Chester
Kallman), and Doone and Medley agreed that he had 'a great
gift for writing a theatrical scene, but no gift for writing a play'. With respect to Doone's working conceptions
of the Group Theatre, moreover, although Auden had written
in the programme for 'The Dance of Death' this maxim –
'Drama is essentially an art of the body. The basis of
acting is acrobatic, dancing and all forms of physical
skill' – he never wholly believed with Doone that actors
are as important as writers. He and Isherwood had none the
less done a great deal to advance the dramatic tenets
enunciated by Doone, to establish the importance of
artistic criteria before propaganda in the theatre, and to
prove the significance of an experimental, expressionistic
drama akin to Brecht's and Toller's. If other members of
Auden's 'Group' demurred to give it their acclaim, the
reason was at least partly because the Auden-Isherwood
plays actually did little to further any supposedly joint
proposals for a revolutionary society, as Julian Symons
has succinctly written: (103) 'The Group Theatre bore
much the same relation to Unity Theatre that 'New Verse'
bore to 'Left Review': that is, its directors and practitioners put aesthetic standards before social ones, although they still wanted to change society.' For a last
word on Auden's engagement with the Group Theatre, Robert
Medley unequivocally recalls that while he and Doone
'accepted Eliot', they 'dreamed of Auden'.

LOVE AND SATIRE: 1936

Auden's non-dramatic work progressed in tandem with the
plays; he published his third collection of poems, 'Look,
Stranger!', within a month of 'The Ascent of F6', in
October 1936.
     Looking pack on the title-poem of 'Look, Stranger!'
(which was published in the USA, at Auden's insistence,
with the title 'On This Island'), George Woodcock remarked that it 'appealed in the thirties because in mood,
in feeling, in image, it trapped so faithfully, outside
ratiocination, the sense of our times. (We did not need it
explained to us then; it spoke directly, literally, to
us!)' (104) Most contemporary reviewers happily noted

Auden's access of clarity, though some of them felt critical and suspicious of the coexistence of satirical verses
and love poems, especially when the latter took such an
impersonal cast. Hugh Gordon Porteus ('Twentieth Century
Verse', January 1937), while acknowledging Auden's versa-
tility and visionary power, found the new work 'time-
marking', and Derek Traversi, perhaps the most antagonistic critic next to Leavis (though the basis of
Traversi's attack was an antipathy to Marxism as a
poetic), (105) thought the satire 'doggerel' and often
'immature buffoonery'. While Janet Adam Smith praised
Auden's ability to describe 'gestures, motions, tics,
which are symptomatic of a state of mind or body' (No. 56),
the 'TLS' (28 November 1936), among other reviews, noted
that it would no longer serve to tag Auden's inclinations
towards negative diagnosis as Communist (after all, he had
purposefully amended 'Comrades' to 'Brothers' in Poem XIV,
first published in 1933). Similarly, while Leavis took the
adverse line that Auden was treating the 'immature' stuff
of 'private neuroses and memories' with self-defensive and
self-indulgent irony, Louis MacNeice took a more positive
if ambiguous view of 'a mix-up of politics and psychology',
and praised Auden as both a religious poet and a legislator. In 'Poetry', January 1937, a special English number
co-edited by Auden and Michael Roberts, C. Day-Lewis gave
hollow applause to Auden's personal poems by proceeding to
forebode, 'the survival-value of his poetry is bound up
inextricably with the survival-value of Freud's teachings'
(No. 55), though several other critics took a more hopeful
and temperate view of Auden's efforts to conflate the public and the private worlds, and of his youthfully peda-
gogic, even bullying, elements. As Laurence Whistler remarked in a balanced but critical review, 'There have
lived on side by side a mature, intelligent, sympathetic
observer of humanity, and a great schoolboy full of bad
jokes and exaggerated opinions ('Poetry Review', January-
February 1937). F.O. Matthiessen, reviewing the American
edition in 'Southern Review' (Spring 1937), found that a
'more mature understanding of personal emotion' had succeeded the autocratic schoolboy tones of the earlier work,
as C. Day-Lewis agreed in a second review, and it was only
later, in an article called W.H. Auden: The Search for a
Public ('Poetry' (Chicago), 1939), that the British critic
David Daiches unironically judged that Auden's best public
'might be called simply the ideal schoolboy'.
    A number of other American reviews praised the work:
William Rose Benét in the 'Saturday Review of Literature'
(13 February 1937) ('Auden's verse has effloresced in
great variety'); Charles Poore in the 'New York Times Book

Review' (7 February 1937) ('stinging and memorable'); and
Eda Lou Walton, who (echoing Gavin Ewart) praised the
manner in which Auden expressed 'the inevitable discord
between the heart's necessities and the mind's convictions' ('Nation', 20 February 1937). The most influential review, however, was Edmund Wilson's sorry piece,
The Oxford Boys Becalmed, in the 'New Republic' (No. 57),
which, far from finding 'On this Island' an advance on
Auden's earlier work, lamented the loose rhythms of both
the lyrics and the satirical verse, and language which
seemed less personal and more derivative (a good number
of other reviews likewise noted borrowings from Yeats,
Eliot, Housman, and Hopkins).

What may be concluded with hindsight is that Auden's
proliferation of modes, his convocation of the public and
the private, and his refusal to consolidate a position as
either a satirist or a lyricist, either a Marxist revolutionary or a prophet of social malaise, disturbed the
critics' impulse to categorize: most were left quite
rightly to applaud his fertility and the variety of his
stylistic accomplishments, even if the poems struck some
of them as irresponsibly eclectic in substance and
direction.

TRAVELS: 1936-9

As Edmund Wilson reported in his review, Auden spent some
weeks early in 1937 in Spain, where the open conflict
between Republicanism and Fascism drew many British
idealists of all classes (half of them, according to
Julian Symons, being Communist) to prove their principles
in active service. Although he had earlier visited Iceland (in 1936), where he and Louis MacNeice had begun an
idiosyncratic travel book commissioned by Faber & Faber,
Auden's pamphlet poem 'Spain' saw print three months before 'Letters from Iceland'. 'Spain' might therefore be
seen as in some sense the product of Auden's attempt to
find an answer to the reflections on morality and contemporary history he had first included in the latter work,
and it needs to be borne in mind that Auden's first
audience was denied that perspective on the two
publications.

In a letter to his friend E.R. Dodds, Auden wrote before journeying to Spain: (106)

    I am not one of those who believe that poetry need or
    even should be directly political, but in a critical
    period such as ours, I do believe that the poet must

have direct knowledge of our major political events.

The pressures on Auden to write a committed statement about the Republican cause must have been enormous, or at least to deliver himself of a Communist viewpoint as most easily defined against Fascism. In an important and influential study called 'Illusian and Reality' (Macmillan, 1937), the Marxist critic Christopher Caudwell (who was himself to be killed in Spain) considered that the Auden group addressed themselves to the subject of the working-class struggle from the base of an endemic bourgeoisie, a view which Auden himself appreciated. (107) Auden accordingly acquitted himself in 'Spain' with an integrity beyond the blunt gestures of propaganda. In his autobiography, Stephen Spender calls 'Spain' 'the best poetic statement in English of the Republican cause', and goes on to argue the moot and possibly sophistic point that Auden could best express Marxist ideology for the very reason that he was not a committed Communist: 'He had a firmer grasp of Marxist ideology, and more capacity to put this into verse, than many writers who were closer to Communism. This led to the legend that he went through a Communist phase. But his poem, "A Communist to Others", is an exercise in entering a point of view not his own'. (108) The suggestion seems to be that disinterested or purely academic understanding could serve the poet better than sincere commitment, but it was Auden's subsequent apperception of his own insincerity which led him to despise and revoke what he came to think of as certain intolerably ignorant and even presumptuously vicious expressions in 'Spain'. In other words, Auden reprehended his youthful utterances for the very posture which Spender found a virtue, the ability to pass off untested opinions as clear-sighted and unemotional judgments. Like Auden, Spender read and accepted Caudwell's analysis of their anomalous position, which he chose to interpret in terms of a creative tension (although Caudwell had essentially defined the social impossibility of speaking for a class that could never be his own), but he saw no reason to modify his view that the appeal of socialism or communism 'involves one in taking sides'. (109)

Writing in the 'Daily Worker', the Communist Richard Goodman set great store by the revolutionary possibilities of Auden's verse, though he had to admit that 'Spain' fell short of being 'true revolutionary poetry' (No. 59) in failing to fuse the personal interpretation with the objective interpretation. Among other critics, only Cyril Connolly, determined that propaganda could not last, inattentively presumed that Auden had written 'Spain' in the service of Communist polemics: 'The Marxian theory of history does not go very happily into verse...' (No. 60) Even Day-Lewis, who wrote from a sense of poetry as a medium responsible to social aims, correctly judged that Auden applied himself more to moral exigencies than to practical politics: 'The poem moves with vivacity and the impersonal tenderness which is so much more effective than any heroics' (No. 58), and Clifford Dyment enthusiastically defined the right point: 'It is not directly concerned with the struggle now in process, but is rather an attempt to use it as a symbol of man's aspiration and man's frailty, and to correlate their present manifestation with the history of today and tomorrow' ('Time and Tide', 12 June 1937). The distinguished Irish poet Austin Clarke, scotching the propaganda value of the poetry of the Auden Gang, applauded Auden's posture in 'Spain' as 'liberal, democratic, and humane' ('Dublin Magazine', April-June 1938). In an essay entitled W.H. Auden and Spanish Civilisation ('Colosseum', September 1937), on the other hand, Bernard Wall cavilled with what he saw as the irrelevance of Auden's response, construing it as 'not so much a hymn to the Spanish revolutionaries as a hymn to the spirit of modern secularism. The Spanish revolutionaries are seen through English eyes...'. To presume that Auden should have identified himself with the Spanish ethos and militancy, which is also to presuppose that the poem is evidence of political action, is actually to judge 'Spain' on anything other than its own terms.

In a famous essay called Inside the Whale (written in 1939, first published in March 1940), George Orwell took a scathing view of the communist sympathies of the Auden 'movement' who 'belonged to the soft-boiled emancipated middle class': 'They can swallow totalitarianism *because* they have no experience of anything except liberalism'. (110) As a damning instance of their culpable inexperience, he cited these lines from 'Spain',

> To-day the deliberate increase in the chances of death,
> The conscious acceptance of guilt in the necessary
> murder:

with the comment that the last phrase 'could only be written by a person to whom murder is at most a *word*.... Mr. Auden's brand of amoralism is only possible if you are the kind of person who is always somewhere else when the trigger is pulled. So much of left-wing thought is a kind of playing with fire by people who don't even know that fire is hot'. (111) It has commonly been supposed that when Auden altered the lines for publication in 'Another

Time' (February 1940), where they read,

> To-day the inevitable increase in the chances of death;
> The conscious acceptance of guilt in the fact of
> murder;

he did so in response to Orwell's sting; but, as Edward
Mendelson has pointed out, (112) he had made the change
before Orwell published his essay. It is quite possible
that Auden came independently to deplore his own phrases,
but it is also possible that he had first been alerted to
their supposed iniquity on reading the 'Criterion' (October 1937), in which Edwin Muir lamented Auden's apparent
advocacy of militancy - albeit 'with restraint and a
natural reluctance' - and pointed to the same specific
lines as showing a connivance in murder. Only once, it
seems, in a letter of 11 May 1963 to Monroe K. Spears,
was Auden moved to protest at Orwell's 'densely unjust'
criticism, and to exonerate the lines with this
explanation: (113)

> I was *not* excusing my totalitarian crimes but only
> trying to say what, surely, every decent person thinks
> if he finds himself unable to adopt the absolute paci-
> fist position. (1) To kill another human being is al-
> ways murder and should never be called anything else.
> (2) In a war, the members of two rival groups try to
> murder their opponents. (3) *If* there is such a thing
> as a just war, then murder can be necessary for the
> sake of justice.

In any event, the bulk of evidence tends to prove that
Auden himself could not finally accept any amelioration
of the sentiments of the poem. When Robin Skelton published his anthology 'Poetry of the Thirties' (Penguin,
1964), for example, he was firmly instructed to put on
record Auden's opinion that he numbered 'Spain' among a
small group of poems he considered 'trash which he is
ashamed to have written'. (114) Likewise, in the fifties,
as Charles Osborne reports, 'Auden crossed out the last
two lines in Cyril Connolly's copy of "Spain", and
scribbled in the margin, "This is a lie." Other friends'
copies were annotated in similar fashion'. (115) The
bland and perhaps sacerdotal tone of the poem certainly
gives it an air of complicity not only with specious postures of militancy but also with a communist revolution
which Auden no longer genuinely credited in the late
thirties. The least that should be said is that Auden's
self-acknowledged penchant for preaching perhaps led him

at the time of writing 'Spain' to compromise his true
convictions, and yet the tenor of the poem as a whole ac-
cords with a remark made towards the end of his life:
'Man must be concerned with understanding things close to
home ... the problems immemorial to man's soul.' (116) It
would certainly have been for him to misgive his temperament to have written a poem about the 'immediacy and actuality' (to use Julian Symons's phrase) (117) of the war in
Spain.

The controversy aroused by 'Spain' continues in later
years. While Dennis Davison (1970) perhaps safely ven-
tures, 'it is clear from the poem itself that Auden's
vision of the future is not the optimistic, socially-
orientated vision of the Marxist', (118) and Bernard
Bergonzi (1978), 'For all its local brilliance, "Spain"
looks strained and unconvincing and, perhaps, unconvinced',
(119) John Wain writes bluntly and, I believe, wrong-
headedly, that 'Spain' 'is a totally and unequivocally
"committed" poem. It is written in support of one side in
a war'. (120)

Visiting Iceland before he went to Spain, and sharing
with Louis MacNeice the task of composing what Edward
Sackville-West (No. 61) called the 'extravaganza' of
'Letters from Iceland', Auden found himself in suspension
- forced, as he put it, 'to reflect on one's past and
one's culture from the outside' (121) - and the work became in large part a deracinated address, wry and witty,
to his own heritage of bourgeois attitudes and what life
had taught him to make of them. Reviewers such as Goronwy
Rees ('Spectator', 3 September 1937), even Christopher
Isherwood ('Listener', 11 August 1937), and, in part,
Sackville-West, who might have expected a more conventional travel book in the vein of Peter Fleming, showed
themselves disappointed with the book. But the good barbed
fun of Auden's light verse appealed to most reviewers
(including Sackville-West) who did not arrive with earnest
expectations - 'This stylish display of markmanship is
equally good for England and for Mr. Auden', wrote the
'TLS' (No. 62) - especially the impressive entertainment
of 'Letter to Lord Byron', which MacNeice himself later
complimented as 'a tour de force'. (122) In an antagonistic essay called The Mind of Mr. W.H. Auden ('Townsman'
July 1938), on the other hand, John Drummond took one cue
from the 'Letter' to instance what he impugned as 'an
important characteristic and popularizing trick, the generalized image ... the statements are at once widely generalized and confined to bourgeois experience', (123) a
view properly corrected in Michael Roberts's characterization of the book's 'good descriptive verse that makes

a scene the starting-point of meditation about the world in general' (No. 63).

The title of Roberts's review, Poets on Holiday, implies what must have been a commonly held view - that 'Letters from Iceland' was a by-product of Auden's career (124) - an inference which might have been supported by the prior publication of 'Spain'. The actual course of events shows that Auden was moving not from involvement to evasion, but from self-admitted exile to engagement. The penultimate poem of the book, 'Auden and MacNeice: Their Last Will and Testament', invokes 'the power to take upon themselves the guilt / of human action...'.

When Auden accepted the King's Gold Medal for Poetry for 'Look, Stranger!' in the autumn of 1937, his obeisance to the Establishment certainly disquieted his more revolutionary associates. Further, 'Letters from Iceland' became a choice of The Book Society, which Geoffrey Grigson reviled as 'a Limited Company pimping to the mass bourgeois mind' (125) (C. Day-Lewis, who had joined the selection committee after much heart-searching, came in for wide traducement), but Grigson none the less proceeded to bestow on Auden the singular accolade of an entire issue (Auden Double Number) of 'New Verse' (November 1937), saluting him as 'the first English poet for many years who is a poet all round ... traditional, revolutionary, energetic, inquisitive, critical, and intelligent'. (126) The issue (see Nos 65-71) contained essays and shorter comments by Isherwood, MacNeice, Spender, Grigson, Kenneth Allott, Day-Lewis, Herbert Read, Edwin Muir, Edgell Rickword, George Barker, Frederic Prokosch, David Gascoyne, Dylan Thomas, Berthold Viertel, Bernard Spencer, Charles Madge, John Masefield, Graham Greene, Sir Hugh Walpole, W.J. Turner, and a curmudgeonly note by Ezra Pound. Though not unequivocally uncritical, the issue did amount to what Robin Skelton has called 'a vote of confidence'. (127)

At the instigation of Bennett Cerf of Random House, Auden's American and British publishers jointly commissioned Isherwood and Auden to write a 'travel book', for which they chose the theatre of the Sino-Japanese war. They visited China in the earlier part of 1938, and though they saw little of the war itself, they produced a fine work, 'Journey to a War', made up of a collaborative 'Travel-Diary' and a sonnet sequence and 'Commentary' in verse entirely by Auden. Only two critics were adverse: the Communist Randall Swingler sniped at the diary for containing 'nothing but accurate superficialities' (No. 77), and at Auden's sonnets for being flat verse 'increasingly abstract and vague', while Evelyn Waugh disdained what he called the 'commercial convenience' of publishing

two books in one, and churlishly and negligently concluded
that Auden's work 'is awkward and dull' (No. 76). (Isherwood's method of presenting the diary led all reviewers to
believe that he alone had written virtually all of it,
which was not the case; for that reason, I have printed the
reviews below in their entirety, not just excerpts on
Auden's poetry.) Less partisan and more responsible critics
very much enjoyed the book. Geoffrey Grigson's valedictory
panegyric (No. 79) in the last issue of 'New Verse' (May
1939) was only rivalled when the American edition inspired
Lincoln Kirstein to a paean (No. 80). Nathaniel Peffer
('New Republic') found Auden and Isherwood 'a bit dégagé',
but if some of Auden's erstwhile fans regretted that he
had moved away from the radical asperity of the earlier
thirties, many other critics were pleased to note that
'Journey to a War' figured a mature voice in broad and
humane contemplation of war and morality.

Grigson's farewell testimonial in 'New Verse' included
these remarks:

> 'New Verse' came into existence because of Auden. It
> has published more poems by Auden than by anyone else;
> and there are many people who might quote of Auden:
> *'To you I owe the first development of my imagination;*
> *to you I owe the withdrawing of my mind from the low*
> *brutal part of my nature, to the lofty, the pure and*
> *the perpetual.'* Auden is now clear, absolutely clear of
> foolish journalists, Cambridge detractors, and envious
> creepers and crawlers of party and Catholic reaction
> and the new crop of loony and eccentric small magazines
> in England and America. He is something good and cre-
> ative in European life in a time of the very greatest
> evil.

EXILE AND A TROUNCING: 1939-41

But Auden had made his own clear withdrawal by removing to
the USA and closing his English chapter. He spelt out his
secession from poetry as political insistence in 'In
Memory of W.B. Yeats' - 'Poetry makes nothing happen' -
first published in full in April 1939, at a time coincid-
ing with Orwell's similar argument for literary disengage-
ment in 'Inside the Whale'. 'September 1, 1939' likewise
reinforced his bias against the 'low dishonest decade' of
the thirties: 'All I have is a voice / to undo ... the lie
of Authority / ...There is no such thing as the State /
And no one exists alone; / ...We must love one another or
die.'

As Samuel Hynes has pointed out, (128) Virginia Woolf's
influential lecture, The Leaning Tower (May 1940) set a
prevailing pattern of enunciating a simplified myth of the
thirties by parcelling up the Auden Generation as self-
divided young writers:

> You cannot abuse that society whole-heartedly while you
> continue to profit by that society.... It explains the
> violence of their attack upon bourgeois society and
> also its half-heartedness.... It explains the destruc-
> tiveness of their work; and also its emptiness. They
> can destroy bourgeois society, in part at least, but
> what have they to put in its place? How can a writer
> who has no first-hand experience of a towerless, of a
> classless society create that society? (129)

In a general way, it is true, Auden's impersonal, diag-
nostic, and satirical gifts (though only one facet of his
output) had looked back in denunciation rather than forward from liberalism, though he had not reckoned, as many
critics pointed out, that he unwittingly identified with
what he condemned. The burden of Virginia Woolf's argument
declared that the group whom Roy Campbell dubbed 'Mac-
Spaunday' was not hypocritical but confused. While she be-
littled their poetry, she seemed ironically to applaud the
group for liberating a new generation - a generation who
might be classless but individual; cultivated, certainly,
but without an inherited culture. 'But the leaning-tower
writers wrote about themselves honestly, therefore cre-
atively,' she observed. (130)

> They told the unpleasant truths, not only the flatter-
> ing truths. The writers of the next generation may in-
> herit from them a whole state of mind, a mind no
> longer crippled, evasive, divided.... For that great
> gift of unconsciousness the next generation will have
> to thank the creative and honest egotism of the leaning-
> tower group.

Auden regarded part of his own past with a regret that
matched Virginia Woolf's generalized and pitying evalu-
ation, for he set out his new terms of reference in an
abandoned book, 'The Prolific and the Devourer', begun in
New York but published only after his death: (131)

> To be forced to be political is to be forced to lead a
> dual life. Perhaps this would not matter if one could
> consciously keep them apart and know which was the
> real one. But to succeed at anything, one must believe

in it, at least for the time being, and only too often
the false public life absorbs and destroys the genuine
private life. Nearly all public men become booming old
bores.

While Left-wing critics had often accused Auden of betray-
ing his origins in his work of the thirties, it is doubly
ironic that he himself subsequently believed that political expectations had led him to betray his gifts.

'Another Time', which gathered up all of Auden's poems
of the later 1930s, reversed the usual order of publication by appearing first in the USA (February 1940), as
did most of his later books. Reviewers certainly took it
as a transitional volume - as David Daiches put it, 'recu-
ler pour mieux sauter' ('Poetry', April 1940). Apart from
poems such as 'Lay your sleeping head, my love' and 'Musée
des Beaux Arts' which came in time to stand among his most
loved and widely anthologized verses, the book contained
a group of lighter poems including 'Miss Gee' (which most
critics considered callous), and other well-known poems on
people and places. The variety compelled almost all reviewers to take careful and extended stock of Auden's
position. Few were as severe as F.R. Leavis: 'That poised
knowledgeableness, that impressive command of the modern
scene, points to the conditions in which his promise has
lost itself. We must still feel that he ought to have been
a poet, but the possibility of development looks very
frail' ('Scrutiny', 9, 1940-1). Richard Church ('Listener',
22 August 1940) also detected an 'emotional starvation',
and Edwin Muir ('Purpose', July-December 1940) thought the
poems unequal in quality, with their feelings being dis-
torted by intellectuality, a view gainsaid by William
Empson's acutely equivocal greeting to 'a wonderful poet'
which feared only that Auden was selling his ideas to simplification (No. 83). Some critics (Michael Roberts, David
Daiches, John Peale Bishop) also found too much triviality,
others (John Lehmann, and the anonymous reviewer for the
'Irish Times') aloofness and technical derivativeness -
most ostensibly from Rilke, whom Roberts (No. 81) considered almost a ventriloquial influence (132) - and the
consensus persisted in complaining about obscurity. Andrew
Wordsworth ('Time and Tide', 20 July 1940), on the other
hand - like T.C. Worsley (No. 82) - happily (though not
unreservedly) registered new levels of fullness, fertility,
eloquence and exuberance: 'much that is eminently beautiful, crystallized in lucid, compelling metaphor'. Michael
Roberts believed that Auden had exhausted his high-
mindedness in 'Spain' and had left himself with cynicism
or pessimism, an opinion echoed by Martin Turnell, who

defined the tragedy of the young generation (in terms perhaps harking to Virginia Woolf's) as being:

> different from that of the older generation whose scep-
> ticism and disillusionment received their final ex-
> pression in 'The Waste Land'. For the tragedy of this
> generation was not the tragedy of too little faith, but
> of too much. It lay in the uncritical acceptance of all
> the revolutionary slogans of its time which led to the
> waste and destruction of its immense abilities.
> ('Tablet', 20 July 1940)

Virtually all critics accordingly concurred in the view
that Auden had obviously reached a divide in his career and
was taking new bearings, the favourable aspect being best
summed up in John Peale Bishop's qualified affirmation:
'It is a heartening rather than a hope, not so much an
overthrowing of negation and despair as a certainty of the
means...' ('Nation', 6 April 1940). The more doubtful
opinion is represented in Kathleen Raine's searching
notice ('Horizon', January 1940), which defines the conclusion Auden should draw, and the move towards Christianity he would actually come to make.

Auden dedicated 'Another Time' to Chester Kallmann, a
young poet he first met in April 1939 who subsequently became his friend, lover, and collaborator, and to whom, as
Robert Craft and Edward Mendelson have testified, (133)
Auden submitted his unpublished work for literary censorship. In a late interview with the 'New York Quarterly'
(Winter 1970, p. 10), Auden acknowledged that he did submit his work to friends whose judgments he valued - 'They
have to be poets because other people's comments wouldn't
be useful'. He also underlined the extent of his personal
and literary reliance on Kallmann (134) in this formerly
unpublished letter to Spender, written in the early 1940s:
(135) 'In Chester's case my mistake, was demanding that he
should be my Mother-Father, and one has no right to ask
that of anyone, least of all someone fourteen years
younger.' In the same letter he implicitly responded to
critics (Julian Symons and John Lehmann among them) who
had complained of a certain technical vagueness and slack-
ness in 'Another Time', and conceded the truth of the
perennial complaint about his immature comportment - which
reviewers had variously found schoolboyish or schoolmasterly (even Empson feared what he called 'a horrid
false note of infantilism') - by accepting that his poetry
should lose 'its whiff of the heartly schoolmaster. Technically this means that I should deprive myself of the
support of strict conventional verse forms...'. (David

Gasgoyne had commented in October 1938: (136) 'Even at the age of 40, he will carry the head of an undergraduate on his shoulders. At 31, he still has an air of disguising only with a difficultly acquired social manner the petulance and embarrassment of an adolescent.')

Asked why he had become an immigrant to the USA, Auden told Benjamin Appel (137), 'The attractiveness of America to a writer is its openness and lack of tradition. In a way it's frightening. You are forced to live here as everyone will be forced to live. There is no past.' (Likewise, in a later interview, he reiterated that 'the difficulty about England is the cultural life - it *was* dim and I suspect it still is' ('Paris Review', 1974.) It would therefore seem that Auden left England for both negative and positive reasons, to deracinate himself from a suffocating culture which had willy-nilly arrogated his poetry to politics, and to enter a new environment with some degree of anonymity.

Reviewers of 'Another Time' mostly restrained themselves from judging the cultural or political repercussions of what had become known as Auden's 'defection'. John Lehmann, who had successfully fostered his contemporaries in 'New Writing', regretted that Auden had removed himself from the possibility of writing 'the poetry of this war we are all waiting for; as it is, there seems to me a danger that a certain vagueness of phrase and a kind of beneficent aloofness that is disturbing in much of his recent work may only increase' (War-Time Poetry, 'Tribune', 6 September 1940), while Julian Symons lamented that Auden had lost his genius with his disinvolvement ('Kingdom Come', Winter 1940-1). But open hostility blazed elsewhere in newspapers and periodicals early in the 1940s at the putative treachery of Auden and others including Isherwood and Aldous Huxley who had left England for the USA, the most indecent shot being fired in a quatrain entitled 'To Certain Intellectuals Safe in America' which appeared in the 'Spectator' (21 June) above the initials of the Dean of St Paul's:

> 'This Europe stinks,' you cried - swift to desert
>   Your stricken country in her sore distress,
> You may not care, but still I will assert,
>   Since you have left us, here the stench is less.

The issue was joined by, among others, Harold Nicolson (condemnation of Auden), Cyril Connolly and Stephen Spender (ambiguous defence), and E.M. Forster (a dignified letter of appeasement to the 'Spectator', 5 July 1940). Sir Hugh Walpole scolded John Lehmann in the 'Daily Sketch'

for continuing to promote the Auden Gang as 'New Writers',
and then again in a private letter:

> I don't think you realize the harm done by Auden,
> Isherwood, MacNeice fleeing to America. I'm not blaming
> them but it has *killed* their influence here. The men
> you write of seem to me to belong in the main to the
> Spanish war. The young writers of this war have an out-
> look quite different. (138)

He added later, 'As to the under *thirties* – Auden seems to
them an ancient schoolboy-joking pedant.' (139) (In 1938,
David Gascoyne had written in his diary, (140) 'More and
more I feel the existence of a great gap between their
generation's conception of poetry and my own, and feel the
need to explain in writing all that this gap means. Auden
I admire because of his mastery over words and because of
the sincerity of the best of his utterances.')

   Auden made no public reply to his critics, not even to
those who slated him for a quisling, as Golo Mann, who
lodged with him in 1940-1, remembers: (141) 'When I showed
him a hostile article in an English paper and said it required some reply from him, he cut me short: "There is no
point." It was another example of his independence, self-
confidence and pride.' He professed not to be hurt by
Cyril Connolly's Comment in the second number of 'Horizon'
(February 1940), an ironic apologia for Auden and his con-
federates in desertion, which he and Isherwood wrongly
assumed had been written by Spender (Isherwood did, in
fact, complain to Spender), but a review Spender wrote of
'Another Time' (in 'Horizon', 3, no. 14, February 1941,
pp. 141-2) provoked Auden to write on 13 March 1941: (142)

> Dearest Stephen,
>   People ring me up from time to time to ask me if I
> am going to answer what they describe as an attack by
> you in 'Horizon'. As I have not read it and don't in-
> tend to, I can't. I did happen by chance to see your
> review of my book ... and was, I must confess, a little
> hurt.
>   Your passion for public criticism of your friends
> has always seemed to me a little odd; it is not that
> you don't say acute things – you do – but the as-
> sumption of the role of the blue-eyed Candid Incorrup-
> tible is questionable. God knows it is hard enough to
> be objective about strangers; it is quite impossible
> with those one knows well and, I hope, loves. Person-
> ally, I will never write a review of a friend's work,
> nor even a review of a contemporary poet if I can

possibly help it. As to your review of me, what you say
is probably accurate enough, but the tone alarms me.
'One is worried about Auden's poetic future.' Really,
Stephen dear, whose voice is this but that of Harold
Spender M.P. [Spender's father] 'I hope, if I am bombed,
he will write some sapphics about me' is funny and a
good criticism, but for you to say it seems to be in
shocking taste, suggesting that my only interest in you
is as potential elegiac material. Your concluding sentence about being tired of receiving vague advice from
America contains more than a trace of *suggestio falsi*.
You know quite well that practically all the poems were
written before the war; even the one you quote was
finished the day before England actually entered the
war, yet you suggest that the book is my American Message to the English people in their Hour of Peril....
     I don't see how my own attitude about the war can be
of any interest except to myself, but here it is. If I
thought I should be a competent soldier or air-warden I
should come back tomorrow. It is impossible for me to
know whether it is a reason or just cowardice that
makes me think I shouldnt be of much military effec-
tiveness. All I can do, therefore, is to be willing to
do anything when and if the Government ask me (which I
told the Embassy here). As a writer and a pedagogue the
problem is different, for the intellectual warfare goes
on always and everywhere, and no one has a right to say
that this place or that time is where all intellectuals
ought to be. I believe that for me personally America
is the best, but of course the only proof lies in what
one produces....

(In a letter to Nicolas Bentley of 12 March 1941, even
Cyril Connolly so moderated his opinion as to agree with
Auden on one point: 'I think Auden here, as Auden, would
be very valuable, in battle dress & so on, quite useless,
much better where he is....') (143)
     In the absence of Auden, as John Hayward reported to
his friend Frank Morley (who was working in the USA), the
literary press returned their attention to T.S. Eliot as
the leading poetic figure: 'there are more and more references in the press and periodicals to his importance as a
poet - obiter dicta provoked, it would seem, by the
failure of the Auden-Spender group to justify their
promise, and by the death of Yeats promoting Tom to Chief
Bard'. (144) What the widely expressed outcry against
Auden does paradoxically indicate is that his literary
prestige still ran high in 1940, that the name of Auden
remained a metonym for a vital force in English life and

letters. That his reputation suffered as a consequence of
his emigration there is no doubt; that the quality of his
work suffered too is another question altogether. On the
first point at least, John Wain, who was associated with
the English 'Movement' in the 1950s, summed up the sorry
reverberations of Auden's shift in an essay called The
Reputation of Ezra Pound (1955):

> After the war, there was a good deal of reconstruction
> to be done in the arts, and the poet who was just set-
> ting out on his life's work had a pretty hard job of
> selection to do... The '30's were no use, at any rate
> as far as the main line was concerned, the Auden line:
> it was worn out even before it got smashed, and what
> smashed it decisively was not the war, but Auden's re-
> nunciation of English nationality.... (145)

THE AMERICAN ANGLICAN: 1941-50

'The Double Man' (1941) showed the world that Auden was
moving towards the logical conclusion of his spiritual
drift, though without yet fully espousing Christianity.
'"The Double Man", written Jan.-Oct. 1940,' Auden wrote
later, (146) 'covers a period when I was beginning to
think seriously about such things without committing myself.' Although Allen Tate irritably rebuked the book for
using language too simply and for failing to resolve a
meaning ('Accent', Winter 1942), most American reviewers
treated it favourably. In England (where the volume bore
the title 'New Year Letter'), R.O.C. Winkler patronizingly
predicted that 'it's only a matter of months before it's
described in one university or another as a 'twentieth
century "Essay on Man"' (No. 89), but Randall Jarrell had
already done so (No. 85). Babette Deutsch, who generally
liked the book, found it 'more engaging as ethics than
as verse', though she did think it too prematurely ambitious an undertaking for Auden (No. 86). Most critics
happily recorded that Auden had departed from politics
for the ethical problems of guilt and evil in the human
soul (Malcolm Cowley, in a well-balanced and clear-sighted
essay (No. 84), doubted that Auden had defined his attitude towards evil with sufficient responsibility as to
disavow 'the passive toleration of evil'), and most, too,
drew up short of acclaiming it as a great or wholly successful work. Cleanth Brooks, Jr, for example, regretted
that 'the general structure of the work is looser than
that which one expects in poetry', but concluded by giving
his qualified approval to 'an important - and readable -

document about Auden and Auden's poetry rather than an extension of that poetry' ('Kenyon Review', Spring 1946),
and Louis Untermeyer had only slight reservations with a
different emphasis: 'it does not (manifestly cannot) resolve the poet's confusions. It persuades, but it does not
over-power. Nevertheless, the poem is unified...' ('Saturday Review of Literature', 17 May 1941). Only Marianne
Moore unreservedly described 'The Double Man' as magnificent ('Decision', May 1941).

English reviewers could in no way equal the fullness of
her praise. The 'TLS', Michael Roberts, and Edwin Muir
('Horizon', August 1941) agreed in criticizing its 'deep
inconclusiveness', lack of imaginative embodiment, and a
reliance on 'undigested abstractions' (a good many other
critics, in fact, disliked the fact that Auden had
apparently renounced a concrete situation for the ab-
stractness of a provisional peroration). George Every SSM,
a friend of Michael Roberts', had no doubt of the real
Christian tenor of the work, and regretted only that Auden
seemed too diffident and detached to have declared himself
('Theology', October 1941). Herbert Read inclined to treat
as a strength the irresoluteness that most critics found a
weakness (No. 87), as did Charles Williams in the 'Dublin
Review': 'it dialectically includes both sides of the
way...' (No. 88). Williams, to whose book 'The Descent of
the Dove' Auden acknowledged his deep indebtedness in 'New
Year Letter', confidently affirmed that 'Its concern is
with the building of the Just City'. (Disagreement about
the quality of 'New Year Letter' continued when it was re-
issued in 1965: (147) while the 'TLS' called it a
'spirited long poem', the Marxist critic Anthony Arblaster
scoffed, 'Like so much of his work, it is glib, often
facile, and intellectually smart, overloaded with pretentious references' ('Tribune', 16 July 1965)).

'For the Time Being' (1944; 1945 in England) - containing 'The Sea and the Mirror: A Commentary on Shakespeare's
"The Tempest"', and 'For the Time Being: A Christmas Oratorio' - Auden's British publishers announced with this
almost backhanded blurb (which T.S. Eliot may have
written):

In the light of 'For the Time Being', Mr. Auden's previous book, 'New Year Letter', has the appearance of an
interim work. It displayed on the one hand great skill
in the management of an antiquated verse form of great
difficulty but narrow scope; and, on the other, a process of development beneath the surface, which adopted
this form only because it had not arrived at the point
of achieving its own form. Mr. Auden's virtuosity has

perhaps been over-emphasized by his critics: it has not
been cultivated for its own sake, and must be viewed in
relation to a profounder evolution. His skill in versification and his personal idiom, are no less vigorous
in 'For the Time Being' than in any previous book; but
they distract the attention less, and interpose less
obstruction between the reader and the meaning, than
ever before. The meaning is not easy, and perhaps not
easily acceptable; but we think that this is the best
book (leaving his dramatic work out of account) that
the author has produced since 'The Orators'.

A good number of critics (including Mark Schorer, Louis
Untermeyer, F.W. Dupee, the 'TLS', Henry Reed, Geoffrey
Grigson, and Louise Bogan) fully agreed with Faber & Faber
that Auden had fulfilled the promise of his rhetoric and
successfully married his wit, intelligence, and bravura
technique, though few were as unreserved in their opinion
as Louise Bogan:

> The two poems, taken together, constitute the most
> minute dissection of the spiritual illness of our day
> that any modern poet, not excluding Eliot, has given
> us.... Auden's change occurred on a non-Romantic level,
> in a region where the beliefs of Christianity and the
> proofs of modern psychological knowledge intersect.
> ('New Yorker', 23 September 1944)

Auden had become Louise Bogan's close friend, and promptly
responded to her review:

> Just a line to thank you for your much too generous re-
> view in the New Yorker.
>   I was particularly pleased at your drawing attention
> to the fact that Oratorios are intended for music, as
> it's just the sort of thing most readers (and reviewers)
> ignore. (Amherst College Library; see also headnotes to
> Nos 41 and 97 below)

Henry Reed, despite his misgivings about the fact that
Auden seemed unable to create character but rather exploited his curiosity about human behaviour in order to
confirm his own knowledge, nevertheless affirmed that 'The
Sea and the Mirror' seemed emotionally genuine ('New
Writing and Daylight' VI, 1945).
   Auden's detractors, though virtually all of them saluted
the ambition and impressiveness of the book, erred on the
side of finding it factitious or disintegrated. While acknowledging passages of magic, brilliance, and tremendous

beauty, they considered Auden's intellectualism, his use of
paradox, abstraction, and irony, all too confusing and depressing. 'For the Time Being' left Sheila Shannon in the
'Spectator', for example, cold, and Harry Levin, in a
dense piece for the 'New Republic', found implausible what
he called the 'evangelical appeal' of Auden's self-
conscious pilgrimage from modernism to mysticism (No. 91).
Most reviewers, including Stephen Spender and Malcolm
Cowley, tended to reiterate David Daiches's uncomfortable
conclusion in the 'Virginia Quarterly Review': 'Auden has
reached the stage where the disparity between his insights
and his poetic feeling has reached disastrous proportions
(disastrous, that is, for his art).' Desmond MacCarthy had
to admit that he failed to comprehend the book (No. 92) and
Hugh Kingsmill attributed to a protracted adolescence
Auden's tendency to distance himself behind intellectually
mystifying barriers or a coruscating technical virtuosity
(No. 93), what W.P.M. in the 'Dublin Magazine' called his
tendency to 'interpose irritating affectations between
the reader and the meaning'. G.W. Stonier ('New Statesman
and Nation', 17 March 1945) and the reviewer for the
'Glasgow Herald' observed that Auden's treatment in 'For
the Time Being' verged on blasphemy. Yet they did not
seriously doubt the reality of Auden's religious experience, as did G.S. Fraser ('I find no evidence anywhere ... of any profound *personal* spiritual experience')
and R.G. Lienhardt in 'Scrutiny' (No. 95). Daniel George
in the 'Manchester Evening News' (22 March 1945) split
the difference and drew an unavoidable conclusion: 'From
this gallimaufry an affirmation of faith emerges, but it
is a faith for a witty intellectual rather than a
humanist.'

The consensus of critical views accordingly held that
'For the Time Being' manifested a rational rather than an
emotional conviction of faith, though F.J.K. ('Irish Independent', 23 April 1945) was alone in being quite sarcas-
tically dismissive: 'Mr. Auden undoubtedly meant well....
Even the best-intentional bull can wreak sad havoc in a
china shop.'

In sum, it seems fair to say, the critics who whole-
heartedly rejoiced in the book were those who both applauded the verbal brilliance and assented to the spiritual dimension of Auden's quest. Those who could not meet
Auden's interest in religion were left either beguiled or
bothered by virtuosity.

'The Collected Poetry of W.H. Auden' (1945), which ap-
peared only in the USA, gave critics, including Donald
Stauffer, F.W. Dupee, F. Cudworth Flint (No. 96), Dan S.
Norton, and Louis Untermeyer, the opportunity to

celebrate the canon of Auden's work so far. John Van
Druten (No. 98) blithely overrode the questions that
critics had elsewhere so hotly debated - 'infinitely more
important than either his technical virtuosity or his
genius for phrase-making is the emotional content of his
work, his complete self-identification with every human
need or perplexity' - and Oscar Williams hailed Auden's
'genuine greatness' with the suggestion that he should be
awarded the Nobel Prize.

Most of the first reviewers dispassionately noted that
Auden had revised or eliminated certain early poems (in
the printer's copy of 'On this Island' he had suppressed
'Brothers, who when the sirens roar', for instance, with
the comment, 'O God, what rubbish') (148), but a number of
other critics came to deplore Auden's prerogative of revising his earlier work, on the assumption that fickle
changes of belief led him to suppress poems which enunciated convictions at odds with his subsequent religious
criteria. Two brilliantly destructive essays by Randall
Jarrell (149), Changes of Attitude and Rhetoric in Auden's
Poetry ('Southern Review', vii, Autumn 1941) and Freud to
Paul: The Stages of Auden's Ideology ('Partisan Review',
xx, 1945), established a trend for discrediting Auden's
revisions by attempting to prove that he changed his mind
so often, capriciously and irresponsibly, as to be fundamentally dishonest and unreliable. Before Jarrell, adverse
critics had blamed Auden for the insincere exercise of
verbal brilliance over genuine feeling; after Jarrell, the
more substantial indictment charged him with untrust-
worthiness. That trend culminated in Joseph Warren Beach's
exhaustive and obsessional spat, 'The Making of the Auden
Canon' (1957), a book which presumably owed much to
Jarrell's example. Professor E.R. Dodds benevolently explained in his autobiography (150) that 'The ruthless
treatment of his own past work which recent critics have
observed and deplored was no new thing in Wystan; it is
the price his readers have to pay for the companionship
of a receptive mind that perpetually judged the past in
the changing light of the present', but Auden himself, in
a number of interviews, always maintained that he revised,
not thought or feeling, but language. The explanation certainly begs questions about the discreteness of language
and thought which no interviewer seems to have pressed.
In any event, his effort to alter what he considered
specious or spurious elements in certain poems has had the
effect of attracting more intense critical attention to
those very poems. His belief that the line, 'We must love
one another or die' (in 'September 1, 1939'), for example,
contained a falsehood led him first to omit the stanza,

then to revise the line, and finally to the conviction
that the poem was irreparably mistaken, (151) but Auden's
scruple has absolutely failed to quash the rhetorical
appeal of the phrase. Trevor Huddleston, Bishop of
Stepney, for example, took the line as a slogan in his
Runnymede lecture: (152)

> The one world to which we all belong is a world in
> which men of different race, colour and creed must, in
> the words of W.H. Auden, 'love one another or die.'
> To turn this message into practical reality is the
> challenge to our generation and is, I believe, pecu-
> liarly the challenge to our own country.

Contemporary reviewers did not extend to 'The Age of
Anxiety' (1947, 1948) the unanimous praise that had
greeted 'The Collected Poetry'. Certain American critics
welcomed the book as a fine achievement: Jaques Barzun
(No. 100); M.L. Rosenthal (No. 99); Louis L. Martz ('Yale
Review', December 1947) ('a gripping poem'); and Marianne
Moore: 'we have in W.H. Auden a master musician of rhythm
and note, unable to be dull, in fact an enchanter, under
the music of indigenous gusto.... "The Age of Anxiety"
assures us that fear and lust have, in faith and purity, a
cure so potent we need never know panic or be defeated by
Self' ('New York Times', 27 July 1947). But their heady
rejoicings seem positively wilful in the face of most
other American and all British reviews, which (with all
due respect and regret) found 'The Age of Anxiety' occasionally adroit and inspired, but mostly dull and emotionless ('TLS', Patric Dickinson, William Elton, Storm
Jameson, Delmore Schwartz), artificial (H. Peschmann),
facetious (Randall Jarrell), or a sterile display of
Auden's own opinions (Wrey Gardiner, Giles Romilly, George
D. Painter). At once damning and extremely disappointed,
virtually all critics reflected Delmore Schwartz's view
(No. 101) that Auden had become self-indulgent and showy
without feeling, the fault being imputed to his failure to
assimilate or even come to terms with the American experience. Just as critics had remarked about earlier
volumes, Auden's work sometimes manifested a puzzling,
occasionally shocking, discrepancy between brilliant intellectual grasp and emotional conviction.

WISDOM OR WAGGERY: 1951-69

'Nones' (1951, 1952) fared somewhat better with the reviewers, though all of them continued to remark how Auden

deployed verbal virtuosity in advance of deep personal
engagement - 'Sometimes one has the impression that Mr.
Auden inhabits an entirely verbal world, and that this
gives the new beliefs which he now holds an effortless
facility', as Spender phrased it ('Spectator', 29 February 1952) (seeming to find reasons for treating as a
strength what he would otherwise have considered Auden's
weakness of detachment or impersonality) - along with an
access of wit or waggery apparently disguising pomposity
or clever solemnity. G.S. Fraser approvingly noted that
Auden 'has never written with more confident ease than
here', yet went on to echo Spender's querulousness,
'What we are left in doubt about, I suppose, is the
nature of Mr. Auden's first-level responses' (No. 105).
Most critics, it appears, could not readily accommodate
themselves to Auden's wry, ironic, meditative tone, which
struck some of them, such as Joseph Clancy ('Thought',
Winter 1952-3), as a kind of ease and tranquillity, but
others as complacency. The majority none the less showed
an astutely high regard for the poem called 'In Praise of
Limestone', which Spender called 'the perfect fusion between Auden's personality and the power of acute moral observation of a more generalized psychological situation,
which is his great gift' ('Poetry', Chicago, September
1951). Daiches alone deprecated it as loose and ultimately
boring.

While Robert Fitzgerald first hopefully discerned the
mature, Horatian mode that would characterize much of the
later Auden -

> It is possible at times, at last, to hear a sincere man
> speaking as a spirit self-known might speak, in an
> idiom which past resources have gone to refine and to
> make dance, so that one listens as to Horatian or
> Mozartian casualness in motion. ('Hudson Review',
> Summer 1951)

- the anonymous critic of the 'TLS' (4 July 1952) expressed a corresponding worry about 'the uneasy mingling
of cleverness and solemnity' which proved just as pre-
cursory.

Saxe Commins, Auden's American editor, provided one of
the fairest and most friendly views of the next volume,
'Shield of Achilles' (1955), in his private notes: (153)

> This is at first glance a demoniacally gifted,
> strangely allusive, witty, brilliant, and tantalizingly
> suggestive collection of poems.... Auden is undoubtedly
> the most gifted of living poets, flawless when he wants

to be and only faltering over his own prodigious virtuosity. One does not remember his poems: one is impressed, overawed and a little dumbfounded by them.
After all the layers are peeled, there remains a core
of solid idea and purpose.

Supportive reviewers like Karl Shapiro (No. 108)
favoured Auden's sage and witty posture, and cheered above
all the new reflective maturity of the Horae Canonicae
sequence. Horace Gregory, in common with Babette Deutsch,
pointed out what he considered the perfectly acceptable
and delightful irony that the sequence seemed 'less religious ... than worldly and adroit' (No. 109), while at
least half the critics, including 'The Times', G.S. Fraser,
Donald Davie, and Philip Larkin, took the contrary view of
questioning Auden's real concern, his lack of personal
immediacy, and what Robert Graves called his 'zinc-bright
influence', (154) his indulgence in playfulness and even
misplaced frivolity. That common view is recapitulated in
Wit and Whimsy ('TLS', 20 January 1956), an article which
points out that 'The chief stylistic link with the earlier
volume ['Nones'] is to be found in a kind of discursive
rumination, slack in form and rhythm and often dangerously
diffuse', and adds that in Horae Canonicae a 'deeper
maturity and insight only control the technique spasmodi-
cally: there is a tendency to lapse back into eclectic
reminiscence, irresponsible smartness, or a display of
miscellanous knowledge'. In contrast, Donald Davie considered that 'this sort of ritual recitative is surely
Auden's best bet for the future; and I hope I am wrong in
suspecting ... that this poet has made his peace with
society too wholeheartedly and too soon' (No. 111).
    Most critics of 'Homage to Clio' (1960) were content
to acquiesce in Auden's combination of the serious and
the silly, what F.W. Dupee called the 'solemn and breezy'
('New York Times', 15 May 1960), and Dom Moraes, 'whimsy
and slight dullness' ('Time and Tide', 9 July 1960).
Ernest Sandeen exercised himself to prove that Auden
showed both the 'gay detachment' of a Christian poet and
the cheerfully cultivated tastes of an English gentleman
('Poetry', March 1961). Donald Hall summed up the well-
disposed reception by terming the book 'a civilised
pleasure' (No. 114), and F.W. Dupee took the most lenient
view of what he called 'a regular variety show'.
    In contrast, from opposite sides of the Atlantic, the
influential voices of Thom Gunn and Philip Larkin seriously refused to share any critical complacency about the
ripening Auden. Writing in the "Yale Review', Gunn (No.
117) severely reprimanded Auden for surrendering 'active

intelligence' to 'the habit of continual trifling ... the acceptance of an attitude similar to Betjeman's appears to have led Auden to write poetry that is both morally and technically frivolous: gracious living has become a moral value in it, and he tolerates the easiest way out with diction and meter except when he imagines he is writing in the eighteenth century'. Larkin, who was to become Betjeman's best advocate, had earlier criticized 'Bucolics' ('Shield of Achilles') - 'They are garrulous, playful-sentimental, and get nowhere' ('Listener', Summer 1956) - and regretfully traced Auden's deterioration 'from the powerfully-suggestive, elliptic originality of 1930 to the silly verbose stew of the present day', which he attri-buted to Auden's departure from England. His opinion of 'Homage to Clio' accorded with Gunn's: 'Auden, never a pompous poet, has now become an unserious one ... lack of serious intention too often means lack of serious effect. In the end that is what our discontent comes down to: Auden no longer touches our imaginations' (No. 115).

With few exceptions - C.B. Cox, for example, who largely felt comfortable with the later Auden (No. 119) - critics were even more saddened by 'About the House' (1965, 1966), mostly for what they considered its cosy, condescending expression of civility, mechanical verse, lack of conviction, and a prevalent silliness. Even his defenders conceded that Auden's discovery of a comfor-table home and a style to match endangered this 'witty, ironic, and skilfully contrived collection', as Howard Sergeant called it: 'its relaxed conversational tone seldom creates the tensions to be found in Auden's earlier work...' ('English', 16). John Press ('Punch', 23 March 1966), who otherwise admired the mature Auden and his 'technical wizardry', spoke for a commonly felt re-gret: 'What grates so often in these poems is the tone, the mixture of portentous dogmatism and arch playfulness'; but John Updike, finding something agreeable about Auden's 'sense of poetry as a mode of discourse between civilized men' and 'a new frankness and a new relaxation in tone', provided the most elegant apologia for the tri-viality and snobbery other critics found indefensible (No. 118), characteristics which the 'TLS' sternly rebuked (17 March 1966) and which John Fuller, like most critics, at once elegized and admonished ('London Magazine', April 1966).

The publication of 'Collected Shorter Poems 1927-1957' (1966, 1967) and 'Collected Longer Poems' (1968, 1969) gave enthusiasts such as John Unterecker ('Massachusetts Review') the opportunity to rehearse their praise for favourite Auden poems, though almost all reviewers took more or less severe exception to the fact that Auden had omitted from the former volume those poems which he considered 'dishonest, or bad-mannered, or boring'. John Whitehead, for example, made a detailed and largely negative examination of what he considered in part Auden's 'curmudgeonly' editing, which Auden himself irritatedly explained in conversation with David Pryce-Jones: 'People got stuck in the Thirties, they want you to go on doing the same kind of thing and they don't like you to do something else. It's my privilege to revise.'(155) He would presumably have endorsed Hugh Kenner's remark that 'When he revises it is to improve the surface', though he might not have been so willing to assent to the unavoidable, if simplistic, postulate, 'The effects are on the surface' ('National Review', 26 December 1967). But Auden's justification for revising his published works fully satisfied no one, and even friendly critics such as Graham Martin found it questionable: 'This separation of thought and language hardly explains earlier revisions, but seems a fair account of the tidying-up spirit at work in this volume, the correction of clumsy grammar, and inexplicable punctuation of many 1950 texts...' ('Listener', 23 February 1967). Francis Berry endorsed Martin's conclusion - 'The vague suggestive imagery of some early poems [has] been given the allegorical explicitness of the post-1948 writing' - with the comment, 'A trouble for the later Auden must be that it is so difficult not to write Audenesque; not to hear and re-write the voice, with its distinctive *timbre*, at a standard parsonical level' ('Tablet', 31 December 1966).

In an effort to isolate and evaluate the 'Audenesque' in Auden (*aet.* 60), reviewers commonly identified parody as a chief constituent, along with what Richard Mayne called 'oddities and lapses' that Auden employed for **fear** of pomposity or self parody (No. 124). Jeremy Robson **des**cribed those very features as 'props' which Auden successfully used to modernize and dramatize his shorter poems (No. 125). Graham Hough, who felt that 'all [Auden's] poems until the war are in a sense parodies', agreed with Robson and other critics in perceiving 'a visible gap between the style and the message' (which Auden's own essays and interviews, after all, curiously confirmed), but radically disagreed with Robson by describing Auden's elements of parody not as 'props' but as positive 'weapons': 'Auden is like Byron in that he is always at his most serious when his manner is most uncommitted. Slapdash, parody, self-parody, are his weapons in a real engagement; and the fanciful self-indulgences always have a moral in attendance' ('Critical Quarterly', Spring 1967).

THE FINAL PHASE: 1969-73

In reviewing 'City Without Walls' (1969), Roy Fuller reversed the terms of Hough's earlier notice: 'Auden, in
fact, is a great comic poet of the Augustan cast. There
has been nothing like him in English since those days,
for the comparison with Byron will not do, the latter being fundamentally slapdash and simple' ('New Statesman
and Nation', 1969). For all the critics who disliked the
work of the 'veteran' Auden (which loosely came to include most of his output of the 1950s and 1960s), its
Augustan or Horatian vein, its Goethean range of interests
(or at least its eclectic allusiveness), and its evincing
of the virtues of common sense and good manners, just as
many critics allied themselves to praise Auden's continuing ability to exercise a many-sided craft. Among his best
advocates was Monroe K. Spears, the author of the first
impartial and thoroughly informed commentary, 'The Poetry
of W.H. Auden: The Disenchanted Island' (1963), a book
which remains invaluable to this day. Spears's review of
'City Without Walls', however, included uncritical mention
of 'Elegy in Memoriam Emma Aiermann' (Auden's Austrian
housekeeper) - 'neither condescending nor sentimental'
(No. 128) - and yet it was that very poem which caused
John Fletcher to smart at its evidence of 'sentimentality'
and 'coyness' (No. 127).
    Critics who deplored the domestic complacency of the
later Auden might have found fuel for their prejudices,
but the more substantial debate latterly focused on
whether or not Auden should be taken as a serious poet,
now or indeed from the beginning. The anonymous reviewer
in 'Time' (26 January 1970) urged that it was Auden's 'refusal to give up possibilities that makes single-minded,
typecasting critics suspect him of essential frivolity....
Today's readers should be more inclined to accept Auden's
virtuosity without imputing shallowness. He is serious,
if not deadly - and who, save [Robert] Lowell perhaps,
can match him for compassion and complexity?' (156)
John Bayley, in an interesting and unprejudiced thesis,
argued to the contrary that Auden is essentially unserious, since his inventiveness is predicated upon lack
of personal commitment or engagement: 'The poetry that
begins in "contraption" ... may ... end in revelation,
but it will not get there by way of seriousness, profound
or otherwise' (No. 126). While Bayley would presumably
have endorsed 'Time's' belief that Auden's 'true voice is
to try all voices', he would have done so with the proviso that such a procedure actually goes against seriousness of purpose. Although it might superficially appear

that critics disputed a semantic scruple, their dif-
ferences of opinion, which caught up a good many voices
reaching back via Beach and Jarrell to the 1930s, in fact
made a fundamental discrimination between Auden as a comic
conjurer and savant and Auden as a frivolous adventurer,
immature and irresponsible.

No critic differed from Martin Dodsworth's view that
Auden had become 'dictionary-drunk' in 'Epistle to a
Godson' (1972), and most reviewers seemed quite content to
accept him as an ageing entertainer, part jester and part
valedictory sage, despite his penchant for being (as
Dannie Abse put it in the 'Sunday Times', 8 October 1972)
'ostentatious' in language, with 'obvious mannerisms' and
'irritatingly camp' remarks. Philip Toynbee spoke for the
favourable consensus in characterizing the latest Auden
persona as 'impeccably good-humoured and kindly, yet
sceptical, caustic, teasing and epigrammatic' ('Observer',
8 October 1972). Christopher Ricks in 'Parnassus' (1, 2,
1972) likewise appreciated Auden's 'new lease of liveliness', as did Robert Nye ('The Times', 12 October 1972),
and Denis Donoghue (No. 131). Norman Nicholson ('Church
Times', 22 December 1972) concurred with Frank Kermode
(No. 129) in cheering Auden as a 'lover of order', and
with Roy Fuller in acclaiming the book as 'dazzling'
(Daily Telegraph', 2 November 1972). John Bayley agreeably
observed that Auden had wed a style of address with a relaxed personality ('Books and Bookmen'). Two strong voices,
however, deplored what they perceived as the radical limitations of the latest Auden manner: Terry Eagleton ('Tablet', 1 December 1972), and Edna Longley in the 'Irish
Times', 4 November 1972:

> Auden seems to have softened into a mellow garrulity,
> his favourite medium uncorseted alcaics which barely
> nudge into shape the flow of chat and reminiscence....
> Today his thematic larder is curiously bare; small
> personal preoccupations rather than a grand imaginative
> urgency seem to have driven him into print ... we ex-
> pect more from Auden than skilful fantasy, humorous
> old fogeyness, and an uncoordinated miscellany of poems
> ranging from one Jabberwocky jeu d'esprit to the pom-
> pous hymn to the United Nations.

Though a majority of reviewers had felt indulgent towards 'Epistle to a Godson', few extended the favour to
'Thank You, Fog', Auden's final, posthumous collection of
poems. Apart from loyal notices by critics like Nigel
Dennis and Geoffrey Grigson, even other supporters such
as Philip Toynbee and John Fuller (No. 133) acknowledged

that Auden had resigned his gifts, though their reservations drew far short of Frederick Grubb's brief, earnest
dismissal ('Tribune', 17 January 1975) of a 'liberal deity
who, unsmart himself, does encourage a certain type of
smart, city rubbish'. Echoing the accusations of Leavis
and Auden's earliest Left-wing critics combined, Terry
Eagleton berated 'an overbred irresponsibility which
threatens to dwindle the substance of a poem to empty
technical acrobatics' and Auden's 'historically obsoles-
cent postures', as well as generally scorning the characteristic late Auden stance ('Tablet', 23 November 1974).
Even Philip Toynbee, however, though on different grounds,
felt he had to 'account for the dismay so many of the
oldest admirers of this marvellous poet have felt at the
note of unreality which had crept into too much of his
later verse' (No. 132).

POSTHUMOUS STANDING AND LONGER STUDIES

Auden's postumous standing has been well served by the
scholarship of his literary executor, Edward Mendelson,
who established the canon with 'Collected Poems' (1976),
a volume which unavoidably roused reviewers to write
sweeping synopses of Auden's career. The majority opinion
- which included Peter Ackroyd ('Spectator'), John Heath-
Stubbs (who was careful to put on record in the 'Tablet',
23 October 1976, that he and his contemporaries at Oxford
in 1939 did not read Auden but preferred neo-symbolism or
the apocalyptic surrealism of Dylan Thomas), Philip
Toynbee ('Observer'), Naomi Mitchison ('Books and Bookmen'),
and David Wright ('Times Educational Supplement') - opted
in favour of Auden's early, 'English' phase over his later
work. The consensus of critical views of 'Collected Poems'
is epitomized in the title of David Bromwich's essay, An
Oracle Turned Jester ('TLS', 17 September 1976). Seamus
Heaney, for instance, spoke for a representative view in
arguing that Auden's 'original clipped and speedy utterance' gave way to 'a flourish of personality and intelligence ... work in which the self is forced to make all the
running' (No. 134).

   Through no fault of his own, Mendelson's next edition,
'The English Auden' (1978), inevitably catered to that
critical weighting in favour of the thirties, despite the
fact that critics such as Geoffrey Grigson and Philip
Toynbee cavilled with the title (others, such as Julian
Symons, approved it). Certainly, Auden did not share the
exclusive partiality most of his critics have come to feel
for his poetry of the 1930s. 'If they want to say I am a

burnt-out old poet, whose best work was done in the
thirties,' he told Tim Devlin (157) shortly after the publication of 'Epistle to a Godson', 'it is their business
not mine', a view he explained by reference to his age:
'My style is bound to be different. As soon as I have
learnt to do a certain thing more or less to my satisfaction, I change to something else, a new form, new
words.'

While there has been no shortage of books devoted
wholly or partly to Auden's poetry, it is significant that
no book has yet satisfactorily treated the entire span.
The foremost study to date is Edward Mendelson's eloquent
'Early Auden' (1981), which provides an authoritative exposition of Auden's poems and plays of the 1930s (he promises a further volume dealing with the later work), and
thanks to Samuel Hynes's admirably lucid 'The Auden Generation' (1976), the broader literary context of Auden's
writings has largely been recovered.

Among the first books, Francis Scarfe's 'Auden and
After' (1942) underlined Auden's indebtedness to Eliot and
relegated Auden in the balance, but it did reaffirm that
'Auden corresponds to a real phase and state of mind in
his generation'. Time has scarcely served, however, to
sustain certain of Scarfe's other interim verdicts, including his opinions that 'Auden is the only young writer
today who has the makings of a first-class dramatist', and
that 'Auden's general position is nearer to Anarchism than
to either Marxism or Christianity'. In view of the fact
that Eliot was one of Auden's models (158) and his first
professional patron, it is curious to discover that Eliot
apparently endorsed Scarfe's off-key conclusions, as John
Hayward recorded at the time: (159) 'Herbert Read, by the
way, is publishing "Auden and After" by Francis Scarfe in
the summer. He recommends it warmly and tells me that Tom
has given it his approval. ("Even Tom growled his
approval"). The book deals with the old Pylon Boys, with
the Surrealist gang....' D.S. Savage, in a chapter of 'The
Personal Principle' (1944) called The Strange Case of W.H.
Auden, wrote what might have struck his less behindhand
contemporaries as this démodé opinion echoing Christopher
Caudwell's criticisms: 'Although he deeply distrusts the
values of his class, he remains tied to it. His weakness
as a poet derives from his lack of a sense of inner validity, that lack which expresses itself negatively in exhortation, satire and moralism.' Still, Auden's critical
stock was somewhat increased by 'Auden: An Introductory
Essay' (1951), the first full-length study of his work,
although Richard Hoggart acknowledged that his view of
what he called 'the rough line of [Auden's] development

(160) derived much from R.G. Lienhardt's critical
'Scrutiny' review of 'For the Time Being'. 'Meanwhile his
achievement is not slight', Hoggart rather half-heartedly
judged. (161)

> He has written a few poems memorable by the strictest
> standards. By his skill and energy he did much to en-
> liven English verse in the 'thirties, and his present
> experiments may well do even more for the 'fifties. He
> has produced some fine songs, and been unusually suc-
> cessful in light ironic verse. Much of his work is
> faulty, but almost all of it reveals important qualities
> of imagination....
>   We may sometimes feel that his view is distorted....
> He is, after all, an 'intellectual of the middle
> classes'; he may possess certain personal character-
> istics which make him hardly a representative contem-
> porary individual. Nevertheless, he is a significant
> figure....

It is not surprising that Auden commented only, 'Oh dear',
when Geoffrey Grigson told him that Hoggart's book had been
published. (162)
    Later books have fortunately been more forceful in
pressing greater claims for Auden. At least three critics –
Gerald Nelson, George W. Bahlke, and Justin Replogle –
have tried to establish the central importance of Auden's
poetry after 1940, Replogle in the eccentric but not unten-
able conviction that 'ideas, personae, and style fit har-
moniously together' in 'his greatest achievement, the late
comic poetry'. François Duchêne, in his intelligent study,
'The Case of the Helmeted Airman', argues that 'Whatever
its superficial temptations, [Auden's art] has been fired
by an underlying conflict to which an artistic ethic of
detachment is a form of adaptation', and likewise concludes
by praising 'the powerful relevance of the comic vision
[and] the scope of Auden's achievement in re-rooting it in
a new environment'. Among other books, John Fuller's valuable 'A Reader's Guide to W.H. Auden' includes a detailed
exegesis of 'Collected Shorter Poems' and 'Collected Longer
Poems'. One other exercise may be mentioned here, an essay
in revisionism by Arnold Rattenbury, (163) who argues:

> The sillinesses, the dog-marx, the simplifications to
> points beyond absurdity which orthodoxy now attacks
> were those of Sentiment then, and were attacked by
> Reason then. So it is Sentiment now that describes the
> way itself behaved in the Thirties, says there was no
> other behaviour than its own, ignores what doesn't
> fit....That the Thirties were made of Auden and friends

and such influences as reached them is as unlikely a
notion as daft.... It's hard for me to say other than
that Randall Swingler wrote from the centre of his
times, while Auden wrote roundabout. His achievement
seems to me - from what and where I was - colossal because of what he attempted; Auden's, at least until his
later academic frivolities, matchless at attempting
less.

Whatever similarly impressive correctives may in time
be offered (164),. however, most witnesses have so far over-
whelmingly proved what impresses me as the more viable
view of another contemporary, Christopher Gillie, that
'talented writers of like sympathies who cohered about
[Auden] ... gave the generation of the thirties - or at
least that part of it that sought a projection of its
moods and preoccupations - a self-diagnosis and a kind of
public confessional'. (165)
The critical issues raised by the kind and quality of
Auden's work assuredly deserve continuing attention, digestion and interpretation. Adverse critics have quarrelled with his subjects and attitudes ever since he appeared to be a gentleman rather than a player in the political contests of the 1930s, and then again when he supposedly turned his coat in the 1940s, but Auden himself
set the greatest store by the aesthetic-technical aspects
of his achievement. It is fair to point out that no critic
has yet emerged to match him on his own provocatively and
indeed irritatingly restrictive terms: 'Every poet has his
dream reader: mine keeps a look out for curious prosodic
fauna like bacchics and choriambs.' (166) It is equally
relevant to say that the vast critical debate in newspapers and little magazines, which is perhaps unprecedented in public influence, will remain indispensable to a
full understanding not only of contemporary literary attitudes but also of the political and social milieu, particularly of the 1930s and 1940s, in which Auden found expression and his audience. To say the least, Edward
Mendelson's scrupulous and excellent editing of 'Collected
Poems' and 'The English Auden' urges the interest of
Auden's honourably Oxonian ordinance that 'You really cannot tell fully about a thing until the man's work is all
there'. (167)

NOTES

1 Letter to Haffenden from Lincoln Kirstein: 'I think
   he liked Edmund Wilson; I know he liked Grigson, but

I don't think their judgement of his writing had much
effect on him' (22 August 1979).

2   Letter to Haffenden from Rex Warner, 17 August 1979.
3   Letters to Haffenden from: Lincoln Kirstein (as note
    1); William Coldstream (31 August 1979); Janet Adam
    Smith (28 June 1979); James Stern (21 June 1979);
    Jason Epstein (27 June 1979); and Dr John B. Auden
    (7 September 1979): 'Wystan's objections were really
    against those critics whose concern was not so much
    to show an understanding of some writing as to ad-
    vertise their own self-inflated importance, and to be
    clever at someone else's expense. That he never did
    himself.'
4   S. Raichura and A. Singh, A Conversation with W.H.
    Auden, 'Southwest Review', 60, 1975, pp. 29-30.
5   Letter, as note 1 above.
6   Ursula Niebuhr recalled, 'He also showed a lordly dis-
    regard for all reviews and criticism. I suggested this
    was sinful pride. Reinhold envied his self-
    sufficiency.... But all this had no effect on Wystan
    whatsoever. He would smile benignly and concede no-
    thing' ('W.H. Auden: A Tribute', ed. Stephen Spender,
    London: Weidenfeld & Nicolson, 1975, p. 115). Like-
    wise, Louis Kronenberger: 'Wystan's response to praise
    was a pleased grunt, with a second grunt to end
    matters...' (ibid., p. 156).
7   V.S. Yanovsky, W.H. Auden, 'Antaeus', Autumn 1975,
    p. 115.
8   Christopher Isherwood, 'Lions and Shadows', London:
    Hogarth Press, 1938; rpt London: New English Library,
    1968, 1974, p. 119.
9   Spender, letter to Haffenden, 10 June 1979.
10 For a stern critical revaluation of Auden's first
    pamphlet, see Moira Megaw, Auden's First Poems,
    'Essays in Criticism', 25, iii, pp. 378-82.
11 'Criterion', ix, 36, January 1930, pp. 268-90.
         C. Day-Lewis wrote to his friend, L.A.G. Strong,
    in January 1930, 'Did you see Auden's play in the
    "Criterion" - balmy, but full of good stuff; his
    style is amazingly homogeneous considering the number
    of his influences...' (quoted in Sean Day-Lewis,
    'C. Day-Lewis: An English Literary Life', London:
    Weidenfeld & Nicolson, 1980, p. 64.
12 See T.S. Eliot, The Criterion (1948), reprinted in
    'Selected Prose', ed. John Hayward, Harmondsworth:
    Penguin, 1953, pp. 228-30.
13 Isherwood, 'Lions and Shadows', p. 119. With respect
    to 'Poems', Auden wrote to another young friend, the
    author Edward Upward, on 6 October 1930: 'I shall

never know how much in these poems is filched from
you via Christopher' (quoted in Alice Prochaska,
'Young Writers of the Thirties', London: National Portrait Gallery, 1976, p. 9. See Upward's interesting
memoir, Remembering the Earlier Auden, 'Adam', xxxix,
379-84, 1973-4, pp. 17-22.

14 Naomi Mitchison, 'You May Well Ask, A Memoir 1920-
1940', London: Gollancz, 1979, p. 119.

15 Ibid.

16 Auden's growing disgruntlement with 'The Orators' culminated in the famous comment, 'My name on the title-
page seems a pseudonym for someone else, someone
talented but near the border of sanity, who might
well, in a year or two, become a Nazi' (Foreward,
'The Orators', 3rd edn., London: Faber & Faber, 1966,
p. 7).

17 Stephen Spender, 'World Within World', 1951; rpt
London: Faber & Faber, 1977, pp. 51, 53, 55.

18 Ibid., p. 115.

19 An Interview with W.H. Auden, 'Arts in Society' (University of Wisconsin), 12, 1975, p. 366. Auden's
literary conservatism has recently been emphasized by
Matthew Hodgart: 'whereas [Dylan] Thomas and [Samuel]
Beckett belonged to the avant garde, Auden and his
friends and followers were literary conservatives.
Their political views and sexual behaviour may have
looked excessively liberated, but they were really
middle-of-the-road, Horace-and-Hardy men at heart...'
(The Age of the Audenesque, 'TLS', 1 December 1978,
p. 1403).

20 John Lehmann, 'The Whispering Gallery', London: Longmans, Green, 1955, p. 171.

21 Lehmann to Julian Bell, 24 December 1931, quoted in
Peter Stansky and William Abrahams, 'Journey to the
Frontier', London: Constable, 1966, p. 76.

22 P. Fry and J.W. Lee, An Interview in Austin with
John Lehmann, 'Studies in the Novel', 3, 1, Spring
1971, pp. 88-9, 96.

23 Stephen Spender, 'World Within World', pp. 138-9.
    In a tribute to Auden, Spender pooh-poohed the very
notion that Auden would have thought of himself as
commanding a group: 'even as an undergraduate he hated
literary movements, manifestos, politics and power.
He thought of nothing corresponding to the Imagism of
Ezra Pound or the Vorticism of Wyndham Lewis. He did
not, like D.H. Lawrence, attempt to run his friends'
lives. He was a bit oracular and something of a
psychoanalyst, perhaps, in the minds of friends who
went to him to show him their poems and to be provided

with the psychosomatic diagnoses of their pimples. In
the psychoanalytic role, however, he was, as a young
man, always extremely funny, buffoon-like, self-
parodying' (W.H. Auden, 'New Statesman', 5 October
1973, p. 478).

Auden's old school-friend John Pudney likewise
quotes one of Auden's letters on the subject of dis-
respecting cliquishness: 'The problem is particularly
bad in a city like London, which is so large that the
only group you can find is living with your own kind,
those mentally like you. This is disastrous, you end
up by hating each other. The whole value of a group
is that its constituents are as diverse as possible,
with little consciously in common, plurality in
unity' ('Thank Goodness for Cake', London: Michael
Joseph, 1978, p. 50).

24 S. Raichura and A. Singh, A Conversation with W.H.
Auden, pp. 28-9.

'Every genuine poet, however minor, is unique, a
member of a class of one,' Auden wrote elsewhere,
'and any trait that two poets have in common is almost certain to be the least interesting aspect of
their poetry' (Introduction, 'Nineteenth Century
Minor Poets', London: Faber & Faber, 1967, p. 20).

25 Edith Sitwell, 'Aspects of Modern Poetry', London:
Duckworth, 1934, p. 239.

26 Ibid., p. 242.

27 Ibid., p. 240.

28 John Sparrow, 'Sense and Poetry', London: Constable,
1934, p. 153.

29 Ibid., pp. 154-5. Having thus pronounced that he was
in no way an adherent of Auden, Sparrow never again
published any view of his work.

30 Charles Osborne, 'W.H. Auden: The Life of a Poet',
London: Eyre Methuen, 1980, pp. 91, 93.

31 If, as seems possible, T.S. Eliot wrote the blurb
for 'The Orators', it is interesting to know that
when Auden submitted the manuscript to Faber &
Faber, Eliot had responded, 'The second part seems
to me quite brilliant though I do not quite get its
connexion with the first' (quoted in Humphrey
Carpenter, 'W.H. Auden: A Biography', London: Allen
& Unwin, 1981, p. 130). 'When "The Orators" had been
seen by Eliot, he told Auden that the first book
"seems to have lumps of St-John Perse embedded in
it"' (Carpenter, 'W.H. Auden: A Biography', p. 121).

Peter E. Firchow provides an uncategorical inquiry
into the poem in Private Faces in Public Places:
Auden's 'The Orators', PMLA, 92, 2, March 1977,

pp. 253-72. Edward Mendelson gives a succinct interpretation in Chapter 5 of 'Early Auden', London:
Faber & Faber, 1981.

32 The 'Glasgow Herald', for example, considered that
'The whole suggests a mind on the brink of collapse
...' (14 July 1932).

33 Mitchison, 'You May Well Ask', p. 121.

34 Ibid., p. 120. '[Auden] wrote to Eliot at Faber's
suggesting that a preface be inserted to apologise
for the fact that, as he put it, "this book is more
obscure than it ought to be". This draft preface also
gave an explanation of "The Orators" which differed
somewhat from the exegesis Auden had given to Naomi
Mitchison:

> The central theme is a revolutionary hero. The
> first book describes the effect of him and of his
> failure on those whom he meets; the second book is
> his own account; and the last some personal re-
> flections on the question of leadership in our
> time.

Eliot advised Auden against printing this preface,
and it was dropped; but Auden remained dissatisfied
with the book as it stood, and wrote in reply to a
reader's letter a few months later: "I didn't taken
[sic] enough trouble over it, and the result is far
too obscure and equivocal"' (Carpenter, 'W.H. Auden:
A Biography', p. 136).

35 In a further review of 'The Orators', Grigson called
it 'a very queer book indeed and very stimulating, he
has revived the virtues of dramatic writing without
its decayed incoherence and length' (Against Vulgarity, 'Yorkshire Post', 14 December 1932).

36 See also Richard Hoggart, The Long Walk: The Poetry
of W.H. Auden - 'an acute, fantastic and vigorous
squib' - in 'Speaking to Each Other' (vol. 2), 'About
Literature', London: Chatto & Windus, 1970, p. 63.

37 Edward Mendelson, Preface, 'Selected Poems', by W.H.
Auden, London: Faber & Faber, 1979, p. xii.
See also: Justin Replogle, The Gang Myth in Auden's
Early Poetry, 'Journal of English and Germanic
Studies', 61, July 1962, pp. 481-95.

38 Hayward Papers, Box 10, King's College Library,
Cambridge.

39 Philip Henderson, 'The Poet and Society', London:
Secker & Warburg, 1939, p. 205.

40 For an apparently independent discussion of the
analogy with Kipling, see Peter E. Firchow, Private

Faces in Public Places, p. 259.

41   Stephen Spender, 'The Destructive Element', London:
     Jonathan Cape, 1935, p. 236.

42   Cf. Barbara Hardy: 'When Richard Ohmann risks the
     generalisation that Auden's "interest in leftish re-
     form movements scarcely went beyond their psycho-
     logical impact on society" (in Auden's Sacred Awe,
     'Commonweal', lxxviii, May 1963) he is ignoring ...
     poems about the relationship of the personal life to
     political action' ('The Advantage of Lyric', London:
     Athlone Press, 1977, p. 101).

43   In the autumn of 1932 Auden categorically told Rupert
     Doone, 'No. I am a bourgeois. I shall not join the
     C.P.' (Berg Collection, New York Public Library;
     quoted in Carpenter, 'W.H. Auden: A Biography', p.
     153). Late in life he argued that he and his contem-
     poraries had not necessarily misapprehended Communism
     as it had been practised in the USSR: 'we thought that
     this was a typically Russian distortion, that our
     communism would be different' (Yanovsky, W.H. Auden,
     p. 127).

44   John Cornford, Left?, 'Cambridge Left', i, Winter
     1933-4, p. 25.
         D.E.S. Maxwell commented, '"A Communist to
     Others" ... is the poem that satisfied John Cornford's
     conditions for true revolutionary poetry. It was an
     essay in dropping the screen of phantasy and parable
     for directly partisan and easily comprehensible verse.
     It is impossible now to be sure whether its feeling
     was wholly and genuinely Auden's.... It is blunt,
     effective satire and worth reading, however callow
     its views' ('Poets of the Thirties', London: Routledge
     & Kegan Paul, 1969, pp. 131-2). Maxwell also argues
     the sensible case that 'Like Yeats's "system",
     Auden's eclectic use of marxist and other ideas tri-
     umphs in the poetry.... They are poems of enquiry and
     oracular reply, of postulates and suggestions, not
     dogma' (ibid., p. 142).

45   Julian Symons, 'The Thirties: A Dream Revolved',
     London: Cresset Press, 1960; revised edn, Faber &
     Faber, 1975, p. 30.

46   Michael Roberts, 'New Country', London: Hogarth Press,
     1933, p. 13.

47   Symons, 'The Thirties', p. 73.

48   In a letter of 11 October 1932 Auden rather de-
     precated Grigson's proposals for a new review which
     became 'New Verse': 'Why do you want to start a
     poetry review. Is it really as important as all that?
     I'm glad you like poetry but cant we take it a little

more lightly' (The Humanities Research Center, University of Texas at Austin; quoted in Carpenter, 'W.H. Auden: A Biography', pp. 153-4).

In 'Auden and MacNeice: Their Last Will and Testament', the authors affectionately bequeathed: 'to Geoffrey Grigson of "New Verse" / A strop for his sharp tongue before he talks' ('Letters from Iceland').

49 Writing within the decade, H.W. Häusermann scarcely discriminated beyond the face values of the politically engaged poems written by Auden and his contemporaries, arguing that a 'process of hardening in doctrine ... threatens to submerge the poetry in propaganda' (Left-Wing Poetry: A Note, 'English Studies', 21, October 1939, p. 207), a reading corrected over thirty years later by A. Kingsley Weatherhead, who reasonably argues for Auden's 'insouciance' and 'the feeling one often derives from the so-called leftish poetry of the thirties that the poetic operation is disengaged from its proper subject matter' (British Leftist Poetry of the Nineteen Thirties, 'Michigan Quarterly Review', 10, Winter 1971, pp. 12-22).

50 See A. Kingsley Weatherhead, 'Stephen Spender and the Thirties', London: Bucknell UP/Associated University Presses, London, 1975, pp. 133-5, for a review of Auden's influence on other poets.

In a letter to Christopher Isherwood Spender himself played down the influence of Auden's poetry: 'I haven't got the style, nor have I got the "tour de force" power of Wystan. Because, honestly, I don't think Wystan's terrific virtuosity quite compensates for his lack of a strong, lucid, objective, free-verse style. All that writing ballads, sonnets, blank verse, rhymed couplets, seems to me a kind of fire works which is marvellous of Wystan, but of no real help to anyone else writing poetry' (Letter 23, March 7 (1935), in Stephen Spender, 'Letters to Christopher', ed. Lee Bartlett, Santa Barbara, Calif.: Black Sparrow Press, 1980, p. 74).

C. Day-Lewis acknowledged his debt to Auden as early as 1929 in 'Letter to W.H. Auden' (subsequently included in 'From Feathers to Iron', 1933), a poem to which Auden responded, 'I liked the poem immensely and was duly flattered' (quoted in Sean Day-Lewis, 'C. Day-Lewis: An English Literary Life', London: Weidenfeld & Nicolson, 1980, p. 55). In submitting the poem for consideration by the 'Realist', Day-Lewis commented to Naomi Mitchison, 'The first two parts of that poem are my "reactions' to the work of a friend

of mine; his writing is very obscure, which perhaps
accounts for the difficulties of my poem' (ibid.,
p. 59), and again to Geoffrey Grigson in 1932: 'I am
stealing some of Auden's thunder for ['The Magnetic
Mountain'], but I don't believe either of us will be
the worse for that' (ibid., p. 72).

Among the offspring of Auden's poetry, Poem XXII
(in 'Poems', 1930) subsequently started William
Empson's famous parody, 'Just a Smack at Auden' ('The
Year's Poetry', 1938, ed. D.K. Roberts and Geoffrey
Grigson, pp. 48-50), a poem which manifestly pays
tribute to the fact that from the first Auden had
attained a personal style and subject, a new voice.
Auden seemed unable to decide whether he approved of
Empson's 'Smack': in one place he called it 'a good
parody' (S. Raichura and A. Singh, A Conversation
with W.H. Auden, p. 35); in another, he commented,
'That was not really a parody; it was written in
Bill's own style' (Michael Andre, A Talk with W.H.
Auden, 'Unmuzzled Ox', 1, Summer 1972, p. 8).

For a verse discourse on Auden's style, language,
and rhetorical abstraction, see Karl Shapiro, 'An
Essay on Rime', London: Secker & Warburg, 1947,
pp. 21, 33, 39-41.

51   'TLS', 18 April 1980, p. 437.
52   British Museum, Add. MSS 53772, pp. 27, 10, 25b
     (a notebook dating from 1947).
53   Rupert Doone, The Theatre of Ideas, 'Theatre News-
     letter', VI, 29 September 1951, p. 5.

Doone's nose for a transformative play was not always infallible, however, for he later turned down
'Waiting for Godot' (interview with Vera Russell,
1979).

54   Christopher Isherwood, The Group Theatre, 'Cambridge
     Review', lix, 19 November 1937, p. 104.
55   Doone, The Theatre of Ideas.
56   See Mirko Jurak, Dramaturgic Concepts of the English
     Group Theatre: The Totality of Artistic Achievement,
     'Modern Drama', 16, June 1973, pp. 81-6.
57   See 'Bertolt Brecht in Britain', ed. Nicholas Jacobs
     and Prudence Ohlser, London: IRAT Services/TQ Publi-
     cations, 1977.

Christopher Isherwood contradicted Auden when
asked if he and Auden had seen 'Die Dreigroschenoper'
in Berlin - 'No, we never did' [the mistake is
Isherwood's, for he arrived in Berlin six months
after Auden had attended the play] - but supported
him in discountenancing the influence of Brecht on
their collaborations: 'I simply didn't know that much

about Brecht at that time. For example, if you go right back to a much earlier period, when Auden wrote "The Dance of Death", he had a speech to the audience about, "We show you death as a dancer," which sounds Brechtian on the surface, but I don't think he could possibly have read this stuff then. I don't think it was physically possible. So that, you know, maybe we influenced Brecht - who knows? If such blasphemy can be permitted' (David Lambourne, 'A Kind of Left-wing direction': an interview with Christopher Isherwood, 'Poetry Nation', 4, 1975, pp. 58, 60).

Donald Mitchell writes, 'when in 1937 Brecht was drawing up a list of people in the theatre, some of them outside Germany, with a view to a pooling of "methods, knowledge and experience", it included the names of W.H. Auden, Christopher Isherwood and Rupert Doone - the director of the Group Theatre' ('Britten and Auden in the Thirties: The Year 1936', London: Faber & Faber, 1981, p. 71). 'It is not known how many of the twenty-odd people on his list Brecht in fact approached with the idea of setting up an international "Diderot Society" to circulate papers on "theatrical science", but it is evident at this period he believed the views of Auden, Isherwood and Doone were compatible with his own. See "Brecht on Theatre, the Development of an Aesthetic". Translation and Notes by John Willett (London: Methuen, 1964), p. 106 (ibid., p. 96 note 19).

58 Interview with Robert Medley, August 1979.
59 Auden, letter to Margrit Hahnloser-Ingold, in 'Das Englische Theater und Bert Brecht', Bern, 1970, p. 87 (cited in 'Bertolt Brecht in Britain', p. 67): Chapter IV, W.H. Auden: Brechtschüler in den dreissner Jahren?, provides an important discussion of Auden's plays. See also: Sigurds Dzenitis, 'Die Rezeption deutscher Literature in England durch Wystan Hugh Auden, Stephen Spender und Christopher Isherwood', Hamburg: Hartmut Lüdke, 1972.
60 In spite of her strong reservations about Auden's work, Auden did personally thank Dilys Powell for introducing his poetry to the review pages of the 'Sunday Times' (interview with Dilys Powell, December 1979). See also headnote to No. 52 below.
61 John Pudney (d. 1977) wrote in his memoirs, 'Some of the work in the 1930 paperback 'Poems'..., which made his wide reputation, had been written and read to me at school. The volume itself made a greater impact on me than any work before or since. The tattered, thumbed text is still treasured not only for itself, but as a

symbol of some magic, bright, quick, hard, which
illuminated the autumn sky in my twenty-first year'
('Thank Goodness for Cake', 1978, p. 52).

62   Robert Medley interview.

63   It is not surprising that Auden joined with MacNeice
to leave 'the mentality of the pit / ...to Ivor Brown'
in 'Their Last Will and Testament' ('Letters from
Iceland').

64   Osborne, 'W.H. Auden', p. 102; Brian Finney, 'Christopher Isherwood: A Critical Biography', London: Faber
& Faber, 1979, p. 157.

65   Despite the mixed interest aroused by Auden's play,
the Group Theatre itself was really put on the map,
according to Robert Medley, by a belated review of
'Sweeney Agonistes' in the 'Listener', 9 January 1935
(complemented by two vivid photographs of the production by Humphrey Spender), in which Desmond
MacCarthy ably evoked the excitement he had experienced - 'the *feeling* of a haunted conscience that is
most powerfully evoked in this strange little piece -
as well as 'the symbolic suggestiveness of the masks,
and ... Mr. Doone's device of turning the audience
itself into a kind of chorus (the actors were sitting
among us)'.

66   Osbert, Edith and Sacheverell Sitwell, 'Trio', London:
Macmillan, 1938, p. 178.

67   Dilys Powell, 'Descent from Parnassus', London:
Cresset Press, 1934, p. 193.

68   'Looking back, it seems to me that the interest in
Marx taken by myself and my friends ... was more
psychological than political; we were interested in
Marx in the same way that we were interested in Freud,
as a technique of unmasking middle class ideologies,
not with the intention of repudiating our class, but
with the hope of becoming better bourgeois...'
(Auden, Authority in America, 'Griffin', iv, 3, March
1955). See also note 43 above.

69   British Museum, Add. MSS 53772, p. 9 (1947).

70   Robert Medley interview. See also Medley's important
memoir, The Group Theatre 1932-39: Rupert Doone and
Wystan Auden, 'London Magazine', 20, 10, January 1981,
pp. 47-60.

71   Osborne, 'W.H. Auden', p. 113, from a quotation in
Catalogue 114, Alan Hancox, Cheltenham. Stephen
Spender also observed, 'I only saw two or three reviews of "The Dogskin". There was a foul one in "The
Spectator". The critics are really disgraceful, because one would have thought that a chance to criticize you and Auden was worth taking seriously; but

instead of that, they chose to pounce' (Letter 26,
August 1 (1935), 'Letters to Christopher', pp. 79-80).
    Shortly after the publication of 'The Dog Beneath
the Skin', on 20 June 1935, T.S. Eliot remarked to
Virginia Woolf: 'Auden is a very nice rattled brained
boy. Some of his plays extremely good, but its superficial: stock figures; sort of Punch figures...'
('The Diary of Virginia Woolf', vol. IV: 1931-1935,
ed. Anne Olivier Bell, assisted by Andrew McNeillie;
London: Hogarth Press, 1982, p. 324).
72   Mirko Jurak, English Political Verse Drama of the
Thirties: Revision and Alteration, 'Acta Neophilo-
logica', i, 1968, pp. 69-70.
    Benjamin Britten attended the first performance of
the play at the Westminster Theatre on 12 January
1936, and recorded in his diary:

> There are some first-rate things in this - Auden's
> choruses are some of the loveliest things I know
> & the best part of the show was the speaking of
> them by Robert Speaight. As a whole the show was
> marred by Rupert Doone double-crossing the 'ts' and
> underlining every point - leaving nothing to the
> imagination - Some of the sets were lovely -
> notably the Red Light scene. Of course it was very
> much cut - but even might be more so - a lot of it
> moves too slowly I feel. [Herbert] Murrill had
> done the music very competently, but adding no-
> thing to the show, I'm afraid. It was just clever
> & rather dull jazz - not as amusing perhaps as the
> original - a common fault with satirists. (Quoted
> in Donald Mitchell, 'Britten and Auden in the
> Thirties: The Year 1936', pp. 119-20)

After seeing the production a second time in March,
Britten commented further,

> It is an excellent show - with glimpses of real
> beauty in the choruses and a lovely sense of wit
> & satire all through. Of course the moral (how
> W.H.A. loves his moral!) is more urgent than ever
> to-day - when the world is sick with fear of war,
> & yet its bloody leaders are dragging it steadily
> into it. (Ibid., p.87)

Edward Mendelson writes, 'In 1935 ... [Auden] was
sent an essay on contemporary drama, especially on
his and Isherwood's "The Dog Beneath the Skin", in
which the author, John Johnson, argued that the new

theatre hoped to change society though psychological revelation rather than by direct social action. Auden told Johnson he meant nothing of the kind: "You must of course saw what *you* think, but I do not think 'an external effort like the Russian Five Year Plan' [Johnson's dismissive reference] is quite as essential if not more so than the inner change. The kind of drama I'm trying to write has a good deal to do with my social views." A reader of "The Dog Beneath the Skin" may doubt this. When, near the end of "The Dog Beneath the Skin", a chorus insists the inner change is not enough, what it means is that the inner change ought not to be limited to the middle class' ('Early Auden', London: Faber & Faber, 1981, p. 186).

73 Lady Diana Mosley, letter to Haffenden, 31 August 1980.

74 Geoffrey Grigson, 'New Verse', 18, December 1935, p. 2.

75 Symons, 'The Thirties', pp. 79-80.

76 Quoted in Finney, 'Christopher Isherwood: A Critical Biography', p. 161. Stephen Spender offered his reading of the published text in a long letter to Christopher Isherwood; see 'Letters to Christopher', pp. 75-6.

77 Michael Newman, W.H. Auden (interview), 'Paris Review', 57, 1974, p. 54. In a letter to Rupert Doone of 5 March 1936, T.S. Eliot very much agreed with Auden's later censure of the choruses: 'What did irritate me was the chorus - not that Veronica Turleigh is not very good indeed: but these interruptions of the action become more and more irritating as the play goes on, and one tires of having things explained and being preached at. I do think Auden ought to find a different method in his next play' (Berg Collection, New York Public Library; quoted in Carpenter, 'W.H. Auden: A Biography', p. 194n).

78 Finney, 'Christopher Isherwood', p. 161.

79 Robert Medley interview.

80 Christopher Isherwood, The Art of Fiction, XLIX (interview by W.I. Scobie), 'Paris Review', 57, 1974, p. 170.

81 Isherwood, 'Christopher and His Kind', London: Magnum/Methuen paperback, 1978, p. 201.

Benjamin Britten, who wrote the incidental music for the play, recorded in his diary on 20 February 1937, 'Rehearsal [of F6] at Mercury all aft - very annoying, Rupert [Doone] is really beyond all endurance sometimes - his appalling vagueness &

quasi-surrealistic directions - & completely impractical for all his talents' (quoted in Donald Mitchell,
'Britten and Auden in the Thirties', p. 97).

Ashley Dukes, the producer, commented in his autobiography, 'Radio speakers and a listening suburban
pair made a double chorus to the tragedy, so that the
authors were able to indulge their satire and their
expressionism at the same time. From this rather uncertain background the group of Himalayan climbers
stood out as remarkable dramatic portraits of boys
one had met at school and never expected to meet
again' ('The Scene is Changed', London: Macmillan,
1942, p. 210).

82 Isherwood, 'Christopher and His Kind', p. 181.
83 Mendelson, Preface, 'Selected Poems', by W.H. Auden,
London: Faber & Faber, 1979, p. xx.
84 Finney, 'Christopher Isherwood', p. 165.
85 Anthony Thwaite, W.H. Auden: 1907-1973, 'Literary
Half Yearly', 15, i, 1974, p. 2.

For a sensible survey of Leavis's position, see
S.K. Pradhan, Literary Criticism and Cultural Diagnosis: F.R. Leavis on W.H. Auden, 'British Journal
of Aesthetics', 12, 1972, pp. 384-94. Auden himself
would not be drawn on Leavis's dismissal of his
work. When S. Raichura and A. Singh asked him in a
late interview, 'Do you think that what F.R. Leavis
wrote about you in the thirties had something to do
with the Oxford-Cambridge "needle"?', he responded,
'Your guess is as good as mine. I wouldn't know, nor
would I care to' (A Conversation with W.H. Auden,
p. 29). Stephen Spender reports, however: 'he once
remarked to me, not about Leavis on himself, but
about Leavis in general, that Leavis was a good
critic of work he liked but totally irresponsible
about work he did not like. The occasion of his telling me this arose because when I first edited
"Encounter" I asked Auden whether he thought it
would be a good idea for me to offer Leavis a column
(I'm pretty sure of course he would have refused) to
write whatever he wished in "Encounter". Auden said
this would be irresponsible on account of Leavis's
hates' (letter to Haffenden, 10 June 1979).

86 13 March 1937; Yeats explained in a further letter
(?18 March):

I did not suggest Britannia to de-bunk the hero.
Remember the English expedition is racing that of
another country because the one who gets first to
the top will, the natives believe, rule them for

a thousand years; remember also what the Abbot has said about will & about government. Brittania is the mother.

> Yrs
> W.B. Yeats

(Both letters in the Berg Collection, New York Public Library.)

Auden explained in a later interview, 'The Ascent of the mountain is a symbol of the *geste*, it can also be a symbol of the act of aggression.... It seems to me that in man's search for God he erects before him a number of images. I believe that the mother-image is one of the last to be outgrown.... In this play the protagonist dies after the appearance of the mother on the mountaintop' (Howard Griffin, A Dialogue with W.H. Auden, 'Hudson Review', 3, Winter 1951, pp. 583, 591).

87 W.B. Yeats, A General Introduction for My Work, 'Essays and Introductions', p. 525; cited in Richard Ellmann, 'Eminent Domain', New York: OUP, 1967, p. 118.

88 Ellmann, 'Eminent Domain', p. 119.

89 Ibid., p. 118.

90 Michael Andre, A Talk with W.H. Auden, p. 9.

Edward Mendelson reports, 'In 1964, when asked by Stephen Spender for a contribution to a book of essays on Yeats, Auden gave this reply:

I am incapable of saying a word about W.B. Yeats because, through no fault of his, he has become for me a symbol of my own devil of unauthenticity, of everything which I must try to eliminate from my own poetry, false emotions, inflated rhetoric, empty sonorities.

> *No poem is ever quite true,*
> *But a good one*
> *Makes us desire truth.*

His make me whore after lies'. ('Early Auden', p. 206)

91 Michael Newman, W.H. Auden, 'Paris Review', 57, 1974, p. 62.

92 J.M. Keynes, letter to Eliot, 10 May 1937; Keynes Papers (10/2), Kings College Library, Cambridge.

93 Keynes, letter to Norman Higgins (Secretary and General Manager of the Arts Theatre, Cambridge), Keynes Papers (10/6), Kings College Library, Cambridge.

94   Keynes, letter to Isherwood, 5 October 1938; Keynes
     Papers (10/8).
95   Keynes, letter to Rupert Doone, 20 October 1938;
     Keynes Papers (10/8). Doone had written to Keynes on
     19 October, 'I personally think it would be best to
     have local representatives see the play & make a
     report rather than a criticism. If it is a good re-
     port, then it will come to London with good publicity
     and with the proper dramatic critics of all the
     English press coming later.... If we only get three
     or four of the London papers, none of the other press
     would be so interested later and the edge is taken
     away for a London opening' (Keynes Papers).
96   Symons, 'The Thirties', p. 81.
97   Isherwood, 'Christopher and His Kind', p. 244.
98   T.S. Eliot, letter to Keynes, 15 November 1938; Keynes
     Papers (10/9). Eliot also suggested, 'I think the part
     of Valerian [Wyndham Goldie] might have been played
     with more subtlety...'.
99   Ashley Dukes, letter to Keynes, 15 November 1938;
     Keynes Papers. See also note 81 above.
100 Isherwood, 'Christopher and His Kind', p. 244.
101 Keynes, letter to Herbert Farjeon, Little Theatre,
     Adelphi, London, 24 November 1938; Keynes Papers
     (10/9). Keynes and Doone hoped to transfer 'On the
     Frontier' to the Little Theatre, but it eventually
     moved to the Globe Theatre in February 1939.
102 Robert Medley interview; other comments in this para-
     graph are also based on Medley's personal
     observations.
103 Symons, 'The Thirties', p. 81.
104 George Woodcock, Auden - Critic and Criticized,
     'Sewanee Review', 82, Fall 1974, p. 696.
105 See D.A. Traversi, Marxism and English Poetry,
     'Arena', 1, October-December 1937, pp. 199-211 (I
     quote from pp. 210-11).
106 Quoted in Osborne, 'W.H. Auden', p. 129.
107 Auden enthusiastically reviewed 'Illusion and
     Reality' in 'New Verse', 25, May 1937, pp. 20-2.
108 Spender, 'World Within World', p. 247-8.
109 Spender, Oxford to Communism, 'New Verse', 26-7,
     November 1937, p. 10.
110 George Orwell, 'Inside the Whale', London: Gollancz,
     1940; rpt Harmondsworth: Penguin, 1962, p. 36.
111 Ibid., p. 37.
112 Edward Mendelson (ed.), 'The English Auden', London:
     Faber & Faber, 1977, p. 425.
113 Monroe K. Spears, 'The Poetry of W.H. Auden: The Dis-
     enchanted Island', New York: OUP, 1963, p. 157.

114   Robin Skelton, 'Poetry of the Thirties', Harmonds-
       worth: Penguin, 1964, p. 41.
115   Osborne, 'W.H. Auden', p. 137.
116   An Interview with W.H. Auden, 'Arts in Society'
       (University of Wisconsin), 12, 1975, p. 366.
117   Symons, 'The Thirties', p. 112.
118   Dennis Davison, 'W.H. Auden', London: Evans Bros,
       1970, p. 51.
119   Bernard Bergonzi, 'Reading the Thirties', London:
       Macmillan, 1978, p. 54.
120   John Wain, 'Professing Poetry', London: Macmillan,
       1977, p. 83. Cf. Edward Mendelson's convincing
       interpretation of the poem in 'Early Auden' (London:
       Faber & Faber, 1981, pp. 315-23), in particular his
       discriminations between the expository and the figu-
       rative arguments of the poem: 'while the poem's mani-
       fest argument asserts that all human actions are
       chosen by the will, the metaphoric argument maintains
       that some special actions in the political realm,
       actions directed at certain social goals, are the
       product not of will but of something very much like
       unconscious instinctive nature' (p. 319).
121   'W.H. Auden to E.M. Auden, No. 2', 'Letters from
       Iceland'.
122   Louis MacNeice, 'Modern Poetry', London: OUP, 1938,
       p. 189. Stephen Spender also gave it perceptive
       praise: 'Wystan was here last night & read his
       "Byron Letter", which is much the best piece of
       political writing & the most enjoyable stuff he has
       done' (Letter 27, November 25 (1936), 'Letters to
       Christopher', p. 127).
123   Cf. 'Robert Conquest ... in the Introduction to
       "New Lines" (London, 1956), makes a vaguely grateful
       gesture about the influence of Auden's "large and
       rational talent" and then converts it into a some-
       what back-handed compliment when he comments, with
       apparent complacency, that his anthology has nothing
       "of the Auden tendency to turn abstractions into
       beings in their own right"' (Barbara Hardy, The
       Reticence of W.H. Auden, in 'The Advantage of Lyric',
       London: Athlone Press, 1977, p. 98).
124   'Though writing in a "holiday" spirit, its authors
       were all the time conscious of a threatening horizon
       to their picnic - world-wide unemployment, Hitler
       growing more powerful and a world-war more inevi-
       table. Indeed, the prologue to that war, the Spanish
       Civil War, broke out while we were there' (Auden,
       Foreword, 'Letters from Iceland', 2nd edn, London:
       Faber & Faber, 1967, p. 8).

125   'New Verse', 25, 1937.
126   Geoffrey Grigson, The Reason For This, 'New Verse',
       26-7, November 1937.
127   Skelton, 'Poetry of the Thirties', p. 35.
128   Samuel Hynes, 'The Auden Generation' (1976), London:
       Faber & Faber, 1979, p. 393.
129   Virginia Woolf, 'Collected Essays', vol. 2, London:
       Hogarth Press, 1966, pp. 171, 175.
130   Ibid., pp. 177-8.
131   W.H. Auden, The Prolific and the Devourer, 'Antaeus',
       21/22, Spring/Summer 1976, pp. 7-23, rpt, Mendelson
       (ed.), 'The English Auden'. pp. 394-406.
132   Auden later commented, 'I think Rilke has had a bad
       influence on me. I had to revise "Sonnets from China"
       to eliminate all the articles which were a result of
       his influence' (Michael Andre, A Talk with W.H. Auden,
       'Unmuzzled Ox', 1, Summer 1972, p. 7). Auden's use of
       the definite article was impugned by G. Rostrevor
       Hamilton in 'The Tell-Tale Article', London: Heine-
       mann, 1949.
133   Robert Craft, The Poet and 'The Rake', 'New York
       Review of Books', 12, December 1974, p. 33; Edward
       Mendelson, The Auden-Isherwood Collaboration,
       'Twentieth Century Literature', 22, 1976, p. 277.
134   Cf. 'One of my problems as a poet is that I don't have
       anyone I can trust fully, and I consequently revise
       and revise without direction' (quoted in André, A Talk
       with W.H. Auden, p. 10). Humphrey Carpenter records
       that 'later in his life, during the 1960s, [Auden]
       developed the habit of sending a copy of a new poem
       to whichever friends he happened to be corresponding
       with. Their enthusiasm, if they expressed it, always
       pleased him more than that of the professional
       critics.... During the 1940s he often showed his work
       in manuscript to Professor Theodore Spencer of Harvard
       University, whom, at Spencer's death, he described as
       a "trusted and not easily replaceable literary confes-
       sor" ("New York Times", 6 February 1949, book review
       section, p. 14)' ('W.H. Auden: A Biography', p. 341
       and note).
135   Auden, letter to Spender, King's College Library,
       Cambridge.
136   David Gascoyne, 'Paris Journal 1937-1939', London:
       Enitharmon Press, 1978, p. 104.
137   Benjamin Appel, The Exiled Writers, 'Saturday Review
       of Literature', 22, 19 October 1940, p. 5.
138   Quoted in John Lehmann, 'I am My Brother', London:
       Longmans, Green, 1960, p. 103.
139   Ibid., p. 104.

140   Gascoyne, 'Paris Journal 1937-1939', p. 55.

141   Golo Mann, A Memoir, in Stephen Spender (ed.), 'W.H. Auden: A Tribute', p. 101.

142   Stephen Spender, quoted in Osborne, 'W.H. Auden', p. 206-7.

143   Cyril Connolly, quoted in Item 474, Catalogue 35, Robin Waterfield Ltd, March 1980.

144   'Letter XXVII', January 1941, Hayward Papers, Box 11, King's College Library, Cambridge.

145   John Wain, 'Preliminary Essays', London: Macmillan, 1957, pp. 158-9.

146   Auden, quoted in Kenneth Lewars, 'The Quest in Auden's Poems and Plays', MA thesis, Columbia University, 1947, p. 104; cited in B.C. Bloomfield and Edward Mendelson, 'W.H. Auden: A Bibliography 1924-1969', Charlottesville: University Press of Virginia, 1972, p. 48.
      Humphrey Carpenter cites an instance of the fact that Auden used Professor and Mrs E.R. Dodds as his preceptors: '"I've finished my long poem (1700 lines)," Auden told Mrs Dodds on 21 April 1940, "and will send it you as soon as I have a rough typed copy. Will you and the Master [Dodds] go through it very carefully for intellectual errors"' ('W.H. Auden: A Biography', p. 294).

147   For what is perhaps the most thoroughgoing exposition of 'New Year Letter' as Auden's 'greatest poem', see Nathan A Scott, Jr, The Poetry of Auden, 'Chicago Review', xiii, Winter 1959, pp. 53-75. See also a notable essay by Samuel Hynes, The Voice of Exile: Auden in 1940, 'Sewanee Review', xc, 1, Winter 1982, pp. 31-52.

148   Auden, quoted in Spears, 'The Poetry of W.H. Auden', p. 154.

149   Stephen Spender observes, 'If [Auden] was virulently attacked he was inclined to diagnose the attack in terms of the attacker's psychology.' In response to Jarrell's critical onslaught, Auden commented to Spender, 'Oh, I think Jarrell must be in love with me' (Letter, Spender to Haffenden, 10 June 1979).

150   E.R. Dodds, 'Missing Persons: An Autobiography', Oxford: Clarendon Press, 1977, p. 123.

151   Auden, Foreword, in B.C. Bloomfield, 'W.H. Auden: A Bibliography: The Early Years through 1955', Charlottesville: University Press of Virginia, 1964, p. viii.

152   Trevor Huddleston, published in an edited version under the title 'Love One Another - or Die, 'Observer', 2 April 1978, p. 11.

153   Saxe Commins, quoted in Dorothy Commins, 'What is an
      Editor? Saxe Commins at Work', Chicago: University
      of Chicago Press, 1978, pp. 137-8.
154   Graves scorned Auden as a 'synthetic' poet whose early
      works had unscrupulously borrowed phrases and effects
      from the poetry of Laura Riding, and who showed his
      real talent in light verse. 'Auden's is now the pre-
      scribed style of the 'fifties, compounded of all the
      personal styles available; but he no longer borrows
      half lines, as for his first volumes. It is word here,
      a rhythm there, a rhetorical trope, a simile, an
      ingenious rhyme, a classical reference, a metrical
      arrangement. Auden's zinc-bright influence is even
      stronger than Yeats's, Pound's, or Eliot's. He has
      been saluted as the Picasso of contemporary English
      poetry; and indeed; if Auden's verse makes me feel
      uncomfortable, so (I confess) does a Picasso design,
      however firmly drawn, when I recognize the source, or
      sources, of his inspiration...' (These be Your Gods,
      O Israel!, 'Essays in Criticism', 5, ii, April 1955,
      p. 147).
          Asked about Graves's criticism late in life, Auden
      gave the cryptic reply, 'He took it back later. I gave
      it to him' (S. Raichura and A. Singh, A Conversation
      with W.H. Auden, p. 29).
155   Conversation with W.H. Auden, 'Daily Telegraph Maga-
      zine', 201, 9 August 1968, p. 22.
          Humphrey Carpenter writes, 'During 1967 the journal
      "Shenandoah" published a *Festschrift* to mark his six-
      tieth birthday; among the contributors was Naomi
      Mitchison, who criticised Auden's omission of what
      she called "essential" poems from his collections of
      his work. Auden drafted a reply, though he did not
      send it: he told her that he considered himself to be
      the only judge of what was essential, and added: "I
      expect personal friends like you, my dear, to respect
      my judgement on poetry, which is a professional judge-
      ment, rather than yours." And, of her accusation that
      he no longer wrote "memorable" poems: "If, by memora-
      bility, you mean a poem like 'Sept 1st 1939', I pray
      to God that I shall never be memorable again"' (W.H.
      Auden: A Biography', p. 418; Auden's draft letter is
      dated 1 April 1967: Berg Collection, New York Public
      Library).
156   Since 'Time' explicitly compared Auden with
      Robert Lowell, it is interesting to know that three
      years earlier Lowell had paid his own respects to the
      elder poet: 'I am most grateful for three or four
      supreme things: the sad Anglo-Saxon alliteration of

his beginnings, his prophecies that seemed the closest
voice to our disaster, then the marvelous crackle of
his light verse and broadside forms, small fires made
into great in his hands, and finally for a kind of
formal poem that combines a breezy baroque grandeur
with a sophisticated Horatian simplicity' (from Five
Tributes, 'Shenandoah', xviii, 2, Winter 1967, p. 45).

157   Tim Devlin, A Poet Out to Cause a Bit of Bother, 'The
Times', 4 November 1972. Ronald Carter compares early
and late poems by Auden in Auden Forty Years On: 'City
Without Walls', 'Agenda', 16, 2, Summer 1978, pp. 63-71.

158   See Morton Seif, The Impact of T.S. Eliot on Auden and
Spender, 'South Atlantic Quarterly', 53, January 1954,
pp. 61-9.

159   John Hayward, letter to Frank V. Morley, 'Letter LIII.
May 1942', Hayward Papers, Box 11 (JDH/FVM/58), King's
College Library, Cambridge.

Mrs Valerie Eliot kindly informs me that there are
occasional critical comments on Auden's work in the
letters of T.S. Eliot, but this material is reserved
for publication in the 'Correspondence' (letter,
7 August 1979). It would appear, however, that in
later years Eliot took a rather canny view of Auden,
as when he commented that 'the representative figure
of the Thirties is W.H. Auden, though there are other
British poets of the same generation whose best work
will I believe prove equally permanent. Now, I do not
know whether Auden is to be considered as an English
or as an American poet: his career has been useful to
me in providing me with an answer to the same question
when asked about myself, for I can say: "whichever
Auden is, I suppose I must be the other"' (American
Literature and the American Language, an address
delivered at Washington University, June 1953; in
'To Criticize the Critic', London: Faber & Faber,
1965, p. 60).

160   Richard Hoggart, 'Auden: An Introductory Essay',
London: Chatto & Windus, 1951, p. 94.

161   Ibid., pp. 217-18.

162   Geoffrey Grigson, letter to Haffenden, 29 June 1979.

163   Arnold Rattenbury, Total Attainder and the Helots, in
John Lucas (ed.), 'The 1930s: A Challenge to Orthodoxy', Sussex: Harvester Press, 1978, pp. 158-60.

164   In The Political Muse ('Books and Bookmen', November
1976, pp. 25-6), for example, Naomi Mitchison is not
merely being captious when she points out that in
'The Auden Generation' Samuel Hynes provides little or
no account of the influential figures of Huxley, Hugh
MacDiarmid, Gerald Heard, or Tom Harrisson. 'He mentions Walter Greenwood once (though not in the index),'
she writes.

'"Love on the Dole" meant far more to a much larger
audience than anything even Auden wrote can have
done.'

165   Christopher Gillie, The Critical Decade 1930-1940,
'Movements in English Literature 1900-1940', Cambridge: CUP, 1975, p. 130.

166   Reply to a Symposium on Auden's 'A Change of Air',
'Kenyon Review', 26, Winter 1964, p. 208. The whole
symposium, reprinted in Anthony Ostroff (ed.), 'The
Contemporary Poet as Artist and Critic', Boston:
Little, Brown, 1964, is uniquely interesting in presenting Auden's extended responses to criticisms of a
specific poem.

167   Remembering and Forgetting - W.H. Auden talks to
Richard Crossman about Poetry, 'Listener', 89, 22
February 1973, p. 239.

Abbreviations

CP(M)   Edward Mendelson (ed.), 'Collected Poems', by
        W.H. Auden, London: Faber & Faber, 1976.
EA   Edward Mendelson (ed.), 'The English Auden: Poems,
        Essays and Dramatic Writings 1927-1939', London:
        Faber & Faber, 1977.

'Paid on Both Sides:
A Charade'

'Criterion', January 1930

T.S. Eliot, who first published the charade in the
'Criterion', evidently placed a high value on its literary
and dramatic qualities, for he wrote to his friend
E. McKnight Kauffer on 6 January 1930,

> I have sent you the new 'Criterion', to ask you to read
> a verse play 'Paid on Both Sides', by a young man I
> know, which seems to me quite a brilliant piece of work.
> I should like to know whether you think the Gate Theatre
> would consider it - and first whether you like it your-
> self. This fellow is about the best poet that I have
> discovered in several years. (Letter in the Pierpont
> Morgan Library, quoted by permission of Mrs. Valerie
> Eliot; a shorter extract appears in B.C. Bloomfield and
> Edward Mendelson, 'W.H. Auden: A Bibliography', p. 3)

Even twenty years later, Eliot still set the greatest
store by Auden's charade as the pioneer of contemporary
verse drama: in his publisher's blurb for Auden's
'Collected Shorter Poems, 1930-1944' (1950), he claimed
that '"Paid on Both Sides" ... may be regarded as the
forerunner of contemporary poetic drama', adding that
Auden's 'influence, on both sides of the Atlantic, has
only increased year by year: he can now be justly called
"a famous poet"; and this collected volume is not only
called for but overdue'.

1. WILLIAM EMPSON ON DEFINING THE ATTITUDE OF A GENERATION
'EXPERIMENT' (CAMBRIDGE)

vii, Spring 1931, 60-1

Renowned both as a poet and as a literary critic, Empson
(b. 1906) is Emeritus Professor of English Literature at
the University of Sheffield, where he held the Chair from
1953 to 1971. During the 1930s he taught at Tokyo National
University and at the National University of Peking. His
publications include 'Seven Types of Ambiguity' (1930),
'Some Versions of Pastoral' (1935), 'Collected Poems'
(1955), 'The Structure of Complex Words' (1951), and
'Milton's God' (1961).

I must first try to outline the plot, as it is not obvious
on one's first reading. There is a blood-feud, apparently
in the North of England, between two mill-owning families
who are tribal leaders of their workmen; it is at the present day, but there are no class distinctions and no police.
John, the hero of the play, is born prematurely from shock,
after the death by ambush of his father; so as to be peculiarly a child of the feud. As a young man he carries it
on, though he encourages a brother who loses faith in it
to emigrate. Then he falls in love with a daughter (apparently the heiress) of the enemy house; to marry her would
involve ending the feud, spoiling the plans of his friends,
breaking away from the world his mother takes for granted,
and hurting her by refusing to revenge his father. Just
before he decides about it, a spy, son of the enemy house
(but apparently only her half-brother) is captured; it is
the crisis of the play; he orders him to be taken out and
shot. He then marries Anne; she tries to make him emigrate,
but he insists on accepting his responsibility and trying
to stop the feud; and is shot on the wedding day, at
another mother's instigation, by a brother of the spy.
     This much, though very compressed, and sometimes in
obscure verse, is a straightforward play. But at the crisis, when John has just ordered the spy to be shot, a sort
of surrealist technique is used to convey his motives.
They could only, I think, have been conveyed in this way,
and only when you have accepted them can the play be recognised as a sensible and properly motivated tragedy.
     The reason for plunging below the rational world at this
point is precisely that the decision to end the feud is a
fundamental one; it involves so much foreknowledge of what
he will feel under circumstances not yet realisable that it

has to be carried through on motives (or by choosing to give himself strength from apparent motives) which do not belong to what is then the sensible world he lives in. For the point of the tragedy is that he could not know his own mind till too late, because it was just that process of making contact with reality, necessary to him before he could know his own mind, which in the event destroyed him. So that the play is 'about' the antinomies of the will, about the problems involved in the attempt to change radically a working system.

He has the spy shot partly to tie his own hands, since he will evade the decision if he can make peace impossible, partly (the other way round) because it will make peace difficult, so that the attempt, if he chooses to make it, will expose him to more risk (for this seems to make it more generous), partly from a self-contempt which, in search of relief, turns outwards, and lights on the man who seems likest to himself, for he too is half a spy in his own camp; partly because he must kill part of himself in coming to either decision about the marriage, so that it seems a first step, or a revenge, to kill by an irrelevant decision the man likest him (for whom he must at the moment, from a point of view which still excites horror in him, feel most sympathy), partly because only by making a decision on some associated matter can he string himself up to know his own mind on the matter in question, partly because what is in his mind makes him feel ashamed and guilty among his supporters, so that he mistakenly thinks it necessary for his own safety to prove to them he is whole-heartedly on their side.

In this way the spy becomes a symbol to him, both of the feud itself, of which he is part, so as to make it seem contemptible, and of his own attempt to escape from the feud, which makes him seem contemptible to his own camp; and in either case the spy is both himself and his chief enemy. And having united himself with the man he despises, he must feel some remorse and self-contempt about killing him for these accidental and neurotic reasons; at any rate it puts him in the wrong, and in part makes him deserve the consequences.

And yet it is precisely the painfulness and dangerousness of these expulsive forces that make it possible for him to give birth to a decision.

Hence we sink down, in this crucial and solvent instant of decision, into a childish scheme of judgment, centring round desire for, and fear of, the mother; jealousy of, and identity with, the brother, who is also the spy; away from the immediate situation, so that younger incidental reminiscences of the author become relevant; below the

distinction between murderer and victim, so that the hero
escapes from feeling his responsibility; below intelligible
sexuality; and in the speech of the Man-Woman (a 'prisoner
of war behind barbed wire, in the snow') we are plunged
into a general exposition of the self-contempt of indecision.   Then the spy is shot, and we return, with circus
farce like the panting of recovery, into the real world of
the play; from then on he knows his own mind, and is fated
to destruction.

One reason the scheme is so impressive is that it puts
psycho-analysis and surrealism and all that, all the
irrationalist tendencies which are so essential a part of
the machinery of present-day thought, into their proper
place; they are made part of the normal and rational tragic
form, and indeed what constitutes the tragic situation.
One feels as if at the crisis of many, perhaps better,
tragedies, it is just this machinery which has been cov-
ertly employed.   Within its scale (twenty-seven pages)
there is the gamut of all the ways we have of thinking
about the matter; it has the sort of completeness that
makes a work seem to define the attitude of a generation.

'Poems'

London, September 1930

2. NAOMI MITCHISON ADVERTISES A NEW GENERATION, 'WEEKEND REVIEW'

25 October 1930, 592-4

Daughter of J.B.S. Haldane, CH, FRS, Naomi Mitchison
(b. 1897) is the widow of G.R. Mitchison (d. 1970), Labour
MP, who was made a life peer in 1964. She is prolific as
a novelist, writer of short stories, playwright, poet, historian, and writer of fiction and non-fiction for children.
     See the Introduction for a discussion of this review,
entitled The New Generation.

The poems of the post-war generation, who were still children, almost undisturbed, in 1918, are, naturally,
only just appearing. We older ones have to find an attitude towards them. A year or two before the war there was
an exhibition of French post-impressionists in London; the
foolish were shocked; the wise were puzzled but excited;
to-day Gauguin and Van Gogh are taken for granted as
masters, while others have utterly vanished.
     Reading Auden's 'Poems' I am puzzled and excited. The
very young, it seems, admire and imitate him. Dare I spot
him as a winner? He is wantonly obscure sometimes. The
'charade' which opens the book is curiously impressive,
more so on a second and third reading than at first; it is
also very dramatic, a quality one does not always find in
poetic plays. But there are passages in the middle which
seem as if they could only be understood by a psycho-analyst.
Again, in the separate poems, numbers VIII and IX, for
instance, are quite unintelligible, though with beautiful

and startling lines, which, if only one could somehow
shake oneself and catch the meaning, might light up like
rockets. But:

> To breast the final hill,
> Thalassa on the tongue,
> Snap at the dragon's tail
> To find the yelp its own.   [EA, 24]

What does that mean? Doubtless it was clear enough when
it was written, but what is the clue? This, though, shows
something of the method, the rhythm, and the rhyme forms,
here rather inchoate, but often the very satisfying con-
sonant rhymes: 'walks-works': which Wilfred Owen first
used, and Auden uses freely and un-selfconsciously. But he
can do much what he likes over rhythms; in the only completely intelligible poem, a protest and a call to action,
he swings straight into 'Locksley Hall' - and why not?

> Lawrence was brought down by smut-hounds, Blake went
>   dotty as he sang,
> Homer Lane was killed in action by the Twickenham
>   Baptist gang.

> Have things gone too far already? Are we done for?
>   Must we wait
> Hearing doom's approaching footsteps regular down
>   miles of straight... [EA, 49]

The whole poem has a young, strong, rebellious he-
quality, and indeed, that is a thing that strikes one over
and over again in the poems. They may be romantic, may be
obscure, but they have the curious, archaic maleness which
seems to me to fit in with three things: the fifth century
before Plato came and muddled it, the heroic age in Iceland
and the modern youth movement in Germany. I like that;
there is nothing anti-feminist about it, but something in
one jumps out to welcome it. The end of the 'charade' is
like a Greek tragedy ending translated into terms of the
Njal Saga, and several other poems have the same effect,
though in entirely modern terms and images, and that is
very exciting and often very beautiful.
    I should like to quote a lot of this heroic stuff,
especially from the poem beginning:

> Which of you waking early and watching daybreak [EA, 41]

But I must instead advise people to read this book and not
to get angry at once with the unintelligibility, but to re-
read and accept it as beautiful and new and a sign of the

times, and hope that Auden will go on and keep unmuddled -
for I am almost sure his ideas are clear, though he chooses
to express them at present in unexplained symbols, perhaps
too economically. If this is really only the beginning,
we have perhaps a master to look forward to. Here definitely is someone perfectly at ease with English words,
ancient and modern, and with the rhythms and rhymes that
for some reason, perhaps physiological, appeal to the
Zeitgeist just now. The country is not going to the dogs
after all.

3. DILYS POWELL, FROM A REVIEW ON NEW POETRY, 'SUNDAY TIMES'

28 December 1930, 8

Dilys Powell (b. 1901) is perhaps best celebrated for her
film criticism in 'Sunday Times' and other periodicals.
Her publications include 'An Affair of the Heart' (1957),
'The Villa Ariadne' (1973), and 'Descent from Parnassus'
(1934), which includes a consideration of Auden on pp.
173-94.

There is some extremely interesting work in a new series
of paper-covered volumes of verse published by Faber and
Faber. Mr. W.H. Auden, for one, is a young poet who commu-
nicates his excitement to his readers. His verse is often
obscure; partly as the result of the compression of heterogeneous images, partly because he does not always give the
link between two disparate thoughts. A 'charade', 'Paid on
Both Sides', reminiscent of the Irish 'troubles', has something of the nightmarish quality of a scene from 'Ulysses'.
It has also a great variety in technique including some
skilful experiments in the kind of dissonances with which
Wilfred Owen was so successful:-

      The Spring unsettles sleeping partnerships,
      Foundries improve their casting process, shops
      Open a further wing on credit till
      The winter. In summer boys grow tall
      With running races on the froth-wet sand,
      War is declared there, here a treaty signed;
      Here a scum breaks up like a bomb, there troops
      Deploy like birds.   [EA, 7]

I shall look anxiously for Mr. Auden's future work.

4. MICHAEL ROBERTS ON AN APPROACH TO INTEGRATION, 'ADELPHI'

December 1930, 251-2

According to T.S. Eliot's blurb for 'Essays' (Spring 1937),
Michael Roberts (1902-48) 'established himself as the most
authoritative critic of contemporary poetry with his
"Critique of Poetry"', and deserved to be called 'not only
a philosophical poet, but a philosopher...'. Equally accomplished as an anthologist, teacher, scientific and social
commentator, ecologist, and mountaineer, he took a principal part in establishing the Movement of the 1930s with
two watershed anthologies, 'New Signatures: Poems by Several Hands' (1932) and 'New Country' (1933) - which together
distributed over 4,000 copies by 1935. In his Preface to
'New Signatures', Roberts commented, 'Mr. Auden's "Poems"
and Mr. Day-Lewis's "From Feathers to Iron" were, I think,
the first books in which imagery taken from contemporary
life consistently appeared as the natural and spontaneous
expression of the poet's thought and feeling'. In addition
to 'Critique of Poetry' (1934), his works include 'Poems'
(1936), 'The Modern Mind' (1937), 'T.E. Hulme' (1938), and
'The Faber Book of Modern Verse' (1936). He worked as a
schoolteacher for most of his adult life, ending as
Principal of the College of St Mark and St John in Chelsea,
London. In a review of the recently issued 'Selected Poems
and Prose', by Michael Roberts (ed. Frederick Grubb, 1980),
C.J. Fox saliently comments:

> The MacSpaundays must have found him an exasperating big
> brother since, despite his intense concern for solving
> the grimly obvious ills of the day, he was deeply sus-
> picious of, in his widow's words, 'the politics of ges-
> ture and emotion, the whole rhetoric of the Left ...
> in so far as they were an easy way out, an excuse for
> not taking the trouble to know, a refuge from hard
> thinking, and an escape from a situation's real com-
> plexity'. (Renaissance Man, 'PN Review', 7, 3, 1980,
> 53)

This review, entitled 'Threshold of the Desert', con-
siders five books of verse, and includes a view of
T.S. Eliot's translation of 'Anabase' ('Anabasis'), by
St-J. Perse, immediately before this comment on Auden.

Mr. Auden's poetry also requires more than one reading, but
for a different reason: it expresses thought stripped to
essentials.   After clothing it in commentary and eluci-
dation, the reader realizes that, after all, the words
themselves gave the exact thought and the strict emotion.
Thus Mr. Auden laments virtues once purposeful, necessary
to life, now revered as decorations, accomplishments, independent and meaningless Virtues:

> And what was livelihood
> Is tallness, strongness
> Words and longness,
> All glory and all story
> Solemn and not so good.   [EA, 34]

He makes no use of facile music or coloured visual imagery but shows 'Life stripped to girders, monochrome.'
Although the syntax and absence of visual imagery often
recalls the work of Miss Riding, Mr. Auden has too strong
a faith in human reason to have any need of the peevish
and sometimes deliberately childish Socratic laughter of
that poet.   Occasionally he makes a futile gesture of
impatience with the old gang, and uses words like 'entropic'
without the appropriate strictness, but in general he
resembles Mr. Herbert Read in integrity, clear-headedness,
and determination not to take shelter in ranting, fine
writing, or weary acceptance of an alien faith:

[Quotes final chorus of 'Paid on Both Sides', EA, 17.]

Mr. Auden approaches that integration, that acceptance
of the dynamic nature of life, which we are all seeking,
but whether we accept or reject his Aristotelianism, we
can enjoy the precision of his writing and recognise the
value of his progress.   We are reminded of Odell's last
sight of Irvine and Mallory on Mount Everest, higher than
man had stood before: 'they were moving expeditiously as
if to make up for lost time'.   These activities may seem
mistaken, irrelevant, but they compel an admiration for
the endurance of human mind and spirit.

5. LOUIS MacNEICE ON 'UP-TO-DATE' AUDEN, UNTITLED REVIEW,
'OXFORD OUTLOOK'

xi, March 1931, 59-61

Poet, playwright, translator, and BBC producer, MacNeice
(1907-63) was born in Belfast. Though associated in the
1930s with Auden, Spender, and Day-Lewis, his poetry was
in fact far less politicized than theirs; always, to use
Auden's phrase, 'beautifully carpentered', rhythmically
live, and humanistic. Before the war he taught classics at
Birmingham University, Greek at Bedford College, London, and
then embarked upon an outstanding career as writer and producer for radio which lasted until his death. In addition
to scholarly translations from the Greek and German which
deserve lasting recognition, his published works include
'Autumn Journal' (1939), 'Collected Poems' (ed E.R. Dodds,
1966), and - in collaboration with Auden - 'Letters from
Iceland' (1937).

God (or Nature) has a diffuse style which poets have often
been busied correcting. Especially modern poets. Mr.
Auden's attempt is to put the soul across in telegrams. But
whereas in the everyday telegram the words tend to be, like
Morse, mere counters, in the poem-telegram the words stand
rather on their own than *for* a meaning behind them. Many
would consider much in these poems to be irrelevant, arbitrary, indifferent.

But in all poetry one feels rather than knows the irrelevance and relevance. Only in new poetry one tends to start
knowing in advance of feeling, because the poems come to
one rather as curios and samples than as something valuable.
And critics, too, are *qua* critics bound to consider what is
curious or typical. Which is why I would rather be a propagandist than a critic.

Mr. Auden, then, uses an up-to-date technique to express
an up-to-date mood (not that either 'use' or 'technique' or
'express' or 'mood' has, in this sentence, any legitimate
sense). Generalisations of this sort are no good except
as rough hints. And special instances are little better.
To detect an 'instance' of the influence of Robert Graves
is little, perhaps, better than an instance of the condit-
ional sentence. A good poet is no more a conglomeration of
the typical and the derivative (and the peculiar) than of
the grammatical. As for bad poets - there are also people
who write solely to write grammar.

Still, though both are conditions and not causes, contemporary literary influence is a more changing condition
than grammar. Which is why it may slightly elucidate these
poems (while having nothing to do with their value) if one
suggests that Mr. Auden is well-read in the 'typical'
'advanced' reading of to-day, that having being helped to
see things newly by modern psychology he is helped to present them in a new and strenuous presentation by, among
others, Eliot, Robert Graves, the later Yeats, G.M. Hopkins
and Wilfred Owen.
We must beware of facile analysis. When Mr. Auden says:

Gannets blown over northward, going home,
Surprised the secrecy beneath the skin,   [EA, 24]

we must not narrow and so destroy his 'gannets' - either by
narrowing them to meaning (as the scientist) or to sound-
value (as, sometimes, Edith Sitwell). We can merely say
that gannet is the right sound (and, incidentally, an Eliot
sound) and that the sound adds to the meaning and by adding
makes a new meaning (= makes poetry = creates). And it is
unjust when Mr. Auden uses a word like 'sessile' to say he
uses it because it is or sounds 'scientific'; more likely
he uses it just because it sounds. Mr. Auden has a remarkable ear which he runs in harness with his mind.
A critic is forced to insult poetry by discussing its
'elements' separately. So now for his 'mood.' Mr. Auden's
mood is that notorious disillusionment of our time which
yet goes forward to realize itself - along roads which its
own bombs have riddled (e.g. Lawrence recognizing sexual
breakdown finds Heaven in sex; Eliot seeing the vanity of
polymathy compiles a solid from vanities; Cummings by and
in disintegrating, aims at new integrities). So Mr. Auden
to pin the flux does not mangle it into something else, but
tries to pin it as it is and yet to pin it, e.g.:

Is first baby, warm in mother,
Before born and is still mother,
Time passes and now is other,
Is knowledge in him now of other,
Cries in cold air, himself no friend.
In grown man also, may see in face
In his day-thinking and in his night-thinking
Is wareness and is fear of other,
Alone in flesh, himself no friend.   [EA, 38]

The Charade which takes up half the book is, as a whole,
his most powerful work (what is not so easy in a short
poem); one knows where one is before the end. And where

one is (usually, in Auden) is in a world without miracles,
which works out always in an equation or bathos. Much modern poetry presents bathos but not mere bathos; for a
bathos which still comprehends the dignity of its precedents
is thereby raised to tragedy.

And one can un-kernel bathos from what is *prima-facie*
triumph. Of such triumphs modern poetry is a criticism –
it discloses a peripeteia not in time but there from the
beginning (there automatically); the stock values are
found facile:

> It is seen how excellent hands have turned to commonness,
> One staring too long, went blind in a tower,
> One sold all his manors to fight, broke through, and
> faltered.   [EA, 26]

Just as art can make of suicide something vital, so here
is the attempt to make of these falterings a rhythm. Hence
he should certainly be read by those of us who are not old
enough to go, or think we go, straight forward.

6. F.R. LEAVIS ON CHAOS AND DEFEAT, IN POETRY AND DISINTE-
GRATION, 'TIMES LITERARY SUPPLEMENT'

19 March 1931, 221

Founding Editor of 'Scrutiny', 1932-53 (an apolitical journal in which all reviews of Auden were written by pupils of
Leavis), Leavis (1895-1978) was a Fellow of Downing College,
Cambridge, 1936-62, and Reader in English, Cambridge University, 1960-2. His other books include 'Revaluation'
(1936), 'The Great Tradition' (1948), 'The Common Pursuit'
(1952), 'D.H. Lawrence, Novelist' (1955), and 'Dickens the
Novelist' (with Q.D. Leavis, 1970).

In the revised edition of 'New Bearings in English
Poetry' (1950; first published 1932), Leavis wrote in a
Chapter entitled Retrospect 1950 that he found Auden's
career

> worth pondering because it is the representative career of
> the nineteen-thirties and has a representative signifi-
> cance. He entered the literary world with a reputation
> made at the university: as a recent critic in the 'Times
> Literary Supplement' puts it, he was 'the Oxford
> intellectual with a bag of poetic squibs in his pocket'.

What this critic doesn't say, or appear to realize, is
that the Auden who conquered the literary world with
such ease was the undergraduate intellectual. The
Oxford valuation became immediately metropolitan....
Auden was accepted as, beyond question, a leading
intellectual and major poet. His admirers spoke of him
as having superseded T.S. Eliot.

Leavis found it ironic that Eliot's 'Criterion', which
had an official bent towards Anglo-Catholicism, readily
accommodated the 'young writers of the Poetic Renaissance'
who were

emphatically Left-inclined - Marxist and Marxizing....
the young poetical Communists and fellow-travellers and
their friends were able to make themselves as much at
home in its review-pages as in the 'New Statesman and
Nation'. For their purposes it became, incongruously,
their organ, and their purposes did not include - did
not permit - the revival of the function of criticism....
And in this way - it is an ironical fact - was ensured,
not only the immunity of these young writers from any
disturbing critical challenge, but that general abeyance
of the function which sufficiently explains why the
influence of T.S. Eliot, out of which a poetic revival
seemed so likely to come, should have been so sadly
defeated.

In a footnote to Retrospect 1950, Leavis took pride in
the sweeping assertion that

this placing of Auden has been enforced in 'Scrutiny' by
detailed criticism in more than half a dozen reviews,
coming from half a dozen different hands. The dismissal
of Spender (once in conventional esteem the Shelley of
the Poetic Renaissance), Day-Lewis, MacNeice, George
Barker, Dylan Thomas, has also been done critically in
'Scrutiny'.

See Introduction pp. 2, 4, 9, 20 and 67 for comment on
Leavis's depreciation of Auden.

A recent writer has remarked that poetry, as a result of
modern mechanization, has become more and more removed from
the external common life of men: that its material is
found more in the inner life of the individual, and its
interpretation depends increasingly upon the individual's
private and personal knowledge. And both these books are

extreme examples of that withdrawal from the objective into
the subjective world. Many passages in each of them are
baffling, if not unintelligible, because they lack that
measure of normality which makes communication between one
individual and another possible. For mental idiosyncrasies,
if they are extravagantly indulged, isolate a writer as
completely as if he spoke in an unknown tongue. Thus in
the first of his poems Mr. Auden invites us, so far as we
understand him, to discover, amid the horrors and humiliations of a war-stricken world, the 'neutralizing peace' of
indifference. But the manner of his invitation is often so
peculiar to himself and so eccentric in its terminology
that, instead of communicating an experience of value to
us, it merely sets our minds a problem in allusions to
solve. For example:-

[Quotes stanzas 5-9 of Poem XXII, EA, 35-6.]

To Mr. Auden himself the meaning of these last three stanzas is doubtless as clear as day, because they fit the
peculiar habit of his mind and his experience. But
although we can sense his general meaning, it requires a
kind of effort to discover the exact relevance of his
allusions which, even when we are sure of having done so,
destroys the possibility of real enrichment. Such poetry,
indeed, completely contradicts Keats's axiom that 'poetry
should surprise by a fine excess and not by singularity':
that it should 'strike the reader as a wording of his own
highest thoughts, and appear almost a remembrance'; and
it fails to make a living contact with us because it is
the fruit of a too specialized kind of concentration. For
intellectual analysis of emotional states, however sharp
its focus, is poetically as barren as emotional diffuseness. And although Mr. Auden can write -

> Coming out of me living is always thinking,
> Thinking changing and changing living,   [EA, 37]

the thinking process in most of his poetry is either arbitrarily imposed upon the living or the living impulse,
weakened by uncertainty and disillusion, begets a symbolism which is full of personal caprice. For a sense of
chaos and defeat not only underlies but determines the very
texture of his verse and particularly of the strange
'Charade', entitled 'Paid on Both Sides,' with which his
book begins and which, in its combination of seriousness
and flippancy, presents in the form of a feud between two
hostile parties, the stultifying division in his own
consciousness which wrings from him the cry -

Could I have been some simpleton that lived
Before disaster sent his runners here;
Younger than worms, worms have too much to bear.
Yes, mineral were best: could I but see
These woods, these fields of green, this lively world
Sterile as moon.   [EA, 7]

7. M.D. ZABEL ON AUDEN'S CERTAIN POETIC GIFTS, FROM A
DAWN IN BRITAIN, 'POETRY'

May 1931, 102-4

Associate Editor of 'Poetry: A Magazine of Verse', 1928-36,
and Editor-in-Chief, 1936-7, Morton Dauwen Zabel (1901-64)
held professorial posts at many American universities. His
publications include 'Craft and Character in Modern Fiction'
(1957).

W.H. Auden has applied himself to a reconstruction of
emotional values, personal and social. He wishes neither
to ignore the motives established by science, nor to lapse
into that lethargy of irony and despair which has overtaken
most of the 'realistic' novelists and life-forcers of
recent years. He hopes to invest with new moral and ethical necessity the ideals of affection, sympathy, and honour
where these have become deflated by psychological and
sociological research:

[Quotes stanzas 9-11 of Poem XXII ('Will you turn a deaf
ear...') EA, 36,]

   Mr. Auden's present volume is hardly more than a pro-
spectus for such a task. Its greatest value lies in the
certainty of his poetic gifts. He has treated the
traditional topics of love, beauty, and delight without
the spurious sentiment which tears the poet out of his
proper mind and his proper age; he has likewise avoided
the scientific jargon which has misled too many dissatisfied modern writers. His style is, in fact, an instrument
subtle enough for greater tasks than have thus far been
exacted of it. The progressive consonance in rhymes and
phrases, the dove-tailing of images, the sometimes solemn
and sometimes ironic juxtaposition of sober words with
comic and of traditional with 'new' - all these combine to

evoke a music wholly beyond the reason, extraordinarily
penetrating and creative in its search of the significance
behind fact.   It has already revealed to Mr. Auden the
saving vision behind such bleak industrial civilizations
as he has pictured in his charade 'Paid on Both Sides'. It
has enabled him to reconstruct his 'ruins' without making
specious glamour out of his memories, and without resort-
ing to remote and unlikely faiths.

8. DUDLEY FITTS, TO KARTHAGE THEN I CAME..., 'HOUND AND
HORN'

Summer 1931, 629-30

Dudley Fitts (1904-72), educator, poet, and critic, won
especial praise for his translations of Sophocles' 'King
Oedipus' (with Robert Fitzgerald, 1949), and Aristophanes'
'Lysistrata' (1954), 'Frogs' (1955), and 'Birds' (1956).
   This Chronicle review discusses eight books of verse,
including volumes by Archibald MacLeish, Roy Campbell,
Horace Gregory, Babette Deutsch, and Robert Graves - whose
work in 'Poems (1926-1930)' he found 'direct'.

Mr. Auden, too, knows how to be direct; but he elects more
often to be oblique. His book opens with a 'charade', a
poetic drama treating a family feud. It is a jerky,
exceedingly bloody curtain-raiser, with considerable sudden
shooting. It is the type of rustic thriller, reminiscent
of nothing so much as of Jacinto Benavente's 'La Malquerida'.
What the symbolology may be, I do not know. There are
excellent passages - lyrics, mostly, in a queer strain
suggestive of early English verse, or of the austerity of
certain choruses of Greek tragedy:

[Quotes final chorus of 'Paid on Both Sides', EA, 17.]

But the 'charade' is so perverse in its melodrama, and so
wilfully obscure (even for a charade!), that the ultimate
effect is one of baffled irritation. And it is this same
obscurity for obscurity's sake that endangers many of the
thirty lyrics which follow. Sometimes Mr. Auden succeeds
in attaining the relaxed toughness, the casual angularity
of improvisation; too often he fails to achieve anything
but a prosaic iteration of incoherencies. The imagery is

not precise, the emotion only partially released. It is
curious to observe that this is nearly always the result
not of slipshod composition, but of composition too sedu-
lously disordered, - too refinedly chaotic. Mr. Auden
stems directly from Gerard Manley Hopkins; and his failures,
like his successes, are those of the earlier poet. The
manner at its best may be observed in the last sonnet:

[Quotes 'Sir, no man's enemy, forgiving all', complete,
EA, 36, and comments in a footnote: 'It is true that
Hopkins' passionate intensity once impelled him, in a
sonnet, to address God as "Sir". It was a good effect,
too; but, I believe, unfortunately unrepeatable.']

'The Orators'

London, May 1932

If 'Poems' had created interest and enthusiasm, 'The Orators' generated still fiercer excitement and perplexity. The American poet John Berryman's testimony that 'When I flew through "The Orators" first / I felt outstretched...' ('Shirley & Auden', in 'Love & Fame', London: Faber & Faber, 1971) is typical of an extremely wide response.

9. WILLIAM PLOMER ON AUDEN'S 'VIGOROUS ATTACK', 'SUNDAY REFEREE'

22 May 1932, 6

Born in South Africa, William Plomer (1903-73) published 'Turbott Wolfe', his pioneer novel on Black Africa, at the age of 22. In his capacity as publisher's reader, he introduced the work of Ian Fleming to the firm of Jonathan Cape, and he later discovered and edited the Kilvert Diaries (3 vols, 1938-40). In addition to his many other books - novels, short stories, autobiographies, and verse including 'Collected Poems' (1960) and 'Taste and Remember' (1966) - he also wrote several libretti for Benjamin Britten, including 'Curlew River', 'The Burning Fiery Furnace', and 'The Prodigal Son'.
This extract is taken from A Poet on English Stateness.

Mr. W.H. Auden may or may not be a great writer; he is certainly an original one. Those who like to keep in touch with the newest developments of English literature have known his name for some time. He is the author of a remark-

able book of poems, and his work has been seen both in
anthologies and in odd corners. Hitherto he has seemed to
some people to be a person with something new to say but
without the certainty of how to say it best. His publishers speak of the excitement caused by his 'unfamiliar
metric' and 'violent imagination.'

How many writers are there at any time who can really
excite us? To some it must have seemed that Mr. Auden was
giving in to a wilful obscurity, but in 'The Orators' the
reader finds his feet much oftener, and concludes that the
writer does the same. This is certainly the work of a man
who knows how to live his own life and think his own
thoughts. From Dante and Blake, from Skelton and Miss
Gertrude Stein, and perhaps Mrs. Woolf, from modern life
and the resources of his own nature, Mr. Auden gathers
materials for a real attempt at 'a constructive policy.'
Vigorous and adventurous, he shows every sign of becoming
a man-with-a-message, and, what is more, an intelligent
message. To begin to find out what his message is or is
likely to become, one must read 'The Orators,' which, in
prose and verse, is strangely beautiful and amuses while it
instructs.

It takes all sorts of people and things to make a world;
do without pity and shame: don't preach more than you can
help; learn to enjoy - these seem to be some of Mr. Auden's
mottoes. An 'English Study'? No, rather a brilliant attack
on English staleness, dullness and complacency. Let us
borrow the methods of the advertiser and say that this book
is a sparkling tonic. It tastes of old wine and new fire.
And it has a new taste all of its own.

10. ALAN PRYCE-JONES PUZZLES OVER MEANING, FROM A POETRY
CHRONICLE, 'LONDON MERCURY'

26, May 1932, 170-1

Alan Pryce-Jones (b. 1908), book critic, author, and journalist, was Assistant Editor of the 'London Mercury' (1928-
32). Then he worked for the 'Times Literary Supplement',
which he edited from 1948 to 1959. He later became Book
Critic for the 'New York Herald Tribune' (1963-6), 'World
Journal Tribune' (1967-8), and 'Newsday' (1969-71). His
publications include 'The Spring Journey' (1931), '27
Poems' (1935), and 'Private Opinion' (1936).

Mr. Auden calls 'The Orators' 'An English Study'; and certainly it would not be easy to find a more precise sub-
title for an essay partly in prose and partly in verse. It
is, in fact, the sort of book which the English are more
accustomed to find in French, and I can imagine that it
might discover a warmer welcome if it were signed by
Raymond Roussel or Louis Aragon - not that their signatures
are interchangeable by any manner of means - than when it
appears under a plainly English name for a proof that the
demon of mental exertion is well in our midst. I choose
Roussel as a possible parent of 'The Orators' because he
shares with Mr. Auden a passion for abstruse machinery.
Dials, pressure-gauges - our author is especially fond of
parts of aeroplanes - and undershot wheels mark or obey
dynamic forces which remain obscure to the reader; and,
beyond this legitimate attempt to create a machina ex Deo,
the reader is saddled with scraps of scientific information, not always, I fear, correct, and rarely more than
elementary.

But what, it may be asked, what is 'The Orators' about?
That is a question I dread. In an earlier article in this
paper I have lamented my inadequacy to share Mr. Auden's
constructive sense; I can only repeat, though with some
indignation, my lament. I do not see why such a tax need
be put upon an intellect which is, at least, average. I
do not see why Mr. Auden should be so preternaturally
endowed that I cannot formulate, in a phrase, the exact
subject of his book. He and I are contemporaries. I am
not in the position of an old gentleman who has always been
a fervent admirer of Lord de Tabley, can tolerate Swinburne,
and once possessed a copy of the first volume of 'Georgian
Poetry'. I have been in an aeroplane quite as often, I
suspect, as Mr. Auden, and when he writes in metaphors of
aerial warfare I further suspect that he gets his knowledge of that art from the same source as I my ability to
criticise his knowledge: a school O.T.C. And yet, before
'The Orators', I find myself nearly as blank as the old
gentleman - vaguely aware that something is going on,
vaguely catching a glimpse of light, and quite unable to
decide in the end what it is all about.

I know, from experience, that nothing is so infuriating
for a poet as that another should fail to grasp a sequence
which is to him perfectly lucid; but I submit, without
wanting to be patronising, that a poet who can write such
a sentence as:

The group snapped at the fifth tee against a background
of Scotch firs, frowning, conscious of their pipes,
cellular underwear, the train whistle in the valley,

> the tall capless one in the back now deliberately half-
> hidden, are taken for ambassadors –   [EA, 82-3]

cannot expect anybody to unravel his intentions. And also
I submit that Mr. Auden must beware of the old enemy of
poets, the catalogue. About a quarter of 'The Orators' is
catalogue – a device which, however picturesque so supple
an imagination as his may make it, puts treacle into the
delicate parts of the machinery once the poem tries to
take flight again; for catalogues end by deadening the
mind.

But what, it may be asked again, what is 'The Orators'
about? I dare not commit myself. The book opens with an
Address for a Prize-Day. The moral of this is easy. Boys,
says the Orator in effect, you must take up a more intelligent attitude to life. The second chapter is like the
explosion of a diamond, but I can find no recrystallisa-
tion. The third chapter is a catalogue; the fourth,
Letter to a Wound, interrupts the book with the appearance
of being impressive on a different plane from the rest;
but really the impression is only a reflex of unfamiliarity,
and on a re-reading the chapter is seen to mean very little.
Book II, the Journal of an Airman, rambles in prose and
verse and a sham-military-notebook style through different
stages of war with 'the enemy,' whom I take to be the
Protean antagonist of an intelligent attitude to life.
More catalogues hold up the war, which, I believe, is lost.
Book III, Six Odes, though individually more intelligible,
leads me to suppose (what would not anyway surprise me)
that my interpretation of the rest is quite wrong.

And yet though the apparent confusion is too great to be
called ambiguity, though I find Mr. Auden's mixing of
planes and styles far more puzzling than Eluard's experiments in a state of artificial paranoia, I cannot throw
away 'The Orators' as worthless bosh. It appears to be
the work of a sane imagination without a mind – a far
more complicated state than the paranoiac's – working on
fragments of knowledge and experience. The interest of
this book, therefore, is purely as a transition to what
the author will do next. If I were thirty years older I
should make myself odious by suggesting that he spend some
months, meantime, turning the earlier poems of Sir William
Watson into Latin alcaics.

11. A.C. BROCK ON MEDIUM BEFORE MEANING, UNSIGNED REVIEW,
'TIMES LITERARY SUPPLEMENT'

9 June 1932, 424

It is not easy to describe this extraordinary composition.
It is written partly in verse, some of which is deliberately free from poetic diction, and partly in prose, some
of which is poetical. In the first part there are three
prose sections and a love-letter; the second part is called
Journal of an Airman, in the form of notes and jottings;
and the third consists of six odes, most of which are
written in free variations of the elaborate metres which
belong more to light verse than to heavy poetry.

In the main the work appears to be an ironical and
satirical description of life in England to-day. But Mr.
Auden's approach is oblique, capricious, and, as it were,
from a distance; he breaks the ordered world of usage into
fragments which he employs both to make a singular pattern
of images and conceits, and also, with a satirical intention, to display the malign absurdity of organized society.
Incongruities and odd juxtapositions are both his artistic
medium and the weapon of his irony. Some of his jokes are
simple and high-spirited, but more often he moves in a
tangle of allusions and images between which the natural
connexions are omitted. He delights in modern slang and
technical diction which is so new that it has not had a
chance to acquire a literary flavour, finding as much
pleasure in these difficult and prickly terms as most young
poets take in the diction of the old masters. In fact, the
words which he seems to like most are those calculated to
knock a sonnet to pieces, not only the technical terms of
wireless, aviation, or war, but even the hidden indecencies
of vulgar speech, of which he uses a good many. He is
insolently but exhilaratingly new, both in his technique
and in the matter of his writing. Unfortunately the usual
resource of quotation is denied to us, for, to be frank,
isolated specimens are apt to sound silly and the quality
of his writing is only displayed in extracts too long for
convenience.

For, it should be said at once, Mr. Auden's composition
is not at all silly. Although it is obvious that this
disintegrated poetry, and still more this 'surrealiste'
satire, might be one of the easiest of all forms of writing,
a mere dribble of disconnexions, and if it were so would
certainly be one of the dullest, this work is neither of
these things. On the lowest level it is very clever, and
Mr. Auden's mind works with a fascinating agility.

Conceits, parodies, and allusions flow in an unceasing
stream from his pen. But, what is more, none of these are
in the least pertly sophisticated or embarrassing. He
never attempts a callow epigram. It is important to recognize this at once, for this is the most common characteristic of such bright young works, and only a mind which is
really sincere and an artistic conscience which is really
scrupulous can avoid it. This is not to say that Mr.
Auden's frequent railings and his persistent air of disgust
with all the complexities of modern life may not sometimes
grow tiresome, but he never commits the artistic faults
which commonly go with such elaborate sophistication. To
make a revolutionary manifesto written in violently
unconventional and unliterary language sound as well tuned,
almost as discreet when it is read as a whole, as an old-
fashioned essay on some safe literary subject is obviously
an unusual feat; and it is certainly something which no
one but a genuine writer could do. For a poet to be able
to say, and to say so persistently, 'I belong to the post-
War generation,' without causing a shudder in every sensitive reader is something of an achievement, especially when,
as one sometimes suspects of Mr. Auden, he would rather like
to cause a shudder in every sensitive reader.

For Mr. Auden's message displays the most thoroughgoing
contempt for all possible conventions and for the general
organization of human life. In the Journal of an Airman he
describes measures of hostility against safe and organized
society so reckless, so violent and so capricious that they
are surely beyond the imagination of any political revolutionary, although, to be sure, he concludes with the observation that he has made a terrible mistake and that ' the
power of the enemy is a function of our resistance,' so
that the only way to remain unspotted from the world is by
complete passivity and retirement. And yet, however stri-
dent his message, it is always of second importance to the
progress and form of Mr. Auden's composition. In his verse
he chiefly uses elaborate metres, not unlike those of
Gilbert, and twists and turns them with a fascinating
effect. And both in his poetry and his prose the quality
of his diction, the adjustment of strange images and the
fall of the sentence have obviously been throughout his
first concern. If his message, his exuberant relish for
the new, have led him into any fault, it is only this, that
we could wish that he had sometimes aimed more deliberately
at beauty and had not always sought to come upon it shyly
and obliquely. For the few snatches of writing which
achieve a calmer beauty suggest that Mr. Auden might well
on occasion attempt a task yet more difficult than such a
composition as this, the extraction of beauty not from the

singular and odd but from the trite associations of classical poetry. This, however, probably could not be such an occasion, and we suppose that Mr. Auden might argue that an opportunity can seldom arise in the world to-day.

12. F.R. LEAVIS, FROM AN UNSIGNED REVIEW, 'LISTENER'

22 June 1932

Auden pointed out with some amusement to Janet Adam Smith that the names Leavis stigmatized as coming from 'a boy's romantic map' were in fact perfectly good place names from Shetland.

Mr. Auden's first book of poems has already won him a reputation; yet it is safe to say that no reader put the book down with a comfortable sense of having understood. The present book makes no easier reading, and, since Mr. Auden obviously has unusual gifts, it becomes important to examine into the nature of the difficulty; for snobbism (such as attends upon every cult) is fickle, and will desert a writer after having encouraged his faults. We expect some measure of difficulty in modern verse; indeed we are suspicious when we find none. But now that fashion has come to favour modernity there is a danger that difficulty may be too easily accepted. The publishers of 'The Orators', on the dust-cover, have almost an air of boasting that their author is obscure. Yet the general nature of what he has to say is plain enough, and the obscurity of the particulars seems to a great extent weakness. 'The Orators', we are told, 'is not a collection, but a single work with one theme and purpose, partly in prose and partly in verse, in which the author continues his exploration of new form and rhythm'. The exploration is still in the early stages, groping and inconclusive, and the roughness of the jottings must not be mistaken for subtlety of charting. The opening piece of prose, 'Address for a Prize Day', is very good, but the standard of precision and coherence introduced here in the part is not maintained generally. Mr. Auden seems apt to set down too readily as final what comes, on the tacit plea that modern poetry has vindicated the right to demand hard work from the reader. But we demand of the poet that he should have done his share, and in Mr. Auden's case we are not convinced. Too often, instead of complex-

ity and subtlety, he gives us a blur; and again and again
it is evident that he has not taken enough trouble to make
his private counters effective currency. One gathers
assurance to put the judgment in this way from the signs,
here and there, that he does not know just how serious he
is: the diagrams, for instance, on pages 42-45 represent
what looks like satisfaction in undergraduate cleverness.
Certain characteristics appear to go back further. The
frequent images of war seem to betray, in part at least,
a romantic habit, deriving from a boyhood lived in the
years 1914-1918.

> Vadill of Uirafirth, Stubbo, Smirnadale, Hammar and
> Sullom, all possible bases: particularly at Hubens
> or Gluss. Survey to be completed by Monday.   [EA, 76]

Those names come from a boy's romantic map.
   But it will not do to condemn the habit as a weakness;
it is associated with a certain strength that makes Mr.
Auden's work remarkable. His imagination tends to the
creation of myth. The hints he drops lead one to dream of
a representative modern English poem - such as it seems
extravagant to hope for. The peculiar bent, as well as
his gift for a kind of satire, is exemplified by the verses
(p. 65):

> Beethameer, Beethameer, bully of Britain, etc. [EA, 86]

These verses exemplify also the technical habits that Mr.
Auden has acquired from the study of Anglo-Saxon.

13. STEPHEN SPENDER EXPLICATES THE EARLY AUDEN, 'TWENTIETH
CENTURY' (PROMETHEAN SOCIETY)

3, July 1932, 13-15

Distinguished poet, playwright, literary critic, autobiographer, and travel writer, Stephen Spender (b. 1909)
was Professor of English at University College, London,
from 1968 to 1973. With Cyril Connolly he founded and co-
edited 'Horizon' magazine from 1939 to 1942, and with
Irving Kristol in 1953 he founded 'Encounter', which he
co-edited until 1965. His publications include '20 Poems'
(1930), 'Poems', which T.S. Eliot accepted for Faber &
Faber (1933), 'Trial of a Judge', a play (1938), 'The

Destructive Element' (1935), 'World Within World', an autobiography (1951), 'Love-Hate Relations: A study of Anglo-
American Sensibilities' (1974), 'W.H. Auden: A Tribute'
(ed., 1975), and 'The Thirties and After' (1978).

See the introduction for a discussion of Spender's continuous commentary on Auden, and their ambiguous confed-
eracy.

This essay is entitled Five Notes on W.H. Auden's
Writing.

---

1. OBSCURITY.

About a year ago, Mr. Auden published a volume of 'Poems'
which contained a long 'charade' and about thirty separate
poems. The chief criticism made against the poetry was
that it was obscure. Mr. Auden's poetry seems obscure
because he uses certain words which rouse familiar associations in us, in contradiction to, or ignoring, those
associations. The difficulty in reading Mr. Auden's poetry
is to accept these words in their relation to the rest of
the poem and nothing else: in other words to accept Mr.
Auden's world. For example, in his new book 'The Orators',
there is a section called the Airman's Journal; in another
section there is a reference to 'Him,' and all through the
book there are numerous references to unexplained persons,
Dick, Gabriel, etc. I notice that one of the critics hasten-
ed to explain that the airman was the poet fighting against
society. It is also tempting to assume that 'He' must be
God, and to think that if we knew all about Dick, Gabriel
etc., the difficult passages in 'The Orators' would immediately become clear to us. But the fact is that the Airman is simply the Airman. Although after we have absorbed
the Journal we may decide that the Airman symbolizes the
poet in conflict with society, this assumption cannot help
us to enter the world that Mr. Auden is creating in the
Journal. If we make the slight effort to accept Airman
simply as Airman, without demanding any further explana-
tions, when we read the poetic journal, the whole world
which Mr. Auden is building up, with all its machinery
of spies, weapons, a caricature society, etc., will begin
to exist for us. Then, afterwards, we may relate it to
our own world, if we wish to do so. It is a world entirely
of his own which we can only enter if we are prepared to
accept it whilst we are reading about it.

The person who when he reads poetry demands an explanation of the use of all the words in the poetry with which
he already has familiar associations, is hampered in exactly the same way as the person who reads a scientific work,

and who insists on loading every reference to atoms, light
waves, etc., with his own visual imagery.

2. 'THE ORATORS.'

The charade in Mr. Auden's first book contained some of his
best poetry but it was disconnected, and it lacked unity.
The new book, 'The Orators,' is divided into three main
sections, the first, the Initiates, containing four
Addresses, the second the Airman's Journal, the third Six
Odes. The form evolved in this book, Addresses, a Letter
to a Wound, a Journal, the Odes, are well adapted to
Auden's style, because his writing does not possess that
driving purposiveness which can give unity to the material
of a poetic drama. His poetry, and his poetic prose, have
rather character or personality, than organic unity. In
this book, in so far as development and unity in each section are achieved, they are achieved only by devices. The
Airman meets with disaster, but the disaster is only imposed, it does not throw out any conflict because there is no
real conflict in him, the disaster that takes place at the
end of the Journal is already there, in effect, on the
first page. As I see it, there is no real problem in the
world which Mr. Auden presents. He writes poetry almost
always about neurotic subjects. His people are, as it
were, transparent. One can see right through them, one
can see why they cannot succeed: things may happen to them,
disaster may fall, but there is no problem about them,
because there is no real conflict in them. Mr. Auden
occasionally asks the world to change:-- 'Drop those priggish ways for ever, stop behaving like a stone,' 'There
isn't going to be very much lunch unless you all wake up,'
but these exhortations are addressed to people who are
mentally children. He *does* feel, very strongly, that if
only people could get rid of their neurotic fears, things
might be different. But 'Who will teach us how to behave?'

3. SATIRE.

Taking a neurotic and almost doomed society as his subject-
matter, Mr. Auden finds only two ways out for us. The first
is satiric. The second is the religious.
   'The Orators' is full of the most original and powerful
satire. If we compare Mr. Auden's satire with that of Roy
Campbell, for instance, we see at once how much Mr. Auden
gains in strength by not projecting a Byronic myth of himself as the toreador, or as King David the psalmist and

bestrider of lovely fillies, or as the only fit companion
for Mr. Wyndham Lewis's eagle-like mental swoopings, etc.,
and by not writing in a style which is pastiche, and which
has already been so superbly used by Pope that it would
be impossible for any imitator to excel in it. Besides
this, Mr. Auden's satire is most original in that it is
hardly at all embittered. The strength of it does not
seem to be derived from any feelings of spite, or even of
very strong moral resentment, but from a most tremendous
sense of fun, fun with a sting in it like the saltness of
the sea. The most personal of the satires is the ballade
'Beethameer, Beethameer, bully of Britain,' but cruel as
this is, here we feel that Auden does not portray the newspaper peer seen from a specially ludicrous angle in order
to ridicule him, but that he really does see Beethameer as
someone who is only ludicrous, and there is nothing more
to it, except that incidentally, for making himself so
prominently nasty, he ought to be whipped. The real
purity of this attitude of mind recalls the satire of
Blake, and we feel that Mr. Auden's scornful amusement,
like that of Blake, has behind it, not feelings of personal
hatred, but the strength of natural elements.

Sometimes, and this is also like Blake, Mr. Auden
will present himself as part of the world that he is
satirizing. 'It is John, son of Warner, who has pulled
my chain,' he writes, completely taking our breath away.
The effect of such a stroke is that he does not stand
romantically aloof from the objects of his satire, and
that he takes us with him as part of the ridiculous fun,
right amongst the 'Majors, vicars, lawyers, doctors,
advertisers, maiden aunts.'

4. THE RELIGIOUS SOLUTION.

The Airman's Journal is the most personally revealing
section of 'The Orators'. The airman in his journal
analyses most carefully the enemy's methods of attack,
what symptoms show that people are on his side, his methods
of propaganda, etc. The enemy does not confine his
activities to any one class of society. The airman is not
fighting for the proletariat, although no doubt he might
be, if he were convinced that the proletariat were free of
enemy traits, of the corruption that is destroying our
society. As we read the journal further we begin to
realize something which is implicit throughout the whole
of 'The Orators.' The difficulty is not in defining the
enemy, but in discovering who is not on the side of the
enemy. The corruption of our society has gone so far (here

I am interpreting Mr. Auden) that the person who is aware
of that corruption and who is fighting it, has inevitably
already been corrupted himself. The Airman is overcome by
a psychological disaster; the nature of this disaster is
not explained, because it is not necessary to explain it,
since it is implicit in the resistance to disaster itself.
The airman at last writes in his journal:.

> 1 The power of the enemy is a function of our resistance,
> therefore 2 The only efficient way to destroy it -
> self-destruction, the sacrifice of all resistance,
> reducing him to the state of a man trying to walk on a
> frictionless surface. 3 Conquest can only proceed by
> absorption of, i.e. infection by, the conquered.[EA, 93]

This is the religious, not the revolutionary state of mind.

5. POETRY AND REVOLUTION.

Poetry is an anti-social activity. The writing of poetry
in itself provides the poet with the solution of his
problems, so that whether those problems are subjective
ones or ones that affect the whole of society makes no
difference, the solution is a personal one. Although a
poet might conceivably write from a truly revolutionary
standpoint, it is unlikely that he would do so, as to the
true revolutionary the creation of poems would seem a
dishonest means of expression. For this reason most poets,
as with Mr. Auden, are forced into an attitude which is
really religious or mystical. If there is no other
religion, poetry itself or 'beauty' will become the
religion.

But in another sense a poet like Mr. Auden is inevitably a revolutionary: that is, because nothing is more
revolutionary than to tell the truth. The journal of
Auden's airman is material for a revolution in the same
way as were Chekhov's plays. Anyone seeing Chekhov's
plays would say 'If these are true, they are true of a
state of society that cannot last.' Anyone reading
'The Orators' will feel that if it is a true picture of
England 'this country of ours where nobody is well, 'then
our kind of civilisation cannot last.

The test of Auden's work lies in the excellence of his
poetry. Nothing, on the face of it, could be less
'proletarian' than this poetry, and yet I am convinced
that if it is as good as I believe it to be no one can
well afford to ignore it; and the proletariat will also
finally be interested in it, in the same way as they will
rediscover the work of Chekhov.

14. GEOFFREY GRIGSON, THE POET AND THE ENEMY, 'SATURDAY REVIEW'

30 July 1932, 131

Auden's most staunch supporter throughout the 1930s, Geoffrey Grigson (b. 1905) founded and edited 'New Verse', 1933-9, which both published and promoted Auden's poetry. Poet, prolific anthologist, literary and art critic, writer on natural history and travel, and of non-fiction for children, he has worked for the 'Yorkshire Post', as Literary Editor of the 'Morning Post', and for the BBC. His publications include 'The Arts Today' (1935), 'New Verse: An Anthology' (1939), and 'The Crest on the Silver: An Autobiography' (1950).

See the Introduction for a discussion of Grigson's stalwart response to Auden.

A book exciting and surprising; and also unique. Mr. Auden is an angry poet who has decided that the poet's place is not rounding off columns in weekly journals or shyly hob-nobbing with Mr. Garvin, a page or two from his six-decker headlines.* He finds no fun in being complacent or lazy-minded over the triumph of mediocrity in all sections of contemporary existence, in being a snail, drawing in horns from the naughty world and sliming a silver path through the cob-nut orchards of Kent or the dahlia-beds of Kensington Gardens. He attacks. In 'The Orators' he is savage, but always with justification; violent, but always in control of his violence. The Enemy is individual (typical, that is) and collective, the whole contemporary situation, the insolence of mediocrity whether in the antics of Beethameer, bully of Britain, whose paper we meet

> Nagging at our nostrils with its nasty news,
> Suckling the silly from a septic teat.
> Leading the lost with lies to defeat;   [EA, 86]

or in the bland evasion of politicians, the smug useless-ness of blind schoolmasters, the unchecked drug-traffic of the writers of fiction. He is the Airman (why attack the Enemy on its own dull mud-level?); and he invests his attack with the clear dream-horror of war, with stark destruction imagery. The delineation of enemy country is sharp and yet muddled like the field frame-work shown in an aerial eye-view or aerial photograph.

* [J.L. Garvin (1868-1947) edited the 'Observer', 1908-42.]

Mr. Auden uses both prose and verse, but there is no
strict separation between them. The prose is closely
rhythmical and breaks easily into verse, in which he has
often gone back beyond Middle to Old English for alliterative emphasis, a justified and excellent excursion. Both
prose and verse are distinguished by the most extraordinary
vigour, by a freshness of vocabulary (much of it stale
words refreshed and much borrowings of technical terminology), by rhythms which are now Mr. Auden's absolute
possession. For method and content, as a creation and as
something new 'The Orators,' I believe, is a book of the
first importance. It has the value of fiction without its
looseness. Where other contemporary poets are fragmentary
(excepting Mr. Eliot and one, or perhaps two, others),
writing little poems each in scarcely connected equilibrium,
where they are static, Mr. Auden has written dramatically.
His writing (as in 'Poems' of 1930) is eventful, full of
act and gesture, without losing its fury of imagination
and pressure. As others have pointed out, it was such
dramatic quality that Donne brought into English poetry.
Mr. Eliot has restored it in our day. Mr. Auden, who is
more free as an inheritor of the difficult hammerings that
Eliot had to do, is carrying dramatic writing further and
(as it seems to me) to great purpose.

15. MICHAEL ROBERTS, UNTITLED REVIEW, 'ADELPHI'

iv, August 1932, 793-6

The poet is under no obligation to provide his own or any
generation with a metaphysical system or a prophetic
message. Sometimes, however, he provides the material out
of which systems and messages are made. He expresses the
sensibility of a generation and, by making experience
communicable, makes it tolerable. He makes it possible to
think what could only be felt before. In poetry of this
kind, narrative interest and logical development, however
valuable they may be as adornments, are no more necessary
than they are to a dictionary.

What hotpotch, giberage doth the Poet bring?
How strangely speakes? yet sweetly doth he sing.

When a good poem does contain an intelligible message
it differs radically from prose propaganda and from its

own prose translation, for it shows not only that an attempt to change a certain situation is a necessary part of the scheme of things, but also that the situation is itself a part of that scheme. It impels the reader to action, but it compels a serenity also, and results in action more finely adjusted to its purpose than the desperate hysteria induced by powerful mob-rhetoric or by the plain, unmediated contemplation of the facts. And whilst we are judging a work as poetry we are more concerned with this serenity than with the nature of the propaganda involved.

Thus in Mr. Auden's 'Prologue,' which, lacking space for quotation or description, I assert to be an excellent poem, there is a fundamental ambiguity of sense but no ambiguity of feeling. The experience, and consequently the poem, may be analysed into 'meaning' in two different and apparently contradictory ways without appreciably affecting the emotional acceptability of the experience or the 'beauty' of the poem.

In praising Mr. Auden's 'Poems' and his new volume of prose and verse, 'The Orators,' critics have made premature attempts to extract specific and familiar messages which would enable them to apply convenient labels, platonist, communist or anarchist. But the important thing about Mr. Auden is not his message, but his manner of writing: indeed it still remains to be seen whether he will be able to organise the material with which his technique enables him to deal. Meanwhile his work, taken line by line, is unquestionably good:

> Next the defective lovers. Systems run to a standstill, or like those ship-cranes along Clydebank, which have done nothing all this year.   [EA, 63]

or again:

> The child's life is intermittent, isolated desultory jerks now and then, which scandalise and alarm its parents, but for the most part it is a motor run off their accumulators.   [EA, 84]

or,

> Going abroad to-day? Under a creaking sign, one yellow leg drawn up, he crows, the cock. The dew-wet hare hangs smoking, garotted by gin. The emmet looks at the sky through lenses of fallen water.   [EA, 65]

More striking than this demonstrable scientific accuracy, is the felicity, undemonstrable yet unquestionable, of other passages:

...another to Cornwall where granite resists the sea
and our type of thinking ends.   [EA, 62]

It is however, on work such as Address for a Prize-Day
that Mr. Auden's popularity will depend. It is here that
his writing hints at a message for it expresses, simply
and unapologetically, Mr. Auden's prejudices:

Three signs of an enemy house - old furniture - a room
called the Den - photographs of friends.   [EA, 82]

There is no pretence at system or correlation in Mr.
Auden's expression of these intuitions, but anyone who is
at all likely to read 'The Orators' will recognise their
accuracy. Mr. Auden does not question his own impulses
and the importance of his future would be more obvious if
it were clear that he had ever done so.

To say this, implies no depreciation of his present
achievement; his self-confidence gives a welcome vigour to
his work. The consequent absence of self-criticism, however, sometimes leads to the making of 'Private faces in
public places' and though the private faces may be, for a
small circle of acquaintances, 'wiser and nicer than public
faces in private places' they are no less irritating to the
stranger than the 'fools' names and fools' faces' which,
the old rhyme assures us, 'are often seen in public places.'

To condemn Mr. Auden's very frequent use of public
school and O.T.C. imagery is, however, unreasonable, for
in addressing the public-schoolboy he is attacking the
creeping timidity and platitudinous conventionality of
English decadence at the crucial point. The Public School
has at the best produced only obedient civil servants
rather than genuine leaders: it has done nothing to check
the gradual atrophy, under democracy, of all sense of
social responsibility in those who still constitute in
effect, the governing classes. Is it too late for public
and secondary schoolmasters to 'Stop the Rot by J.L. Garvin'
as the 'Observer's' poster recently advised?* Whilst the
vestiges of an aristocratic system linger as social
snobbery, the middle-class shirking of social responsibility,
the acceptance of convention in place of independent and
impersonal judgment, and the degenerate 'Safety First'
tradition, may still be attacked through the public schools.
This attack, of which Mr. Auden's book is symptomatic, is
important; for the English middle-class, unlike that of
pre-revolutionary Russia, is not the by-product of an
economic system, it is an expression of the English
character. In an industrialised country such as England a
bourgeois standard of living is quite possible: the

*   [See footnote on p. 106 above.]

labouring class is a by-product of capitalism and the
middle-class is the true proletariat. But if the English
tradition is to survive, the attack on 'Beethameer,
Beethameer, bully of Britain' must be intensified a
thousandfold. Mr. Auden's work is of general interest
because it seems as relevant to the contemporary situation
as that of Shaw and D.H. Lawrence once appeared to be.
Further, even though its admirers do not find in it the
organisation which they would like to see, it is remarkably sensitive and acute writing, it is good fun, and
incidentally it is practical politics.

16. BONAMY DOBRÉE, PROVISIONAL PRAISE, 'SPECTATOR'

cxlix, 20 August 1932, 239

Bonamy Dobrée (1891-1974) was Professor of English
Literature at the University of Leeds from 1936 to 1955.
His books include 'Restoration Comedy' (1924),
'Restoration Tragedy' (1929), 'Modern Prose Style' (1934),
'The London Book of English Verse', with Herbert Read,
(1949), 'Alexander Pope' (1951), 'Rudyard Kipling' (1967),
and 'Milton to Ouida: A Collection of Essays' (1970).

Literary historians of the future are going to have a bad
time of it: periods are contracting from half-centuries
or generations to decades. Perhaps, even schools of poetry
will come to be known by years, like vintages. It will
certainly seem incredible that Mr. Auden should be a
contemporary of Mr. Humbert Wolfe.* Yet it will not be
enough to explain Mr. Auden to say that he is one of those
whose boyhood coincided with the War; it must be added
that the tradition to which he belongs is that of the new
current of metaphysical poetry, of which Mr. Eliot and
Mr. Read are among the elder - but not yet old - writers;
there is in him something of the revolt of Rimbaud; the
chief influence, one would say, is that of St. J. Perse;
technically he has learnt from Wilfred Owen. This is not
to say that Mr. Auden is unoriginal; he is certainly so.
It is merely an attempt to place him in the flow to which
he belongs.
    How deeply Mr. Auden differs from the Georgian poets
(they are still with us) might be expressed by saying that
whereas the Georgians sing from their lips, Mr. Auden sings

*   [Wolfe (1886-1940) was a Civil Servant, poet and trans-
    lator.]

from his viscera, as Donne did. It is perhaps, doubtful
if he sings at all, except occasionally; his words are
utterances rather than song. His book, indeed, is written
largely in prose, prose which has the logic, the sequences
of poetry, its stresses, its concentration. It is, like
most modern poetry that is worth anything, extremely
difficult: the links connecting thought with thought are
omitted: much, indeed too much, in the way of allusion
is taken for granted. That it is an important poem there
can be no doubt; how good it is it will be impossible to
say, not only until it has been read several times, but
until one has had considerable time to digest it, to let
it sink in. It is not to be immediately apprehended
intellectually, though much can delight at once both in
the prose and the verse (both are poetry), by the sound of
the words and the succession of images, and the assonances,
often internal. It is unfair to quote extracts from what
must be read as a whole, but small passages of each may
give something of the flavour:

> On the steps of His stone the boys play prisoner's base,
> turning their backs on the inscription, unconscious of
> sorrow as the sea of drowning. Passage to music of an
> unchaste hero from a too-strict country. March, long
> black piano, silhouetted head; cultured daughter of a
> greying ironmaster, march through fields. The hammer
> settles on the white-hot ingot. The telescope focuses
> accurately upon a recent star. On skyline of detritus,
> a truck, nose up. Loiterer at carved gates, immune
> stranger, follow. It is nothing, your loss. The
> priest's mouth opens in the green graveyard, but the
> wind is against it.   [EA, 69]

> Not, Father, further do prolong
>   Our necessary defeat;
> Spare us the numbing zero-hour,
>   The desert-long retreat.   [Ode VI, EA, 109]

It is, no doubt, the business of a reviewer to try to state
what a poem is about; it is useless (though true) to say
that a poem is its own explanation. Any attempt must be
crude, not to say lop-sided; but if one were to try to
state the fundamental theme of 'The Orators', one might
suggest that Mr. Auden is intent to explode fear,
especially the fear of what might happen to the individual
if all the old assumptions were broken down: it is here,
and in his contempt for 'safety first' that he is nearest
Rimbaud. One large section of the book consists of the
Journal of an Airman, a fantasy; the airman, the modern,

daring everything in his eternal campaign against 'the
enemy,' the Old Adam of fear, of safety first, of easy
compromises, which is as strong as the Devil himself
because it is the masses, the respectable masses. Those
who have read Mr. Auden's 'Poems' will recognise him in
'The Orators', but it is a Mr. Auden who has made strides
not only in his craft, but in the development of his
attitude towards a coherent whole.

17.   JOHN HAYWARD ON OBSCURITY AND STIMULUS, UNTITLED
REVIEW, 'CRITERION'

xii, October 1932, 131-4

Editor, anthologist, bibliographer, and literary critic,
John Hayward (1905-65) first won praise for his precocious
editions of Rochester, Donne, and Swift, and occupied an
influential place in English letters from the late 1920s
until his death. He became the confidant and adviser of
numerous writers, as well as a prolific reviewer, and
provided creative advice on the plays and poems (especially
'Four Quartets') of T.S. Eliot, with whom he shared a
Chelsea flat from 1946 to 1957. In his last years, as the
erudite and astringent editor of the 'Book Collector', he
made that journal pre-eminent in the field of bibliography.
His own anthologies include the 'Penguin Book of English
Verse' and the 'Oxford Book of Nineteenth-Century Verse'.
Auden, with whom he became acquainted in the 1930s, placed
some confidence in his criticism, as this note from the
1940s (dated New York, 25 October) confirms: 'The opera
['The Rake's Progress'] whose libretto you so kindly vetted
is going well - the second act nearly finished' (Hayward
Papers, King's College Library, Cambridge).

The generation, for whom the last war is a confused memory
of darkened windows, margarine and fearful visions in the
pages of the 'Illustrated London News'; of fathers and
elder brothers returning on leave with bits of shrapnel
and pressed wild flowers; of drawing-rooms littered with
cretonne bags and skeins of wool; that generation has
grown up since the publication of 'The Waste Land', ten
years ago. It has not been an easy or a happy apprenticeship.
      Mr. Wystan Auden belongs to that generation; he is, I

suppose, about twenty-five years old. He has already
published a book of poems, unlike any written before
the war or since. His second book is longer and much more
ambitious. There are others, I feel, more competent to
discuss it than I am; I find it exceedingly difficult to
understand, but in spite of this, extraordinarily stimulating. Nor am I certain that I have grasped the significance
of 'the single theme and purpose' that run through it.
'The Orators' is divided into three books: (1) The
Initiates; (2) Journal of an Airman; (3) Six Odes; and a
short prologue and epilogue. The first book is further
divided into four sections: Address for a Prize Day;
Argument; Statement; Letter to a Wound. The book is a
mixture of prose and verse.

I think it is obvious that Mr. Auden is profoundly dissatisfied with the present state of civilization in this
country; it is a natural attitude for his generation to
adopt. But he is not content to express his disgust and
to leave it at that. He feels the need for a complete
regeneration of society, and at present he is still at the
stage of groping for a formula. In so far as he is under
the necessity of adjusting himself to post-war society, he
is concerned with a personal problem, and most of the
obscurity of 'The Orators', I feel, is the consequence of
his failure to find a complete, that is to say, a satisfactory solution; and it is this also, which tends to make
'The Orators' an interior monologue. But he is deeply
concerned with the much wider, or more complicated problem
of society itself. It is the moral aspect of this problem
that lends itself to satire, satire keener and more
effective than Mr. Roy Campbell's belated pastiche of Pope,*
and incomparably more witty, in the 'metaphysical' sense.
Indeed much of Mr. Auden's writing has the merits and
defects of 'metaphysical poetry'; his conceits, though far-
fetched, are often worth the carriage, though sometimes
they are so remote that they never arrive, or their source,
the substance from which they derive, like a star, is dead
before the light reaches us.

Another and more obvious cause of obscurity is the
exploitation of the private joke, which can only be
appreciated by the initiated, that is to say, by Mr. Auden's
personal friends, sometimes, perhaps, only by Mr. Auden
himself; and references to personal adventures, which are
unintelligible to the ordinary reader, however painstaking
he may be. Indeed Mr. Auden expects far too much of the
uninitiated; he expects them to understand the incomprehensible. It is a serious fault in a writer who has something important to say, and is experimenting in new forms
of expression, which, in themselves, demand, as I think

*   [Roy Campbell, 'The Georgiad', London: Boriswood, 1931.]

they deserve, the reader's closest attention. There is a
point beyond which ingenuity ceases to please; the poets of
the first half of the seventeenth century frequently
exceeded it, and so does Mr. Auden three centuries later.
There are too many 'Clevelandisms' in his verse, and their
presence may well injure his reputation, as they have
Cleveland's, Cowley's and even Donne's. They tend to reappear, whenever poetry becomes over-intellectualized.
The ordinary reader cannot relate them to his experience
of the external world, and I still believe, old-fashioned
as it may seem, that it is the poet's business to interpret
this world in terms that educated people can understand
and to give us the emotional and intellectual experience
of sharing what our own feeble gifts of sensibility and
intelligence cannot provide on their own account.

'The Orators', nevertheless, does give us something.
It is, as I have said, an extraordinarily stimulating book,
and if Mr. Auden's imagination lights up strange and
surprising scenes, it does so with astonishing brilliance.
His technique is still experimental, and often produces
grammatical ambiguities, but it is evidently in the highest
degree active. Indeed, without grasping his meaning, we
can still admire the variety of his verse-forms, and the
subtle effects he creates by employing such devices as
internal rhymes, alliteration and assonance. The only
modern poet I know of, whose skill in this respect was
comparable to Mr. Auden's, is Wilfred Owen, and I presume
that Mr. Auden owes something of his impulse to experiment
along these lines to Owen.

After two readings, I do not feel that I have grasped
the 'single theme and purpose' of 'The Orators' sufficiently
firmly to be able to summarize it in a few words. The
theme may be one of three: The value of Leadership;
Society; The importance of group organization over the
individual: or it may be a mixture of them. It is clear
that there is a leader, and that he comes to disaster,
some rather obscure psychological disaster at the end of
Book II. Presumably he is the speaker at 'The Prize Day'
in the first part of Book I, and he re-appears later as
'Him' to his disciples, the regenerators of society - the
opponents of 'The Enemy'. He is also, I presume, the Airman, the author of the most brilliant pages of the book;
and he is an aviator, I venture to suggest, because mastery
of the air implies indirectly a mastery of the situation
below; he is, that is to say, in a position to observe
everything. 'The Enemy' is the society, whose mental,
emotional and physical habits Mr. Auden deplores and
detests. 'Beethameer, bully of Britain' - the newspaper
magnate - is one of its most obviously repulsive members,

as he is also an opportunity for an excellent piece of satirical writing. The final book – the Six Odes – containing the best poetry in the whole work, is an account, I dare say, of the Leader's disciples; John Warner, to my mind, is the most interesting of them.

It might be possible to improve upon this very inadequate exegesis by quotation. But 'The Orators', though, in my opinion, it lacks organic unity, is yet so closely interwoven that no short passage can be isolated with advantage. It is a book which must be read patiently and with care; and it is worth reading more than once, for I have no doubt that it is the most valuable contribution to English poetry since 'The Waste Land'. The last ten years have been singularly unfruitful; the next ten years will show whether the promise, contained in 'The Orators' and in Mr. Auden's first volume of poems, published eighteen months ago, is fulfilled, as I believe it will be.

18. GRAHAM GREENE ON AUDEN'S VIRTUOSITY, THREE POETS, 'OXFORD MAGAZINE'

1i, 10 November 1932, 158

Graham Greene (b. 1904) is the author of over thirty novels – including 'Brighton Rock' (1938) and 'The Heart of the Matter' (1948) – 'entertainments', plays, children's books, travel books, and collections of essays and short stories. In the later 1930s he was film critic of the 'Spectator'.

'The Orators' is an astonishing advance on Mr. Auden's first book. The first section is written in a bastard (though sometimes effective) prose too close to poetry; the second section, Journal of an Airman, is a scrappy blend of prose and verse and biological formulas. But the six odes and epilogue justify his being named in the same breath as Lawrence. The subject of the book is political, though it is hard to tell whether the author's sympathies are Communist or Fascist; they seem a little vaguely and sentimentally directed towards a 'strong man,' a kind of super-prefect, for the book has a slight smell of school changing-rooms, a touch of 'Stalky.' But Mr. Auden's virtuosity is amazing. He uses the whole language without self-consciousness. Take, for example, the Ode dedicated to the Captain of Sedbergh School XV:

> Sandroyd - what of their side? -
> In jerseys of chocolate and white
> Prancing for prowess, posh in their pride,
>   Unbeaten last night:
> No changing-room clapping for them, no welcoming
>   dazzle,
> But a hushed school receives them in a drizzle,
> Clambering, sodden, from a maundering chara., licked
>   to the wide.[Ode II, EA, 97]

And take the close of the noisy farcical boastful ode
to John Warner, which rouses and repels and finally intoxi-
cates like mob enthusiasm, as an example of how he can
stretch and contract his metre to include the opposed
emotions drawn from a political close-up and from a remote
shot of quiet countryside:

[Quotes last 17 lines of Ode IV ('Roar Gloucestershire, do
yourself proud...'), EA, 105-6.]

19. HUGH GORDON PORTEUS ON VALUE AND INFLUENCE, 'TWENTIETH
CENTURY' (PROMETHEAN SOCIETY)

iv, February 1933, 14-16

Porteus is author of 'Wyndham Lewis: A Discursive
Exposition' (1932) and 'Background to Chinese Art' (1935).
Samuel Hynes describes the Promethean Society as

> an organization of young radicals that met to discuss
> politics, 'sexology', philosophy, religion, and art, and
> published its own journal, the 'Twentieth Century'....
> certainly the Promethean Society represented some
> definitive currents in the generation.... the eclectic
> politics, the faith in science, and the pacificism are
> all there, and give to the time a sense of disorganized
> good intentions that have not yet been exposed to
> reality.
>   The 'Twentieth Century' ran for two years, from March
> 1931 to May 1933. During that time it published some
> of the generation's leaders, including Auden ...
> Spender ... and Michael Roberts, as well as an odd
> mixture of elders - Havelock Ellis, Wyndham Lewis, and
> Trotsky. And it caused enough stir to be noticed by
> the 'Daily Express' ('250 Young Rebels Challenge the

Whole World. Down with Everything. Marriage, Morals,
Parliament' the headline read). But in 1933 the notion
that civilization could be saved by scientific research
and eclectic radicalism was dead, and the journal and
its Society were dead, too. ('The Auden Generation',
pp. 83-4)

For better or for worse, upon Mr. Auden appears to have
devolved the head gardenership of our contemporary
nursery of poetry. In attempting to account for this we
must consider (a) the climatic and meteorological conditions which permitted or forced his work to attain its
present prominence, then (b) the relation between these
conditions and (c) the intrinsic value, so far as we can
assess it, of what he has produced to date. When Auden's
unusual and poetic name first began to sound, fashion had
already deserted the made reputations. A decade of
Eliotolatry, accompanied by more and more pallid imitations,
had prepared us to receive sympathetically almost anything
which should succeed in combining vitality with a modicum
of novelty. 'Paid on Both Sides,' monopolising the better
part of the whole issue of the 'Criterion,' answered this
demand; and was for at least one reader an event and an
experience of some magnitude. Then came the 'Poems,' and
afterwards 'The Orators' and the eager chattering of
apostles in quads and drawing room corners. From the moment
I for one began to subdue my enthusiasm and adopt a
severely critical attitude towards, not: Mr. Auden and his
work, for I can pretend to know neither, but: my own reactions and the *voix d'enfants chantant*. Auden is one of
those figures (and it is evidence of his personality) that
drive one to extremes in conversation. I have sometimes
caught myself abusing his work with a vehemence as astonishing, in retrospect, as that with which in different circumstances I shall probably continue to praise it. The
wise, no doubt, will keep silence. The Chinese say of the
Tao that those who understand it never speak of it, and
those who speak of it have never understood it. Talking
or writing about art is admittedly a drivelling occupation.
And it is almost certain that we exaggerate the ultimate
significance, virtuous or vicious, of most contemporary
phenomena. Yet even if I have overstated the importance of
(for example) Mr. Eliot or Mr. Wyndham Lewis, it is very
certain that a majority (whose silence is not a function
of its wisdom) continues grossly to underestimate it.
Auden anyway, thank heaven, is neither so absolutely
important nor so absolutely obscure as the Tao. Meanwhile his work is supposed to possess a specifically

contemporary importance. To investigate it in the light
of the claims made for it is one of the purposes of this
note: I am attempting to disentangle the value of the
work itself from its alleged value as tendency or influence.
    Auden's work seems to me valuable because he is
primarily a poet with a fine critical apparatus, in
contradistinction to that much commoner type: a critic
with an itch to manufacture occasional verse. He has
abundant resources: a fertile invention, a great facility
in coining and effectively juxtaposing images, a power over
language to make it do unusual tricks, considerable
technical virtuosity (as in the use of half-rhymes,
Mauberleywise), and enough intelligence and sensibility
to make the job worth while -- the job, I mean, of ordering
and recording what looks like a genuine and consistent
vision. Now the sophisticated writer has a choice today
of two methods. He can write in a formal, 'mannered'
fashion, which will enable him to *display* his sophistication; or he may write with complete *in*formality in a
publicly accessible medium of which he has complete mastery.
'Snooty Baronet' is a good example of the latter; the (sic)
'transitionists' afford a few good, and many bad, instances
of the first method. And it is only natural, if deplorable,
that young writers should choose the first method; it gives
more immediately impressive results with considerably less
expenditure of effort. (Given the requisite degree of
sophistication, to forge a passable 'surréaliste' picture
or poem is a good deal easier than it looks). Attempts to
combine the two methods - (for convenience: 'subjective'
and 'objective' respectively) - have not met with great
success; and the measure of success appears to depend on
which happens to be in the ascendant. The interminable
polyglot sagas of Joyce ('Work in Progress') and Pound
('Cantos from a Poem of Some Length') are intolerable except
in short snatches; even the parody-prattle in the
'Childermas' can become exhausting. In combination, the
virtues inherent in either method are liable to cancel out,
leaving a sum of vices. Mr. Auden's importation of a
modified surréaliste technique, even though it is employed
in a comic capacity, seems to me to spoil large tracts of
his two major works: first by depriving them of definition
and intellectual clarity, secondly by rendering them
inaccessible to the general reader. (I find it impossible
to agree with the critic who maintained that Auden had in
his Charade 'put surréalism in its place'; for I contend
that surréalism's place is roughly Montparnasse or more
precisely the beloved 'unconscious' of some not very
interesting Franco-American minds).

Mr. Auden owes much of his prestige to something else beside the aesthetic merits of his work: viz., to certain doctrines with which (very strangely, I think) his name has become associated. No need to repeat the doctrines; enough to say that they have a political origin and purpose. Let us suppose, then, that we are nice simple 'Twentieth Century' plain readers, all waxing ecstatic over the doctrines said to animate, and emanate from, the material marshalled above New Signatures. Opening the latest work of Mr. Auden - say, The Diary of an Airman - we shall (if we are playing Plain Reader properly) rub our innocent eyes very hard indeed. The doctrines surely promised us, among other boons: No Isolation, No Egos, 100% All Popular. Whereas we find what looks like obscurity and 'subjectivity' as never before! The most we shall see is a man in a trap. We shall feel fooled. We have paddled for miles in our bare feet only to hear Mary call the cattle home across the Sands of Dee. Of course, the plain reader would be wrong. Mr. Auden's practice does not entirely contradict the theories: but he brings us bang up against a nest of paradoxes that are the very devil to dismantle. One thing can be put down now: Auden's obscurity is not a *poetic* obscurity; poetically his work always has the clarity of the equally, but differently, difficult writing of Eliot. But Auden, continually succumbs to the temptation to be too original - a common complaint. Eliot wrote lately: 'the poem which is absolutely original is absolutely bad; it is, in the bad sense, 'subjective,' with no relation to the world to which it appeals.' Auden's work is always related to his own world, but not always to the world to which it should appeal; he is, in fact, and against the current doctrine, guilty of 'isolation.' (We must be careful to distinguish between: the admirable and necessary solitude of the objective artist and: the vicious privacy of the too-subjective artist). The 'Times Literary Supplement' reviewer of Auden's poems even saw in them an 'extreme example òf that withdrawal from the objective into the subjective world' which can 'isolate a writer as completely as if he spoke in an unknown tongue.' Auden's 'subjective' world is insubstantially furnished and peopled with private spooks which he too often fails to 'materialise' satisfactorily. A subjective world is worse than merely inaccessible: it lends itself to any and every misinterpretation by readers who impregnate the thin visible fabric with their own thinner private dream.

The relation between the Self and the Not-Self - (or if you prefer the dress-clothes phrase of the signatories - including Mr. Auden - of the 'Oxford Poetry' Manifesto: 'the psychological conflict between the self as subject and

the self as object') - is not best stated in terms of the
'subjective' self; and 'The Enemy of the Stars', for all
the wildness there, is perhaps still the most vigorous
attempt to state it objectively. Elsewhere I have lately
written all I wish to write, for the moment, about these
matters, and about another matter - satire. But Mr. Auden
has already acquired some hardly-deserved renown as a
satirist. How far he may be held responsible for the
expository remarks of his colleague Mr. Spender, I do not
know, but this is how the latter describes him: 'Mr. Auden
will present himself as part of the world he is satirising
. . . he does not stand romantically aloof from the objects
of his satire . . . he takes us with him as part of the
ridiculous fun, right amongst the "mayors, vicars, lawyers,
doctors, advertisers, maiden aunts."' Pray Mr. Spender
what is wrong with 'Punch'? 'Romantic' in the above quotation is a pejorative; but the opposite of 'romantically
aloof' is 'classically submerged' - surely a difficult
position from which to write effective satire. All
successful satirists have at least had the conviction, and
given the illusion, of an absolute superiority (in some
sort) over their chosen victims: a satirist must in *one*
particular (it matters little what) be master of his world.
Auden is not, to my mind, a satirist at all. He (to enlist
a congenial figure) simply 'rags.' But he rags the whole
school - blows down the bunsens, stops the drains, cuts
the buttons off every pair of pants in his dormitory.
Incidentally it is impossible not to remark on Mr. Auden's
curious obsession. More than half his imagery, it is
little exaggeration to say, is drawn from the rugger field,
the labs, and the O.T.C. His poetry continues to insist,
in a most disquieting manner, on its unimpeachable schoolboy complexion. A parallel disease seems often to inflict
his verse, and when both appear simultaneously you get
such things as the idotic refrain:

We'll give you the thrashing you richly deserve.[EA, 86]

Mr. Auden's one real service to contemporary poetry has
been his invention of a medium or solvent capable of
assimilating much new and hitherto intractable material.
He has thus, for us, extended the boundaries and enriched
the potentialities of poetry. In doing this he has not
ignored the value of 'the dramatic' and 'conversational'
ingredients insisted on by Mr. Eliot, nor the latter's
recipe for durability, well given by Mr. Michael Roberts
when he reminds us that 'A poem which survives does so
either because of its elegance (in the mathematical sense)
or because its symbolism will bear a variety of different

interpretations, and therefore solve a variety of emotional problems.' But imitations of Auden (of which lately we have seen too many) appear to be more pernicious than imitations of Eliot (which at the worst tend merely to dessication and dullness). Auden's poetry (again, this is evidence of his personality) is charged with an irresistible power; and his novel mannerisms are extremely infectious.

The nimble fume of the Audenary Manner is apt to run to weak heads in the form of a fiat roughly as follows: 'Verse will be worn longer this season and rather red. More vocatives will be used, with verbs invariably imperative; all questions rhetorical, rude and abrupt. Articles definite and indefinite will be almost entirely dropped.' Imitation of the Manner (the insincerest form of flattery) is harmless compared with imitation of the Matter, however. The subjectivity of an interesting mind has its place and value - extra-aesthetically. The subjectivity of an uninteresting mind is nothing but a stinking specimen excretion. As an influence, Auden's work is likely to produce nothing but disasters; the value of his work surely lies, as Mr. Spender says, 'in the excellence of his poetry.' The best of it, parts of the two ambitious pieces and such single poems as Nos. II, and IX, and XI, and XII, and XX, and XXX, is definitely among the best poetry this century has produced. It would be impertinent to complain that it lacks solidity, the really satisfying substance, of the greatest poetry: it has other qualities which, equally uncommon in contemporary writing, could never have emerged in any age but our own.

20. HENRY BAMFORD PARKES, AN EXPATRIATE VIEW, 'SYMPOSIUM'

iv, April 1933, 245-8

Born in Sheffield, England, Henry Bamford Parkes (1904-72) emigrated to the USA in 1927, and was naturalized in 1940. He became Professor of History at New York University in 1949, and was Chairman of the Graduate Division of American Civilization from 1944 to 1968. His books include 'Jonathan Edwards' (1930), 'Marxism: An Autopsy' (1939), 'The American Experience' (1947), and 'The United States of America' (1953).

Parkes took his cue for declaring that Auden had become a Communist from a misleading letter Auden himself had

written him in December 1932: 'The book is, as I didn't
realise when I was writing it, a stage in my conversion to
Communism' ('Colby Library Quarterly', December 1977,
p. 276; cited in Humphrey Carpenter, 'W.H. Auden: A
Biography', London: Allen & Unwin, 1981, p. 152). Cf. Introduction note 43 above.

Mr. Auden is a young Englishman - too young to have been
directly affected by the war. He belongs to a group of
writers with similar methods and beliefs, the most important of whom, in addition to Auden himself, are probably
Stephen Spender and Cecil Day-Lewis. The appearance of
this group is perhaps the first convincing indication that
the epoch of 'The Waste Land' in England is near its end.

'The Orators' is about the attempt of the young and
idealistic individual, who does not find in society the
kind of assistance which he requires in achieving emotional
integrity, to assert himself in rebellion against society.
Such a person necessarily dramatizes himself as a hero, and
thinks in terms of heroes and hero-worship. Mr. Auden's
theme is the futility of this kind of rebellion and of the
heroic idea; the individual cannot destroy all his connections with society without destroying himself as a consequence.

Book One is about a group of hero-worshippers who, under
the leadership of a kind of Messiah, have set out to
regenerate society. In Address for a Prize-Day the leader
describes the failure of the present inhabitants of
England; borrowing the method used in the 'Purgatorio,'
he classifies them as excessive lovers, defective lovers,
and perverted lovers. Argument deals with his followers,
their reverence for the leader and the progress of their
campaign. At the end of this section they hear, however,
that he has come to some kind of disaster. In Statement
they mortify their pride and learn to accept themselves
and other people for what they are. In Letter to a Wound
one of them realizes the educative value of the experience.
Book Two, which shows us the hero, is the Journal of an
Airman, who is perhaps identical with the leader of Book
One. He wishes to achieve a true organic integrity by
allowing passional impulses to express themselves freely.
He is hindered by persons who inhibit impulses by imposing
on them an abstract system of moral laws and habits; these
persons dominate English society and are known, collectively,
as 'the enemy.' The airman organizes an elaborate campaign
against the enemy. His separation from society, however,
causes him to have feelings of persecution and strange
fears - presumably of madness. His campaign results in

general chaos and destruction - apparently in his own mind.
He then realizes that his methods have been wrong from the
beginning: warfare against an abstract system of values
increases the evil which it is designed to cure. The
result (Mr. Auden seems to imply) is merely to substitute
one set of abstract values for another; emotional integrity
cannot be achieved by such methods. He therefore learns
humility and abandons the struggle. Book Three is a series
of odes which develop the consequences of surrender. The
writer resigns himself to what is inevitable. He knows,
however, that the struggle was necessary and that, in other
forms, it will be continued.

'The Orators' is written partly in prose and partly in
verse. The prose has, however, rhythms which are close to
those of verse. It also has a sensuousness and a compact-
ness which the verse does not always achieve. One can
easily illustrate its precision:

> Going abroad today? Under a creaking sign, one yellow
> leg drawn up, he crows, the cock. The dew-wet hare
> hangs smoking, garotted by gin. The emmet looks at
> sky through lenses of fallen water.   [EA, 65]

The felicity of its rhythms:

> Next the defective lovers. Systems run to a standstill,
> or like those ship-cranes along Clydebank, which have
> done nothing all this year.   [EA, 63]

Its colloquial quality:

> Then the excessive lovers of their neighbors. Dare-
> devils of the soul, living dangerously upon their nerves.
> A rich man taking the fastest train for the worst
> quarters of eastern cities; a private school-mistress
> in a provincial town, watching the lights go out in
> another wing, immensely passionate. You will not be
> surprised to learn that they are both heavy smokers.
> That one always in hot water with the prefects, that
> one who will not pass the ball; they are like this.
> You call them selfish, but no, they care immensely, far
> too much. They're beginning to go faster. Have you
> never noticed in them the gradual abdication of central
> in favor of peripheral control? What if the tiniest
> stimulus should provoke the full, the shattering
> response, not just then but all the time.   [EA, 62-3]

Mr. Auden's verse is not always so successful. At his
best, as in two or three of the odes, he can create rapid

movement or massive simplicity. But his rhythms frequently lack subtlety; and he has a fondness, not obviously justifiable, for imitating Anglo-Saxon, chiefly by making excessive use of alliteration. His natural bent is towards a refinement of ordinary speech: he is in the tradition of Wordsworth and Robert Frost rather than in that of the Metaphysicals.

'The Orators' has obvious signs of immaturity. It has neither the concentration of feeling nor the verbal and metrical skill of, for example, 'The Waste Land.' There are passages which need a drastic pruning and others which show a schoolboyish crudity. There is a persistent ambiguity of mood which suggests that Mr. Auden, while writing it, was still in process of deciding whether individualist revolt was to be glorified or rejected. But though it is inferior to 'The Waste Land' as a poem, it may prove to be of similar importance in helping to formulate the spiritual tone of an epoch.

If 'The Orators' is considered purely as literature, then it is important chiefly because of Mr. Auden's success in expressing himself wholly through imagery derived from contemporary life. English poets of the twentieth century have mostly evaded the task of presenting an honest record of their reactions to the world around them. But when poetry loses its connections with contemporary life, it ceases to be alive; any reform of poetry usually takes the form of abandoning a conventional rhetoric and finding a more natural medium through which to express honest, instead of second-hand, emotions. Mr. Auden, unlike his predecessors, is saturated in contemporary English life. His metaphors are taken mostly from modern warfare, the modern English countryside (not the fake countryside of the Georgian poets), and the English public school; his rhythms and vocabulary are close to those of English speech. Yet, though his mind is open to impressions, he is not overwhelmed by them; he has sufficient energy to organize for his own purposes the material which they give him.

The attitude implied in 'The Orators' is also of unusual interest. One guesses that D.H. Lawrence has been a strong influence in Mr. Auden's development. But, to Lawrence's insistence that passional impulses must not be impeded by abstract values, he adds a realization of the utility of tradition. One of the most prominent motifs in 'The Orators' is that the struggling individual can derive guidance and encouragement from 'ancester-worship'; the war with 'the enemy' began in the distant past and is continued in each generation. Mr. Auden seems in fact to have realized that the Lawrentian doctrine of obedience to

passion can be regarded as a rediscovery of the Greek and
Catholic doctrine that every organism is moved by instinct
towards the actualization of its nature.

The individual who aspires to be an integrated organism
is hindered by the bourgeois society which is organized
mainly for the encouragement and satisfaction of the
acquisitive instinct; other human impulses cannot usually
be expressed in forms provided by society and are therefore liable to be frustrated. The conflict with society,
which is the theme of 'The Orators,' has been the normal
experience of the sensitive individual during the past century or century and a half. Mr. Auden states the problem
in universal terms, avoiding aspects of it which are peculiar to himself; but, unlike most of his predecessors
(except, possibly, Rimbaud, who, however, did not explain
his surrender), he realizes the futility of the romantic
revolt. The individual needs an appropriate environment in
which to exercise his powers; he cannot achieve harmony and
integration except in a regenerated society.

Since writing 'The Orators' Mr. Auden has become a
Communist. Communism, perhaps, if it is accepted as a
technique for making the necessary changes and not as a
dogmatic religion, is the best available method of regeneration; it does, at least, aim at prohibiting individual
acquisitiveness. But it remains to be seen whether artistic
honesty and the organic growth of the individual, with
which Mr. Auden is chiefly concerned, can be reconciled
with its present intolerance.

21. JOHN GOULD FLETCHER ON A POET OF COURAGE, 'POETRY'
(CHICAGO)

xlii, May 1933, 110-13

Fletcher (1886-1950), American poet and author, lived in
Europe from 1908 to 1933. His early poetry earned praise
from Ezra Pound; later works include 'The Epic of
Arkansas' (1936), 'Life Is My Song' (autobiography, 1937),
and 'Selected Poems' (1938), which won a Pulitzer Prize.

Despite Fletcher's welcoming appraisal of the early
Auden (and his preference for Auden's viewpoint to
Eliot's), it is reasonable to infer that by the mid-1940s
his tolerance for Auden had declined so far as to share
the sentiments of this extract from a letter (dated 6
December 1946) by his contemporary Conrad Aiken:

Yes, the Auden influence has been lethal: I respect
the guy, but I can't like him. The poetry of undigested
intellectual formula, with its ever-so-casual off-hand
psychological-economical-sociological aggregates, and
its typically homosexual fear and shame of love - to
think that we should be delivered over to *this* generation for slaughter! ('Selected Letters of Conrad
Aiken', ed. Joseph Killorin, New Haven and London: Yale
University Press, 1978, p. 277)

(Aiken's own generation had included T.S. Eliot, Van Wyck
Brooks, and Walter Lippmann, who were his contemporaries in
the Harvard Class of 1911. His own poetry and prose gradually, though belatedly, won a high reputation, as did his
idiosyncratic 'autobiographical narrative' 'Ushant' (1952).
Throughout the 1930s he lived in England, where he was for
some time London correspondent of the 'New Yorker'.)

From its promising beginnings, our age has rapidly degenerated into an epoch of poetic timidity. The fact that
for the first time in human history a society has evolved
which possesses no common intellectual or spiritual focus,
may be the reason why the best poetry that has been produced in the last twenty years or so, often seems by comparison with the best of the past, to be shallow in impulse
and insufficient in technique. During the lifetime of the
present generation, the interest of the most advanced
poets seems to have shifted from the external world to the
inner world, and it now seems about to shift back to the
external world again. The enormous advance of science, of
rapid communication, of short cuts to knowledge, of book
and periodical publication, have not clarified our situation, have only left us with a deeper degree of mental and
spiritual indigestion. Of this indigestion, everything,
from our muddled economics to our periodical political
crises, have become dangerous symptoms. In such a state of
affairs, courage is more necessary to the poet than ever
before, courage to be obscure, unpopular, courage to
attempt some linkage between the older world of spiritual
appeals and loyalties that we are so rapidly losing and the
new world of inhuman and naked scientific entities that we
are so rapidly entering.
     Mr. W.H. Auden is a courageous poet. He is trying to
find some way of living and of expressing himself that is
not cluttered with stale conventions and that is at once
intellectually valid and emotionally satisfying. In order
to do so, he is obliged to hack his way in zigzag fashion

through a stifling jungle of outworn notions which obstruct progress. Hence his 'Orators,' which may be read as a satire on the English public-school system (Mr. Auden is himself a schoolmaster) or as a piece of buffoonery in the Joyce and Wyndham Lewis manner, or as a fragmentary auto-biography, or as a sort of manifesto for an unwritten poem. In any case, Mr. Auden is undoubtedly obscure, in the sense that it is most difficult to see precisely what it is that he is getting at from page to page of his book. All that one can say is that in range and felicity of utterance he yields to none among present-day poets. The only difficulty in following him is that he seems to be perpetually mixing up two levels of experience, private and public. Publicly he tries to persuade us that the world is a farce, pri-vately we feel that he regards it largely as a tragedy. And this results in a great confusion of symbols and of meanings in his work. If one adopts the theory put forward by Mr. Empson, that a great deal of the world's best poetry rests on ambiguity of meaning, and that the task of the poet consists in finding and stressing this ambiguity, then one can say of Auden that his object is to extend this am-biguity from words to events themselves, so that for him there is scarcely a happening that does not bear two meanings. And in this way he both gets around and overleaps the position established by Mr. Eliot, for whom there is only one interpretation of today possible, and that a highly disillusioning one. Mr. Auden, on the other hand, suggests that we should suspend our judgment, and allow events to speak for themselves.

Apart from this curious division of impulse itself, there is still in Mr. Auden, despite his obvious and honest attempt to come to terms with this age, still too much of the matter and manner of other poets. A careful reader of his work cannot fail to be struck with the obvious echoes of Rimbaud, St. John Perse, de Gourmont and Pound with which it is sprinkled. Indeed, in some cases he carries imitation to the point where it becomes pedantry. Yet it remains clear that he is at his best wherever he is least 'up to date,' and most 'Saxon'; that is to say, where he is least ingenious in constructing verbal puzzles. Here we get, as is frequent in many modern poets, something that suggests less the Renaissance, than a new kind of mediaeval poetry. His alliterative measures, in particular, have a swing, a stroke about them that goes back direct to Langland. For instance:

Came summer like a flood, never did greediest gardener
            Make blossoms flusher;
Sunday meant lakes for many, a browner body

Beauty from burning:
Far out in the water two heads discussed the position,
Out of the reeds like a fowl jumped the undressed German,
And Stephen signalled from the sand dunes like a wooden
madman
'Destroy this temple'.   [Ode I, EA, 95]

Anyone who thinks that poetry as austere and as complete
as that particular stanza is easy to write, let him try!
Mr. Auden, for all his frantic attempts to out-do the
moderns, is really at bottom a Puritan; that is to say,
something not so much anathema to the present day, as
totally out of place in it - and for that very reason, more
afraid to speak out fully than many people without a tithe
of his honesty. Here is no 'satiric' poet in the Sitwellian
sense: no breaker of the Victorian butterfly on a crude and
clumsy wheel. It seems that Mr. Auden has scarcely heard of
Victorians at all. Where they mistook sentiment for morality, he gives us morality raw: 'Destroy this temple.' He is
a fanatic. Why he has not succeeded oftener in making his
meaning clear, why he has not written what this book occasionally hints at, an epic of the 'holy war' of the spirit
against the combined stupidity and self-satisfied vulgarity
of this age, must remain a matter of conjecture. Perhaps
his failure is due to ill-health, or overwork, or too great
a fear of possible popularity. All that we can say is that
he still convinces us that he is the one man best equipped
to attempt such a thing at the present day. Perhaps in a
few years' time he will have assimilated better what he has
learned from other poets and will hammer out a philosophy
that is less purely negative. Meantime, he still remains
about the most interesting poetic 'possibility' that England has produced since the war.

22. ROBERT PENN WARREN ON THE ENGLISH 'POETICAL
RENASCENCE', FROM TWELVE POETS, 'AMERICAN REVIEW'

May 1934, 221-7

A distinguished poet and novelist, Robert Penn Warren (b.
1905) was Professor of English at Yale University (1961-
73). His most recent books include 'World Enough and Time'
(1950), 'Incarnations' (1968), 'Democracy and Poetry'
(1975), 'Selected Poems 1923-75' (1977), and 'Now and Then:
Poems 1976-8'.

W.H. Auden has been termed the satirist of the English
'poetical renascence'. The basis of this reputation is
'The Orators, an English Study,' a very perverse, obscure,
somewhat exciting, and at times powerful poem. It is composed of three books: the Initiates, Journal of an Airman,
and Six Odes. Most of the first two books is in prose, the
third entirely in verse. It has been attacked by John
Sparrow in his study 'Sense and Poetry' as an example of
unintelligible writing. The construction is by some principle of association which, except in its broadest outline,
generally defies definition. It is more difficult, perhaps
more confused, than 'The Waste Land,' its most likely prototype. It is more difficult because the basic symbolism of
'The Waste Land' was more apparent, and the mechanism of
its system of ironic reference more accessible. The system
of reference and symbol in 'The Orators' is a personal, if
not arbitrary, matter.

In the first section of Book I, Address for a Prize-Day,
the tone of the work is set in the speech of a visiting
celebrity to the boys, a speech which moves from the clever
innocence of parody to the question: 'What do you think
about England, this country of ours where nobody is well?'
Then for conclusion:

> Draw up a list of rotters and slackers, of proscribed
> persons under headings like this. Committees for muni-
> cipal or racial improvement - the headmaster. Disbeliev-
> ers in the occult - the school chaplain. The bogusly
> cheerful - the games master. The really disgusted - the
> teacher of modern languages. All these have got to die
> without issue.... Quick, guard that door. Stop that man.
> Good. Now boys hustle them, ready, steady, - go.[EA, 64]

This parable of revolution is followed by two sections of a
highly personal nature which are hard to relate to the re-
mainder of the poem except by the tone of disorder and despair pervading them. The fourth section, Letter to a Wound,
effects a sort of ironic resolution for Book I. The victim
has fallen in love with his own mortal hurt, takes a solace
in its intimacy, and concocts from despair a contentment:
'Nothing will ever part us. Good-night and God bless you,
my dear. Better burn this.'

Book II, Journal of an Airman, is a *mélange* of prose and
verse. From its essential confusion two or three suggestions
emerge. The Airman is preparing for, or is already partici-
pating in, a civil war. Fragments similar to the material
in the second and third sections of Book I, some of which
hint at the Airman's personal curse, sexual in character,
appear at intervals in Book II, but are subordinated to the

preoccupation with the objective facts of his business, the stabilizing element in his despair. These facts are the 'Airman's Alphabet':

> *Ace* -   Pride of parents
>   and photographed person
>   and laughter in leather....
>
> *Death* -   Award for wildness
>   and worst in the west
>   and painful to pilots....
>
> *Wireless* - Sender of signal
>   and speaker of sorrow
>   and news from nowhere.

The six odes of Book III are, in detail at least, the most interesting part of 'The Orators', the most pointed, most intense, and best constructed. They are, one might say, a distillation of the foregoing sections. The first five are primarily a definition of that country 'where nobody is well':

> I saw the brain-track perfected, laid for conveying
>   The fatal error,
> Sending the body to islands or after its father,
>   Cold with a razor:
> One sniffed at a root to make him dream of a woman,
> One laid his hands on the heads of dear little pages;
> Neither in the bed nor on the *arête* was there shown me
>   One with power.   [Ode I, EA, 96]

And there is the brooding expectations of violence, certain and aimless, in the ode 'To My Pupils':

> You've a very full programme, first aid, gunnery,
>   tactics,
> The technique to master of raids and hand-to-hand
>   fighting;
> Are you in training?   [Ode V, EA, 107]

The last ode, probably the most conventional in technique but an excellent poem, concludes the volume on another note:

> Not, Father, further do prolong
>   Our necessary defeat;
> Spare us the numbing zero-hour,
>   The desert-long retreat....

     Be not another than our hope;
        Expect we routed shall
     Upon your peace; with ray disarm,
        Illumine, and not kill.   [Ode VI, EA, 109-10]

   The 'Poems' exhibit the same obsessions and same temper
as 'The Orators'. 'Charade', a dramatic fable of the collapse of civilization, is really 'The Orators' in little.
Other pieces, such as X, XI, XII, or XXIX, are equally
specific; and even in most of the others a constant reference for image and metaphor is found in the same background, the broken minehead, the dead mill, the half-
finished culvert, the fortified farm. The 'explosion of
mania' is imminent: 'It is later than you think.' Satire in
these poems has replaced the irony of the preceding decade,
the tone defined by Eliot and Pound. The temper is more
drastic and morose, more specifically critical. If Eliot,
for instance, has certain technical obligations to the
Jacobean dramatists, Auden has a nearer affinity in his
materials and attitude. He is obsessed with the confusion
of his world, with the confusion of issue under the level
of conventional life, with sexual frustration and homosexuality (which, it seems, bears some relation to his
notion of revolution), with the stop-gap futilities and
windiness of the world's rulers.

     If we really want to live, we'd better start to try;
     If we don't, it doesn't matter, but we'd better start
          to die.   [EA, 49]

For violence is a kind of cathartic. It is probably to
be preferred to the alternative, a 'classic fatigue'. And
afterwards,

     The few shall be taught who want to understand,
     Most of the rest shall love upon the land;
     Living in one place with a satisfied face
     All of the women and most of the men
     Shall work with their hands and not think again.[EA, 105]

Meanwhile for the individual

     ...there is left remaining
     Our honour at least,
     And a reasonable chance of retaining
     Our faculties to the last.   [EA, 27]

That is, if the individual has will enough.
     Auden is a stylist of great resourcefulness. He has

undoubtedly drawn heavily on the experimenters of the past decade, Eliot, Pound, Graves, and Riding in verse, and Joyce and Woolf (especially 'The Waves') in prose. But he is not an imitator, for very rarely has he failed to assimilate completely what the model had to give. He is not a writer of one style. The lyrics written in short lines display an aptitude for economy of statement that is almost ultimate; he has sometimes paid for this by an insoluble crabbedness or a grammatical perversity in the unsuccessful pieces, but a few of this type are among his best poems. On the whole, he is most effective in the poems using a long line, poems where the difficulty his verse offers is more often legitimate, that is, derives from an actual subtlety of thought and effect rather than from a failure in technical mastery. Some of this type, however, suffer, as does 'The Orators', from an excessive obliquity or purely arbitrary construction. It may be that a strong talent engaged in the process of experiment and self-discipline must almost of necessity be prodigal of such half-realized fragments. There is no reason, nevertheless, for Auden to be shy of the broad, direct effect in poetry, for his talent has enough vitality to support the naked statement.

Auden, I am fairly confident, may be trusted to solve a good many of his stylistic problems as they arise unless he is deluded by the worship of obscurity for obscurity's sake. The graver problem that may confront him is the one of theme. His present preoccupations, if their treatment remains naïve and overt, may well result in something like a formula, a danger which both Eliot and Pound have frequently succumbed to. Satire, undertaken on his present premise, might mean a mere multiplication of instance; as a matter of incidental reference, as it occurs in much of Donne's work where it is absorbed into the tissue of the poetry, it might be a source of strength and enrichment. For the present it seems that the most constantly satisfactory poems may be pieces of that nature, for instance, II, III, XI, XV, XVI, and XXIV. But it is useless to prescribe or predict.

Auden *is* the advertised English 'poetical renascence', although Stephen Spender is claimed on the jacket of his 'Poems' as its 'lyric poet'. In the short period since the publication of that volume his work has already been considerably over-rated. What is best is deeply indebted to Auden's influence; at least I assume this to be the case because of Auden's infinitely greater force and fertility. As a matter of fact, Spender is probably an inferior poet to John Pudney, whose work 'Spring Encounter' is practically unknown in this country and who seems to have

profited more in a small field from some of the suggestions
of Auden's poetry. Space has compelled me to be thus dogmatic about Spender. From those enthusiastic about his work
I can only ask pardon for my dogmatism and a re-inspection
of his performance, a re-inspection of his thoroughly conventional, 'poetical' idiom, his relaxed rhythms, and his
thin, almost feminine, subject matter.

As for the 'renascence', it remains to be seen whether a
swallow can make a summer.

23. STEPHEN SPENDER ON PSYCHOLOGY AND REVOLUTION

1935

From The Airman, Politics and Psycho-Analysis, 'The Destructive Element', London: Jonathan Cape, 1935, 267-76.

Rilke, in his journal - like all the great aesthetes: like
Joyce, and Henry James, and the early Yeats - is occupied
with the problems of individuals. The aesthetic fulfilment
of the individual soul is what occupies him, as apart from
the personal salvation which concerns Eliot, or the personal damnation of Baudelaire. In Auden's work the emphasis
is quite different: the interest is the relation of the
individual to society....

Combined with Marxism is psychology, and a very acute
analysis of the behaviour of individuals. The 'enemy'
sections are the strength and also the weakness of the
Journal. They are strong because they contain the same true
vision as does the wider, social observation. The weakness
is, firstly, that the enemy tends to be too easily recognizable as one of several public school types. Secondly,
that in this context, psychology combined with Marxism
tends to produce a peculiarly ingenious form of heresy-
hunting.... it justifies narrow personal dislikes, uni-
versalizes petty criticism, and because in many cases it
encourages a kind of masochistic self-abuse....

The principle of the airman is, of course, to shock, although his methods are also partly a satire on established
Fascist methods: it is an extension of Baudelaire's mockery
of everything bourgeois....

The airman, being who he is, is bound to fail, because
he is alone. So long as he is alone he is bound, like paci-
fists, to answer war by non-resistance of a kind which he

believes to be anti-toxin. That is, as long as the airman's observations, whilst they make an enemy of the governing class, do not find an ally in any other class. There is never any really revolutionary issue in The Airman's Journal, because the airman has no friends.... The airman and the artist is, like Roderick Hudson, apart from the rest of the world, isolated by his sensibility. Yet without him civilization is only a name.

One sees then in 'The Orators', the victory of the idea of a psychological cure, which is always predominant as an aspect of Auden's work. But this is followed in 'The Dance of Death' by a violent swing-over to the other, the revolutionary idea.

The position of this play then is complementary, but not contradictory to 'The Orators'. What the play does is not to make a propagandist assertion, but to state a situation. The statement is not irreconcilable with the position of 'The Orators'. Each book states, as it were, a hypothesis, and the two hypotheses enable a writer to achieve his picture of the whole contemporary scene. If one asks at what point that synthesis is achieved, I think the answer is that it rests in a loving attitude of mind: the writer does not write from hatred, not even when he writes satire, but from a loving understanding. His gift is the peculiar gift of a writer who does not write from rejecting his experiences, nor from strict selection amongst many experiences, but accepting more and more of life and of ideas as he goes on experiencing. His danger is that sometimes he adopts the too facile formula of regarding all the world as ill, so that he expresses a philosophy as soothing as that of a nurse. The peculiar kind of experience which his poetry offers is an organic, living experience, made up sometimes of contradictions, and which is sometimes irresponsible and evasive. It is a mistake to suppose his poetry is primarily one of ideas.... It is a poetry of life which deals in ideas, but which is not ruled by them.

An uncompleted 'epic'

1932-3

'I am very hard worked but am pegging away at my epic,'
Auden wrote to Naomi Mitchison in 1932 ('You May Well Ask,
A Memoir 1920-1940'. London: Gollancz, 1979, p. 123). This
unfinished narrative, which consists of two cantos (the
first running to 925 lines, the second to 310 lines), has
recently been transcribed and published, together with an
informative preliminary discussion, by Lucy S. McDiarmid -
W.H. Auden's 'In the year of my youth...', 'Review of
English Studies', new series, xxix, 115, 1978, pp. 267-
312 - who quotes this comment by Auden from an interview
conducted long afterwards: 'It was part of a long poem I
started to do around 1930, a very long dream sequence
something like the "Roman de la Rose" or the "Hous of
Fame" or "The Pastime of Pleasure".' Strongly influenced
by Dante, Langland, and Pope, the draft poem presents an
alienated vision of a valueless city. McDiarmid also comments:

> Long sections of it went into an unpublished play, 'The
> Chase', which was then rewritten as 'The Dog Beneath
> the Skin', and individual lines and phrases turn up
> throughout the poems in the volume 'Look, Stranger', in
> the 'verse commentary' of 'In Time of War', and in mis-
> cellaneous short lyrics. The alliterative metre makes
> lines from the poem recognizable in the midst of
> choruses in 'The Dog Beneath the Skin'. But the more
> remarkable aspects of the poem - the use of epic models,
> the narrative structure, a few incidents and images -
> are not evident from any of the published fragments....

The influence of Gerald Heard , whom McDiarmid describes as
'a popularizer of historical theories', figures in Auden's
largely unavailing efforts to assimilate to the poem the
positive arguments - for a 'new direct sense of social

135

communion' - of Heard's 'The Social Substance of Religion'
(1931).

24. HAROLD NICOLSON ON AUDEN'S DERISION AND INTEGRITY

August 1933

Author, diplomat, politician, lecturer, and journalist, Sir
Harold Nicolson (1886-1968) began his career in the diplomatic service. In 1913 he married the Hon. Victoria (Vita)
Sackville-West, the poet and novelist. After failing as a
parliamentary candidate for Sir Oswald Mosley's New Party
in 1931, he won a seat for the National Labour Party, 1935-
45. He joined the Labour Party in 1947, but unsuccessfully
contested a by-election the next year. Lacking the temperament to become a wholly successful politician, he exercised
both before and after the war a far greater talent for
writing literary and historical biographies, his later
achievements including the splendid 'George V: His Life and
Reign' (1952). He was knighted in 1953, and in 1956 stood
for the Chair of Poetry at Oxford, which Auden won by
twenty-four votes (see Evelyn Waugh's comment in headnote
to No. 76 below).
    From an entry for 4 August 1933, 'Harold Nicolson's
Diaries and Letters, 1930-1939', ed. Nigel Nicolson,
London: Collins, 1966, p. 153.

Wystan Auden reads us some of his new poem in the evening.
It is in alliterative prose and divided into Cantos. The
idea is Gerald Heard as Virgil guiding him through modern
life. It is not so much a defence of communism as an
attack upon all the ideas of comfort and complacency which
will make communism difficult to achieve in this country.
It interests me particularly as showing, at last, that I
belong to an older generation. I follow Auden in his
derision of patriotism, class distinctions, comfort, and
all the ineptitudes of the middle-classes. But when he
also derides the other soft little harmless things which
make my life comfortable, I feel a chill autumn wind. I
feel that were I a communist the type of person whom I
should most wish to attack would not be the millionaire
or the imperialist, but the soft, reasonable, tolerant,
secure, self-satisfied intellectuals like Vita and myself.
A man like Auden with his fierce repudiation of half-way

houses and his gentle integrity makes one feel terribly
discontented with one's own smug successfulness. I go to
bed feeling terribly Edwardian and back-number, and yet,
thank God, delighted that people like Wystan Auden should
actually exist.

'The Witnesses'

'Listener', x, 12 July 1933, Poetry Supplement, ii-iii

25. T.S. ELIOT ON AUDEN, FROM A REPORT ON POEMS PUBLISHED
IN THE 'LISTENER', 1931-3

Autumn 1933

When Auden's 'The Witnesses' appeared with poems by other
poets in the 'Listener's' poetry supplement, Sir John
Reith, Director-General of the BBC, catechized the editor
Janet Adam Smith on the supplement, and especially on 'The
Witnesses'. 'The D.-G. wanted to know why there was so
much that seemed odd, uncouth, "modernist", about our
poems,' she recalled. 'He was not choleric ... but
puzzled' (T.S. Eliot and the 'Listener', 'Listener',
lxxiii, 21 January 1965, p. 105). T.S. Eliot was accordingly asked to deliver a verdict on the new poetry.
    Classicist, royalist, and Anglo-Catholic, Eliot (1888-
1965) was in a strong position to answer for the younger
generation of poets. 'Prufrock and Other Poems' (1917),
'Poems' (1920), and 'The Waste Land' (first published in
1922) had secured his own reputation as a creative writer.
He was equally distinguished as an essayist - 'The Sacred
Wood' (1920) and 'For Lancelot Andrewes' (1928) - as editor
since 1922 of the 'Criterion' and as a publisher with the
firm of Faber, which he had joined in 1925. He could therefore speak with authority in his report, though he could
not pretend disinterest (since he had already adopted the
'Auden Generation' in his capacity as editor and
publisher).
    Three years earlier, in a letter of 11 December 1930,
Eliot had written to Herbert Read, 'I chiefly worry about
Auden's ethical principles and convictions, not about his
technical ability; or rather, I think that if a man's ethical and religious views and convictions are feeble or

138

limited and incapable of development, then his technical
development is restricted' (quoted in Humphrey Carpenter,
'W.H. Auden: A Biography', London: Allen & Unwin, 1981,
p. 137).

A few of the writers have appeared in the 'Criterion': two
of them, W.H. Auden and Stephen Spender, have had volumes
published on my recommendation by Faber & Faber. Of all the
younger poets, Auden is the one who has interested me most
deeply, though I feel that it is impossible to predict
whether he will manifest the austerity and concentration
necessary for poetry of the first rank, or whether he will
dissipate his talents in wit and verbal brilliance.

'Poems', second edition

London, November 1933

26. F.R. LEAVIS REPLIES TO WILLIAM EMPSON, FROM AUDEN, BOTTRALL, AND OTHERS, 'SCRUTINY'

iii, June 1934, 76-80

The second edition of 'Poems' gave F.R. Leavis the opportunity to scout Auden by way of a reply to Empson's essay
on 'Paid on Both Sides' (see No. 1). Leavis further explained in Retrospect 1950 why he had included no criticism of Auden in the first edition of 'New Bearings in
English Poetry' (1932; revised edn. 1950): he believed that
the 'curious and youthful' 'Paid on Both Sides'

> might have represented the very green immaturity of a
> notable creative talent.... The childlike vividness of
> imagination was accompanied by ... an obscurity of the
> wrong kind ... a surprising radical adolescence that
> should have been already well outgrown. It seems to me
> that Auden has hardly come nearer to essential maturity
> since, though he made a rapid advance in sophistication.

The second edition of Mr. Auden's 'Poems' is an opportunity
for reconsidering his 'Charade,' which still, I think, represents his talent at its most impressive. I remember the
prolonged indecision with which I read and re-read 'Paid on
Both Sides' when, three years ago, I was writing the last
chapter of a book on modern poetry. It seemed impossible to
offer an account of it that shouldn't have the effect of
taking away more than it granted, so in the end I said nothing. That was perhaps too easy a solution, though even
now critical appraisal presents itself as a delicate undertaking. Fortunately I have turned up an appraising comment

by Mr. Empson (it appeared in a Cambridge organ, 'Experiment,' in Spring, 1931), and see a possible approach by
comment on that.
    Mr. Empson starts by outlining the plot, which, he
justly observes, is not obvious on first reading, so that
we may gratefully accept his help:

[Quotes first two paragraphs of Empson's essay, omitting
the first sentence.]

    'The play,' Mr. Empson says (the author's word, I think
it worth noting, is 'charade'), 'is "about" the antinomies
of the will, about the problems involved in the attempt to
change radically a working system'; and the analysis in
which he elaborates this account is characteristically
subtle. But I must, at the cost of unfairness, pass it
over, and come to Mr. Empson's concluding paragraph:

[Quotes the final paragraph, complete.]

    The work that could evoke this response is beyond ques-
tion a remarkable one. But - all that in twenty-seven
pages! And, going back again and again to the Charade, I
found that the process of applying Mr. Empson's eluci-
cation remained preponderantly one of adding it on. In
short, it is one of those cases in which the strength of
the author of 'Ambiguity' (and that handful of remarkable
poems) appears as a weakness. I do not, while thus making
a critical convenience of Mr. Empson, throw out an un-
gracious reflection as a mere wanton aside, but because I
see in it a means of doing critical justice to Mr. Auden.
Mr. Auden's strength, then, is to have just what Mr.
Empson appears to lack: a profound inner disturbance; a
turbid pressure of emotions from below; a tension of impulsive life too urgent and shifting to permit him the
sense of intellectual mastery. As a poet he is too immediately aware of the equivocal complexity of his material,
and too urgently solicited by it, to manipulate it with
cool insistence into firm definition and deliberately coherent elaboration. He has nevertheless achieved enough
in the matter of technique to impress upon the reader a
highly individual sensibility.
    But Mr. Empson's account, though it testifies to the
force of this impression, extravagantly overstates the
achievement - misrepresents, indeed, the pretension. 'So
that the play is "about" the antinomies of the will, about
the problems involved in the attempt to change radically a
working system.' - This doesn't misrepresent the nature of
Mr. Auden's preoccupations, but it is not for nothing that,

as noted before, he calls 'Paid on Both Sides' not a 'play' but a 'charade.' The term intimates plainly enough that the claim to dramatic status is not to be taken too seriously; the preoccupations are serious enough, but Mr. Auden does not deceive himself as to the degree in which he has attained dramatic projection, dramatic impersonality. A 'charade' is for domestic performance - 'domestic,' here, in a very special sense: to attempt actual stage-production would be to misconceive the strength of what is offered.

This is not to deny that Mr. Auden has achieved a certain dramatic impressiveness - he has; but the drama remains not much more than merely schematic. Moreover, it appears to owe its vigour largely to a set of interests that have a romatic tinge - that belong less to maturity than those indicated by Mr. Empson. That blood-feud, those 'tribal leaders,' and the action among those taking northern place-names retain something of the spirit of the schooldays to which they clearly point back. Not that maturity cannot draw upon such sources; that he can do so, indeed,is one of the most promising things about Mr. Auden's talent. The criticism is that he has not sufficiently organized his interests; that they are not sufficiently subordinated to his most serious intention; and, in short, that 'Paid on Both Sides' expresses an essential uncertainty of purpose and of self in a very different way from that suggested by Mr. Empson.

It is an immediately relevant observation that the obscurity Mr. Empson notes in Mr. Auden's verse is very different from that of Mr. Empson's. The difference might be described as that between working things out (Mr. Empson's way) and letting them work themselves out. It is Mr. Auden's advantage that he can so much (as it were) leave things to happen. Nevertheless, there must be intensive critical labour if such problems as his are to be solved - 'Probably, indeed, the larger part of the labour of an author in composing his work is critical labour; the labour of sifting, combining, constructing, expunging, correcting, testing....' (T.S. Eliot). It is impossible to avoid the conviction that Mr. Auden is prone to be too easily satisfied with what comes. An intensity of feeling carries off the obscurities in the best verse of the Charade, but in the accompanying poems the freedoms of transition and private association appear altogether too casual, and there is no evidence of any sustained intensity of preoccupation with technique.

A certain assured personal manner Mr. Auden has indeed invented, but the assurance seems to me to cover something very different. It may be examined in 'The Witnesses,' a poem specified by Mrs. Monro for its seriousness. On me the

effect is disquietingly analogous to that of Rupert
Brooke's irony. Auden, it need hardly be said, works at
a very much higher level; the distinction of his talent is
nowhere more apparent than in this kind of work. But so
subtle a blend of surface poise and fundamental self-
mistrust would seem to indicate the need for a peculiarly
resolute critical effort on the part of the poet. Of 'The
Dance of Death' one can only say that it emphasizes this
conclusion. Auden can seldom have written more easily and
his subtlety has never been the servant of a more indeterminate intention. He appears to know little better than the
characters of his drama what the point of it is; to be, as
far as significance is concerned, along with them. And this
is proletarian speech: ''E's a bit of orlright, ain't 'e
Bill?'. That's how 'Punch' spells what the proletariat
'sez.' The point may seem a trivial one, yet I think a
radical criticism of Mr. Auden's attitude in the matter of
'class' is involved.

'The Dance of Death'

November 1933

A. THE TEXT

27. JOHN PUDNEY, FROM POETRY AND SATIRE, 'WEEK-END REVIEW'

vii, 16 December 1933, 670

John Pudney (1909-77), who had been a friend and contemporary of Auden's at Gresham's School, Holt, worked as a
BBC producer and writer from 1934 to 1937, then as a correspondent of the 'News Chronicle' (1937-41); later as a
Director of Putnam's, publishers, from 1953 to 1963. His
published books include 'Ten Summers' (1944), 'Collected
Poems' (1957), and 'Lewis Carroll and his World' (1976).

Poetry and Satire includes comments on books by
Siegfried Sassoon and Herbert Read.

'The Dance of Death', Mr. Auden's poetic play, presents 'a
picture of the decline of a class, of how its members
dream of a new life, but secretly desire the old, for there
is death inside them'. Within limitations, which his
earlier work disregarded, it is an interesting production.
There is efficiency of action and simplicity of speech
throughout. There are comic cadences and rhythms which are
new. One feels, however, lacking in sympathy with the class
he so exquisitely offers for sacrifice. Remembering one of
his own poems which begins:

What's in your mind, my dove, my coney...

it is dull to listen to the syncopated satire of this chorus of young men in silk dressing-gowns. There is always Noel Coward.

The second edition of his poems provides an opportunity of reassessing a change which he has influenced to a considerable degree. The publication of his 'Poems' in 1930 was one of the first signs of a movement now apparent in English poetry. It is not so much a fashionable change in technique or language as a new filtration of energy, rain to roots, causing new grass to appear, which is sensitive to wind's direction or the temperature of the season. At a first reading the book had qualities of assurance, technique, and athletic sensibility that commanded surprise and interest. The reading of this second edition renews one's convictions.

28. D.G. BRIDSON AWAITING THE FULFILMENT OF PROMISE, 'NEW ENGLISH WEEKLY'

iv, 21 December 1933, 234-5

D.G. Bridson (1910-80) worked for thirty-five years as one of the most creative and innovatory writer-producers on BBC radio, for which he produced two authoritative series, 'The Negro in America' (1964) and 'America since the Bomb' (1966), as well as broadcasts with Auden. His early writing figured in Ezra Pound's 'Active Anthology' (1933), and he formed friendships with both Pound and Wyndham Lewis, despite the fact that his own political affiliations lay with the radical liberal left. His books include 'The Filibuster: A Study of the Political Ideas of Wyndham Lewis' (1972), 'Prospero and Ariel: The Rise and Fall of Radio' (1971), and 'The Quest of Gilgamesh' (1956).

A re-issue of Auden's 'Poems' in the perfect format which only Messrs. Faber and Faber could give them is well worth buying. So many dabblers get their limited editions de luxe, that satisfactory setting of the few poets still with us is very near being a cultural necessity. Auden, of course, would be worth reading if printed only upside down and backwards - especially when presenting, as he now does, seven new poems in thirty. At his best, he is a poet worth quoting seriously; and he is at his best in at least one of the seven.

It is three years since the first edition of his
'Poems' appeared, and since then his reputation has grown
a lot and shrunk a little - both justly. His style, in
those three years, has been modified considerably - and not
always for the better. His earliest work, in fact, shows a
promise which is still to be fulfilled. On the other
hand, as most of his later work has been a matter of experiment, the promise cannot be regarded as thus far
broken.

The chief objection to the earliest work, of course,
was the trivial fact of its being consistently unintelligible. He suffered from what Dr. Leavis described as a
mind of 'undoubted subtlety.' Auden himself knew what he
was writing about, perhaps, but very few other people did -
in particular, that is to say. He suggested a mood which
could be appreciated easily enough: as Dr. Leavis complained, he 'excited' and 'stimulated' in a general way.
He created the impression of being a poet brimful of ideas,
but quite unable to get them across clearly. This was all
the more remakable in view of his command of language.
The inference was that he knew what he was doing - as he
probably did. Certainly, he could knit his verse unusually
close when he chose, and was well in the knack of constructing his own constructions. Perhaps, indeed, he took
his construction rather too seriously at times. The opening
stanza of that 'Poem' so justly admired by Mr. Herbert
Palmer is a case in point:-

      For what as easy
      For what though small
      For what is well
      Because between
      To you simply
      From me I mean.   [EA, 113]

But if this is not good poetry in itself, it at least
suggests a technique capable of writing it. Which Auden's
undoubtedly is.

A fair amount, obviously, could be said in extenuation
of such - or any - obscurity. As Mr. Eliot has decreed,
we should be glad that a poet expresses himself at all.
But for a poet writing, as Auden professes to do, of the
death of one world and the birth of another, obscurity of
a wilful order destroys a desired effect. One might say of
'The Hollow Men' 'how depressing' and of Auden's 'Poems'
'how exciting' - there being quite enough rarefied Nancy-
boys about to twitter enthusiastically about generalities
and moods. But a poet claiming any sociological importance
at all must be far more definite.

The difficulty which Auden and his hangers-on appear to be up against is one of time. Events move too slowly for them. They can prophesy the end of an order in five minutes, and must then wait indefinitely for the coming of a new. They are all very much alive to the decay of the world as we know it: they all insist on a change in attitude. They are aware of the general trend which will probably bring the change about. They fully appreciate the necessity for a new morale - even have some idea of the new morale necessary. But when it comes to detailed instructions and definite statements, not being technicians or wanting to be, they simply fall back upon generality. They don't really wish to commit themselves, even if the canons of good poetry would admit of their doing so gracefully. They cannot quite escape the atmosphere of the Common-room, or its usual specious talk of increasing production, digging ditches, building roads, etc.

Admittedly, one cannot blame Auden for the vagueness of Day-Lewis. He has never, as yet, turned himself to plans of war and blue-prints of revolution; there is no reason to think why he should. His work is primarily satiric, and as such is to be considered. But even as a satirist his work suffers from the same lack of directness and particularity. He blows his man down with the draught from shot fired past him: he never aims at the navel. The net result is that he does less damage than we might wish he did.

Apparently, he is becoming rather more conscious of the necessity to be understood and felt. Hence the 'curious psychological document' of the 'simple' poems, which might not seem so curious to anyone who had read Shelley's 'Song to the Men of England' and other such. It might now be said, indeed, that a fair proportion of Auden's poetry is sufficiently straightforward to be understood by an average Bootee. He has even taken to writing pseudo sonnets. But the unfortunate fact emerges that whenever Auden writes his poetry straightforwardly, he writes it badly. His ideas, when understood fully, are not so very exciting after all. They are almost as ordinary as some of his refrains. His verse loses its poetry when it loses its idiosyncracies: one might almost say that it reads best when taken the wrong way.

It remains to be seen, in fact, whether he can combine the *feeling* for poetry manifested in his early obscurity with the directness of his later, using the later form with the earlier gusto. If he can, there seems to reason why he shouldn't lead the field - to use a metaphor probably his own. On the other hand, if he can only follow out his present tendency towards the weakly sing-song, he most certainly won't.

His new piece, 'The Dance of Death,' does not settle the
matter either way. While never obscure, it is never more
than efficiently versified in a catchy manner. The manner,
however, being one traditionally adapted to the scheme he
had in mind, cannot be blamed so much upon him as upon
others. It is the manner used in 'Sweeney Agonistes,' and
one rather more reminiscent of Mr. Aldous Huxley than of
serious poetry. That fact apart, 'The Dance of Death' can
be praised as sound enough of its kind. Its satire, if
still more precious than damaging, is satire of the kind
accepted to-day, and better written than most. If not so
interesting as the Charade which put Auden on the map, it
is neverthless worth reading for one reason or another.
And in any case, one can always stand and wait.

29. C. DAY-LEWIS ON THE DANGERS OF DILETTANTISM

Poet, critic, novelist, and writer for children, Day-Lewis
(1904-72) was the eldest of the *soi-distant* 'Auden Generation'. In spite of being naturally more conventional in
diction and sensibility than Auden, his work during the
thirties came under Auden's influence; but unlike Auden, he
committed himself to the Communist Party for a while. Beginning with 'Transitional Poem' (1929) his work in poetry
won wide critical attention, and he also enjoyed great
popular success as a writer of detective novels under the
nom-de-plume 'Nicholas Blake'. Accomplished as a lecturer
and recitalist, he was appointed Clark Lecturer at Cambridge in 1946; subsequently Professor of Poetry at Oxford.
He became a Director of Chatto & Windus, and served, too,
as Chairman of the Arts Council Literature Panel and, from
1958, as Vice-President of the Royal Society of Literature.
In 1968 he succeeded John Masefield as Poet Laureate.
  See Introduction, pp. 5, 12-13, 26, 31-2, and 61-2, for
comment on Auden and Day-Lewis.
  This is taken from 'A Hope for Poetry', Oxford: Blackwell, 1934, pp. 46-64.

[Auden] is an expert at diagnosis, but has only one treatment for all ailments: we should feel happier if he evinced
a love of health and a knowledge of its nature equivalent
to his love and ability of diagnosis. In the second place
his treatment, his method of satire is apt to defeat its
own ends. Spender has correctly called it 'buffoon-poetry';

and in guying his victims Auden too often becomes identified with them, so that, instead of the relationship between satirist and victim which alone can give significance
to satire we get a series of figures of fun into each of
whom the satirist temporarily disappears.... If Auden could
maintain an objective attitude to his victims, if the part
of him that writes buffoon-poetry could be brought into
closer relationship with his positive poetic force and be
modified by it - or, in other words, if he had a coherent
philosophy at his back, nothing could stop him from writing
major poetry. At present he suffers from an extreme sensitiveness to the impact of ideas combined with an incapacity
to relate them to any scheme of values, which is apt to
give his work a flavour of intellectual dilettantism....

'Poems' and 'The Orators' are didactic from an individualist psychological viewpoint. 'The Dance of Death' is an
attempt at didactic writing from a Marxian viewpoint. If
it fails, the failure must be imputed to the fact that the
classless society is not established in England, for we
have seen that social satire requires an established system
from which to work: the poet cannot satirize the present in
the uncertain light of the future.... The poet is a sensitive instrument, not a leader. Ideas are not material for
the poetic mind until they have become commonplaces for
the 'practical' mind....

...English revolutionary verse of to-day is too often
neither poetry nor effective propaganda for the cause it is
intended to support. Its vague *cris-de-coeur* for a new
world, its undirected and undisciplined attack upon the
whole broad front of the status quo, are apt to produce
work which makes the neutral reader wonder whether it is
aimed to win him for the communist or the fascist state.
Here again the influence of D.H. Lawrence assists to confuse
the issue. We find, for instance, in Auden's preoccupation
with the search for 'the truly strong man,' Lawrence's
evangel of spiritual submission to the great individual....
And though this does not necessarily contradict communist
theory, it is likely to give a fascist rather than a communist tone to poetry....

...when the post-war poet is successful in his use of
concentrated images and paradoxically juxtaposed ideas,
the effect is generally a dramatic one: this is especially
noticeable in Auden's work.

B. THE PRODUCTIONS

30. A. DESMOND HAWKINS ON AUDEN'S DRAMATIC DYNAMITE, 'NEW ENGLISH WEEKLY'

iv, 12 April 1934, 617

Novelist, critic, broadcaster, A. Desmond Hawkins (b. 1908) worked in the 1930s as Literary Editor of the 'New English Weekly', then of the quarterly 'Purpose' (where T.S. Eliot persuaded the owner-editor to allow Hawkins a free hand), and as Fiction Chronicler of the 'Criterion'. In 1946 he became Features Producer, BBC West Region, and Head of Programmes in 1955; he founded the BBC Natural History Unit in 1959. His publications include 'Poetry and Prose of John Donne' (1938), 'Stories, Essays and Poems of D.H. Lawrence' (1939), 'The BBC Naturalist' (1957), and 'Hardy the Novelist' (1965).

This is taken from Recent Verse, a review of two 'club' performances.

The 'Dance of Death' has been published for some months, so I may assume a degree of intimacy with the text. It is a Marxist morality play, eschewing 'natural' representation, and using a chorus (embodying the Bourgeois principle) as the central player with Death the Dancer. Lacking the literary virtues of the same author's 'Charade' it was clearly written for an immediate dramatic purpose, and its performance makes plain that there is sufficient dynamite in Mr. Auden to destroy the sad garbage of the contemporary theatre. To have verbal dexterity, poetic quality, and metrical resourcefulness allied to studied and significant movement on a stage was a pleasure made almost uncritical by its rarity. The play was eager, vivid, and full of movement; the players among the audience had an infectious energy; and Mr. Rupert Doone achieved in his dancing the macabre quality of the speech context.

My main criticism is directed to the chorus, who deluged the stage with the hearty good-humour of a party charade. Faced with Mr. Doone and his attendants they moved and spoke with evident relish, and never ceased to be a crowd of very jolly young men and women having a lark. I am convinced that verse drama must beget a new acting technique of limited, deliberate gesture, occasional stylised

movement and disciplined utterance. The present attempt
was necessarily crude and the experience will doubtless be
of great value. As an alternative, Mr. John Allen's rigid
carriage and monotonous delivery seemed to be too narrow in
scope.

Within its limits, as a kind of satirical masque, presenting a panorama of comic situations which must be kept
free of pathos, the play has, I believe, been underrated.
There are surprisingly juvenile patches, and one would
gladly forego an occasional revue-brightness of the surface; while the general bias of caricature sweeps Marx
away with his victims. Nevertheless it is as a whole an
original and fertile work *in the theatre*, giving hope that
we may again infuse vitality into our decrepit Drama.
Mr. Auden has sharply opposed the accepted clutter, and
the audience rose to demonstrate that something had at
last HAPPENED on a London stage.

31. MICHAEL SAYERS, THEATRE AT LAST!, 'NEW ENGLISH WEEKLY'

vii, 10 October 1935, 435

A review of the Group Theatre's performance in a season
which opened on 1 October 1935.

A. Desmond Hawkins (see No. 30 above) responded to
this review with a letter to the 'New English Weekly' complaining about the Group Theatre's bad production and bad
acting, 'a *stench* of pseudo-artiness' and its 'dangerous
fashions in technique' (24 October 1935, pp. 39-40).

'Sweeney Agonistes' and 'The Dance of Death' (Westminster
Theatre). Nothing since the advent of Ibsen has so successfully exposed the wretched incompetence of the majority of
our dramatic critics as these first productions of the
Group Theatre. The best we get from our popular papers is
the sort of 'criticism' that will damn a new play because
Sarah Bernhardt could not have acted in it; and the vilest
is the dogmatic obscurantism that abominates anything new
simply because it *is* new and disquieting. And again we
have the type of sincere ignoramus, one of these downright
fellows who in any sane community would be much better and
happier at carting coal, but in England, writes dramatic
criticism for the 'Morning Post,' and dictates to thousands
of theatregoers that they are to consider Mr. T.S. Eliot's

'Sweeney Agonistes' 'crude and sordid and pretentious,' and that it is 'an attempt to prove that Life is Death.'

I have not the space here (though I hope to do it elsewhere) to discuss these plays at length. All I can say is that no one who professes (or, as it may be nowadays, confesses) an intelligent interest in theatre can afford to miss the present productions by Rupert Doone and Tyrone Guthrie at the Westminster. I say it without exaggeration: here at last, in an experimental form that is bringing about results, and despite its occasional *brashness*, is modern presentational theatre art as I have been attempting to describe it to you for the past year. Here is theatre springing from the rhythms and idiom of your own life, the only life you know, with its slang and jazz heightened into poetry, your own fevers and languours made tragic, pathetic, comic, so that the action seems familiar, and at the same time disturbing, almost an exposure of your thoughts, a satire of your secrets. And sometimes at the Westminster the other evening one could feel the audience setting itself *against* the show - especially during Mr. Auden's 'Dance of Death.' The audience, whose spokesman is the 'Morning Post,' had come expecting the usual dreary character-studying post-Ibsenite *drame,* and it, or at least part of it, really resented being involved in the action. The middle-class element loathed it. Much preferable, in its opinion, to be the Peeping Tom who pays for the privilege of prying through the fourth wall - one is unconcerned - one can cuddle one's sweetie (God, one's *sweetie!*) - 'only a play, after all.' It is against this attitude that the Group Theatre has to fight, and is fighting; and I for one am at its service.

Room must be found to mention the acting of Isobel Scaife and John Moody in 'Sweeney'; and Rupert Doone, John Allen, Stefan Schnabel, and Arabella Tullock and Hedli Anderson, in 'Dance of Death.'

32. A.L. MORTON ON THE DEATH OF A CLASS, 'DAILY WORKER'

10 October 1935, 4

Arthur Leslie Morton (b. 1903) began his career as a schooltecher, including a spell at A.S. Neill's progressive school, Summerhill. He joined the Communist Party in the late 1920s, and went to work for the 'Daily Worker' - as Proprietor, and as a reporter and sub-editor among other

capacities - from 1934 to 1937. Soon afterwards he wrote
his pioneer Marxist study, 'A People's History of England',
which has gone through many printings since Victor Gollancz
first published it as a Left Book Club choice in 1938. In
addition to distinguished service in Communist Party activities and Marxist education, he has published many further
books including 'Language of Men' (essays, 1946), 'The
English Utopia' (1952). 'The British Labour Movement 1770-
1920' (1956), 'The World of the Ranters' (1970), and
'Collected Poems' (1977). 'Rebels and Their Causes', a
festschrift for A.L. Morton edited by Maurice Cornforth,
appeared in 1978.

Although the Left trend in literature was welcomed in a
general way as bringing possible new allies, A.L. Morton
recalls, very few of the staff of the 'Daily Worker' (with
the exception of Tom Wintringham and Morton himself)
showed any real interest in poetry (letter to Haffenden, 24
November 1980).

This review appeared above the nom-de-plume 'Martin
Marprelate'.

'You have forgotten death, but death has not forgotten
you,' declaims Fate, the announcer over the doomed
bourgeoisie.

In 'The Dance of Death,' by W.H. Auden, which seems to
me to be politically, poetically, and dramatically the most
effective play produced in London for years, this doom
works itself out in detail to an accompaniment of spasmodic
efforts at evasion.

We see the class which death has marked out pursue one
Utopia after another without conviction 'because secretly
they desire the old.'

Auden presents a list of modern movements, not for the
sake of a satiric catalogue, but because these movements
illustrate his thesis, the quest for life in death of a
dying class.

We can see how the cult of bodily fitness can lead to
the creation of a fever of militarism. We see how the
aftermath of war leads to discontent easily diverted into
Fascism by appeals to national sentiment.

Later a more subtle scene shows us how the desire for
death inspires a mysticism of action, desire for action
for its own sake, for the thrill the individual soul experiences in the conquest of some untrodden peak or in
moving faster than anyone has ever moved before.

And we see the complement and degeneration of this in
the quest for sensuous gratification symbolised in the
night club scene.

Through it all dances the figure of Death, now appearing
as a gymnastic instructor, now as sergeant-major, now as
Fascist 'Leader.'

But Auden does not allow us to see this disintegration
as an automatic process. In the body of the theatre the
voice of the revolutionary working-class grows menacingly
till their appearance as an active force ends the play.

In the Fascist scene, placed on a ship the waves rise.
'We are the Waves' chorus the workers.

The ship strikes a rock. 'We are the rock.' Fascist
demagogy is punctuated by the slogans of the United Front.

And as death dies Fate announces his will, in which the
whole technical and cultural heritage of capitalism passes
into the hands of the proletariat.

The Group Theatre are to be congratulated upon a courageous and highly accomplished performance. Rupert Doone as
Death, John Allen as the Announcer (he really knows how to
speak verse) and Hedli Anderson as a singer show something
more than ability.

You have two more days to see this play. There are seats
as cheap as 9d. The Westminster Theatre is close to
Buckingham Palace.

And the audience is invited to participate in the action
of the play – which anyone who has 'assisted' at a Fascist
meeting or taken part in demonstrations should find it easy
enough to do.

33. HAROLD HOBSON APPLAUDS A PIONEER, 'CHRISTIAN SCIENCE
MONITOR'

22 October 1935, 12A

Sir Harold Hobson (b. 1904) was Assistant Literary Editor
of the 'Sunday Times', 1942-8, TV Critic of the 'Listener',
1947-51, and Drama Critic for the 'Sunday Times' from 1947
to 1976. In 1976 he became a member of the National Theatre
Board. His books include 'The Theatre Now' (1953), 'The
French Theatre of Today' (1953), 'The French Theatre since
1830' (1978), and 'Indirect Journey', an autobiography
(1978).

'The Dance of Death,' Mr. W.H. Auden's brilliant, and in my
opinion, entirely successful, attempt to work out for the
theater a new, significant art-form, may, in the strictest

sense of the term, prove epoch-making. This, however, depends far less upon its intrinsic merits than on what is to be done in the same line in the future by Mr. Auden and his followers.

At the moment Mr. Auden belongs more to the pioneers than to the masters of drama. His achievement consists rather in pointing out a fresh road than in traveling down it very far himself. The development of the theater is made up, on the one hand, of the discovery of original methods of expression, and, on the other, of the using of these means of expression to communicate a new content.

Originality of the latter kind Mr. Auden does not claim. In fact, his theory of drama expressly forbids the search for new and unaccustomed ways of thinking. The subject of drama he maintains, is the commonly known, the universally familiar stories of the society or generation in which it is written. The audience, he declares, ought, like the child listening to the fairy tale, to know what is going to happen next. In looking for the sort of fable which would fulfill his own conditions, however, Mr. Auden evidently has not been completely successful, since, for the sake of clarity, he has found it advisable to include in the program a short analysis of the theme of his drama. But he not only tells us what is going to happen before it takes place; on the stage he puts an announcer (Mr. John Allen) who tells us what is happening while it is happening.

Briefly, his conception is the decline and fall of the middle class. According to the strictest sect of his economics, Mr. Auden is a Communist, and his play ends with the triumphant storming of the stage by a band of Bolsheviks who irrupt out of the audience, singing the Internationale, and waving a Red flag of truly magnificent proportions.

To enjoy Mr. Auden's play, and to perceive its importance in the development of the theater, one need not agree with the thesis which he uses it to expound, though such agreement would not, I suppose, hinder one's appreciation. In any case, if a workers' revolution is inevitable in Great Britain, it is highly unlikely that its approach will be officially heralded by clever young men from Oxford and Cambridge, of whom Mr. Auden and his colleagues may be taken as representative and attractive examples.

No - it is not what Mr. Auden says, but the way he says it, that is supremely interesting. He takes that most frivolous of entertainments, the musical comedy, and transforms it so that it becomes an instrument for the serious drama

of which the potentialities, in his skilful handling,
seem illimitable. It is an extraordinary achievement,
as though one were to see 'No, No, Nanette' taken, without incongruity, as the mouthpiece for a twentieth-
century 'Convrat Social.' When Scott took the flimsy,
sensational, pasteboard, romance of Mrs. Radcliffe and
'Monk' Lewis, and changed it into the serious historical
novel, he hardly did a more remarkable thing than has Mr.
Auden in 'The Dance of Death.'

The play, which is a short one, is continuous. The
action opens on a bathing beach, where young representatives of the bourgeoisie are pursuing the current cults of
sun-bathing and athletics. To them, and their songs and
games, enters a dancing Figure (Mr. Rupert Doone) which
symbolizes the dissolution of their class. Sharply cutting
into their uselessness come cries from the audience demanding a workers' revolution, which the Announcer quickly
takes up, and uses as an excuse for fomenting a rising
which will be more particularly suited to English conditions. Meanwhile, the Theater Manager suavely begs the
audience to be quieter, and a budding Fascist organization
forms itself upon the stage. As soon as it is established,
this organization, with an effect at once surprising and
extremely vivid, turns upon the Theater Manager, who is a
Jew, and beats him up.

From then on, the transitions from one phase of sociological development to another are cunningly and smoothly
arranged, while the dramatic effect is elicited and pointed
by a singularly skilful use of all the instruments of theatrical expression - song and dance, speech and action,
mime and decoration and grouping. The Central Figure of Mr.
Doone is always dramatically adequate in holding the piece
together, whilst Mr. John Allen as the Announcer and
several other members of the company considerably distinguish themselves.

34. ASHLEY DUKES PREDICTS A POET'S THEATRE, 'THEATRE ARTS
MONTHLY'

xix, December 1935, 906-8

Dramatist, critic, and theatre manager, Ashley Dukes (1885-
1959) first acted as Drama Critic for A.R. Orage on the
'New Age' in 1909, and later collected his essays in
'Modern Dramatists' (1911). In addition to writing a number

of original plays including 'The Man with a Load of Mis-
chief' (1924), he successfully adapted for the English
stage much of the European theatre he loved, in particular
plays by Toller, Bruckner, Kleist, and Wedekind. He
opened the Mercury Theatre in 1933 as a workshop for
poets' drama and for his wife's Ballet Rambert, and later
staged T.S. Eliot's 'Murder in the Cathedral' (1935) as
well as 'The Ascent of F6'. He was co-editor of the international 'Theatre Arts Monthly'.

The article is entitled The English Scene, and it includes comment on the expressionist methods of the Jooss
Ballet before this review of 'The Dance of Death'.

It was particularly interesting to go the next night to
the opening of the Group Theatre with W.H. Auden's 'The
Dance of Death'; for here a young dramatic poet (raw and
not too level-headed, but still a dramatic poet) was trying to say in a 'political musical comedy' the same things
that Jooss had tried to say in movement. I take it their
philosophy of life and politics is much the same; certainly Auden is explicit enough in his attack on 'the
middle class' (not perhaps the best verbal translation of
the *bourgeoisie* that is the communist bugbear). Admitting
that the piece breathes a hatred of this middle class
which is unknown in proletarian circles, but confined to
the world of well-nourished intellectuals, I should admit
also that it is pointed, theatrically effective, and sometimes humorous as well as witty. I cannot recall being
bored by it for an instant, and therefore assume it to be
original musical comedy as well. If this is an example of
spoken ballet - which may be as good a description of it
as any other - then in expressiveness it stands far above
the silent form employed by Jooss or for that matter
Massine. The actual choreography in 'The Dance of Death'
is not important, though Rupert Doone (who is the prime
mover in the Group Theatre organization) contrives to make
his silent figure the most significant of the play. What
is important is a correlation of acting, movement and
words unlike anything else in to-day's theatre experience.
And stangely enough (especially for those who see the
cloven hoof of the director in every new theatre form)
this harmony of effort is traceable directly to the dramatist. Here is a writer for a future poet's theatre who
knows what is dramatically right and leads his company on
to the realization of his own knowledge. It is not surprising to learn that the play itself sprang from his
association with the company and that all his dramatic
writing is adapted to its needs. And if this time the

result is a blend of some inspiration and much nonsense, that is no fault of the way of going to work.

In such enterprises as this, theatre programs are made the medium for manifestos. Here is W.H. Auden's manifesto, which may be preserved as a record of a young impatient poet's dramatic creed in the year 1935. Under the heading 'I Want the Theatre to Be', it reads:

Drama began as the act of a whole community. Ideally there would be no spectators. In practice every member of the audience should feel like an understudy.

Drama is essentially an art of the body. The basis of acting is acrobatics, dancing, and all forms of physical skill. The music hall, and Christmas pantomime, and the country house charade are the most living drama of to-day.

The development of the film has deprived drama of any excuse for being documentary. It is not in its nature to provide an ignorant and passive spectator with exciting news.

The subject of drama on the other hand is the commonly known, the universally familiar stories of the society or generation in which it is written. The audience, like the child listening to the fairy tale, ought to know what is going to happen next.

Similarly the drama is not suited to the analysis of character, which is the province of the novel. Dramatic characters are simplified, easily recognizable and over life-size.

Dramatic speech should have the same self-confessed, significant and undocumentary character as dramatic movement.

Drama in fact deals with the general and universal, not with the particular and local. But it is probable that drama can only deal, at any rate directly, with the relations of human beings with each other, not with the relation of man to the rest of nature.

Read this again in 1950, and you will find that it explains much of the dramatic history of the intervening fifteen years. Loose and fragmentary as the creed may be, it affords a basis for dramatic writing - and a basis such as was understood, consciously or unconsciously, by the dramatists of every great age. It positively opposes every tendency of to-day's theatre, from drawing-room realism to Shavian intellectualism, and from spectacular production to coterie symbolism. I am particularly interested in Auden's reference to dramatic speech, for it is clear that he thinks of the verse-play in one shape or

another as the natural dramatic medium – and not only
the medium of re-telling legendary or historical tales,
but the dramatic language appropriate to themes of modern
life. The verse-play, whether tragic or comic, is destined to be the form of the immediate future. And where-
ever a small stage raises itself in revolt against the
screen-ridden mentality of the larger stages, it will discover that dramatic speech, 'self-confessed, significant
and undocumentary', is most readily related to dramatic
movement through poetic expression. This does not imply
by any means a revival of 'poetic' drama as the prose
audience of to-day understands it, but rather the contrary. Many people will strenuously deny that the new
dramatic poetry is poetry at all, just as they once denied
that impressionism was painting. The battles of the new
movement will have to be fought over again, and last
generation's pioneers will be this generation's reaction-
aries; there is no help for it.

'Poems', American edition

New York, September 1934

35. JAMES BURNHAM ON CHANGE AND REORIENTATION, 'NATION'
139, 8 August 1934, 164-5

James Burnham (b. 1905), Professor of Philosophy at New
York University from 1929 to 1953, became editor of the
'National Review' in 1955. His books include 'The Machi-
avellians' (1943), 'The Coming Defeat of Communism'
(1950), and 'Congress and the American Tradition' (1959).
  Using the English editions of 'Poems', Burnham anticipated the American publication by just a month.

The peculiarities of the depression book business in
this country have prevented American readers from learning
about a group of young English writers whose development
is of considerable literary importance. No book of
theirs has been published here, and only a few magazines
(notably 'Poetry,' the 'Hound and Horn,' and the 'Symposium') have given them serious attention.
  The easiest approach to these writers as a group is
through two anthologies, 'New Signatures' and 'New
Country,' which include samples in both prose and verse
of the ablest representatives. They should be approached
as a group, for in this way we can see them to be part of
a definite movement that is somewhat more than literary.
Like young French writers, they publish manifestoes, and
proclaim themselves. They want very much to know what they
are doing.
  All of them, in spite of sound Public School training,
are or claim to be communists, at least to the extent of
acccepting, and wishing to work in their own way toward, a
classless society. 'I think,' Michael Roberts writes in
the preface to 'New Country,' ' and the writers in this

160

book obviously agree, that there is only one way of life
for us: to renounce that [capitalist] system now and to
live by fighting against it.' They are all, moreover,
acutely conscious of the problem of the relation of their
social views to their creative writing. Indeed, their current writing is a series of experiments probing various
solutions of this poet-breaking problem.

More technically, this revolution of the social spirit
has, in the group, its stylistic parallels. These writers
have managed to take a hurdle that has been standing for
some time impassable in the literary way. They have absorbed the lessons of Joyce in prose, and of Pound and
Eliot in verse, and have gone on from there. I don't of
course mean that any one of them has yet shown himself the
equal of Joyce or Pound or Eliot. I mean simply that
whereas before them writers either didn't know what Joyce
and Pound and Eliot were about and thereby belonged to a
past generation or were forced to be imitators, these
young men do know, and knowing go about their own business.
Their newness comes out in a number of ways: in the influences they draw from - Gerard Manley Hopkins and the English eighteenth century, for example, instead of the
French poets and the seventeeth century; new enthusiasms,
the very willingness to be enthusiastic, in contrast to
sterility and despair; a looking forward, instead of
chiefly back; and, as always in a genuinely new development, the direct thrust for metaphors into immediate personal experience.

There are several promising writers by whom the group
can be tested: Stephen Spender, Cecil Day-Lewis, Michael
Roberts, William Plomer, Richard Goodman. So far, however,
W.H. Auden is the most considerable. He has published more
than the others: a volume of 'Poems' (besides those appearing in the anthologies and in magazines), an unclassi-
fiable work in both verse and prose called 'The Orators,'
and, most recently, a kind of masque called 'The Dance of
Death.' The sometimes startling figures, the intricate
structure, and the often fascinating semi-rhythms of the
early poems -

[Quotes ll. 1-11 of 'Which of you waking early and watching daybreak', EA, 41.]

these are frequently more accomplished than his recent
verse, with its jog-trot rhymes and the attempt to translate prose rhythms directly into verse forms - an attempt
that sometimes ends simply in flat verse. Indeed, oddly
enough, though primarily a poet and known as such, Auden
has perhaps written more successful prose than verse, a

prose that at its best is colorful, swift, and flexible -

> Next the defective lovers. Systems run to a standstill,
> or like those ship-cranes along Clydebank, which have
> done nothing all this year. Owners of small holdings,
> they sit by fires they can't make up their minds to
> light, while dust settles on their unopened correspon-
> dence and inertia branches in their veins like a zinc
> tree.   ['The Orators', EA, 63]

However, the reason for Auden's uneven development is
the reason why he is a writer of potential importance.
He has not been content to master the technical surface,
nor to fall back on a 'message' and let the surface go.
His social vision is for him more than the formula it has
become for so many of our literary racketeers. He finds
that he must reintegrate his personality in its light; and
re-fuse his personality and his art. This is not an easy
job for a writer who takes writing seriously.

'The Orators' marks for Auden the change and the reorientation. It is his intellectual and emotional break
with the present order, his realization of the intensely
personal problem this break involves for the poet, and
his statement of certain prerequisites of a solution.
Partly through elaborated symbols (many of them recurring
in his poetry) and partly by sharply direct observation,
he surveys once more the spiritual wasteland of contemporary civilization. In the longest section, Journal of an
Airman, he seems to be examining the possibilities of the
romantic attitude, summed up in the figure of the airman,
as a way out of the wasteland. (Nearly all this group, together with a number of the younger English novelists, in
their early writing assert a romanticism in modern dress
against both the neo-classicism of Eliot and the fashionable low realism of the 'twenties.) But the airman, though
noble as an isolated individual and embodying certain
values that must be part of the cultural solution, is inadequate, and before the end himself realizes the inadequacy ('Three days to break a lifetime's pride'). He takes
off into what is clearly his last journey.

It was, I am told, just after completing 'The Orators'
that Auden became a convinced communist. And it should be
noticed that Auden, like the others of the groups, sees
in communism not a destructive force nor a mere economic
revolution. They find it valuable, as poets should, 'in
so far as it removes the vested interests which by enforcing
standardization, oppose all genuine education, the full
development of the individual....' It is this that concerns them.

36. RUTH LECHLITNER, NEW POETS HEARD IN ENGLAND, 'NEW YORK HERALD TRIBUNE'

23 September 1934, section 7, 8

Ruth N. Lechlitner, poet and critic, is author of 'Tomorrow's Phoenix' (1937) and 'Only the Years' (1945).

This review compares 'Poems', by Auden, with 'Poems', by Stephen Spender.

Among the younger generation of English poets - sometimes called the radical group - whose work has incited great interest recently, are W.H. Auden, Stephen Spender, William Plomer, Richard Goodman, William Empson and Cecil Day-Lewis. Auden and Spender, acknowledged in England to be the most important of the group, now appear in book form for the first time in this country.

Spender, who draws from a more familiar tradition and who possesses the superior lyrical impetus, is likely to be the more popular of the two. But in a larger and more signficant sense, W.H. Auden stands at the head of the group. Not since the publication of T.S. Eliot's 'Poems,' fifteen years ago, has there appeared poetry of such dynamic originality and potentiality for influence upon a new school of modern poetic thought and expression. Like Spender, Auden acknowledges his debt to Eliot. But he has more to say than Eliot has said. Making a cleaner break from the self-absorbed participation (as individual and as artist) in the chaos of our present social order, he directs his more robust energies toward not only an attempted analysis but solution of that chaos through mass as well as through individual action.

Yet only in a transitional sense can Auden be considered as a propagandist for advanced socialistic ideas. In his brilliant satirical masque, 'The Dance of Death.' this is made clear. Because he can no more completely identify himself with the 'proletariat' than with the 'decaying aristocracy' of the middle classes, he will be condemned by the strictly left-wing critics. On the other hand, he has - with almost too clever insight and with needle-thrust irony - punctured the masks of hypocrisy and indifference worn by so-called modern activity; activity that, to him, is tottering upon its two outworn, age-feeble stumps: religion and aristocratic tradition.

Auden owes more, in the above connection, to D.H. Lawrence (and both, in turn, to 'the dark, satanic mills of Blake') than to Eliot. When Lawrence affirms that 'man

is only perfectly human when he looks beyond humanity,'
Auden can say (in a reiterated jazz refrain):

Here am I, here are you:
But what does it mean? What are we
          going to do?   [EA, 42-3]

Auden and Lawrence have other points common: each is
balked by a kind of spiritual onanism; each longs for
the assurance of the triumph of the body over death -
though each in his heart is aware that this, as well as
the thing men call progress, is illusory; each decries
the worship of ancestors (cf. Auden, Poem XX); and each,
cherishing moon and stars (being among those 'self-lovers'
of whom Auden speaks in the master's address to the boys
in 'The Orators') hates the sun-followers, the sun-
bathers:

Europe in a hole
Millions on the dole
    But come out in the sun

It is Joyce, however, whom Auden has most wisely assimilated. Witness the superbly compressed and integrated
rhythmical patterns of many of his prose passages (as
shown in parts of 'The Orators' and in the dramatic skit
'Paid on Both Sides'); the exact beauty of his imagery.
For example: The 'dew-wet hare hangs smoking.' 'garroted
by gin,' and the Joycean double-entendre in the 'Enemy'
signs and the Alphabet in the 'Journal of an Airman.'
Auden's prose, at its best, is superior to much of his
verse, particularly his rhymed verse. While he has for
the most part mastered a modern, flexible technique, his
work is highly uneven: in a few of the poems he does
approach, for instance, the sheer excellence of that
brief description of his meeting, as a child, with his
uncle. ('Journal of an Airman.')
    Some of his best work, in verse, is to be found in the
six concluding Odes. But probably the most interesting inclusion in the volume is the play, 'The Dance of Death.'
This cannot be adequately described. It must be read. And
there is no reason why it might not be staged with striking and amusing effect. It is, in brief, a satire depic-
ting the decline of the capitalistic system (represented
by the Dancer), together with the decline of a class (represented by a Greek chorus in two-piece bathing suits),
the whole motivated by an Announcer before a microphone.
When the Dancer finally dies, Mr. Karl Marx is ushered in
to the tune of Mendelssohn's Wedding March and pronounces

the funeral oration:

> The instruments of production have been too much for
> him. He is liquidated.

> There is some real danger that Mr. Auden may be much
> too clever a young man for his own good: the people whom
> he attacks may actually read and understand him. For 'this
> is the dragon's day. the devourer's' - and, verily, the
> teeth of the dragon are sharp!

37. MALCOLM COWLEY ON EMBATTLED PARABLES, FROM SPENDER AND AUDEN, 'NEW REPUBLIC'

lxxx, 26 September 1934, 189-90

Poet, editor, literary critic, and historian, Cowley (b.
1898) was Literary Editor, 1929-40, and Staff Critic,
1940-53, of the 'New Republic'; President of the National
Institute of Arts and Letters, 1956-9 and 1962-5; and
Chancellor of the American Academy of Arts and Letters
from 1967 to 1976.
  Since Random House issued Auden's 'Poems' and Spender's
'Poems' at the same time, Cowley, like most American
critics, reviewed them jointly. Like a number of other
English critics, John Hayward regretted what appeared to
be their obligatory mating: 'By the way, I should like to
support a plea, wittily made in a recent New Yorker editorial, that Auden and Spender should be treated as individuals instead of a kind of tandem combination' (A London
Letter, 'New York Sun', 1 December 1934).

There has been a great beating of drums and clashing of
cymbals to announce these two poets; perhaps there has
been more noise than is justified by their work so far.
Neither Stephen Spender nor W.H. Auden has yet written a
long poem that belongs with the English classics, even
with those of the second rank. But they have done something else, something that seemed next door to the impossible: they have brought life and vigor into contemporary
English poetry.
  They appeared in a dead season when all the serious
young men were trying to imitate T.S. Eliot and weren't
quite bringing it off. Eliot himself, after writing

'The Waste Land,' had entered a territory that was supposed to be watered with springs of spiritual grace, but
most travellers there found that the waters were subter-
ranean and the soil brittle with drought. Reading his new
poems was like excavating buried cities at the edge of
the Syrian desert; they were full of imposing temples and
perfectly proportioned statues of the gods, but there was
nothing in the streets that breathed. Say this for Spender
and Auden: they are living in an actual London; they walk
over Scotch moors that are covered with genuine snow; they
are not in the British Museum pressed and dried between
the pages of a seventeenth-century book of sermons.

Still more important, they do not stand alone. They are
merely the vanguard of a group that includes Charles
Madge, John Lehmann, Cecil Day-Lewis (in some ways the
most promising of all), Richard Goodman, Julian Bell and
others. All of these poets are young, gifted in their
various fashions, and seem to know what they are doing.
All of them are able to write about political issues, not
dryly or abstractly, but in terms of human beings. Most of
them are radical without being proletarian. It is a matter
of simple good sense that a proletarian poet ought to
begin by being proletarian, just as a Catholic poet ought
to be Catholic; otherwise he runs the risk of becoming as
empty and affected as the hangers-on of the Oxford movement. These young men, graduates of the English universities, don't pose for the newsreel men in the role of
mechanics, dressed in greasy overalls; but neverthless
their sympathies are with the workers, and their sympathies have sharpened their perception of what is going on
in the world around them. They are able to convey the
sense of violence and uncertainty that we gulp down with
the headlines of our morning papers, and of disaster
waiting, perhaps, outside our doors.

So far Auden and Spender are the only members of the
group whose work has appeared in this country (and incidentally their publisher deserves credit for giving
them two handsome volumes). In a curious way they remind
me of two recent American poets. Auden suggests E.E.
Cummings: he has the same crazy wit, the same delight in
playing with words and the same indifference to whether
he is being understood. Spender suggests Hart Crane, more
by a quality of outpouring emotion than by any specific
mannerism. Auden, with his sharper tongue and quicker
eyes, has more to teach his fellow poets, but Spender, on
second reading, is the one I prefer.

W.H. Auden is a battle poet. His boyhood was spent
among rumors of war, troop movements, lists of officers
dead on the field of honor; his career as a poet belongs

to the gray depression years. In his poems he has made a
synthesis of these two adventures. The results of unemployment are projected forward into another war, this
time a war between social classes fought against a background of decaying industrialism. He gives us a sense of
skirmishes in the yards of abandoned factories, of rail-
roads dynamited, ports silted up, high-tension wires
fallen to the ground, of spies creeping out at night or
stumbling back to drop dead of their wounds (it is curious
how often he mentions spies) and always a sense of mystery, of danger waiting at the corner of two streets:

> But careful; back to our lines, it is unsafe there,
> Passports are issued no longer; that area is closed.

Along with this goes a sanguinary sort of wartime
humor that is best illustrated in his burlesque account
of a revolution in England. On the second day of fighting, 'A white-faced survivor informs the prison governor
that the convicts, loosed, storming the execution shed,
are calculating the drop formula by practical experiment,
employing warders of various weights.' On the third day,
famine attacks the upper classes - 'For those who desire
an honorable release, typhoid lice, three in a box, price
twopence, are peddled in the streets by starving corner
boys.' There are pages of Auden that have the irresponsible savagery of the Dada Manifesto.

His principal fault, I think, is his damnable and perverse obscurity. Partly this is the result of his verse
technique, of his habit of overusing alliteration and
thus emphasizing the sound of words at the expense of what
they signify. Partly it is the result of literary tradition - the famous tradition of 'opacity' that Eliot and
Pound did so much to spread, and the plain-reader-be-
damned tradition that was part of Dadaism and Super-
realism. There are times when Auden deliberately befogs
his meaning, and other times when he obviously doesn't
mean anything at all; he is setting down his perceptions
for their value in themselves and if they don't fit together into a unified picture, well, so much the worse for
the reader. But there is another reason for his obscurity,
a psychological reason having to do with his own position
in that class war about which he is always writing. By
birth and training Auden belongs with the exploiters. When
he says 'we,' the people to whom he refers are the golf-
playing, every-morning-bathing, tea-at-the-rector's-
taking type of Britons. When he says, 'they,' he is thinking of the workers; but he admires 'them' and despises
'us.' He believes that his own class is decaying from

within, is destined to be overthrown, and he looks forward to this event with happy anticipation:

> If we really want to live, we'd better start at once to try;
> If we don't, it doesn't matter, but we'd better start to die.   [EA, 49]

And that, I think, is the principal source of his ambiguity: he regards himself as a class traitor, a spy, a Copperhead. For this reason he is forced to speak in parables, to use code words like a conspirator in a Vienna cafe who wants to deliver a message but knows that the bulls are listening. He is on his guard, wary - till suddenly he gets tired of being cautious and blurts out a condemnation of everything he hates. I like him best when he is least self-protective.

What shall we say of both these poets? They have a good many obvious faults, their appeal is partly a snob appeal (and this is true of Auden in particular), but there is life in them always, and reading them is a stimulating experience. They are opening up a new territory. The best of them is the feeling that they will call forth other poets, not merely to follow in their footsteps, but perhaps to go beyond.

'The Dog Beneath the Skin'

(with Christopher Isherwood)
London, May 1935; New York, October 1935

A. THE TEXT

published seven months before the first stage performance

38. I.M. PARSONS ON 'A HALF-BAKED LITTLE SATIRE',
'SPECTATOR'

cliv, 28 June 1935, 1112, 1114

Ian Parsons (1906-80) became a Director of Chatto &
Windus Ltd in 1953, and was Chairman from 1954 to 1974.
He was President of the Publishers Association from 1957
to 1959. His own publications include 'The Progress of
Poetry' (ed., 1936), 'Men Who March Away' (1965), 'Poems
of C. Day-Lewis' (1977), and 'The Collected Works of
Isaac Rosenberg' (1979).

This extract is taken from Poetry, Drama and Satire,
which includes comment on Eliot's 'Murder in the
Cathedral'.

Auden, together with Louis MacNeice, retaliated upon
this review in their Last Will and Testament: 'May the
critic I.M. Parsons feel at last / A creative impulse...'
('Letters from Iceland').

In contrast to 'Murder in the Cathedral', 'The Dog Beneath
the Skin' is a shoddy affair, a half-baked little satire
which gets nowhere. If it had been written by Mr. Brown
and Mr. Smith, instead of by two intelligent young men

like Mr. Auden and Mr. Isherwood, nobody would have
bothered to publish it, and nobody would have been the
loser. For of all the dreary jokes imaginable it must
surely be the dreariest, the flattest, and the stalest
that has managed to get into print for some time. Dreary,
because it is set out with a great deal of extravagant
pretension; flat, because the satire is so crude that it
completely misses fire; and stale because the objects
against which it is directed have been objects of ridicule
for the last ten years or more. The target, in fact, has
been so consistently shot at that only a direct hit can
nowadays produce any noticeable effect. Messrs. Auden and
Isherwood never, it seems to me, register so much as a
lucky 'outer.'

Take, for example, the passage in which philistinism is
in the stocks. The scene is the restaurant of the Nineveh
Hotel (plutocracy) during a cabaret performance. Destructive Desmond, 'dressed as a schoolboy, with ink stains
on his cheeks, a crumpled Eton collar,' &c., produces first
a Rembrandt and then a third-rate Victorian landscape. An
Art Expert among the audience is invited on to the stage
and pronounces the Rembrandt genuine and the Victorian
landscape an inferior reproduction of a revolting picture;
upon this Destructive Desmond produces an enormous pen-
knife and prepares to slash the Rembrandt to pieces. The
Art Expert protests, appeals to the audience, is shouted
down and rushes from the scene while Desmond merrily puts
his fist through the masterpiece. Could anything be more
clumsily ineffectual? Or more untrue to life? And this is
important, because satire depends upon the recognition of
incongruities, through the simultaneous presentation of
truth and absurdity. Without a basis of truth there is no
scale of actuality against which to measure the pretensions which are the objects of satire. If the audience had
shouted down Desmond instead of the Art Expert, not because they liked the Rembrandt better than the Victorian
landscape but because (a) they knew it was worth more,
and (b) they knew they *ought* to like it better, then the
scene might have contained a flicker of satire. As it is,
its grotesqueness effectively kills such humour as it
might have had.

And this is largely true of the rest of the play, of
the jibes directed against the press, the pulpit, the
politician and the retired general, not to mention the
public school system and the arms manufacturer. Only in
these cases the jibes are not only poor but stale. One
wonders what fun an audience not entirely composed of
morons could conceivably extract from so much knocking
about of battered Aunt-Sallies, and so much preaching to

the converted. The play, incidentally, is to be produced
in the autumn by the Group Theatre under the direction of
Mr. Rupert Doone, to whom Mr. Eliot also acknowledges
help. If the same ladies who at Canterbury so successfully
ruined the Becket choruses by their drawing-room melo-
dramatics are included in the caste of 'The Dog Beneath
the Skin,' a very good time should be had by all.

39. A.L. MORTON, SHOCKED SATIRISTS, 'DAILY WORKER'

3 July 1935, 4

'It's an awful shock,' as Francis observes, 'to start seeing people from underneath,' and this is an experience
which many, like the writers of this fantastic, satirical
play, are now seeking.
   The result here is criticism, often pointed and effective, of a Europe distracted by Fascism and crisis. But
for the most part this criticism just misses the centre of
the target. For this there seem to be two reasons.
   First, Auden as in 'The Orators' and elsewhere, concentrates his fire upon the secondary characteristics of the
enemy. He hates the bourgeoisie not because they are the
bourgeoisie, but because they have the qualities which as
members of the class to which they belong they must necessarily have.
   The result is individual criticism and satire trying to
become social.
   And, secondly, there is no sign that Auden is by nature
a satirist at all. He is (at moments) a superb lyrical and
descriptive poet, capable of mapping a whole landscape or
situation in a few sentences. Even when he is his most
fantastic his geography is never at fault.
   But here the satire has crowded out the geography to
produce a blazing phantasmagoria.

40. MONTAGU SLATER, TWO REVIEWS IN 'LEFT REVIEW'

1935

Poet, novelist, librettist, critic, and writer for films

and television, Slater (1902-56) worked early in his
career for the 'Observer' and the 'Daily Telegraph'. He
had joined the Communist Party by 1930, and in 1934 became Editor-in-Chief of the 'Left Review', to which he
also contributed when it was later edited by Edgell
Rickword (see No. 70) and by Randall Swingler (see No. 77).
During the war he was Head of Scripts in the Film Division
of the Ministry of Information. He co-founded the periodical 'Our Time' in 1940, and founded the quarterly 'Theatre
Today' in 1947. In addition to numerous plays and film
scripts, and novels including 'The Inhabitants' (1948), he
also wrote the libretto for Benjamin Britten's opera
'Peter Grimes' (see 'Peter Grimes and Other Poems', 1946).
Slater's creative work is well represented by Poems and a
Play in John Lucas (ed.), 'The 1930s: A Challenge to
Orthodoxy', Hassocks, Sussex: Harvester Press, 1978.

Slater published two notices of 'The Dog Beneath the
Skin' in the 'Left Review', the first critical, the second
much more favourable. In a paragraph immediately preceding
the first extract below, he praised the 'sense of history'
in Auden's earlier poems, but added the sorry observation
that 'what has been disconcerting, as time goes on, is
that this sense of the outward world seems to have
thinned not thickened.... introspection still rules'.

---

i. From the Fog Beneath the Skin, 'Left Review', July 1935,
429

'The Dog Beneath the Skin' is a satirical musical comedy
interspersed with serious poetic choruses, some of them
as memorable as that which W.H. Auden chose for publication in 'Left Review' No. 8. I do not know how the
authors divided the work between them. Auden evidently
wrote the choruses. The unfunny practical-joking extravaganza of the piece should perhaps be blamed on the difficulties of collaboration. The piece again shows Auden's
power of giving morbid neuroses an objective and even
amusing life of their own (though this sounds like a
contradiction in terms). Yet the dramatic ingenuity which
he showed in 'The Dance of Death' is not so evident. The
piece seems to have been planned in confidence that anything goes in a charade among friends. A sense of history
gives place to an eye for tabloid headlines. We labour
through wastes of depression to reach the glow of a faint
but more cheerful dawn.

> Mourn not for these; these are ghosts who choose their
>   pain,

Mourn rather for yourselves; and your inability to
     make up your minds
Whose hours of self-hatred and contempt were all
     your majesty and crisis,
Choose therefore that you may recover: both your
     charity and your place
Determining not this that we have lately witnessed:
     but another country
Where grace may grow outward and be given praise
Beauty and virtue be vivid there.

'Your inability to make up your minds' - is that it? For
surely the truth is that after the first brilliant promise
of these young poets there has followed too long a period
of hope delayed. They are still poets of an indeterminacy
principle.

ii. From The Turning Point (which includes notice of 'The
Poet's Tongue', an anthology edited by Auden and John
Garrett, London: G. Bell & Sons, 1935), 'Left Review',
October 1935, 20

The first item in Auden's first volume of Poems is 'a
charade,' intended apparently to be acted by the group in
a drawing-room, like Yeats's 'Four Plays for Dancers.'
Yeats who also used to hope for community art out of group
art, was already an influence. A stronger influence were
the English pre-Renaissance things like the 'Mummers'
Play' and 'The Revesby Play,' two folk plays reprinted in
'The Poet's Tongue.' In time the idea grew more sizeable.
The group grew big enough to swallow the ballet. 'The
Dance of Death' was written for the Group Theatre. In turn
the Group Theatre grew more ambitious. This season it is
going to the Westminster Theatre. And now it has a full
length play - full-length musical comedy even - 'The Dog
Beneath the Skin,' by W.H. Auden and Christopher
Isherwood.
  My first impressions of this play recorded in the July
'Left Review' were unfavourable and partly mistaken. There
is a difficult leap to make in the synthesis: for the
Group Theatre now swallows not only the ballet but ironically makes a meal of the red plush seats and valanced
scenery of the musical-comedy theatre; makes a meal too
(and still half ironically) of the basic English dramatic
conventions (themselves almost folk-conventions). It has
even occurred to me that the authors had been often among
the audience of 'Young England.' Irony makes this full
meal and keeps it down though the reader sometimes suffers

heavings. After a little training it is possible to revel in the risk of dyspepsia. A man can eat this meal, the first time suffering indigestion, the second belching pleasurably in the Eastern fashion.

The poets are not satisfied to arrange with irony the heavy plush furniture of their theatre. They give their theatre intelligent decoration, give it poetic choruses which (especially the final chorus) are exhilarating positive pieces of writing. So we have an added risk and an added glory. Bravery is added glamour. 'Comedy,' quotes Bukharin, 'is for criticizing men, tragedy for praising them.' Yet this comedy ends in a tremendous pæan of praise for men who are not there and have not been mentioned. The praise is subtle and deep, though abstract as poetry dare be. And certainly it is right in the English tradition to mingle magnificent poetry with the most ironical comedy. The truly marvellous is put beside the too marvellous and - well there it is....

41. LOUISE BOGAN ON THE CONVICTION AND CHARITY OF A GOOD PLAY, 'NEW REPUBLIC'

85, 27 November 1935, 79

Louise Bogan (1897-1970) seems to have been encouraged to appreciate Auden by Edmund Wilson, who wrote to her on 12 December 1933:

> Auden seems to me really good. I think you said you'd read his poems and didn't think very highly of them; but 'The Orators' and 'The Dance of Death' are more interesting.... Why don't you write a *confession d'un emfant du siècle*? - maybe Auden's 'Orators' would give you a cue. ('Letters on Literature and Politics 1912-1972', ed. Elena Wilson, 1977, p. 234)

Her own lasting enthusiasm for Auden evidently began, however, only with 'The Dog Beneath the Skin'. Well-known as a poet, critic, and translator, her publications include 'Body of This Death' (1923), 'Selected Criticism' (1955), 'The Blue Estuaries: Poems 1923-68' (1968), and 'A Poet's Alphabet' (1970).

This article is entitled Action and Charity.

W.H. Auden has emerged rapidly from the soliloquy
darkened by private associations, a form that might
have hampered him for a longer time. His first dramatic
efforts, 'Paid on Both Sides' and 'The Dance of Death,'
were founded on the feeblest possible dramatic framework:
the charade. He has written, in the present play, with
the competent aid of Christopher Isherwood, a long,
highly amusing revue, whose satire is so deft that it may
stand, without cutting a sorry figure, beside the early
Gilbert. Along with the satirist's wit, the imagination
of a poet and the broad humor of a sane young man are
also involved.

Auden's play is closer to the original music-hall
entertainment so admired, in the nineties, as a refuge
from the torpid, affected art and literature current at
that time, than Eliot's 'Sweeney Agonistes' or Cocteau's
'Orphée,' derived from the same source. It is less dependent on pure queerness than Cocteau's play, and it is not
heavily symbolic, like Eliot's. It is a light-hearted yet
fundamentally grave parable of the noble youth who des-
cends from his class to give humanity in general a hard
and unprejudiced stare....

Auden and Isherwood are by no means the first young
members of the English upper class who have pilloried
their caste. Even the rather unsettled Sitwells have put
down, in terms far from uncertain, the grotesque antics
of members of the three estates. The most noticeable in-
gredient in Auden's attitude is his lack of hatred; he
has much pity and strong anger, but he is not blood-
thirsty and he does not blame. He surveys the scene from
above and below; he gives it elevation, section and plan,
but he does not rant against it. The hysterical, the
gloomy, the portentously righteous and solemn note is
missing, yet the power of his indictment is not diminished
because of its absence. And there is a hint given from
time to time that it is man's present (and perhaps future)
partial capacity for sense and for good, his defective
and divided nature, that helps to distort the scene.

To men of action, pity is sentimental and insight into
the human heart unnecessary. To a poet, pity and insight
may also kindle the fire of action and sharpen the pen in
the hand. Auden fearlessly incites to action, after he has
shown that what must be fought are not only the outer
horrors but also the flesh on the bones and the stupidity
in the veins:

You have wonderful hospitals and a few good schools:
Repent.
The precision of your instruments and and the skill of
    your designers is unparalleled:

Unite.
Your knowledge and your power are capable of
    infinite extension:
Act.

Auden has now proved himself capable of real power
over his material. His poetic endowment, remarkable from
the beginning, is gaining in depth and scope. He is a fine
poet and he has written a good play, his convictions and
his charity within it.

42. JOHN LEHMANN ON A CAREER IN PROGRESS, 'INTERNATIONAL
LITERATURE'

4, April 1936, 69-74

Poet, critic, biographer, and publisher, Lehmann (b. 1907)
was founding Editor of 'New Writing'. 1946-50, and of
'London Magazine', 1954-61; Partner and General Manager of
the Hogarth Press, 1938-46, and Founder and General
Manager of John Lehmann Ltd, publishers, 1946-52. His
publications include 'Collected Poems' (1963), 'A Nest of
Tigers' (1968), and three volumes of autobiography, 'The
Whispering Gallery' (1955), 'I Am My Brother' (1960), and
'The Ample Proposition' (1966). His 'New Writing in
Europe' (Harmondsworth: Penguin, 1940) ably reviews the
literary culture of the 1930s.
    This is an extract from Some Revolutionary Trends in
English Poetry: 1930-1935.

W.H. Auden is undoubtedly the most interesting mind in the
'New Country' group, and it is not too great a claim for
his powers to say that, if his 'Poems' had not appeared
in 1930, none of the poets, including Spender and Day-
Lewis, would be writing precisely as they are. It is not
merely that his fertility and invention, in images,
phrases, rhythms, is enormous and scarcely equalled in
modern English poetry, but also that he has managed to
present consistently through a long collection of poems,
with these technical powers, a remarkable dramatic sense
of a collapsing culture, a civilization desperately ill
beneath an imposing exterior. It was this new way of looking at the world, which Eliot has prepared though it is
profoundly different from his own which startled into

fresh creative activity many minds already sensitive to
the volcanic tremblings through the soil of everyday
life. Auden brings a psychological X-ray to bear on contemporary society revealing fundamental weaknesses, in-
hibitions, streaks of madness, which, through individuals,
are acting destructively beneath the surface of life. He
sees these weaknesses, too, as historically conditioned;
there are forces working in us, from one generation to
another, which he calls 'love,' 'the enemy,' 'death,' developing an extraordinary mythology around them. For a
generation determined to accept nothing easy or un-
complex, nothing that yielded its meaning at first glance,
his frequent obscurities, and his love of mystification,
private jokes, invocations to names and symbols that could
have little sense to those not 'in the know,' were by no
means an obstacle to admiration. Through his early work he
seems to be speaking to an elect few, salvaged from the
general wreck of civilization, his friends. Another trait
that makes of him a peculiarly 'intimate' poet, a poet
for a private circle of friends, is his love of charades
and clowning - the very first work in 'Poems' is a
charade, where Father Christmas appears suddenly in the
middle of a tense scene. His work is, indeed, extraordinarily complex - one is reminded of Ilya Ehrenburg's
observation apropos of Malraux's 'La Condition Humaine,'
that just such a complexity is characteristic of a culture
in its decline, - and brilliant satirical flashes follow
passages where a curious religious note predominates; in
his style there are traces of Eliot, G.M. Hopkins (from
these two perhaps comes the religious note), Wilfred
Owen, Anglo-Saxon poetry, Jazz Songs, and in his ideas,
not only of Marx, but also of Freud and Lawrence, to name
only a few.

'Poems' (which four years later was issued in a revised edition,) is probably his finest work. In comparison with the best in this book much of his later work
seems to show a drying up of inspiration, a failure to advance to new positions, and a technical looseness which is
disappointing. In 'Poems' we see his favorite, North
Country landscape of industrial decay:

> Smokeless chimneys, damaged bridges, rotting wharves
>   and choked canals,
> Tramlines buckled, smashed trucks lying on their side
>   across the rails....   [EA, 48]

At the same time he is continually introducing his
favorite symbolic landscape of frontiers, lurking enemies,
and passes difficult to cross:

> Crossing the pass descend the growing stream
> Too tired to hear except the pulses' strum,
> Reach villages to ask for a bed in
> Rock shutting out the sky, the old life done....[EA, 12]

'Paid on Both Sides,' the charade, and some of the
poems with their background of feud and shooting, show how
living in Germany had affected him, but on the whole the
poems are extremely English in their background, and in
the particular kinds of psychological illness which he
fastens upon. The sense of belonging to a generation
brought up in a tradition that had suddenly shown itself
to be inadequate, is everywhere:

> ...They taught us war,
> To scamper after darlings, to climb hills,
> To emigrate from weakness, find ourselves
> The easy conquerors of empty bays:
> But never told us this....   [EA, 7]

> Their fate must always be the same as yours,
> To suffer the loss they were afraid of, yes,
> Holders of one position, wrong for years....   [EA, 45]

> We know it, we know that love....
> Needs death, death of the grain, our death,
> Death of the old gang....   [EA, 40]

His most remarkable quality, his sense of this cultural
decay as a historic phenomenon, is presented in many dis-
guises, the progress of life, or the historical process
appearing as 'love,' or as 'I':

> Since you are going to begin today
> Let us consider what it is you do.
> You are the one whose part it is to lean,
> For whom it is not good to be alone....
> But joy is mine not yours - to have come so far,
> whose cleverest invention was lately fur....
> Nor even is despair your own, when swiftly
> Comes general assault on your ideas of safety....
> Your shutting up the house and taking prow
> To go into the wilderness to pray,
> Means that I wish to leave and to pass on,
> Select another form, perhaps your son....   [EA, 44-5]

In writing like this he shows that he had passed well
beyond the negative pessimism of Eliot. A clinical sense
(it is difficult to call it anything else) of the

possibility of being cured of psychological illness, as
well as a historic sense of life moving on to new hope in
new shapes, gives his work a definite optimism. Witness
his more direct satirical manner:

> Financier, leaving your little room
> Where the money is made but not spent,
> You'll need your typist and your boy no more;
> The game is up for you and for the others.... [EA, 47]

And the passage already quoted:

> Send to us power and light, a sovereign touch
> Curing the intolerable neural itch,
> The exhaustion of weaning, the liar's quinsy,
> And the distortions of ingrown virginity....
> Cover in time with beams those in retreat.... [EA, 36]

In 'The Orators,' published in 1932, two years later,
the same themes are to be found, the same brilliant imagery
and unexpected angles of approach. The poetry proper is
in this book less important; the set of Odes which come
at the end are rather long and rambling, introduce very
little that is new, and are almost entirely personal in
allusion. The paraphernalia of a schoolmaster's life, and
the tone of the games-master giving the boys a talk before
the match, make a rather overwhelming appearance. Auden,
Day-Lewis, Warner, Upward, are, or have at one time been,
schoolmasters, and this style now spreads very rapidly,
even to their followers, which gives their work of this
period an unfortunately cliquish, even semi-fascist
flavor. Much more interesting in 'The Orators' is the
prose, particularly the Address for a Prize-Day and the
Letter to a Wound, which brilliantly develop the ideas of
the 'Poems,' and more explicitly:

> What do you think? What do you think about England,
> this country of ours where nobody is well?...
>   Next the defective lovers. Systems run to a stand-
> still, or like those ship-cranes along Clydebank, which
> have done nothing all this year. Owners of small hold-
> ings, they sit by fires they can't make up their minds
> to light, while dust settles on their unopened corres-
> pondence and inertia branches in their veins like a
> zinc tree....   [EA, 62-3]

There are other prose pieces, more obscurely written,
in which the religious note appears. There is an attempt
to state a philosophy in private symbols and a style like

the litany, which seems curiously passive in comparison
with, for instance, the Address for a Prize-Day. That
passages like:

> Speak the name only with meaning only for us, meaning
>   Him,
> a call to our clearing....   [EA, 64]

still occur in his writings, seems to indicate that as yet
a profound decision between passivity (religion) and activity (revolution) is unresolved in his nature. The remarkable psychological and historical intuition, one feels, is
being wasted for lack of clear rational direction.

The Journal of an Airman is the pièce de resistance,
and an examination of its curious symbolism and myth-
making makes one feel all the more strongly that there is
a confusion in Auden's ideas. It is a work which no one
but Auden could have written, dramatizing in an extraordinary way one of his fundamental ideas, that of 'the
enemy,' with moments of deep insight into personal and
social psychology. There is scattered evidence of Marxian
thought:

> The effect of the enemy is to introduce inert velo-
> cities into the system (called by him laws or habits)
> interfering with organisation. These can only be re-
> moved by friction (war). Hence the enemy's interest in
> peace societies....   [EA, 73]

But at the same time potentially fascist thought,
hitherto latent in his work, comes out now like a measles
rash. The curious doctrine of 'ancester-worship,' which
Day-Lewis has maintained is so important to the group,
now makes its appearance, and the fondness for clowning, practical jokes and private allusions runs riot.
There is to be a transformation of society, but it is to
be carried out by the Airman and his friends, and followed
by an orgy of private revenge, with a mixture of public
school high spirits and vicious cruelty. In the section
called 'After Victory' the Airman notes:

> Few executions except for the newspaper peers - Viscount
> Stuford certainly, The Rev. McFarlane?
> Duchess of Holbrook for the new human zoo.
> Tom to have the Welsh Marches.
> Ian a choice of Durham and Norfolk.
> Edward for films....   [EA, 91]

His decriptions of traits by which the enemy can be recognized are a mixture of clever insight and comic allusions
to purely private dislikes:

> Three kinds of enemy walk - the grandiose stunt - the
> melancholic stagger - the paranoic sidle.

> Three kinds of enemy clothing - fisherman's
>   pockets -
> Dickens' waistcoats - adhesive trousers....   [EA, 81]

Stephen Spender has written, in 'The Destructive Element', at some length on the Airman:[see No. 23 above].
Spender has put his finger on the crucial problem for
the writer of bourgeois origin who is dissatisfied with
the present state of society, and sees that it must be
radically altered; unless he in some way can make contact
with the masses, he is lost. This is a point which must
be dealt with again later.
'The Dance of Death' (1933) shows that Auden has for
the moment swung right over to an infinitely clearer
Marxian position. The theme is clearly stated and worked
out, and the satiric verse is perfectly straight-forward.
It has considerable dramatic, even propaganda value as a
lively and concise presentation of the present sickness
of capitalist society. It is more a dramatic ballet than
a play, and is very swiftly moving. The reader, or spectator, is not left this time to deduce for himself who
symbolizes what; Auden this time approaches closer than
ever before to popular writing. At the very beginning, the
Announcer says:

> We present to you this evening a picture of the decline
> of a class, of how its members dream of a new life, but
> secretly desire the old, for there is death inside
> them. We show you that death as a dancer....

The chorus is then shown going through a variety of
phases typical of post-war bourgeois society. Sun-bathing
is first of all the cure for all their ills; then the
Dancer by a trick sets them off on the road to war; at the
moment, the audience which represents the proletarian
masses threatens revolution, in which the Chorus (which
can be taken to represent the middle classes) shows signs
of taking part:

> One, two, three, four
> The last war was a bosses' war.
> Five, six, seven, eight

Rise and make a workers' state.
Nine, ten, eleven, twelve,
Seize the factories and run them yourself....

At this point, the growth of fascism is very cleverly
parodied. The Announcer hurriedly makes a speech to confuse the revolutionary impulses that have been aroused,
and persuades both Chorus and Audience to follow him on
an extremely vague adventure for an 'English' revolution.
They finally join him with enthusiasm, but the adventure
ends in shipwreck, and the Dancer collapses. The Chorus
then turns to a sort of mystic nature worship, followed
by an even more mystic flight from the 'alone to the
Alone.' By this time the Dancer is ready for a further
effort, but almost at once he collapses again, half-
paralysed. It is here that the piece seems to weaken. The
Manager with his Alma Mater night club does not seem to
have so clear a place in the argument as what preceded it.
There are also passages where characters speak to one another in an English that is a literal translation of
German; it is difficult to see the point, or even the
humor of these. However, as the Dancer is dying, the
Chorus sing a history of the development of society, in
which there are some excellent verses:

The feudal barons did their part
Their virtues were not of the head but the heart.
Their ways were suited to an agricultural land
But lending on interest they did not understand....

The Dancer suddenly dies, and at that moment there is
a noise without:

Quick under the table, it's the 'tecs and their narks,
O no, salute - it's Mr. Karl Marx.

The play ends as Marx enters, with two young Communists,
and says:

The instruments of production have been too much for
him. He is liquidated.

'The Dance of Death' showed that Auden could write, to
appeal to the widest circles of his own class, direct
propaganda that is at the same time art. But the contradictions do not yet seem to be resolved in his nature; the
next work, 'The Dog Beneath the Skin' (1935) written in
collaboration with Christopher Isherwood, is also a kind
of play. The satirical comedy, in prose and verse, is here

broken by choruses which are as serious as any poems of
Auden's. But there is no new advance; private allusions,
the schoolmaster touch reappear, the satire is not so
cleverly written or so clear in analysis as parts of 'The
Dance.' There are long rather tedious passages, which
give the impression of having been hurriedly written, and
one feels that from the revolutionary point of view, one
is back again with the Auden of 'The Orators,' brilliant
as the choruses are. The future direction which Auden will
take remains extremely problematical.

B.   THE PRODUCTION

43. DEREK VERSCHOYLE ON AN UNCONSTRUCTIVE TALENT,
'SPECTATOR'

clvi, 7 February 1936, 211

Derek Verschoyle (d. 1973) was Literary Editor of the
'Spectator' from 1932 to 1940, and First Secretary, H.M.
Embassy, Rome, 1946-50. His books include 'The English
Novelists' (ed., 1936).

'The Dog Beneath the Skin' is in every respect a much more
impressive work than Mr. Auden's earlier play, 'The Dance
of Death.' It is more precise, and therefore more pointed,
in its choice of subject-matter, more consistent and (for
the most part) more mature in its satire, and, apart from
its rather embarrassing conclusion, much less naïvely
evangelistic in its political attitude. It takes its form
from musical comedy and revue, and differs from everyday
revue (which it occasionally challenges on its own ground)
chiefly in its assumption of a comprehensive moral outlook. The choruses, in which the authors underline the
purport of their satire, are eloquent and often moving,
the dialogue has a competence of wit, and the prose
scenes, which range from the burlesque to the gravely
ironic, bear the mark of a genuine dramatic talent. Nevertheless it is far from being a completely satisfactory
play.
    'The Dog Beneath the Skin' has it in common with its

predecessor that it is a satirical study of a society
which has surrendered to unreason and attempts to conceal
from itself the symptoms of its own decadence. The examination of this society is made inclusive by a device borrowed from everyday musical comedy. Alan, the hero, is an
unsophisticated village youth who is chosen by lot to conduct a search for the lost heir of the local landlord,
the promised reward for success being the hand of Sir
Francis's sister. He is accompanied on his journey by a
woolly dog, an animal of remarkable intelligence but with
a regrettable habit of lapping whisky incontinently from
a bowl, who more than once manages to extricate him from
a dangerous situation. The moral indignation of the
authors directs the pair through the representative institutions of a decaying continent. The countries which have
succumbed to Fascism are shown as giant lunatic asylums,
a decrepid monarchy as a gilded brothel, and England as a
feckless suburb in which the population attempts to escape
from reality through athleticism, æstheticism, eroticism,
hypochondria, or intellectual suicide in a herd. In the
last scene the lost heir, who has emerged from his hiding-
place under the dog's skin, delivers a sermon on the ini-
quities of contemporary society to the massed inhabitants
of his native village, who have been mobilised into a
patriotic organisation by the vicar and a choleric
colonel, and is promptly shot for his pains.

It seems to have become a commonplace of criticism that
an author who exposes social evils is under no obligation to suggest a remedy. But the validity of this assumption surely depends on the amount of novelty in the
exposure. So far from being new, many of Mr. Auden's tar-
gets - the press, the pulpit, the armament-manufacturer,
the party-politician and the rest - have been familiar
objects of intellectual ridicule for a decade. One has no
objection to his attack on them on this occasion, beyond
being rather bored by so assiduous, and sometimes so
feeble, a pelting of already battered Aunt Sallies. But
one rather expects that, by way of compensation for the
lack of novelty in his attack, Mr. Auden will make some
attempt to prescribe a constructive substitute. It is a
grave fault in the play, as much considered purely dramatically as in its capacity of social analysis, that it
provides no more to this point than a vague and doctrinaire
outline of a priggish and watery Utopia.

There is no space in which to discuss the Group
Theatre's production in detail. As a whole, it showed almost as great an improvement on the production of 'The
Dance of Death' as the play itself showed on its predecessor. Mr. Rupert Doone appears to have learned that

it is not the most effective method of staging a revue
to be ironically apologetic about that unexalted but ex-
pressive dramatic form, and his direction is much more
balanced and less inclined to force after freakishly nervous effects. The best performances came from Mr. John
Moody as the hero, and from Mr. John Glyn-Jones and Mr.
Desmond Ellis as two journalists who accompany and complicate his search; the worst from Mr. Gyles Isham, who
declaimed the choruses with a painfully gentlemanly air.
Mr. Auden's speech contributed greatly to the gaiety of
the evening.

44. CYRIL CONNOLLY, RELUCTANTLY DEPLORING POPULARIZATION,
'NEW STATESMAN AND NATION'

xi, 8 February 1936, 188

Sometime Literary Editor of the 'Observer' and regular
Book Reviewer for the 'Sunday Times', Connolly edited
'Horizon' magazine from 1939 to 1950. He wrote one novel,
'The Rock Pool' (1935), and other books including 'The
Unquiet Grave' (1944-5), 'The Condemned Playground'
(1944), and 'Enemies of Promise' (1938).
    Connolly later commented,

    I did not much like 'The Dog Beneath the Skin' perhaps
    because I had found the hero, Francis Turville Petre,
    a little too much....
        One of the drawbacks of being a professional critic
    is that one sometimes cannot get out of reviewing a
    friend's books although one is disappointed. I once
    apologized to Wystan for one of these infrequent dis-
    paragements, 'O that's all right', he answered, 'I
    didn't mind. I thought "It's just Cyril".' 'And is
    that what you would have said if I had praised it?'
    (Some Memories, in Stephen Spender (ed.), 'W.H. Auden:
    A Tribute', London: Weidenfeld & Nicolson, 1975,
    p. 68)

Apparently Auden would have agreed with Connolly's disparagement of the bare stage, for John Hayward reported
that Rupert Doone 'intends to produce ["The Dog Beneath the
Skin"] in a very bare, formal fashion, without decor or
costume, though Auden tells me that it was written with a
view to an elaborate production along the lines of an

Edwardian musical comedy' (London Letter, 'New York Sun', 12 October 1935).
Late in life Connolly (1903-74) recalled:

I belonged to the tail end of the Twenties myself; my contemporaries were a little older - Evelyn Waugh, Graham Greene, Kenneth Clarke [sic].... At that time I was a kind of Clapham Junction where various literary lines crossed, partly through my work on the 'New Statesman', partly through my eclectic temperament and my position as a renegade from the Sitwellian aesthetes trying to pass as one of the 'Pylon Boys', though it was I who named them as that. ('English Poetry', ed. Alan Sinfield, London: Sussex Books, 1976, pp. 201, 203)

He also remembered,

I first heard of Wystan through Tom Driberg's column in the 'Daily Express' when he required of his large pub-lic 'Awareness of Auden', referring, I think, to the 'Poems' of 1930, but it was the 'Orators' (1932) which deeply moved me, while I found the chilly Marxism of 'The Dance of Death' rather intimidating. (Some Memories, 'W.H. Auden: A Tribute', p. 69)

In 'Enemies of Promise' he categorically recorded:

We have one poet of genius in Auden, who is able to write prolifically, carelessly, and exquisitely, nor does he seem to have to pay any price for his inspir-ation. It is as if he worked under the influence of some mysterious drug which presents him with a private version, a mastery of form and of vocabulary.

Auden read the book with considerable appreciation, as he told Connolly in a letter of 15 November 1938:

I think 'E. of P.' is the best English book of criti-cism since the war, and more than Eliot or Wilson you really write about writing in the only way which is interesting to anyone except academics, as a real occu-pation like banking or fucking with all its attendant egotism, boredom, excitement and terror. (quoted in 'W.H. Auden: A Tribute', p. 72)

This extract is taken from a review entitled The Muse's
Off Day.

Those who have read the book of this play will remember
that it is two-thirds heavily rhyming Gilbertian charade,
with a few fine prose speeches, to one-third chorus, the
choruses being typical ascetic examples of Auden's verse,
though not his best. If a play has got to be written in
doggerel which often breaks into song, the only thing to
do is to treat it as comic opera, and make it more Gilbertian still. Handed over to Messrs. Cole Porter, Cecil
Beaton, and Oliver Messel with a cast of singers and a
lavish production something might be made of it. As it
was, the bareness of the stage reflected the poverty of
the lines - such death scenes as

ALAN: You shall not die!

CHIMP: No, Alan, no.
        The surgeon now
        Is ignorant as a dove.
        To Iris my love   [Dies]

are either satirical (if so, of what?) or intentional, in
which case no acting can disguise their banality. The
play in fact must disappoint any who were not disappointed
by the book. The charades are average undergraduate
satire, a scene in a red-light district, where pity is
the prevailing emotion, a Hitler skit, a hospital skit,
a gala night at a big hotel ('Children of the Ritz' was
better), a village fête. In between the charades came the
spoken chorus. Mr. Gyles Isham and Miss Turleigh came before the curtain and harangued the audience with a fine
austerity. It was irritating to note the didactic quality
of these choruses, the authentic rallying cries of homo-
communism, and also their slightly forced lyricism, in-
sisting on the beauty of birds and the tragedy of de-
parting puberty after each roistering scene. Of course,
Auden's diction and imagery are always fresh and tonic,
but I think the note of intention, the 'You there with
a lotus, you will learn to get used to bloaters' type of
thing comes out much more when the choruses are spoken
than when read. The play, unfortunately, is somewhat
altered from the script, the censorship would have appeared to have operated almost entirely on religious
grounds, and a different and unsatisfactory ending has
been substituted. One misses the magnificent sermon (previously published as the sermon of an armaments

manufacturer) which was the best thing in the script,
and also Destructive Desmond which I am sure would have
been admirable 'theatre.' There was no scenery, the
lighting and grouping were excellent. It is hard to
criticise the actors, for their roles gave them little
opportunity and their lines less, but Mr. Schnabel was
charming as Grabstein, Mr. Glyn-Jones and Mr. Walter
Ellis life-like as the two reporters, and Mr. Wincott
spoke well as the Dog. The women made the best of their
small derogatory roles. The fault of 'The Dog Beneath the
Skin' (whose wanderings I took to symbolise the cynical
interlude in a young man's life, before the romanticism
of adolescence is converted into the Communist ideal of
service) lies deep, and is based on a misconception of the
role of the poet. I think Auden is the only poet of any
real stature since Eliot, but he is essentially an obscure, difficult, personal writer. His muse resembles that
of Yeats, Blake, Donne, not that of Kipling and Tyrtaeus.
He may be a better man and will certainly be a happier
man for trying to get in touch with the masses, but his
work will suffer. I know this is the point of view of the
anarchic 1920's about the political 1930's - but there
are younger writers: Dylan Thomas, Barker, and Sykes
Davis, who couldn't be more esoteric if they tried - and
they don't have to try. I conclude with an example -
quotation one is from a sonnet sequence of Auden's ('New
Verse' 1933), quotation two, from the play, shows the
effect of making the discreditable experience of escapist
love more palatable to the comrades:

    (i) I see it often since you've been away:
        The island, the veranda, and the fruit;
        The tiny steamer breaking from the bay;
        The literary mornings with its hoot;
        Our ugly comic servant; and then you,
        Lovely and willing every afternoon.
        But find myself with my routine to do,
        And knowing that I shall forget you soon. [EA, 423]

    (ii) 1st Mad Lady. 'Seen when night was silent,
                  The bean-shaped island
                  And our ugly comic servant
                  Who is observant.
                  O the veranda and the fruit
                  The tiny steamer in the bay
                  Startling summer with its hoot.
                  You have gone away.'

So our happy life of shame is still safe for a while.

'The Ascent of F6'

(with Christopher Isherwood)
London, September 1936; New York, March 1937

A. THE TEXT

45. E.M. FORSTER ON FOCUSING 'THE ASCENT OF F6',
CHORMOPULODA, 'LISTENER'

xvi, 14 October 1936, supplement 31, vii

Distinguished both as a novelist and as a critic, E.M.
Forster (1879-1970) was an Honorary Fellow of King's
College, Cambridge, from 1946 until his death.

This play is not easy to focus. It is quite short and
straightforward, yet at least four pairs of spectacles
are necessary before we can examine it properly. Let us
start by looking at it through a heroic pair.

Behold Michael Ransom, known to his friends as M.F.!
He is a gifted, sensitive, ascetic, altruistic mountaineer, who crowns a noble life with a glorious death.
Aeroplanes locate his body on the summit of the virgin
peak known as F.6, which he alone has scaled. His body
perishes, his name liveth for evermore. A national hero,
akin to Colonel Lawrence in temperament and to Captain
Scott in fate - that is what we see through this pair of
spectacles, but the play is by Messrs. Auden and
Isherwood, and the spectacles soon slip off the nose and
smash into nasty splinters. Try another pair.

Try the politico-economic outlook. F.6 now appears to
be situated on the boundary of two colonies, British
Sudoland and Ostnian Sudoland, and the expedition to scale

189

it is really a political ramp. The British and the
Ostnians are racing one another to the top, for reasons
of prestige, and if the British lose they will have
trouble with the natives down in the coffee plantations,
and no dividends. Thus viewed, the play becomes a satire
of familiar type, the type instituted over thirty years
ago by Hilaire Belloc in his brilliant and memorable
novel 'Mr. Burden'. The situation is old, the machinery
up to date, for Auden and Isherwood can show us the working up of public opinion through broadcasting. Little Mr.
and Mrs. Everyman in their poky flat - they are caught by
the F.6 propaganda, they listen spellbound to the important personages who come to the microphone; as they hear
about the terrible mountain and the glorious young man,
their own lives become less drab and boring, and they
actually dash off and have a week-end at Hove, though
they can ill afford it, as they realise on their return.
'He belongs to *us* now', they cry, as they gaze at the
obelisk erected to Ransom, after his death, by Big Business. Sudoland is safe. The natives work. The coffee
comes. The curtain falls.

But focus again; this time upon Ransom himself. F.6 now
appears as a test for his character, which he fails to
surmount. He suffers from the last infirmity of noble
minds; thinking he pursues virtue and knowledge, he really
pursues power. And at the crisis, in the nightmare-cloud
on the summit, he sees that his motive has been impure,
and, as evidence of this, the ghosts of the friends whom
he has killed. He has sacrificed them in devoting himself.
He had tried to turn back, but as soon as he set foot on
the mountain all were doomed.

Why is F.6 so fatal? Chormopuloda the natives call it,
and it is haunted by a demon, they say. There is a monastery on the upper glacier, and the monks there spend their
time less idly than might be supposed, restraining the
demon by their meditations from irrupting on to the
plains. The abbot explains to Ransom that the demon takes
different forms for its temptations; he does not reveal
that to Ransom himself it will take the form of his own
mother. Mrs. Ransom has appeared earlier in the play. It
is she who made her son go, when he shrank from the temptation of Power. She wants him to be brave, for her sake,
and to be happy, provided she supervises his happiness.
Cornelia, the mother of the Gracchi! For her other son,
James, is the politician who organises the ramp. Cornelia-
Jocasta! For our final pair of spectacles is provided by
Freud. When the cloud lifts from the summit of the mountain, Ransom finds his mother waiting for him, reabsorbing
that which she has created. He has never escaped her. He

re-enters the womb. The lyric final suggests 'Peer Gynt',
but there is a bitterness in it which neither Ase nor
Solveig conveys. She sings to her little boy:

> Reindeer are coming to drive you away
> Over the snow on an ebony sleigh,
> Over the mountains and over the sea
> You shall go happy and handsome and free.

But the chorus retorts:

> True, Love finally is great,
> Greater than all; but large the hate,
> Far larger than Man can ever estimate.

Mother-love, usually sacrosanct, becomes a very nasty cus-
tomer in this exciting play.

'The Ascent of F.6' is a tragedy in a modern mode, full
of funniness and wisecracks. It is not an entertainment
for all its lightheartedness, because its details fit in
to its grave general plan. It is a tragedy. Unlike its
predecessor, 'The Dog Beneath the Skin' it moves onward
instead of after its own tail; the changes from poetry to
prose, from monastery to mike, advance the action, the
subordinate characters, amusing as they are, never blur
the genius and the pathos of Ransom. It makes excellent
reading. It should act excellently. Will it ever be broadcast? Putting on one pair of spectacles, I say 'In view of
the diverse needs of listeners, it would not perhaps be
wholly suitable for this purpose, despite its unquestionable sincerity and impressiveness'. Putting on another
pair, I say 'I don't think'.

46. STEPHEN SPENDER ON DISAPPOINTING SIMPLIFICATIONS,
FROM FABLE AND REPORTAGE, 'LEFT REVIEW'

ii, November 1936, 779-82

Spender wrote two letters to Christopher Isherwood by way
of prefacing this review:

> About the 'Ascent.' I liked it very much. It's impossi-
> ble to say much more than this until I see it performed
> as all the points I am unclear about would either be
> cleared up or made defects by the acting. On a first

reading, I was slightly disappointed because I judged
it on the one hand by Wystan's single poems & on the
other by your novels or stories. To me, it isn't as
interesting as either but I dare say that is inherent
in what you are trying to do. It strikes me that you
both, as it were, draw too much on your ample resources. Wystan's psychology comes pat, the son is in
love with his mother, there are lots of striking bits
of annotation & psychological observation; this is a
currency on which Wystan can draw whenever he likes.
The same with characterization - your hallmark - which
is altogether well done.

I think that probably a play is bound to be a display of 'effects,' so this is not criticism at all.
I only say it to show my state of mind. Anyhow, there
are very beautiful & interesting scenes, it is an improvement on 'Dogskin,' and Ransom is very moving.
I think Wystan's versification now has a light style
of its own, which is quite distinct from jazz or
doggerel.

When I have seen the performance, I shall know my
mind. Louis MacNeice says you have re-written a lot,
in which case I have no doubt that you will have removed my objections! (Letter 34, October 5 (1936),
'Letters to Christopher,' Santa Barbara, Calif.:
Black Sparrow Press, 1980, pp. 121-2)

I'll send you today or tomorrow 'Left Review' with my
article on the 'Ascent,' which you may not have seen.
When it actually comes on, one of us will write it up
again to do it the justice it deserves. I hope you
won't feel I've been unfair. Really my only objection
is that at the end of the play instead of giving the
consequences of Ransom being the kind of person he is,
you give an acute piece of analysis. To my mind the
most interesting thing about Ransom is that he is a
prig; perhaps that is even more important than his
fascism, which is after all a doctrinaire point. I am
sure it is more important than that he is in love with
his mother. I can't help taking it for granted that all
Wystan's & your heroes are in love with their mothers.
An American friend of mine, called Lincoln Kirstein
[see No. 80 below], wrote to me how much he admired the
'Ascent' which seems to be very successful over there.
(Letter 35, October 30 (1936), Ibid., p. 123)

Spender did not after all review the production, but gave
extended consideration to both 'The Dog Beneath the Skin'
and 'The Ascent of F6' in his long essay The Poetic Dramas

of W.H. Auden and Christopher Isherwood (see No. 49 below).

Whilst the Novel and the Stage run efficiently along their
sterile but well-oiled grooves, the Poetic Drama offers
herself to the writer as the most problematic and perhaps
the most fertile of forms. What are her special
attractions? Well, she has connections with the audiences
of the Music Hall and Variety Stage, tougher collabor-
ators than those of the novelist who attains the gilt-
edged visiting cards of the Book Society or the Hawthorn-
den Prize. Moreover, in the theatre, the audience is
notoriously both critic and creator: it applauds or throws
eggs: it identifies itself with the hero.

Yet perhaps even more important than the over-discussed
relationship of the audience as a 'group' to the actors
and author of the play (for, after all, not even Auden
and Isherwood have as yet, in any wide and established
sense, found their audience), is the solution which the
theatre offers to the poet simply of the problems of
writing contemporary poetry. I see the poetic drama above
all as a way out of isolation and obscurity. There are a
dozen forces in modern life which tend to make the single
poem, in which the poet is 'aware' of this complexity of
impulse, more and more difficult. To mention only two
factors, there is the distraction of the surface of the
whole modern world of frustrated appearances: the traffic
moving without any very evident benefit to anyone, each
path of specialised living – the bank clerk, the scientist, the poet, the unemployed – becoming boxed away from
all others. Next, there is the isolation of the individual
in this world; his very perception of the significance of
what is going on round him often becomes a means of im-
prisoning him in his own personality.

The single poem then – and to some degree the single
work of fiction when it attains to the highest kind of
art – tends simply to express this isolation: a negative,
ingrown attitude which finally bores the poet himself.
'Dramatise, dramatise,' is the cry of Henry James throughout the prefaces of his immense life-work of described
poetry – which is what his novels are – and he was right.
The most successful modern poets have nearly all been
highly dramatic. 'Prufrock,' 'The Waste Land,' 'A Communist to Others,' the later poems of Yeats. Yeats wins the
victories of a lifetime devoted to poetry in an unashamed
passion of self-dramatisation. Auden is most simple, passionate and effective when he can present the attitude of
the communist poets to the workers on the one hand and,
on the other, to the bourgeiosie; the earlier Eliot when

he can contemplate a Prufrock who is not so much himself
as a groove of life down which some phantom, in whom he
can recognise his own features, is forced.

Yet the author of 'The Tower' or the hero of 'Prufrock'
is only one voice and his drama is a monologue. When the
poet begins to lose confidence in his own egotism, or
when he has no political or religious belief, the single
voice of the prophet becomes dissected into several voices
of doubt, self-accusation. It is at this moment that obscurity sets in, because the single poem is no longer a
monologue, it is an introspective inquiry: unless, indeed,
the poet is able to project from his own inner conflicts
the several voices of a poetic drama.

All this is only to state some of the poet's private
problems which make him turn to the stage. Once he begins
to write poetic drama, the state of the contemporary
theatre, the mood of audiences, the condition of acting,
become practical problems, demanding immediate solution.

If one is unaware of these factors, one's judgment of
'The Ascent of F6' by W.H. Auden and Christopher
Isherwood - or, indeed, of any other contemporary poetic
drama - is likely to be abstracted and unhelpful. On the
one hand, then, the poet takes to poetic drama with a
widening of the impulse that leads him to write single
poems: on the other, he is faced with the enormous difficulty of entertaining an audience brought up to appreciate
drawing-room comedy, romance or tragedy. His first aim
must be to entertain, amuse, terrify the audience: the
main fatality is to bore them.

Allowing for all this, how much should one expect, and
what does one get, from Auden and Isherwood? In the first
place, one expects and gets a more realistic grasp of the
practical problems of entertainment and production than
has been shown in earlier attempts to 'revive' poetry on
the stage. Secondly, much as one would like it, one
doesn't get any very striking development of Auden and
Isherwood's ideas and writing. In short, this play, in the
total impression which it produces, is inferior to Auden's
best poems or to Isherwood's two novels, 'Mr. Norris
Changes Trains' or 'The Memorial.'

If one judges this book simply from reading it, one is
rather disappointed. Yet I think that when the play is
performed the authors will be justified in having sacrificed so much which they can obviously do in the way of
poetry, subtle characterisation and brilliance, to simplicity of theme, caricature, and occasional lapses into the
humour of an undergraduate smoker. For I believe the play
will act well, and that remains at present the most important consideration. Also, it is an advance on 'The Dog

Beneath the Skin,' than which it is far better constructed. Some of the poetry is very good indeed: at
times the action is tragic and moving: the doggerel of the
earlier play has been replaced by the light passages,
capable of rapid transitions on to a different plane of
seriousness, of the dialogues between the two characters
who are choric spectators, Mr. and Mrs. A.

The story is the ascent of a mountain called F6 on the
English maps, and Chormopuloda by the natives, lying
between Ostnia and British Sudoland. The Ostnian colon-
isers are conducting a rival expedition from their side,
and Imperial interests - prestige, coffee, domination,
etc. - make it essential that the British expedition, led
by Michael Ransom, should win. The public, represented by
Mr. and Mrs. A, seated in boxes near the stage, follow
broadcast accounts of the expedition with varying degrees
of interest as it stimulates or depresses them in conducting their private affairs. These choric passages are excellently done, with a sureness of touch which makes the
characters of the booby political magnates, Lady Isobel,
Lord Stagmantle and Michael's brother James, seem almost
clumsy.

The centre of the play is Michael Ransom, and it is in
his character that the strength and the weaknesses of the
whole conception become evident. The other characters are
all presented either satirically or else with great objectivity: but Michael is the hero, and although his tragedy
is that of his failure as a personality, he is presented
sympathetically and his characteristics are evidently meant
to be those of someone possessing a certain nobility of
character. Ransom is a colossal prig, a fact of which the
authors seem insufficiently aware. He behaves in the way
in which one projects behaviour when one does not think of
any way of living, but simply of ways of behaving in a
given situation. He is a born actor: he is very, very calm
when he is with the other members of the expedition, whom
he regards rather as if he were the author of a play and
had written their parts for them, which is, of course,
exactly how everyone regards other people in heroic day-
dreams. In a sly way he manages the lives of everyone
round him. He is always smiling with a kind of sympathetic
superiority when other people are upset.

DOCTOR: And if it's bad down here, what's it going to
        be like up there on the arête?

RANSOM (*smiling*): Worse.

There is a lot of this kind of thing.

Ransom also has delusions of grandeur which are revealed to him in a vision which he receives when crystal-gazing:

Bring back the crystal, let me look again
And prove the former vision a poor fake:
The small gesticulating figure on the dais
Above the swooning faces of the crowd
And the torrential gestures of assent -
Was it myself? Was it for me the band
Far down the road distended their old cheeks?
The special engine barnacled with flowers,
The clashing salutations from the steeple?

Auden and Isherwood do not conceal in these remarkable, visionary monologues that their hero is a Fascist type. Nor is the fact that they deal with this type sympathetically a fault. The weakness of the play is that the drama does not realise and externalise in action the most important implications of Ransom's character. I cannot help feeling that the final tragic realisation of the last act should have been that Ransom was a prig, a fact, after all, even more significant than that he was in love with his mother. As it is, when the mother is revealed on the mountain top to croon over her dying son, one is left feeling that instead of the truth about Ransom having been realised, it has only been explained: the tragedy culminates in an acute piece of analysis.

I think it is this climax - making one feel that one has climbed to the top of a mountain for something which one might have learned more easily down below - that makes the play far less satisfactory than a poem like XIV (originally called 'A Communist to Others') in 'Look, Stranger!,' where the three forces of the two worlds of rich and poor and the individualist regarding them are perfectly balanced. The writer might very well have twisted this poem inside out to show that the individualist addressing the two worlds is himself a neurotic: actually, where the poem is so sure, we are, of course, aware of the psychological mood which conditions the poetry so that an account of it, like that of Ransom's relations with his mother, would not add to our knowledge. What does add to it is the statement which the individualist from his isolated height is able to make about the exploiting class, a statement such as Ransom's tragedy does not rise to, because the interest turns in on itself -

> Their splendid people, their wiseacres,
> Professors, agents, magic-makers,
>   Their poets and apostles,
> Their bankers and their brokers too,
> And ironmasters shall turn blue
> Shall fade away like morning dew
>   With club-room fossils.

The poems in 'Look, Stranger!' show a remarkable development from Auden's first book of poems. Obscurity has
almost vanished. In addition to his psychological observation, his power of inventing beautiful lines and memorable parables, his poetry now has the consistency of a
powerful diction which immensely broadens its range, enabling him to write of material which his earlier poems
could not have included. We are too near these poems to
make any critical estimate of them: all I can urge is that
they should be read.
    Perhaps the best feature of the Auden-Isherwood dra-
matic style in 'The Ascent of F6' is the rhythmic contrast
which the writers maintain between two entirely different
methods of presentation: firstly, realistic scenes of
political reportage; secondly, fables. There are two approaches to the contemporary political scene: the one is
direct, or partially satiric, external presentation; the
other is fantasy or allegory.

47. BEN BELITT ON 'FARCE FOR THE SALON', FROM RUGBY AND
THE TRAGIC MUSE, 'NATION'

cxliv, 17 April 1937, 439-40

Ben Belitt (b. 1911) was Assistant Literary Editor of the
'Nation', 1936-7, and became a Professor of the Department
of Literature and Languages at Bennington College, Vermont,
in 1938. In addition to numerous translations from the
works of Pablo Neruda, he is the author of 'A Preface to
Translation' (1978).

According to the title-page, the authors of 'The Ascent of
F6' reckon their newest offering a 'tragedy in two acts.'
Its stock of choruses, corpses, and soliloquies is consequently impressive, and there is abundant talk concerning
'the destructive element of the will'; yet the play is

essentially a piece with its satirical predecessor, 'The Dog Beneath the Skin.' It offers, again, polite, 'revolutionary' farce for the salon rather than the open market, conceived on the principle of the rugby match, wherein a symbol serves the function of a football, in contest of endurance between the actors, the authors, and a handful of selected visitors including Shakespeare, Noel Coward, W.S. Gilbert, and T.S. Eliot.

The unpardonable sin of the satirist is perhaps mere silliness, which defeats not only the author but the critic as well; and 'The Ascent of F6' is a continuous offender. The most useful comment which suggests itself is that the protagonists, in a moment of stress during which they are rapidly turning into symbols and helping themselves to Eliot's epilogue to 'Murder in the Cathedral,' are instructed to 'behave, in general, like the Marx brothers.' Similarly, the performance as a whole is executed in the temper of a comic strip fallen by some odd chance among homilies. Even 'tragic' protagonists like Lamp, the botanist, with his chatter of *'Stagnium menengitis,' 'frustrax abominum,'* and other 'rare specimens' are cartoons which border upon the infantile. It is less than astonishing under the circumstances that the play should eventually stiffen under its own paltriness and expire in a clutter of allegorical visitations. Auden and Isherwood are not the first of their calling who have omitted to go to school to the playwright before sitting down to their poetic tragedy; but few have further encumbered themselves with the baggage of a symbol so spurious and noncommittal that it overturns the vehicle it is intended to propel. The final word, perhaps, must be reserved for Walter de la Mare, who in a lecture before the British Academy suggested not long ago that 'satire and poetry, the one destructive, the other creative, in intent, are unusually uneasy bedfellows.' Certainly 'The Ascent of F6' is one of their bad dreams.

48. WYNDHAM LEWIS ON 'MARXIAN PLAYBOYS', FROM 'BLASTING AND BOMBARDIERING'

1937, 340-1

Percy Wyndham Lewis (1882-1957), who is rated perhaps more as an artist than as a writer, first exhibited his work in 1911, then at the Post-Impressionist exhibition organized

by Roger Fry in 1912. In 1914 he brought out the first of
only two issues of 'Blast', the Vorticist review, and
later edited the equally short-lived 'Tyro' (1921-2) and
'Enemy' (1927-9). Acidulous and extravagantly contentious,
he attacked his friends T.S. Eliot, Ezra Pound, and James
Joyce; reasonably regarded as Fascist in his opinions, he
contributed to Oswald Mosley's 'Action', though he never
joined the quasi-Fascist 'New Party' and described himself
in 1931 as 'partly communist and partly fascist, with a
distinct streak of monarchism in my marxism, but at bottom
anarchist, with a healthy passion for order'. His books
include 'Tarr' (1918), 'Hitler' (1931), 'The Apes of God'
(1930), and 'Men Without Art' (1934).

Although he does not specifically refer to 'The Ascent
of F6', Lewis is clearly adverting to Auden's and
Isherwood's collaborations in this passage of disgruntled
recognition. In Part V of 'Letter to Lord Byron' (EA, 198)
Auden dubbed Lewis 'That lonely old volcano of the Right'
(see also 'The Letters of Wyndham Lewis', ed. W.K. Rose,
London: Methuen, 1963, p. 214).

Is he [Auden] *the new guy who's got into the landscape?*
No: but he's got the technique of a new guy. I like what
he does. He is all ice and woodenfaced acrobatics. Mr.
Isherwood, his *alter ego*, is full of sly Dada fun too.
Both pander to the uplifted, both flirt robustly with the
underdog, but both come out of Dr. Freud's cabinet....
If I have mentioned these Marxian playboys first, it is
not out of bias for the rebellious mind. It is because the
right-wing never 'creates', for some reason, in England.

49. STEPHEN SPENDER, THE POETIC DRAMAS OF W.H. AUDEN AND
CHRISTOPHER ISHERWOOD, 'NEW WRITING'

New series 1, Autumn 1938, 102-8

This essay was reprinted with revisions in 'The Thirties
and After', London: Collins, 1978, pp. 54-61.

The Elizabethan drama was aimed at a public which
wanted *entertainment* of a crude sort, but would *stand*
a good deal of poetry; our problem should be to take
a form of entertainment, and subject it to the process

which would leave it a form of art. Perhaps the music-
hall comedian is the best material. I am aware that
this is a dangerous suggestion to make. For every person who is likely to consider it seriously there are a
dozen toymakers who would leap to tickle æsthetic
society into one more quiver and giggle of art debauch.

So wrote Mr. T.S. Eliot in 'The Sacred Wood,' outlining
a tactical programme for writers of poetic drama which has
been carried out more exactly by Auden and Isherwood in
'The Dog Beneath the Skin' and 'The Ascent of F6' than by
himself in 'Murder in the Cathedral' and 'The Rock.'
The problem was to write plays in verse which would
interest an audience large anough to justify their presentation on the stage, and which attracted this audience by
entertainment rather than by the sense of piety which
still attracts people to pay a bored homage to the holy
muse. In this, these writers have admirably succeeded;
and one can criticize their plays as experiments which
are entirely successful. The faulty Group Theatre productions have shown that it is possible to interest a growing
audience in a type of play rather resembling the revue or
even the musical comedy, but which has a serious subject
and contains excellent poetry. 'The Ascent of F6' had a
successful run in London at the Mercury Theatre throughout
the Coronation Season. There is little reason to doubt
that, given sufficient commercial backing, plays of this
kind could be as successful as any popular revue, and
would command a great deal more attention from their
audiences.
The victory has not been gained without a certain number of concessions which amount perhaps to a loss to
modern poetry. Most of the poetry in these plays is inferior to the poetry of Auden's single poems; no character
in them has the subtlety and profundity of characters in
Mr. Isherwood's novels. The fact that a collaboration produces results so strikingly inferior to the separate works
of either collaborator is rather disappointing. Lastly, I
doubt whether, considered as a purely literary influence,
the effects of these plays have been altogether good on
writers younger than Auden and Isherwood who imitate them.
What a relief it must have been to the undergraduate admirers of Auden's difficult 'Poems' to discover that Mr.
Auden had started writing in the manner of Cole Porter!
How easy to imitate him! Backed up by a misunderstanding
of Mr. Auden's statement that he considers 'Lear,' jazz
lyrics and rhymes in Kennedy's Latin Grammar all as
'poetry,' his influence has produced a kind of Lowest Common Multiple of his own work written by his followers who

find that after all it is not so difficult to attain
Auden - at any rate at certain levels. The magazines devoted to new verse are full of such imitations.

Still, Auden's jazz lyrics are extremely effective.
Isherwood, on the other hand, when he depreciates his
style is not so successful. In the parody of various public figures in 'The Ascent of F6,' he fails, because he
does not succeed in making one think that any set of
people talk so exactly like the parodist's idea of them.
Colonels, newspaper proprietors, Lady Houstons, cabinet
minsters, are so unconvincing if one hears them in real
life (for example, I have heard Sir John Simon give a
perfect Auden-Isherwood talk in his club, on Red Gold)
that if they are presented on the stage something has to
be done to prevent them appearing as the stuffed dummies
which, in fact, they are. C.K. Munro's play, 'The Rumour,'
fails for the same reason as Isherwood's dialogue in 'The
Ascent of F6'; huge maps are put on the wall, everything
is made as important and public as possible, all the elements of publicity are exaggerated to an extent which is
incredible in real life (although true) and therefore
doubly incredible on the stage. For that matter, I have
failed in the portrait of Hummeldorf in Act II of 'Trial
of A Judge,' for the same reasons. There is one example
of a completely successful solution of the problem; and
that is Bernard Shaw's portraits of Asquith and Lloyd
George in 'Back to Methuselah'; they provide a wonderful
combination of private motives with public ridiculousness.
The absurdity of the public man's position lies in the
perpetual interplay between the pettiness of the man and
the grandiosity of his position. Most successful publicists
have succeeded in concealing their private personalities
and in becoming entirely public; the clue for the satirist
lies not in emphasizing the public qualities of public
figures, but in stripping them away so that one can see
the private weaknesses behind.

Other critics have remarked on adolescent qualities in
the satire of the Auden-Isherwood plays. I think we have
a clue to it here. They have fallen into the trap of making the absurd, of setting down what is ridiculous or
horrible in real life, copying it directly from life, just
as a schoolboy caricatures the most obviously ridiculous
defects of his masters. The schoolboy's caricature appears
impotent, because it is weaker than the defects themselves, and it therefore remains merely spiteful, it draws
our attention to the schoolboy's own weakness in being
subject to the absurdities of others. In the same way as
Isherwood produces a mere flat representation of Lord
Stagmantle the newspaper proprietor, without analysing his

motives, so in 'The Dog Beneath the Skin,' both writers
present pictures of a world in decay, which are really not
nearly so fightening as that world itself. The scene in
which the inmates of a lunatic asylum of Westlanders applaud a broadcast speech by the Leader and behave in the
way that Nazis behave is inept because the alarming fact
about Nazi Germany is that the Nazis are *not* lunatics.
Merely to say, 'Oh, the Germans are lunatics' (which is
the effect of this scene) so far from being satire is complacency; it is like the schoolboy calling the master who
sneaks 'Slimy' or the French master 'Froggy.' On the
whole, the effect of such a scene cannot be to increase
the spectator's realization of what fascism signifies, but
to decrease it by making him reflect that after all his
compatriots are not lunatics like the inhabitants of Westland. The satire of 'The Dog Beneath the Skin' suffers
through the approach of the writers to European problems
being much too direct. You cannot reproduce chaos by buffoonery chalked on a school blackboard.

This is not to say that all - or nearly all - of the
satire in 'The Dog Beneath the Skin' is ineffective. For
example, the satire on the invalids in the hospital where
an operation performed by a famous surgeon is extremely
successful. With a sure touch, it probes beneath the
hygienic surface of the whole atmostphere of the sick bed
and reveals an egotism on the part of the patients, a
superstition attached to the medical profession, which are
not generally recognized, but which, once pointed out, the
audience recognizes as true. Satire must probe, it must
present new and striking surfaces; that is why the obvious
subjects of satire - the ludicrous behaviour of public men
in public life - are difficult to satirize, whereas there
is always something new to learn about the 'manners' of an
age - the fashionable vices and diseases - which are skins
grown over passions of vanity and egotism underneath.

'The Dog Beneath the Skin' succeeded, in spite of its
faults, by the persistence of high spirits and great
energy. Although some of the visits of Alan, the hero, to
different parts of Europe in search of the long-lost heir
Francis, who is disguised in the skin of the dog which
accompanies him, are like the visits of a schoolboy to an
International Exhibition, the total effect of a long and exhilarating journey made and a large and varied scene created, does get across. It is at the end of the play, when
we are presented with a moral, that our worst misgivings
arise. The dog, having returned home with Alan, whose
search seems to have proved fruitless, reveals himself to
the villagers of his home estate Pressan Ambo as their
long-lost heir, and makes a sermon. Hearing this sermon,

one wonders whether after all this enormous journey and
this animal disguise was not rather a circuitous route by
which to have arrived at conclusions which the Vicar of
Pressan Ambo himself could scarcely have regarded as astonishing. 'As a dog,' says Francis to the villagers, 'I
learnt with what a mixture of fear, bullying, and condescending kindness you treat those whom you consider your
inferiors, but on whom you are dependent for your pleasures. It's an awful shock to start seeing people from
underneath.' The real moral then emerges. Francis re-
nounces all claim to his inheritance because he has decided that the inhabitants of Pressan Ambo are part of an
army. He belongs to another army - the Workers - which he
is now going to join. As this is the first we have heard
of the army 'on the other side' throughout the play, this
conclusion may seem rather surprising. But it is not
really so, because the satire has been directed from 'the
other side' throughout the play. The reason why the
writers fail to present that 'other side' whose point of
view they implicitly accept is because whereas they know a
great deal about the side of the bourgeoisie - from which
they consider themselves disinherited - they know far less
about the workers' side which they believe themselves to
have joined. 'The Dog Beneath the Skin' is a picture of a
society defeated by an enemy whom the writers have not put
into the picture because they do not know what he looks
like although they thoroughly support him.

'The Ascent of F6' is far the most successful of these
plays, partly because the characterization of the members
of the mountaineering expedition, is extremely successful,
partly because the fable of the expedition which is at
once a pure attempt by Ransom the hero to excel (like the
writing of a pure poem) and at the same time an important
turning point in the struggle between two imperialisms, is
true and convincing. Ransom is, of course, a prig; but the
struggle which takes place in his mind is a serious and
important one. This struggle is really religious, though
it is set against the background of politics and commer-
cialization, on the one hand, symbolized by the struggle
between two imperialisms to ascend the mountain first, and
by the broadcasting of every phase of the climb, listened
to by the petit-bourgeois Mr. and Mrs. A; and against, on
the other hand, Ransom's own psychology - his rivalry with
his brother James, the successful politician, for the love
of his mother. When the mother turns out to be the demon
at the top of the mountain who is the final goal of
Ransom's achievement at the moment of his death, the
legend ceases to be altogether satisfactory; one feels
that this may be the final solution, but the religious

theme of the struggle going on in Ransom's own soul, has
not been fully worked out. The conversations with the
Abbot on the mountain do not lead to a satisfactory solution, and a convention of modern psychological ideology is
mechanically substituted for lack of some organic ending
to the play which the authors have not been able to find.

If one looks closely at the actual writing of the play,
one wonders whether there is not a lack of organic structure in the speeches themselves. A very ingenious framework has been contrived, some natural characterization
and dialogue written, and into this a number of speeches
are fitted which are not always closely enough related to
the action of the play. Here Auden particularly seems content to throw in too much 'stuff' which is what Mr.
Geoffrey Grigson would call 'good Auden' but which does
not have an essentially dramatic bearing on the action and
thoughts of 'The Ascent of F6.' More than any other form,
a play must be coherent to itself and be stamped throughout with its own unique and confining atmosphere; but the
following might be an extract from 'The Orators' or any
other of Auden's prose speeches: 'Virtue. Knowledge. We
have heard these words before; and we shall hear them
again - during the nursery luncheon, the prize-giving
afternoon, in the quack advertisement, at the conference
of generals or industrial captains; justifying every base-
ness and excusing every failure, comforting the stilted
schoolboy lives...' etc. Now this speech - which should
certainly create an atmosphere, since it opens the play -
lives within the body of Auden's Collected Works, but does
nothing to suggest the key symbols of the play. There are
far too many disintegrated references to a scene of activity outside the theatre, which have nothing to do with
the evening's performance. Of course, I am not suggesting
that a play's imagery should be entirely self-reflecting,
but I think that there is a tendency in this play to invoke far too wide a range of references. It may be said
that it is impossible to write poetic prose speeches without a very wide range of reference to an emotional background outside the play. If the reader thinks this, I beg
him to read that great and fantastic masterpiece, 'Dantons
Tod,' by Georg Buechner which, although written in the
early nineteenth century, is a play suggesting a solution
of nearly all the problems of a modern poetic drama.

It is not only the prose speeches which are 'good
Auden' but not so necessarily good for the play; the blank
verse speeches suffer excessively from being written in
the Shakespearean manner. The speeches by Mr. and Mrs. A
do produce exactly the suburban atmosphere which Mr.
Auden intends; but Michael Ransom slides off into patches

of 'Lear' which are even more disconcerting to hear on
the stage than to read:

>O senseless hurricanes,
>That waste yourselves upon the unvexed rock,
>Find some employment proper to your powers,
>Press on the neck of Man your murdering thumbs
>And earn real gratitude!

An encouraging start has been made by Auden and
Isherwood to solve the problems of creating a contemporary
poetic drama. The most important of these problems - that
of finding an audience -- they have solved better than anyone for a generation. They have concentrated - quite
justifiably - on providing entertainment; but since they
are also creating a form and presenting a view of the
world, one has to realize how many of the problems of presentation they have evaded. The most obvious failure is the
failure to write satisfactory endings to their plays: but,
where an ending cannot be found, one may suspect that
there is a lack of organic growth throughout the play and
something is wrong from the start. One may suspect that
the collaboration itself is responsible for some of these
faults: each writer hopes that the other is going to try
harder than himself; when a difficulty is encountered by
one writer the other suggests a solution which is really an
an evasion; neither writer feels as responsible for the
criticism which the play may arouse as he would if the work
were entirely his own. More important, it must be very
difficult in a collaboration to construct the unique,
hemmed-in and claustrophobic atmosphere, which is essential to a play.
  So far, these writers have been content to throw fragments of good stuff into a loosely constructed play, without concentrating their abilities on making the whole conception of the play rank with their own most serious work.
For them, the problem is largely an æsthetic one - to
write a play which is as satisfactory as 'Mr. Norris
Changes Trains,' or any single poem in 'Look Stranger!'
For their audience the problem is neither simply æsthetic,
nor simply a question of increasing the prestige of poetry
by restoring the spoken word on the stage. It is really a
question of reviving the drama itself, which has fallen
into a decadent 'naturalistic' tradition, confining itself,
for the most part, to the presentation of faked-up photographic vignettes of the life of a small section of the unemployed rentier class. If we think of the realities of
the world to-day - using the word reality in a sense little
known to the West End London stage - we see that there are

great conflicts and a moral and material struggle involving the birth of a new world, which poetry is peculiarly qualified to deal with, since a poetic use of
language is the only literary medium which can deal
realistically with a wide and generalized subject without
being overloaded with details of naturalistic representation. The Auden-Isherwood plays are only the beginning
of a movement far more significant than any 'revival' of
the poetic drama or even any sudden flourishing of advanced poetry; for what is required and what we may get
during the next years is a revolution in the ideas of
drama which at present stagnate on the English stage, and
the emergence of the theatre as the most significant and
living of literary forms.

B.   THE PRODUCTIONS

50. A.R. HUMPHREYS ON VITALITY AND CONFUSION, 'CAMBRIDGE
REVIEW'

58, 30 April 1937, 353-5

A.R. Humphreys (b. 1911) was Professor of English at the
University of Leicester from 1947 to 1976. His publi-
cations include 'William Shenstone' (1937), 'The Augustan
World' (1954), and 'Steele, Addison, and their Periodical
Essays' (1959), as well as editions of Shakespeare, Defoe,
and Fielding.
    This review of 'The Ascent of F6' considers the Group
Theatre's productions both at the Arts Theatre, Cambridge,
where the play opened on 23 April 1937, and earlier at the
Mercury Theatre, London.

There can be no doubt of the vitality of the Auden-
Isherwood contributions to poetic drama, a species too
often anaemically ritualistic. Their plays in performance
hold the attention, not merely because they bewilder and
fascinate, but because they seem to be saying something
important in an inherently dramatic way, through character
which appears to be solid, and in speech which has an
assured manner. It is when one asks just what has been

said that the difficulties arise, and this is due, unfortunately, to the obscurity rather than the complexity
of the content. 'The Ascent of F6' inevitably raises
these questions again.

Six years ago, in 'Experiment,' Mr Empson produced a
brilliantly suggestive analysis of Auden's 'Paid on Both
Sides.' 'The Point of the tragedy,' he wrote, 'is that he
[the hero] could not know his own mind until too late, because it was just that process of making contact with
reality, necessary to him before he could know his own
mind, which in the event destroyed him. So that the play
is "about" the antinomies of the will, about the problems
involved in an attempt to change radically a working
system.' But the union of intense pressure of feeling
with complex psychological analysis which was excitingly
foreshadowed in 'Paid on Both Sides' has not materialised;
the new play makes more of an attempt to realise it than
did 'The Dance of Death' and 'The Dog Beneath the Skin,'
but a large element in the complication is taken over
bodily from T.S. Eliot and only adds to the confusion -
'Mr Ransom, beware of spiritual pride. It is not for us to
put an end to the Demon, and the desire to do so is, to
brave and good men like yourself, the Demon's most powerful and insidious temptation.'

To turn for a moment to the satirical elements; 'to
those who feel that perhaps the Communist does not hold
all the cards,' Auden himself wrote not long ago, 'the
most disquieting fact is that the armament firms, the
yellow and gutter press, the advertising agencies are
staffed not by monsters, but by extremely intelligent
young men of liberal opinions,' Yes. But caricature is
easier than serious analysis, and the satirical comment
conveyed in glib doggerel in 'The Dance of Death' and
(with Isherwood) in 'The Dog Beneath the Skin' and 'The
Ascent of F6' has been no more than a superficial amusement. And at the same time the psychological preoccupations which gave 'Paid on Both Sides' its potency have
resulted in obscurity and indecision. The recurrence of
Marx and Freud (under the shadow of Eliot) has a suspiciously fashionable air.

Perhaps the spectator expects too much of a poet whose
capacities are so extraordinary and who has proved able,
in the choruses of 'The Dog Beneath the Skin' and 'The
Ascent of F6,' to grip so intensely what he sees and express it in incomparably vivid phrase. Such achieved mag-
nificence makes one greedy for more. The trouble is not,
of course, that the plays as a whole fail to maintain the
level of their highest excellences - that must be true of
any drama, however great - but that their shape and

intentions are so Protean. At first, in 'The Dance of
Death' and 'The Dog Beneath the Skin,' this was due to
the vague object of the main satire and the peripheral or
excursive nature of the subsidiary satire; the latter
play, despite its occasional poetic splendours, was little
more than a fun fair as Alan Norman (the ordinary man)
wandered among the formalised fragments of degenerate
capitalism in search of the Redeemer, who turns out, as
might be expected from the speech of 'The Two' at the beginning, to be the unobserved observer ('It's an awful
shock to start seeing people from underneath') and who,
when found, leaves the culture into which he was born 'to
be a unit in the army of the other side.' The intermittent suggestions of sickening evil - not merely social
wrong or cultural mistakes - have the promise of unusual
power:

> Here too corruption spreads its peculiar and emphatic
>   odours
> And Life lurks, evil, out of its epoch....
>
> So, under the local images your blood has conjured,
> We show you man caught in the trap of his terror,
>   destroying himself.
> From his favourite pool between the yew-hedge and
>   the roses, it is no fairy-tale his line catches
> But grey, white and horrid, the monster of his child-
>   hood raises his huge domed forehead
> And death moves in to take his inner luck.

But these hints are not substantiated with the concentration they call for.
  'The Ascent of F6' opens admirably; there is no hint of
the unctuousness which later creeps into Ransom's part in
his first superbly controlled speech - 'the web of guilt
that prisons every upright person and all those thousands
of thoughtless jailers from whom Life pants to be delivered - myself not least; all swept and driven by the
possessive incompetent fury and the disbelief. For of that
growth which in maturity had seemed eternal it is now no
tint of thought or feeling that has tarnished, but the
great ordered flower itself is withering; its life-blood
dwindled to an unimportant trickle, stands under heaven
now a fright and ruin, only to crows and larvae a gracious
refuge.' But the crows and larvae are not so convincing as
Ransom's legitimate despair about them; the stock comic
general, the specious politician, the greasy-voiced newspaper magnate. Their delusive air of authenticity is conveyed by the effective use of the cliches in which they

speak - witness their broadcasting manners; otherwise
they are no more than voices, which is too low an estimate
of their real significance.

Nevertheless, the first act undoubtedly moves, partly
because of its brisk counterpoint of scenes, partly because of the effective, if glib, satirical comment. Easily
the weakest moment on the stage was the 'throwback' to
Ransom's childhood (not included, it may be noted, in
the published text) to link more explicitly the son's and
mother's will (cf. the cry 'It's the Demon, Mother.'). But
the play hereabouts is already explicit enough, and the
over-emphasis is nearly disastrous. For the rest, the interest, mainly on the plane of political satire, is
straightforward; F6 is a mountain and an imperial symbol.

The second act is another matter. It is simplest to say
that the mountain becomes oneself, the Demon the ultimate
power in that self. (This impression is over-simple, and
may be wrong, but it is better to be simple, even at the
risk of being wrong). The superimposition on a realistic
physical adventure of a symbolic spiritual adventure does
not make for clarity. F6 therefore, and the Demon, are
different matters for each of the climbers; 'the Demon is
real,' declares the Abbot, 'only his ministry and his
visitation are unique for every nature.' For Gunn, as
Ransom explains (obviously authoritatively), F6 represents
the maximum terror-thrill ('Being frightened is his chief
pleasure in life.... At present he prefers mountaineering
because it frightens him most of all'); for Lamp, the at-
tainment of passionately desired specimens; for Shawcross
the ultimate knowledge of the self, which yet, suspecting
his inadequacy, he fears to investigate. ('The Ascent of
F6 represents, for Ian, a kind of triumph which he not
only desires but of which he is desperately afraid.... He
wants me to order him to face it. But if I do, it will
destroy him'). Gunn, however, 'is not afraid of F6; nor
of himself' - the two being, in one aspect of the symbol,
identical. This is elementary. For Ransom himself, the
symbol is more confused, because the mountain is what he
both fears and loves. He refuses, and agrees, to climb it;
he dreads and desires the power it gives; loathes and
cherishes the fame it brings; is simultaneously victor and
vanquished in the struggle. His mother, making him
stronger than his brother, makes him weaker too; his fixation on her is both a necessity and a fatality. The
Demon, his mother's power, is that farthest reach of his
own will, and the discovery that this is not his own destroys him; the fatality is simultaneously pleasurable and
terrible - terrible in that the struggle to complete the
exploration is bitter and ends in the horror of

discovering his final dependence on another; pleasurable
in that the dependence and surrender are a relief and release. The last chorus emphasises this. His will to power,
revealed in the crystal, sacrifices his companions to his
pride (which is also weakness, involving two surrenders,
first to his mother, second to imperialist necessities),
and then sacrifices himself because he cannot, at the
Abbot's invitation, accept the abnegation of the will.
Jealousy of his brother is too an important motive; yet
because he co-operates in the political intrigue he
shares the same guilt, and though he seems the Deliverer
and his brother the destroying Dragon, yet his brother
wins at the end as he won in the Lakeland inn.

The phantasmagoria which conveys this is extremely confused - apparently a surrealist presentation of Ransom's
hysteria under the stress of approaching the summit. So
complex a theme could hardly be solved. What is disturbing, however, is the authors' hesitancy; there are at
least three extant conclusions. The first is that of the
book, outlined above, including also a reference to the
imperialist satisfaction of Stagmantle and James, for
Ransom has permanently established British prestige.
His success on this low level contrasts ironically with
his spiritual defeat. The Mercury Theatre performance,
however, omitted the phantasmagoria and everything following his immolation before his mother's spirit. The
ironies here are quite different; British prestige gains
nothing, since the expedition is presumed lost in the
blizzard - his physical victory and spiritual defeat both
amount to failure. The Arts Theatre performance admitted
the 'political' conclusion and left the last words with
Mr. and Mrs. A, incidentally deflating the play like a
pricked balloon. Dramatically, the second ending was
easily the best, in simplicity, unity of theme, and dignified economy; but the fact that conclusions with very
different implications are apparently thought interchangeable is alarming. Apart from this, the play loses grip at
the end; the jazz interlude is dreadfully wrong. A symbol
must present two or more meanings simultaneously, but the
individual meanings should not be foggy, as they are here,
nor should the shifts of meaning suffer from the irresponsibility to which plays produced by a dual authorship
would seem naturally susceptible. The intention may have
been to produce a modern 'Everyman'; the result is more
like that 'flight into the Heart of Reality,' which was
satirised in 'The Dance of Death.' If the final impression
is one of exteme confusion, the blame should not be laid
on the reader or spectator.

51. G.W. STONIER ON A SUCCESSFUL REVIVAL, 'NEW STATESMAN
AND NATION'

xviii, 1 July 1939, 13

Born in Australia, G.W. Stonier (b. 1903) was Raymond
Mortimer's Assistant Literary Editor on the 'New Statesman
and Nation' from 1928 to 1945. C.H. Rolph recalled

> that quiet, elusive and enchantingly inventive writer
> G.W. Stonier; whose work seemed to some of us like a
> specially lucid kind of modern verse pushed into
> conventionally-shaped 'New Statesman' paragraphs....
> He is one of the older 'Statesmen' to whom, in the
> estimation of most people who know the paper's history
> - and certainly in Kingsley's - much of its early suc-
> cess was due. ('Kingsley: The Life, Letters and Diaries
> of Kingsley Martin', Harmondsworth: Penguin, 1978, pp.
> 236-7)

Stonier's books include 'Gog Magog' (1933), 'The Shadow
Across the Page' (1937), 'Shaving through the Blitz'
(1943), and 'Rhodesian Spring' (1968).
    Stonier's reference to the final appearance of Ransom's
mother sitting 'on a Gothic peak in white' suggests that
the Group Theatre had gone some way to heed W.B. Yeats's
advice (see Introduction, pp. 20-1 and 67-8) in this
revival at the Old Vic on 27 June 1939.

The Group Theatre have taken the plunge. By renting the
Old Vic during its close season they not only provide us
with unexpected pleasure at the one place where we can
consistently see good plays and good acting, but they are
also, I hope, doing themselves a good turn. There is much
to be said for the _théâtre intime_ in introducing works of
a new kind; and it is always a risk to transplant them
from the hothouse. 'The Ascent of F6,' whatever misgivings
one may have had about its appeal with a large audience,
succeeds brilliantly. There was a full house, and I was
astonished to notice how quickly jokes were taken up by
the gallery. I do not intend this as any reflection on the
gallery - my surprise, I mean - for it is often the most
intelligent part of theatre. But the Old Vic is a roomy
building; words must get lost up there under the rafters.
But everything went tip top: the poetry of F.M. and his
companions, the broadcaster's prose, the jingle of the
suburban couple always at table - all came over perfectly.

I had not seen 'The Ascent of F6' performed before, though of course I had read it, and I was delighted to find how admirably it is suited to the theatre.

The stage at the Old Vic is large enough to divide into two. On the left, we have the scenes in Wastdale, White-hall, Ostnialand; on the right the breakfast parlour of the little couple who listen in. Thus, there is no wasted time of scene-shifting; one set of curtains draws, the other opens. Mr. Rupert Doone has provided a small brightly lit room for the chorus. The rest is done with lights and curtains.

One can never say exactly how a play read will act. If it is a good play it of course gains; and 'The Ascent of F6' gains a great deal. The fine quality of the prose emerges; when Ransom, for example, sitting on the top of the Pillar Rock, looks into the valley below –

Beyond the Isle of Man, behind the towers of Peel
Castle, the sun slides now towards the creasing sea;
and it is into a Wastwater utterly in shadow that the
screes now make their unhalting plunge. Along the
lake shores lovers pace, each wrapped in a disturbing
and estranging vision. In the white house among the
pines coffee will be drunk, there will be talk of art
at the week-end. Under I cannot tell how many of
these green slate roofs, the stupid peasants are making
their stupid children.

It is curious that in this play all the poetry should be written in prose and the verse should be jaunty and prosaic. The actors went against this: Ransom and his companions speaking often as though in metre, and the suburban couple sliding over their couplets as conversationally as possible. At times the second of these tricks proved irritating. If only, one felt, the verse had been a little more skilful or the authors had kept to the conversational accents of prose. An acid note introduced into a Wilhemina Stitch was the effect.

The biggest surprise, though, of seeing this play acted is the character of the leader, Ransom. No doubt the authors intended this character as a tribute to T.E. Lawrence, and on the stage he is extraordinarly impressive. Alec Guinness conveyed the ascetic qualities of a modern saint and man of action with superb quiet. Faced at the beginning with his brother (Gyles Isham) and the newspaper peer (Ronald Adam), conversing with the Abbot (played with admirable dignity by Francis James), fighting the jealousies of his companions, he was a dramatic without being a ranting figure. The scenes of the ascent – despite

the fact that they were carried out on the flat - were
remarkably tense and exciting, and the characters of the
different climbers struck one as being very true. What
was less admirable was the relationship between Ransom
and his mother, and the surfeit of boring comment from
suburbia.

The mother is the one unfocused point of the play.
Several appearances have been cut out from this new version at the Old Vic and the final scene rewritten, so
that she does not speak, but only sits, on a Gothic peak
in white, like Dickens's mad old bride among the cobwebs.
But that last scene is still a failure. The expressionist
tricks spoil the simplicity towards which the play has
been moving and it would be infinitely better to cut out
the scene altogether, substituting for it a single speech
or merely the tableau of the climber motionless. All we
should miss would be the march past of Ransom's dead men
and their criticisms. The mother theme is implicit and
would be better left unstressed.

The other fault which emerges in performance is the
weakness of much of the satire. The whine of complaints -

The boarding-house food, the boarding-house faces,
The rain-spoilt picnics in the windswept places,
The camera lost and the suspicion,
The failure in the putting-competition.

go on far too long. The two speakers are not convincing:
no more say than the unfortunate Miss Edith Gee of Auden's
ballad. Nor are the capitalists - the foreign office and
the newspaper peer. When you are out to make propaganda,
as Auden and Isherwood are here, against Imperialism it is
a mistake to set up guys as adversaries. The little
general would never have won Egypt and India, the Foreign
Office official would never have brought off a treaty with
anyone. They serve to throw into relief the humanity of
the mountaineers, but at the expense of the authors' crusade against authority.

But, with all these faults, some of which could be removed (and one would like to see a new production with
other ideas than Mr. Doone's), 'The Ascent of F6' is a
fine play. It deserves a run at the Old Vic, and to judge
from the first night audience it is likely to get it.

'Look, Stranger!'

London, October 1936; New York (as 'On This Island'),
February 1937

Combined reviews with 'The Ascent of F6'

52. DILYS POWELL ON THE POEMS AND THE PLAY

October and November 1936

Dilys Powell wrote separate reviews of 'Look, Stranger!'
and of 'The Ascent of F6', but they are grouped together
in this section because they elicited from Auden this uncharacteristic response:

> Dear Miss Powell,
> I want to thank you for your generous and acute re-
> views of F6 and my poems.
> You are quite right in saying that some of the dif-
> ficulties in the first book were due to punctuation.
> I never have understood that art. Now I make someone
> else do it for me.
> The non-dramatic quality of the poems is of course
> intentional. I want lyric verse to be really lyrical,
> because at least in my own work when I get into the
> dramatic lyric I hear far too often the shrill tones
> of the hockey-mistress.
> In theatrical drama, as you said, I want to objectify
> the images, in symbols of action. I do want the drama
> I write to become more and not less like a boy's adven-
> ture story. The significance on the external plane must
> be as childishly simple as possible. Till I have really
> learnt to do that properly (because at present my

trouble is not that the behaviour of my characters is
too schoolboyish, but that their schoolboyishness is
sometimes only that, i.e. the real significance has
failed to get itself projected into terms of their behaviour), I feel that I must soft pedal the poetry a
bit.... (n.d. (November 1936), The Humanities Research
Center, the University of Texas at Austin; a shorter
extract figures in Mendelson, 'Early Auden', p. 264)

---

i. On 'The 'Ascent of F6': Heroic Tragedy, 'London Mercury', xxxiv, October 1936, 561

This piece, though it has the satirical interludes and the
indirect comments from stage-box which are still apt to
flummox the general public, is in essentials a direct
heroic tragedy. It is the tragedy of a man sacrificed for
the people (the hanged god again?): a man, however, at
fault in allowing himself to be sacrificed. The colonial
rivalry of England and Ostnia demands the ascent of the
haunted mountain, F6; Michael Ransom is prevailed upon to
lead the English expedition. Like Becket in Mr. Eliot's
play, he is four times tempted; unlike Becket, he yields
to the fourth temptation, the temptation of spiritual
pride; and he dies on the summit of F6 after a phantasma-
gorical scene which contrasts with, while it recalls, the
the realistic scenes which precede it. There is a moment
of serene and noble reflection on the tragedy of man
self-destroyed; then the ironic comment, the clichés of
obituary; the tragedy is general as well as individual,
the tragedy of the false cause as well as of the hero
lost.
     There are some superifical resemblances to Eliot's
verse, early and late: phrases in the stage-box duologues
between Mr. and Mrs. A., such as 'yet another shop-soiled
day,' might come from the 'Prufrock' volume, and one might
easily assign the line

     Sitting in the crowded restaurant, I have
     overheard the confabulations of weasels

to 'Murder in the Cathedral.' Generally Mr. Auden's verse
wants the richness of the choruses in 'The Dog Beneath
the Skin'; the prose rhetoric, however, is admirable. The
play shows a more successful synthesis of literature and
propaganda than anything Mr. Auden, or Mr. Auden and Mr.
Isherwood, have yet done; pity, irony, and contempt are
less obviously apportioned; and there is no scramble to
wind up with a change of heart. For the moment the poetry

has lost something in the process of fusion, but this may
be regained later. Meanwhile, it is interesting to note
that Mr. Auden tends more and more to communicate his
ideas through symbols of *action*; literature assumes more
and more the external characteristics of a boy's adventure
story.

Next month he is publishing a book of verse; comment on
that will allow at the same time further comment on this.

ii. On 'Look, Stranger!': Mr. Auden's New Poems, 'London
Mercury', xxxv, November 1936, 76-7

It is six years since Mr. Auden published his first book,
'Poems,' and immediately established a reputation. In the
interim he has produced a denunciatory 'English study' in
prose and verse, 'The Orators' (1932); a rather papery
satirical play; and, in collaboration, a far solider play
with some fine verse choruses, and an heroic tragedy. The
plays, though they have widened his reputation, have not
always strengthened it; admirers are apt to look to the
'Poems' and 'The Orators' for his most remarkable work.
But Mr. Auden always keeps us guessing; the vitality of
his talent, and its extraordinary suppleness and variety,
make him one of the few young writers worth watching. He
gives a singular sensation of power; one feels that if
that power were rightly controlled and directed, something
of first-rate importance would emerge. The publication of
'Look, Stranger!,' his first volume of poems since his
appearance as a poet, interests both those who respect his
work and those who believe that the group he leads is
something more than a bunch of literary *enfants terribles*.

A good many of these poems are familiar from their
publication in periodicals and anthologies, so that the
development from the style and mood of 'Poems' and 'The
Orators' is less immediately striking than it might have
seemed. But the development is there. The book opens with
a 'Prologue' to which one can properly apply a word often
degraded by misuse, beautiful.

O love, the interest itself in thoughtless Heaven,
Make simpler daily the beating of man's heart;
    within,
There in the ring where name and image meet,

Inspire them with such a longing as will make
    his thought
Alive like patterns a murmuration of starlings
Rising in joy over wolds unwittingly weave;

Here Mr. Auden handles the long line as he has always
handled it, with easy generous mastery; but its movement
is more fluent than in the earlier verse or in the dramatic choruses; and the poem as a whole commands by its
own excellence and not by means of the military exhortations of 'The Orators.' 'Prologue' has none of the rough
and choppy effect, stylistically and in mood, of much previous work; intellectually it is far less difficult. But
it still has the ability to surprise and excite by its
images and metaphors. And everywhere in these poems we
find the apt sudden phrase: 'Crooked to move as a money-
bug or cancer'; 'ocean's quaking moor'; a tide-stranded
monster's 'whorled unsubtle ears'; June evenings when

> Fear gave his watch no look;
> The lion griefs loped from the shade
> And on our knees their muzzles laid,
> And Death put down his book.   [EA, 137]

But the dramatic phrases which Mr. Auden so effectively
handles are less frequent. This is a collection of non-
dramatic verse; but one of the remarkable things about
the first poems and 'The Orators' was their dramatic
quality. This volume is far more truly lyrical and reflective. The title poem is a piece of precise description
with carefully descriptive technique:

> Here at the small field's ending pause
> Where the chalk wall falls to the foam, and its
>   tall ledges
> Oppose the pluck
> And knock of the tide,
> And the shingle scrambles after the suck-
>   ing surf, and the gull lodges
> A moment on its sheer side.   [EA, 158]

The dedication of the book indicates a move from 'the external disorder' to 'a narrow strictness'; and there is a
poem, 'Casino,' which with its exquisitely imaged grief
reminds one of Baudelaire. And two or three pieces have
something of the quality of a seventeenth-century lyric -
the address to the sulking lover, the contrast of human
with non-human lives:

> Fish in the unruffled lakes
> The swarming colours wear,
> Swans in the winter air
> A white perfection have,
> And the great lion walks

Through his innocent grove;
Lion, fish, and swan
Act, and are gone
Upon Time's toppling wave.   [EA, 162]

Other poems return to the familiar themes - approaching
disaster, 'the dangerous flood of history,' the will-to-
death, the hope of new life. And here, as in the new
Auden-Isherwood play, 'The Ascent of F6,' published a
month ago, there is a more satisfactory fusion of poetry
and propaganda; the sense of direction is less erratic,
the changes of mood are better controlled. Mr. Auden is
perhaps growing more self-critical; he has revised some
of the poems, and many passages in the earlier versions
are here omitted; for instance, of the poem 'A Happy New
Year,' which appeared in 'New Country,' only the latter
section, and that shortened, is here printed. Even 'Prologue' has undergone slight revision; its changes in punctuation, indeed, are a little disturbing, since they suggest how much of Mr. Auden's difficulty may be caused by
a misplaced or a capriciously placed full-stop; the sense
of verses 9, 10, and 11 is entirely changed by the new
punctuation.

The mood of these poems is less crudely prophetic and
minatory than that of his other books, (with the exception
of 'The Ascent of F6'). Mr. Auden still offers a choice
between life and death, between individual and universal
love, but it is offered without truculence. The note of
warning still sounds - sometimes with grandeur, sometimes
with the sententiousness of moral exhortation; occasionally it becomes mere moralizing.

But the book as a whole, despite at any rate one poem
which seems to me ill-judged (No. 18), gives an impression of increasing stability. Whether this kind of
poetry shows Mr. Auden at his best is another matter. His
virtuosity is singular, but I feel that so far his
greatest talent has been seen in dramatic verse.

...For the wicked card is dealt, and
The sinister tall-hatted botanist stoops at the
      spring
  With his insignificant phial, and looses
The plague on the ignorant town.   [EA, 165]

Sometimes, as here, a reflective poem takes on a dramatic
quality through images of action. The decay of poetic
drama is due to the inability of poets to write verse
which is dramatic; here for once is a poet with the
ability. 'The Ascent of F6' is in some ways disappointing -

theatrically effective, but with a slightly schoolboyish
appeal. But in this piece and the earlier, 'The Dog Beneath the Skin,' is a hope, not for poetry only, but also
for drama.

53. GAVIN EWART ON THE UNACCOMMODATING PLAY AND THE POWER-
FUL POEMS, UNTITLED REVIEWS, 'UNIVERSITY FORWARD'

iii, November 1936, 16

After working for the British Council, 1946-52, Gavin Ewart
(b. 1916) was an advertising copywriter from 1952 to 1971.
His poetic virtuosity can be seen in 'The Collected Ewart
1933-1980' (1980).

   Always a firm admirer of Auden's verse, Gavin Ewart
had been introduced to the early poetry by T.C.
Worsley (see No. 82 below) at Wellington College. 'Like
many other young admirers of the obscure and cryptic but
fascinating early verse I wasn't ready for the burlesque
simplifications of the plays' (letter to Haffenden, 30
October 1980). In a recent profile Alex Hamilton remarked
to Ewart that Leavis had 'disparaged Auden's setting up of
a team, like a 1st XI'. Ewart appropriately observed,
'Leavis had liked Auden's early poems, but later went off
him - Leavis's opinions on Auden were wrong. Auden was a
great poet, and it says a lot against Leavis that he didn't
recognise that' (The Poet Loves Putting on the Style,
'Guardian', 10 June 1980, p. 9). In an earlier review of
'The Dance of Death', published in 'New Verse' 1934, Ewart
had regretted the limp versification which lacked 'any
touchstone by which the various degrees of stupidity and
vulgarity' could be gauged.

---

i. On 'The Ascent of F6'

This play contains the same three main ingredients as its
predecessor by the same authors; the adventure story, the
political satire and the psycho-analytical interpretation
of action. The story is about a mountain peak known as F6,
which lies on the frontier between British and Ostnian
Sudoland. The natives believe that the first man to reach
the top will rule both the Sudolands, with his descendants,
for a thousand years. Rival expeditions from the two countries set out to climb the mountain and there is a race to

reach the top first. This is the adventure story. The
satire is mainly directed against imperialism; a newspaper peer called Lord Stagmantle states the facts which
it is not policy to print. 'The truth, Lady Isabel, is
that the natives of Sudoland would like us to go to hell -
pardon my language - and stay there. The truth is that
we've got ten millions invested in the country and we
don't intend to budge - not if we have to shoot every
nigger from one end of the land to the other.' The analysis of the motives of the various characters is perhaps
fairly true but becomes too complicated and the symbolism
and the occasional visionary mysticism are too muddled or
too subtle for a stage play.

There are also scenes between Mr. and Mrs. A., who represent the average man and woman. A good deal of the
authors' own political insight is projected onto these two.
For instance they speak of members of the cabinet as:-

> Smiling at all the photographers, smoking, walking in
>   top hats down by the lake.
> Treating the people as if they were pigeons, giving the
>   crumbs and keeping the cake.

The climb and the scene in the monastery are exciting,
the dialogue excellent, and the long set speeches everything that readers of Auden have come to expect. The verse
is competent but not much different from anything in 'The
Orators' of 1932 except for passages written against the
background of the dance lyric; some of it has a beautiful
fluidity. The hero is rather a prig and his mother is too
much a maternal symbol. The play should certainly be read,
and if possible seen, when the Group Theatre act it in the
near future.

ii. On 'Look, Stranger!'

Here is a selection of the poems which Mr. Auden has published in various anthologies and periodicals since 1930.
There are one or two omissions but the best of the recent
poems are included. Since his first book, Mr. Auden's
verse has undergone a considerable simplification and a
more severe formal discipline, emerging both concise and
emotive, in the political poems of very great powers and
in the love poems and in general of very great sympathy
and tenderness. The power is in poems about the middle
classes:-

> And you, the wise man, full of humour
> To whom our misery's a rumour
>   And slightly funny;
> Proud of your nicely balanced view
> You say as if it were something new
> The fuss we make is mostly due
>   To lack of money.   [EA, 122]

And the Cambridge economists:-

> Let fever sweat them till they tremble
> Cramp rack their limbs till they resemble
>   Cartoons by Goya:
> Their daughters sterile be in rut,
> May cancer rot their herring gut,
> The circular madness on them shut,
>   Or paranoia.   [EA, 123]

Most of the poems are about life and love in the twentieth century, and it says a lot for Mr. Auden's poetic gift that even the most personal will easily carry the reader's own emotions.

> But love, except at our proposal,
> Will do no trick at his disposal;
> Without opinions of his own, performs
> The programme that we think of merit,
> And through our private stuff must work
>   His public spirit.   [EA, 153]

The width of ground covered by this poetry is one of the most remarkable things about it. It is strongly social, with definite ideas about society, conscious of everything that goes to make up the world we live in. The attitude is always that of the middle-class intellectual with a public school education, but this is not really a fault because a viewpoint is necessary in order to see anything and this is always recognized and discounted in the poetry itself. The private and public worlds are a constant antithesis in Mr. Auden's work, so that the love poems often contain political metaphors, like Donne writing of love in terms of religious experience and religious poems in terms of love. It only remains to say that these poems with their fine organization and human understanding make the critical vocabulary of praise look silly, that their faults are few and negligible and that anyone even remotely interested in poetry or modern England should read the book:-

Peter, Pontius Pilate, Paul,
Whoever you are, it concerns you all
   And human glory.

54. F.R. LEAVIS ON IRRESPONSIBLE IMMATURITY, MR. AUDEN'S
TALENT, 'SCRUTINY'

v, December 1936, 323-7

'Since the publication of 'Poems' in 1930, which immediately marked the author as a leader of a new school of
poetry that has since established itself...' Mr. Auden
(one may go on, while questioning whether a school that
springs up as immediately as the publisher reports is
properly to be described as a 'school of poetry') has certainly been a significant and representative figure, a
figure to watch. One has watched him for signs of development. His talent was indubitable; one has waited for him
to begin to do something with it. Those who open 'Look,
Stranger!' in hope will be once again disappointed - which
doesn't make him the less significant and representative.
   The talent, an impressive one, is apparent here in the
familiar ways. There are those striking and so characteristic phrases and images. For he certainly has a gift for
words; he delights in them and they come. He continues,
in a way that would be very promising in a young poet, to
be happily in love with expression. But Mr. Auden cannot
now be far short of thirty, and he is still without that
with which a poet controls words, commands expression,
writes poems. He has no organization. He hasn't, at any
rate, the organization corresponding to his local vitality,
to the distinction of his phrasing and imagery at their
best. This lack comes out very obviously, as before, in an
embarrassing uncertainty of tone and poise, an uncertainty
not the less radical and disquieting for his tendency to
make a virtue of it. He no doubt knows that he is writing
doggerel in XVIII. But he does the same kind of thing in
pieces that beyond any doubt ask to be taken seriously -
as seriously as anything he offers asks to be taken.
   He is, of course, a satirist, and we know that there is
such a thing as irony. But his irony is not the irony of
the mature mind - it is self-defensive, self-indulgent or
merely irresponsible; and his satire is fairly represented
by his imitation of Burns (XIV):

[Quotes stanzas 13-14 of 'Brothers, who when the sirens roar...' (originally titled 'A Communist to Others' when published in 'New Country', 1933), EA, 122-3.]

- Those stanzas might, by themselves, be serious (and they are certainly popular among Cambridge undergraduates). But (not to mention what goes before) they are followed by:

> Let fever sweat them till they tremble
> Cramp rack their limbs till they resemble
>   Cartoons by Goya:
> Their daughters sterile be in rut,
> May Cancer rot their herring gut,
> The circular madness on them shut,
>   Or paranoia.

Mr. Auden's irony, in fact, is a matter of his being un-certain whether he is engaged mainly in expressing *saeva indignatio* or in amusing himself and his friends. And there is habitually in him a similar uncertainty.

It is significant that he should in this book borrow the show of a mature poise here from Burns and there from Yeats - see for instance, III and XXIV. (There are other curious literary reminiscences; among them - though this doesn't illustrate the immediate point - an elaborate echo, in VII, of those sestines from 'Arcadia' that Mr. Empson quotes in 'Ambiguity'). Since so much of his emo-tional material and his poetic aura, glamorous or sinister, comes fairly directly from childhood and schooldays, the borrowing can hardly have any other effect on us than that of implicit self-diagnosis. For Mr. Auden still makes far too much of his poetry out of private neuroses and mem-ories - still uses these in an essentially immature way. He has, of course, his social preoccupation, and he still habitually makes his far too easy transitions between his private and his public world:

> And since our desire cannot take that route which is
>   straightest,
> Let us choose the crooked, so implicating these acres,
> These millions in whom already the wish to be one
>   Like a burglar is stealthily moving,
>   That these, on the new façade of a bank
>   Employed, or conferring at health resort,
>   May, by circumstance linked,
>   More clearly act our thought.   [EA, 118]

The sinister glamour that so often attends his premonitory surveys of the social scene is transferred too directly

and too obviously from the nameless terrors of childhood
or their neurotic equivalent.

But is what is implied here more properly to be called a
public world or a private?

> The Priory clock chimes briefly and I recollect
> I am expected to return alive
> My will effective and my nerves in order
> > To my situation.
> 'The poetry is in the pity,' Wilfred said,
> And Kathy in her journal, 'To be rooted in life,
> > That's what I want.'   [EA, 144]

'Wilfred,' it would seem, is Wilfred Owen, and 'Kathy'
Katherine Mansfield. It is a significant habit that is betrayed in this mode of referring to them.

For corroboration of the surmise that the habits of the
group-world are intimately associated with the failure of
Mr. Auden's talent to mature we have the new play that he
has written with Christopher Isherwood. The talent, the
striking gift of expression, appears in the opening
soliloquy of Michael Ransom, and here and there in other
places. But more generally it is Mr. Eliot's gifts that we
are aware of, for the play is heavily parasitic upon both
the Eliot of 'Sweeney Agonistes' and the Eliot of the
Choruses. But the hero, Michael Ransom, is not one who can
be brought into any comfortable relation with any manner of
Mr. Eliot's. Ransom says ('*smiling*') to one of his group
(the dialogue is in the authors' own style): 'You haven't
changed much have you, Ian, since you were head Prefect
and Captain of the First Fifteen?' Ian might have retorted
in much the same formula. They have none of them, in fact,
in Ransom's group, changed much since they were at school
- at their Public School. And it is clearly assumed that
the audience will not have changed much either. For we are
unmistakably expected to feel towards the school hero (the
school, of course, being the class in which mountaineering
is a normal interest) the respect and awe felt by his
school-fellow followers. How seriously we are to take him
we may gather from the Abbot of the Great Glacier who,
offering him a place in the Monastery as one of the élite
of the earth (Ransom has studied the Book of the Dead)
speaks of 'your powers and your intelligence.'

But powers and intelligence cannot be injected into
the drama by the mystico-psychological hocus-pocus of the
Monastery and of the death scene. There can be no significance in the drama that is not active in the dramatist's
words. Well, the realistic dialogue of 'The Ascent of F6'
is simply and unironically Public School, and for the lift

into verse we have:

> I have no purpose but to see you happy,
> And do you find that so remarkable?
> What mother could deny it and be honest?
> .   .   .   .
> May not a mother come at once to bring
> Her only gift, her love? When the news came,
> I was in bed, for lately
> I've not been very well. But what's a headache
> When I can stand beside my son and see him
> In his hour of triumph?

That is the Tennysonian pathetic.* And Ransom at the moment of high tragic realization breaks into the solemn Shakespearian parody of this:

[Quotes last 17 lines of Ransom's speech, from 'O Senseless hurricanes' onwards, Act II, scene IV (cf. C. Day-Lewis's comments on the same speech, No. 55 below.]

It was necessary, in order to make the point, to suggest effectively both the pretensions and the kind of badness of this play. That kind of badness, when a writer of Mr. Auden's gifts is led into it, implies not only a complete absence of exposure to criticism, but also a confident awareness of an encouraging audience. In other words, the present is the time when the young talent needs as never before the support of the group, and when the group can, as never before, escape all contact with serious critical standards. In such a time it often seems a hopeless undertaking to promote by criticism the needed critical stir.

Note

* Cf.   I would you had a son!
>   It might be easier then for you to make
>   Allowance for a mother - her - who comes
>   To rob you of your one delight on earth.
>   How often has my sick boy yearned for this!
>   I have put him off as often; but to-day
>   I dared not - so much weaker, so much worse
>   For last day's journey.   [Tennyson, 'The Falcon']

55. C. DAY-LEWIS ON A CLASSIC OR A CURIOSITY, PAGING MAN-
KIND, 'POETRY'

xlix, January 1937, 225-8

'The Ascent of F6' shows a marked forward development from
the authors' last play, 'The Dog Beneath the Skin': the
construction is firmer, the verse is quite as fine, and
the morality is rendered more explicit without loss of
balance or inconsistency of texture.

F6 is a haunted mountain on the frontier between
British Sudoland and Ostnian Sudoland. The natives in the
British colony, unsettled by Ostnian propaganda, have 'begun telling each other that the white man who first
reaches the summit of F6 will be lord over *both* the Sudolands.' Ostnia has just sent an expedition to conquer the
mountain. The British government, represented by Sir James
Ransom, Lord Stagmantle, a newspaper proprietor, and the
third Houston sister (under the stage name of Lady Isabel
Welwyn), appeals to Sir James's twin brother, Michael, to
lead an expedition. Michael - a character with certain obvious affinities to the late T.E. Lawrence - at first refuses, realizing that his love of climbing is to be exploited for a political manoeuvre. Later, however, he
succumbs to the blandishments of his mother, who plays
upon his unconscious jealousy of James:

> ...She had died
> To make him free; but when the moment came
> To choose the greatest action of his life
> He could not do it, for his brother asked him
> And he was padlocked to a brother's hatred.

In the second act, Michael is again offered a choice -
this time by the Abbot of the monastery on the mountain
side: a choice between 'the life of action and glory and
the life of contemplation and knowledge.' The Abbot warns
him against spiritual pride, against the temptation to put
an end to the Demon of the mountain by confonting him.
But it is too late to turn back: Michael, by making the
'wrong' choice originally, has made himself responsible
for his friends, who would now go on without him should he
back out. The climb begins. One by one his friends are
killed. At last Michael reaches the summit, and seeing in
a vision his own real defeat, understanding the will-to-
power which has finally destroyed him, dies there.

This is a moving climax to a most interesting play.
Technically, few faults can be found. The chorus - a

suburban couple, Mr. and Mrs. A. - is an excellent device.
The way Michael's broadcast exploits first stir them to
romantic day-dreams and then purge them with pity and
horror to an acceptance of their own humdrum life ('Our
moments of exaltation have not been extraordinary but they
have been real'), is admirable. There are also some passages of superb rhetoric, such as -

[Like Leavis (see No. 54 above), Day-Lewis quotes last 17
lines of Ransom's speech, from 'O senseless hurricanes'
onwards, Act II, scene IV.]

The morality is much more questionable. As far as I
have understood it, by erecting a colossal bogy out of
Lord Acton's words, 'power corrupts ... all great men are
bad,' it asserts that the good man's responsibility must
begin and end with his own soul. The implications of this
are at best Oxford Group and at worst Fascist. One revealing line, 'There is always a wicked secret, a private
reason for this,' seems to involve a belief that, since
the source of every action is poisoned, the safest place
for everyone is a monastery. The authors' preoccupation
with motives is consistent; but when the interpretation of
motives is elevated into a morality, that morality is apt
to be negative, defeatist, and dangerous.
     That Auden is obsessed with the idea of personal sal-
vation is contradicted, however, by several passages in
his new volume of verse, 'Look, Stranger!'

     Dare-devil mystic who bears the scars
     of many spiritual wars
          And smoothly tell
     The starving that their one salvation
     Is personal regeneration....   [EA, 122]

In poem *30*, which presents an autobiography of Auden's
ideological growth, we read

     Five summers pass and now we watch
     The Baltic from a balcony: the word is love.   [EA, 156]

Auden has been repeating this word for several years now,
with variations of extraordinary beauty, strength, and
understanding, but at times he still seems a poet in the
aristocratic tradition, urging himself not to be exclusive.
Consequently, his strictly personal poems are still on the
whole his most successful. One must except, however, the
two excellent ballads - 'O for doors to be open and an invite with gilded edges,' with its Yeatsian refrain, and

the one that begins

> O what is that sound which so thrills the ear
>   Down in the valley drumming, drumming?
> Only the scarlet soldiers, dear,
>   The soldiers coming.

Here Auden's remarkable dramatic power is accentuated by
a subtlety of meter and a formal coherence which his verse
has sometimes lacked before. Yet Auden is putting all his
eggs in one basket: the survival-value of his poetry is
bound up inextricably with the survival-value of Freud's
teachings. If the latter are destined to be built into the
structure of civilization, then Auden will be without the
least doubt a classic: but to a generation that knew not
Freud, his work would appear - with the exception of a few
'anthology pieces' - a literary curiosity.

56. JANET ADAM SMITH ON COMPLEX ACCURACY, 'CRITERION'

xvi, January 1937, 329-32

Janet Adam Smith (b. 1905) was Assistant Editor of the
'Listener', 1930-5; then Assistant Literary Editor, 1949-
52, and Literary Editor, 1952-60, of the 'New Statesman
and Nation'. In 1935 she married Michael Roberts (see Nos
4, 15, 63, and 81). Her publications include 'Poems of
Tomorrow' (ed. 1935), 'R.L. Stevenson' (1937), 'Mountain
Holidays' (1946), 'Collected Poems of Michael Roberts'
(ed., 1953), and 'John Buchan and his World' (1979).
    This is taken from an untitled review which includes
criticism of volumes of verse by Richard Eberhart and
William Plomer.

'The Dog Beneath the Skin' was a simple narrative: one
thing happened after another. In 'The Ascent of F6'
several things are happening at the same time. English and
Ostnian climbers are attacking F6, the Haunted Mountain,
from different sides (coffee plantations and the control
of Sudoland are the stakes); Mr. and Mrs. A. in the
suburbs are following their fortunes by newspaper and wireless, and finding in their exploits compensation for their
own dull work and duller holidays; Michael Ransom is pursuing virtue and knowledge, and discovering that he longs

for power; Michael Ransom is in love with his mother. The
first two themes make an excellent satiric play. Different
lights are thrown on the action, it is talked of in different tones of voice. The professional politician is heavy
('The future of England, of the Empire...'); the newspaper
peer, blunt ('The truth is, we've got ten millions invested
in the country'); the BBC talker, suave ('The natives are
delightful people, of wonderful physique'); the climbers,
practical ('How many tins of malted milk?'); Mr. and Mrs.
A., grandiose ('He belongs to us, now'). The reader gets a
lesson in seeing through wireless and newspaper ballyhoo,
and a warning of what happens to his private pleasures
when they are exploited for political ends.

The two dramas of Ransom's private life are hardly so
successful. We are meant to see all round and through the
hero - he is the only person allowed to soliloquize - but
compared with the flat, easily recognized characters of the
politicians and the other climbers, he remains misty and
unsubstantial, a collection of attitudes rather than an integrated personality. His virtue-power struggle is partly
externalized in the scene at the glacier monastery, when the
Abbot asks him to give up the climb and take his place with
the monks in a life of prayer and contemplation (though even
here his motive for going on seems to be a wish not to disappoint his friends rather than a craving for power); but
the drama of his relations with his mother remains a thing
of words, it never becomes action. When Mrs. Ransom persuades him to lead the F6 expedition, after he had refused
his brother's appeal, she does nothing but speak at him,
telling him that all these years he has been her darling
though for his own good she concealed her love. If her
power over him had been implied in action his changeover
might seem less arbitrary. Again, her appearance on the
summit of F6 at the end of the play is only convincing in
so far as we are persuaded that a mountain really is a
mother to him; but his dealings with her have been too
shadowy for us to accept this meeting as the inevitable
climax of his personal tragedy as readily as we accept his
death on the mountain-top as the climax of the political
drama.

The question implicit in 'F6', and in several poems of
'Look, Stranger!' is one which Mr. Auden has asked explicitly elsewhere: What shall the self-conscious man do
to be saved? There is no hint that Ransom's friends were
wrong in climbing the mountain, that it offered them any
temptation; it is Ransom, who comes to know himself and his
motives, who is judged and condemned. He turns all his
energy and intelligence to solving a problem outside himself, he is willing to give his life for a cause - climbing

F6, conquering the Demon who lives on the summit; but he cannot escape his own nature. The mother to whom he is tied waits for him on the top of the mountain, by his death he wins the power he had longed for, and his brother sees that it is turned to political profit. The alternative way of life is stated in the play by the Abbot, and is indicated in a number of the poems. The poet, the artist, the self-conscious thinking man, must first leave his isolated personal life; he must be assimilated by his fellow-men, joined to them in love, no matter how futile or maddening many of them may be –

> Pardon the studied taste that could refuse
> the golf-house quick one and the rector's tea.

There is sympathy and understanding for at least one of the villains of 'F6'; Stagmantle, the newspaper peer, is a comic and likeable person as soon as he stops talking in headlines, not at all like Beethamer and the other butts of Mr. Auden's earlier work. But love can only be learnt by saving and helping, not by leading and ordering – Auden admires men like Nansen and Schweitzer, who while capable of founding movements and heading crusades, have chosen to serve their neighbour rather than lead him and use him. (But surely Nansen had many of Michael Ransom's qualities; it is not made clear at what point the power to lead becomes dangerous.) The strong man's influence must be pervasive and insidious:

> And since our desire cannot take that route which is
>   straightest,
> Let us choose the crooked, so implicating these acres,
> These millions in whom already the wish to be one
>   Like a burglar is stealthily moving,
>   That these, on the new façade of a bank
>   Employed, or conferring at health resort,
>   May, by circumstance linked,
>   More clearly act our thought.   [EA, 118]

It is a difficult doctrine; it may mean accepting, for a time, an order of things which is felt to be wrong (as, for instance, Wilfred Owen was against war, but he knew that his place was with his company), it lays down no precise rules for behaviour, and it demands not a surrender of the intelligence, but a sharper use of it:

> The Priory clock chimes briefly and I recollect
> I am expected to return alive
> My will effective and my nerves in order
>   To my situation.   [EA, 144]

The difficulty of the doctrine is reflected in several of
the poems. 'Our hunting fathers', for instance, is ambiguous not because it says one thing obscurely, but because it says at least three things simultaneously, and it
is impossible to say which of them is the 'right' meaning.
The truth of the poem lies somewhere between them, and depends on their co-existence.

On the other hand, those two books have far fewer puzzles in the way of private meanings than 'Poems' or 'The
Orators.' All his readers may not attach Mr. Auden's significance to weasels and botanists; but there are very few
allusions that would not be quite clear to anyone who had
read the same books. No doubt there is a Ph.D. waiting for
the industrious student who in fifty years' time grubs up
Auden's sources, tracking certain of his phrases back to
Irving's 'Romance of Mountaineering,' Collett's 'The
Changing Face of England', and the works of Lenin, but
what is more important to us now is to find out what use
he makes of his borrowings. He collects phrases, gestures,
actions like a magpie; and his hoard always provides him
with the effective word and image;

Taking our premisses, as shoppers take a tram....

Worlds as innocent as Beatrix Potter's....

Saussure, whose passion for Mont Blanc became a kind
     of illness....

When inland they are thinking their thoughts but are
     watching these islands,
As children in Chester look to Moel Fammau to decide
On picnics by the clearness or withdrawal of her tree-
     less crown....

What matters is not where Mr. Auden found the phrase or
image, but the accuracy with which it states a situation.
Metres and stanza-forms are collected and produced in the
same way; not out of technical virtuosity, but because the
situation demands a tone of voice which another poet has
already produced. For the chorus of monks who comment on
Ransom's final struggle with the mountain, Auden needed
the tone in which the elders speak in 'Judith of Bethulia';
so he takes over John Crowe Ransom's stanza.

Mr. Auden describes gestures, motions, tics, which are
symptomatic of a state of mind or body....

57. EDMUND WILSON REGRETS THE RETROGRADE, THE OXFORD BOYS
BECALMED, 'NEW REPUBLIC'

xc, 24 February 1937, 77-8

Famed as a literary critic, cultural commentator, and
memoirist, Edmund Wilson (1895-1972) is generally regarded
as the pre-eminent American man of letters of his time.
His many influential books include 'Axel's Castle' (1931),
'The Wound and the Bow' (1941), 'To the Finland Station'
(1940), and the posthumous 'Letters on Literature and
Politics 1912-1972' (ed. Elena Wilson, 1977).

   Wilson admired 'Poems' and 'The Orators' (see headnote
to Louise Bogan's review of 'The Dog Beneath the Skin',
No. 41 above), and obviously felt dismayed to discover
that by the mid-1930s Auden had in his view become stag-
nant and imitative. Thereafter he became keenly appreciative of Auden's work, especially of his achievements in
the USA after 1939 (see No. 113).

I confess to being rather disappointed by these last two
books of W.H. Auden's. It looks as if the group to which
he belongs - the school of young Oxford poets which includes C. Day-Lewis, Stephen Spender and Louis MacNeice -
had lapsed, after their first lift of enthusiasm for the
clean sweep of society promised by communism, of repudiation of the world to which they belong, into a period of
relaxation into vagueness, of cooling down and marking
time.

   W.H. Auden has presented the curious spectacle of a
poet with an original language apparently in the most robust English tradition, whose development has seemed to
be arrested at the mentality of an adolescent schoolboy.
His technique has seemed to mature, but he himself has not
grown up. His mind has always been haunted, as the minds
of boys at prep school still are, by parents and uncles
and aunts. His love poems seem ambiguous and unreal like
the products of adolescent flirtations and pre-school
homosexuality. His talk about 'the enemy' and 'their side'
and 'our side' and 'spying' and 'lying in ambush' sounds
less like something conceivably to be connected with the
psychology of an underground revolutionary movement than
like the dissimulated resentments and snootiness of the
schoolboy with advanced ideas going back to his family
for the holidays. When this brilliant and engaging young
student first came out so strongly for the class struggle
it seemed a bold and exhilarating step; but then he simply

remained under the roof of his nice family and in the
classroom with his stuffy professors; and the seizure of
power which he dreams of is an insurrection in the
schoolroom by the students:

> I should like to see you make a beginning before I go,
> now, here. Draw up a list of rotters and slackers, of
> proscribed persons under headings like this. Committees
> for municipal or racial improvement - the headmaster.
> Disbelievers in the occult - the school chaplain. The
> bogusly cheerful - the games master. The really dis-
> gusted - the teacher of modern languages. All these
> have got to die without issue. Unless my memory fails
> me there's a stoke hole under the floor of this hall,
> the Black Hole we called it in my day. New boys were
> always put in it. Ah, I see I am right. Well look to it.
> Quick, guard that door. Stop that man. Good. Now boys
> hustle them, ready, steady - go.   [EA, 64]

With all this - and out of all proportion to the interest of what he has had to say - Auden's imagery and
speech have had an energy, a felicity, a resource, a
nerve, which have made him a conspicuous figure. He certainly has more of what it takes than anybody else of his
generation in England or, as far as I can remember, in
America. And in one department he is entirely successful:
he has invented a new satire for the times. The most satisfactory part of his work seems to me such skits as 'The
Dance of Death,' with its cheap and weary rhythms; the
satiric-elegiac choruses of 'The Dog Beneath the Skin'; and
such poems as that in this new collection in which he describes the Cambridge intellectuals,

> Who show the poor by mathematics
>   In their defence
> That wealth and poverty are merely
> Mental pictures, so that clearly
> Every tramp's a landlord really
>   In mind-events.   [EA, 123]

He is especially good at calling the roll of the lonely,
the neurotic, the futile - of all the queer kinds of individuals who make up the English upper middle class. No one
else has given us just this sense, at once pathetic and
insipid, of the slackening of the social body and the falling apart of its cells.

But once having taken this stand, once having put themselves on record, we get the impression that Auden and his
associates are at a loss as to what to do next. In some

ways they appear to be retrograding. Thus the language of
Auden in this new book seems to me to be actually less
personal than it was in his earlier poetry. He seemed in
his earlier work to have revived the traditional language
of English poetry at its most vigorous, its most lively
and most free, telescoping the whole tradition from the
emphatic alliteration of Anglo-Saxon through the variety
and ease of the Elizabethans to the irony and bizarre
imagination of the generation just before his own. But in
'On This Island' it seems to me that the rhythms of the reflective and lyrical poems approach too close to the deliberate looseness of the satirical ones; and the off-rhymes
begin to get on one's nerves. (Negligent rhythms and near
rhymes, I suppose, are a symptom of blurred emotions. There
are moments when Louis MacNeice sounds like a serious
Ogden Nash.)

And it has come to be a depressing feature of the
literary scene at the present time (noticeable also in
this country) that writers who had hitherto seemed able
to stand on their own feet have begun flopping over on one
another and imitating one another's idiom - without there
necessarily being any question of the normal attraction of
the weaker toward the stronger. Thus Auden, whose voice we
knew and liked, disconcerts us by suddenly falling into
the accents of Housman or Yeats or the palest of the later
Eliot. And thus MacNeice, who seems to me with Auden the
most gifted of the Auden group, with a lyric impressionism
quite different from the rest, appears in a recent number
of 'New Verse' to have toppled over upon Auden and to have
become almost indistinguishable from him. (Louis MacNeice's
book, by the way, ought to be brought out in America. His
north-of-Ireland accent and material make him stand out
from the Oxford lushness, and in his best moments he has a
combination of intensity with felicity which makes much of
the work of the school sound synthetic.)

And the second of the Auden and Isherwood plays, 'The
Ascent of F6,' is certainly very much inferior to 'The Dog
Beneath the Skin.' 'The Dog Beneath the Skin' had its
shortcomings: a good deal of its satire was banal - it
sounded as if the clever schoolboys had just discovered
some of the stalest jokes of Marxism and worked them up
for a school entertainment. But the first part, at any
rate, was very funny; and the choruses, as I have said,
were of Auden's best. 'The Ascent of F6' suffers even more
from the flimsiness of amateur theatricals; and here Marxism itself has been forgotten for a relapse into Freudianism. The theme is a sort of psychoanalytic version of a
career like that of Colonel Lawrence. It has the peculiarly exasperating defect of appearing to be padded in a

tiresome way and yet at the same time to be too short and
not to exploit the possibilities of the subject.

Not, however, that Auden and his group are any worse off
than other Left intellectuals. And they have given expression to their plight and their time much more brilliantly and honestly than most. The combination of communism
with homosexuality, of an England suburbanized and Ameri-
canized in the peculiarly dreary English way, with an English university culture as rich as the richest fruitcake,
is something which has never before been seen in the history of English literature and which it took some courage
and genius to get there. Besides, MacNeice and Auden are
only thirty, Day-Lewis thirty-two, Spender twenty-eight.
They are remarkable at that age for having been able to
say so well something which had not been said before at
all:

[Quotes last two stanzas of 'August for the people and
their favourite islands', EA, 157.]

'Spain'

London, May 1937

58. C. DAY-LEWIS, UNSIGNED REVIEW, 'LISTENER'

xvii, 26 May 1937, 1050, 1053

This poem of a hundred and four lines can be called with
accuracy and no depreciation an occasional poem. It differs
from what we should normally understand by 'occasional
verse' in being neither trivial, pompous, sycophantic, nor
dull: it relates a present issue with the past -

> Yesterday all the past. The language of size
> Spreading to China along the trade-routes; the diffusion
>   Of the counting-frame and the cromlech;
> Yesterday the shadow-reckoning in the sunny climates.

and with the future hoped-for -

> To-morrow the rediscovery of romantic love,
> The photographing of ravens; all the fun under
>   Liberty's masterful shadow;
> To-morrow the hour of the pageant-master and the musician.

In spite of this oblique approach to its subject and the
relative deepening of its significance thereby, the poem
is essentially a poem for the moment dealing with a
straight issue - the struggle in Spain. No doubt this
struggle will affect the future course of Mr. Auden's work,
as it will affect the lives of all of us: but poetry may
have short-term as well as long-term obligations, and it
is to Mr. Auden's credit that he can use it also in the
acceptance of 'Today the makeshift consolations'. He realises that we stand at a crucial point of history, and
that poetry can help man to choose his destiny and shape

the future:

> To-day the deliberate increase in the chances of death,
> The conscious acceptance of guilt in the necessary
>   murder;
>   To-day the expending of powers
> On the flat ephemeral pamphlet and the boring meeting.

Mr. Auden's method here is that of a news-reel contrasting dark motive and brilliant event: image and commentary are blended with that skill, vividness and unfailing interest which we have come to expect from this poet. At times the cataloguing in detail becomes a little monotonous, and occasionally he comes near to guying his own idiom - as in 'Today the makeshift consolations: the shared cigarette, The cards in the candlelit barn, and the scraping concert'. But the poem moves with vivacity and the impersonal tenderness which is so much more effective than any heroics towards its final admonition:

> The stars are dead. The animals will not look,
> We are left alone with our day, and the time is short,
>   and
>   History to the defeated
> May say Alas but cannot help nor pardon.

59. RICHARD GOODMAN FORESEES TRUE REVOLUTIONARY POETRY,
FROM PERSPECTIVES FOR POETRY, 'DAILY WORKER'

2 June 1937, 7

Poet and Communist, Goodman (1911-66) contributed to 'New Country' (1933), and published 'Poems' (1931), 'A Footnote to Lawrence' (1932), and 'Britain's Best Ally' (an appeal for alliance with the Soviet Union, 1939).

'Spain' - the best poem that Auden has yet written and, with Spender's 'Vienna,' the only poem by an Englishman anywhere near being a real revolutionary poem - still deals with Auden's own personal reactions and personal interpretation of the Spanish struggle, although it is very near realising the fusion of this personal interpretation with the objective interpretation,

which is essential for the realisation of true revolutionary poetry.
How near this poem is to bringing about this fusion will be appreciated:-

[Quotes lines 45-6, and 56-68, of 'Spain', EA, 211-12.]

Perhaps almost the fusion is complete. At moments throughout the poem I am inclined to believe that it is....

That the progress made by Auden - and the much smaller progress made by Spender in 'Vienna' - is due almost entirely to the fact that they have been in contact with a mass struggle, confirms the impression that only when the British Labour movement has developed a really fighting unity and so a really mass movement in this country will it be possible for really revolutionary poetry to be written.
That Auden - and to a less extent Spender - are by now more or less technically equipped for immediately seizing upon such a movement when it comes is obvious, at least in Auden's case, from 'Spain.'
It is to him, perhaps more than to any other British writer, that one must look as the first revolutionary British poet, once the objective conditions are realised which will make revolutionary poetry possible in Britain.

60. CYRIL CONNOLLY, FROM TO-DAY THE STRUGGLE, 'NEW STATESMAN AND NATION'

xiii, 5 June 1937, 926, 928

'Spain' is a hundred-line poem by Auden; it is good medium Auden in a good cause - the Spanish Medical Aid. The Marxian theory of history does not go very happily into verse, but the conclusion is very fine.... Literature is something which is just as good in ten years' time, propaganda is not, and the contrast is acute for many.

              To-day the struggle,
    To-day the deliberate increase in the chances of death,
    The conscious acceptance of guilt in the necessary
                  murder;
          To-day the expending of powers
    On the flat ephemeral pamphlet and the boring meeting.

So writes Auden in 'Spain' and Milton, Marvell and
Shelley all wrote pamphlets. But Auden's non-pamphleteering
love lyric ['Lay your sleeping head my love / Human on my
failthless arm'] is by far the best thing in ['New Writing',
3, Spring 1937] and utterly without political purpose.

'Letters from Iceland'

(with Louis MacNeice)
London, August 1937; New York, November 1937

Auden recorded in August 1937 that he had written two-thirds of the book; all the photographs were his. According to Auden's New York agent, the Faber edition, of which 10,240 copies were printed, had an advance order of 8,000 copies.

61. EDWARD SACKVILLE-WEST ON BEING MAINLY AMUSED, 'NEW STATESMAN AND NATION'

xiv, 7 August 1937, 226

Edward Sackville-West (1901-65) was 5th Baron Sackville. His publications include 'Piano Quintet' (1925), 'The Sun in Capricorn' (1934), 'Inclinations' (1949), and 'The Record Guide' (with Desmond Shawe-Taylor, 1951).

This review is entitled Public and Private Schools.

In a letter to 'E.M.A.,' in the middle of the book, Mr. Auden describes his and his collaborator's intention thus: 'This letter ... will be a description of an effect of travelling in distant places which is to make one reflect on one's past and one's culture from the outside. But will form a central thread on which I shall hang other letters to different people more directly about Iceland.' Accordingly, the authors have thrown loosely together everything that happened to occur to them in the course of their desultory journey, from serious poems to menus. The method undoubtedly has its virtues, and the resulting extravaganza makes very easy reading: one is no longer surprised

that the Book Society should have selected this book when
one discovers that it contains nothing obscure or 'profound'; no message, though the point of view is naturally
leftish (poor Jane Austen is made to exemplify the economic basis of society), and no really virulent satire.
The authors are out to amuse and (very mildly) instruct;
they succeed in the main very well. And they are funny,
whether they are quoting from other books on Iceland or
describing their own experiences; and Mr. Auden's Byronic
stanzas are brilliant light verse. The same cannot be said
for Mr. MacNeice's heroic couplets, which are exceedingly
slovenly: this is not a form which is tolerable except
when highly polished. When I was at Oxford, we used to
play a game - a form of Consequences - called Communal
Verses, in which each player wrote two lines 'blind.'
The result was very like Mr. MacNeice's; but such things
are scarcely worth publishing. On the other hand, Mr.
Auden contributes three serious poems which are of real
beauty, though I doubt if Book Society members will make
much of them.

I found the long satire on the schoolgirl style over-
done to the point of dullness; but some of the straight
description is very good indeed:

Mysterious violent figures rise out of the background
slashing at prisoners without looking at them. Im-
passive horses survey another world than theirs. One of
the thieves has his head thrown right back and on his
forehead dances a bear holding a child. Serried figures, the Queen of Heaven with a tower, St. Peter with
no back to his head, etc., rise like a Greek Chorus,
right and left of the main panel.

Then there is a collection of proverbs à la Blake, of
which I select the following: 'Gifts should be handed, not
hurled'; 'Men fight by day, devils by night'; 'The meanest
guest has the keenest eye.'

The authors have found a certain difficulty in making
Iceland itself seem interesting. In this they suffer from
the same trouble which besets all modern explorers: that
of finding little-visited spots of the earth to write
about, the trouble which drove Mr. Peter Fleming to the
most meaningless part of Central Asia. Perhaps this is why
they found it necessary to eke out their book with such a
very large quantity of private jokes and references to un-
described friends of whom the ordinary reader will have no
knowledge whatever. Thus, the Last Will and Testament, with
which the book ends, is a veritable orgy of this kind of
game, no doubt extremely amusing to the other members of

the Upper Fifth, but scarcely to anyone else.
The photographs are sometimes beautiful and invariably
disarming.

62. UNSIGNED REVIEW, COOLING WATERS, 'TIMES LITERARY SUP-
PLEMENT'

7 August 1937, 572

This review is subtitled A Byronic Interlude in Iceland.

Mr. Auden is at the stage when one wonders with a lively
expectation whether the next fork in his road will take
him towards poetry or the drama, or whether he will now go
ahead in his own right, rediscovering a track which makes
the best of both these worlds. But he is full of surprises; and this time he disappears, with a new companion,
round a bend which seems at first to be hairpin but turns
out to have the virtue of an S. His new book begins with
the first canto of a letter to Byron written in a form and
spirit with which his correspondent would be dangerously
familiar; it contains an extraordinary Last Will and Testament which may amuse everybody but its innumerable lega-
tees; and it ends with statistical graphs showing the dis-
tribution of population, industry and foreign trade of
Iceland.
    No one will be more suprised at this than Mr. Auden was.
He went to Iceland with a contract to write a travel book
and with no idea how this should be done. (Authorship as
an exacting affair of dates and delivery is a modern development about which Byron might have been glad to receive a stanza or two.) However, he read 'Don Juan' on the
way out, and received a challenge of virtuosity. To accept
was a different matter, but Housman is not the only poet
who has been spurred up Parnassus by a minor ailment:-

        Indeed one hardly goes too far in stating
    That many a flawless lyric may be due,
    Not to a lover's broken heart, but 'flu.

Mr. Auden, gloomily nursing a cold in an Icelandic bus,
suddenly saw, streaming before him, Byron as his way out.
He would chat to Byron about cabbages and kings, and to
other more accessible correspondents about Iceland. Light

verse, poor girl, practised as she is only by 'Milne and
persons of that kind' and confined 'to the more bourgeois
periodicals,' is in a poor way: she will be all the better
for some fresh air:-

> And since she's on a holiday, my Muse
> Is out to please, find everything delightful
> And only now and then be mildly spiteful.

So he takes her, keeping his promise fairly well, for five
longish cantos. These have no relevance to Iceland except
in so far as the poet, with glacier on one hand and a gey-
ser on the other, has put so much cooling water between
him and England - and even between himself and his habitual
life - that he can laugh at her absurdities (and his) and
grumble at her plight (and his) with as much wit as he can
muster, and without the anger of close-quarter fighting.
This stylish display of marksmanship is equally good for
England and for Mr. Auden. He accepts the discipline of the
Byronic stanza (less, it is true, one line) with fine and
gleeful virtuosity, and has some glorious adventures in
rhyme. 'My trouble is that the excitement of doing a kind
of thing I've never tried to do before keeps making me
think it's better and funnier than it is.' Precisely; Mr.
Auden tries for a bull of autobiographical, social or
aesthetic criticism in every stanza, and often scores at
least an inner, as in this preliminary to a description of
the change from John Bull to 'the little Mickey with the
hidden grudge':-

> We've still, it's true, the same shape and appearance,
>   We haven't changed the way that kissing's done;
> The average man still hates all interference,
>   Is just as proud still of his new-born son:
>   Still, like a hen, he likes his private run,
> Scratches for self-esteem, and slyly pecks
> A good deal in the neighbourhood of sex.

Mr. MacNeice is a more morose rebel. His contributions
stand beside Mr. Auden's intermittent instruction of Byron
like desolate pools unmoved beside a volcano five times in
eruption. Both authors are rather sheepish about their
presence in Iceland when Europe wants such careful attention. Mr. MacNeice in a rhymed letter to N.W.8 describes
with desperate wit 'the obscure but powerful ethics of
Going North.' Is it possible, horrid thought, that these
poets are becoming escapists? No, answers Mr. Auden categorically, when Mr. Isherwood asks him about life on small
islands:-

We are all too deeply involved with Europe to be able,
or even wish, to escape. Though I am sure you would enjoy a visit as much as I did, I think that, in the long
run, the Scandinavian sanity would be too much for you,
as it is for me. The truth is, we are both only really
happy living among lunatics.

The cat in the last sentence comes out of Mr. MacNeice's
bag as well, except perhaps for the world 'happy.' He faces
the question in a powerful Eclogue from Iceland in which
two tourists, hoping for solitude on an Icelandic heath,
are lectured by the ghost of Grettir,

> The last of the saga heroes
> Who had not the wisdom of Njal or the beauty of Gunnar,
> I was the doomed tough, disaster kept me witty;
> Being born the surly jack, the ne'er-do-well, the
> > loiterer.
> Hard blows exalted me.

A voice from the macabre dancing floor of Europe is enough
to keep the travellers where they are, but Grettir sends
them back:-

> Minute your gesture but it must be made -
> Your hazard, your act of defiance and hymn of hate,
> Hatred of hatred, assertion of human values,
> Which is now your only duty.

One must correct the impression that in this book Iceland is only the point of departure for gunman journeys of
the spirit. Mr. Auden's photographs are usually good and
always intelligent. He is knowledgeable, concentrated, exact and pungent on cost, transport, food and clothes, and
has a humility and brevity unusual in a three months'
visitor when he tells an Icelander what he thinks of his
country. Perhaps this was written after compiling
'Sheaves from Sagaland,' in which he gathers a pretty harvest from the writings of a long line of distinguished - or
at the least eccentric - predecessors in plodding across
Iceland.
  Finally there is 'Hetty to Nancy,' the only letter whose
author and recipient are not clearly indicated. It is apparently the diary of a lady who travelled painfully, on
horseback, round Langjokull, in the company of a school-
mistress and four schoolgirls. This joyous document is what
the good travel book is like when it is not written by Mr.
Auden. There are unfortunately only forty pages of it, for
Mr. Auden thinks that such humours grow monotonous. It

might, indeed, have been written by Hetty, but her sex
is strongly suspected to be male, her surname Auden.

63. MICHAEL ROBERTS ON USEFUL ENTERTAINMENT, POETS ON
HOLIDAY, 'LONDON MERCURY'

xxxvi, September 1937, 483-4

Mr. Auden and Mr. MacNeice are turning an honest penny in
an honest way:

> In the 'bus to-day I had a bright idea about this tra-
> vel book. I brought a Byron with me to Iceland, and I
> suddenly thought I might write him a chatty letter in
> light verse about anything I could think of, Europe,
> literature, myself. He's the right person, I think, be-
> cause he was a townee, a European, and disliked Words-
> worth and that kind of approach to nature, and I find
> that very sympathetic.

Mr. Auden and Mr. MacNeice are both honest townees: they
do not profess to use landscapes as symbols for a state of
mind, as Wordsworth did, but that does not prevent them
from writing good descriptive verse that makes a scene the
starting-point of meditation about the world in general.
They profess to dislike hardship, but they deliberately
land themselves in situations where some hardship is inevitable:

> Wystan has butted in again
> To say we must go out in the frightful rain
> To see a man about a horse and so
> I shall have to stop. For we soon intend to
> go
> Around the Langjökull, a ten day's ride,
> Gumboots and stockfish. Probably you'll
> deride
> This sissy onslaught on the open spaces.
> I can see the joke myself....

There appears to be a fair amount of mud and corrugated
iron in Iceland, but the chief hardships are gastronomical:
'Dried fish is a staple food in Iceland. This should be
shredded with the fingers and eaten with butter. It varies
in toughness. The tougher kind tastes like toe-nails, and

the softer kind like the skin off the soles of one's feet.'
By the way of delicacy there is 'Hakarl, which is half-dry,
half-rotten shark. This is white inside with a prickly horn
rind outside, as tough as an old boot. Owing to the smell
it has to be eaten out of doors. It is shaved off with a
knife and eaten with brandy. It tastes more like boot-
polish than anything else I can think of.'
    Practical advice to travellers is not perhaps the main
intention of this collection of letters, but a good deal
of it creeps in, and there is a useful bibliography, as
well as an entertaining anthology of the observations and
inanities of previous travellers. Mr. Auden's Letter to
Byron is divided into five parts: it forms the recurrent
theme of the book, and in between there are prose narratives (including some Cambridge-and-Gordon-Squareish 'letters from Hetty to Nancy,' whose authorship the reader
can, from internal evidence, guess), and a number of
oddments:

> Every exciting letter has enclosures,
>   And so shall this - a bunch of photographs,
> Some out of focus, some with wrong exposures,
>   Press cuttings, gossip, maps, statistics, graphs;
>   I don't intend to do the thing by halves.
> I'm going to be very up-to-date indeed.
> It is a collage that you're going to read.

Towards the end of the book the authors set out their
'Last Will and Testament' in loose *terza rima*: if everybody mentioned in it buys a copy, the book ought to do
well, and if they ever receive their legacies the world
will be considerably livened up.
    The whole book is entertaining, useful, and light-
hearted. It expresses a great number of Mr. Auden's private judgments and some of Mr. MacNeice's; the reader will
probably applaud most of them all the more heartedly because they are not disguised as moral principles. It contains some of the liveliest light verse that Mr. Auden has
yet written, and two of his best and most characteristic
poems. Since the early work of Chesterton, light verse has
mostly been limited to inoffensive exercises: there is no
venom in the present book (after all, the authors were on
holiday), but there is enough tune and jingle to please
the ear and help the memory, and enough punch to cause a
few sore heads and bloody noses.

64. EDWIN MUIR, UNTITLED REVIEW, 'CRITERION'

xvii, lxvi, October 1937, 154

Scottish poet, critic, translator, and novelist, Muir
(1887-1959) was born and spent his early years in rural
communities in the Orkneys. After a period as A.R. Orage's
assistant on the 'New Age', he devoted his life to poetry
and translation, and to prolific articles which contained,
according to T.S. Eliot, 'the best criticism of our time'.
With his accomplished wife, Willa, he translated into English numerous works including those of Kafka and of
Hermann Broch. His poems (collected in 1960) grew steadily
in maturity, and express a humane vision of life which is
underlined by his celebrated autobiography (1954).

'Letters from Iceland' is mainly entertainment, and mainly
good entertainment. Mr. MacNeice seems to have liked the
island better than Mr. Auden, and also to have taken it
more seriously. The best single items in the book are, I
think, an account of an eruption in 1727 by the Minister
of Sandfell, and a fairy tale, Gellivör, retold by Mr.
Auden. After that comes the long 'Letter to Lord Byron',
written in instalments by Mr. Auden, in which he catches
with astonishing skill the mood and style of 'Don Juan'.
This poem is vigorous, careless, amusing, altogether enjoyable, and considerably more than an exercise. The one disappointing feature in the book is Auden and MacNeice's
Last Will and Testament at the end, which is dull and
laboured. Altogether it is a pleasantly formless book.

From Auden Double Number

'New Verse', Nos 26-27, November 1937

'We salute in Auden', Geoffrey Grigson wrote in his editorial to this special issue of 'New Verse', 'the first
English poet for many years who is a poet all the way
round.... He is traditional, revolutionary, energetic, inquisitive, critical, and intelligent.' While acknowledging that there was much both to praise and to criticize in
Auden, he explained further, 'there are plenty of writers
who do recognise Auden's broad power of raising ordinary speech into strong and strange incantation....'

65. CHRISTOPHER ISHERWOOD, SOME NOTES ON AUDEN'S EARLY
POETRY

4-9

Novelist, dramatist, translator, and writer on religion,
Isherwood (b. 1904) published his first novel, 'All the
Conspirators', in 1928, and collaborated with Auden on
'The Dog Beneath the Skin', 'The Ascent of F6', 'On the
Frontier', and 'Journey to a War'. His autobiographical
novel 'Lions and Shadows' (1938) contains a vivid portrait
of the young Auden under the guise of 'Hugh Weston'. This
essay is reprinted in 'W.H. Auden: A Tribute' (ed. Spender,
1975), where Isherwood adds a Postscript containing important third thoughts and corrections (pp. 78-9).

If I were told to introduce a reader to the poetry of W.H.
Auden, I should begin by asking him to remember three
things:

First, that Auden is essentially a scientist: perhaps I should add 'a schoolboy scientist.' He has, that is to say, the scientific training and the scientific interests of a very intelligent schoolboy. He has covered the groundwork, but doesn't propose to go any further: he has no intention of specialising. Nevertheless, he has acquired the scientific outlook and technique of approach; and this is really all he needs for his writing.

Second, that Auden is a musician and a ritualist. As a child he enjoyed a high Anglican upbringing, coupled with a sound musical education. The Anglicanism has evaporated, leaving only the height: he is still much preoccupied with ritual, in all its forms. When we collaborate, I have to keep a sharp eye on him - or down flop the characters on their kneees (see 'F6.' passim): another constant danger is that of choral interruptions by angel-voices. If Auden had his way, he would turn every play into a cross between grand opera and high mass.

Third, that Auden is a Scandinavian. The Auden family came originally from Iceland. Auden himself was brought up on the sagas, and their influence upon his work has been profound.

Auden began writing poetry comparatively late; when he had already been several terms at his public school. At our prep-school, he showed no literary interests whatever: his ambition was to become a mining-engineer. His first poems, unlike Stephen Spender's, were competent but entirely imitative: Hardy, Thomas and Frost were his models:

THE CARTER'S FUNERAL

Sixty odd years of poaching and drink
And rain-sodden waggons with scarcely a friend,
Chained to this life; rust fractures a link,
      So the end.

Sexton at last has pressed down the loam,
He blows on his fingers and prays for the sun,
Parson unvests and turns to his home,
      Duty done.

Little enough stays musing upon
The passing of one of the masters of things,
Only a bird looks peak-faced on,
      Looks and sings.

ALLENDALE

The smelting-mill stack is crumbling, no smoke is alive
          there,
Down in the valley the furnace no lead ore of worth burns;
Now tombs of decaying industries, not to strive there
    Many more earth-turns.

The chimney still stands at the top of the hill like a
          finger
Skywardly pointing as if it were asking: 'What lies there?'
And thither we stray to dream of those things as we
          linger,
    Nature denies here.

Dark looming around the fell-folds stretch desolate,
          crag-scarred,
Seeming to murmur: 'Why beat you the bars of your
          prison?'
What matter? To us the world-face is glowing and flag-
          starred,
    Lit by a vision.

So under it stand we, all swept by the rain and the
          wind there,
Muttering: 'What look you for, creatures that die in
          a season?'
We care not, but turn to our dreams and the comfort we
          find there,
    Asking no reason.

The saga-world is a schoolboy world, with its feuds,
its practical jokes, its dark threats conveyed in puns
and riddles and understatements: 'I think this day will
end unluckily for some; but chiefly for those who least
expect harm.' I once remarked to Auden that the atmosphere
of 'Gisli the Outlaw' very much reminded me of our schooldays. He was pleased with the idea: and, soon after this,
he produced his first play: 'Paid on Both Sides,' in which
the two worlds are so inextricably confused that it is impossible to say whether the characters are really epic
heroes or only members of a school O.T.C.
    Auden is, and always has been, a most prolific writer.
Problems of form and technique seem to bother him very
little. You could say to him: 'Please write me a double
ballade on the virtues of a certain brand of toothpaste,
which also contains at least ten anagrams on the names of
well-known politicians, and of which the refrain is as

follows....' Within twenty-four hours, your ballade would
be ready - and it would be good.

When Auden was younger, he was very lazy. He hated
polishing and making corrections. If I didn't like a poem,
he threw it away and wrote another. If I liked one line,
he would keep it and work it into a new poem. In this way,
whole poems were constructed which were simply anthologies
of my favourite lines, entirely regardless of grammar or
sense. This is the simple explanation of much of Auden's
celebrated obscurity.

While Auden was up at Oxford, he read T.S. Eliot. The
discovery of 'The Waste Land' marked a turning-point in
his work - for the better, certainly; though the earliest
symptoms of Eliot-influence were most alarming. Like a
patient who has received an over-powerful inoculation,
Auden developed a severe attack of allusions, jargonitis
and private jokes. He began to write lines like: 'Inexor-
able Rembrandt rays that stab...' or 'Love mutual has
reached its first eutectic...' Nearly all the poems of
that early Eliot period are now scrapped.

In 1928, Spender, who had a private press, printed a
little orange paper volume of Auden's poems. (This book-
let, limited to 'about 45 copies,' is now a bibliophile's
prize: the mis-prints alone are worth about ten shillings
each.) Most of the poems were reprinted two years later,
when Messrs. Faber and Faber published the first edition
of their Auden volume: here is one of the few which were
not:

> Consider if you will how lovers stand
> In brief adherence, straining to preserve
> Too long the suction of good-bye: others,
> Less clinically-minded, will admire
> An evening like a coloured photograph,
> A music stultified across the water.
> The desert opens here, and if, though we
> Have ligatured the ends of a farewell,
> Sporadic heartburn show in evidence
> Of love uneconomically slain,
> It is for the last time, the last look back,
> The heel upon the finishing blade of grass,
> To dazzling cities of the plain where lust
> Threatened a sinister rod, and we shall turn
> To our study of stones, to split Eve's apple,
> Absorbed, content if we can say 'because';
> Unanswerable like any other pedant,
> Like Solomon and Sheba, wrong for years.   [EA, 438]

I think this poem illustrates very clearly Auden's

state of mind at that period: in this respect, its weakness is its virtue. Auden was very busy trying to regard things 'clinically,' as he called it. Poetry, he said, must concern itself with shapes and volumes. Colours and smells were condemned as romantic: Form alone was significant. Auden loathed (and still rather dislikes) the Sea - for the Sea, besides being deplorably wet and sloppy, is formless. (Note 'ligatured' - a typical specimen of the 'clinical' vocabulary.)

Another, and even more powerful influence upon Auden's early work was non-literary in its origin - in 1929, during a visit to Berlin, he came into contact with the doctrines of the American psychologist, Homer Lane. (Cf. Auden's own account of this, in his 'Letter to Lord Byron', Part Four.) Auden was particularly interested in Lane's theories of the psychological causes of disease - if you refuse to make use of your creative powers, you grow a cancer instead, etc. References to these theories can be found in many of the early poems, and, more generally, in 'The Orators.' Lane's teachings provide a key to most of the obscurities in the Journal of an Airman (Mr. John Layard, one of Lane's most brilliant followers, has pointed out the psychological relationship between epilepsy and the idea of flight.)

The first collaboration between Auden and myself was in a play called 'The Enemies of a Bishop.' The Bishop is the hero of the play: he represents sanity, and is an idealised portrait of Lane himself. His enemies are the pseudo-healers, the wilfully ill and the mad. The final curtain goes down on his complete vitory. The play was no more than a charade, very loosely put together and full of private jokes. We revised the best parts of it and used them again, five years later, in 'The Dog Beneath the Skin.'

It is typical of Auden's astonishing adaptability that, after two or three months in Berlin, he began to write poems in German. Their style can be best imagined by supposing that a German writer should attempt a sonnet-sequence in a mixture of Cockney and Tennysonian English, without being able to command either idiom. A German critic of great sensibility to whom I afterwards showed these sonnets was much intrigued. He assured me that their writer was a poet of the first rank, despite his absurd grammatical howlers. The critic himself had never heard of Auden and was certainly quite unaware of his English reputation.

The scenery of Auden's early poetry is, almost invariably, mountainous. As a boy, he visited Westmorland, the Peak District of Derbyshire, and Wales. For urban scenery, he preferred the industrial Midlands; particularly in districts where an industry is decaying. His romantic

travel-wish was always towards the North. He could never
understand how anybody could long for the sun, the blue
sky, the palm-trees of the South. His favourite weather
was autumnal; high wind and driving rain. He loved industrial ruins, a disused factory or an abandoned mill: a
ruined abbey would leave him quite cold. He has always had
a special feeling for caves and mines. At school, one of
his favourite books was Jules Verne's 'Journey to the
Centre of the Earth.'

A final word about Influences - or perhaps I should say,
crazes. For Auden is deeply rooted in the English tradition, and his debt to most of the great writers of the
past is too obvious to need comment here. The crazes were
all short-lived: they left plenty of temporary damage but
few lasting traces. The earliest I remember was for Edwin
Arlington Robinson. It found expression in about half a
dozen poems (all scrapped) and notably in some lines about
'a Shape' in an Irish mackintosh which malice urges but
friendship forbids me to quote. Then came Emily Dickinson.
You will find her footprints here and there among the
earlier poems: for example,

> Nor sorrow take
> His endless look.   [This lunar beauty, EA, 52]

Then Bridges published 'The Testament of Beauty,' and
Auden wrote the poem beginning: 'Which of you waking early
and watching daybreak...' which appeared in the first
Faber edition, but was removed from later impressions.
Finally, there was Hopkins: but, by this time, Auden's literary digestive powers were stronger: he made a virtue of
imitation, and produced the brilliant parody-ode to a
rugger fifteen which appears at the end of 'The Orators.'

66. STEPHEN SPENDER, OXFORD TO COMMUNISM

9-10

I first knew Auden during his last year and my first year at
Oxford. Then he had a rather sinister public reputation for
keeping a revolver in his desk and for working at midday
in artificial light with all the blinds of his room drawn.
He had comparatively few friends, but I believe he influenced them greatly; perhaps more in the conduct of their
lives than in their work. Amongst these were Cecil

Day-Lewis and Rex Warner. I may add that, although
Auden's, Day-Lewis's and my name have been linked together ever since the publication of 'New Signatures,' I
had never met Day-Lewis or read any of his work until
some time after my own 'Poems' were published: so that if
there is a common factor in Day-Lewis and me, it must be
the influence of Auden.

When I was at Oxford, I did not understand Auden's
poems, yet they gripped my imagination, and, although I
have a very bad memory for poetry, I found myself involun-
tarily remembering lines and phrases of his. It was something analytical, objective, self-consciously clinical,
deliberately impersonal which fascinated me. In those days,
his fantasies of the necessary impersonality of poets led
him at once to a distrust of politics and to extravagance.
I remember him once saying that 'the poet' would 'enjoy,'
in a civil war, lying on a roof and shooting at his best
friend, who was on the other side. I was always interested
in politics, but his interests were poetry, psycho-analysis
and medicine. I think he disapproved of my politics, just
as, at that time, he disapproved of my writing prose or
going to concerts to hear classical music.

Auden 'arrived at' politics, by way of psychology. His
early poems begin by being preoccupied with neurosis in
individuals, but this gradually extends (at the time when
he had left Oxford and gone to live in Berlin) to an interest in the epoch and capitalist society. At first though
this interest was clinical; he was content to state what
he beautifully and profoundly saw without implying an
attitude or a remedy.

Yet the strength of socialism or communism and its appeal to the poet lies in the fact that the mere statement
of social realities today, if it goes far enough, both
suggests a remedy and involves one in taking sides. For
example, in post-war and pre-Hitler Berlin, one began by
noticing symptoms of decadence, suffering and unemployment;
one looked further and one saw beneath the decay of the
liberal state, the virulent reaction of the Nazis and the
struggle for a new life of the Communists. The one side
stood for the suppression of the very objectivity which
the poet required, perhaps also his life, certainly his
intellectual standards; the other, however painful and
disillusioning its birth pangs, promised finally a world
in which one could see and tell the truth.

From the point of view of the working-class movement
the ultimate criticism of Auden and the poets associated
with him is that we haven't deliberately and consciously
transferred ourselves to the working class. The subject of
his poetry is the struggle, but the struggle seen, as it

were, by someone who whilst living in one camp, sympathises with the other; a struggle in fact which while existing externally is also taking place within the mind of the poet himself, who remains a bourgeois. This argument is put very forcibly by Christopher Caudwell in the last chapter of his book 'Illusion and Reality.' Whilst accepting its validity as a critical attitude, may we not say that the position of the writer who sees the conflict as something which is at once subjective to himself and having its external reality in the world - the position outlined in Auden's Spain - is one of the most creative, realistic and valid positions for the artist in our time?

67. LOUIS MacNEICE, LETTER TO W.H. AUDEN

11-13

October 21st, 1937.

DEAR WYSTAN,

I have to write you a letter in a great hurry and so it would be out of the question to try to assess your importance. I take it that you are important and, before that, that poetry itself is important. Poets are not legislators (what is an 'unacknowledged legislator' anyway?), but they put facts and feelings in italics, which makes people think about them and such thinking may in the end have an outcome in action.

Poets have different methods of italicisation. What are yours? What is it in your poetry which shakes people up?

It is, I take it, a freshness - sometimes of form, sometimes of content, usually of both. You are very fertile in pregnant and unusual phrases and have an aptitude for stark and compelling texture. With regard to content, the subject-matter of your poems is always interesting and it is a blessing to our generation, though one in the eye for Bloomsbury, that you discharged into poetry the subject-matters of psycho-analysis, politics and economics. Mr. Eliot brought back ideas into poetry but he uses the ideas, say, of anthropology more academically and less humanely than you use Marx or Groddeck. This is because you are always taking sides.

It may be bad taste to take sides but it is a more vital habit than the detachment of the pure aesthete. The taunt of being a schoolboy (which, when in the mood, I should

certainly apply myself) is itself a compliment because it
implies that you expect the world and yourself to develop.
This expectation inevitably seems vulgar to that bevy of
second-rate sensitive minds who write in our cultured
weeklies.   .

'Other philosophies have described the world; our business is to change it.' Add that if we are not interested
in changing it, there is really very little to describe.
There is just an assortment of heterogeneous objects to
make Pure Form out of.

You go to extremes, of course, but that is all to the
good. There is still a place in the sun for the novels of
Virginia Woolf, for still-life painting and for the nature-
lover. But these would probably not survive if you and your
like, who have no use for them, did not plump entirely for
something different.

Like most poets you are limited. Your poems are strongly
physical but not fastidiously physical. This is what I
should expect from someone who does not like flowers in his
room.

Your return to a versification in more regular stanzas
and rhymes is, I think, a very good thing. The simple poem,
however, does not always wear too well. At first sight we
are very pleased to get the swing of it so easily and
understand it so quickly, but after first acquaintance it
sometimes grows stale. A.E. Housman, whom I join you in admiring, was a virtuoso who could get away with cliché
images and hymn-tune metres, but, as you would, I think,
admit, his methods are not suitable to anyone who has a
creed which is either profound or elaborate.

I am therefore a little doubtful about your present use
of the ballad form. It is very good fun but it does not
seem to me to be your *natural* form as I doubt if you can
put over what you want to say in it. Of course if you can
put over half of what you want to say to a thousand people,
that may well be better than putting over two thirds of it
to a hundred people. But I hope that you will not start
writing down to the crowd for, if you write down far
enough, you will have to be careful to give them nothing
that they don't know already and then your own end will be
defeated. Compromise is necessary here, as always, in
poetry.

I think you have shown great sense in not writing 'proletarian' stuff (though some reviewers, who presumably did
not read your poems, have accused you of it). You realise
that one must write about what one knows. One may not hold
the bourgeois creed, but if one knows only bourgeois one
must write about them. They all after all contain the germ
of their opposite. It is an excellent thing (lie quiet

Ezra, Cambridge, Gordon Square, with your pure images,
pure cerebration, pure pattern, your scrap-albums of orna-
ment torn eclectically from history) that you should have
written poems about preparatory schools. Some of the Pure
Poets maintained that one could make poems out of anything, but on the ground, not that subject was important,
but that it didn't matter. You also would admit that anything can go into poetry, but the poet must first be interested in the thing itself.

As for poetic drama, you are now swinging away from the
Queer Play. This, like the formal change in your lyrics,
is also a good thing and also has its danger. But the danger is not so great for you as it would be for some. Whatever the shape of your work, it will always have ideas in
it. Still, when authors like Denis Johnston, who can
write excellent straight plays, feel impelled to go over
to crooked plays and 'poetic writing,' there must be some
good reason for it and it may appear perverse in you to
forget your birthright and pass them in the opposite direction to a realism which may not be much more natural to
you than poetry is to them.

These are the criticisms which occur to me at the moment.
I have no time to expand on your virtues, but I must say
that what I especially admire in you is your unflagging
curiosity about people and events. Poetry is related to
the sermon and you have your penchant for preaching, but it
is more closely related to conversation and you, my dear,
if any, are a born gossip.

Yours ever,

68. GEOFFREY GRIGSON, AUDEN AS A MONSTER

13-17

Auden does not fit. Auden is no gentleman. Auden does not
write, or exist, by any of the codes, by the Bloomsbury
rules, by the Hampstead rules, by the Oxford, the Cam-
bridge, or the Russell Square rules. Auden writes about
boys at school. Auden bites his nails. Auden uses rhymes.
Auden uses any kind of form. Auden does not dislike A.E.
Housman. Auden resembles Kipling more than he resembles
William Carlos Williams. Auden prefers Daumier to Mondrian.
Auden would sooner read the Laxdœla saga than 'The Waves.'
And so on.

Auden is a monster:

> The sad and bearded fires, the monsters fair,
> The prodigies appearing in the air...

It is a long time since an able monster has been included among English poets, and since monsters are beings
extremely difficult to measure up or confine, I shall only
write a little about a monstrous quality in Auden's verse.
One of the most frequent images used by Auden is the image
of the frontier, the line between the known and the feared,
the past and the future, and the conscious and everything
beyond control, the region of society and the region of
trolls and hulders (and Goebbelses). Auden lives very much
in this frightening border territory (Dover is a border
town). The uses of it as a symbol, at the present time,
are so obvious that I do not understand why so many of
Auden's critics - even Mr. Edgell Rickword - so incongruously treat it as the consequence *only*, and the expression
only, of Auden's middle-class position.

There is much of it in one of the poems by Auden I like
best - 'The Witnesses' (it would be worth while working
out just why this poem has been scrapped). I read 'The
Witnesses' once in a paper on Auden to a women's club.
Afterwards a Russian woman in exile came up, much excited
and moved:

> The bolt is sliding in its groove,
> Outside the window is the black remov-
>   er's van,
> And now with sudden swift emergence
> Come the women in dark glasses, the hump-backed surgeons
>   and the scissor-man.

This is Auden on the dangerous side of the frontier, and
the woman held her hands together tightly, and said how it
reminded her of a Russian poem in which a child is ill in a
room. By the window a clock is tick-tocking, with a long
pendulum. The moment the dwarf comes to the window, and
puts his hand in, and catches hold of the pendulum, the
child dies. If you are neither a poet just of form and
ideas - an 'embodied mind' is the only mind we know and
Auden would agree that 'Man's spirit will be flesh-bound
when found at best' - nor a poet just of objects, then you
can be most effective if you are able to combine two
'magics,' if you are able to combine images of the frontier
with the right incantation, symbol with sound:

> In his green den the murmuring seal
> Close by his sleek companion lies....

The cocks did crow to-whoo, to-whoo
And the sun did shine so cold!

Coleridge noticed a passage in Scott's 'Pirate,' 'Many
prodigious stories of these marine monsters (the Kraken
and the sea-snake)...were then universally received among
the Zetlanders, whose descendants have not as yet by any
means abandoned faith in them,' and he wrote in the margin
'No wonder! for *I* believe in the Sea-snake; Robert Southey
in the Kraken; and Linnæus in both.' Auden believes in
the troll:

Starving through the leafless wood
Trolls run scolding for their food;
And the nightingale is dumb,
And the angel will not come;

and no doubt, if the belief fitted them, he and Coleridge
and Southey would equally have believed in Eskimo eye-
goblins whose eyes open from top to bottom. There is something about Auden of the benign wizard casting out devils,
but enjoying the devils and the wizardry.

If Auden was only a monstrous (if you like call it 'romantic') phrase or line or passage maker, there would not
be much more to say about him. Then he would be small and
simple, and patchy, like Christopher Smart, or Clare, or
Darley or Edward Thomas. The frontier images are natural
to Auden, but Auden is an energetic intelligent explorer
who is always filling himself with observations and ideas,
and so he uses images of the kind deliberately as well as
naturally. Also he can manage patterns and forms, and so
one of his best poems can produce the full effect of
poetry. If you have, then, a medical, moral and practical
view, more or less, about the arts, if art is a releaser
of tension, something which cleans and polishes up the
raggedness of the soul, something which 'can help us immensely by casting light upon the ground on which we stand,
and dissolving by its warmth the cold mist of indifference
and unconscious falsehood in which we are all more or less
enclosed,' then you must find Auden perhaps the most valuable poet alive.

Mr. Herbert Read complains further on in this number
that in Auden's work there is 'a backsliding in the technique of verse,' that 'artificial verse [but is there a
natural verse?] is only worth doing if done supremely well,
as by Pope,' that Auden apes the antics of Kipling and
Byron. The liberation of verse form, he thinks, from Blake
through Whitman and Lawrence has something to do with political, moral and intellectual liberation. This is not easy

to understand. Strict verse form has never made anyone a
worse poet. If there is liberation, there is also anarchy.
Human physiology has not changed, and rhythmical repe-
titions and variations are as much desired by us now as by
Esquimaux or Melanesians. It is hard to see (i) how liberation could go any further, or just continue, (ii) how
Auden's monstrous image-making could work in 'liberated'
forms, which are all very well for generalising statements
or simple statements with little more than their first
meaning. When Lawrence is a good image-maker and is most
moved by what he is saying, he is least free in his form,
as in the 'Ballad of Another Ophelia.'

Peace be with Mr. Read, but he reminds me in his complaint of Carl Sandburg, one of whose favourite remarks is
said to be 'Think what Shakespeare could have done with the
emotion behind the sonnets if he had been free, not bound
by any verse form.'

Also I am glad that people disparage Auden by means of
Kipling. It is a compliment. Kipling was an Auden gone
wrong. (When I read 'Danny Deever' the other day I thought
just how Auden would have made it exactly right.) The
fault of the celebrated Kipling was not exuberance or
energy. It was falsity of premiss, cheapness of feeling,
atrophy of morals, mistraining of intellect and inef-
ficiency of technique. Kipling was a remarkable human being
wrong, Auden is a remarkable human being right, more or
less; many worse poets than Auden who are 'better' poets
than Kipling are only pencils and pens.

Auden does not obey the codes. But when a monster who
writes so much is so fidgety and inquisitive, so interested in things and ideas, so human and generous, and so rude
to the infinite, it does not matter at all if the lines of
his development are twisted and obscure, if he writes
plenty of verse which is slack, ordinary, dull, or silly,
or if for a year, or two, he seems to be no poet at all.
I wish some critics of Auden would remember this. One expects ignorance and impudence from 'Evening Standard' reviewers (Mr. Howard Spring wrote 'Mr. W.H. Auden, I understand, is a celebrated young man. Mr. Louis MacNeice, I
believe, is also not unknown to juvenile cognoscenti') or
scurfy rudeness from an old bull like Mr. St. John Irvine,
but the authors of the malignant and silly ineptitudes
thrown from Cambridge and the weeklies are educated men:
'The Ascent of F6' 'should be very successful, but it looks
unpleasantly like the end of Auden's talent.' A wet day in
April is not the end of the summer. Will these proud persons look through the collected writings of good poets or
the paintings and sketches of good painters? Then they will
know that life is not over at thirty, that great men can at

times be as otiose and empty as if they lacked all their
abilities.

It is much to Auden's honour that he is so entirely and
successfully a poet. Coleridge said about Milton that 'the
age in which the foundations of his mind were laid was congenial to it as one golden aera of profound erudition and
individual genius.' The era in which Auden has grown up has
been one of bewildered mediocrity, triviality and fudge.

69. KENNETH ALLOTT, AUDEN IN THE THEATRE

17-21

Allott (1912-73), who was Assistant Editor of 'New Verse'
from 1936 to 1939, became A.C. Bradley Professor of Modern
English Literature at Liverpool University in 1964. His
publications include 'Poems' (1938), 'The Ventriloquist's
Doll' (1934), 'The Art of Graham Greene' (1951), 'The Penguin Book of Contemporary Verse' (1950), and 'Complete
Poems of Matthew Arnold' (1965).

We should leave theory about the contemporary drama until we have produced some contemporary drama to theorise
about.

I do not believe that the dramatic pieces of Auden, or of
Auden and Isherwood, are good plays: but 'The Dog Beneath
the Skin' and 'The Ascent of F6' are exciting and interesting (if mainly for irrelevant reasons) and as good plays
as we can expect to see on the English stage today. I am
not going to use the yardstick of Shakespeare to beat
Auden with - as Humphrey Jennings did in the special
theatre number of 'New Verse.'* I want to show that the
plays would be better if Auden and Isherwood were free of
certain pre-conceptions. I am sure Auden is a good poet.
I am equally sure that he is a wrong-headed dramatist.

A word about 'Paid on Both Sides' and 'The Dance of
Death' - Auden's solo flights in the vacuum of the modern
theatre. Isherwood explains the genesis of the former. It
is fun to act (I suppose), but too puzzling for anything
except an audience of personal friends - this frame of
mind is not one you can reasonably expect 'anybody' to
assume. It is written in the telegraphese of Auden's early
period: a clipped utterance, without colour, without

amazing news. The 'Manchester Guardian' dialect of the
'Poems' as against the 'Daily Express' gaiety of 'Look,
Stranger!' 'The Dance of Death' is what the Group Theatre
imagines to be 'good theatre.' It satisfies all Auden's
precepts for drama printed in a Group Theatre programme.
There is a myth, acting in the auditorium, plenty of dancing and dance lyrics. I think it is the worst thing Auden
has done.
    The precepts. They are an attempt to define what areas
of experience can be realised on the stage. Like the
Thirty-Nine Articles these dogmas often contradict each
other. They are best considered as the Auden antithesis to
current theatrical superstitions - nothing in the theatre
rises to a belief - e.g., that the realistic theatre is
the only one, that gesture and rhetoric are funny in themselves, that Gielgud is a good actor. 'Drama is essentially an art of the body.' Auden means acting. 'Drama began as the act of a whole community. Ideally there would
be no spectators.' This is a matter of degree of attention.
A man may participate in and be a spectator of different
parts of a single play. Even at High Mass (community drama
in excelsis) the most recollected come down to earth as
the plate goes round, when the drama is broken for the
sermon, when a dog runs up the aisle. Origins are not always helpful. Must we strum a ukulele as we read 'The Witnesses,' because Jubal struck the corded shell?
    'The Way of the World' and 'The Cherry-Orchard' (best
plays by Congreve and Tchekov) were flops. The success of
'Murder in the Cathedral' and the Auden plays is due to
the fact that they are 'modern' and 'experimental.' Leave
experiment to stage-hands and phoneys like Gordon Craig. A
play which needs an oval stage is probably a bad play. No
good dramatist has ever gone outside the dramatic conventions of his time. N.B. Almost every good dramatist has
opposed the dramatic taste of his own day. This is quite
another matter.
    Auden would leave documentation to films, character to
the novel. The theatre should deal with the familiar
stories of the generation (We should know what is going to
happen next). Characters should be simplified and over
life-size. This is conceding too much. The real limitations
of the stage are that it is dangerous to monkey with space
(and to a less degree with time) without the sacrifice of
illusion. A true objection of genre can be made against
'The Ascent of F6,' where B.B.C. announcers, the Press and
the Government are part of a sub-plot (Mr. and Mrs. A are
a chorus) only linked to the main action because Sir
James (the Colonial Office) and Michael (Hero) are
brothers. Graphically the play is a phrase of morse - a

series of dots and dashes representing a broken continuity
line. This is film technique.
The lack of character-drawing is plain in the poverty
of the speeches between Michael and his mother in the Lakeland inn. Stagmantle, Lady Isabel (neé Houston) and the
General are broad, adequate caricatures, but the main
characters are only mouthpieces for poor rhetoric. 'I have
no purpose but to see you happy...James! Was there no
other name you could remember...?'
In 'The Dog Beneath the Skin' (graphically a straight
line) Auden makes up for lack of character-drawing (1) by
the caricatures being an integral part of the picaresque
progress - there is no plot, (2) by his excellent understanding of *things* - *e.g.*, in the choruses:

Paddington. King's Cross. Euston. Liverpool Street.
Each hiding behind a Gothic hotel its gigantic green-
house.

(Trains are much more real to Auden than people. *Cf.*
the commentary to 'Night Mail' with its pleasing anthro-
pomorphism.)
'I cannot believe,' says Auden, 'that any artist can
be good who is not more than a bit of a reporting journalist.' I agree with this and I appreciate the speech
about Sudoland by the B.B.C. lecturer, the chatter of
medical students in 'The Dog Beneath the Skin': but they
gainsay Auden's statement that the theatre should leave
documentation to the film. They are pure documentary,
like so much of 'The Orators.'
'The familiar stories of our generation' are not yet
myths. Cocteau uses classical myth, Yeats Irish heroic
legend, for the support given by tradition and to reduce
surprise - old wine in new bottles. The search for an
heir, and the Everest expedition, are only in the process
of becoming myths *in* the plays. We cannot foresee the
endings. We can only guess them. It is new wine.
'The Ascent of F6' is poorer entertainment than 'The
Dog Beneath the Skin.' The latter has some of the life of
a good musical-comedy and it has the advantage of Auden's
magnificent choruses. The plays justify themselves by the
poetry they evoke. A situation is an excuse for a poem for
which it would be hard to find an excuse in the economy of
life outside the stage-door. N.B. This is not parallel to
liking the plays of Yeats for the songs they contain. The
insignificance of character in some of Yeats' plays is
fully justified (1) by the distance of the fable from reality, (2) by the element of formal plot. Aristotle v.
Coleridge. Auden's plays, like most Elizabethan and

Jacobean plays, invite the realistic criterion. William
Archer and 'the naughty life-forcer in the Norfolk Jacket'
are as often right as wrong in attacking Webster or Shakespeare. 'The Ascent of F6,' although poorer entertainment,
is a better play than 'The Dog Beneath the Skin' because,
for one thing, the conflict is kept steadily in view all
the time. In the earlier play there is no actual conflict
till the discovery of Francis.

'The Dog Beneath the Skin': man and society.
'The Ascent of F6': man and his own conscience.

Cheaply, Marxist man and Freudian man.
'The Dog Beneath the Skin' has several very effective
scenes: the hero undressing the dummy (excuse for a superb
epithalamium), the palace executions of the workers to
church music, the Destructive Desmond cabaret turn (echoing 'Which shall I release unto you? Christ or Barabbas?').
It is interesting that in production the last two scenes
were omitted, the point of the first stupidly missed by
the substitution of a real woman.

The thesis of the second play gives less opportunity for
twopence-coloured scenes. Three scenes are of importance:
the interview with the mother, the interview with the
abbot, the interview between Ransom and his own fears –
the subjective nature of the last scene is suggested by the
repetition of scraps of previously used dialogue, a device
employed extremely well in the brothel scenes of 'Ulysses'
and here adapted to the cruder substance of the stage.

Of course we have not seen the plays yet. The Group
Theatre productions have been notable only for slack production, poorish acting and too much art and craftiness.
Mr. Rupert Doone claims 'I serve art in the Gothic mode.'
So did Pugin. If Auden and Isherwood would only forget
that they are amateurs, would only remember that, however
little they may know about the theatre, all actors and
most producers know less, their plays would begin to become
expert.

I have an idea that poets still feel uneasy in the
theatre, and still trust some 'man of the theatre' to put
them right about craftmanship.

Note

*   The projection of horrid self into hateful works is true
    of any play or poem ever written. It is a matter of how
    consciously the thing is done, and of the size and
    amiability of the resulting world.

70. EDGELL RICKWORD, AUDEN AND POLITICS

21-2

Edgell Rickword (1898-1982) is widely acclaimed as one of
the most important and influential critics and editors of
the twentieth century. As editor of the 'Calendar of Modern
Letters', 1925-7, his rigorous and discriminating criticism
set an acknowledged precedent for F.R. Leavis's work in
'Scrutiny'. Leavis himself published in 1933 a selection
from the 'Calender' under the title 'Towards Standards of
Criticism' (republished with new introduction, 1976). In
the 1930s Rickword joined the Communist Party and worked
for 'Left Review' (1934-8), which he edited with an inter-
nationalist awareness from January 1936 to June 1937; he
later edited the Communist cultural periodical 'Our Time',
1944-7. Though well received as a poet in early years, he
ceased to write lyric poetry on joining the Communist
Party (from which he withdrew after the Soviet invasion of
Hungary in 1956). His publications include 'Invocations to
Angels' (poetry, 1928), 'Essays and Opinions 1921-1931'
(1974), 'Behind the Eyes: Collected Poems and Translations'
(1974), and 'Literature in Society: Essays and Opinions
1931-1978' (1978). (See also 'PN Review', 6, 1, 1979, for
Edgell Rickword: A Celebration, an informative collection
of memoirs and opinions.)*

Auden expresses, more poetically than any of his contemporaries, the feeling of insecurity that afflicts a section
of the middle-classes as the ceaseless concentration of
capital into fewer hands undermines their comparatively
privileged position. His early verse prophesies and
threatens the imminent downfall of a system which has become inimical to good living. Ruined boys, handsome and
diseased youngsters, stupid valetudinarians, implacable
gangsters in a meaningless feud, these are some of the
symbols that haunt his first volume of poems. They show
the impact of after-the-war reality in a certain environment on the dream-world of the growing boy.

'Ours was a Renaissance, we were going to have lovely
fun,' but something has happened; that world of culture,
of the free exercise of the mind and body which seems a
possibility for those brought up in a well-to-do household, has collapsed, and the poet sees round him only
deadly dulness or cocktail corruption. His whole dream
cannot be salvaged, so he jettisons the need for intellectual standards. 'Knowledge no need to us...' (Poem

xviii.) and in 'The Orators'

> Living in one place with a satisfied face
> All of the women and most of the men
> Shall work with their hands and not think again...[EA, 105]

I don't for a moment suggest that Auden followed out the implications of that last couplet, the essence of Nazi demagogy with its degradation of women and regimentation of the 'Strength through Joy' variety. Perhaps that is to take a 'mere poem' too seriously, for Auden has expressed his detestation of Fascism definitely enough, but his failure to analyse the social movement which so profoundly affects his work often leads him into emotionally irresponsible statements. In his poem 'Spain' he says:

> To-day the expending of powers
> On the flat ephemeral pamphlet and the boring meeting,

which is an extraordinary example of what used to be accepted as the aloofness proper to the intellectual, in one who has recently been to Spain and had the opportunity of observing the immense vitality which the people are bringing to the task of simultaneously defeating the invaders and creating a free culture. 'To-day the struggle, to-morrow the poetry and the fun,' that attitude of Auden's would be completely incomprehensible to the Spanish intellectuals to-day.

The setting-up of a pamphlet-poem antagonism, *i.e.*, social struggle *versus* inner struggle, is a reflection of the poet's continuing isolation, falsifying the perspective of social development and delaying the re-integration of the poet into the body of society. It is that need of re-integration, I feel, which underlies the neurotic character of the dramas Auden and Isherwood write, and they are really evading the issue by tackling the problem in psychological terms.

The lyric grace of Auden's later poems is achieved at the expense of that sensuous consciousness of social change which made his early poems such exciting discoveries. Auden is too good a poet to fall back into the simple exploration of individuality, after having originated a poetry of the social type along the lines of which there are so many fertile experiments to be made.

Note

*   John Lucas's decent revaluation of Rickword's verse, A

Tribute to Edgell Rickword ('Poetry Review', 72, 3,
September 1982, 46-9), appeared too late to mention in
the headnote.

71. TWELVE COMMENTS ON AUDEN

23-30

Grigson originally organized sixteen comments, including
contributions from Berthold Viertel, Bernard Spencer, W.J.
Turner, and two curt sentences from Ezra Pound in effect
declining to comment because he felt that English reviews
paid insufficient attention to E.E. Cummings, William
Carlos Williams, 'etc.'.

---

i.   EDWIN MUIR

Apropos Muir's remark about Auden belonging 'in too particular a sense to his age', it is worth noting that when
Auden was appointed to the Chair of Poetry at Oxford University Muir wrote: 'I think it will be good for Auden to
be back in England again: I don't think America has been
good for his poetry: it has been getting more and more
rootless' (letter 114, 10 April 1956, 'Selected Letters of
Edwin Muir', ed. P.H. Butter, London: Hogarth Press,
1974, p. 185).

Auden has imaginative and intellectual power, moral passion, and wit. I should range his gifts in that order. His
imagination, which is mainly grotesque, is, I think, of
the finest quality, his intellect subtle but circum-
scribed, his moral passion less subtle and more circum-
scribed, and his wit of a lower order altogether. Where
the first three qualities come together, his poetry has
the natural fullness and intensity of major poetry. His
intellectual view of the contemporary world is, nevertheless, I think, vitiated by fashion and mass feeling, and
his morality a morality of emergency, derived from that
view; on the other hand his imaginative picture of the
world always strikes me by its profound truth. I often find
myself therefore disagreeing with his particular statements,
while assenting to something beneath them. It may be that

he belongs in too particular a sense to his age, but such direct control of language and boldness of imagination are given only to poets of genius.

ii.   GEORGE BARKER

George Barker (b. 1913) is a poet, novelist, playwright, and essayist. Since 'Collected Poems 1930-1955' (1957) he has published several more volumes of verse, the latest being 'Villa Stellar' (1978).

I like Auden's work because it exhilarates me in a way which height, ozone, speed, love, drink, and violent exercise do not: I mean it has the singular effect of poetry upon my senses. I dislike aspects of it because behind or through the poetry I discern a clumsy interrogatory finger questioning me about my matriculation certificate, my antecedents and my annual income. I sense also a sort of general conspiratorial wink being made behind my back to a young man who sometimes has the name Christopher, sometimes Stephen, sometimes Derek and sometimes Wystan. Briefly I criticise its snobbery of clique - which in itself is not much, but which indicates a definitely restricted angle of glance at things.
    This, however, seems to matter not much in the long run, since I find that in reading a good or goodish poem by Auden my responses experience an exhilaration and excitement in a way, as I say, which only poetry, and by this I mean calling things felicitous names, can give.

iii.   FREDERIC PROKOSCH

Prokosch (b. 1908) is a poet, novelist, and translator. His publications include 'The Asiatics' (1935).

The big thing about Auden is the quality of his memory. The roots of all poetry, presumably, dwell in memory: in Auden's case, the memory is of an oddly limitless and invigorating kind. It constitutes a sort of 'negative capability' - at any point the impulse, the thought, calls forth a whole vista of objects - phrases from other poets (even Shakespeare), fears, hallucinations, aspirations. Sometimes this gives a surrealist sheen to his poetry,

more often to his prose. But the mode of resuscitation is
the opposite of that employed by surrealists, as far as I
can see: not the process but the stimulus is important,
the unity of the décor and not the discordance.

He does, thus, juxtapose tradition and actuality in a
startling and often moving fashion. The process is dangerous; but he, more than anyone I know, has created for himself a fairly natural and decently authentic, if wildly
uneven, path between past and present. The future is always intruding, of course, and always unsolved (v. the bad
endings to his plays, the badness of the Iceland book).
There is something a bit wrong about it all, I suspect:
and he knows it: the feelings of guilt, of withdrawal, of
self-pity, of hysteria, creep in. There are technical dangers too - glibness, theatricality, cocksureness, oppor-
tunism, laziness - to put it harshly. But the talents are
really immense.

iv. DAVID GASCOYNE

Gascoyne (b. 1916) is a poet, playwright, novelist, and
literary critic. His publications include 'A Short History
of Surrealism' (1935), 'Collected Poems' (1965), 'Collected Verse Translations' (1970), and 'Paris Journal 1937-39' (1978).

There is such a thing as lyrical complacency, lyrical irresponsibility. It would be a great deal better for poetry,
for both its readers and its writers, if nine out of every
ten contemporary poets became silent. W.H. Auden is one of
the rare exceptions.

The traditional wisdom of the poet is that of one who
stands outside; it is 'unfairly' won; and, though vaguely
comforting, impractical. As soon as the purely lyrical
poet becomes implicated in real life, he loses this wisdom,
to find that what he has learnt through struggle, instead
of grasped through intuition, he cannot write about. W.H.
Auden is one of the rare exceptions.

One has only to compare such widely varied poems as 'A
Bride in the 30's,' 'Casino,' and 'Spain,' for instance,
with the efforts of most of Auden's contemporaries to deal
critically and constructively with other people's problems,
or even with their own, to see that strength of character
and depth of experience are inseparable, ultimately, from
important poetry. Without them, poetry may be ravishingly
beautiful, but *merely* decorative, *merely* lyrical.

v.   DYLAN THOMAS

Thomas (1914-53) published 'Eighteen Poems' at the age of
twenty, 'Twenty-Five Poems' in 1936. Other works include
'Deaths and Entrances' (1946), 'Portrait of the Artist as
a Young Dog' (autobiography, 1940), 'Under Milk Wood'
(1954), and 'Adventures in the Skin Trade' (1955). 'Collected Poems 1934-1953' appeared in 1966.

In 'A Letter to my Aunt Discussing the Correct Approach
to Modern Poetry', a poem which dates from the early
1930s, Thomas observes that 'Few understand... / ...young
Auden's coded chatter...' ('Dylan Thomas: The Poems', ed.
Daniel Jones, 1971).

I sometimes think of Mr. Auden's poetry as a hygiene, a
knowledge and practice, based on a brilliantly prejudiced
analysis of contemporary disorders, relating to the pre-
servation and promotion of health, a sanitary science and
a flusher of melancholies. I sometimes think of his poetry
as a great war, admire intensely the mature, religious,
and logical fighter, and deprecate the boy bushranger.

I think he is a wide and deep poet, and that his first
narrow angles, of pedantry and careful obscurity, are worn
almost all away. I think he is as technically sufficient,
and as potentially productive of greatness, as any poet
writing in English. He makes Mr. Yeats's isolation guilty
as a trance.

P.S. - Congratulations on Auden's seventieth birthday.

vi.   C. DAY-LEWIS

It is a good thing when writers can express in public their
affection and respect for a distinguished colleague. I met
Auden first at Oxford eleven years ago: I knew very soon
that he was and would be the best poet of my generation,
and I have never had any reason to change my mind. Other
contributors will no doubt be calling attention to his unusual powers of assimilation, to the vigour of his personal idiom and its revolutionising effect upon the verse
of our day, to the extraordinarily consistent development
of his own work - a true imaginative growth emerging at
each stage without precociousness or hesitation from the
previous stage. I would like to add this note on the revolutionary content of his writing. His satire has been
criticised at times as irresponsible: this is to

misunderstand its motive and aim: in so far as it proceeds
from the life of one social class, a class which has lost
its responsibility and civilising impetus, the terms of
this satire are bound to be superficially irresponsible.
But no contemporary writing shows so clearly the revulsion
of the artist from a society which can no longer support
him, his need to identify himself with a class that can
provide for his imagination.

vii. ALLEN TATE

Allen Tate (1899-1979), eminent poet, novelist, playwright,
literary critic, esayist, and historian, was founding Editor of the 'Fugitive', 1922-5, edited 'Sewanee Review' from
1944 to 1946, and was Professor of English, 1951-66, and
Regents' Professor, 1966-8, at the University of Minnesota.
His publications include 'Memoirs and Opinions 1926-1974'
(1975) and 'Collected Poems' (1978).

I haven't read any of Auden's new work, that is, in the
past two years. Of course, I admire very much what I do
know, but I have never rated him as highly as, I suppose,
you do. He is the best of his 'group,' but not much ahead
of MacNeice. As of two years ago I may say that both Auden
and Spender seem to be caught in a juvenile and provincial
point of view. The well-brought up young men discovered
that people work in factories and mines, and they want to
know more about these people. But it seems to me that instead of finding out about them, they write poems calling
them Comrades from a distance. But they are excellent
technicians, and Auden and MacNeice, at least, are both
tough minds and real poets.

viii. CHARLES MADGE

Charles Madge (b. 1912) is a poet and sociologist, and
also writes on politics and the Third World. He worked as
a reporter on the 'Daily Mail', 1935-6, founded Mass Observation in 1937, and was Professor of Sociology at the University of Birmingham from 1950 to 1970. His publications
include 'Mass Observation' (with T. Harrisson, 1937), and
'Art Students Observed' (with B. Weinberger, 1973).

His energy is admirable. As when I first read it, 'Paid on
Both Sides' seems full of this energy. Since then, there
has been a diffusion of it. The original, but gawky, style
has not developed. Its immature quality, once an attraction, becomes an embarrassment. There is too much morality
extraneous to the poetry. The 'Hope for Poetry' is too
conscious. The plays are catch-penny without being truly
popular. But there is still so much energy left that his
personality, if not his poetry, is certain to have an increasing effect. For myself, I would like to ask him to
help with a Mass-Observation survey of Birmingham, his
native city.

ix.   HERBERT READ

Sir Herbert Read (1893-1968), celebrated as a literary
critic, critic and champion of modern art, poet, novelist,
autobiographer, and educationalist, held various professorial posts in both poetry and the fine arts in England
and the USA. With Roland Penrose in 1947 he founded the
Institute of Contemporary Arts, of which he became President. His numerous books include 'Art Now' (1933), 'The
Green Child' (1935), 'The Art of Sculpture' (1956), 'Collected Poems' (1946), and 'Henry Moore: A Study of his
Life and Work' (1956).

For. Auden has brought a new vitality into English verse,
an exuberance and inventiveness which it has lacked since
Browning's death. His idiom is contemporary, his outlook
is revolutionary. He is human and observant, witty and
masculine. He has an honest handshake. He is fond of fells,
fosses and screes; his landscape is northern, his mind cosmopolitan. His poetic diction is good speech, as Montaigne
would have it: rather difficult than tedious, void of affection, free, loose, and bold; not donnish, nor marxian,
nor neo-catholic, but downright, comrade-like. Fondled by
fortune, but not likely to be fuddled by praise.
   Against. A certain retardation in growth. Schoolboy
jokes and undergraduate humour. A cruel handshake. But
more seriously: a definite backsliding in the technique of
verse. The 'evolution' of verse form is a doubtful historical phenomenon; but I personally cannot help regarding
a certain tradition in poetry which begins perhaps with
Blake, and passes through Whitman and D.H. Lawrence as an
important liberation (very intimately related to liberation in the political, moral and intellectual spheres).

It is sad, therefore, to see a poet of Auden's ability
aping the antics of Kipling and Byron. It is good enough
as a pastime, but we have no time to pass. Artificial
verse is only worth doing if done supremely well, as by
Pope. He is a little sentimental and indifferent to objective beauty. He has a dangerous memory. A little too
teutonicising; has probably never read 'Les Liaisons
dangereuses,' and wouldn't like it if he had. Climbs
mountains.

x.   JOHN MASEFIELD

Masefield (1878-1967) won lasting popular acclaim with
'Salt-Water Ballads' (1902), followed by other books in-
cluding 'The Everlasting Mercy' (1911). Appointed Poet
Laureate in 1930, he also became President of the Society
of Authors in 1937. He told I.A. Richards that he con-
sidered Auden 'a man of genius ... a dynamic person'
(Constance Babington Smith, 'John Masefield: A Life',
London: OUP, 1978, p. 202).

All good wishes for the success of your tribute to Mr.
Auden.

xi.   GRAHAM GREENE

No room for criticism, only for the personal statement -
that to me Mr. Auden is a long way the finest living poet -
and a few personal notes. Mr. Auden, unlike the other members of the famous trio, has developed away from politics.
There is no reason why a poet shouldn't share a political
or any other ideology, but he shouldn't preach it: among
the preachers Browning and - lately - Eliot. Unlike Allen
Tate he has become more lucid on the surface with every
book he has published. A popular poet - as distinct from a
popular versifier - is probably, at this time of day, a
fabulous creature, but at any rate Mr. Auden puts no barrier between himself and his public. The obscurity is
where it should be, in the layers of suggestion under the
lucid surface. A last personal statement: that, with the
exception of 'The Tower,' no volume of poetry has given me
more excitement than 'Look, Stranger!' One is the more
grateful, because with every year that passes one finds
that the capacity for any fresh æsthetic appreciation
weakens.

xii.   SIR HUGH WALPOLE

Prolific novelist, man of letters, bibliophile, and
generous patron, Sir Hugh Walpole (1884-1941) became first
chairman both of the selection committee of the Book
Society and of the Society of Bookmen. His many novels include 'Mr. Perrin and Mr. Traill' (1911), 'The Cathedral'
(1922), and the Herries saga (1930-3).

I delight in Auden's poetry, and for the reasons, I don't
doubt, of which he would himself least approve.

It is as Teacher and Reformer - as a leader of the
children of darkness into light - that he sees himself appointed, not too solemnly, because his sense of humour is
constant and there is as much of the schoolboy in him as
the teacher.

In this rôle, though, he is superior, a little arrogant,
thinking well of himself and speaking 'above the Battle.'
Here he is not truly himself which was why 'Letters from
Iceland' so grievously disappointed.

When he forgets that he is a schoolmaster he is a wonderful companion, making discoveries, seeing beauty,
happily forgetful of everything but his vision.

So forgetful he *does* become a leader and writes some of
the finest poetry of our time.

'On the Frontier'

(with Christopher Isherwood)
London, October 1938; New York, March 1939

72. UNSIGNED REVIEW, A POETIC DRAMA OF TO-DAY, 'TIMES
LITERARY SUPPLEMENT'

29 October 1938, 689

This is the third play of the Auden-Isherwood collaboration; and achieves more effectively, more assuredly what
had been tentative in the earlier plays. Their dramatic
genre here reaches complete power, which fact is worthy
of praise and also enables criticism more justly to estimate the *genre* so brilliantly established. What does it
mean to the theatre?

Certain points appear. There are no characters, no individuals; only types. 'The drama,' Mr. Auden wrote in
1935, 'is not suited to the analysis of character, which
is the province of the novel. Dramatic characters are simplified, easily recognizable and over life-size.' The
types are here less cartoon-like than formerly, but they
remain, at most, shaded in two dimensions rather than
penetrated. An impersonal psycho-analytic depth is sometimes there, but the dimension of personal depth is
omitted. All are mass-people, mass-leaders or mass-
exploiters. Nearest to a character is Valerian, the Westland industrialist, endowed with a Shavian effrontery,
whom we see, in different scenes, having the Leader to
lunch, lulling the tired Leader with music and being shot
by a sacked employee. Interlarded are scenes of the two
family groups of the opposed countries of Westland and
Ostnia, visible on either side of the stage but unaware
of one another, except for a boy and a girl in contrary
groups, who yearn for each other and are frustrated in a
war.

As irresponsible and generalised phantoms
In us love took another course
Than the personal life...

Europe lies in the dark
City and flood and tree;
Thousands have worked and work
To master necessity.
To build the city where
The will of love is done
And brought to its full flower
The dignity of man.

Serious poetry, such as in these lines, is used to mark
a certain type; it is the tone of the lovers. But most of
the rest of the play is in prose, except for the popular
jingles which are used in short scenes of soldiers or
factory-workers. The text is alive; the authors are not
exclusively 'literary,' but aware of other theatrical aspects - a result of their collaboration with an actual organization, the Group Theatre. The piece is called a melodrama, but the horror of international events, surrounding
the persons, is given an atmosphere of farce, and is perhaps the more horrible for that. Life is shown as a monstrous Kafka-like absurdity, overwhelming a few green loves
of younglings.

For years we have complained, concerning the average
modern drama, that it has not been contiguous with modern
life. It has been a drama of little detached intrigues,
usually erotic. Here is the swing of the pendulum - a
drama so much absorbed with characteristic world events
that the play hardly stays in the theatre at all. Its
whole reference is outside. We, the audience, are present
at a running commentary. Working always by allusion, the
persons remain all the time, as it were, members of a
chorus annotating something 'off.' There is no *inner* development in the course of the acts. We might parallel it
in some ways with the morality play. The response to be
evoked is 'This is wicked. It ought not to be.' It is
also like a superb parody of public life, where Truth is
borne through the theatre on a placard.

73. KINGSLEY MARTIN ON HONEST, OUTSPOKEN TOPICALITY, 'NEW STATESMAN AND NATION'

xvi, 19 November 1938, 826-7

After an early career as an assistant lecturer in political science at the London School of Economics, followed by a spell as leader writer on the 'Manchester Guardian', Kingsley Martin (1897-1969) began his long and brilliant career as editor of the 'New Statesman' in 1931, the year when the liberal 'Nation' was amalgamated with the socialist 'New Statesman' (Beatrice and Sidney Webb and Bernard Shaw had been closely involved in the first planning and production of the 'New Statesman' in 1912). Martin fashioned 'New Staggers and Naggers', as it became widely known, into a paper of candid Left-wing dissent, and fostered such a high standard of literary criticism that it attracted readers who otherwise balked at its political committment. 'Under Martin's editorship', 'The Times' obituary records,

> the circulation of the 'New Statesman' rose from about 15,000 in 1931 to 30,000 in 1939 and then to about treble that figure by the end of the Second World War... It was not his view that the literary side of the paper should square at all points with the Socialist doctrine of the editorials. He rightly let his brilliant writers - and they included Raymond Mortimer, Desmond MacCarthy, V.S. Pritchett, G.W. Stonier, Robert Lynd, Edward Sackville-West, and T.C. Worsley - have their heads.

C.H. Rolph adds that Martin

> soon came to know ... that he was editing what was at that time the best *literary* weekly in the English-speaking world; though he was not always ready, I believe, to acknowledge the extent to which the literary half secured attention for the political, especially in America. ('Kingsley: The Life, Letters and Diaries of Kingsley Martin', Harmondsworth: Penguin, 1978, p. 204)

Martin's books include 'The Triumph of Palmerston' (1924) and 'Father Figures' (1966).

This review was published under the evocative name of 'Tom Paine', one of Kingsley Martin's many pseudonyms (see Introduction, p. 23).

The first night of 'On the Frontier' was a great success
at the Cambridge Arts Theatre. The play is precisely topical; for it deals not only with dictators and war, but
boldly and sincerely with the problems which dictatorship
and war have set for every member of the audience. The
verse is admirable and the music effective. The play is
well acted and beautifully staged; it is dramatically much
more mature than 'The Ascent of F6.' For several scenes
the stage is divided into two rooms separated by a symbolic frontier. We see the bourgeoisie of Ostnia, a democracy, and Westland, a dictatorship, passing through the
same grim cycle of war fever and war agony. Symbolically
the frontier is bridged by the love of an Ostnian girl and
a Westland boy; in their frustrated lives we are shown the
urge of the young and the thoughtful to unite across the
barrier and to struggle, not against each other, but
against the forces of violence that ruthlessly separate
them.

There are limits to this expressionist drama, which
Toller and others developed so successfully in Germany.
It may be that great drama can only be achieved through
the full and intimate characterisation of individuals. In
this technique, so much influenced by the cinema, the
forces of the world are presented to us through types and
choruses, not through the conflict they cause in particular individuals, and because no problem is competely resolved in any one personality, such plays leave one imperfectly satisfied. They should be considered and judged as
pamphlets are judged – but some pamphlets that made history
remain to be read as the best expression of troubled
periods. In this play the dilemma of the idealist in war is
intellectually worked out in the case of Eric Thorvald, but
the stages by which he reaches his conclusion, and the
emotions he passes through, cannot be revealed by more than
hints. The choral interludes are designed to carry the
imagination to the wider political battle. Four men,
shadowy figures behind prison bars, breathe defiance from
a concentration camp:

Perhaps we shall die by a firing-squad,
Perhaps they will kill us, that wouldn't be odd,
But when we lie down with the earth on our face
There'll be ten men much better to fight in our place!

Then there are the dancers, who discuss with their partners
their individual problems if there is war and will not heed
those who call upon them to unite to prevent it, and there
is a jolly interlude of fraternisation in the trenches.

The best scenes are those in which the Guidanto

(esperanto for leader) postures and raves before the contemptuous captain of industry who thinks he controls his
puppet dictator until he finds himself helpless to stop the
war which the Guidanto's hysteria makes inevitable. The
Guidanto is admirably played by Ernest Milton, and Wyndham
Goldie is a powerful and cynical king of industry. Perhaps
the best acting of the evening is Everley Gregg's characterisation of the thwarted maiden aunt, who finds an out-
let for her emotions in a religious adoration of the Guidanto. In the flesh, the Guidanto whose voice over the
wireless is a terribly accurate reminder of the voice from
Nuremberg, is discovered as a persecuted and miserable man
in an agony of indecision; shall he go down to history as
a great leader in war or as a great maker of peace? The final decision, on which the survival of civilisation may
depend, is purely subjective; an hysterical mood of horror
at the responsibility thrown upon him is stiffened by sentimental music into a decision for a great gesture for
peace, which is transformed with equal suddenness into a
plunge into war when he is told that a provocative incident has occurred on the other side of the frontier. In
their less hysterical way most people are like this: the
great life and death decisions are made by most of us,
not as a result of the deliberate balancing of facts, but
by the sudden shift when the unstable equilibrium of our
minds is changed at a critical moment by a delusion or an
accident.

The play ends in a poem, recited by the young man and
the girl who have loved across the frontier and been destroyed in the conflict. The man has striven as a pacifist
to hold aloof from the dark forces of the world. He has
been to prison and in prison reached a new decision. This
poem is the most remarkable in the play and must be read
at length in the book. He declares that he was wrong to
hope to maintain his independence 'as the sane and innocent student aloof among practical and violent madmen.'

Yet we must kill and suffer and know why.
All errors are not equal. The hatred of our enemies
Is the destructive self-love of the dying,
Our hatred is the price of the world's freedom.
This much I learned in prison. This struggle
Was my struggle. Even if I would
I could not stand apart.

The conclusion of this? That national frontiers are artificial nonsense and the real struggle that between common
people and those who rule them by money and fraud; that the
individual who understands this is confronted with a

terrible choice of evils and may be compelled to submit to
the 'necessary wrong' of killing his friends; but that he
can always remember what he is fighting for and who his
real enemies are; so that when the chance does come, hands
may be joined across the trenches and a new world be
founded out of common suffering and bitter experience. It
is an infinitely tragic, but not a wholly pessimistic conclusion; the civilisation we know may die, but a new one
may arise and those who would build it must take the path
that brings them into contact, even though it is the contact of murder, with their friends in the trenches opposite to them. Many questions arise - one is whether we
must wait for universal murder before we can speak to our
friends? But Auden and Isherwood are postulating war, and
their conclusion is as honest and outspoken as it is memorably phrased.

74. C. DAY-LEWIS ON UNSUCCESSFUL SINCERITY, UNSIGNED RE-
VIEW, 'LISTENER'

xx, 24 November 1938, 1145

The gist of this new play is a war-crisis between two countries, Westland and Ostnia, which represent the totali-
tarian and the monarchist-democratic state. It is not entirely the dwarfing effect of the recent crisis which
makes 'On the Frontier' seem the least successful of the
Auden-Isherwood plays: it possesses neither the vitality
and invention of 'The Dog Beneath the Skin' nor the deeply
realised moral conflict of 'The Ascent of F6'. Through the
character of Valerian, the Westland industrialist, we are
given a different but less subtle aspect of the problem of
power than was offered by Michael Ransom in 'F6'. Charming,
ironic, the complete a-moral Superman, Valerian is equally
contemptuous of the common herd ('The truth is, Nature is
not interested in underlings - in the lazy, the inefficient, the self-indulgent, the People'), and of the neurotic Leader whom his own wealth and cleverness have
raised to power. The best scene in the play is the one
where this Frankenstein loses control over his monster. A
moment after deciding that he will propose to Ostnia a non-
aggression pact, the Leader gets word of an incident on
the frontier and declares war instead: up to this moment
Valerian has been the absolutely dominant figure: now, in
a flash, all his apparently infallible calculations fall

to the ground; the episodes of war and revolution that
follow show him to have been wrong all along the line -
his self-interest is proved as gullible as that of the
underlings he so much despises. This is an admirable dramatic turn. But it cannot quite rescue a play in which almost all the other characters appear as the nonentities
that Valerian considers them. The Westland-Ostnia Room, a
stage device by which the authors present the reactions of
ordinary people on either side of the frontier, is occupied for the most part by stock figures or abstractions:
Colonel Hussek, for instance, is no better than any Indian
Army Colonel in a school-magazine skit. The change of key
in Act 2, Scene I, where, after an orgy of patriotism on
the part of their elders, Anna and Eric, two lovers of the
opposed nations, come together, is a dramatic trick which
only the most careful production will save from obviousness, just as the dialogue that follows between them is
only just saved from sentimentality by sacrificing every
ounce of rhetoric. Throughout the play, in fact, the
authors have consistently rejected the rhetorical openings
that their theme offers them. While sympathising with
their motive for doing so, we are likely to feel that they
have sacrificed too much: the texture of the verse-passages
is often thin, the effect sometimes banal: lines such as
the following have nothing but their sincerity to recommend
them: 'For Truth shall flower and Error explode And the
people be free then to choose their own road'.

75. JULIAN SYMONS REVIEWS THE DRAMATIC CANON, 'LIFE AND
LETTERS TODAY'

February 1939, 71-9

Critic, biographer, and writer of crime fiction, Symons
(b. 1912) edited 'Twentieth Century Verse', 1937-9, and
has been a 'Sunday Times' reviewer since 1958. His books
include 'The Tell-Tale Heart: The Life and Works of Edgar
Allan Poe' (1978), 'Conan Doyle' (1979), and 'The Thirties:
A Dream Revolved' (1960; rev. edn, 1975), which includes
extensive discussion of Auden's work and influence.
    This is taken from an article entitled Auden and Poetic
Drama 1938.

One of Mr. Eliot's most valuable achievements as critic

has been to make clear our special problems in the theatre;
'We admit that we cannot expect to produce a new dramatic
literature until we have the audiences and also the producers capable of helping the poets to write for the
theatre. On the other hand the producers are checked until
they have enough dramatic repertory with which to feed and
train the audience. *I believe that the deficiency of plays
is more serious at present than the lack of producers or
of possible members of audiences* (My italics). We need not
assume that the possible audiences represent one class
rather than another, or one political tendency rather than
another. So far as the dramatic artist is concerned "the
people" is everybody except the present occupants of the
stalls at the more expensive theatres.' 'The audience does
not come to see what he (the dramatist) does, in order to
rally round a theory, but to be interested and excited.
The indispensable merit of a verse play is that it shall be
interesting, that it shall hold the audience all the time.
And it will not do that, if the audience is expected to do
too much of the work.' The poetic drama has very great possibilities, it is the most effective way in which poetry
can be put before a considerable public: but it is *the
poet* who will have to unbend and do the work - the audience
will not do it. The poetic playwright's task now is to
write a play which shall be able to compete on one level
with Mr. Noel Coward and Mr. Robert E. Sherwood and on another with Sophocles and Shakespeare. It is from this
standpoint that poetic playwrights now must be judged.
From this standpoint we must judge Mr. Auden.

The influence of Eliot the critic on Auden the playwright has been very great. Auden's plays conform more or
less to Eliot's precepts; in addition Auden has (or had) a
theory of his own that Drama is the 'art of the body'. In
some notes called I Want the Theatre To Be... in the Group
Theatre Programme of 'The Dance of Death' Auden says:
'Drama is essentially an art of the body. The basis of
acting is acrobatics, dancing, and all forms of physical
skill. The music hall, the Christmas pantomime, and the
country house charade are the most living drama of to-day.'
'The subject of Drama ... is the commonly known, the universally familiar stories of the society or generation in
which it is written. The audience, like the child listening to the fairy tale, ought to know what is going to happen next.' 'Similarly the drama is not suited to the analysis of the character, which is the province of the novel.
Dramatic characters are simplified, easily recognizable
and over life-size.' Auden's five plays (five if we count,
as I think we should, 'Paid on Both Sides' and 'The Dance
of Death' as plays) show a constant endeavour to reconcile

Eliot's ideas with his own. The reconciliation has not
been successful: 'The Dance of Death' , the only play in
which Drama as 'the art of the body' is given a prominent
place, is very bad indeed. Yet I would agree that *movement*
on the stage is in itself a good thing; even in 'The
Dance of Death' the acrobatics, the people running about,
walking about, leaping about, doing physical exercises,
lend the play a liveliness which is not possessed by
'Murder in the Cathedral', in which a sermon is preached
on the stage and the only action in the whole play - the
murder - is symbolic action, which might as well be done
in the wings.

'Paid on Both Sides' is a short unactable play. The
charade form was used, one guesses, because Auden was not
sure enough to attempt anything orthodox, so this odd one-
act form was chosen, a form in which he could make his own
rules. The quality of the verse is high: but one could not
follow the speeches successfully without a book.

> To throw away the key and walk away
> Not abrupt exile, the neighbours asking why,
> But following a line with left and right
> An altered gradient at another rate
> Learns more than maps upon the whitewashed wall
> The hand put up to ask; and makes us well
> Without confession of the ill.   [EA, 12]

This is not difficult, but it would not be grasped easily
by any listener who had not read the book: and since almost the whole of the charade is written in this, or more
compressed language, the total effect is one of confusion,
even to a reader in the swing, who knows just what to expect. It may be objected that 'Paid on Both Sides' was
called a Charade, and was meant to be played in those
country houses where the 'living drama of to-day' is to be
found. But still, it is published in a book, it has been
much praised (and the verse rightly praised): it is a contribution to drama, and as such the complaint must be made
that it could only be acted by a circle of friends who
would understand all the little jokes.

'Paid on Both Sides' has never been staged publicly.
'The Dance of Death' was shown by the Group Theatre in the
same programme with 'Sweeney Agonistes'. As Mr. Kenneth
Allott has pointed out, it satisfies Auden's requirements
for the theatre (see the quotations above) - acting in the
auditorium (the audience should join in the play), dancing
and dance lyrics. I have mentioned the acrobatics; there
is also a Jew hunt, a revolver shot, people shouting 'Red
Front'; all this is good, makes it less likely that the

audience will be bored. Yet 'The Dance of Death' is emphatically an entertainment for highbrows, it does not 'entertain'; it is too consciously written down to audience-
level. The action, if not quite all the speeches, could be
understood by a child of six and for a child of six it
would be a nice pantomime. But not for us.

With 'The Dog Beneath the Skin', Mr. Isherwood comes
on the scene officially (rumour has it that he was there
before in an unofficial way): and the question of Isher-
woood's part in the Auden-Isherwood productions is bound
to be raised. For the purpose of this article it is necessary only to point out the increased technical skill, the
increased suavity of the jokes, the attempt at some sort
of plot - by Auden's principles a plot is not needed at
all, a myth is enough, but still we have arrived at a plot
in 'On the Frontier'. I think all these things may be attributed chiefly to Isherwood: it does not seem advisable
to go beyond that in guesswork.

The 'audience' problem is solved in 'The Dog Beneath
the Skin' by the use of Gilbert and Sullivan passages:

General Hotham is my name.
At Tatra Lakes I won my fame,
I took the Spanish lion.
In Pressan now my home I've made
And rule my house like a brigade
With discipline of iron.

by the superb choruses, and by giving the play a thin surface of comic icing to sweeten the solid cake of the collective gospel. (The comedy is in the *acting* as much as in
the speeches - for example, Act 1, Scene 2, when the Dog
laps up whisky, becomes drunk and is sick, and the two
journalists and Alan give a comic song and dance.) There
is no particular objection to this, except that the comic
scenes are dramatically static - they are amusing to
listen to, but do not help the play - and a good deal of
the serious action is carried on in the choruses! Only two
or three of the scenes, notably those in the Lunatic Asylum and the Operating Theatre, really make part of the
play: and the choruses are much more than (what they
should be) a comment and judgment on the action. Without
the choruses there would not be much action to judge, or
at least the action would be seen as wholly incoherent.
And there are too many choruses, too much verse that contains nothing but plain statement or description; I saw
'The Dog Beneath the Skin' three times, and every time the
impatience of the audience with the choruses was plainly
discernible; more than twelve rows back it was difficult

to follow everything that was said, or rather recited, by
the two Witnesses. The play is an admirable failure, in
which the dramatist's problem is solved by evasion (Auden
the moralist and poet letting himself go in the choruses,
and larding the rest of the play with more comedy than it
can bear, to make up).

'The Ascent of F6' is a better constructed piece, the
choruses have been kept down to a reasonable length, each
scene follows logically from the last, the broadcast announcer is used very well, a 'character' (Ransom) is created. It is perhaps in Auden theory a good play (you know
what is going to happen next, there is a good deal of
action, the play is based on a myth): in practice (that
is, seen on a stage) the rhetoric turns out to be uncom-
monly poor, very nearly fake-Elizabethan, the mountain
myth is boring because it was foreseen, the Boy Scout seriousness is often unintentionally comic. 'F.6' has incidental virtues, but they are closely bound up with its pretentiousness; in conception it is a highbrow play for
Mayfair.

'On the Frontier' has a discernible plot, partly spoilt
by the splitting of the cast into two parts, Ostnians and
Westlanders, joined by the very thin connecting link of the
war. Auden as a writer is in everything except his most
personal lyrics a split-man; he needs to develop *two sides*
of everything. (There are two Witnesses, the charade is
called 'Paid on Both Sides', there is a similar, though
inferior, double-plot in 'F.6': these examples could be
multiplied.) But the play has now become the thing; except
for the choruses, verse is spoken in only two scenes. And
the verse of the choruses is strictly subdued to the needs
of the play:

The clock on the wall gives an electric tick,
I'm feeling sick, brother; I'm feeling sick.

The sirens blow at eight; the sirens blow at noon;
Goodbye, sister, goodbye; we shall die soon.

Mr. Valerian has a house on the hill;
It's a long way to the grave, brother, a long way still.

This verse has no other merit than as part of a play; I
think it effects its purpose as a workers' chorus. 'On the
Frontier' has an air, in one way distressing, of maturity;
some of Auden's faults have been got rid of, one or two
have elevated as nearly as possible into virtues - the
radio has a lot of work to do, and the use of broadcasting
in a play is at best a trick, a short cut which leads

nowhere, though it may be a good trick, avoiding a deal
of tediousness; the 'characters' are still the 'easily
recognizable, simplified and over life-size' sketches de-
siderated in I Want the Theatre To Be.... Nothing else in
the Notes on the Characters which precede the play is so
accurate as 'Col. Hussek: An old lobster'. Auden likes
lobsters; but when it come to writing about 'Mrs. Vrodny:
Embittered by poverty and household responsibilities; but
with considerable reserves of power. The Vrodny-Hussek
family has aristocratic traditions', we have only Auden's
word for this. There is no indication of it in the play;
and of course it is a confession of weakness to append
notes on characters at all.

The merits of 'On the Frontier', compared with Auden's
other plays, are considerable: and they are as likely to
be seen by lowbrow as highbrow critics. This is the first
time that Auden's serious dramatic purpose has been expressed seriously. I assume that Auden, as a Communist,
wishes to convince his audience that Communism is necessary and good; and for every person converted by 'The Dog
Beneath the Skin' and 'The Ascent of F.6' ten will be
converted by 'On the Frontier'. The fact that the play is
topical, a piece of *reportage* instead of a myth, is a
help; Auden's precepts are not much use in making a play.
And the schoolboy jokes, entirely permissible in a poem
but to be regretted in a play intended for the biggest
possible audience, an audience which simply cannot understand what is beyond its nose, have been pruned down. In
the last scene of 'The Dog Beneath the Skin', after
Francis has revealed himself, he calls upon the lads of
Pressan to follow him. Five of them walk across the stage
to join him, and he warns them: 'We're not going on a
treasure-hunt, you know, or looking for pirates.' The
warning is salutary; but seriousness is improper in so frivolous a play, and the reader (or listener) is not convinced - a treasure-hunt or something like it is the
right ending, this seriousness must be itself a kind of
joke! The end of 'On the Frontier', the shooting of the
cultured capitalist Valerian, the newspaper-chorus her-
alding the coming revolution, the death of Eric and Anna,
are, however crude, not directly contradictory to the progress of the play.

The difficulties facing a poet who wishes to write verse
for the stage to-day are tremendous; if I seem over-
critical of Auden's achievement, it is fair to say that
among the younger poets there is *no one else,* no one who
has shown any signs of being able to write a poetic play.
Mr. Spender's 'Trial of a Judge' is watched, indeed, with
almost equal admiration of the author's courage in writing

it and the audience's courage in sitting it out: and Mr.
MacNeice's 'Out of the Picture' is merely flippant. No one
but Auden has observed Eliot's injunction:

> 'You have got to keep the audience's attention all
> the time.'
> 'If you write a play in verse, then the verse ought
> to be a medium to look *through* , and not a pretty dec-
> oration to look *at*!'

Those are the important things for us: the rest can
come later. The crudity and blunders of 'On the Frontier'
do not much matter: its immediate value is considerable
and to the point. To master the public the poetic dramatist must first be its servant. Writing for posterity is
the quickest way to the scrap heap.

'Journey to a War'

(with Christopher Isherwood)
London, March 1939; New York, August 1939

Auden wrote to Mrs E.R. Dodds on 5 September 1938, 'Are
the enclosed trash, or not? I am much too close to them to
know.... They are the first part of a sonnet sequence for
the China book. Please let me have them back, with comments, as they are the only copies' (quoted in Humphrey
Carpenter, 'W.H. Auden: A Biography', London: Allen &
Unwin, 1981, p. 240), and then again in the autumn, en-
closing his Commentary for the volume: 'Please let me have
your comments. I am very uncertain whether this kind of
thing is possible without becoming a prosy pompous old
bore' (ibid., p. 242).

Edward Mendelson writes, '"In Time of War" - the sonnet
sequence, not the verse commentary - is Auden's most profound and audacious poem of the 1930s, perhaps the greatest
English poem of the decade' ('Early Auden', London: Faber &
Faber, 1981, p. 348).

76. EVELYN WAUGH ON A PANTOMIME APPEARANCE, MR. ISHERWOOD
AND FRIEND, 'SPECTATOR'

clxii, 24 March 1939, 496, 498

Waugh (1903-66) won high praise as a novelist, biographer,
and autobiographer, and posthumously as a diarist and
letter-writer. His novels include 'Decline and Fall' (1928)
and 'Brideshead Revisited' (1945). Waugh's depreciation of
Auden lasted for many years: during the electioneering
skirmishes for the Chair of Poetry at Oxford, which Auden
won in 1956, he recorded:

There is keen excitement about the election of the
Professor of Poetry - Auden and Nicolson, both homo-
sexual socialists, and an unknown scholar named Knight.
I wish I had taken my degree so that I might vote for
Knight. John Sparrow and Maurice Bowra have put up
Nicolson, Enid Starkie and David Cecil, Auden. (20
January 1956, 'The Diaries of Evelyn Waugh', ed. Michael
Davie, Harmondsworth: Penguin, 1979, p. 753)

'Journey to a War' represents an experiment in publishing
that should attract notice, and may set a fashion. Poetry
has always been a worry to the trade; it will not sell;
not only does an annual slim volume fail to support the
author, it barely covers the modest expenses of its production. Hitherto poets have been credited with private
means or alternative, prosaic occupations, and poetry, for
the publisher, has been treated as a source of honourable
loss, a form of conscience-money paid from less noble
sources, the gangsters' wreath at the funeral of literature. Now, however, Messrs. Faber and Faber have hit on a
new dodge of incorporating the slim volume in a more solid
and marketable work, and have attached 43 pages of Mr.
Auden's verse to a substantial travel diary of Mr.
Isherwood's, nearly 200 pages in length. The mutual esteem
of the two writers has apparently survived the vexations
of hard travel, and - a far more severe test - they have,
without dissension, been jointly fêted by their oriental
admirers; so one may reasonably hope that this pantomime
appearance as hind and front legs of a monster will not
embarrass their happy relationship. It is impossible,
however, to treat this publication as a single work; it is
two books which for purposes of commercial convenience
have been issued as one.
    Mr. Isherwood's diary covers the spring of 1938, and is
for the most part in the form of a day-to-day record. He
and Mr. Auden travelled from Hong-kong to Canton, thence
to Hankow and Chengchow, where the railway branches East
and West to Suchow and Sian; here they visited the North
battle-line; thence they returned to Shanghai, visiting
the South front on their way. It is needless to say that
their journey involved many inconveniences and some danger;
at one stage they fell in with Mr. Peter Fleming, and with
him evacuated Meiki a few hours before the Japanese moved
in. There are inevitably a few passages of the kind which
begin: 'My feet now utterly collapsed,' but the majority
of the pages deal with sleeping-cars, mission-stations,
consulates and universities. They travelled in a sensible
way, accepting the comforts that were offered. These

comforts have now become tolerably familiar to English
readers; we have already shared the kindly domestic life
that flourishes in the missions among bombs and bandits;
we know that the papists will give you a drink, and the
adventists will not; we have, vicariously, fumbled for
adequate courtesies to exchange with Chinese officials.
There is only one portrait in Mr. Isherwood's collection that does not recall a familiar type; that is the
host of the Journey's End Hotel, Mr. Charleton, and for
the few pages of his appearance the narrative suddenly
comes to life, and one is reminded that Mr. Isherwood is
not only the companion of Mr. Auden, but the creator of
Mr. Norris and Miss Bowles. Not that his work ever falls
below a high literary standard. It is admirable. The style
is austerely respectable; not only does he seldom use a
cliché, he never seems consciously to avoid one; a distinction due to a correct habit of thought. Anyone of
decent education can revise his work finding alternatives
for his clichés; a good writer is free from this drudgery;
he thinks in other terms. Mr. Isherwood writes a smooth
and accurate kind of demotic language which is adequate
for his needs; he never goes butterfly-hunting for a fine
phrase. It is no fault of his technique that 'Journey to a
War' is rather flat; he is relating a flat experience, for
he is far too individual an artist to be a satisfactory
reporter. The essence of a journalist is enthusiasm; news
must be something which excites him, not merely something
he believes will excite someone else. Mr. Isherwood - all
honour to him for it - has no news sense. In particular,
he is interested in people for other reasons that their
notoriety. The quality which makes Americans and colonials
excel in news-reporting is the ease with which they are
impressed by fame. Mr. Isherwood met nearly all the public
characters in his district; he felt it his duty as a war
correspondent to be interested in them. But they were
bores - or rather the kind of contact a foreign journalist
establishes with a public character is boring - and he is
too honest a writer to disguise the fact. Nowhere in China
did he seem to find the particular kind of stimulus that
his writing requires.

Mr. Auden contributes some good photographs and some
verses. The English public has no particular use for a
poet, but they believe they should have one or two about
the place. There is an official laureate; there is also,
always, an official young rebel. I do not know how he is
chosen. At certain seasons the critics seem to set out
piously together to find a reincarnation of Shelley, just
as the lamas of Tibet search for their Dalai Lama. A year
or two ago they proclaimed their success and exhibited

Mr. Auden. It is unfair to transfer to him the reproach that properly belongs to them. His work is awkward and dull, but it is no fault of his that he has become a public bore.

77. RANDALL SWINGLER ON BEING UNINVOLVED, TWO INTELLECTUALS IN CHINA, 'DAILY WORKER'

29 March 1939, 7

Randall Swingler (1909-67), poet and editor, joined the Communist Party in 1934 (which he left in 1952), and became closely involved with the Workers' Music Association, the Left Book Club, and the Unity Theatre. His editorial career spanned the 'Daily Worker' book page, 'Left Review' (of which he was the last editor), 'Poetry and the People', 'Our Time', 'Arena', 'Circus', and the 'New Reasoner'. His books include 'Poems' (1932), 'The Years of Anger' (1946), and 'The God in the Cave' (1950).

Many people will, I think, be annoyed by this book. There are only two good reasons for journeying to a country wracked with war: to find out what is really happening and to report it or to participate. Here are one or two brilliant little pictures, as of their first experience of a Japanese air-raid, and an occasional good dramatic line of verse. But on the whole the authors are too preoccupied with their own psychological plight to be anything but helplessly lost in the struggle of modern China.

We learn nothing but accurate superficialities about the course of the war and the various unimportant people they met. When they encountered anyone in an important position, they always asked 'the routine questions.' It is impossible to escape the impression that the authors are playing: playing at being war correspondents, at being Englishmen, at being poets.

Auden's sequence of sonnets at the end is more serious, but flatter verse than most of what he has written. The subjects of them are unspecified 'he' and 'they,' and the expression increasingly abstract and vague. All of which seems to typify their feeling of being left out, on the fringe of things, and their helpless contemplation of a history that passes their closed window and their comprehension, and 'may say Alas, but cannot help nor pardon.'

78. WILLIAM PLOMER, UNTITLED REVIEW, 'LONDON MERCURY'

xxxix, April 1939, 642-4

Commissioned by their publishers to write a travel book
about the Far East, Messrs. Auden and Isherwood chose to
go to China, and spent four months there last year. They
now offer the reader who has never been there 'some impression of what he would be likely to see, and of what
kind of stories he would be likely to hear.' The book
contains a travel diary by Mr. Isherwood, and poems and
many excellent photographs by Mr. Auden.

That these two writers were enterprising goes without
saying. Starting from Hong Kong, they journeyed by way of
Canton, Hankow, and Sian, and ended up at Shanghai. They
travelled by boat, by car, by train, by rickshaw, on
horse-back, on foot. As guests, as interviewers, as English
visitors, as fellow-travellers, they encountered all kinds
of people, ambassadors, beggars, an American bishop,
Chiang Kai-Shek and his wife, doctors, missionaries, Mr.
Peter Fleming, servants, soldiers, intellectuals. They
visited hospitals and film-studios, dealt with bugs and
dysentery, air-raids and ennui, and made their way to the
front, or perhaps we had better say the scene of military
operations.

All this has resulted in a various and lively commentary; no bouquet of recollections in tranquillity; not the
work of someone with a knowledge of the Chinese language,
or of Chinese or Japanese history and culture; but a collection of snapshots by two extremely animated minds, and
like any collection of snapshots uneven and miscellaneous.
Without being a trained journalist (thank goodness) Mr.
Isherwood is a brilliant reporter. His fictional writings
are the work of a brilliant reporter who can lend a kind
of mythological importance to the people that interest him,
and through his eyes we can see 'ordinary' or shabby individuals brought into a startling and memorable focus
against the background of some complex phase of society,
more or less corrupt. In this travel-diary, for all its
diversity and entertainment, he has been handicapped. The
rapidly travelling Western intellectual in the Far East
(Cocteau is a recent example) seldom has the chance or the
time to do his best. He rushes through a strange world, is
too close to strange things and people, and then instantly
close to differently strange things and people, is a little
on the defensive, asserts his Western-ness, and sometimes
has to try and make up for superficiality, and for being
unable to learn and to collect his thoughts, by a telling

descriptive passage or a satirical conversation-piece.
Highly observant, intelligent, and good-humoured, Mr.
Isherwood has grappled wonderfully with a difficult situation. There is an occasional lapse into portentousness
('Auden, with his monumental calm...') but that is a
detail. He has known how to seize a point in every situation and has conveyed with freshness the impact upon himself and his companion of a strange world. He has even
conveyed the slight forlornness that accompanies the European traveller (however bold) in the Far East, that air of
an exile, of being different and hairier, of strain in
adapting oneself and failure to merge into one's surroundings. He gives us, so to speak, a feature-film of China at
war, the sense of distances, of millions of people very
much at sea, of political cross-currents, of chaos, and
reminds us continually that 'war is untidy, inefficient,
obscure, and largely a matter of chance.' In the end one
is left, perhaps inevitably, with a clearer impression of
the Europeans and Americans encountered than the Chinese,
and there are two passages in particular where Mr.
Isherwood gets a chance to be completely himself. One is
a very diverting description of a hotel called Journey's
End in the hills near Kiukiang ('Up here,' said an advertisement, 'all is fresh, clean and beautiful') and of its
highly original proprietor, who, we feel, might have
formed the central figure in a novel: Mr. Isherwood was at
home with Mr. Charleton. The other is a description of
Shanghai, where the eyes that missed so little in Berlin
ten years ago instantly gave their owner his bearings.
    Neither Mr. Auden nor Mr. Isherwood attempts at all to
account for the behaviour of the Japanese or to make the
least allowance for that race, which like every other, has
its virtues - and its liberal intellectuals. They are
satisfied to see China as a 'cultured pacific country'
attacked by a 'brutal upstart enemy.' A dangerous simplification. In the days when they were at preparatory
schools it used to be said that 'plucky little Belgium'
had been trampled on by 'those vile Huns.' We live to face
the consequences of that attitude. Culture, a love of
peace, brutality, pluck, vileness, are monopolies of no
race, and the inner turmoil that leads an individual or a
race to aggressiveness will never be allayed by mere condemnation. Some recognition of the danger of being
'closeted with madness' appears at the beginning of the
book in a dedicatory poem to E.M. Forster (one of the very
few English writers of his generation loved by Auden's and
Isherwood's generation) and in the other poems by Mr.
Auden the deeper, 'ideological' issues emerge. In a sonnet
sequence he traces the strayings of humanity from a proper

way of life:

> ...our star has warmed to birth
> A race of promise that has never proved its worth,[EA, 256]

either in the East or the West. In the subsequent verse
'Commentary' it is emphasized that the war in China is 'a
local variant of a struggle in which all ... are profoundly implicated'; that ours is 'a world that has no
localized events'; and finally that

> among the just
> And only there, is Unity compatible with Freedom.[EA, 269]

In this poem Mr. Auden speaks with power and eloquence,
with the skill of an artist and the idealism of an anarchist.

79. GEOFFREY GRIGSON ON HUMANE AND POWERFUL POETRY, TWENTY-
SEVEN SONNETS, 'NEW VERSE'

n.s.2, May 1939, 47-9

All who have believed in Auden are by this time a hundred
times justified. This strange creature, this monster out
of Birmingham and the middle classes, flying about at
night like the owl's ear in his own poems, has seemed to
many of us at times likely to fail. The ear might catch
sounds, the photo-electric cell might react, the lense
might gather in a scene, the seismograph might detect a
shiver, but now and then it looked as if we were going to
get nothing but the fragments, the sensations, the brilliant summaries here and there in an image, the brilliant
buffoonery, the excitement, the animal manoeuvres which
have sometimes been pastiche, sometimes mannerism of
Auden's own extravagant and excellent manner. But we are
in luck. Auden has already written poems in which his
power to catch things is equalled by his power to give
them meaning and shape, and the twenty-seven sonnets
called 'In Time of War' are more, and some of the best of
this humane poetry in which goodness becomes actual,
delightful and persuasive.
    In poems written during the last two years by Auden one
could see certain distortions, which were caused by Auden's
desire to write formally and clearly. He had more idea of

the forms he wanted to use than of how to put into them
his particular language and observations and images; and
as these forms were traditional, he was apt to falsify his
language by giving it the traditional turns of speech
which had already been fitted into the forms by other
writers. He wrote poems in compact stanzas in which occasional scraps of vision were joined up by lengths of pastiche, or he avoided the difficulty by writing slightly
flat and long-lined poems, such as 'Dover'. The twenty-
seven sonnets are neither flat nor pastiche. The form
hardly ever distorts the language, and the language, which
is mostly the natural Auden language, does not burst out
of the form; and there are few or none of those old Auden
tropes which are too grand (geography or the whole-history-
of-mankind) for their interior meaning.

Auden has not brought off this success just because he
has learnt how it should be done: he has brought it off
because he was so much impelled by what he was feeling and
thinking. He was feeling and thinking about human history,
about war and about the crisis politics of bullying the
possibility of freedom out of the indifferentiated masses
of men; about history particularly exemplified in China,
about war particularly exemplified in the Chinese War,
about crisis politics particularly exemplified in the
action he was witnessing, about the masses particularly
examplified in the Chinese masses all round him. Some
people have quoted from the sonnets the end of Number 16:

> And maps can really point to places
> Where life is evil now:
> Nanking; Dachau –   [EA, 257]

I would rather quote:

> We envy streams and houses that are sure:
> But we are articled to error; we
> Were never nude and calm like a great door,
>
> And never will be perfect like the fountains;
> We live in freedom by necessity,
> A mountain people dwelling among mountains,   [EA, 262]

because that shows better what kind of subject he has
taken. Think of a poem like 'Anabase': a disarticulated,
grand image of human history lying about rather carelessly
in time. Auden's Sonnets are like an 'Anabase' formalised
and made more effective and presented *now* in the time of
the badness of Europe; yet they are not a 'Daily Telegraph'
leading article, 'right' this morning and wrong to-morrow.

They are immediately but also perpetually relevant, since
men can never defeat, but only modify, imperfection.
    I first read these sonnets after hearing the speech by
Chamberlain on March 17th, in which he dealt with the
occupation of Prague. For Chamberlain, it was a clear and
moving speech, rising above the low point of his 'freezing
gift of understatement.' But it was a pure example of
political mediocrity, at a time when even a Chamberlain
might have *felt* human history, even if he had mixed his
feelings with economic self-interest. One thought of
Chamberlain what Coleridge thought of Pitt. Then reading
these sonnets, I did feel life instead of death. I was
surprised, and delighted, and possessed; and I still am.
The owl's ear catches the sounds and the sounds have been
made full of meaning. The meaning remains full, with
little repetition, the excitement continues high with only
a gap or two through all the sonnets; and right into the
Verse Commentary at the end:

                ...and in the silence
    The cry that streams out into the indifferent spaces,
    And never stops or slackens, may be heard more clearly,

    Above the everlasting murmur of the woods and rivers,
    And more insistent than the lulling answer of the
        waltzes,
    Or the hum of printing presses turning forests into
        lies;

    As now I hear it, rising round me from Shanghai,
    And mingling with the distant mutter of guerrilla
        fighting,
    The voice of Man: 'O teach me how to outgrow my
        madness.'

    The power of these poems obviously comes out of their
totality as a collection. They must not be condemned from
faults in any one line or excerpt.
    Good as Isherwood's prose travel-diary is, as a des-
cription of the *bigness* of China and the War, not jazzed
up into the dramatic, know-all, pseudo-significant pattern
of the journalist, it is really rather small beside the
moral and imaginative weight and tenderness of Auden's
poems; but I am sure it is a good thing that the poems
have come out in this way with photographs, a map, and a
war story. They will be read by people who might not have
bought them in a separate book.
    I do not know any poems written in the last forty years
by Yeats, or Eliot, or any Englishman which are superior

to some of the best of Auden's recent poems; and I say
that after allowing for any bias of feeling I might have,
going back to the first poem I ever read by Auden when we
were both undergraduates.

'New Verse' came into existence because of Auden. It
has published more poems by Auden than by anyone else; and
there are many people who might quote of Auden: 'To you I
owe the first development of my imagination; to you I owe
the withdrawing of my mind from the low brutal part of my
nature, to the lofty, the pure and the perpetual.' Auden
is now clear, absolutely clear of foolish journalists,
Cambridge detractors, and envious creepers and crawlers
of party and Catholic reaction and the new crop of loony
and eccentric small magazines in England and America. He
is something good and creative in European life in a time
of the very greatest evil.

80. LINCOLN KIRSTEIN ON THE GREATEST POETRY OF OUR SPEECH,
POETS UNDER FIRE, 'NATION'

cxlix, 5 August 1939, 151-2

Lincoln Kirstein (b. 1907) is the founder and Director of
the School of American Ballet. He edited 'Hound and Horn'
from 1927 to 1934, and has published numerous books and
monographs on art, dance, and ballet.

This book is ostensibly a record of a trip through war-
torn China by two of the most talented young English
writers of our day. But primarily it is a book about the
conscience of a Western ruling class faced with the agony
of an Oriental people to whom they feel responsibility. It
is funny, brilliant, fierce, tragic, and technically
superb. It is entirely in another class of usefulness from
Agnes Smedley's, Edgar Snow's, or John Gunther's books.
Reading these other remarkable records does not obviate
the necessity of owning 'Journey to a War.' Less encyclo-
pedic, less factually inclusive than any of the others, it
is nevertheless perhaps the most intense record of China
at war yet written in English.

It is a diary, with photographic and verse commentaries.
The initial shock is Isherwood's. His 'Good-bye to Berlin'
suffered a curious fate in America. Brilliantly reviewed,
as it well deserved, it was nevertheless allowed to lapse

almost unadvertised, as if its publishers were upset by
the attitude of the author toward pre-Hitler Berlin. This
attitude was different from the loose and merely indignant
expressions which are currently fashionable in liberal
literary circles. It is Isherwood's particular talent to
hunt deeper than apparent outrage or obvious injustice. He
tries to find the root of terror and frequently does. The
actual search is disturbing, but what he finds is more so.

His prose is full of the dry crackle of witty short
circuits. His humorous exasperation has the fascinated
gaze of a patient watching the surgeon operate on him
under local anaesthetic. He is soberly lyrical over the
veiny glories of a superb sarcoma. During a permanent
nervous breakdown he nicknames his naked nerve ends. His
irony springs from the dichotomy of an excellent education
and a realization of where such conditioning has served to
place that class which he cannot choose but represent. It
is the self-accusation tormenting a middle-class Englishman at this juncture, in this place: China, 1938. With dry
anger and antiseptic self-exposure, he uncovers his own
moral sickness and hence his country's. This involves
Hamlet doubts concerning his own or any writer's usefulness. He is of use in direct proportion to the intensity
of his awareness, which is deep. His manners are those of
the stock English gentleman, reversed. A lurid rat-like
politeness is sprayed all over himself and particularly
over such others as young Peter Fleming, the streamlined
Etonian, the dazzling special correspondent who, bred to
the modern sciences of appeasement and face-saving, has
inevitably elevated himself from 'The Times' closer to the
Foreign Office. Isherwood awards all honors to the adversary. How droll the courtesies of the permanent duel; how
comic the steady treachery. It is as if in some music-hall
undertaking parlor he spiritually arranged the suicide of
the English so that the removal of their living corpses
might make it somehow easier for China. His diary makes
the tiresome war glow with klieg-lit back-stage reality.
The actors by some cosmic vaudeville turn are murdering
their audiences.

With Auden it is different. He is a poet and, to a
degree, apart. In fact, he is a monster of verse, or
rather a monstrous genius inhabits him. He pilots his
large instinctive talent, which he increasingly masters,
around the big fresh graveyards of our world, and it produces for him with funereal splendor. Since Yeats's death
he has taken his place as the first poet writing in English. At the sick breast of fact he taps for fault,
extracts the limping organ, inspects it and puts it back.
The disease has advanced too far for one pair of fingers

to heal - he knows it - though if he were a surgeon he
would be another Cushing. Yet he is always suspect - a
really dangerous person, in so far as anyone is dangerous
- for he threatens even our most recent and difficultly
intrenched ideas. He also employs pragmatic treachery to
every preconceived poetic formula. In this treachery he
uses as forced allies any English poet from Beowulf to
Byron. He scraps these allies, one after the other, to
found a new front which may have certain special uses.
Unlike others of his publicized group, his talent proceeds
in spite of direct experience with violence or politics.
It is not arrested in the rut of comfortable memoirs, on
account of it. He has too much respect for poetry not to
be interested in his own genius and proper personal survival. It is his good fortune that he can make poetry out
of realizing what sort of man Chiang Kai-shek really is
from having seen him, rather than from hoping what Chiang
Kai-shek might under optimistic circumstances do for new
China. Frequently a talent has been 'greater' than a given
artist's 'behavior' under certain trying social and economic circumstances: one remembers Wordsworth, or maybe
Courbet. Auden is obviously a brave man physically, if
that is significant, in so far as he neglects his fear
under gunfire. But he has the fiercer courage of being
able to state disagreeable truth about even our lives, and
those who are on 'our side.' He can be hateful. He is the
relentless adversary of the kind of weak conscience-money
conspiratorial optimism which now identifies so many of us
within the fringes of protest and action - where we have
our precarious moral safety just under the angle of the
guns of our real defenders.

The distinction of his writing, the disciplined
felicity of his simple metrical surprises, are the combination of human indignation with his energetic and solitary gift. No longer does one find the private jokes or
the ex-don's wry humor. If the sonnets are difficult, they
are difficult as Rilke's are, since the thought they embody
is hard for all of us to comprehend. Once they are understood, they make it even more difficult to proceed with
that understanding in us. The twenty-seven final sonnets
have, as a group, a cumulative connection for which one
must return to the Elizabethan sonneteers for comparison.
If one doubts this as facile praise, read XVI, XVIII,
XXVII, or 'The Sphinx.'

For, as in Rilke, so beautifully celebrated in XXIII,
the object of Auden's verse is love and praise. The 'Commentary' with its opposition of great epitaphs, its
fountainous eruption of unforgettable images, its sober,
musical probity and vivid finish, reads like our epoch's

last will and testament. It is the index of Auden's greatness that he realizes the exact degree of finality of his
or anyone else's poetry, and that such a will as he signs
must have more to do with the living than with the dead.
The reason Auden is writing the greatest poetry of our
speech is because his one subject is personal responsibility. He assumes for himself, as a man, the entire load,
the whole blame. His service is in that it is ours also,
and his accusation ennobled by his colloquial disdain
somehow can hearten us by its fragmentary vision of an
absolute diagnosis.

'Another Time'

New York, February 1940; London, June 1940

81. MICHAEL ROBERTS ON A FAILURE TO AFFIRM, NOT THIS TIME?,
'SPECTATOR'

clxv, 26 July 1940, 100

Mr. Auden has always been fluent, he has always been ready
to turn out a piece of slack, gossipy verse for a social
or political occasion, and he has always shown a remarkable capacity for picking up odds and ends of other
people's styles. The present volume is, on the whole,
trivial or skilfully imitative, although it opens with a
very effective dedicatory poem in Mr. Auden's most characteristic Blake-ish manner:

> Every eye must weep alone
> Till I Will be overthrown -
>
> But I Will can be removed
> Not having sense enough
> To guard against I Know,
> But I Will can be removed.   [EA, 456]

In the poems that follow, the predominating influence is
that of Mr. Leishmann's excellent early translation of
Rilke. 'Perhaps I always knew what they were saying,'
'Brussels in Winter,' 'Herman Melville,' 'The Capital,'
'Pascal,' 'Voltaire at Ferney' and other poems all have so
much of Mr. Leishmann's characteristic idiom, rhythm and
syntax, that it is difficult to judge them as independent
works: the reader is left wondering how much of Rilke's
vision ought to be read into these poems and whether Mr.
Auden really means anything by the mythology that he
borrows from Rilke. ('Where do They come from? Those whom

we so much dread....') It is not easy to accept these
personifications as reality, or images of reality, from a
poet who at other times talks with far more confidence in
terms of Freudian analysis and discusses patriotism, religion and disinterested labour as if they were the result
of some fixation about The Father that could be avoided,
and ought to be.

Mr. Auden at times believes that the poet's business is
to 'Show an affirming flame' and to 'Teach the free man
how to praise.' And yet there is little praise in this
book, little of the affirming flame:

> The fishes are silent deep in the sea,
> The skies are lit up like a Christmas tree,
> The star in the West shoots its warning cry:
> 'Mankind is alive, but Mankind must die.'   [EA, 209]

Mr. Auden writes with an acute sense of the evil and
suffering of the world: he is not sure that all our
troubles 'are from eternity, and shall not fail'; but his
remedy is love and understanding, and at his worst (in the
'Lighter Poems') he is cruel, uncomprehending and unjust.
The religious poet, the man with a clear vision of good
and evil, can afford to be a satirist: the apostle of love
without responsibility and understanding without humility
has no standards by which to condemn. He can only poke fun,
like W.S. Gilbert, at the weak, the unhappy, and the unsuccessful. Some of Mr. Auden's popularity may be due to
his ballads, dismal rather than tragic, his jaded songs,
his funeral blues: here they are, a little wordy, but still
the familiar mixture, and with no adequate contrast of
positive faith. This book gives the impression that Mr.
Auden used up all his emotional energy in treating the
Spanish Civil War as a crusade, and cannot now bring himself to form anything but a cynical and pessimistic judgement on a world in which the cause of honesty and justice
is tainted with dishonesty and injustice. But in one of
the best of these poems, in which he breaks away from
imitation and triviality, he tries to apply his own lesson
of universal love and understanding not to a world of
illusion but to the real, imperfect, and active world of
people:

> O stand, stand at the window
>   As the tears scald and start;
> You shall love your crooked neighbour
>   With your crooked heart.   [EA, 228]

82. T.C. WORSLEY ON UNDERSTANDING THE LIFE OF OUR DAY,
MAJOR POET, 'NEW STATESMAN AND NATION'

xx, 27 July 1940, 92

T.C. Worsley (b. 1907), novelist, theatre critic, and
autobiographer, was Literary Editor and Drama Critic of
the 'New Statesman', 1948-60; Drama Critic, then Television Critic, of the 'Financial Times' from 1960 to 1972.
His books include 'Behind the Battle' (1939), 'The Fugitive Art: Dramatic Commentaries 1947-1951' (1952),
'Flannelled Fool: A Slice of Life in the Thirties' (1967),
and 'Fellow Travellers' (1971).

The great merit of W.H. Auden's poetry is that it is
written out of the centre of our cultural pattern. Neither
narrowly local nor obsessively personal, it speaks the
language of our time, and expresses, more fully than any
other living poetry quite does, as well the roots and the
flowers of the civilisation in which we live. That civilisation is predominantly urban and industrialised, and even
the constants in it, like love and the landscape, hardly
avoid those characteristics; so that the imagery of his
love poetry has in it an echo of the clinic, and he cannot
describe a countryside or a resort without seeing behind
them the slag-heaps and the factory chimneys by leave of
which they now exist. Reading Auden, even at his most
obscure or his most silly, enlarges our understanding of
what the life of our day is really like. His favourite mode
is, it seems, the analytical, where the analysis is on
several different levels; his eye is the movie-camera's
eye, which moves not only in space but in time, unpeeling
the layer upon layer of history, and displaying the moti-
vation no less than the movement. At its simplest this
will combine into such a poem as 'The Capital' (No. 14 in
this collection):

[Quotes 11. 1-6 and 13-20 of 'The Capital', EA, 235-6.]

In 'Another Time' this analysis is turned with acute
penetration on a number of the great dead: Housman,
Rimbaud, Voltaire, Freud, Yeats, etc. The shortest of
these poems are also the best, where in a few strokes the
character is placed among the impulses which formed it and
drove it to its particular conclusion; and one notices
among them, too, the memorable, universal phrases - in the
Housman, for instance:

> In savage footnotes on unjust editions
> He timidly attacked the life he led.   [EA, 238]

or in the Yeats:

> And the seas of pity lie
> Locked and frozen in each eye.   [EA, 243]

Where the poems pass over into a more difficult territory of speculation, they seem to be less successful; they
are either extremely obscure still, like the poem on
Pascal, or they offer too baldly simple a solution: 'We
must love one another or die' - when no one knows better
than Auden that the ways of love are as crooked as a card-
sharper's. The problem which has been engaging his attention lately - the problem which an older mythology described in terms of Original Sin and which he has indicated
in the phrases 'Men are not innocent as the beasts, and
never can be.' 'Man, the only animal aware of lack of
finish' - this problem still seems to be too unclear in
his own mind to be stated, much less solved. We are left,
for the present at any rate, with some fascinating hints
and teasing phrases:

> O the striped and vigorous tiger can move
> With style through the borough of murder; the ape
>   Is really at home in the parish
>   Of grimacing and licking; but we have
>
> Failed as their pupils. Our tears well from a love
> We have never outgrown; our cities predict
>   More than we hope; even our armies
>   Have to express our need of forgiveness.   [EA, 244]

In the territory which he knows well, however, what is
remarkable is the clarity of the language and the statements, and the new life which he has forced into traditional forms. Here might be the basis for a belief that
his poetry may become what he has always wanted it to be,
popular. But his deliberate experiments to that end have
never really come off - the dance lyric examples here, for
instance, are not a noticeable advance on, say, Cole
Porter; and the three ballads which he reprints are another failure. They have certain qualities, the quick
ballad movement and a sardonic naivety, and they were
funny enough sung in the author's peculiar voice slipping
up into falsetto above his peculiar accompaniment; but in
print they carry overtones of that undergraduate superiority which ruined the plays. The best parts of them, in
fact, are those which relate most nearly to folk poetry,

and this effect he now achieves as spontaneously in his serious poems as in those which are labelled 'Lighter' in this volume:

[Quotes stanzas 8 and 10-11 of 'As I walked out one evening', EA, 228.]

There is no technical reason why such a poem as that from which these verses are taken should not be popular; the metre and the rhythm are easy and helpful, and the symbols have reference to a world of experience common to every inhabitant of these islands. Here (and in a number of other poems in this collection, such as the Refugee Blues) the poet has gone as far as he can along the road to creating a popular poetry; the other necessary condition, the change in society which will remarry culture with everyday life, is another problem, and does not belong to him as a poet.

'Another Time' is certainly rather a miscellaneous collection, less sustained and brilliant than his section of the China book. The best, most of which have been published before in journals in this country, are very good indeed. But Auden is, and always will be, a very uneven poet. He cannot, to begin with, resist the small boy's impulse to throw a stone at Solemnity's window. When it is most seriously aimed, this urchin humour comes off delightfully as in the sonnet on The Fall:

They wondered why the fruit had been forbidden;
It taught them nothing new....   [EA, 251]

but too often it falls very wide of its mark. Then again, the eraser is not his favourite tool; there are many lines here which (as we remember was said of another poet) a stricter self-criticism might have blotted, and whole poems which second thoughts might have excluded. But this carelessness is the complement of his fertility and exuberance and we cannot have it both ways.

Most of the poems date from before the war and it is too early to say what effect migration will have on his work. I cannot believe that it will be detrimental, for he is the least provincial of poets. The Capital of the poem quoted above might be Paris, Brussels, Budapest - or equally New York. The stuffy vertical barriers are down; even as we fall back in defence of our tight little island we proclaim it the bridgehead of a larger freedom. Today's struggle is world-wide - and America is as much a part of it as we are. Internationalism of one kind or another is included in everybody's war aims. If one succumbed to the

Philistine habit of demanding a message from our poets, one would find it in the last poem of 'Another Time' which celebrates as a symbol of 'the planting of human unity' the marriage of a famous Italian with a famous German exile.

83. WILLIAM EMPSON ON SIMPLIFYING THE MACHINERY, UNTITLED REVIEW, 'LIFE AND LETTERS TODAY'

1 August 1940, 178-80

He is a wonderful poet, and I cannot see this falling off that people talk about. Wyndham Lewis has a phrase 'the surge and roar that greets a reader approaching one of the great Shakespearean tragedies'; that is, I take it, a whole cycle of ideas and feelings has been connected to the main theme so that even the casual phrases of the play seem to hint at a great deal. Certainly if you compare Auden with almost all his contemporaries it is clear that they have hardly anything to say. You often find that he has taped firmly what you had been dumbly feeling; for instance, I have found myself saying weakly in the recent disasters, 'I don't know why, but I feel it's somehow all my fault,' and I had forgotten how Auden can always say this with a bang:

> Out of the mirror they stare,
> Imperialism's face
> And the international wrong.   [EA, 245]

The sheer ability of the thing (for instance in the Housman sonnet) is enormously cheerful for a critic; he is free to talk about the opinions, fully expressed, instead of some failure to express them.

At the same time you are afraid on every page that a horrid false note of infantilism will poke up its head. The poems here about famous men give striking cases of it. Voltaire, we are told, 'cleverest of them all, He'd led the other children in a holy war Against the infamous grown-ups.' About Freud, on the other hand, and the voice of the poet breaks at the thought, we are told 'He wasn't clever at all' (he was just such a *good* boy, your heart aches to think of it). No doubt Freud himself is largely respons-ible for this idea that people are best understood by seeing them as children; and yet this curious line of

sentiment about the word 'clever' would, I suppose, be as
hard to translate into German as into French. It is something to do with the English system of education; it
throws absolutely no light on Voltaire. At the end of
'Spain' the poet describes an ideal state, with the rather
puzzle-headed introduction 'To-morrow, perhaps the future',
and it is a boys' school; there would be no room for Auden
himself except as one of the masters. I see that some of
the verses have been cut out; 'the eager election of
chairmen / By the sudden forest of hands' is no longer put
forward as a scene that Auden would take part in gleefully.
He has also, very oddly, cut out the best and most characteristic verses, the comparison of aspects of suburban
fretfulness with the instruments of war which they are
supposed to have engendered. And 'the conscious acceptance
of guilt in the necessary murder' has become 'in the fact
of murder'. We are still though to have 'all the fun
under - Liberty's masterful shadow'; it is a very Fascist
picture. I can't myself feel that the race of man is like
this at all. What is heartening about people is their
appalling stubbornness and the strong roots of their
various cultures, rather than the ease with which you can
convert them and make them happy and good. Probably a
whole political outlook can turn on this. The poem
'Schoolchildren' is fine because there Auden finds it
natural to admit that men are a bit different from schoolchildren. Maybe you could connect the utopian note of the
politics with a remark in one of the love-poems:

> I believed for years that
> Love was the conjunction
> Of two oppositions;
>   That was all untrue....   [CP(M), 207]

You can over-do it, to be sure, but things can't be all
kiss and make friends either. Auden's later poetry, I
think, gains by simplifying its machinery, but wouldn't
gain if it came to simplify the ideas in the background.
    The text, by the way, is bad. I am not at all opposed
to honest farce on the part of a printer:

>   all our whiteness shrinks
> From the hairy and clumsy bridge-room   [EA, 243]

seems to me a pretty line, if you see what has gone wrong
with it. But take the last verse on the death of Freud:

> One rational voice is dead; over a grave
> The household of Impulse mourns one dearly loved.

> Sad is Eros, builder of cities,
> And weeping anarchic Aphrodite.   [CP(M), 218]

In the Faber text the entrancing rhythm of the last line has been murdered by the insertion of the word 'of'.

'The Double Man'

New York, March 1941; London (as 'New Year Letter'),
May 1941

84. MALCOLM COWLEY ON THE IDEA OF GUILT, AUDEN IN AMERICA,
'NEW REPUBLIC'

civ, 7 April 1941, 473-4

W.H. Auden's new poem is the most ambitious he has so far
written, and in many ways the most successful. People who
haven't followed his recent development will find on reading it that they are entering an unfamiliar and uncomfortable but stimulating world of ideas.

'The Double Man' is a work in three parts, consisting
of 1,707 numbered lines, followed by 87 pages of notes,
quotations and comments in prose and verse. The poem itself is written in four-beat iambic couplets. This is a
pattern that has generally been used for satires, epigrams
and brief narratives - Dean Swift, for example, was fond
of it - and when followed too faithfully in longer poems,
it runs the risk of becoming monotonous. Auden avoids that
danger by the alternation of moods, by headlong rhythms
and hairbreadth rhymes, so that 'The Double Man' is technically a considerable achievement. It is much more
interesting, however, for what it has to say - in other
words, for the element in poetry that is generally disregarded by reviewers.

Auden says, like others before him - beginning perhaps
with Berdyaev in 1919 - that our society is now convul-
sively dying. The Economic Man created by the Renaissance
is ending his days, after finding himself enslaved by the
machines that he invented. We who survive know that a
crime has been committed, and all are seeking for the
criminal; even the Men of Good Will are now eager to em-
bark on a crusade against Hitler. The real guilt, however,
rests on all of us; it cannot be confined to politicians,

even the worst of them, since they are merely the voice of
the crowd. In appearance, the modern tyrannies have a
double source, being partly derived from Plato's idea of
philosopher-kings, and partly from Rousseau's idea of man
as a naturally good animal. But in reality, both these
misconceptions have an identical basis - that is, the cold
spiritual pride that leads each separate man to believe he
is all-important. Being lonely, the ego has become monstrous; being monstrous, it has become terrified of itself,
and in terror it is plunging toward self-destruction. We
can avoid that fate for ourselves by deciding that although the old bonds of family and locality have been destroyed and each of us is totally alone, still we can form
what Auden calls 'a purely personal confederation.' As
discrete persons, we must learn to love one another....
And the poem ends with a deeply felt prayer for humility
and strength.

The various sections of 'The Double Man' are not
equally good. Sometimes Auden so involves himself in
ethical distinctions that he seems to be pulling hairs
from imaginary heads in order to split them into four
equal parts. Other passages are full of a fanciful but
fundamentally serious eloquence - as, for example, his
picture of how living poets are judged by a tribunal of
the dead and his fine tribute to Karl Marx as one of the
'great sedentary Caesars.' Meanwhile the poem as a whole
keeps its unified framework and an uninterrupted movement.

There are three respects in which it seems fundamentally different from most of the poetry we have been
reading.

In the first place, its subject is moral rather than
political. All during the 1930's, poets were preoccupied
with the possibility of social changes, but Auden wants to
begin by changing the inner world. He has lost most of his
faith in the fruitfulness of political action, and all of
his faith in writers as political agents. Like the English
poets of the 1790's who began as fellow travelers of the
French Revolution, but were alienated by the reign of
terror and the conquests of Napoleon, Auden and his
friends have been alienated from communism and are now
preoccupied with the problem of evil in the human soul.
And they are fully conscious of this historical parallel.
Auden, for example, is determined not to follow the example of Wordsworth, who ended as a devout supporter of
the English squires. He is more attracted by the example
of Blake, who wanted to change the political revolution
into a revolution of love. But perhaps he most resembles
the later Coleridge - the prose Coleridge - being inclined
like him toward theological speculations and being

nourished on German metaphysics.

And the word 'German' suggests the second novelty in his work. The authors quoted in his eighty-seven pages of notes include Goethe, Wagner, Nietzsche, Kierkegaard (a Dane adopted by the Germans), Freud, Jung, Thomas Mann, Kafka, Rilke, Groddeck, Jaeger - to mention only a few of those belonging east of the Rhine. Twenty years ago, a young man writing poetry was likely to borrow his ideas from the French Symbolists, beginning with Baudelaire and ending with the latest disciple of Dada encountered in a Montparnasse café. Ten years ago, the source of ideas was the communist tradition, from Marx to Bukharin. As for Auden, he quotes a little French, but to judge from his rhymes he badly mispronounces it; and when he speaks of Marxian ideas, it is as if he were writing a charitable epitaph. His real interest is in the priests, prophets and healers who were admired in the Reich before Hitler.

And Auden is German not only in his sources, but also in his manner of writing poetry. He delights in the Germanic abstractions of which Edmund Wilson said that they convey 'almost the impression of primitive gods. They are substantial, and yet they are a kind of pure beings; they are abstract, and yet they nourish.' His poems, like the works of German philosophers, are rich in nouns and poor in verbs of actions. And although many of the nouns at first glance appear to be concrete rather than general - being words like valley, mountain, water, islands - one discovers that they have lost their common meanings and stand for abstract principles - the islands, for example, being places of dream and refuge. Such nouns are not so much signs for *things* as the symbols or statues of ideas. And reading some of Auden's poems is like wandering at dusk through a gallery of white marble statues that dissolve before one's eyes into white mists - and sometimes take shape again as their own opposites.

But besides being German in spirit, Auden is also - and this is the third novelty in his work as compared with that of the past decade - a profoundly Christian poet. His new book is preoccupied with the problem not only of war guilt but of guilt in general. The chief lesson it teaches is the Christian lesson of humility based on a conviction of original sin (for the pride of the ego, on which he places the ultimate blame for the state of things, is exactly that sin). Some of his best and more of his worst verse deals with fundamentally theological questions. And yet, though Christian, he also seems to be agnostic. He allows the Devil to be present in his narrative - if only as a mental concept - but he insists on disguising God under a series of symbolic or naturalistic names; usually

he is Life or Love. It is only in the final prayer - and
only after invoking Him as the Unicorn, the Dove, Ichthus,
the Voice, the Keeper of the Years, the It without Image -
that Auden, in a quotation from St. Augustine, uses the
Latin vocative form of God's name: 'O da quod jubes,
Domine.'

But even if this indicates that his Christianity may
cease to be Christless, still it would remain somewhat
heretical. For, in the midst of all its subtle differen-
tiations - between tribulation and temptation, between
doing evil and sinning - it fails to draw the customary
and orthodox distinction between sin and guilt. It fails
to recognize that although all men are sinners in the
sight of God, some men are guiltier than others. It refuses to admit that Christians have the right and duty to
oppose those of greater guilt. On this point I think that
Reinhold Niebuhr - to mention a recent example - is the
better moralist. The danger in a philosophy like Auden's,
quite apart from any question of its truth, is that it
might lead him and has already led some of his disciples
into an attitude of pure passivity - and this at a moment
when the passive toleration of evil may prove to be a form
of collective suicide.

85. RANDALL JARRELL ON A LIMITED SUCCESS, 'NATION'

clii, 12 April 1941, 440-1

Distinguished poet and critic, Jarrell (1914-65) was
author of several books including 'Poetry and the Age'
(1953) and 'The Complete Poems' (1969). 'The Third Book of
Criticism' (1969) and 'Kipling, Auden & Co.' (1980) collect together Jarrell's several articles on Auden.

See Introduction, p. 44, for a discussion of Jarrell's
views on Auden's 'changes' in technique and ideology.

In 1931 Pope's ghost said to me, 'Ten years from now the
leading young poet of the time will publish, in the
"Atlantic Monthly," a didactic epistle of about nine hundred tetrameter couplets.' I answered absently, 'You are a
fool'; and who on this earth would have thought him anything else? But he was right: the decline and fall of
modernist poetry - if so big a swallow, and a good deal of
warm weather, make a summer - were nearer than anyone

could have believed. The poetry which came to seem during
the 'twenties the norm of all poetic performance - experimental, lyric, obscure, violent, irregular, determinedly
antagonistic to didacticism, general statement, science,
the public - has lost for the young its once obsessive
attraction; has evolved, in Auden's latest poem, into
something that is almost its opposite. 'New Year Letter'
(which, with many notes and a few lyrics, forms 'The
Double Man') is a happy compound of the Essay on Man and
the Epistle to Dr. Arbuthnot, done in a version of Swift's
most colloquial couplets. Pope might be bewildered at the
ideas, and make fun of, or patronizingly commend, the
couplets; but he would relish the Wit, Learning, and
Sentiment - the last becoming, as it so often does,
plural and Improving; and the Comprehending Generality,
Love of Science, and Social Benevolence might warm him
into the murmur, 'Well enough for such an age.' How fast
the world changes! and poetry with it! What he would have
said of the more characteristic glories of 'Gerontion,'
the 'Cantos,' or 'The Bridge,' I leave to the reader's
ingenuity.

  'New Year Letter' contains Auden's ideas about everything (Life and the Good Life, Art and Society, Politics,
Morals, Love, the Devil, Economic Man), organized inside
a successfully concrete framework of what he has read and
seen and met with. Auden's ideas once had an arbitrary
effective quality, a personality value, almost like ideas
in Lawrence or Ezra Pound. They seem today less colorful
but far more correct - and they are derived from, or are
conscious of, elements over most of the range of contemporary thought. Sometimes the reader exclaims delightedly,
'What a queer thing for a *poet* to know!' (This replaces
the resentful remark of the 'twenties: 'What a queer thing
for anybody to know!') The poets of the last generation
were extremely erudite, but their erudition was of the
rather specialized type that passed as currency of the
realm in a somewhat literary realm. About Darwin, Marx,
Freud and Co., about all characteristically 'scientific'
or 'modern' thinkers most of them concluded regretfully:
'If they had not existed, it would not have been necessary
to ignore them.' (Or deplore them.) In their comparison of
the past and the present, the present came off, not even a
poor, but a disgraceful second; 'and this was not surprising,' as Carroll says, since the values by which they
judged - the whole climate of their judgment - were desperately and exclusively those of the past. They constituted a forlorn hope we must admire but understand.
Auden's culture and doctrines are more accessible and
plausible than theirs to the ordinary cultivated person,

whose thought is not now essentially religious, literary, reactionary, or anti-scientific. And the manner of Auden's knowledge surprises as much as the matter; there is none of the atmosphere of stupefying scope and profundity of information that has accompanied Pound's and Eliot's application of the methods of the industrial revolution to literature: so far as Auden's tone is concerned, London and Rome are still untouched by American hands, the great *Volkerwanderung* of the barbarian scholars has never occurred.

'New Year Letter' seems to me, within certain limits, a great success. It is thoroughly readable: Auden handles with easy virtuosity humorous and serious material – sometimes his method of joining them verges on simple Byronic alternation, but they tend to be swept together by the tone and verse-movement, rapid, informal, and completely adaptable. The poetry, strained through so many abstractions, is occasionally a little pale; but it *is* poetry. Auden has accomplished the entirely unexpected feat of making a successful long poem out of a reasonable, objective, and comprehensive discussion. It is kept concrete or arresting by many devices: wit, rhetoric, all sorts of images (drawn from the sciences, often); surprising quotations, allusions, technical terms, points of view, shifts of tone; he treats ideas in terms of their famous advocates, expresses situations in little analogous conceits; and he specializes in unexpected coordinates, the exquisitely ridiculous term – he is remarkably sensitive to the levels and interactions of words. The poem is not quite first-rate. It lacks the necessary finality of presentation; it is at a remove; the urgency and reality have been diluted. Evil is talked about but not brought home; there is a faint sugary smell of *tout comprendre est tout pardonner*: everything is going to be all right in the end. When one remembers his earlier poetry at its best, one feels unreasonably homesick for the fleshpots of Egypt. But these are almost too many qualifications: it is a valuable, surprising poem.

In the notes there are quotations, aphorisms, exposition, verse, a few poems: if not God's plenty, at least, plenty. Some notes are valuable in themselves, some amplify or locate the poem's ideas; but these water a positive desert of Good Sense: machine-made parables, forced definitions, humorless half-truths, with which we wearily dissent or impatiently agree. (The notes specialize in neither the High nor the Low, but the Mean Sublime.) To the question, 'What is the only thing that always remains work, that can never give us aesthetic satisfaction?' Auden replies, *the ethical*; the victims of his insistent

raids on the Moral can ruefully agree. The lyrics called
The Quest (conscientiously flat, abstract, and characteristic parables) seem to me rather uninterestingly unsuccessful.

I've made my review general because I wanted to em-
phasize, like the advertisements: 'This poem's *different*';
some people who don't ordinarily read modern poetry might
enjoy 'New Year Letter.' Since I've no space for what I
should like - a careful discussion of its ideas and technique - let me finish simply by saying that it is worth
buying.

86. BABETTE DEUTSCH ON AUDEN'S ANALYTIC ETHICS, 'SIRS,
WHAT MUST I DO TO BE SAVED?', 'POETRY'

lviii, June 1941, 148-52

Babette Deutsch (b. 1895), poet, critic, and writer for
children, is a Chancellor of the Academy of American
Poets, and taught poetry at Columbia University from 1944
to 1971. Author of several volumes of verse, she has also
published translations of Alexander Blok, Puskhin, and
Rilke. 'The Collected Poems of Babette Deutsch' appeared
in 1969.

One of the young Auden's most notable poems was a religious sonnet, addressing God with Emily Dickinson's
directness as 'Sir,' and praying for 'New styles of architecture, a change of heart.' The significance of this poem
was somewhat eclipsed by the fact that so much of his
early work showed him as a rather naive Marxist and a
decidedly boyish *épateur*. It strikes the keynote, however,
for the extensive and pregnant piece which forms the body
of his latest book. The new styles of architecture, which
were so often his chief concern, have become less important to him than the change of heart. As the title indicates, he is sharply aware of human ambivalence, though it
is of an intellectual rather than an emotional kind, and
it is with painful cognizance of the difficulties involved
that he demands that we set our house in order, substituting for a barren *ordre logique*, which cannot bring salvation, that *ordre du coeur* which promises the full fruition
of sympathy and intelligence.

The poem is in the nature of a letter to a friend, and

rambles on, as letters do, offering a happy example of free association. But it is governed throughout by the fact that the poet is preoccupied with man's divided mind and interested in the achievement of integration. So that although he may wander into all manner of curious by-paths - and how many and how odd they are is attested by the voluminous notes to the poem - he never loses sight of the main road, and he comes out into the open at the end.

These notes, which occupy twenty more pages than does the poem itself (and that runs to over 1700 lines), are of doubtful value. Aside from the fact that the reader is distracted by being compelled to page back and forth as though he were reading a scholarly treatise, there is the further objection that the note is not seldom a gratuitous reference to a familiar quotation, or a slightly musty anecdote, or an exposition which does not explain. It is not clear why the essential matter was not incorporated into the body of the text, especially as many of the notes are already in verse, and the poem is furnished with a brief bibliography of its modern sources, which range from Thucydides' 'History of the Peloponnesian War' to Whitehead's 'Process and Reality' and the Lynds' 'Middle-town in Transition.'

Its dubious construction notwithstanding, for a post-script should not exceed the length of the letter to which it is appended, the poem falls into three fairly well defined sections. The first serves as an introduction and concludes by stating Auden's personal predicament as a poet. He observes neatly that

> The situation of our time
> Surrounds us like a baffling crime,

and proceeds to work out this image with telling precision. Under such circumstances, what can the writer do? He knows that

> ...language may be useless, for
> No words men write can stop the war
> Or measure up to the relief
> Of its immeasurable grief.

Yet he hopes that his private communication to a friend, reaching a disheartened public, may renew its faith in those humane ideals by which, with the help of modest rations, men live. The second part of the poem is a dis-quisition on the evil forces that have put us where we are. Auden's Devil is not Milton's, nor even Blake's. He is the opponent, as he is also the creature and servant of

that God to whom the sonnet mentioned above was addressed.
He is, in short, 'the Spirit-that-denies.' He is also that
state 'Of fear and faithlessness and hate' which, when
properly subdued, can 'push us into grace.' Not the least
interesting passages of this section are those which deal
with the distinction between sin and evil-doing, a distinction elaborated in the notes. The first is defined as
acting consciously in defiance of necessity; the second as
acting contrary to self-interest, and unlike sin, as inevitable, because our self-knowledge is not sufficient to
permit us to do otherwise. Auden rests in the comforting
reflection that the devil deals not in lies but in half-
truths, which we can synthesize so as to illuminate our
muddled world, and bring order out of chaos. Particularly
to this part of the poem belongs the epigraph from
Montaigne on the title-page: 'We are, I know not how,
double in ourselves, so that we believe we disbelieve, and
cannot rid ourselves of what we condemn.' The third and
final part resolves the discords examined in the previous
section. 'O once again,' pleads the poet, 'let us set out,

> Our faith well balanced by our doubt,
> Admitting every step we make
> Will certainly be a mistake,
> But still believing we can climb
> A little higher every time,
> And keep in order, that we may
> Ascend the penitential way
> That forces our wills to be free.

Condemning alike Plato's reliance on the elect philosophers and Rousseau's exaltation of the noble savage,
confirmed in his belief that 'Aloneness is man's real condition,' he concludes that

> ...true democracy begins
> With free confession of our sins...
> And all real unity commences
> With consciousness of differences.

The substance of the poem is, in fine, an analysis of
man's divided soul, and an insistence that salvation lies
in acknowledging our weaknesses, and in recognizing and
loving the uniqueness of each individual.

    In an early passage, speaking of the ideal audience
that each poet sets himself, Auden confesses that his own
is composed of Dante, Blake, the young Rimbaud, Dryden,
Catullus, Tennyson, Baudelaire, Hardy, and Rilke, among
others. In describing Dante he says that the great

Florentine grasped the complex 'Catholic ecology.' One
might say that Auden in this poem attempted to grasp the
ecology of man in contemporary society, with special
reference to the ethical implications of his survival.
Auden has come a long way since he first dazzled his
public with the exploits of an extremely clever and rather
naughty boy, but he is not yet prepared for so ambitious a
task as this. His adoption of the epistolary form allows
him a good deal of leeway, and he makes full and effective
use of it. Indeed, the poem might be described as an
interior monologue intended to be overheard, centering
upon the theme of an ordered mind in an ordered world,
which is also more or less the subject of the lively
sonnet sequence at the end of the volume. It is nearly
always interesting, not least as an instance of the intellectuals' trend toward religiosity, with its concomitant
sense of guilt and desire for penance, though Auden wears
his rue at different slant from T.S. Eliot. It is sometimes wise, often witty, and occasionally, especially when
the passage has to do with music, delightful poetry, but
it remains more engaging as ethics than as verse. A long
poem made up entirely of couplets in iambic tetrameter
palls on the ear, and when it deals largely in abstractions there is little room for imagery that will compen-
sate for the lack of melody. One could wish that Auden had
found a new style of architecture to house such pertinent
ideas, yet one cannot but welcome so entertaining an argument for a change of heart.

87. HERBERT READ ON MISUSE OF FORM, HUDIBRASTICKS,
'SPECTATOR'

clxvi, 6 June 1941, 613-14

When a poet has the will to write poetry and poetry does
not come, he has two alternatives before him: he can relapse into silence, or he can find a substitute for poetry.
If he cannot experience poetry, he can at least poeticise
experience; and the result, though it does not contain a
single line of poetry, may nevertheless be significant
(a word for which reviewers can never be sufficiently
grateful). But should it then be called poetry? That excellent critic Oliver Elton, in discussing this question
in relation to a poet whose work has some parentage to
this new poem of Mr. Auden's, remarked that

> While poetry has no upper limit (for it may soar as
> high as it can), its lower limit is harder to define.
> There is a no-man's-land, without fixed frontiers, over
> which hangs ambiguity; and a new name is wanted for the
> verse of Samuel Butler or of Swift. If we call it
> poetry, we seem to be setting it in the same rank as
> the work, let us say, of Dryden. Yet so sure is the
> reaction of metre upon syntax and idiom, and so power-
> ful the consequent 'medication of the atmosphere,' that
> the result is more than a prose which merely rhymes and
> rattles. ['The English Muse', 1932; repr., 1937, 256-7].

That Mr. Auden himself is aware of the problem is evident
from his introduction to 'The Oxford Book of Light Verse,'
and he himself is content to call such writing 'light
verse,' with the proviso that light verse can be serious.
    Professor Elton's remarks were prompted by Butler's
'Hudibras,' and in diction, method and intention Mr.
Auden's new work closely resembles that odd and isolated
masterpiece. One wonders whether, before embarking on his
imitation, Mr. Auden considered why Butler's burlesque had
remained so odd and isolated. It was Johnson, who on the
whole liked Butler, who said, 'Nor even though another
Butler should arise, would another Hudibras obtain the
same regard.' His argument is interesting, and of direct
application to the present case.*

> Burlesque consists in a disproportion between the **style**
> and the sentiments, or between the adventitious **senti-**
> ments and the fundamental subject. It therefore, **like**
> all bodies compounded of heterogeneous parts, contains
> in it a principle of corruption. All disproportion is
> unnatural; and from what is unnatural we can derive
> only the pleasure which novelty produces. We admire it
> awhile as a strange thing; but, when it is no longer
> strange, we perceive its deformity. It is a kind of
> artifice, which by frequent repetition detects itself;
> and the reader, learning in time what he is to expect,
> lays down his book, as the spectator turns away from a
> second exhibition of those tricks, of which the only
> use is to show that they can be played.

Light verse can be serious, says Mr. Auden, but what in
effect Johnson is saying is that serious verse cannot be
light. It depends partly on the question of metre. Common
to both 'Hudibras' and 'New Year Letter' is a short four-
foot line with double rhyme. Johnson described it as
'quick, spritely, and colloquial, suitable to the vulgarity of the words and the levity of the sentiments.'

Dryden thought that 'it turns earnest too much to jest, and gives us a boyish kind of pleasure.'*For example, here are a dozen lines from Auden:

[Quotes 11. 399-410, beginning 'Poor cheated MEPHISTOPHELES', CP (M), 168.]

And here are a similar number of lines from 'Hudibras' which will serve for criticism as well as for comparison:

It was a parti-colour'd dress
Of patch'd and pyball'd languages:
'Twas English cut on Greek and Latin,
Like fustian heretofore on satin.
It had an odd promiscuous tone,
As if h'had talk'd three parts in one.
Which made some think when he did gabble,
Th' had heard three labo'rers of Babel;
Or Cerberus himself pronounce
A leash of languages at once.
This he as volubly would vent
As if his stock would ne'er be spent. [Canto I, 95-106]

There is no denying the wit and the learning of Mr. Auden's poem. As for the former, to quote Johnson once again, inexhaustible wit cannot give perpetual pleasure, and after 1,707 lines of it, the mind is dazzled into a kind of stupor. For our aid and refreshment there are eighty pages of footnotes, some of them in verse, many of them quotations (from poets, philosophers, scientists, theologians, anthropologists and statisticians), and a few of them - in my own opinion, the most valuable part of the the book, original comments on life by Mr. Auden himself. It does not seem to me that any very clear philosophy emerges from the book - Mr. Auden is still in the process of digesting Kierkegaard, and is therefore faced by a dilemma which will determine the rest of his life. But he represents the modern intelligence in all its acuteness and confusion, and his present misuse of a medium (misuse rather than abuse, for it is fundamentally a failure in communication) does not affect our faith in his genius, and our expectation of its eventual expression either in verse that is 'simple, clear and gay' (his own demand), or in prose that is clear, simple, and serious.

* [Read's quotations from Johnson's Life of Samuel Butler are taken from G.B. Hill's edition of 'Lives of the English Poets' (Oxford: Clarendon Press, 1905), which also cites Dryden's comments on 'burlesque writing' on p. 217 n. 2.]

88. CHARLES WILLIAMS ON LIFE AND MR. AUDEN, UNTITLED
REVIEW, 'DUBLIN REVIEW'

ccix, July 1941, 99-101

Charles Williams (1886-1945) won great prestige as poet,
novelist, playwright, biographer, literary critic, theological exegete, and conversationalist. His works include
'The English Poetic Mind' (1932), 'Thomas Cranmer of
Canterbury' (1936), 'War in Heaven' (1930), and 'The
Descent of the Dove' (1939), to which Auden acknowledged
his indebtedness for 'many ideas' in 'New Year Letter'
(note to l. 1600).

The fact that Mr. Auden has included a reference to the
present writer in his notes need not perhaps prevent this
review. I should have preferred to write about the book in
octosyllabic verse as near to Mr. Auden's own as I could
manage, were it not for the space involved. That measure
has always been a habit of English light verse, using
those two words as Mr. Auden does in his own anthology of
such verse; it has a continuous speed that conceals, sometimes, its intensity, except to the careful ear. Mr.
Auden's has both speed and intensity; he is, as he always
has been, more vital with verse than most of us, and that
vitality has here free range.

The book contains a 'Prologue', the 'Letter', eighty
pages of notes, a number of shorter poems called the Quest,
and an 'Epilogue'. The notes are, on the whole, unnecessary to the poem, which is as it should be, but they are
fascinating in themselves; they contain a number of remarks by Mr. Auden, and some more poems by him, and a
large number of quotations out of other writers from
Horace to Mr. C.S. Lewis. I cannot resist quoting one or
two: from Baudelaire - 'La vrai civilization n'est pas
dans le gaz, ni dans le vapeur, ni dans les tables tour-
nantes. Elle est dans la diminution des traces du péché
original'; and almost as a companion piece, A.E. Housman's
'comment upon a certain textual editor: "He is like a
donkey between two bundles of hay who fondly imagines that
if one bundle of hay be removed he will cease to be a
donkey."'

The publishers say that this 'is the most important
statement Mr. Auden has made for a long time', and this is
so true that I do not propose to try and rewrite it, less
nobly, here. Its concern is with the building of the Just
City, but 'its architecture is its own'. It would be as

true to say that it was a poem about Life; it would be
even truer to say (and it is no small compliment) that it
sometimes gives the impression of being a poem written by
Life about Mr. Auden, written about him by the universe
which he, like each other man,

> Must carry round with him through life
> A judge, a landscape, and a wife.

In the course of what, from that point, is almost an
erotic love poem, and from Mr. Auden's opposite point is
almost a logical love-poem, high coincidences of the two
occur. As, for example, the description of the devil:

> By every name he makes a note
> Of what quotations to misquote,
> And flings at every author's head
> Something a favourite author said;

or the lovely descriptions of England, which remind the
reader of a serious mystical geography:

[Quotes ll. 1096-104, from 'Whenever I begin to think...',
CP(M), 182.]

or the description of Pride:

> A witch self-tortured as she spins
> Her whole devotion widdershins;

or the very fine conclusion:

> O every day in sleep and labour
> Our life and death are with our neighbour
> And love illuminates again
> The city and the lion's den,
> The world's great rage, the travel of young men.

Mr. Auden is a little hard in his notes on the Romantic;
or rather he uses the name only for the kind of mind I
should call the pseudo-Romantic: he defines Romanticism as
'unawareness of the dialectic'. With that this poem certainly cannot be charged. It is, after its own manner, a
pattern of the Way; that is dialectically includes both
sides of the Way only shows that it is dealing with a road
and not a room; in its own quotation - 'da quod jubes,
Domine'. I think perhaps, for once, the Lord has done so
here.

89. RAYMOND WINKLER, MR AUDEN'S WELTANSCHAUUNG, 'SCRUTINY'

x, October 1941, 206-11

Simplicity, it will be recalled, was habitually Mr.
Auden's strength and virtue. He was not, in fact, generally
classed as one of the 'simple' poets: in verse, complexity
of attitude towards a given situation on the one hand, and
simplicity of attitude towards a complex situation on the
other, have both given rise to accusations of obscurity.
Mr. Auden's method was ordinarily the second of these, and
by sticking firmly to a handful of easily-grasped principles, he steered his verses through the intricacies of
contemporary existence and produced some interesting
patterns of experience. The resultant scope constituted
the virtue; the fact that he felt no compulsion to modify
his attitudes under the stress of experience enabled him
to explore a wide field of phenomena without confusion.
The weakness of the plays sprang from the same source -
this insistent singularity of outlook and intention was
fundamentally undramatic: the apparent interplay of personality was soon revealed as the unsubtle clash of propaganda and counter-propaganda.
      The present work consists of a 'Prologue,' the 'Letter'
itself, eighty-two pages of notes in prose and doggerel
verse, a series of twenty sonnets, and an 'Epilogue.' The
'Letter' is described on the wrapper as 'a long philosophical poem in a regular metre,' and my guess is that
it's only a matter of months before it's described in one
university or another as a 'twentieth century "Essay on
Man"' or 'another "First Anniversarie."' The simplicity of
Mr. Auden's ideas persists; indeed, deployed as it is over
some eight hundred and fifty octosyllabic couplets, it can
fairly be considered obtrusive. The central conception of
modern social life as a kind of tribal war of scattered
groups, enunciated so effectively in 'Paid on Both Sides,'
reappears; though in the interval, under the tuition of
Kafka and others, Mr. Auden has discovered that each of
these groups has only one member -

      For the machine has cried aloud
      And publicized among the crowd
      The secret that was always true
      But known once only to the few,
      Compelling all to the admission
      Aloneness is man's real condition...   (11. 1537-1542)

And this is seen as the natural result of the process that

began with the Renaissance, leading the individual into
self-contradictions from which art provides no escape, and
to which (roughly) the solution is universal love:

[Quotes lines 1589-602 of 'Letter', CP(M), 191.]

This is a representative quotation. It has all the persistent qualities of the poem as a whole. Robbed of the concrete situation to serve as an agent for precipitating his
ideas, Mr. Auden has to rely on personification to give
them body, and metre and rhyme to give them sinew - an
inversion of the usual practice of good verse (Mr. Auden's
own practice in the best of the 1930 'Poems'), where the
idea crystallizes the imagery and modulates the rhythm;
and the effect is to hang a curtain between author and
reader. The method implies reaction in Mr. Auden's system
of ideas. His solution to the predicament in which
Renaissance man finds himself at the latter end of his
pilgrim's progress is to return to the attitudes which
were revolutionary at the beginning of that pilgrimage,
and establish them in the appropriate verse-form - indifferent to the fact that personifications, for example,
that were disturbing at a time when scientific quanti-
fication was giving a new point to the figures of the
moralities are now, after three centuries of logical
sophistication, as ineffectual and forlorn as a Britannia
in a 'Punch' cartoon.

The 'wit' too, which was at once evidence of resilience
and the cutting-edge in the arguments of the seventeenth-
century practitioners in Mr. Auden's adopted verse-form,
is here jam to mix with the powder, and every now again
quips are inserted, rather like daring sallies in the
college magazine by a theological student at a Scottish
university -

> In Ireland the great *Berkeley* rose
> To add new glories to our prose,
> But when in the pursuit of knowledge,
> Risking the future of his college,
> The bishop hid his anxious face,
> 'Twas more by grammar than by grace
> His modest Church-of-England God
> Sustained the fellows and the quad.   (ll. 459-466)

One is reminded that the Ministry of Information has
lately found the same verse-form a convenient vehicle for
National Savings propaganda -

So why don't you do like your mates
And purchase some certificates?
They're free from fire and flood and crime,
- And only fifteen bob a time!

(I quote from memory.)
It is only (too rarely) when a physically-conceived
situation dramatizes the idea that the verse abandons its
bludgeoning and momentarily acquires the kind of subtlety
which might have been its staple quality.

O but it happens every day
To someone. Suddenly the way
Leads straight into their native lands,
The Temeno's small wicket stands
Wide open, shining at the centre
The well of life, and they may enter.   (11. 860-865)

But Philosophy is at hand (Nietzsche this time), and Mr.
Auden reverts to the planchette again almost immediately -

Though compasses and stars cannot
Direct to the magnetic spot,
Nor Will nor willing-not-to will,
For there is neither good nor ill
But free rejoicing energy....

The notes to the 'Letter' are, in bulk, considerably
more extensive than the poem itself. At first reading I
had the impression that they were intended to be read together with the poem more or less as a single unit, which
would provide some justification for their bulk; but the
patent irrelevance of many of them discredited this view
on subsequent readings. They are intended, I think, to
give an impression of the diversity of material from which
the poem itself was distilled. If one accepts this account,
it isn't altogether surprising to find that some of the
bones contain more nutriment than the soup. They are,
however, generously assorted. Some of them serve the same
purpose as those to 'The Waste Land,' and merely supply
the source for a quotation, or cite a reference for some
piece of information of which the reader might otherwise
have been ignorant. Many of them, though, demonstrating a
less healthy aspect of Mr. Auden's naiveté, are quotations
from suspiciously fashionable authors like Kafka,
Kierkegaard and Rilke, whose connection with the matter in
hand is little more than generic. Other notes are prose
aphorisms dealing with Sin, Forgiveness, and kindred
matters, in the Emersonian 'Thought for To-day' tradition.

The remaining main class of notes is a number of verses
(modelled, possibly, on Swift's epigrams), incidental to
the central pattern, and most of which could have been
omitted without loss. A quotation will indicate that when
I referred to them earlier as 'doggerel,' I was expressing
not a spirit of disparagement but a matter of fact; it is
a note on the couplet (1. 961)

> Once again let us set out
> Our faith well balanced by our doubt

and runs,

> With what conviction the young man spoke
> When he thought his nonsense rather a joke:
> Now, when he doesn't doubt any more,
> No-one believes the booming old bore.

The 'Prologue' and the sonnet sequence (called The
Quest) engage the attention more fully than the 'Letter.'
The Quest is a series of twenty sonnets mostly about a
generalized 'He,' somewhat in the manner of Kafka's 'Notes
from the Year 1920.' With less space at his disposal for
the manoeuvering of his attitudes, Mr. Auden here finds
the specific situation (though allegorical) a convenient
vehicle, and the verse and the words of which it is constructed display considerably more animation as a result.
But the tendency to accept the easy solution (of the moral
problem and the problem of composition, which I take to be
continuous) persists, and musty personifications reappear:

> And when Truth met him and put out her hand
> He clung in panic to his tall belief
> And shrank away like an ill-treated child.   (VI)

The ghost of Herbert in Freudian uniform doesn't really
offer one a technical or ethical solution, but, on the
contrary, points the inadequacy of any attempt to make
ends meet that ignores the nature of the material between
the ends. It is in keeping with this too easy simplification that the Boy Scout earnestness of 'The Ascent of F6'
reappears in the Excelsioresque tones of the 'Epilogue':

> Let the lips do formal contrition
>   For whatever is going to happen...
> That the orgulous spirit may while it can
> Conform to its temporal focus with praise,
>   Acknowledging the attributes of
>   One immortal, one infinite Substance;

       And the shabby structure of indolent flesh
       Give a resonant echo to the Word which was
          From the beginning, and the shining
          Light be comprehended by the darkness.   [CP(M), 223]

    The 'Prologue' comes closer than anything else in this
book to the best of Mr. Auden's earlier work. The standpoint is more mature, by about three hundred years, and
the reminiscences of Eliot* are indicative, not of pla-
giarism, but of contemporaneity. The 'Letter' really adds
little to the exposition of the problem in the 'Prologue,'
and I would suggest that another edition of this book
omitting the 'Letter' and the notes would detract less
from Mr. Auden's deserved reputation.

Note

*   Cf. the passage beginning 'Only on battlefields...' with
    'The Waste Land,' 1. 415, and the specific reference to
    'Ash Wednesday,' II, in the passage beginning, 'For, how-
    ever they dream they are scattered, Our bones cannot help
    reassembling themselves....'

'For the Time Being'

New York, September 1944; London, March 1945

90. MARK SCHORER ON AUDEN'S BEAUTIFUL FLIGHTS, 'NEW YORK
TIMES'

17 September 1944, section 7, 4

Mark Schorer (1908-77), critic, biographer, novelist, and
writer of short stories, became Professor of English at
the University of California at Berkeley in 1947. His
books include 'Sinclair Lewis: An American Life' (1961)
and 'The World We Imagine: Selected Essays' (1968).
     This review is entitled Auden, Shakespeare and Jehovah.

'New Year Letter,' W.H. Auden's last long poem, brilliant
and demonstrative yet again of his extraordinary virtuosity, seemed nevertheless, with its heavy packet of notes
on its back, like an exercise in the poet's education
rather than as a document in his poetic progress. It was
a most instructive poem, for it presented the spectacle of
a distinguished poet in the act of pushing out his intellectual limits, putting new questions to himself and, in
the verse itself, arguing their answers; it gave the
reader the best illustration up to that time of the Auden
logic, which is the logic of paradox, and it supplied him
besides with a considerable reading list. But its total
impression was of a poem in which formal considerations,
for the moment, had been put aside. The year, after all,
was 1940.
     Looking back at 'New Year Letter' from the point of
view of the new Auden book, 'For the Time Being,' it seems
more than ever like the 'Biographia Literaria' of our time;
yet, the 'Biographia Literaria' of a poet who is not, like
Coleridge, reviewing the history of his mind, but rather

of one who is charting his mind for new excursions. The
two long poems which make up the new volume are beautiful
flights which carry with them effortlessly all that was
learned in the school of the poem before. Each of them
takes a paradox as its center, and each of them has as
theme one of the two major themes of 'New Year Letter':
the relation of art and life, and the problem of evil.

'The Sea and the Mirror,' Auden's 'commentary' on 'The
Tempest," is, to the present reviewer, one of the most
purely delightful of all modern poems. From the ingratiat-
ing relaxation of the first lines spoken by Prospero -
'Stay with me, Ariel, while I pack' - to its last lovely
lyric, a 'Postscript' addressed to Caliban by Ariel (and
for forcing the Elizabethan note, even to the particular
manipulation of the refrain, which here is merely 'I,'
into his own exquisitely ambiguous purposes, this lyric
represents Auden's virtuosity at its highest) - from
beginning to end, the sense is of enchantment. Not, naturally, of the explicit enchantment of 'The Tempest,' for
Auden's poem takes up after the last speech of the play,
when the spell is broken and the mood is of disillusion
(the mood which Auden himself identifies with imagination),
but enchantment arising from the zest of the poetry.
    There is space to examine only the organization of the
poem. It has two centers: Antonio, who betrayed his
brother Prospero, and Caliban, the natural beast. The
first, one might describe as the dramatic center, and he
is involved in the moral problem, the problem of action;
the second, as the reflective center, is involved in the
esthetic problem, the problem of meaning. Antonio and
Caliban, it will be remembered, are the two characters who,
in the casual resolution of Shakespeare's play, are 'rejected,' as it were: Antonio, from the moment of the
accusation to the curtain, says nothing at all - his
culpability is too grave for the increasingly lyrical note
of the drama to take into account, and he is left to
silence; Caliban, too gross for any climate but the most
mysterious, is abandoned to the deserted island.
    These two Auden takes up. In a series of dramatic
lyrics which may well be the best that have been written
since the early Eliot poems, each of the characters of the
play contemplates his future in terms of Antonio's ego-
ism, a moral defect which continues and which will determine not only Prospero's life -

    As I exist so you shall be denied,
    Forced to remain our melancholy mentor,
    The grown-up man, the adult in his pride -

but, in the pervasive, indirect manner of evil, the lives
of all.

> Happy Miranda does not know
> The figure that Antonio,
> The Only One, Creation's O
> Dances for Death alone.

The irony is patent in her protest, as it is in that of
each of the others.

Then Caliban takes over. More than half the poem is
devoted to his address to the audience, in prose quite as
brilliant as the verse. He talks abstractly, with almost
no direct reference to the action of the play and with
mention, among the characters, of Ariel alone. Yet he
brings along into his discourse the problem of evil which
Antonio has dramatized, and much more. First he speaks for
the audience to Shakespeare (the objection is that the
playwright has introduced life into art, and possibly art
into life!), then for Shakespeare to any aspiring artists
in the audience (the lesson is that at last art discovers
the very worst in life, and must live with it), and
finally, for Ariel and himself to the audience, pointing
out that they are aspects of the same. And the whole ends
in the lyric already mentioned, in which Ariel addresses
Caliban ('Helplessly in love with you'), and in which, by
a paradox of verse-making which must leave its author
rejoicing, Caliban is also addressing Ariel.

On the second poem, 'For the Time Being,' a Christmas
oratorio, which is perhaps the more 'serious,' we do not
have space to comment. Here the poet pursues that greatest
of all paradoxes, the Incarnation, and the most devious of
all questions, the relation of God to man, of good to evil.
This poem, like the first, mingles verse and prose, but
perhaps more arbitrarily; yet certainly Herod's prose
soliloquy, for example, is, as a thing in itself, wonderful. This poem, too, contains a number of answers, and the
poet forces none of them. As his logic rests on paradox,
and his method on irony, so his art itself rests on a form
of withdrawal, which one might also describe as a recognition of all the possibilities:

> Follow him through the Land of Unlikeness;
> You will see rare beasts, and have unique adventures.

91. HARRY LEVIN, THROUGH THE LOOKING GLASS, 'NEW REPUBLIC'

cxi, 18 September 1944, 347-8

Levin (b. 1912) became Irving Babbitt Professor of Comparative Literature at Harvard University in 1960. His books include 'The Overreacher: A Study of Christopher Marlowe' (1952), 'The Power of Blackness: Hawthorne, Poe, Melville' (1958), and 'The Question of Hamlet' (1959).
He has recalled:

> Once I reviewed a book of [Auden's] poems, respectfully though not ravingly, and he was gracious enough to send me a postcard of thanks. To my cavil - that certain lines had sounded oversimplified - his answer was lucidly practical. He had been writing for music in this case, and had discovered that the lyricist was lucky if he could emphasize one word in a single line. We had further opportunities to discuss the question, and I realized how much thinking and reading and listening he had spent upon it. It was his conclusion that Ben Jonson and Thomas Moore had fitted words to sounds most effectively in English, and many of his own experiments may profitably be scanned for such effects. In a less technical vein, I retain a letter which reads like an apologia for his increasing conservatism. Though I have no copy of what I had written to him, I must have echoed the common charge that he had been abandoning his earlier sociocritical stance. He begins by expressing skepticism toward all literary ideologies - a view which then was prompting him to revisions and excisions, and which would leave him more of a virtuoso than an iconoclast. He was careful to keep his religion in a separate category, deprecating the pseudo-mysticism of Aldous Huxley. For Fascism and other modes of authoritarianism his contempt remained intransigent, because he could not see such absolutes imposed upon the fallibilities of man's Augustinian condition.
> (Harry Levin, Recollecting W.H. Auden, 'Memories of the Moderns', London: Faber & Faber, 1981, p. 154)

Poetic justice, with its attendant ironies, must have presided over the mutually rewarding interchange that sent T.S. Eliot to England and brought W.H. Auden to this country. Eliot, whose preaching has never quite rationalized his practice, has retained a peculiarly individual talent. Auden, whose iconoclasm has merely tested his

loyalties, has not broken with tradition. Craftsmanship
is a surer link than manifestos and genuflections, and
Auden's skill is linked with the odes of Dryden and the
patter of Gilbert, with the varied masters and characteristic journeymen of English prosody. He has taught much,
and can teach more, to our native poets: few of them have
really mastered the technical requirements of their craft,
and those who have spend most of their efforts reminding
us of the fact. A book which - despite its temporizing
title - takes in its stride the ballade, the villanelle,
the sestina, sapphics, elegiacs and *terza rima*, while
making words a vehicle for ideas instead of the contrary,
is more than a current event; it is an enduring delight.
When poetry is as topical and colloquial, as pregnant with
issues and idioms as Auden's, it cannot be transplanted
without undergoing some abstraction of matter, some
intensification of manner. Imagery becomes less immediate,
diction more macaronic. Gorgeous dames have Oxford accents
and juke-boxes play Handel. The old familiar-exotic contrast between a concrete little England and the big abstract globe gives way to the broader antitheses of art
versus nature and naturalism versus supernaturalism. But
the *discordia concors*, whereby they are resolved, is still
the dominant mode; Auden and Eliot can still meet, if not
on the common ground of the vernacular and contemporary,
then in the rarefied atmosphere of the literary and
philosophic.

The perpetual aspiration of poetry toward the condition
of drama, which Eliot has bravely expounded and weakly
exemplified, finds further expression in the two long
poems that compose Auden's latest volume. Since his province is not dramatic characterization, but lyric speculation and satiric generalization, he has wisely allowed
Shakespeare and the gospels to provide the text for his
comments. 'The Sea and the Mirror' is a commentary on 'The
Tempest' and 'For the Time Being' is a Christmas oratorio.
Taken together, as mystery and masque, they represent the
alpha and omega of the theatrical cycle. The last comes
appropriately first, for Shakespeare's ending is far too
happy to be conclusive: it suggests disparities between
literature and life which neither Prospero's magic nor the
audience's make-believe can altogether reconcile. By
singling out the unreconciled character, by harping on the
discordant note, Auden bespeaks our attention for 'The
drama that Antonio Plays in his mind alone.' But it is
Caliban who provokes Auden, as he did Browning and Renan,
to the most interesting afterthoughts. The servant-
monster, gesturing with the hands of Sweeney and speaking
in the voice of Henry James, expresses the paradoxical

'relationship between the real and the imagined.' If he is
nature, art is his mirror, and Ariel is the artist's
tricksy genius, 'the spirit of reflection.' If Ariel is
the idealized image of Caliban, Caliban is the gross echo
of Ariel, and metaphysical reality lies behind the pros-
cenium - on the other side of the mirror. Life is
ultimately envisaged, not as Plato's cave nor Bede's
sparrow, but as 'the greatest grandest opera rendered by a
very provincial touring company indeed' - a mock-heroic
metaphor which Trotsky once applied to the social-
revolutionary government.

> It's as if
> We had left our house for five minutes to mail a letter,
> And during that time the living room had changed places
> With the room behind the mirror over the fireplace....

Thus the oratorio picks up the whimsical theme of the
commentary, and carries it through a series of resourceful
modulations to a music-hall finale, setting the Flight
into Egypt - 'the Land of Unlikeness' - against a real-
estate development of the Waste Land. The perplexities and
strivings of the intellectual, the man with the mirror,
are profoundly grasped and impressively orchestrated: 'How
can his knowledge protect his desire for truth from
illusion?' The response, prompted by the occasion, is the
Good News from Bethlehem, refulgent against the bad news
of modern civilization. Herod, the very pattern of a
modern liberal, is outheroded by Simeon, prototype of the
convert. Auden, like most intelligent believers, affirms
a positive faith by a kind of double negation, a denial of
doubt, a questioning of skepticism. He is more adept at
burying Caesar than at praising Christ, more anxious for a
Messiah than confident in the Revelation. When his libretto calls for a paradisiacal strain, he touches the
quavering reed-organ of revivalism: 'There's a Way.
There's a Voice.' The medieval nativity plays, *sancta
simplicitas*, could mix slapstick with piety; but the mixture of satire and theology, as Dostoevsky shows, is diabolically complex. Sin is notoriously easier to dramatize
- or believe in - than grace; hence Freud is a more pertinent guide that Beatrice. The rhyming clichés of the
romantics, 'love' and 'dove,' are displaced by the
Freudian be-all and end-all, 'womb' and 'tomb.' The cult
of Mary is treated as the supreme mother-fixation, and
Joseph is seen as a comic degradation of the superflous
husband. Nostalgia conjures up expressionistic visions of
the sea-changed past and the air-conditioned future.
Belief is a god in the machine, who sublimes private and

public problems, and by whom Imagination is redeemed from
'promiscuous fornication with her own images.'

That this is all done with mirrors, that poetry which
aspires to prophecy is even more paranoid that art for
art's sake, the skeptical reader can neither affirm nor
deny. But he cannot help observing a narcissistic tendency
to escape through the looking-glass into an island kingdom
or desert exile. Auden's parenthetical remark '(there is
probably no one whose real name is Brown)' seems very
revealing; it reveals the 'contrived fissure' between the
poet and his audience. His function - for we have almost
lost sight of Shakespeare's definition - is to hold the
mirror up to nature, not to denaturalize Caliban or super-
naturalize the White Knight. 'Our wonder, our terror remains,' to be sure, but it is more fully explained by
today's headlines than by Auden upon Setebos. Though so
sincere and talented a writer is not fairly to be compared
with Aldous Huxley, their self-conscious pilgrimages from
modernism to mysticism run curiously parallel. And latterly their insight into our follies and weaknesses has been
made the sudden pretext of an evangelical appeal which,
for those of us who do not happen to be going their way,
is more embarrassing than convincing. Huxley was always a
glib faddist, whereas Auden drew energy from his social
convictions. To have exhausted them so quickly, while the
circumstances they faced are more pressing than ever, does
not heighten the plausibility of his present credo. To be
stalemated by the false dichotomy between a subjective Us
and an objective Them, a sentimental notion of culture and
a naive prejudice against science, is hardly the way to
protect a desire for truth from illusion. It is what we
have learned to expect from our academics and clericals,
our all-too-humanists and quack angelic doctors. But we
still expect something more truly humane from a poet whose
writing has been so lucent and polished a mirror of the
time being.

92. DESMOND MacCARTHY, BEAUTY AND BUGBEAR, 'SUNDAY TIMES'

11 March 1945, 3

Sir Desmond MacCarthy (1877-1952), literary and dramatic
critic, became Drama Critic of the newly established 'New
Statesman' in 1913, and Literary Editor from 1920 to 1927.
From 1928, as well as editing 'Life and Letters' for five

years, he succeeded Sir Edmund Gosse as Senior Literary
Critic on the 'Sunday Times', a position he held until his
death. G.E. Moore, G.M. Trevelyan, Henry James, Shaw, and
the members of the Bloomsbury circle figured among his
early friends and acquaintances. His books include 'Shaw'
(1951), 'Portraits' (1931), and the posthumous 'Memories'
(1953).

I sit down to write a review of this book in a rage - with
it, with myself, and the whole business of reviewing. My
business as a reviewer is to inform others what the two
long poems (made up of dialogues, choruses, prose interludes and soliloquies) which 'For the Time Being' contains,
are about - and I can't; to convey what they are like -
and I can't do that properly either, for that would entail
copious quotation; and, lastly, to estimate how far the
author has succeeded in doing what he set out to do. But
how can a reviewer do that if he has not understood an
author's intentions? Well, I must fumble about as best I
can.

The first poem is concerned with 'The Tempest' in the
sense that here verse and prose are put into the mouths of
characters in that play, but only occasionally are the
words spoken in character. Shakespeare's characters have
turned into symbolic figures defined, as far as they are
defined, so as to be mouthpieces for what Mr. Auden has to
say about - alas, there I am rather stumped - about love?
life? art? I confess I have not grasped his main theme. At
the end Caliban comes forward and in a long prose epilogue
of astonishing virtuosity, full of fascinating and
vigorous phrases, explains - alas, again I fail you. I
think he was sometimes talking, and talking brilliantly,
about Mr. Auden's style and literary methods - at least,
to begin with 'our native Muse' is mentioned, and

> her amazing unheard of power to combine and happily
> contrast, to make *every* shade of the social and moral
> palette to contribute to the general richness, of the
> skill, unapproached and unattempted by Grecian aunt or
> Gaelic sister, with which she can skate full tilt to-
> ward the forbidden incoherence, and then, in the last
> split second, on the shuddering edge of the bohemian
> standardless abyss effect her breath-taking triumphant
> turn.

I must say that, and a great deal more too long to
quote, reminds me of Mr. Auden's poetry at its best
moments. Only in my opinion, his own Muse all too

frequently fails to swerve from the abyss in time. The
chariot of his verse is again and again dashed to pieces
by cutting too fine the corner of nonsense. I know his
generation delight in verbal smithereens, and I admit they
can be exciting.

> He who of these delights can judge and spare
> To interpose them oft, is not unwise;

especially any poet who is also set upon thinking down
into the depths of life. What strikes me as amiss with
'For the Time Being' as a whole, and on the whole, is that
Mr. Auden has not balanced truly his dual allegiance; his
message as a mystic and his devotion to particular aesthetic effects. With the result that he is far more incoherent and allusive than even the difficult nature of
his themes compels him to be. He cannot resist trying to
be mysteriously impressive when it would be in the end
more impressive to try to be clear, even if it is almost
impossible. It would be at any rate more sincere, and in
religious poetry sincerity is of the first importance.

A large part of 'The Sea and the Mirror' is written in
conversational verse, which as Mr. Auden's readers know is
his favourite medium out of which he suddenly breaks into
lofty or ultra-learned diction. There are occasional lines
with a Shakespearean ring:

> O blessed be bleak Exposure on whose sword,
> Caught unawares, we prick ourselves alive!

He triumphs in the drinking song or crazy lyric. Few have
matched him in blending rough humour with flashes of high
imagination. If only the whole poem were as successful as
the song of Master and Boatswain!

[Quotes the song, 'At Dirty Dick's and Sloppy Joe's...',
complete, 18 lines, CP(M), 322-3.]

The second and longer poem is a transposition of the
Gospel story of the Nativity and the flight into Egypt
into terms symbolising Mr. Auden's mystical philosophy. It,
too, contains gleams of surprising beauty, but again what
I call bugbear predominates - the suggestion of some portentous significance which melts when examined. The star
of the Nativity portends 'the doom of orthodox suphrosyne,'
whatever that means. The shepherds, wise men, angels, Mary
herself and Joseph speak, Simeon and Herod also; the two
last in prose. In 'a recitative' I take the poet himself
to be speaking:

Therefore, see without looking, hear without listening,
breathe without asking:
The Inevitable is what will seem to happen to you
purely by chance;
The Real is what will strike you as really absurd;
Unless you are certain you are dreaming, it is certainly a dream of your own;
Unless you exclaim - 'There must be some mistake' - you
must be mistaken.   [CP(M), 274]

That is familiar mystical rhetoric, and that, no doubt, is
sincere.

93. HUGH KINGSMILL ON AUDEN'S SELF-CONSCIOUSNESS, OCCLUDED
PASTURES, 'NEW ENGLISH REVIEW'

xi, May 1945, 79-81

Hugh Kingsmill (1889-1949), born Hugh Kingsmill Lunn,
unillusioned biographer, essayist, novelist, and parodist,
was Literary Editor of 'Punch' and, for twenty years, of
the 'New English Review'. His books include 'Matthew
Arnold' (1928), 'Frank Harris' (1932), 'The Table of Truth'
(parodies, 1933), and 'The Progress of a Biographer'
(1947). See also 'The Best of Hugh Kingsmill' (ed. Michael
Holroyd, 1970).

This volume takes its title from the second of the two
dramatic pieces it contains, perhaps because 'For the Time
Being' aims higher than 'The Sea and the Mirror', being
transcendental in intention and ending on a note of joyful
acceptance which might be convincing if anything in the
poem had led up to it. The vein of genius which runs through
Mr. Auden's work is richer in the first piece than in the
second. Two quotations will show its nature, one from some
verses spoken by Trinculo, the other from a speech
delivered by Caliban.
    The characters in 'The Sea and the Mirror', which has
for its sub-title 'A Commentary on Shakespeare's "The
Tempest"', are Shakespeare's characters reinterpreted by
Mr. Auden, a legitimate device used also by Shakespeare in
his borrowings from other writers. In 'The Tempest'
Trinculo is a brutish clown designed to amuse the pit and
help the story along. Auden's Trinculo is a poet whose

imagination has lifted him into the clouds out of the
world in which once he felt secure and at home.

[Quotes stanzas 1, 3 and 4 of Trinculo's speech, CP(M),
324.]

This longing for the world of childhood is expressed by
Caliban too: 'Give me my passage home, let me see that
harbour once again just as it was before I learned the bad
words. Patriarchs wiser than Abraham mended their nets on
the modest wharf; white and wonderful beings undressed on
the sand-dunes; sunset glittered on the plate-glass windows of the Marine Biological Station; far off on the
extreme horizon a whale spouted. Look, Uncle, look. They
have broken my glasses and I have lost my silver whistle.
Pick me up, Uncle; let little Johnny ride away on your
massive shoulders to recover his green kingdom, where the
steam-rollers are as friendly as the farm dogs....'
There are exquisite touches in these two passages,
which express the nostalgia for childhood as poignantly
as anything in Hans Andersen or 'David Copperfield'. Yet
beautiful though the fruits of this nostalgia are, it is
a limiting emotion which, in spite of a surface likeness,
differs profoundly from the way in which Wordsworth or
Traherne recollected his childhood. For Traherne and
Wordsworth the first years of life were spent not in paradise, but in sight of it: 'Something infinite behind
everything appeared: which talked with my expectation and
moved my desire.' There is a hint of this feeling in
Auden's 'white and wonderful beings', but essentially
childhood is for him, as it was for Dickens or Andersen,
a lost Eden, a state not of promise but of possession, not
of expectancy but of enjoyment. It is true that his intelligence, much more sophisticated than Dickens's or
Andersen's, tells him that this is an illusion, for he
makes Caliban speak of the Eden which memory 'falsely con-
ceives of as the ultimately liberal condition'. But
emotionally he believes in this lost Eden, 'that solid
world these hands can never reach'. Life is for him a
journey away from Eden, not towards it, a retreat into an
always deeper isolation and an increasingly intensified
self-consciousness.
Self-consciousness, with its feeling, partly complacent,
partly self-pitying, of difference from others, is strongest in adolescence, and Auden, though now in the late
thirties, is still adolescent. He uses his imagination not
to unite him to life, but to isolate him from it, drama-
tising himself, according to his mood, as a lost and
lonely figure, like Trinculo, or a forlornly knowing and

devil-may-care one, like Caliban, or even as a - what? How
characterise Antonio, whom Auden invests with an occult
significance and a secret superiority to the others for
which Shakespeare has in no way prepared us? In 'The
Tempest' Antonio is a villain who has dispossessed his
brother Prospero of his dukedom and, after being bewitched
and plagued on Prospero's magic island, is cursorily and
contemptuously pardoned by his injured brother: 'I do for-
give thee, unnatural though thou art.' Shakespeare's
Prospero is to a large degree an agent through whom Shakespeare revenged all the humiliations he had endured as
an actor and playwright from kings and courtiers, and one
can understand Auden being moved to adjust the balance in
favour of Antonio. But the self-love which moulded Shakespeare's conception of Prospero is mild indeed compared
with the self-love which has inflated Auden's Antonio.
Shakespeare's Prospero returns to reality at the close of
'The Tempest':

> Now I want
> Spirits to enforce, art to enchant;
> And my ending is despair
> Unless I be relieved by prayer....

Auden's Antonio dismisses Prospero as 'our melancholy
mentor, the grown-up man, the adult in his pride' who,
unlike Antonio, can 'never enter The green occluded pas-
ture as a child', and then proceeds to distinguish between himself and the rest of the cast in a series of
stanzas, one of which terminates each of the monologues
spoken by the other characters. For example:

> ...Dying Alonso does not know
> The diadem Antonio
>   Wears in his world alone.

> ...Hot Ferdinand will never know
> The flame with which Antonio
>   Burns in the dark alone.

> ...Happy Miranda does not know
> The figure that Antonio,
> The Only One, Creation's O
>   Dances for Death alone

All this is the poet whistling, very melodiously, to
keep up his spirits in the dark. In 'For the Time Being',
his courage suddenly collapsing, the 'alone' with which
each of the ten Antonio stanzas defiantly closes reappears

to express the horror of isolation:

> Alone, alone, about a dreadful wood
> Of conscious evil runs a lost mankind,
> Dreading to find its Father lest it find
> The goodness it has dreaded is not good:
> Alone, alone, about our dreadful wood.

This is moving, but there is little else in 'For the Time
Being' which is not either factitious or trivial. Clearly
Auden is well read in metaphysics and mysticism, but to
write a religious poem it is not enough to look up the
answers; one should also understand the questions. Auden
has spared no expense on his Christmas Oratorio, as he
calls 'For the Time Being'. The characters bear well-known
names - Joseph and Mary, Herod and Simeon, the Wise Men
and the Shepherds; and there are choruses of angels, fugal
choruses, chorales, recitatives, and other garnishings,
the total effect of which is most depressing. No amount of
ingenuity can make good an absence of inspiration, as one
example will be enough to show:

> Our Father whose creative Will
> Asked Being for us All,
> Confirm it that Thy Primal Love
> May weave in us the freedom of
> The actually deficient on
>   The justly actual.

To balance this complicated inanity we have such jets of
silly-simple rapture as -

> Let us run to learn
> How to love and run;
> Let us run to Love

and a great deal of colloquial prose and verse written in
the vein of jaunty disillusion which used to charm Auden's
less intelligent admirers, and perhaps charms them still.

   The general impression left by this volume is that
Auden is at present revolving in a circle; and the circle,
in spite of Antonio, is a symbol of limitation and repetition, not of freedom and creation.

94. STEPHEN SPENDER ON ARGUMENT OR EXPERIENCE, AUDEN,
'TIME AND TIDE'

xxvi, 25 August 1945, 711-12

This is the third volume by Auden containing poems published during the war and since his own departure to
America. He has now returned to Europe, to investigate,
with an American mission, conditions in Germany. The
wheel has come full circle, and it is possible tentatively to consider what has been the profit and loss
account in his poetry of his translation to America.

The first of his American volumes 'Another Time' is
the most miscellaneous collection he has published. Of the
poems written in America, 'September 1st, 1939', with its
famous lines beginning 'All I have is a voice' and ending
'We must love one another or die', is very beautiful and
amongst his best work.

'New Year Letter' opens wonderfully and brilliantly,
then it settles down to being a kind of roving commentary
by an extremely intelligent observer on what might be
called 'contemporary trends'. In this poem one is brought
up immediately against Auden's weaknesses which are of a
kind it is difficult to criticize because they often
appear to be the weakness of the reader, who feels like a
schoolboy who is missing all the interesting things which
the one really important teacher in the school is saying.
Yet perhaps it is Auden's weakness that his range is far
too wide and his conclusions are far too remote from any
vision of how they might be applied. It is not, of course,
that I disagree with the conclusion, frequently reached in
his poems, that we must love one another, but that I think
the really important question is to know how we are to do
so, given the various kinds of physical and intellectual
necessity in which we are all involved. Never was the
situation of the preacher more complicated by the conditions which separate him from his audience than it is
today. One may or may not (for example) accept D.H.
Lawrence's philosophy: but what makes most people indifferent to it, is that Lawrence had to run round the
world in circles in order to practise it himself. Auden in
America may still be developing the ideas which he had in
England but the fact that he has conditioned his own circumstances in such a special way is bound to influence the
content of his work on some level which is not exactly
what he says nor even his technical means of saying it.

The effects of his decision to stay in America are,
indeed, immediately observable. For one thing, he has been

able to produce far more than any poet in England. For another he has become a technical master in the way that Pope and Tennyson were masters. The range of his technique is amazing. He is able to write in any form that he chooses to use, he is always perfectly sure of his effects, he is sometimes full but he never stumbles. One has the impression that Auden is the master of far more forms than he needs ever to use in his writing: whereas Eliot, a great technician also, is only master of a form which he has evolved for the peculiar purposes of what he has, on occasion, to say.

It was surely worth while proving that a modern poet in the English language could acquire a complete mastery of form. Obviously Auden had to stay in America in order to prove this, since he would never have been allowed to write poetry under English mobilization.

The loss, as revealed in these American poems, is a lack of a centre of the poet's own experience from which to write, the lack of a direct and simple relationship with what he writes about, a growing inability to experience things in his poetry. 'New Year Letter' fails because the poet substitutes lots of opinions, lots of prejudices, some principles, and a great deal of miscellaneous reading, for a point of view derived from an integrated and whole experience which includes all that he is writing about. T.S. Eliot has a good many things to say about life in 'Four Quartets' but his comments are the fruit of experience, they are related to what the poet himself *is* after, a lifetime of endeavour; and this existence of the poet is supreme, the knowledge and reasoning which he uses are secondary to it. Auden is a dazzling observer and enormously clever but one relates the conclusions of his poetic arguments to some rational argument or to some book, nearly always, hardly ever to the poet's deepest experience. For this reason, although he is a master of formal patterns, his books themselves are almost entirely lacking in form, they are ideas of a brilliant mind strung together, because they lack that wholeness and depth of form which comes from an inner and complete experience which moulds a work of art into an organic unity.

'For the Time Being' in its strength and in its weaknesses brings all these considerations to mind. 'The Christmas Oratorio' contains very fine passages, is amusing as well as being serious, and, whilst it is impossible to imagine its being set to music, has the power in some of the choruses, of bringing to mind the mighty chorales of Bach. However, the total impression left by the play is not that Christianity is part of Auden's experience, but rather, that he admires tremendously the Christian myth, because he finds it possible to interpret so much of his own myth into it.

The most important part of 'For the Time Being' is (as all the critics seem agreed) the first section, called 'The Sea and the Mirror', which is a kind of poetic commentary on Shakespeare's 'Tempest'. The idea of the poem is that the play is over, the magic island has been abandoned, Prospero's wand cast away, and all the characters are on a boat returning to Milan. Each of them is allowed to utter a lyrical speech in which his innermost mystery, the symbolic meaning of his role in life and his relation to the other characters, are revealed. 'The Tempest' is Shakespeare's most mysterious play and it admits of such interpretation, or rather of such trans-formation: for nothing could be more different than Auden's from Shakespeare's approach. The essence of Shake-speare is surely that he reveals people from the outside, that he believes in the separateness of every person from every other person, the solid and intrinsic and separate reality of every human passion. Auden, on the other hand, tends to expose every motive in terms of every other motive; he inhabits, apparently, a transparent or semi-transparent universe in which all feelings and ideas can be related to each other, in which everything can be ex-plained, and nothing is respected as having a kind of final inexplicable irreducible concrete reality which is not symbolic but which is just itself. Thus it is curious to compare the attitude of Shakespeare's Prospero with that of Auden's. Shakespeare's certainly has magical powers in the sense that he sees everything: nevertheless, things are real to him, he is mystified by Ariel, the evil of Caliban makes him indignant, he can do reverence to Miranda's love, he respects Gonzalo. Auden's Prospero *sees through* everyone, which is quite different. He psycho-analyses Ariel, to him Miranda and Ferdinand are passing through a 'phase':-

> Will Ferdinand be as fond of a Miranda
> Familiar as a stocking? Will a Miranda who is
>   No longer a silly lovesick little goose,
> When Ferdinand and his brave world are her profession,
>   Go into raptures over existing at all?

No wonder that Antonio, reflecting on Prospero's resig-nation of the symbols of power, sighs:-

> Break your wand in half,
> The fragments will join; burn your books or lose

Them in the sea, they will soon reappear,
Not even damaged....

Prospero is the headmaster with the eagle eye who sees
through the motives of all the boys, so it is no use his
breaking up his cane.

Yet the transparency of Mr Auden's analytic method produces the most charming and beautiful results here. The
music of much of this poetry is magical, the imagery
fantastic, and the power of expressing clearly and con-
cretely the most subtle and difficult ideas gives constant
delight. This poem is a masterpiece, and it is difficult
to think that future generations will not discover new and
ever deeper meanings in it.

95. R.G. LIENHARDT, AUDEN'S INVERTED DEVELOPMENT,
'SCRUTINY'

xiii, September 1945, 138-42

Ronald Godfrey Lienhardt is Reader in Social Anthropology,
and a Professorial Fellow of Wolfson College, University
of Oxford; author of 'Social Anthropology' (1964).

It is becoming apparent that any claim to poetic importance which Auden may have in the future will rest upon
effects produced almost casually in his early work. His
experiments have been immensely more promising than his
achievement, and the fact that his poetry has not profited
by them rather indicates that his efforts have not been
directed towards improving his poetry, but towards something at the best extraneous to it, and at the worst extremely damaging. It has become increasingly obvious with
each new publication that this poet's greatest difficulty
lies in determining quite what he wishes to express and in
formulating an appropriate attitude towards it, and that,
at any time, his equipment for dealing with his matter, in
a technical sense, is vastly in excess of what is required.
The correct answer to this problem, for Auden, would have
been to admit to himself that he could range safely only
in a limited field, and to confine himself to saying the
comparatively little that he could say personally, and to
reduce and refine his effects to the minimum necessary for
complete individual expression. Instead of this, he has

attempted to assimilate more and more general ideas, to
write verse based upon human experience quite outside his
individual scope, and hence to write at second-hand. His
technical facility has been lavished upon the expression
of sentimental regrets, boyish fantasies and unbalanced,
immature enthusiasms. Few poets can have started writing
with such superficial promise of accomplishment, have
developed so completely their early weaknesses, and
shelved so definitely their early strength. One is thus
forced to the conclusion that Auden has occasionally
written a few lines worth preserving as a bye-product of
his conscious application to his task - a view which is
supported by a glance through his work. For only such a
series of casual successes will explain the absence of any
single, successful poem, and yet the appearance throughout
of occasional successful passages. Further, it will be
noted that those qualities which make for success remain
undeveloped throughout - that the better parts of his
later work are not an advance on the better parts of his
earlier work, whereas his faults develop in a predictable
way and connect quite simply with weaknesses already
revealed. He has thus undergone an inverted process of
development, natural enough in a poet impervious to criticism from outside the group which formed his ideal public,
and which existed on a basis of mutual admiration which a
more independent poet would have found an embarrassment.

Reading 'Paid on Both Sides', one becomes aware of
moral issues suggested but not fully defined or worked out
in the poetry - there is a residue which one feels one has
not quite grasped, a meaning beyond the literal meaning of
the words on the page, suggested, but persistently elusive.
Images come to have enormous symbolical significance, an
action appears to be in progress between protagonists of
immense importance.

[Quotes 9 lines, from 'O how shall man live...', 'Paid on
Both Sides', EA, 7.]

Here there appear to be possibilities; a situation is
partly realized in an urgent and supple idiom, and there
appears to be a reserve of meaning which might eventually
make itself apparent. But as one reads on one discovers
that the qualified success of this and later poems depends
upon ambiguity - that when a point is reached at which a
definite formulation of an attitude or an issue is made,
one is confronted with a shallow commonplace, something
vaguely defined in terms of 'love', 'beauty' or 'good'.
Just as throughout his work the indefinite evil forces, to
which he seems extremely sensitive, resolve themselves

into nothing more than a succession of images of disease,
sterility or cruelty, so his positive values are the
merest indications of conventional virtues. In fact, there
is no imaginative life whatsoever in Auden's treatment of
moral conflict, and it is a verbal fluency, incorporating
a number of effectively juxtaposed images, appearing to
make a general impression by putting together a number of
smaller impressions united at the most by compatible moods,
which gives a specious vitality to much of his earlier
work. He is consequently at his weakest when he is most
explicit, when the suggestiveness of his language has to
give way to a bald statement. Then the alarming paucity of
an idea beneath the surface of his impressionistic
facility reveals itself, and in his yearning for

New styles of architecture, a change of heart   [EA, 36]

one realizes that Auden is attempting to diagnose the
spiritual malady of an age with the experiential equipment
of the man in the street. Again, it becomes more and more
obvious throughout Auden's work that his morbidity and
disillusion, which have always the insecurity of pose, are
in fact nothing more than a fashionable accretion, perhaps
unconscious and unavoidable, and that fundamentally he is
committed to an easy materialistic optimism, that somewhere and somehow agents for good are at work, though what
the 'good' is and how these indefinite virtuous ends are
to be achieved is more than he can tell us. We know that
'It is time for the destruction of error', but after the
inevitable, and sometimes effective, sequence of related
images which follow that announcement in the poem from
which it is extracted, all we discover is that the 'death
of the old gang' is a necessary preliminary, and that
after

The old gang to be forgotten in the spring,
The hard bitch and the riding-master,
Stiff underground...

we may see

deep in a clear lake
The lolling bridegroom, beautiful, there.   [EA, 40]

What success this has depends upon its lack of explicitness, and it is therefore not surprising that 'For the
Time Being', which is in places the most explicit work he
has produced yet, if in places the most ambiguous, should
also be much the least satisfactory.

'For the Time Being' consists of two compositions of
indeterminate genre, with a persistent suggestion of
having been adapted for broadcasting. The first, called
'The Sea and the Mirror', is an attempted extension of
'The Tempest' into regions more uncertainly defined, both
geographically and philosophically, than Prospero's island.
The second is the title-piece of the whole and is described as 'A Christmas Oratorio'. Both are dramatized and
have prose inserts of considerable length, in which the
essentials of the situation being treated are discussed
very tediously with the audience. Here, much of the poet's
intention, already apparent from the verse, is unnecessarily emphasized, and much that remained obscure in the
verse is presented with no added clarity in laboured and
ungainly prose. In both works he indulges his increasing
taste for general philosophical propositions, concerns
himself with much deeper issues than he is at all competent to do justice to, and becomes involved in a complex
of ideas which he has neither the intellectual sweep nor
the emotional integrity to assimilate as a poet. The first
poem is much the less explicit of the two, and is accordingly the more successful; but here the allegorical
figures have such a wide possible field of reference, and
the indication of any definite level at which the poem is
to be understood as a whole is so vague, that the whole
point of allegory is lost, the meaning too dependent on
individual construction. (A reviewer in one of the
literary weeklies, for example, connected Prospero with
Democracy). Instead of working out his general ideas in
particular and concrete terms throughout the poem, so that
the interplay of concepts and qualities becomes something
accessible to the mind and feelings at once, the poet
provides his familiar association of images and metaphors,
but with no suggestion of any coherent imaginative scheme
for the whole. In consequence, there is a superficial
suggestion throughout that some impressive action is being
worked out, but on closer examination the significance of
it evaporates, and one is left with the theme of the resolution of the duality of Ariel and Caliban, with other
characters from 'The Tempest' who may mean this, that or
the other according to the general construction which the
reader puts on the main theme. There are occasional
passages of pleasant imagery which excite no complaint,
unless it be that even here Auden's rhythms are becoming
flaccid and his language more reflective than active.
Above all, there is a persistent inflated manner which one
can trace back without difficulty to earlier work in which
the poet permitted himself to preach too unguardedly.
Compare, for example:

> Greed showing shamelessly her naked money,
> And all Love's wondering eloquence debased
> To a collector's slang, Smartness in furs,
> And Beauty scratching miserably for food...   [EA, 157]

with his more recent

> O blessed be bleak exposure on whose sword
> Caught unawares, we prick ourselves alive!
> Shake Failure's bruising fist....

There can be few clearer signs of lack of poetic vitality
than these automatically produced catalogues of abstract
qualities, all doing something conventionally appropriate
or with conventionally suitable attributes, but no more
vivid or disturbing than if they had remained in the
dictionary. At the best, they are dull; at the worst, they
are absurd, as when the Star of the Nativity in the second
poem invites one to

> Hear tortured Horror roaring for a Bride....

The habit of using capital letters for emphasis, where
true emphasis would be achieved by a well-managed sentence
construction and rhythm, is one which has grown on Auden.
It results not infrequently in an appearance of extraordinary pretentiousness, emphasized by the complete flatness of the straightforward, unambiguous statement, as in
the following:

> Sin fractures the Vision, not the Fact; for
> The Exceptional is always usual
>   And the Usual exceptional.
> To choose what is difficult all one's days
> As if it were easy, that is faith...

'A Christmas Oratorio', from which the last quotation
comes, is an example of how bad Auden can be when it comes
to treatment of clearly defined moral issues - in this
case the theme of the Nativity, with comments by a
Narrator who is, presumably, the detached observer of the
action, pointing the moral but by no means adorning the
tale. There is no place here to quote examples of his
lapses of taste, his lack of proportion which makes him
self-important when he wishes to be serious, frivolous or
even nasty when he wants to be witty. His values, uncertain and unsystematized, represent nothing appreciably
solid or coherent. This subject, if it is to be treated
tolerably, demands either genuine simplicity or genuine

sophistication in the artist. The poet who writes at one
end of the scale

> Come to our well-run desert
> Where anguish arrives by cable
>   And the deadly sins may be bought in tins
> With instructions on the label...

and at the other

> He is the Way.
> Follow him through the Land of Unlikeness;
> You will see rare beasts, and have unique adventures

has neither qualification. For it is in just that irresponsible spirit, of undefined but 'unique' adventure, that
he approaches his material - The Nativity, 'The Tempest',
the Oedipus legend in 'The Ascent of F6'.

That Auden started his career with apparently unusual
gifts cannot be denied; and even this volume displays, in
places, snatches of his old accomplishment. But it has no
chance when set against his determination to write on a
grand scale with the mental equipment only of a minor poet.
If his seriousness of purpose were part of his nature
instead of yet another, if unconscious, attitude, his
tendency to the cheap, commonplace and exhibitionistic
might not persist. But it is clear from this volume that
his separation from the circle in which that tendency was
formed came too late to enable him to discard his public
character and see what values of his own he could substitute for those of the group which made his reputation.

'The Collected Poetry of W.H. Auden'

New York, April 1945

Auden urged Saxe Commins at Random House to issue a one-
volume collection of his poems as early as 16 January
1942: 'I hate to behave with the traditional petulant
vanity of the author, but I *should* like people to be able
to get hold of my work' (quoted in Humphrey Carpenter,
'W.H. Auden: A Biography', London: Allen & Unwin, 1981,
p. 329). In a letter of 10 June 1951 he explained to
Stephen Spender why he had chosen to order the poems ach-
ronologically by first lines: 'My reason for doing that
was not to pretend that I have gone through no historical
change, but because there are so very few readers who can
be trusted to approach one's poems without a preconceived
notion of what that development has been. I wanted to test
the reader who believes that my earliest poems are my
best; e.g. make him read a poem and then guess its date'
(ibid., p. 331).

96. F. CUDWORTH FLINT REVIEWS 'AN AGILE INTELLIGENCE',
'NEW YORK TIMES'

8 April 1945, section 7, 1, 28-9

After beginning the Nineteen Twenties by luxuriating in
post-war disillusionment, intellectuals began to look
about for a less empty topic. Those who were poor and indignant took up Marxism. The wealthy and exhausted took up
Freudianism. Only poetry lagged behind. The newest star -
T.S. Eliot's - had risen over a Waste Land. It did move on,
but to take its stand above a secluded garden dedicated to
the pruned Catholicism of the High Anglicans. The times

were not going that way. What poet would be their fellow-
traveler in their pilgrimage away from Canterbury?
    In 1930 appeared in England the 'Poems' of W.H. Auden,
and the answer had been found. Here was a mind energetic,
inquisitive, modern; a technique dexterous and Protean; an
interest in, if not exactly an espousal of, the Communist
principles, and an imagery and vocabulary so permeated by
the materials and terms of psychoanalysis as at times almost to seem 'clinical' - thereby realizing an announced
aim of the author. Perhaps this young poet, late of Oxford and just returned from the spiritual Babel of Berlin,
would, as soon as his first enthusiasm for collecting information and styles had sobered somewhat, achieve the
fusion of Marx and Freud, of the outer revolution and the
inner purge, which might be the religion of the era to
come.
    But Mr. Auden was not going *that* way. As book followed
book - the curious medley of verse, prose and diagrams
called 'The Orators'; in a collaboration with Christopher
Isherwood, the satiric extravaganzas, 'The Dog Beneath the
Skin' and 'The Ascent of F6'; in collaboration with the
poet Louis MacNeice, a medley in verse and prose of travel
and comment on civilization in general entitled 'Letters
from Iceland,' and a similar book (with Isherwood) about
China called 'Journey to a War'; another collection of
poems, 'On this Island' (the English title is 'Look,
Stranger!'); several anthologies, including the 'Oxford
Book of Light Verse,' and, after his coming to America in
1939 to live, further collections of poems - 'Another
Time,' 'The Double Man,' and his recent brilliant 'For the
Time Being' - from all these it became clear that even his
style had been wrongly perceived. Sheer variousness was not
its chief characteristic.

It is true that a line here, a phrase there, may record
some one or another of Auden's numerous momentary flirtations: with the style of T.S. Eliot, the later Yeats,
Emily Dickinson, A.E. Housman, Gerard Manley Hopkins, and
perhaps some of Auden's more elaborate stanza-patterns -
molds into which the material is neatly fitted rather than
consummations of the rhythms of the lines - derive from his
early interest in Thomas Hardy. In spite of all such surface influences, however, he has developed a way with words
which is recognizably and emphatically his own.
    This way is constituted by a vocabulary rather than a
single style. Auden dislikes what he called 'damp' poetry;
that is to say, romantic or emotionally resonant or 'pure'
poetry. He even has recipes for avoiding it; he mostly ex-
cludes colors and scents from his poems, and emphasizes

shapes. His vocabulary ranges from terms of abstract analysis to homely epithets of contemporary realism, as in

> Abruptly mounting her ramshackle wheel,
> Fortune has pedaled furiously away

And Auden's movements back and forth along this range are
managed with easy swiftness. One, for instance, might not
expect a poem entitled 'Heavy Date' and beginning in the
neutral center of the range

> Sharp and silent in the
> Clear October lighting
> Of a Sunday morning
>   The great city lies,

to pass easily to

> Love has no position,
> Love's a way of living,
> One kind of relation
>   Possible between
> Any things or persons
> Given one condition,
> The one sine qua non
>   Being mutual need.

But in some of the poems from his earliest book (which
can usually be spotted at a glance by their short lines
and lack of a stanza-pattern) a terseness of syntax, even
though the diction is simple, involves the reader in
puzzles. There are too many alternative meanings which will
account for all the words set down on the page. Auden may
have been emulating the riddling brevity of the Icelandic
sagas, which have impressed him - he is of Icelandic descent; but, at least to the non-Icelander, an Icelandic
riddle is a riddle still. In his later books he has relaxed this terseness, and none of his more recent poems
say too little to tell their tale. It is mostly these
earlier poems that gave given him the reputation of being
'difficult.'

Obviously, a vocabulary such as Auden's is well adapted
to satire, and Auden at his best can be an excellent satirist - when the demands of neatness imposed by satirical
point are not overcome by his tendency to slapdash improvisation. He himself has recognized this tendency, and
some of the longer poems in the 'Collected Poems' have been
pruned of superfluous stanzas and merely personal
allusions.

Come to our bracing desert
Where eternity is eventful,
    For the weather-glass
    Is set at Alas,
The thermometer at Resentful.

Come to our well-run desert
Where anguish arrives by cable,
    And the deadly sins
    May be bought in tins
With instructions on the label

is pointedly satiric. But it will serve as a transition to
another of Auden's main accomplishments, which might not be
expected from what I have said of his vocabulary.

This is his success in creating a sense of the ominous.
Building in his earlier work on his researches into the
dreads of the neurotic - he is the son of a physician -
and in his later work on a realistically religious estimate of the role of Possibility in man's fate, Auden has
become almost a specialist in the terror-to-come. Sometimes such warnings are expressed in the language of psychoanalysis or abstract discussion, but more often they
are conveyed through scenes in which, by a method akin to
that of Chirico, the portrayed detail becomes ominous because it is portrayed in isolation from its expected ac-
companiments. In a Chirico painting, what is that building which exists only to block our view around a corner,
whence not even a shadow suggests what may lie beyond?
Who is that single figure running in the distance down the
deserted street? Similarly, in Auden

        behind you without a sound
The woods have come up and are standing round
        in deadly crescent.

The bolt is sliding in its groove,
Outside the window is the black remov-
            er's van.   [The Witnesses, EA, 130]

These scenes implying peril are usually compounded of a
rugged countryside and ruined mines and factories (reflecting Auden's early acquaintance with Derbyshire and Yorkshire) and with the distresses of industrialism in the
English Midland counties. It is noticeable that since he
has come to America this scenic element has faded from his
poetry.

About the time Auden came to the United States it became
quite evident to any reader that he was not traveling, as
I have mentioned, toward any fusion of Marx and Freud.
In his 'New Year Letter' appears a passage discriminat-
ingly appreciative of Marx, but none of his earlier 'Communist' poems – few at best – have been retained in this
latest collection. For Auden, economic distresses have
been rather symptoms than causes; or at least, he had not
thought of them as total or chief causes. He has latterly
passed on from psychology by the frontier away from economics; the frontier bordering religion. Isherwood was too
hasty when he wrote in the 'Auden Number' of 'New Verse'
(November, 1937) that from Auden's High Anglican rearing
the only remains were a tendency to ritualism in constructing plays, and a good ear for music. To be sure, it is not
as a disciple of Anglican theologians, nor as a proponent
of that visible Catholic Church, that Auden has come to reaffirm the Christian position. Judging by references in his
poetry and criticism, I should say that the Danish theolo-
gian Kierkegaard had been the strongest influence; and his
present position is not unlike the 'Neo-orthodoxy' connected in this country specially with the influence of
Reinhold Niebuhr.

In brief, in addition to the world as a spectacle known
to art, and the world as a terrain for improvement by reg-
ulation known to ethics, Auden adds another interpretation
of life: the world as the perpetual invitation and intention to choose love. The primacy and validity of this ideal
has been made known to mankind by the transit of the Eternal into the temporal in the Incarnation. But this choice
will never – for the individual – be completely successful,
completely realized. For it is carried out in the presence
of necessities which sometimes confuse and sometimes pre-
clude a proper choice. Again, this choice is carried out
within time, and we cannot be certain of all the consequences in future time of our particular choices. Finally,
every successful choice has been achieved by skirting at
least two opposite errors, even when there are no more.
The most generalized forms of error Auden finds to be dualism, which suggests that there is a valid realm where
Truth has no validity; the kind of monism which insists
that all manifestations in human life of reality must follow a single pattern or kind – esthetic or ethical – of
pattern, and atomism: the idea that each human being can
create his own universe for himself, and there's an end
on't.

It is in 'For the Time Being: A Christmas Oratorio' –
one of the two poems making up the book so titled – that
this religious position receives its fullest statement, in

what most critics agree is a brilliant poem. In it Auden does not forget to present in a delightful prose address the feelings of the outraged scientific liberal, Herod, to whom the Incarnation is the lapse of enlightenment back into superstitious barbarism. But Auden takes his stand with Simeon, who in his meditation finds in the Incarnation the interpretation and support of history, art, science and the redemption of man.

In the just-published 'Collected Poems' Auden has preserved most of what has appeared in the earlier books of poems, except that very little of 'The Orators' has been retained: some of the Six Odes and a few shorter pieces, but of the prose in that book, only the Letter to a Wound. Poems appearing first in the two books of travel are reprinted here, and there are twenty-four poems previously uncollected. This is a convenient edition of Auden, and those previously unacquainted with him would do well to begin with it. However, persons wishing to make a thorough study of him must still obtain the earlier separate volumes.

Nobody has any business to presume to sum up a poet until the poet is dead. In fact, a complete summing up might be achievable only as the terminus of a complete losing of interest. In one passage of the 'New Year Letter' Auden, speaking of Art, says of its manifestations

> Now large, magnificent, and calm,
> Your changeless presences disarm
> The sullen generations, still
> The fright and fidget of the will,
> And to the growing and the weak
> Your final transformations speak,
> Saying to dreaming 'I am deed.'
> To striving, 'Courage. I succeed.'
> To mourning, 'I remain. Forgive.'
> And to becoming 'I am. Live.'

This is not a complete theory of all Art; indeed, Auden has elsewhere, through the person of Caliban, who is using the idiom of Henry James, gone into the matter more fully, more delightfully, and with needed extensions of doctrine. Still, the quoted lines express what is true of much art. But not, I think, quite of Auden's. It is not full of presences that are magnificent and calm. On the contrary, most of it is full of the fright and fidget, the striving and the weak. These, however, are fixed by the poet's scrutiny, immobilized for our inspection by the novel tactic of the really just phrase.

Hence, we grow familiar with our fright and fidget; we
see just what these are; we come to the realization that
we are not, we cannot continue to be, like *that*; and so,
in its own way, Auden's poetry carries out its admirable
therapy. Nevertheless, it would be a great mistake to con-
centrate solemnly on the therapy. For though we now see
that Auden is one of the most seriously intelligent minds
of his generation, he remains deft, agile, dexterous. And
joy in dexterity is a right kind of morality also. So let
us be joyful in it.

97. LOUISE BOGAN, UNTITLED REVIEW, 'NEW YORKER'

xxi, 14 April 1945, 78, 81

Auden prefigured his efforts to revise early poems in this
letter of 18 May 1942 to Louise Bogan:

> Now and then I look through my books and is my face red.
> One of the troubles of our time is that we are all, I
> think, precocious as personalities and backward as cha-
> racters. Looking at old work I keep finding ideas which
> one had no business to see already at that age, and a
> style of treatment which one ought to have outgrown
> years before.
>   I sometimes toy with re-writing the whole lot when
> I'm senile, like George Moore. (Amherst College Library;
> a shorter extract figures in Carpenter, op. cit., p.
> 330)

He responded to this review on 13 April 1945, 'What a
swell write up you gave me in the New Yorker this week.
Thanks a lot. The only thing that makes me feel uncomfortable are the references to the Master of Russell Square.
I shall never be as great and good a man if I live to be a
hundred' (Amherst College Library). See also Introduction
and No. 41 above.

A moment occurs (or should occur) when the growing artist
is able to bequeath his tricks to his imitators. The mature
writer rejects the treasured 'originality' and the darling
virtuosities of his apprenticeship in art, as well as the
showy sorrows and joys of his apprenticeship life, often
just in time. 'How they live at home in their cozy poems

amd make long stays in narrow comparisons!' Rilke once
said, speaking of the run of versifiers, who never change
or grow. Once youth's embroidered coat is cast aside, what
is left? Only imagination, ripened insight, experience,
and the trained sense of language, which are usually
enough.

'The Collected Poetry of W.H. Auden' is a sizable volume
for a poet born in 1907 to have credited to him in 1945.
Auden, it has for some time been apparent, has succeeded
Eliot as the strongest influence in American and British
poetry. And he has managed, in this collection, by skill-
ful arrangement and deletion, to present himself to the
reader as he exists at this moment. He does not draw attention to his growing pains or take us step by step
through stage after stage of his development. He begins
the book with one of those poems ('Musée des Beaux Arts')
which announced, a few years ago, the beginnings of his
maturity - a poem that seems as simply composed as a passage in conversation. It is not filled with Anglo-Saxon
compression, or clogged with modern apparatuses and
machines, or trimmed with off-rhymes. Earlier poems on
his favourite subjects and in the special manner of his
youth are included in the book. But they never leap out at
us. The general tone is one of composure and simplicity,
of that ease wherein, for a time, a young master can rest.

The collection gathers up, fortunately, poems that have
so far been scattered in plays or books of prose. The fine
sonnet to E.M. Forster once served as the dedication for
'Journey to a War,' which was written in collaboration with
Christopher Isherwood. Other sonnets and a verse commentary come from the same volume. The fine 'Journey to Iceland' is out of 'Letters from Iceland.' written in collaboration with Louis MacNeice. Some choruses from plays
turn up as separate poems, now with titles. The volume
also contains two prose passages - the early Letter to a
Wound and a new 'sermon' entitled 'Depravity.' Last
autumn's 'For the Time Being' is reprinted complete, and
there are several new poems.

What is the particular thread that runs through this
collection, the clue to Auden's importance and power?
In what way is his great gift different from Eliot's, and
in what way is it of importance to Auden's contemporaries?
Auden shares with Eliot a sense of his time. He is, however, much more exuberant, restless, sanguine, and unself-
conscious than the older poet. And he is a natural dramatist in a degree surpassing Eliot. Eliot can dramatize his
lyrics but cannot project real dramatic action with force.
Auden dramatizes everything he touches. He is wonderfully
effective with that most dramatic of lyric forms, the

ballad. At the same time, his purely lyrical endowment   is
so deep and so natural that many of his songs sound as
though they had been worked up at a moment's notice as im-
provisations. He can sing about as many things as the Elizabethans, and with the same disregard for the demands of
the high literary line and the 'refined' literary tone.
Eliot's importance is based on the fact that he had the
sensitiveness and the melancholy foreboding to sense the
general tragedy of his period when that tragedy had not
yet impressed other observers. Auden, nearly twenty years
Eliot's junior, stands farther from the shadow of the nineteenth and early twentieth centuries; he is more able,
therefore, to deal with particulars. He is conscious of
his physical surroundings down to the last contraption of
'light alloys and glass;' conscious of his spiritual scene
down to the last sob of modern self-pity, down to modern
brutality's last threat. He has smashed the 'tabu against
tenderness,' as someone has said, he is not afraid or ashamed either to laugh or weep. (How gloomy everyone was,
after Eliot!) He knows what Rilke felt and foresaw, what
Kierkegaard rebelled against, what modern psychiatry has
plumbed. He is not ignorant of facts or clumsy in dealing
with them. He is able to absorb and speak of any item in
the extraordinary crowd of objects and techniques he finds
on all sides. He is able to define and present a range of
ideas, passions, compulsions, manias, anxieties, fears,
and intuitions that at present float about, only half-
perceived by many people and most poets, in our intellectual and emotional climate. He is at once able to act and
to imagine, to formulate and interpret.

Behind him stand exemplars he acknowledges - Rilke and
Henry James, Freud, the Symbolists and post-Symbolists,
and Surrealism at its most effective. Part of the excitement in reading the volume through derives from the fact
that we are dealing with a poet one of whose inner urges
will always be to transcend himself, that we are reading
the work of one who is still a young man, and that there
will be more to come.

98. JOHN VAN DRUTEN, HE BRIDGED THE ATLANTIC, 'KENYON
REVIEW'

vii, Summer 1945, 507-11

Born in England, Van Druten (1901-57) wrote numerous plays,

among them 'I Am a Camera' (adapted from Christopher
Isherwood's Berlin stories), the basis for the musical
'Cabaret'.

The publishers' jacket tells us he is 37. It is a figure
which lies transparently coded in every line he has
written, not only as the product, but also as the mouthpiece, the oracle and the prophet of his generation, to
whom the world before or immediately after the last war -
the background of security, real or imagined, to the
Georgian poets, for example, exists only as the memory of
a childhood that betrayed its promises and now excites mistrust rather than nostalgia. Auden's sympathetic understanding, expressed through his poems, operates almost exclusively on the certainties of the classics or the doubt-
ings of the world in which, since, 1918, he grew up, the
storm clouds darkening the sky with each year of advancing
awareness. The war that broke out in 1914 took its poets
by surprise, if one is to judge from their poems; the war
of 1939 is foreshadowed in almost every line that Auden
wrote before it cracked his world open.
    Now in 1945, gathering 'all that he wishes to preserve'
of his poetry, he sits in judgment on his own achievement,
and passes what must seem to his admirers a harsh sentence.
The bulk of this book, if one is to believe his brief preface, consists of pieces 'which he has nothing against except their lack of importance.' That is an utterance which
would seem to indicate an excess of sensibility, but if it
tempts one to the question: 'Why reproduce them, then?'
the poet has his answer ready. 'Because,' he says, 'were
he to limit his book to those poems for which he is honestly grateful, his volume would be too depressingly slim.'
One wonders faintly about this preface, matching the word
'importance,' used when he denies it to his work, against
its evasion in the second half of the sentence when logic
would seem to demand it. Modesty can lead one onto equivocal ground.
    Two classes of poem he tells us he has omitted alto-
gether; those which he frankly regrets as pure rubbish;
and those in which the vision outran performance, and so
disappointed him. Curious always as to the man behind the
writer, one turns, detective-like, to see what he has left
out, gasps at the amount, and then begins to speculate on
why, trying to assign each missing poem to one or other
of the classes. The cabaret song 'Tell Me the Truth About
Love' belongs, one supposes, to the first class, though
why it, more than some of the other lighter pieces, is
hard to know. The more serious discarded poems one must

believe to have been disappointments to the author, but their rejection seems in many cases something of a rebuke to one's own taste for having admired them. I have looked for what I have always thought an exquisite poem, beginning: 'Here on the cropped grass of the narrow ridge I stand,' and failed to find it; although, as there is lamentably no index of first lines, as chronology has been disregarded and half the poems have new titles assigned to them, it is possible that I have overlooked it. If it is not there, it seems a pity; more than a pity; its absence damages the book like a torn-out page.

The poem on A.E. Housman, with its bitter, brilliant couplet:

Deliberately he chose the dry-as-dust,
Kept tears like dirty postcards in a drawer

- that is omitted, too. Again one must suppose it to come into the second category, unless some scruples of taste have provided a third. Why is the ballad of James Honeyman not here, when its companion ballads of Victor and Miss Gee are included? Can it have something to do with the use or non-use of poison gas in this war? That makes a fourth reason for omissions. One wishes he had not done this, had not paid court to the moving finger, luring it back to cancel whole poems, and in other cases literally washing out one word of them. In 'A Bride of the Thirties,' the phrase: 'The new pansy railway' has been changed to 'the strategic railway.' Still, the new way is the better, and perhaps it is only envy that wonders about an author's right to the *esprit de l'escalier*.

And the bulk of the poems are here untouched, together with a handful of new ones. They remain brilliant, provocative, often - to use his own phrase - 'amazing as thunderstorms' - and often more than a little obscure. The obscurity would seem to spring from two causes, one legitimate, the other perhaps more questionable. The omitted thought-links, that ask the reader to make great chamois-leaps of association; the transferred metaphors that demand of him an alertness and ingenuity equal to the poet's own - these are the idiom and the privilege not only of Auden, but of all his generation who have discarded the direct statement and the frank simile. But there are times, too, when one senses some family joke, some personal allusion to an incident or occasion known only to the person for or about whom the poem is written, and one longs for footnotes to explain them.

But he is a magnificent poet, earning both our gratitude and our pride that these years of dreadfulness should have

produced a figure so likely, as far as one can read the
signs for his contemporaries, to rank with those who speak
truth for all times as well as for their own. Technically,
he is amazing, both in his facility and fertility which
seems so inexhaustible that one can relax to them as to
some kind of natural bounty, and in his colossal range that
covers and is at home in half a dozen different styles.
He has an electrifying gift of phrase, of which some of
the most beautiful and dazzling examples occur in: 'Dover
1937,' and in the really lovely poem called 'A Commentary.'
In other places, it occasionally produces lines like this:

O little restaurant where the lovers eat each other,[EA, 235]

which, though it will recur to the mind for quotation in
every bistro in the world, yet has a little more the ring
of prose than poetry.

But beyond that and infinitely more important than
either his technical virtuosity or his genius for phrase-
making is the emotional content of his work, his complete
self-identification with every human need or perplexity,
willing to trace back in himself the whole chain of caus-
ation to its obscurist roots in the sub-conscious. In his
later poems, the note has changed and deepened; the faculties of sympathy, reason and analysis fuse into a spiritual seeking and awareness, colored with mysticism. The
'Christmas Oratorio' with which this book ends has all the
brilliance of his earlier verse (and some magnificent prose
as well), but also a humility of spirit, never so clearly
seen in him before, that causes a new radiance to arise
from off the printed page.

Reading as much of any poet at one time as a collected
volume necessitates is never quite fair to the subject.
Echoes begin to sound in the ear, suggesting habits; and
the mind inclines itself mechanically to parody or imitation. There is in Auden a note of awful warning, a series
of symbols of doom and disaster hidden in the innocent and
humdrum trappings of material living, which are so recurrent that one finds oneself automatically improvising more:

And Hell is under the Hydro,
And the Front where the Nannies sit,
And the dropped stitch in the knitting,
Looks straight into the pit.

It would not seem too hard to go on.

This sinister motif is, to me, the most insistent sound
in all of Auden's work, ringing from the moment when I heard
it in the first poem of his that I ever encountered. This

was the poem now entitled 'The Witnesses,' which I have
previously thought of as 'The Two.' It is typical of him
(and again of his generation) that he never identifies
this grim pair. I was amused recently to find Walter de
la Mare's poem 'The Listeners' reprinted in an American
School Reader, and below it a series of questions, of
which the first was: 'Who do you think the Traveller might
have been?' Now I had once been worried by this, myself,
having first read the poem at an age when I was accustomed
to the symbolism of poets whose figures were strictly allegorical, either announcing themselves as Love, Death or
Chastity in the last line, or else being unmistakably
recognizable as such from the beginning. A flippant friend
to whom I read aloud the question, answered: 'Jesus Christ,
of course. It always is.' The point of the story, however,
is that when I asked the schoolboy to whom the Reader belonged to put the question to his English teacher, the
answer was just that. 'She said she thought it might have
been Jesus Christ.' Poetry, to most of her generation - to
most of any generation before the present one - had to be
specific, cut to certain standard moulds, as Rupert Brooke
indicated when he discovered that the Browning family's
poems all suddenly referred to God in the last line. The
larger unspecified implications of Auden's prophecies and
pronouncements are as typical as anything about him of the
poems of the men of 37 or under.

There is one last thing to be said about him, so obvious
as to account perhaps for its being so often overlooked or
taken for granted, which is to me almost his most important claim to merit. As far as I am aware, he is the only
poet to have bridged the Atlantic, to have absorbed completely the essence of both England and America, and to
have made himself bilingual and bi-sensual as artist and
as human being. If the airplane has shrunk the 3000 miles
that separate them in distance to a day's division, it
seems to me that Auden's beautiful and deeply-searching
poetry has drawn them to a span no larger than the space
between the covers of this book. And that, in these days
especially, is something for which both we and he may be -
to use the words of his preface - 'honestly grateful.'

'The Age of Anxiety'

New York, July 1947; London, September 1948

99. M.L. ROSENTHAL, SPEAKING GREATLY IN AN AGE OF CON-
FUSION, 'NEW YORK HERALD TRIBUNE'

20 July 1947, section 7, 3

M.L. Rosenthal (b. 1917), poet and critic, has taught at
New York University since 1945. His publications include
'The Modern Poets' (1960), 'The New Poets: American and
British Poetry since World War II' (1967), and 'Sailing
into the Unknown: Yeats, Pound, and Eliot' (1978).

This is the first poem, in English at any rate, that speaks
boldly, greatly and at length of our sick, desperate confusion in this era of the second world war. It will give
sharp reminder to our numerous talented minor poets that
there can be strength and responsibility in their art:

> All that exists
> Matters to man; he minds what happens
> And feels he is at fault, a fallen soul
> With power to place, to explain every
> What in his world but why he is neither
> God nor good....

The vigor, even the quality, of the ideas in 'The Age of
Anxiety' must obviously be tested by their influence on its
readers, many of whom will doubtless find Auden's diagnosis, with all its pessimism, infinitely superior to his
suggested cure. But no one who takes up this emotionally
stunning work is likely to concern himself immediately with
whether or not he agrees with the author. Rather, his attention will be absorbed by the various centers of

concentration along which the 'plot' is strung, each of them one aspect of a continuous, straining effort to get at the heart of the human condition and trace the lines of possible (or impossible) salvation. He will be carried along, too, by the muscular alliterative sweep of the lines, subtly and marvelously varied from the simple basic pattern to fit a number of modes, from sweet lyric to intellectualized argument, from sharp satire to poignant introspection.

Auden calls his poem 'a baroque eclogue,' because, says the jacket, it adopts the 'pastoral convention in which a natural setting is contrasted with an artificial style of diction.' (But I fear there is a sad pun in that 'baroque,' considering the setting of most of the poem!). On All Souls' Night, in a war year, four people - an elderly intellectual, a cynical old failure who knows a great deal of mythology, an idealistic young sailor who lacks self-confidence, and a day-dreaming Jewish girl whose 'experiences' and success as a department store buyer cannot rid her of her feelings of guilt and shame - find themselves in a Third Avenue bar. War news on the radio throws their thoughts in the same channels, and soon they are discussing the terrible moral ambiguities of the war.

From this point on, in three allegorical sequences, the poem explores every man's guilt, in terms of the 'seven ages' of Shakespeare and the personal lives of the characters; takes us on a journey in search of that impossible 'prehistoric happiness which, by human beings, can only be imagined in terms of a landscape bearing symbolic resemblance to the human body'; and dismisses the great romantic love-dream as a way out of the trap which man, with helpless yet evil foreknowledge, sets for himself. The world is too much, in different ways, for the youth and the old cynic; but the girl and the intellectual, in burning assertions of their separate faiths, accept suffering and the grim task of reconciling 'the clock we are bound to obey. And the miracle we must not despair of.'

This poem is so rich, has so many facets, that no brief review can be just to its meaning or technique. It appears, at first reading, to be one of the splendid poems of our language; it convinces, it moves, it dazzles; It is hardly time to quibble with this work, and I doubt that it will ever be. One does not quibble with 'The Waste Land,' whatever one's ideas, and this is another such case.

100. JACQUES BARZUN ON A PHILOSOPHICAL POEM, 'HARPER'S
MAGAZINE'

cxcv, September 1947, back matter, i-ii

A distinguished scholar and author, Barzun (b. 1907) first
taught at Columbia University in 1927, concluded as Uni-
versity Professor Emeritus, and has been Literary Adviser
to Scribner's, New York, since 1975. He was awarded the
Legion of Honour, and is an Extraordinary Fellow of
Churchill College, Cambridge. His books include 'The French
Race' (1932), 'Berlioz and the Romantic Century' (1950),
'Classic, Romantic and Modern' (1961), 'Clio and the
Doctors' (1974), and 'Simple and Direct' (1975).
This extract is taken from Workers in Monumental Brass.

When the house is cleared, that is, when the important figures have been shoveled under at public expense, and the
world-shaking events are forgotten, especially and repeatedly by schoolboys, and the big books that everyone had to
read are offered for ten cents on sidewalk stalls, the one
thing left by the scavengers of waste is usually a small
volume of shorthand notes on what took place, written by an
obscure young man who posthumously grows into a great poet.
Only through Homer or Blake, Shelley or Milton, Villon or
Hardy, do we seem to be able to find out what happened. We
learn much else from knowing them, but surely the most remarkable thing is the discovery that the ideal substance
for taking and holding the impress of time is poetry - particularly when it is not purposely trying to do it.
   These reflections occurred to me as I read the last
prose words in Mr. W.H. Auden's new poem, 'The Age of
Anxiety': 'he returned to duty, reclaimed by the actual
world where time is real, and in which therefore poetry
can take no interest.' The magnificent semi-pastoral, semi-
naturalistic drama which ends thus stands of course in
direct contradiction to what has just been quoted from it.
The very title, 'Age of Anxiety,' roots it in our generation; the scene is wartime New York, and the four characters speak the speech of their decade, be it slang, advertising slogans, or military allusion. One says 'Time flies.'
'No,' rejoins the other,

        Time returns, a continuous Now
   As the clock counts.

The paradox of a continuous Now that grows dim and has

to be recorded perhaps explains how it is that poetry is
at once so absurd and so imperishably truthful a medium.
What distinguishes poetry from poetastering is that it
uses, not description, which is single-eyed and flat, but
vision, which is binocular. The poet always keeps half of
himself elsewhere than in the present scene, and sees
things as they must be rather than as (we say) they are.
This is why we do not recognize them - or him. Having
also kept his tongue uninhibited, the poet speaks of
things with analogical freedom. He does not go after
images, but prevents his local mind from excluding the obvious ones that come. To take a simple example, Mr. Auden
lights up a dark side of our paper-fed civilization when
he includes the (italicized) 'vision' in a commonplace
'observation':

> ...forward into
> Tidy utopias of eternal spring,
> Vitamins, villas, *visas for dogs,*
> And art for all...

Or again, what Darwin spent a lifetime stuttering:

> The corporate greed of quiet vegetation

I have called poetry absurd as well as truthful because
it is continually taking a chance that its vision and its
speech shall turn out nonsensical and false. The poet is
ridiculous or sublime as the figure skater would be who
was never allowed to practice, but must skim for his life
over untried surfaces and hidden perils. Do we not say the
poet *falls* into bathos, prose, sententiousness, gibberish?
Language betrays him. Why then does he tamper with it so
childishly - rime, alliteration, inversion, mixed metaphor,
knotty syntax? But this is a question we no longer dare
ask when every jive gabbler, columnist, thief, and advertiser usurps the right to make new words or twist old ones.
The drugstore can flaunt 'cheeseburger'; why shouldn't Mr.
Auden say 'hideola'? We can understand him with a little
effort akin to digestion. All poetry is difficult because
it tries to thicken again, and restore, the experiences we
dilute and distort through habit and conventional speech.
Whence it is the fate of certain poems to become shorthand notes on history. I have not the slightest doubt that
when books analyzing our plight are read only by candidates
for degrees, Auden's eclogue will be quoted, in bits, as a
sufficient token of our times. His very forms and turns will
mean all that we try to say in long chapters. And this implies that besides knowledge he gives pleasure. Fashioned

as a dialogue in various settings, real and imaginary, the
poem contains songs of all kinds, soliloquies, catalogues,
transformation scenes, action and philosophizing in prose.
The bulk of it is written in alliterative verse with four
accents to a line, handled with such virtuosity that it
never drums in your ear: just compare it with 'Beowulf.'
The substance is enormously rich in allusion, sound, and
intellectual power. There has been nothing like Auden's
shower of ideas in poetry since Hardy's death, and it is
no wonder that the competition he represents for his admiring colleagues has sometimes made them live beyond
their intellectual income.

This is not to say that 'The Age of Anxiety' preaches
or teaches. It is a philosophical poem as 'Hamlet' is, or
'The Darkling Thrush.' Its purport, or rather its preoccupation, is stated in these lines about man:

[Quotes 15 lines of Malin's speech, from 'That field of
force where he feels he thinks...' onwards, CP(M), 355-6.]

This concern is a modification of the dogma of original
sin, and though Auden makes his attitude toward it seem at
times perversely helpless ('Many have perished, more will')
it is so productive of poetry and truth that one gladly
yields the doctrinal point. It is in any case personally
felt, as I often suspect that another attitude of Auden's
is not. I mean the relapse into the too-easy humor of our
modern egotists, as for instance, in speaking of the beast
within us:

> each contributes his
> Personal panic, his predatory note
> To her gregarious grunt as she gropes in the dark
> For her lost lollipop.

The lollipop is a leftover of Eliotish conceit, a sign of
our contemporary mind in a very different sense from the
poetical. Of such images future readers will say what we
say of certain annoying tricks in earlier poets - word-
play in the Elizabethan, nature-mongering in the Romantic -
'there they go again.' It is only fair to add that this
fault occurs but seldom in Auden, and that he atones for
its affectation by triumphs of simplicity which, again,
only Hardy could encompass. Imagine getting away with the
commonplace *and* the pedantry of:

> Past vice and virtue, surviving both,
> Through pluvial periods, paroxysms
> Of wind and wet....

Thanks to just this unrivaled ear for the blessedly vulgar
in vocabulary and rhythm, Auden can modulate from bawdy
songs (which the censor will not catch) to the involved
pessimism of the climacteric question, how shall we end:

> By any natural
> Fascination of frost or flood, or from the artful
> Obliterating bang whereby God's rebellious image
> After thousands of thankless years spent in thinking
> about it,
> Finally finds a solid
> Proof of its independence?   [CP(M), 381]

For pessimism and naturalism and virtuosity, 'The Age of
Anxiety' makes one think of Shakespeare's 'Tempest,' but
one hopes that it will not hold the corresponding, that is,
final place in the canon of Auden's works. From the greatest living poet in English, we expect, we require, in his
mid-flight, numerous, vast and unpredictable conceptions.

101. DELMORE SCHWARTZ ON AUDEN'S 'MOST SELF-INDULGENT
BOOK', 'PARTISAN REVIEW'

xiv, September-October 1947, 528-31

Schwartz (1913-66), a poet and critic, was an editor,
1943-7, and associate editor, 1947-55, of 'Partisan Re-
view'; and Poetry Editor and Film Critic of 'New Republic'
from 1955 to 1957. Auden's work strongly influenced
Schwartz's early poetry collected in 'In Dreams Begin
Responsibilites' (1938), which was hailed by the elders of
American letters - Eliot, Pound, Tate, Stevens, Ransom, and
William Carlos Williams - and led to his being styled 'the
American Auden'. Other publications include 'Genesis:
Book One' (1943), 'Summer Knowledge: New and Selected Poems
1938-1958' (1959), 'The Selected Essays of Delmore
Schwartz' (ed. Donald A. Dike and David H. Zucker, 1970),
and 'What is to be Given' (sel. Douglas Dunn, 1976).
    This is an extract from Auden and Stevens, Stevens's
work under review being 'Transport to Summer'.

The scheme of Auden's new long poem is clear enough and
rich in possibility. Four human beings meet in a Third
Avenue bar, drink, discuss the seven ages of existence,

get drunk, and become or discuss states of prehistoric happiness, go to the apartment of Rosetta, the one girl among
them, and continue to drink until one of the men starts to
make love to Rosetta just before he passes out. The poem
concludes with a long passage of vague affirmation, an affirmation of Christianity which is no more convincing than
Auden's rejection of Christianity twelve years back when,
for example, he spoke of cathedrals as 'luxury liners for
the self-absorbed.' Within this framework, which might be
very dramatic, Auden inserts juke-box lyrics, parodies of
the radio, and exercises in the seven or eight poetic
styles of his career.

What this work comes to, at least for me (and perhaps I
should say that no one else has spoken of it with anything
but admiration), is the most self-indulgent book Auden
has written. It is far more self-indulgent than 'The
Orators.' Here the seeming order is merely contrived and
allows for all kinds of gratuitous excursions. In 'The
Orators' the seeming disorder was produced by the sub-
liminal character of the subject matter, by the fact that
very important unconscious material broke through to consciousness. It can be said that the most unique quality of
modern literature is the eruption of the unconscious within
areas of the conscious mind, which is not quite able to
understand and control all that has forced its way up. It
is significant that Auden now regards 'The Orators' as a
failure while in writing 'The Age of Anxiety' he strives
to renew communication with the subject matter which
made 'The Orators' one of his most exciting books.

In this new work, Auden's technical skill, which is as
various as any poet's, and his easy virtuosity, which is
at times too easy, show in full stength. The use of alliteration here is a beautiful addition to his enormous bag
of tricks. But the result is a plethora of effects which
for the most part get in each other's way. The possibility
of a narrative line is muffed throughout. And the eloquent
dialectic inherent in the use of dialogue comes to almost
nothing because each character often speaks as if he had
not heard what the previous character just said. The Third
Avenue bar does not really exist in the poem, despite the
juke box. There is no real anxiety in the poem, but merely
the discussion of anxiety. And the characterization of the
four persons is blurred or blotted out again and again
when each one makes speeches which cannot be said to be out
of character because they have nothing to do with character
at all. Just before the end of the poem, for example,
Rosetta suddenly turns out to be Jewish for the sake of a
speech about the nature and the destiny of Jews; nothing
whatever in Rosetta's previous remarks has prepared the

reader for this revelation about Rosetta's origins and her
views of them.

The poem as a whole simulates narrative, drama, and
philosophical dialogue. In actuality it is hardly more than
a suite of expositions, alternately discursive, allegorical,
and lyrical, of Auden's thoughts and opinions. Perhaps the
cause is Auden's mixed and contradictory intentions. His
chief motive is now didactic. He has become a teacher,
father, and prophet; he began as a subversive satirist,
dissident son, and *enfant terrible*. He is now trying to
write in the didactic mode while at the same time retaining the idiom of his early work, which was most successful
when it was a fusion of the ominous, the flip, the colloquial, and the intuitive. In this new work, Auden attempts
to use phrases such as 'You're not my dish really,' in the
same kind of context as 'His Good ingressant on our gross
occasions.' The effect on one reader at least can only be
compared to hearing that there's going to be a hot time in
the old town tonight chortled in an extremely English
accent. Perhaps it is possible to write in a style which is
at once full of colloquial diction and philosophical terminology (and this work might very well be a stage in
Auden's development of such a style); and perhaps it is
also possible to be didactic, dialectic, lyrical, dramatic,
narrative, philosophical, concrete, and abstract in the
same poem. But Auden has not succeeded in doing so. There is
nothing wrong with being a didactic poet, if one has a coherent set of ideas which one has lived with for a long
time. But Auden is not really a didactic poet, he is something better and more important.

One also senses much that is uncertain and unclear in
the ideas of which Auden now writes so fondly. It is as if
he were not really sure that they were true, despite the
schematism and the capitalized abstractions by means of
which he presents them. Whether this be an accurate impression or not, we have from years back a good example of how
easy it is to be lucid, eloquent, and utterly wrong. When
Auden came to America, his coming was compared to James's
and Eliot's departure for England as if it were the same
kind of migration and not absolutely different: to go to
Europe from America is obviously to go in the opposite
direction from going to America from England. There is
much to suggest that an insensitivity to this overwhelming
difference may explain the quality of Auden's recent work.
His genius depends upon England, upon the English scene,
upon perceptions and emotions inspired by being English.
It is in America that he must become a poetic teacher who
versifies doctrines picked up carelessly and uncritically
from a dozen heterogeneous and unexamined sources. In

America too Auden has taken some of his most beautiful and
serious poems and in his collected volume attached to
these poems titles which are facetious and silly: 'Shut
Your Eyes and Open Your Mouth,' 'Heavy Date,' 'Such Nice
People,' 'Please Make Yourself At Home,' 'Do Be Careful,'
'It's So Dull Here,' 'Nobody Understands Me.' These are
representative instances of the kind of tourist slanginess
which has infected Auden's style as a whole and which is
far from being the same thing as the colloquial actuality
which gave his work of ten and fifteen years ago so much
emotional force. There is nothing in this new book which
comes near the prophetic power of such a passage as this,
from his first book:

[Quotes last 14 lines of 'It was Easter as I walked in the
public gardens...', EA, 40.]

102. GILES ROMILLY, THE AGE OF DESPAIR, 'NEW STATESMAN AND
NATION'

xxxvi, 30 October 1948, 376

An author and journalist, Romilly (1916-67) cut short his
undergraduate career at Oxford to fight in the Spanish
Civil War, and subsequently worked for the 'Daily Express'.
During the Second World War he was arrested by the Germans
in Norway while on his way to cover the Russo-Finnish war
and spent some years as a prisoner of war, partly in solitary confinement and eventually at Colditz.

The effect produced by Mr. Auden's poem is one of desolating sadness. He might, indeed, have named it 'The Age of
Despair.' Anxiety, with its psychiatric associations, suggests something curable; but here no cures are offered,
and palliatives are put forward only to be rejected. Here,
I think, is a fundamental difference between this poem
and all of Mr. Auden's earlier work. 'If we want to live
we'd better start at once to try'; and Mr. Auden used to
indicate that we could live if only we would try intelli-
gently. He prescribed and he diagnosed; often the diagnosis was the prescription, a sort of salutary shock. In
'Spain' he concluded with the sternest of all his
warnings:

> The stars are dead. The animals will not look.
> We are left alone with our day, and the time is
>   short, and
>   History to the defeated
> May say Alas but cannot help nor pardon.

But it was impossible then to feel, however the pulse
might flicker and the temperature soar, that Mr. Auden
despaired of the fate of his patient. He seemed at times
too frivolously light-hearted, a medicine-man rather than
a doctor. In later poems, 'The New Year Letter' and 'For
the Time Being,' when all the warnings had come horribly
true, there still appeared the Micawber-like feeling that
'something would turn up' - even if now it was to be something vaguer and larger, a spiritual revelation rather
than a trend or a Beveridge Plan. Through all that time
of productive and optimistic resilience Mr. Auden continued to be a very good, sometimes great, and always unequal poet.
    In 'The Age of Anxiety' all that is changed. It takes
a little time to realise quite how despairing this poem
is, for it is a very forbidding work, both in metre and
diction, and a first reading gives one nothing except an
unpleasant sensation, like that of eating an omelette made
with egg-shells. On page 54, after a long discussion about
human life between four people who have met casually in a
New York bar, Quant (elderly widower) says to Rosetta
(buyer for a big department store):

[Quotes 10½ lines of Quant's speech, 'Come, peregrine
nymph...', CP(M), 370.]

The words 'delight your shepherds' and the few lines immediately following, seem to sound a new note in Mr.
Auden's work. It is as if he was standing quite suddenly
blank and helpless, with no feeling other than a sag and a
slump. The words 'and a shame surely' have this curious
sick deadness. It is never possible to predict or to understand the moment of illumination, which comes to a scientist, we do not see the hundreds of scrapped experiments.
Mr. Auden has never spared us his. Here it has taken him
fifty pages of litter to tell us, in a handful of sad
lines, that human beings are in a bad way, and that he no
longer has the slightest idea what is to be done about it.
    The four persons of the poem - the other two are Malin,
a middle-aged scientist, and Emble, a young man afraid of
failure - attempt to escape their plight by a search for
a 'prehistoric happiness.' 'May our luck find the Regres-
sive road to Grandmother's House,' says Rosetta; and this

hideous way of putting it foreshadows the arid futility of
the attempt. They are conducted on an imaginary journey of
seven stages, through a landscape 'bearing a symbolic resemblance to the human body.' Whichever way they go, disappointment awaits them. For example, it is tempting to
stop in the 'hermetic gardens' -

> With their smirk ouches and sweet-smelling borders,
> To lean on the low
> Parapet of some pursive fountain....

But the loitering in these gardens - it is sex which is
represented here - quickly calls out the form of anxiety
special to each. Dionysus fails; guilt and conscience will
not be silenced, the real world returns upon them more
terribly as the Bar closes. Their last bid to stave off
despair, by the consecrating of an improvised liaison
between Emble and Rosetta, fails also.

'The Age of Anxiety' has already come in for some severe criticism nor is it difficult to understand why.
Linguistically this is by far the least attractive poem
which Mr. Auden has ever written, a desert with scarcely
an oasis, with great stretches which seem pointlessly repellent, over which Mr. Auden scurries like a distracted
red ant. No single passage has the felicitous memorability
of his earlier work. 'Arm in arm with their opposite type,'
The eye stops; 'type' is one of those slick, smirky words,
which Mr. Auden throws at us far too insensitively.
'Deuce,' 'Lonelies,' 'your dish really' - there have never
been so many , so offensively used, as in this poem. And
they proliferate into those horrid little sequences, in
which Mr. Auden parades all his old favourites, as 'types,'
with the tired slickness of a commercial traveller who has
just a few 'lines.' From 'type' on page 54, for example,
he goes on:

> Like dashing Adonis dressed to kill
> And worn Wat with his walrus moustache
> Or one by one like Wandering Jews,
> Bullet-headed bandit, broad churchman,
> Lobbyist, legatee, loud virago,
> Uncle and aunt and alien cousin...

and so on; and the nastiest feeling one has about these
little lists is that they are simply not true; and that
the man who palms them off on us is not entitled to be
taken seriously, when he wishes to put a grave case. The
fault, a juvenile and cock-snooking facetiousness, was
there earlier, but here it quite sets one's teeth on edge:

> And Caustic Keith grows kind and silly
> Or Dainty Daisy dirties herself....

Apart from the language, it is difficult to believe that the intention and content of the poem justify its enormous length. It is not that Mr. Auden says very little, but that what he says is tremendously diffused. For example, the discussion on the Seven Stages of man, pages 33 to 54, seems to me almost entirely otiose; it is all personal psychologising, of the sort which Mr. Auden has done before with much greater precision and point. As verse it is remarkably unenticing, and we would be quite happy to take it all as said, or compressed into a single prose paragraph. The argument of the poem, all that which is at all fresh about it, begins with Quant's invitation to Rosetta on Page 53, and with her doubting and tentative answer. Thereafter, one feels, the poem would still have gained by compression. Its love scene, in particular, is drawn-out, facetious, and dull. It is possible to be wrong; and what we cannot doubt, I think, is that Mr. Auden intended these disagreeable effects. His teeth have chattered, and he wants ours to chatter. He has left his powerful observatory, and set himself down shivering in the wreckage like some Hiroshima victim. There is little doubt either, despite all linguistic excrescences and trivialitites, of the fundamental earnestness and thoroughness with which he has set about it. It was a dangerous attempt for an artist to make, and almost certainly, in the present instance, a mistaken one. Chattering teeth do not make good poetry, even in The Age of Despair.

103. PATRIC DICKINSON, UNTITLED REVIEW, 'HORIZON'

xix, May 1949, 377-8

Patric Dickinson (b. 1914) is a poet, playwright, and freelance broadcaster.
    This extract is taken with the author's consent from an untitled review which includes discussion of volumes of verse by John Crowe Ransom, Allen Tate, and John Berryman.

W.H. Auden's long poem 'The Age of Anxiety' ... is written in a language somewhere between English and American or translation. It is Mr. Auden's first American production

and for an English critic there are certain obvious
sources of irritation which must be overcome before the
work can be judged objectively. The first thing to surprise, even to alarm, is that the piece is persistently
boring. It is hard to believe that Mr. Auden could be
boring, but so it is. The poem is described as a *baroque
eclogue* so that one may expect a grotesque extravagant and
artificial affair, and this is set in the opposite of pastoral circumstances - a New York bar, in wartime, on All
Souls night. But soon it is apparent that the naturalistic
setting does not signify at all, and that All Souls is a
euphemism for All Psychologists. So we are left with four
idola or 'personifications of abstract ideas' - by no
standards can they be called characters - getting drunk in
a baroque. It is clear from this poem that Christopher
Isherwood supplied the dramatic element in the late collaboration, for these four circumambulate only in the poet's
mind: their artificial dialogue never reaches a real interplay of thought, but only a loose nexus of ideas. Though
they are given four names and two and a half sexes there is
no tension between them. Sex does not apply.
 The poem must therefore stand by its rhythmic impulse
and its language. Mr. Auden has chosen for the artifice of
the eclogue to use a loose alliterative line, lumpy as
school porridge, and rhythms which bump and thud like a
poltergeist - out of which occasional pieces of coal, and
teacups, so to speak, describe their queer inhuman para-
bolas. The poem is carefully, painstakingly written, but it
has an air of strain alien to its convention and the insistent hammering of the consonants has a sad undertaking
sound.
 Then, what has the poem to say? It is unthinkable that
Mr. Auden could have sat down to this long work without a
genuine purpose. Three men and a woman get slowly drunk
in a bar, they talk, their personalities merge, they go
back to the woman's flat, the two elder men leave, the
younger passes out on the woman's bed and cannot sleep with
her, as she had hoped. The purpose is to show what is going
on in four separate minds. But what does go on is a rehash
of Auden's psychology divided by four, and multiplied by a
great many of his older clichés. Even for what they are
these idola have little validity - they are impure superficial conceptions....
 It is unfair perhaps to cite the poet himself, but to
have heard him read an extract from this poem recently was
illuminating. The accent - save for short 'a' sounds, as in
fast - was still English, but the determination was to be
American. So in the poem the local allusions stick out like
a porcupine's quills from a tiger's paw. The setting, the

putting of Emble and Malin into uniform, the fact that
Rosetta recalls an England that has only existed as a silly
literary convention (a Mrs. Miniver England), that Quant
has child-dreams of Ireland all testify to the poet's embarrassment; and calling the piece a *baroque eclogue* only
the more exposes it. We know too much of Auden's history
as a man: what is distressing about this poem is the very
attempt of the poet to project his privacies into it.
Purely as a work of art it seems utterly remote from living
experience; quite emotionless; full of carefully written
words and carefully contrived ideas, but all *in vacuo* - and
it is difficult not to conceive that this vacuum has been
created by the poet's life. When he really has become American, inside as well as out, in diction, in rhythm, in
feeling, in thought (as Mr. Eliot has become English) surely
he will again produce living work?

'Collected Shorter Poems, 1930-1944'

London, March 1950

Substantially the same collection as 'The Collected Poetry' (New York, 1945), though with certain omissions, additions, and changes of poem titles in Part I.

104. GEORGE D. PAINTER, LETTERS FROM WASTELAND, 'LISTENER'

xliii, 20 April 1950, 705-6

George D. Painter (b. 1914), prize-winning biographer, was Assistant Keeper in charge of fifteenth-century printed books at the British Museum from 1954 to 1974. His books include 'Marcel Proust, A Biography' (2 vols, 1959, 1965), 'William Caxton: A Quincentenary Biography' (1976), and 'Chateaubriand: A Biography', vol. I: 'The Longed-for Tempests' (1977).

There is a well-known photograph in which Auden leans with Isherwood from a train-window. A cigarette droops from his friendly grin, his eyes go one better than being visionary, by being knowing: it is a latterday Childe Harold with Polidori, bidding a long farewell to perfidious Albion, because he is

> set on the idea
> Of getting to Atlantis.

Auden is the chief romantic of Freudian love, the Byron of the unconscious mind: his clubbed foot is the wound to which he once wrote a letter, his Italy is America, and he

is in perpetual quest of Missolonghi. From a spiritual
outpost further than Marshall-Land, from the Ibsen's
glacier or Eliot's desert that make a modern poet's
Cockayne, he has sent us the regular postcards of his poems:
the present volume is the first of his collected
correspondence.

He would hardly send us *that* unless he felt that at last,
not another time, nor for the time being, but now, he has a
right to our answer. And the question of questions a poet
asks his readers is the one set by the dwarf in the fairy-
tale: we have to guess his name. Auden's critics for these
twenty years have mostly preferred collecting the stamps,
or cataloguing the blots, to deciphering the proud identity
of the sender. But the blots, I should say, are hardly
those specific to bad poets. He has borrowed from everyone
he ever read? Good! His influence on his imitators has
been pernicious? Splendid! He is prolific, likes assonance
and private faces and horizontal man? Exc- but is it in any
case relevant to look, strangers that we are, for his defects? Strictly speaking, a poet can have only one serious
fault, that of not being great; and a great poet, strictly
speaking, doesn't have faults, but qualities. Isn't it
possible now, in the light of this collection, to call
Auden great, to see that, as he once predicted they would,
his features shine, and his name is Star?

As early as twenty years ago Auden invented, or rather
was the first to detect under the scientific conditions of
poetic imagination, that sense of guilt which has been our
generation's characteristic rearward approach to eternal
verities. The early

> Sir, no man's enemy, forgiving all
> But will his negative inversion

posits the same means of salvation that preoccupy his
latest work: he invokes (and so, in their ways, did Pascal
and Kierkegaard before him) the help of God as a supreme
mental healer. Auden's task has been to retranslate the
lawless language of the unconscious - with extreme caution,
so that there may be no mistake about it this time - back
into the sermon on the mount. For he sees Freud not only
as the exposer of the shocking and true, not only as an inexhaustible suggester of knock-down poetic imagery, but as
one of a line of healers and saviours.

Probably, too, his powers have been less stationary than
meets the eye. While part of him remains at base, excavating for the good of us all ever deeper layers of his

fissured self -

> Rummaging into his living the poet fetches
> The images out that hurt and connect -

another presses forward through the so-far endless gla-
ciers, the ever-derelict power-houses of his universal
landscape; and another undergoes new literary influences,
falls in love, and ripens with age. He climbs, too, the
infernal escalator on which most stand unaware they are
moving:

> History
> That held one moment burns the hand -

how often has he formed and found the resolution to grip
its fiery banister! The time has gone when Isherwood, with
'squat spruce body and enormous head', could

> make action urgent and its nature clear.

Mr. Leishman's great translation of Rilke helped Auden to
endure and accept a journey to a war that now seems minor:
now, the leading sin-eater of his age, he is masticating a
greater, for which acceptance may prove neither possible
nor appropriate, and all literary and personal influences
powerless.

If the assemblage of his poems makes it possible, however tentatively, to call him great, it is unfortunate
that their new order should conceal how he became so. Re-
arrangement of a poet's works in any other order than that
in which they were given to him, can only doubly hide their
veiled and perhaps most important subject, the life-line
of a horizontal man. The time will come when

> a shilling life will give you all the facts.

It will then become of immense importance to know out on
whose lawn he lay in bed, or to read

> Symondson - praise him at once!
> Our rightwing threequarter back

on 'How Auden struck me as an English master'; but of comparatively little to know that the poet chose to arrange
his work in a punctured oval, when he had completed only
two sides of an as yet unpredictable figure.

'Nones'

New York, February 1951; London, February 1952

105. G.S. FRASER, THE CHEERFUL ESCHATOLOGIST, 'NEW STATES-
MAN AND NATION'

xliii, 1 March 1952, 249

After several years as a freelance literary journalist and
broadcaster in London, Fraser (1915-80) took up university
lecturing in his early forties and in 1964 became Reader in
Modern English Literature at the University of Leicester.
His publications include 'The Traveller has Regrets and
Other Poems' (1948), 'The Modern Writer and His World'
(1953, revised ed 1964), 'Vision and Rhetoric: Studies in
Modern Poetry' (1959), and 'Lawrence Durrell: A Study'
(1968).

Nones is the daily office of the Church originally said at
the ninth hour, or three o'clock in the afternoon; it was
between the sixth and the ninth hour, while Christ hung on
the cross, that there was a darkness over the earth, the
sun was darkened, and the veil of the Temple was rent.
There is, however, another meaning of the word that is
also relevant to Mr. Auden's new book. 'Nones' is the old
spelling of 'nonce.' Many of these new pieces are nonce-
poems (poems inspired by unrecurring occasions or written,
in some cases, for public declamation at American gradu-
ation ceremonies). They are also full of nonce-words:

> On the mountain, the baltering torrent
> Shrunk to a soodling thread,   [CP(M), 417]

for instance; the once battering but now faltering torrent,
I suppose, sunk to a soothing and dawdling thread. One is

half tempted to say that Mr. Auden's inspiration has itself begun to soodle, but, if there is nothing here in
the old, urgent, hortatory vein, that is because Mr.
Auden now feels that 'all sane affirmative speech' has been so
'pawed-at' and 'profaned' by newspapers and politicians
that the only civilised tone of voice for the poet to-day
is

> the wry, the sotto-voce,
> Ironic and monochrome.   [CP(M), 472]

And, in fact, Mr. Auden has never written with more confident ease than here. He hits just the note he wants to,
even when he is seeking to hold the attention of a throng
of undergraduates:

> Between the chances, choose the odd;
> Read *The New Yorker*, trust in God;
> And take short views.   [CP(M), 263]

Whether under the ease of the surface there is a slack-
ness of will is another question; also, how far irony and
humour at this level betray a fundamental undue complacency. The recipe for the 'New Yorker' type of humour,
I think, is to step far enough back from the routines we
are all immersed in to feel sophisticated about them; but
not far enough back to cease to be one of the boys. But
Auden can be one of the boys at several levels, and there
is quite a different snob highbrow pleasure, for instance,
in recognising the tesselations of Horatian syntax in
these lines addressed to Mr. Brian Howard:

> ...what bees
> From the blossoming chestnut
> Or short but shapely dark-haired men

> From the aragonian grape distil, your amber wine,
> Your coffee-coloured honey...   [CP(M), 417]

Auden, in fact, is more unscrupulously adroit in the
range of his appeal than anyone else writing now. He can
be back-slapping, ominous, port-winy, or abstruse, as the
occasion demands. But if these new poems mostly do not aim
at major statements, there are major themes, above all the
Christian theme, in the background; the frivolity is in a
sense permissible because the last things, death, judgment,
hell, heaven, are always in mind, and the worldly hopes men
set their hearts upon have been rejected. In the interim,

there is nothing against harmless enjoyment. What we are left in doubt about, I suppose, is the nature of Mr. Auden's first-level responses, if any. His type of Christianity, I would say, is a sophisticated Lutheranism. He does not exactly say to us, *Pecca fortiter,* but to avoid despair he has to put most of his money on Grace since he knows he is going to fall down on Works. The trouble about such a type of Christianity is that to the outside observer it might appear to make no practical difference:

> But that Miss Number in the corner
> Playing hard to get...
> I am sorry I'm not sorry...
> Make me chaste, Lord, but not yet.   [CP(M), 466]

Humility consists of recognising one's impurity, but also provides an excuse for going on being impure:

> The Love that rules the sun and stars
> Permits what He forbids.   [CP(M), 466]

Stated at that level, even allowing for the not very biting satire, the attitude is a little vulgar: Dante and St. Augustine at the cocktail party, or soulfulness as adding to the kick. But stated with more personal conviction, it can be moving and dignified, as in the last lines of the loveliest poem here, 'In Praise of Limestone':

>   Dear, I know nothing of
> Either, but when I try to imagine a faultless love
>   Or the life to come, what I hear is the murmur
> Of underground streams, what I see is a limestone
>   landscape.

Deliberately slackening down a little when everybody else is keyed up, taking a humorous view of guilt and anxiety as part of the set-up - 'throwing it away,' as the actors say of a strong line - is, after all, a defensible human attitude when everybody else is getting shrill, frightened, and nasty. This is a continually disconcerting book, but I would say it more often embodies positive values (it is certainly a value that someone can go on unashamedly enjoying himself to-day, as Auden seems to) than 'The Age of Anxiety' where the theme of our awkward *malaise* was all too faithfully mirrored in the tone and handling. I suppose from all sorts of official and respectable points of view 'Nones' is a quietly outrageous little book; my own kind of fundamental doubts I have tried to indicate; but I have enjoyed the poems more than anything Auden has written in a good many years.

106. ROBIN MAYHEAD, THE LATEST AUDEN, 'SCRUTINY'

xviii, June 1952, 315-19

Mayhead is Reader in English at the University of Stirling;
author of 'Understanding Literature' (1965), 'John Keats'
(1967), and 'Walter Scott' (1973).

'Mr. Auden's readers', the dust-jacket informs us, 'know
him as an intellectual poet whose technical resourcefulness
is always equal to the ceaseless development of his mind
and sensibility; a poet who never arrests his progress or
repeats himself...'. That might seem to be a challenge to
those people who have from time to time had occasion to
declare their disappointment at the stasis, the failure in
fulfilment, of a poet who, amidst an arid literary scene,
appeared in his early work to have the virtues of intelligence and vigour and a real, if at times irresponsible,
feeling for language. A failure of growth, an absence of
anticipated soundness and maturity, have for a number of
readers seemed to mark the volumes published since the
early 'Paid on Both Sides'; yet many must have hoped that
Mr. Auden might suddenly, somehow, find himself again,
might after all justify their early interest and expectation. It is well to say directly that 'Nones' does not
give evidence of a turn for the good. Indeed, it gives the
impression of being in the nature of a full-stop; or
rather, perhaps, a path from which it seems improbably that
Mr. Auden will ever wish really to stray.
    Perhaps the best way to lend support to this view is to
take the hint of the blurb. If. Mr. Auden's 'technical resourcefulness' is the correlative of his 'mind and sensibility', to what conclusions will an examination of his
'technique' lead us? One may begin by looking at the opening lines of the first poem, 'Prime':

> Simultaneously, as soundlessly,
>   Spontaneously, suddenly
> As, at the vaunt of the dawn, the kind
>   Gates of the body fly open
> To its world beyond,

Here, I think it will be agreed, there is a sense of strain,
a sense that the poet is trying artificially to inject life
into verse that resolutely refuses to leave the ground. For
what can the first two lines be said to have achieved? Do
the four adverbs, words with a rich potential of

associations, signify as much in the context as the attention drawn to them by the alliteration would suggest? Does
it not seem as though the choice of those particular words
has been dictated less by a concern for precision and
rightness than by a preoccupation with alliteration and internal rhyme? To me, at any rate, they seem little more
than gestures towards a desired illusion of portentousness.
A further source of the lack of conviction one feels behind the lines is a certain rhythmic awkwardness and inex-
pressiveness - not, it must be said, anything like so prevalent in this poem as it is in 'The Managers' or 'Pleasure
Island':

> To send a cry of protest or a call for
>   Protection up into all
> Those dazzling miles, to add, however sincerely,
>   One's occasional tear
> To that small volume, would be rather silly,

Those few lines were picked at random from a poem running to
some eighty. The monotony of reading verse of that kind, it
will readily be appreciated, the effort involved in dragg-
ing the apprehension from one line to the next, is such as
to make it necessary positively to drive oneself through to
the end. The words seem to be strewn haphazardly, tortu-
ously, over a rigid framework which sternly forbids any
subtlety of intonation or suppleness of movement. Not that
the arrangement of words has been haphazard. The first and
second lines of the extract end where they do in order
that the words 'Protection' and 'all' may receive some
sort of stress. I say 'some sort of stress' because the effect obtained is purely ocular. A quite unwarrantable effort of 'interpretation' is required if it is to be brought
out in a live reading. Mr. Auden ought to know by this time
- indeed, I am sure he does know - that one does not obtain
effects of speech-stress and rhythm merely by chopping the
lines.
    Mr. Auden, we have already recalled, was distinguished
in his early poetry by a feeling for language; that is to
say, his language had pliability, at times a cumulative
suggestiveness, that went appropriately with very real, if
limited interests. But even then there was a tendency, more
insistent as volume succeeded volume, to indulge in verbal
virtuosity for its own sake. The results were often striking and amusing, but hardly what one expected from a
responsible man growing older in an age growing simultaneously more and more barren and disheartening. His taste
for verbal ingenuities persists in 'Nones', though it has
become a very feeble sort of juggling:

Sometimes we see astonishingly clearly
The out-there-now when we are already in;
Now that is not what we are here-for really.[CP(M), 474]

Or there is the bad, unfunctional use of pun, as in 'Prime':

Holy this moment, wholly in the right,

Mr. Auden has always been fond of coinages and slangisms,
a schoolboy habit that one had hoped he would grow out of.
'Nones' shows us that he is not tired of them yet. Whereas
in the earlier work, however, one tended to regard them as
excrescences on more solid substance, they figure here
rather as substitutes for genuine verbal vitality. Essentially they are a means of escape from the responsibility of
integrating language and experience; of deciding, in other
words, exactly what, if anything, the experience amounts
to. I do not think that any very convincing case could be
made out to justify the following lines, even though the
poet might claim the sanction of Browning. The reader who
is interested in poetry is likely to feel that his intelligence is being insulted:

                      the orchestral
    Metaphor bamboozles the most oppressed
        - As a trombone the clerk will bravely
    Go oompah-oompah to his minor grave -   [CP(M), 264]

Such devices, far from being a sign of fertile verbal invention, manifest an essential tiredness, an inability
clearly to focus the poetic object. They are protestations
of a vitality that does not exist.
    'Tiredness' would also seem to be a descriptive word
for the staple of Mr. Auden's imagery. Much of it has a
faded, second-hand air, a suggestion of having been drawn
from some property-cupboard of modern poetical cliché:

    As disregarded as some
    Discarded artifact of our own,
        Like torn gloves, rusted kettles,
    Abandoned branchlines, worn lop-sided
        Grindstones buried in nettles.   [CP(M), 481]

(The passage is an extremely felicitous commentary on itself.) With that kind of thing, as might be expected, there
goes a persistent habit of reminiscence. Yeats is a fairly
constant presence:

> Speak well of moonlight on a winding stair,
> Of light-boned children under great green oaks;
> The wonder, yes, but death should not be there. [CP(M), 475]

So, in various guises, is Mr. Eliot, from echoes of
'Triumphal March' in 'Ischia' to reminiscences of 'Four
Quartets' in 'The Chimeras'. But the most surprising pre-
sence of all is that of Mr. Walter De la Mare, whom Mr.
Auden's would-be ironic surface cannot hide:

> Their learned kings bent down to chat with frogs;
> This was until the Battle of the Bogs.
> *The key that opens is the key that rusts.* [CP(M), 258]

Such 'influences' are not in the nature of the fertile suggestion that leads to fresh poetic creation quite distinct
from the original, but rather testify to a want of personal
idiom, which in itself is but a local sign of lack of urgency, lack of conviction, lack of real interest.

An air of boredom and lassitude, indeed, broods over the
whole volume. Not infrequently Mr. Auden seems to be trying
to atone for this by indulging in slightly *risqués* side-
glances:

>   The boiling springs
>   Which betray her secret fever
>   Make limber the gout-stiffened joint
>
> And improve the venereal act;   [CP(M), 416]

That might be likened to a faintly salacious smile. At
other times it becomes a more decidedly unpleasant snigger,
like this 'spicing' of the tedious straggle of 'Pleasure
Island':*

>   As bosom, backside, crotch
>   Or other sacred trophy is borne in triumph
>   Past his adoring by
>   Souls he does not try to like;

Disgust, of course, is the impression intended by the poet,
but the pleasure taken in enumerating its objects is unmistakable. In any case, that kind of disgust, if genuine disgust it be, can hardly be called healthy or mature. It is
little more than the disgust of the sensitive adolescent
schoolboy, outraged by his gross contemporaries.

An unresolved ambiguity of attitude, manifesting itself
locally in a corresponding uncertainty of tone, has for
long been a characteristic of Mr. Auden's work. One

remembers the satiric gestures at the expense of the Public School ethos, which oddly enough seemed at the same
time to be an endorsement of the very prejudices they were
apparently intended to undermine. The same kind of ambiguity characterizes such poems as 'The Managers' or 'A
Household'. It is hard to say exactly how we are supposed
to take the business-man of the latter poem, who, in order
'to disarm suspicious minds at lunch', or to mollify those
with whom he has just driven a bargain, paints a false and
glowing picture of his home. Never, '(A reticence for which
they all admire him)', does he speak of his early-deceased
wife,

> But proudly tells of that young scamp his heir,
> Of black eyes given and received, thrashings
> Endured without a sound to save a chum;

That, in whatever spirit it was offered, could not but be
embarrassing.

It should by now be apparent that 'Nones' represents no
new departure, no fresh mustering of forces. It is significant that the less tiresome poems in the volume, (though
they cannot for all that be called good), are mildly amusing squibs in the familiar manner of the earlier Auden,
like 'The Love Feast', or 'The Fall of Rome', dedicated to
Mr. Cyril Connolly:

> Fantastic grow the evening gowns;
> Agents of the Fisc pursue
> Absconding tax-defaulters through
> The sewers of provincial towns.

And yet he confesses himself, in 'A Walk after Dark', to be

> already at the stage
> When one starts to dislike the young

The volume shows early irritating mannerisms persisting
without even the irresponsible vitality that once went with
them. Maturity of years has brought no maturity of outlook,
no deepening and broadening of the interests, but merely
weariness and boredom. For that is the abiding impression
of these poems. Not one of the poems gives evidence of any
urgency, any real pressure or personal engagement. The defence could no doubt argue that the volume is a testimony
to the variety of Mr. Auden's interests. He certainly writes
on a number of subjects, if that is the criterion, but his
attitude to all of them is external and superficial. The
dust-jacket tells us that 'Nones' has 'an underlying unity

that makes it more than a collection of scattered verse':
yet one looks in vain for any dominant impulse controlling
the heterogeneous mass. For what has Mr. Auden positively
to offer? There is, to be sure, a kind of fashionable
metaphysical aura:

> Somewhere are places where we have really been,
> dear spaces
> Of our deeds and faces, scenes we remember
> As unchanging because there we changed,   [CP(M), 413]

Then 'Memorial for the City', with an epigraph from Juliana
of Norwich, reminds us that Mr. Auden is a Christian. But
this lengthy poem has no more vitality than the rest; it
does not persuade one that the poet's religious preoccupations have prompted him to live creation any more than
his other sources.

'Nones', then, is far from being an encouraging volume.
Mr. Auden has for some time now been academically respectable, and the present volume bears unmistakably the marks
of academic enshrinement. It has the right kind of stol-
idity, and a fundamental inoffensiveness to the comfortably
prejudiced but *soi-disant* 'open' mind. That being so, there
is little prospect that Mr. Auden will in the future choose
to alter his course. 'Nones' has the variety of deadness
that passes very well for 'ripeness' and 'serenity'. But to
have pronounced all these strictures on a poet who once
evinced such distinct ability, is no laughing matter , no
occasion for complacent self-congratulation. To anyone
really concerned about the health of contemporary literature, such a spectacle of dissolution must be profoundly
depressing, even tragic.

Note

* It is apposite to remark here that 'Pleasure Island',
  in common with other poems in the volume, oddly suggests
  inspiration from Hollywood. Much of 'Not in Baedeker'
  could be the commentary of a 'serious' travel film.

107. UNSIGNED REVIEW, DIVERSE OCCASIONS, 'TIMES LITERARY
SUPPLEMENT'

4 July 1952, 432

'Nones' is the first new volume consisting entirely of
shorter poems that Mr. Auden has given to us since 'Another Time,' 12 years ago. It is described on the wrapper
as a sequence 'with an underlying unity,' but there is
certainly no obvious unity on the surface: many of the
poems have previously appeared in a wide variety of periodicals and they celebrate diverse occasions, moods and
themes. The first general impression may well be of a certain diffuseness and lack of vitality, qualities which
appeared in some extent in 'The Age of Anxiety.' In form
and style there are examples of several earlier manners -
the six-lined stanza, recalling Burns, for light satire;
Yeatsian rhyming trimeters, portentous lines in *terza rima,*
slick trochaic quatrains, gnomic songs and sophisticated
adaptations of classical elegiacs and ode forms. There are
also various freer and looser patterns, while Mr. Auden's
customary technical ingenuity appears with assonance and
internal rhyme, in particular the rhyming of the last word
of a line with the penultimate syllable of the one before
(see 'Pleasure Island,' 'The Managers'). While for the
most part comparatively unobtrusive, these devices do not
seem to have any very positive function, and they hardly
impose themselves as the inevitable expression of new ways
of feeling.

In a dedicatory poem to Reinhold and Ursula Niebuhr the
poet apologizes for his addiction to 'the wry, the sotto-
voce, Ironic and monochrome,' explaining that

> All words like peace and love,
> All sane affirmative speech,
> Had been soiled, profanced, debased
> To a horrid mechanical screech.   [CP(M), 472]

The excuse is easier to accept than the perfunctory bathos
of that last line, especially when it is taken with the
conventional opening reference to 'golden hours, When body
and soul were in tune.' There is, of course, nothing to
prevent wryness and irony from becoming automatic and habitual, and there are poems in this volume which come peri-
lously near to self-parody - see, for example, 'The Fall of
Rome' and 'Love Feast' (both of which also have marked reminiscences of the Sweeney poems), 'Music Ho' and 'To Mr.
T.S. Eliot on his Sixtieth Birthday.' Images of doom and

decay, in particular, have become poetic commonplace, as
Mr. Auden is well aware when he stops to think, but he
still turns too readily to 'abandoned trains,' 'flu-
infected cities' and 'worn lopsided Grindstones buried in
nettles.' It seems inevitable that he should locate an
airport 'where two fears intersect.' At times he drops
into the older glib smartness of phrase and rhythm: this
is all very well in such an academic squib as 'Under Which
Lyre,' to which, though overlong and a trifle laboured,
much may be forgiven for its commandment,

> Thou shalt not sit
> With statisticians, nor commit
> A social science.

- but as a whole the poem hardly suggests maturity.
The more characteristic tone of this volume, however,
is meditative and discursive. Mr. Auden reflects on the
nature of consciousness ('Prime'), on the senses ('Precious
Five'), on music ('Music is International'), on the modern
wielders of power ('The Managers') and in a number of poems
on the 'spirit of place.' This last group contains some of
the most successful in the collection: 'Ischia,' with its
sophisiticated use of the Horatian convention, has an attractive lightness; 'Airport' conveys effectively the sense
of rootlessness and 'In Praise of Limestone' links a
favourite symbol of Mr. Auden's with deeper insights into
psychology, history and man's place in the scheme of
things:

> Not to lose time, not to get caught,
> Not to be left behind, not, please! to resemble
> The beasts who repeat themselves, or a thing like water
> Or stone whose conduct can be predicted, these
> Are our Common Prayer....

Readers of 'The Enchaféd Flood' will recognize in this poem
some of the interests pursued in that study. They appear
even more clearly in 'Memorial for the City' - with the
title poem, perhaps the most ambitious in scope in this
volume. The first contains a rapid sketch of the history
of Western civilization and an evocation of our present
plight, with an epilogue spoken by 'Our Weakness'; the
feeling that in spite of striking phrases it does not succeed as a whole is produced partly by its over-conscious
rhymes and assonances and partly by the uneasy mingling of
cleverness and solemnity. 'Nones' plays round the themes
of the Crucifixion, generalized crime and guilt and perhaps the use of the atomic bomb: it recalls some parts of

'The Family Reunion' and altogether leans rather heavily
on Mr. Eliot:

> Behind the rapture on the spiral stair,
>   We shall always now be aware
> Of the deed into which they lead, under
>   The mock chase and the mock capture,
> The racing and tussling and splashing,
>   The panting and the laughter....

The poem lapses too often into a symbolism of facile melodrama, though it recovers in the last stanza.
  Mr. Auden has always been a moralist, and a strongly
marked moral concern appears in several of these poems, implicit in 'Pleasure Island,' more directly didactic in
'Cattivo Tempo,' with its prescription for 'outwitting hell
with human obviousness.' Here, indeed, we seem to be almost
in the world of 'The Screwtape Letters,' while 'The
Chimeras' has suggestions even of 'The Great Divorce.' Of
all this group the most impressive is 'Under Sirius,' with
its vaguely late-Roman setting and its theme of religious
choice:

> How will you answer when from their qualming spring
>   The immortal nymphs fly shrieking,
>   And out of the open sky
> The pantocratic riddle breaks -
> 'Who are you and why?'

It is difficult to detect much that is specifically
American in this volume, apart from occasional terms or
slang words and the curiously rhetorical conclusion to the
final poem as the poet wonders

> what judgment waits
> My person, all my friends,
> And these United States.   [CP(M), 268]

'Their Lonely Betters' makes attractive use of Mr. Frost's
manner, and elsewhere there are occasional phrases recalling Miss Marianne Moore.
  In general the less ambitious of these poems are the
most successful. Mr. Auden's work always shows a mind susceptible to the widest possible variety of intellectual interests, and a keen sensitiveness to the contemporary cultural flux. But his talent is continually dissipated in irresponsible facility and incidental cleverness: when these
fail he is capable of a somewhat humourless solemnity.
There are poems in this volume for which the reader will be

justly grateful, but little sign of that sustained discipline and concentration which alone can give the deepest
imaginative intensity.

'The Shield of Achilles'

New York, February 1955; London, November 1955

108. KARL SHAPIRO, W.H. AUDEN VERSUS..., 'NEW YORK TIMES'

20 February 1955, section 7, 6

Shapiro (b. 1913), a poet and critic, edited 'Poetry: A Magazine of Verse', 1950-6, and has been Professor of English at the University of California at Davis since 1968. His books include 'V-Letter and Other Poems' (1944), 'The Poetry Wreck, Selected Essays 1950-70' (1975), 'Collected Poems 1940-1978' (1978), and 'An Essay on Rime' (1945), which includes an anatomy of the Auden mode (see Introduction, note 50).

Auden is the Great Ruminator of modern poetry. In many ways he is also the typical poet of our age. In him are the rare words no one really wants to look up. In him are the negative convictions which are the trade-mark of modernism. Over most of the land of modern poetry he maintains his grumpy proprietorship. He is smugly unhappy. His whole work is a schoolroom, his universe a blackboard filled in with phyla, genera and species - all human types. His poems are playful games of Personification or the small Allegory, or colloquies of Ideas. His main theme is the quest for the Authentic City, a city neither in heaven nor earth, not the Unreal City and not the Accursed City of the self-damned poets, but the city in which human excellence is possible. Auden long ago gave up the conventional romantic visit to the New Jerusalem, but one still senses his nostalgia for it. Nowadays when Auden talks about the Good City or the Just City it is as if he were telling a story about a wonderful place where something terrible happened.

393

The shield of Achilles in Homer has emblazoned upon it
the triumphs of the future. Auden, looking into the shield,
sees the horrors of the modern state. But such a pattern,
perfect though it is, seems to be too simple for the Auden
of today.

Take, for example, the opening stanza of 'Fleet Visit':

The sailors come ashore
Out of their hollow ships,
Mild-looking middle-class boys
Who read the comic strips;
One baseball game is more
To them than fifty Troys.

The romantic agonizing is almost gone from Auden's
poetry. In its place we find a disarming first-person-
singular Auden, almost as small as Cummings' little 'i.'
This friendly, witty, serious, tutorial Auden chats
comfortably of literary manners and the psychological
phases of the mind. How he loves the dedicated man, the
precise man, the productive man - those who have found
their vocations! And how he splutters with impatience
for the others - 'all poor s-o-b's who never Do anything
properly.' In this role of teacher Auden uses a strangely
intimate vocabulary, as if he were always among old
friends. And one is aware that his idiom has returned
quietly to the most official English.

His new book contains two sequences of poems and one
middle section made up of assorted pieces, several of which
are superb examples of Auden at his most urbane. The
opening sequence, called Bucolics, is one of Auden's best
works. The poems are named 'Winds,' 'Woods,' 'Mountains,'
'Lakes,' 'Islands,' 'Plains' and 'Streams.' Auden's
bucolics, naturally, are those of the city man. When he
goes to the country he wonders how long he can stand it.
The poem 'Plains' would make a good chapter for his
autobiography: 'If I were a plainsman I should hate us
all.' And 'I should also like to own a cave with two exits.'
The poem 'Streams' is one of the most beautiful pieces of
writing in modern literature.

The other sequence, which ends the book, is Horae
Canonicae. Auden changes the canonical hours of prayer
into seven periods of the day in which the poet examines
his consciousness. He does this not in a clinical manner
but with personal warmth, like an analyst who has fallen
in love with the patient. In these poems we see Auden
versus the crowd, Auden versus the world, Auden versus
others. Like the Bucolics, the seven poems of the
canonical hours reveal the Auden Type. He is an Arcadian;
his Anti-Type is a Utopian. Auden plays with these terms,

creating himself phase by phase. We see the Arcadian,
simple, peace-loving, good. And we see the Anti-Type,
science-ridden, exacerbated, haughty. And everywhere in
the poems we see a master of English poetry, whose stature
increases with each new work.

109. HORACE GREGORY, AUDEN'S NEW POEMS INVOKE ECHOES OF
DON GIOVANNI, 'NEW YORK HERALD TRIBUNE'

27 February 1955, section 6, 4

Gregory (b. 1898) is a poet, critic, and translator. His
publications include 'Collected Poems' (1964), and 'Spirit
of Time and Place: Collected Essays of Horace Gregory'
(1973).

Auden's book of poems I think is among his best, and the
poems which show brilliance are at a far distance above
the writtings of his imitators. He has written somewhere
that he is befriended by a gift - and so he is, and no poet
of the last quarter century has ridden the wild Zeitgeist
with more spectacular success than he. More than half of
his gift was an early present from the goddess Minerva.
    Since no one can paraphrase a poem, much less a book of
poems, one can only say in prose what his latest book is
like; to me it is very like a performance of Mozart's and
da Ponte's 'Don Giovanni.' Nor is this analogy as far-
fetched as it may seem. Some years ago Auden wrote his
'Letter to Lord Byron' in the manner of 'Don Juan.' The
double, now triple affinity of Don Juan, Byron and Auden
is a consistent strain throughout Auden's verse. In the
new book of poems the theatrical character of the
Mozart-da Ponte hero, his wit, his laughter, his moments
of downright hokum or 'corniness,' his touch of genius, his
marvelous arias are all there.
    The book is divided into three sections: Bucolics,
In Sunshine and in Shade, and Horae Canonicae; and in
keeping with 'Don Giovanni' itself, its undertones are of
the eighteenth century: that is, eighteenth-century titles
and themes appear in twentieth-century dress - and the best
of the verse retains an air of eighteenth-century formality.
It is between Auden's Bucolics and the hours of canonical
retreat that the magnificent arias occur. Auden's
thoroughly urban Bucolics are conversations in what have

become near parodies of his own style, resulting in lines
like these: 'Five minutes on even the nicest mountain /
Is awfully long' - which are cute, but not as clever as
they may seem. These are not the high reaches of his gift,
but rather the quick turns of his facility. The actual
poetry in the book begins with the title poem, 'The
Shield of Achilles': it continues in 'The Willow-Wren and
the Stare,' in 'The Proof,' has excellent wit in certain
lines of 'The Truest Poetry Is the Most Feigning,' and
rises again in 'Nocturne I.' All these are poems of a
quality that has given Auden his place in contemporary
poetry, a place that would be extremely dull without him.
  Auden's meditations in his hours of retreat are less
religious (in any sense of the word I know) than worldly
and adroit, closing with the remarkable 'Lauds,' an aria.
They show rather that Auden has steered his Zeitgeist into
recognition of the Christian world - but how can one
expect Don Giovanni to be possessed by moments of religious
feeling? If one recalls the last scenes of Mozart's opera
(the threat of hell receiving the brilliant hero) and
as one listens, reads the last section of Auden's book,
one has an image of his goddess Minerva descending to the
stage, stepping out of her machine and rescuing him
before the devils come. The play is over and a voice is
singing the refrain of Auden's 'Lauds': 'In solitude, for
company.' The gift has saved him.

110. RANDALL JARRELL ON MITIGATED TRIUMPHS, 'YALE REVIEW'

xliv, June 1955, 603-8

This is taken from Recent Poetry, a review of eleventt books.

'A culture is no better than its woods,' Auden writes.
Fortunately for him, a book of poetry can be better than
its poems. Two-thirds of 'The Shield of Achilles' is non-
Euclidean needlepoint, a man sitting on a chaise longue
juggling four cups, four saucers, four sugar-lumps, and
the round-square: this is what great and good poets do
when they don't bother even to try to write great and
good poems, now that they've learned that - it's Auden's
leit motif, these days - art is essentially frivolous.
But a little of the time Auden is essentially serious, and
the rest of the time he's so witty, intelligent, and
individual, so angelically skilful, that one reads with

despairing enthusiasm, and enjoys Auden's most complacently
self-indulgent idiosyncrasy almost as one enjoys Sherlock
Holmes' writing *Victoria Rex* on the wall in bullet-holes.
After a couple of decades of moralizing us to the top of
our bent, Auden has finally - in half the poetry of these
last two books - given up morality: 'In my Eden,' he writes
now, 'each observes his compulsive rituals and superstitious tabus but we have no morals.' And Auden's old, superstitious, compulsive readers - I'm one - are that way,
almost necessarily, about Auden: you can't argue with a
hog, a Senator, the Epicurean Gods, or the retired Talleyrand - we don't judge Auden, we just enjoy him. (He's over
on the other side of Judgment, in a wordy, worldly Limbo of
his own.) As we read that 'in my Eden a person who dislikes Bellini has the good manners not to get born,' we
just say, 'I'm glad I like Bellini'; when we read that 'I
stand in Eden again, welcomed back by the krum-horns,
doppions, sordumes of jolly miners and a bob major from
the Cathedral (romanesque) of St. Sophie (*Die Kalte*),' we
murmur only: 'What orchestration! Nothing like it since
Mahler!' It is, in a sense, a waste of great, the greatest
powers; but who wastes powers if he can keep from wasting
them? better for us to smile back, wondering, at the last
of the great English eccentrics. Yeats said that he had had
everything he wanted, done what he had meant to do, and
still was haunted by Plato's ghost crying, 'What then?'
Auden, it's plain, is never haunted by Rilke's. But now
I'm doing what Auden's readers don't do, I'm moralizing.

A third of 'The Shield of Achilles' consists of seven
poems about Winds, Woods, Mountains, Lakes, Islands, Plains,
and Streams: these exercises in viewing landscape quasi-
morally are learned, masterly, charming, complicatedly
self-delighting, trivial. 'Lakes' ends: 'It is unlikely
I shall ever keep a swan / Or build a tower on any small
tombolo, / But that's not going to stop me wondering what
sort / Of lake I would decide on if I should. / Moraine,
pot, oxbow, glint, sink, crater, piedmont, dimple ...? /
Just reeling off their names is ever so comfy.' Comfy,
that's it! just reading the poems is ever so comfy.

'The Shield of Achilles,' an impressive, carefully
planned, entirely comfortless poem, is the best thing in
the book's miscellaneous middle third. 'The Truest Poetry
Is the Most Feigning' (the most wishful title eyes e'er
saw or pen e'er wrote) is done according to a formula
Auden's become fond of: be as cynical as you can for a
couple of pages and then, in a couple of lines, tell
people it was all for the deepest and highest ethical and
religious reasons. *Lie to them, do as you please, tell
them anything,* this poem tells poets, with knowing
contempt, and then finishes about the poet, about Man:

'What but tall tales, the luck of verbal playing, / Can trick his lying nature into saying / That love, or truth in any serious sense, / Like orthodoxy, is a reticence?' I know that I ought to respond, 'True, true! I'll never tell the truth again. Anybody like to join me in some tall tales and verbal playing?' But what I really say is - but I'll be reticent. The poem made me think of this rhetorical question: 'If a shoemaker doesn't stick by his last, will he stick by anything else?' If Auden thought a little worse of himself, and a little better of poetry, how different Auden and his poetry would be!

And yet, how witty, how elegant, how altogether charming the best parts of this very poem are! When the poet, converting his love-song to the Triple Goddess into an ode to Mussolini, is made to change *Goddess of wry-necks and of wrens* into *Great Reticulator of the Fens,* I am wax, I am putty. In Spring, Auden says, 'leaves by the miles hide tons of / Pied pebbles that will soon be birds.' When our Mother, Earth, 'joins girl's-ear lakes / To bird's-foot deltas with lead-blue squiggles she makes, / Surely, a value judgment, / "Of pure things Water is the best."' At this point, reading 'Ode to Gaea,' I've no more morals, I murmur only, 'Now who else on all this earth -' whether they write poems or don't write poems, poets are best.

And in the last third of the book, a sequence about the crucifixion, there are certainly some real poems. The best two are reprinted from 'Nones.' This new book is, essentially, a kind of appendix to 'Nones,' a still later stage of this very late poetry of Auden's. *Nones* means "the office of the church said at the ninth hour, three in the afternoon." In the real dark day or white night of the soul, Auden seems to feel, it is always three o'clock in the afternoon: you can see everything that is there, which is what was there, which is what will be there - there is nothing else to see, and you do not see it; it is the hour when you used to despair and, now, take your nap. It is the hour of an accustomed disenchantment, of an anticlimax which smiles indifferently at its own old absurd climaxes: as Auden says, 'the wind has dropped and we have lost our public.' The public is still there, of course, but Auden has become surprisingly indifferent to it. The most professional magician is the one who gets bored with magic, who at last really has nothing up his sleeve, not even his arm; the most professional orator is the one who gets tired of pleasing and moving his audiences - and who, then, does as *he* pleases, talking slowly and steadily and unemotionally, with learned fantastic elaboration, reversing or inverting

half his old devices, delighted that the fools no longer
cheer, no longer cry. At this hour, Auden says, we cannot
'remember why / He shouted or what about / So loudly in the
sunlight this morning ... We are left alone with our feat."
The word *feat* is as calm and deadly as the 'dead calm'
of this hour; the feat, we realize as we go on into 'Nones',
is the crucifixion. But this is a crucifixion without
cross, Christ, crowd - everthing is already over; nobody
is left in the stadium but the janitors picking up the
cushions and Coca-Cola bottles. The poem gives us 'the
plain sense of things,' a residuum. It is a strange poem
to have been written by everybody's *enfant terrible*, by
the man who wrote that he supposed 'My friends will say
until I turn my toes up ... why *doesn't* Wystan ever
grow up? Wystan has grown up; has grown old - as old as
Talleyrand, as Disraeli, as that 'tired old diplomat'
who's become a stock figure in the poems. People used to
resent Eliot's 'Why should the aged eagle stretch his
wings?' but Auden has got over on the shady side of so
much, has become so convincingly old, so irrevocably,
inexorably middle-aged, that we wouldn't resent his telling
us that he is the Wandering Jew. And the change in the
Auden of the poems prepares us for the change in the everyday Auden, who is no longer a lank, tow-headed, slouching
boy, but who looks at you with a lined, sagging, fretful,
consciously powerful old lion's face.

Auden said in 1940, 'For I relapse into my crimes, /
Time and again have slubbered through / With slip and slapdash what I do, / Adopted what I would disown, / The
preacher's loose immodest tone.' He said this, and it
was so; and for five or six years afterwards it kept on
being so. During the last half of the 'thirties he had
preached, with slip and slapdash, the Popular Front; during
the first half of the 'forties he preached, with as much
slip and as much slapdash, as many tricks and as much
talent, his own idiosyncratic version of Barth and Niebuhr
and Kierkegaard. He disapproved of his crimes, perhaps,
but how he enjoyed committing them! And yet one day he
stopped enjoying it; he was tired. How much of his
moralizing, and stained-glass attitudes, and Moving
Rhetoric, he also began to be tired of! In fact, disin-
genuous creature that he is, he began sometimes to pretend
that there was nothing to *be* tired of - began to
pretend that he had always been on the other side, the side
of the resistance, in the great war between Morality and
Fun, between Doing as We Ought and Doing as We Please.
He began to specialize (whenever he wasn't regressing
into sermons) in witty and scornful denunciations of
'pompous Apollo' and all his works; *he* was - had always

been - on the side of Hermes, god of thieves and business-
men.

One of Housman's poems tells how, long ago, 'couched
upon her brother's grave / The Saxon got me on the slave' -
and how now, along the 'marches of my breast,' the
'truceless armies yet / Trample, rolled in blood and
sweat; / They kill and kill and never die / And I think
that each is I.' Auden is writing about a war which has
gone on for many years along the marches of *his* breast;
often the Unconscious, the Original, the Inside Auden must
have smiled mockingly, demonically, at what the Conscious
Outside was telling everybody else to do - smiled, and
gone about its living. In many of these last poems the
Conscious and Moral Auden is, quite consciously and
immorally, coming to terms with the Unconscious Auden by
going along with it, letting it have its way - and not
just in life, where we can do and gloss over anything, but
in poems, which are held against us by us and everyone else.
Perhaps Auden had always made such impossibly exacting
moral demands on himself and everybody else partly because
it kept him from having to worry about more ordinary,
moderate demands; perhaps he had preached so loudly,
made such extraordinarily sweeping gestures, in order to
hide himself from himself in the commotion. But he seems,
finally, to have got tired of the whole affair, to have
become willing to look at himself *without doing anything
about it,* not even shutting his eyes or turning his head
away. In some of the best of his later poems he accepts
himself for whatever he is, the world for whatever it is,
with experienced calm; much in these poems is accurate just
as observed, relevant, inescapable fact, not as the journa-
listic, local-color, in-the-know substitute that used to
tempt Auden almost as it did Kipling. The Poet is a man
of the world, and his religion is of so high an order, his
morality so decidedly a meta-morality, that they are more
a way of understanding everybody than of making specific
demands on anybody. Auden, in most of this last book,
lies back in himself as if he were an unmade bed, and
every line in his sleepy, placid face seems to be saying:
'But whoever makes beds'?

Auden has become the most professional poet in the world;
there is a matter-of-course mastery behind the elaborate
formality, the colloquial matter-of-factness, of these last
two books - after reading 'Under Sirius' another poet is
likely to feel, 'Well, back to my greeting-cards.' But to
be the most professional poet in the world is not necessarily to be the best: Minerva says, 'But *you* don't need
me.' Auden is using extraordinary skill in managing a
sadly reduced income. There is a tiredness and flatness

about much of 'Nones,' a comfortable frivolity about much
of 'The Shield of Achilles,' that give the accuracy and
truthfulness and virtuosity of the best poems a lonely,
disquieting ring. (And it is strange to see, among so
many strongly individual poems, three successful ones - 'A
Household,' 'The Chimeras,' and 'Cattivo Tempo' - that are
characteristic less of Auden than of Graves.) These best
poems are a triumph - mitigated, as triumphs are. One is
delighted at the slower and drier excellence that has
replaced the somewhat flashy and ambiguous excellence of
what Auden wrote during the later part of the 'thirties,
the earlier part of the 'forties; but has Auden ever again
written quite so well as he was writing at the beginning of
the 'thirties, in 'Poems ' and 'Paid on Both Sides'? He
wrote, then, some of the strongest, strangest, and most
original poetry that anyone has written in this century;
when old men, dying in their beds, mumble something
unintelligible to the nurse, it is some of those lines that
they will be repeating.

111. DONALD DAVIE ON AUDEN'S PLAYFULNESS, FROM AN UNTITLED
REVIEW, 'SHENANDOAH'

vii, Autumn 1955, 93-5

Davie (b. 1922), a poet and critic, is Andrew W. Mellon
Professor of Humanities at Vanderbilt University. His
publications include 'Purity of Diction in English Verse'
(1952), 'Thomas Hardy and British Poetry' (1972), and
'Collected Poems 1950-70' (1972).

Auden's new volume begins with seven Bucolics, entitled
(the solemn catalogue is itself a joke) 'Winds,' 'Woods,'
'Mountains,' 'Lakes,' 'Islands,' 'Plains,' 'Streams.' In
the last of these, addressing the streams, he writes:

And *Homo Ludens*, surely, is your child, who make
Fun of our feuds by opposing identical banks,
    Transferring the loam from Huppim
        to Muppim and back each time you crankle.

And as we read on, we realize that this is the latest
Audenesque persona. Homo Ludens, incorrigibly playful,
preferring the bad pun to the good one, the arbitrary

connection to the smooth, the conspicuously wrong word -
waters 'chortling,' echoes that 'trundle,' streams that
'canter' and 'slog forward' and 'sprint' - to the inconspic-
uously right one. This was always a prominent feature of
Auden's manner, but now it is the chief controlling principle. And one could applaud it - though without the poet's
authority - as the conscious choice of a strictly limited,
superficially an all but trivial objective. The Tennysonian
discrepancy between the elaboration of the artifice and
the lack of urgency in the matter would then be no cause
for complaint, since the poet by his deliberately casual
idom admits as much and seeks our approbation only on
those deprecating terms. Certainly this is what he asks
in the Bucolics and a related piece, 'Ode to Gaea,'
where the lack of any real concern is made insolently
patent and therefore in itself innocuous. The joke, the
playfulness, is in the tacit admission that the true form
of all these pieces is the improvisation, whereas the
form that they seem to have, in print on the page, is
austerely and intricately regular, just as the facetious
diction denies precisely those 'transports' by which,
traditionally, the improvisatore justifies his perversities.

Fair enough, so far. All one asks is that the joke be
good enough, sustained and elaborated with some invention.
Unfortunately, the playfulness turns out to be ponderously
coy ('I wish I weren't so silly...,' 'Five minutes on even
the nicest mountain / Is awfully long'); and what we get
isn't Homo Ludens after all but only Auden Ludens - Auden
in short pants, acting the little horror. One realises in
fact that there is no question of a *persona*; far from wanting to efface himself behind a mask, this is the rhetorician, using language only to sell to the public his own
endearing uniqueness.

Auden's problem is clear enough: he has to find a form
for the relaxed and fluently expert writing which he now
favours, or which now favours him - a form in which he does
not have to fake the tensions and transports that are no
longer his. The form of the Bucolics - improvisation
turned inside out - was a good idea, but it let him in for
the other thing he has to guard against, pirouetting and
posturing in the public eye. A better idea was the ritual
sequence, which could serve him much as 'The Rock' served
Eliot - as an honest and proper form for poetry at a low
tension. This is what we get in Horae Canonicae, the
sequence which closes this volume. Here too, unfortunately,
in the section headed 'Vespers,' the poet finds room to
posture in; but 'Prime' (which we have seen already in the
volume 'Nones') is musical, lucid and original, and another
section, 'Sext,' though in a style nearer oratory than

poetry, is similarly controlled and memorable. In fact,
this sort of ritual recitative is surely Auden's best bet
for the future; and I hope I am wrong in suspecting, from
the 'New Yorker' tone and from one of the epigraphs ('Guard,
Civility, with guns / Your modes and your declensions'),
that this poet has made his peace with society too whole-
heartedly and too soon.

112. ANTHONY HARTLEY ON AUDEN'S TOTAL COSMOS, 'SPECTATOR'

9 December 1955, 816

Hartley (b. 1925) has worked for the 'Guardian', 'The
Economist', the 'Spectator' (as Diplomatic Correspondent
and as Deputy Editor), and 'Encounter' (as Assistant
Editor); edited 'Interplay Magazine', New York, 1967-71,
and since 1971 has been Executive Director of the Committee
of Nine of the North Atlantic Assembly. His publications
include 'A Study of England' (1963) and 'Gaullism: The Rise
and Fall of a Political Movement' (1971); he edited the
Penguin books of nineteenth and twentieth century French
verse, and the Penguin 'Mallarmé'. The largest part of
Empson and Auden, the review from which this extract is
taken, discusses Empson's 'Collected Poems'.

It is true that Mr. Empson's achievement is a limited one.
If he is compared to a poet like W.H. Auden, whose latest
collection of verse has just appeared, it is easy to see
just how limited it is. To be an *honnête homme* is, from
one point of view, simply a way of lessening the risks of
living, and, as a poet, Mr. Empson takes very few risks
indeed. His means are perfectly adapted to his aims. The
tensions may be there, but he has them well under control.
There is nothing beyond him in his world, nothing with
which he cannot cope. Mr. Auden, on the other hand,
identifies himself with the humanity of suffering, neurosis
and fear. He is a tragic poet who does not particularly
care about the dignity of tragedy. His poetry, by turns
rhetorical and colloquial, is always about to slip into
bathos. Like its creator it is not concerned with correct
attitudes. I hope I shall not be misunderstood if I say
that it is Mr. Auden's readiness to risk a thoroughly bad
poem that makes him a far greater poet than Mr. Empson,
the most original English poet, in fact, to appear during

the last thirty years.

This last volume of poems shows no sign of a deterioration in his talent. Two of the poems in it we have seen
already in 'Nones,' but they are now replaced in the
sequence for which they were intended. There is also a
series of landscape poems, which continue the note struck
in 'In Praise of Limestone' in the same collection. Once
again in these poems it becomes apparent how extremely
concrete Mr. Auden's poetry is without, curiously enough,
being at all visual in its approach. The title poem of the
book is intended to consist of a set of tableaux, but,
in fact, simply gives the impression of a set of moral
judgements:

> A ragged urchin, aimless and alone,
>   Loitered about that vacancy, a bird
> Flew up to safety from his well-aimed stone:
>   That girls are raped, that two boys knife a third,
>   Were axioms to him, who'd never heard
> Of any world where promises were kept.
> Or one could weep because another wept.

This is also a moral epistle, but of a more affective
character than Mr. Empson's, for the poet is far more
committed to a realisation of the horror of what he is
describing. Add to this less detached attitude the
anarchistic virulence of Mr. Auden's tone and imagery,
and it is quickly apparent why he has the makings of
greatness in poetry.

For, after all, poetry, like all forms of creative
activity, does involve being interested in people. You
cannot make poetry with a head full of Wittgenstein and
a rhyming dictionary. If some of Mr. Empson's poems come
off, it is because he allows his natural lyrical gift full
play. If Mr. Auden is a better poet than Mr. Empson, it
is because his poetry is more dramatic, has a wider human
range, while penetrating as deeply beneath the surface
of emotion. In this particular human activity there is
no room for an *a priori* conception of limits. Poetry
is not observation of a sector of the universe, but the
creation of a total cosmos around the poet.

113. EDMUND WILSON, W.H. AUDEN IN AMERICA, 'NEW STATESMAN AND NATION'

li, 9 June 1956, 658-9

After a temporary disaffection with Auden's work in the late 1930s (see No. 57 above), Wilson became highly enthusiastic over the poetry Auden produced after his removal to the USA in 1939. Although he criticized Auden in a letter of 9 October 1947 for the following 'sin' in particular -

> Your regurgitation in 'The Age of Anxiety', in the girl's speech over the sleeping boy, of the last pages of 'Finnegans Wake'. This is the only misstep in this poem, in which the influence of Joyce, where it elsewhere appears, is pretty completely absorbed by your own style -

he was otherwise wholly admiring -

> Aside from the echo of Joyce, I thought 'The Age of Anxiety' was wonderful - as an exploit in language and imagery, it really rivals 'Finnegans Wake'. Don't let anybody tell you that your recent work isn't your best. ('Letters on Literature and Politics', ed. Elena Wilson, London: Routledge & Kegan Paul, 1977, p. 431).

Likewise, in a letter of 10 October 1946, he stressed to William McFee that Auden

> has a much bigger public than you realize. His collected poems, published last year, sold in an amazing way. The truth is that, unlike Eliot, he represents a reversion to the old-fashioned 'family' poet - Longfellow, Wordsworth, Browning - who can be kept around and read in bulk and who provides a kind of moral pabulum. (ibid., p. 432)

In 1956, when he published this essay, Wilson also collaborated with Louise Bogan (see Nos 41 and 97) in writing a jocular poetic tribute - To Wystan Auden on His Birthday - published in 'Shenandoah', xviii, 2, Winter 1967, p. 43.

It is interesting to go back over Auden's books and to try to trace the effect on his work of his residence in the United States, to which he first came in 1939 and which, now an American citizen, he has made his headquarters ever since. Let me say at the outset that this influence of America does not seem to me in the least to have diluted the Englishness of Auden or to have changed its essential nature. Auden's genius is basically English – though in ways which, in the literary world, seem at present rather out of fashion. He is English in his toughness, his richness, his obstinacy, his adventurousness, his eccentricity. What America has done for Auden is to help him to acquire what is certainly today one of the best things an American can hope to have: a mind that feels itself at the centre of things. It has given him a point of view that is inter- or super-national.

One can see now, in re-reading Auden, that he had always a much more widely foraging habit of mind than most English writers of his generation. The chief theme of his early work was, to be sure, a British schoolboy conspiracy in which the Marxist crusade against capitalism was identified with the revolt of the young against schoolmasters and parents and their governments. The economic crisis of the Thirties gave rise to such protests everywhere and inspired such subversive hopes, but the rebellion of Auden and his friends was so much in terms of the English world – of public-school, university and Bloomsbury – in which they had grown up and been educated and in which they now felt themselves imprisoned – as scarcely to be intelligible elsewhere. A brilliant poem such as the Last Will and Testament of Auden and Louis MacNeice, included in their 'Letters from Iceland', will need eventually as many notes to explain its innumerable references to the Oxford-Cambridge-London group as the Testaments of Villon that suggested it (though it should always be able to speak for itself as the Testaments of Villon do). Yet there was more in this early Auden than the schoolboy loves and hates and the private jokes. The writer of this article, who first read Auden's poems at a time when he had seen very little of England since the beginning of the first world war in the summer of 1914, was largely unaware of their interest as a commentary on English life. It was only in 1945, when, returning to the United States after spending some time in England, he looked into these early poems of Auden again, that he found in them an illuminating picture of an England he had not known till he saw it, in a further phase, at the end of the second war: an England suburbanised, industrialised, considerably Americanised, impoverished and sadly crippled

but pretending that nothing had happened. One could see
how young men in England, in the years just before the war,
might have thought they would be happier in the United
States, where you had the whole thing on a bigger scale -
the excitements of the machine age and its bankruptcies,
the vulgarities as well as the freedoms of an era of social
levelling - and with not so much of the past to act as a
drag on new departures. Those who criticised Auden and his
friends in the Thirties for not outgrowing their schoolboy
mentality should not blame them for breaking away and
betaking themselves to a country where hardly half-a-dozen
names in the Iceland Testament would even be recognised.
They had already begun to explore: Spain and Germany as
well as Iceland. Auden and Christopher Isherwood had
made, in 1938, a journey to Hongkong and Shanghai, then had
crossed the Pacific to Vancouver and ended up in New York.
They returned at that time to Europe, but the following
year came back to live permanently here in the United
States. With Auden the process of Americanisation had
already begun in England. He had been reading American
writers, had tried his hand at American ballads, and had
shown, in these and in 'The Dance of Death', published in
1933, that he had already - in rather a surprising way -
got the hang of the American vernacular.

The first fruits of Auden's American period - especially
'New Year Letter' of 1941, which contains the long poem of
that title and the sonnet sequence The Quest - are already
in certain ways quite distinct form anything he had written
in England. The poet is more alone. 'Derek' and his other
allies as well as 'the enemy' of 'The Orators' have disappeared in The Quest.

> What is the greatest wonder in the world?
> The bare man Nothing in the Beggar's Bush.

These strange *dépaysés* sonnets seem to me unique and
enchanting - their fairy-like phantoms that alternate with
commonplace down-to-earth phrases, their images that dilate
or wobble, the mysterious concluding poem with its blur of
beginnings and endings:

> The gaunt and great, the famed for conversation
> Blushed in the stare of evening as they spoke,
> And felt their centre of volition shifted.

It was in connection with 'New Year Letter' that the writer
of this article first noticed a certain characteristic of
Auden's writing. If one was baffled by a passage in one
of his poems, one was likely to become aware soon after-

ward that what the poet had been saying was something that, precisely, one had just felt oneself but that one had hardly expected to find expressed in poetry so promptly.

If the hero of The Quest seems stripped of old friends, the longer poem, 'New Year Letter', addressed to a refugee from Germany, opens on a larger vista than those of the earlier poems:

> Across East River in the night
> Manhattan is ablaze with light...
>
> More even than in Europe, here
> The choice of patterns is made clear
> Which the machine imposes, what
> Is possible and what is not,
> To what conditions we must bow
> In building the Just City now.

The last lines of this poem give voice to the poet's exhilaration in moving about the world and the conviction of solidarity with companions in anxiety everywhere that was justified by such a response on the part of the foreign reader as, in my own case, I have mentioned above:

> O every day in sleep and labour
> Our life and death are with our neighbour,
> And love illuminates again
> The city and the lion's den,
> The world's great rage, the travel of young men.

He touches here on American history, but he makes no attempt to talk American. He speaks of 'East River' without the article, as no New Yorker would do. One finds in the 'Letter', as in The Quest, an accent of loneliness. Yet one feels that the poet is now, as he was not in his earlier poems, a completely free-swimming organism; and he has created his extraordinary new language, a brilliant international English, which may drop into French or German or carry along bits of Latin and Greek, and which is presently to absorb much American. He is not here any longer rebelling against British institutions that have irked his boyhood. He is dealing with the whole modern world: its discomforts, its disquiets, its crimes, its myths - 'the city and the lion's den'; with the problem of how to live in it, to get out of it what it can give, to avoid being paralysed or bought by it. It may well be that this aspect of Auden is more intelligible to an American than to an Englishman, for this feeling oneself a member of a determined resistant minority has been now for

nearly a hundred years a typical situation in America.
Such people in the later nineteenth century were likely to
be defeated or embittered. In our own, they have felt
the backing of a partly inarticulate public who are not
satisfied with the bilge that the popular media feed
them in their movies and magazines, and who are grateful
to anyone who will make a stand for that right to think
for themselves which is supposed to be guaranteed us by
the Bill of Rights and that right to a high level of
culture which the framers of the Constitution - taking
it so much for granted - would never have thought to
include. These American writers of which I speak do not
constitute a group, they do not frequent an official café;
and on this account, the visitor from Europe is likely to
come to the conclusion that, except in the universities,
we have no intellectual life. He cannot conceive that the
American writers are functioning in the crevices of cities,
on the faculties of provincial colleges or scattered all
over the country in the solitude of ranches and farms.
This kind of life was now to be Auden's lot, and he must
have had some desolating experiences:

> Some think they're strong, some think they're smart,
> Like butterflies they're pulled apart,
> America can break your heart.
> *You don't know all, sir, you don't know all.*

But I have always been struck by the naturalness with which
Auden took things here for granted and - though I thought
there was a good deal he did not understand - with the
perfect propriety of his being here. One felt this
especially when one noticed how easily he was able to
incorporate the American colloquial speech, American
allusions and customs, into the marvellous amalgam of his
language, along with his foreign quotations, his technical vocabulary of botany, psychology and metallurgy
(that sometimes derail the reader) and all those toothsome
old British words - such as *mawmet, faffle* and *balter* -
that turn out, when you look them up, to be Prov. Eng.
or Dial. Eng., Archaic or Obsolete. It is not a question
here of a successful American impersonation, as in the
case of those stories of Kipling's that are supposed to be
told by Americans or of those parts of Isherwood's
'The World in the Evening' in which the narrator's
American aspect is supposed to be uppermost. Such performances are *tours de force,* in which the least slip
will jar. But in Auden an 'East River' or two does not
matter, since it is not an imaginary American who is
speaking - and even when Auden has assigned his lines to

some invented being (he has little dramatic sense) -
it is the language of Auden that is speaking, and this
language has breathed in its Americanism as easily as its
Oxford gossip, its country talk of '*leats*' and '*eagres,*'
its Horatian and Anglo-Saxon metres. The poem called 'The
Unknown Citizen', contributed to the 'New Yorker' at an
early stage of Auden's American residence, was a satire on
standardisation of a kind of which we had already had a
good deal and which it did not take Auden to give us; but
by the time he did his Phi Beta Kappa ode for Harvard in
1946, he had a quite intimate knowledge of the special
world to which he was addressing himself, and had something of his own to tell it. [Under Which Lyre, CP(M), 259]

It is curious to compare Auden in his London dress of
the 'Poems' of 1930, published by Faber & Faber, one of
their thin and distinguished volumes that all the smart
people read, with Auden in American homespun - or at least,
in a New York suit - the 'Collected Poetry' of 1945, published by Random House. Hardly can we recognise here the
young man, just up from Oxford, who appeared, under Eliot's
patronage, in company with a few select friends. The
friends are no longer present; the poems that seemed to
herald the British revolution - including some very good
ones - have for the most part been pitilessly scrapped.
We find a volume printed on not good grey paper, of over
four hundred pages, in which the poems are all run together,
not beginning on separate pages, and in which old poems
have been given new titles of a colloquial, even folksy
kind: 'Please Make Yourself at Home', 'It's Too Much',
'Something is Bound to Happen', 'Venus Will Now Say a Few
Words'. Here are most of our favourite old friends, along
with a lot of new ones, sitting around in New York or
strolling on the college campus. One saw with surprise
that Auden - so far from being a rarity that could only be
appreciated by a few - was the old-fashioned kind of poet,
like Browning or Henry Wadsworth Longfellow (not that I
would compare him with the latter), who is at his best when
printed and read in bulk. He amuses us, converses with
us, does his best to give us good advice; he sings us
comic songs, supplies us with brilliant elegies on the
deaths of great contemporaries; he charms us, he lulls us
to sleep; he lifts us to a moment of inspiration. In
metrics, in architectonics, as well as in handling of
language, he is, of course, an incredible virtuoso - the
most accomplished poet in English since the great
nineteenth-century masters; Tennyson, Browning and
Swinburne; he does not call attention to this, and many
people who read him do not even know it. If he is not
precisely a 'family poet' like Longfellow, Wordsworth,

and Tennyson, the fact that he is one of the most edible,
one of the most satisfactory of contemporary writers in
verse is proved by the sales of the 'Collected Poetry',
which have reached, in the United States, the almost
unprecedented figure of over thirty thousand copies.

I have had lately a little the feeling that the
interest for Auden of the United States is not now quite
so lively as it once was. His last book, 'The Shield of
Achilles', seems less localised than any of its predecessors. One of its most attractive features is the
sequence of lovely Bucolics that consists - under such
bald titles as 'Mountains', 'Lakes', 'Islands' and so on -
of generalised pieces about landscape, about landscape
presented in a novel but very characteristic way that is
at once geological and subjective. Since becoming an
American citizen, the poet has not ceased to explore, to
roam - he has covered more ground in this country than
most Americans do, and he now spends every summer in
Italy. This spring he returns to England to be lecturer
on poetry at Oxford. It is a part of his role to go
everywhere, be accessible to all sorts of people, serve
interestedly and conscientiously in innumerable varied
capacities: on the staff of a Middle Western college;
at a cultural congress in India; on a grand jury in New
York City, deciding the fate of gangsters; on a committee
of the American Academy, making handouts to needy writers.
He has above all withstood the ordeal of America through
a habitation of seventeen years; he has even 'succeeded'
here. And he has made all these exploits contribute to
the work of a great English poet who is also - in the not
mondain sense - one of the great English men of the world.

'Homage to Clio'

New York, April 1960; London, July 1960

114. DONALD HALL, DRY FARMING, 'NEW STATESMAN'

9 July 1960, 61-2

Hall (b. 1928) taught at the University of Michigan,
Ann Arbor, from 1957 to 1977, and has been Poetry Editor
of 'Paris Review', 1953-61. Author of several volumes
of verse, he has also edited the 'Faber Book of Modern
Verse' (1966).

W.H. Auden begins his latest collection with four lines on
the dehydration of land, which ends, 'Methods of dry
farming may still produce grain.' If the analogy is intended to apply to the poet in his fifties, good work behind
him and old age ahead, one can at least report that
'Homage to Clio' fills the barn with a healthy crop. One
may be irritated at Auden for a variety of reasons but one
must admit at the very least that he has an interesting
mind and that his language is adequate to it. 'Homage to
Clio' is a civilised pleasure, like the 'good dinner'
which Auden hopes for, 'Should the night come when comets
blaze and meres break.'
   It is true that the pleasure is 'dry', if by that adjective we mean that the pleasure occurs largely in Lawrence's
'upper cerebral regions'. The two big poems on which the
book chiefly depends - 'Homage to Clio' and 'Good-bye to
the Mezzogiorno' - are roughly in the manner of 'In Praise
of Limestone', which is I suppose Auden's most successful
poem of the recent past. They are written in a syllabic
stanza which alternates lines of eleven and nine syllables.
(In fact Auden allows himself considerable variation in
the count, but there is so much consistency that we must

call the form syllabic. Strictness of number is less
relevant in long-lined syllabics than in most metres,
because the ear cannot count over five or six without
concentrating on the count rather than on the sense.)
Auden performs the peculiar tone of the syllabic with his
customary light skill. Make a new fiddle and he'll be its
master. Syllabics are hard to describe: they give a sense
of randomness within control. One poet has borrowed
Leavis's phrase, 'creative exploration', to explain the
sensation; another once said, with an irony which he intended, that they conveyed 'the authority of prose'. Here
is Auden's chatty, inclusive, anti-rhetorical manner, from
'Goodbye to the Mezzogiorno':

[Quotes from the first 10 lines of the poem, CP (M) 486.]

His wit, which rhyme can make flashy, stands unaided by
gimmicks, and is all the more effective.
   As usual, he does a variety of things well. His
'Metalogue to the Magic Flute' is an occasional poem done
in Augustan pastiche, and it is full of asides and allusions: 'Even *Macaulay's* schoolboy knows today what
Robert Graves or *Margaret Mead* would say About the
status of the sexes in this play...' Auden rhymes brilliantly on the off-stress in 'Dame Kind', writes a fine
sonnet in 'Objects', and applies for membership in The
Movement in 'Words'.

   A sentence uttered makes a world appear
   Where all things happen as it says they do;
   We doubt the speaker, not the tongue we hear:
   Words have no word for words that are not true.

Some of his best short lyrics in recent years are
'Makers of History' and 'There will Be No Peace'.
Finally we have a section of thirty-two clerihews, two
limericks and a tribute to Canon Jenkins of Christ Church.
   The theme of the book is history, and the theme occurs
throughout; even the dull stretch of prose notes - a sort
of a diary kept while not writing a love poem - brings
up the subject. Clio here is not merely the muse of
armies and senates - though Auden fears, like any sane man,
that our civilisation is done for; she is the sense of
time passing and time past. Auden is a nostalgic
historian and his attitude toward history is paradoxically
sustained by his desire for change. Northern visitors to
Italy want to understand 'from / What we are not what we
might be next...' Auden has always looked in the mirror
to see who he is. The pathos, for the reader, is that he

is always the same. He learns new ways of writing or
abandons old ones; he reads a new book, he picks up a new
idea. He resembles the creature of the limestone
landscape: intelligent, not terribly committed, restless, and unable to break out of his own detachment.

Of course this is why Auden irritates us. Also, he
irritates us because, as a literary influence, he has been
responsible for so much which is sloppy and specious and
semi-accomplished. One cannot blame a poet beçause his
followers are bad; one may blame him for the *way* they are
bad. His own affectation of carelessness (I assume that
he knows he is outrageous) produces real carelessness in
others. In his 'Goodbye to the Mezzogiorno', after witty
and splendid lines he suddenly uses cliché dead metaphors
of the grossest sort: '...there *yawns a gulf* / Embraces
cannot *bridge*.' (My italics.) One imagines W.H.A. telling
W.H.A. 'Watch out. You're being too bright. Be modest.
Muck it up a bit.' Or maybe W.H.A. would only quote a
line from W.H.A.'s 'Homage to Clio' (torn protesting from
its context): 'Banalities can be beautiful.'

115. PHILIP LARKIN, WHAT'S BECOME OF WYSTAN?, 'SPECTATOR'

ccv, 15 July 1960, 104-5

Larkin (b. 1922) is Librarian of the Brynmor Jones
Library, University of Hull. Poet, novelist, and critic,
his books include 'Jill' (novel, 1946), 'A Girl in Winter'
(novel, 1947), 'The Whitsun Weddings' (verse, 1964), 'High
Windows' (1974), and the 'Oxford Book of Twentieth Century
English Verse' (ed., 1973).

I have been trying to imagine a discussion of Auden between
one man who had read nothing of his after 1940 and another
who had read nothing before. After an initial agreement
by adjective - 'Versatile,' 'Fluent,' 'Too smart sometimes'
a mystifying gap would open between them, as one spoke of
a tremendously exciting English social poet full of
energetic unliterary knock-about and unique lucidity of
phrase, and the other of an engaging, bookish, American
talent, too verbose to be memorable and too intellectual
to be moving. And not only would they differ about his
poetic character: there would be a sharp division of
opinion about his poetic stature.

Only an experiment of this kind could bring home how little the last twenty years have added to Auden's reputation. Why should this be so? He has remained energetic and productive; his later work shows the same readiness to experiment coupled with new and (in theory) maturer themes; he has not lost his sense of humour. And yet no one is going to justify his place in literary history by 'The Shield of Achilles' any more than Swinburne's is justified by 'Poems and Ballads: Third Series.'

The appearance of his latest collection 'Homage to Clio,' marks the end of the third decade of Auden's poetic life and does not alter the fact that almost all we value is still confined to its first ten years. We need not remind ourselves of his virtues - the wide-angled rhetoric, the seamless lyricism, the sudden gripping dramatisations - but to understand what succeeded it we must understand to what extent his poetry was of its time. He was, of course, the first 'modern' poet, in that he could employ modern properties unselfconsciously ('A solitary truck, the last Of shunting in the Autumn'), but he was modern also by embracing a kind of neo-Wordsworthianism which, in an effort to put poetry at the service of the working-class movement, called it 'memorable speech' and made no theoretical distinction between 'Paradise Lost' and 'The Young Fellow Called Dave.' This view held that if the poet were not concerned with the historic necessities of the age and akin to the healer and the explorer (typical figures!) his work would be deservedly disregarded.

Few poets since Pope have been so committed to their period. It is not only that to be at home in Auden's poetry we must recognise Bishop Barnes, Coghlan's coffin, Van der Lubbe and all the personalia of 'Last Will and Testament' ('Letters from Iceland,' with Louis MacNeice); we shall also find the depression, strikes, the hunger marchers; we shall find Spain and China; and above all we shall encounter not only the age's properties but its obsessions: feeling inferior to the working class, a sense that things needed a new impetus from somewhere, seeing out of the corner of an eye the rise of Fascism, the persecution of the Jews, the gathering dread of the next war that was half projected guilt about the last:

The chairs are being brought in from the garden,
The summer talk stopped on that savage coast
Before the storms, after the guests and birds:
In sanatoriums they laugh less and less,
Less certain of cure; and the loud madman
Sinks now into a more terrible calm.   [EA, 40]

It is precisely this dominant and ubiquitous unease
that lay at the centre of Auden's verse and which he was
so apt to express. How quickly, for example, he seized on
the symbol of 'the Struggle,' 'the game ... that tends to
become like a war'; in other writers as well as Auden this
concept of the 'Two Sides' was used time and again to
represent the young against the old, the poor against the
rich, the healthy against the diseased, the class struggle,
Spain, the coming war. And whereas the conflict was
originally seen as victorious ('The Orators'), as the
Thirties wore on disaster became more and more likely.
It was in this atmosphere that Auden's sensitivity was
quickened and his perceptions heightened, perceptions not
only of
    Ten thousand of the desperate marching by
    Five feet, six feet, seven feet high,

but also how

        in the houses
    The little pianos are closed, and a clock strikes.

I have stressed this identification not for its own sake
but to make clear why Auden's outlook was completely dis-
located when it ceased. As everyone knows, this came about
in two ways - by the outbreak of war in 1939, and by Auden's
departure for America a few months earlier. At one stroke
he lost his key subject and emotion - Europe and the fear
of war - and abandoned his audience together with their
common dialect and concerns. For a different sort of poet
this might have been less important. For Auden it seems to
have been irreparable.
    His immediate reaction was to take a header into litera-
ture. Previously few writers had been named in his pages -
Lawrence, Owen, Katherine Mansfield - which was eloquent
of his 'deep abhorrence'

    If I caught anyone preferring Art
    To Life and Love and being Pure-in-Heart.   [EA, 195]

Now there came a whole flood. One cannot but notice the
shift in tone from the disrespectful reference in 1937 to
'Daunty, Gouty, Shopkeeper, the three Supreme Old Masters'
to the eulogistic invocation in the 'New Year Letter' of
1941:

> Romance? Not in this weather. Ovid's charmer
>   Who leads the quadrilles in Arcady, boy-lord
> Of hearts who can call their Yes and No their own.
>   Would, madcap that he is, soon die of cold or sunstroke:
> Their lives are in firmer hands: that old grim She
>   Who makes the blind dates for the hatless genera
> Creates their country matters.   [Plains, CP(M), 432]

Such is, explicitly, the kind of thing he likes:

> Be subtle, various, ornamental, clever.
> And do not listen to those critics ever
> Whose crude provincial gullets crave in books
> Plain cooking made still plainer by plain cooks.[CP(M), 470]

This view must be what permits lines like 'Just reeling off
their names is ever so comfy' or:

> She mayn't be all She might be but
>   She *is* our Mum.   [CP(M), 503]

Are there people who talk this dialect, or is it how Auden
talks to himself?

Secondly, one cannot escape the conclusion that in some
way Auden, never a pompous poet, has now become an unserious
one. For some time he has insisted that poetry is a game,
with the elements of a crossword puzzle: it is 'the luck
of verbal playing.' One need not be a romantic to suspect
that this attitude will produce poetry exactly answering
to that description. Here again it seems that Auden was
happier when his work had an extraneous social function,
and if he feels that poetry is fundamentally unserious
otherwise it is a pity he parted from it, for lack of
serious intention too often means lack of serious effect.

In the end that is what our discontent comes down to:
Auden no longer touches our imaginations. My guess is
that the peculiar insecurity of pre-war England sharpened
his talent in a way that nothing else has, or that once
'the next War' really arrived everything since has seemed
to him an anti-climax. But these are only guesses. Something, after all, led him to write 'A poet's prayer' in
'New Year letter': 'Lord, teach me to write so well that
I shall no longer want to.' In any case it is our loss.

116. GRAHAM HOUGH ON TALENTED GLIBNESS, FROM AN UNTITLED REVIEW, 'LISTENER'

lxiv, 28 July 1960, 159-60

Hough (b. 1908), Professor of English at the University of Cambridge from 1966 to 1975, is author of 'The Last Romantics' (1949), 'The Romantic Poets' (1953), 'The Dark Sun' (1957), 'Image and Experience' (1960), and 'Selected Essays' (1978).

There are times when one suspects Professor Auden of being less than wholly serious. Whoever it came from this would be a slimmish collection. It is filled out with limericks, clerihews very much like other people's clerihews, and a piece of academic compliment that might have been written by anybody at all. There is also a long prose apologia for a poem that did not get written; and this is probably the key to the book. The poem is one that has never really been written, though half the European lyric is concerned with making approximations to it. It is the poem that would express exactly what it means to say 'I love you'. By now the approximations to it are so numerous that hardly anyone dares to attempt it at all. Auden made his own beautiful attempt once, years ago (in 'Lay your sleeping head my love'), and now instead he writes a penetrating set of aphorisms and reflections around it. The other poems in this volume, many of them concerned with the ironies of fame and history, are as usual dazzlingly intelligent, genially witty, and formidably well read. But these admirable and enviable qualities are not in the end those which produce poetry. He has almost said so in his dedication:

> Bullroarers cannot keep up the annual rain,
> The water-table of a once green champaign
> Sinks, will keep on sinking: but why complain?
>   - Against odds,
> Methods of dry farming may still produce grain.

We should be the last to complain; the grain produced by Auden's dry farming, even the occasional patches of corn, make a better harvest than the well-irrigated crops of most other cultivators. Some of these pieces are written in that wonderful spoof form that American Creative Writing teachers call syllabic verse.* It consists of chopping up a passage of prose into symmetrical lengths;

but when Auden does it one's irritation at the imposture is quite overcome by admiration for the impudent dexterity. In many places there is a glib familiarity with the big ideas that treads dangerously near to vulgarization. But after all there is nothing like talent; and when the deeper springs of poetry fail there is no writer who has so much of it to fall back on as Auden.

Note

*   [In his essay Marianne Moore ('The Dyer's Hand', 1962) Auden acknowledged that for a long time after first reading Miss Moore's work in 1935 he had failed to 'hear' her syllabic verse but had lately come to appreciate its qualities.]

117. THOM GUNN ON AUDEN'S TIRED MANNERISMS, FROM MANNER AND MANNERISM, 'YALE REVIEW'

Autumn 1960, 133-5

An English poet long resident in the USA, Gunn (b. 1929) is the author of several volumes including 'My Sad Captains' (1961), 'Moly' (1971), 'Jack Straw's Castle' (1967), and 'Selected Poems 1950-1975' (1979).

The most solid performance in W.H. Auden's latest book is the 'Metalogue to "The Magic Flute."'

[quotes 11. 86-91 from 'A work that lasts two hundred years is tough...', CP(M), 442.]

These lines are characteristic: workmanlike and witty. At the same time, the poem's limitations are so obvious that they scarcely need mentioning; it is an excellent pastiche of eighteenth-century poetry from beginning to end, down to the italicized proper names. Very good in its way, but the rest of the book doesn't rise even to the level of a pastiche. He addresses the Muse Clio in these terms:

> ... I have seen
> Your photo, I think, in the papers, nursing
> A baby or mourning a corpse: each time
>
> You had nothing to say and did not, one could see,
>   Observe where you were, Muse of the unique
> Historical fact, defending with silence
>   Some world of your beholding, a silence
>
> No explosion can conquer but a lover's Yes
> Has been known to fill...

There is some kind of idea behind this passage, but the writing is so tired that it has no chance to emerge. Almost everything possible is wrong with it: the style is recognizably Auden - too recognizably, for he is using his own mannerisms like an imitator; 'a lover's Yes' is a sentimental indulgence worthy of Cummings; the movement is dull, the meter being impossible to identify; and I suspect that the identation of alternate lines serves no purpose at all. The passage is typical of the serious verse in the new volume, though not so bad as 'There Will Be no Peace,' perhaps the worst of Auden's poems I have seen in book form. Besides the serious verse, there is a collection of semi-epigrammatic prose notes which amount to a confession of inadequacy and nothing much more, and a lot of comic verse which is pretty light-weight compared with his other work of this kind.

I cannot agree with the critics who find a progressive deterioration in every successive volume of Auden's poetry. He has written a great deal, and has published much that is carelessly executed. But most of his weakest poetry was written in the middle 'thirties: the later 'For the Time Being' has all the vigor of 'Poems' and 'The Orators', and is written with a good deal more cunning. And many of the poems in the recent books have been excellent, showing a calm thoughtfulness that I personally prefer to the excitement of the earlier poems. But 'Homage to Clio' is probably his worst book since 'The Dance of Death'.

What, then, has happened? I think we may find the answer, indirectly, in four lines from the 'Magic Flute' poem:

> It makes a servantless New Yorker sore
> To think sheer Genius had to stand before
> A mere Archbishop with uncovered head:
> But *Mozart* never had to make his bed.

The implication is that Mozart's time was superior to ours
for two reasons: the representatives of orthodox religion
were properly respected, and there were plenty of servants.
The lines are intended as a kind of epigram, of course,
but the epigram is seriously meant. Auden has in fact
reached a stage of belief, or lack of belief, very similar
to Betjeman's attitude of High Church snobbery. The
trouble is that High Church snobbery tends to repress the
active intelligence, replacing it with the habit of
continual trifling. You cannot even, finally, be sure
whether the trifler is a snob or not, he is so lightheartedly evasive in his tone. And the acceptance of an
attitude similar to Betjeman's appears to have led Auden
to write poetry that is both morally and technically
frivolous: gracious living has become a moral value in it,
and he tolerates the easiest way out with diction and
meter except when he imagines he is writing in the eighteenth century. In the past, he has shown magnificent
resourcefulness in his powers of recovery: I hope it does
not seem presumptuous in an admirer half his age to
suggest that it is now time for him to call on all his
resources once more.

'About the House'

New York, July 1965; London, January 1966

118. JOHN UPDIKE ON AUDEN'S HUMANISTIC RELAXATION,
UNTITLED REVIEW, 'MOTIVE'

xxvi, November 1965, 50-2

A novelist, writer for children, poet, and playwright,
Updike (b. 1932) has published many books including
'Couples' (1968), 'The Centaur' (1963), 'Midpoint and
Other Poems' (1969), 'The Coup' (1979), and 'Picked-Up
Pieces' (1975), which reprints this review on pp. 248-54
under the title Auden Fecit.

[Quotes 11. 1034-7 ('There are two atlases...'),
and 11. 1047-52 ('The other is the inner space...'), of
'New Year Letter', CP(M), 180-1.]

Thus, in his great 'New Year Letter' of 1940, Auden distinguished between the two realms explored by his lifelong
search for civilization. As a young man, his concern was
more with 'public space,' and he remains *the* poet of the
foreboding that preceded World War II, the lucid
exhausted voice of 'September 1, 1939' and of the elegies
to Freud and Yeats, both dead in 1939. As an aging post-
war man, he has turned more toward the 'inner space,' the
landscape of his will and need and (from the same poem)
'the *polis* of our friends.' His latest collection,
'About the House,' celebrates this intimate city, the
microcosm of his privacy, in almost doting detail. But the
best of the poems are redeemed from triviality by the
seriousness with which Auden considers his own comfort an
episode in civilization.
    The first, and superior, half of the book is a sequence

of twelve poems inspired by the rooms of his recently acquired house in Austria. Each poem carries a personal dedication, and though the anonymous reader may be charmed by intimations of custom-tailored pertinence (a husband and wife get the cellar and attic respectively, and Christopher Isherwood is awarded the toilet), he is more likely to feel merely excluded; what with the Kennedys, the Glasses, the Sinatra Clan, the friends of Norman Podhoretz, and the Pop-Camp-Hip crowd, there seem enough in-groups in the western world without a formal roll-call of Auden's acquaintanceship. Plato's vision of the Perfect City ruled by philosopher-kings seems somewhat impudently transmuted into genial snobbery:

> The houses of our City
>   are real enough but they lie
> haphazardly scattered over the earth,
>   and her vagabond forum
> is any space where two of us happen to meet
>   who can spot a citizen
> without papers.   [CP(M), 531]

Technically, the sequence is marred by the erratic interruption of 'Postscripts' - short poems in another meter, often in the irksome form of *haiku*, tacked on wherever (however vaguely) appropriate. And it must be said that Auden, in developing each room into a cosmic instance and drawing significance from every nook, does not always avoid his besetting sin of, well, silliness. The steamy bath is extolled in an uncharacteristic non-meter which he explains as a 'mallarmesque / syllabic fog,' and the stanzas to excrement include:

> Freud did not invent the
> Constipated miser:
> Banks have letter boxes
> Built in their façade,
> Marked *For Night Deposits,*
> Stocks are firm or liquid,
> Currencies of nations
> Either soft or hard.   [CP(M), 527]

But in sum the twelve poems comprise an impressive essay upon Man the domestic animal; his domesticity is felt as a consecration of his animality.

> city planners are mistaken: a pen
>   for a rational animal
> is no fitting habitat for Adam's
>   sovereign clone.   [CP(M), 520]

Precise biological terms - clone, conurbation, neotene -
insist on humanity's living context. The poem on the
dining-room with high wit summarizes the full organic
history of dining:

[Quotes from 'Tonight at seven-thirty', 11. 1-8 ('The life
of plants ... more terrified...'), and 11. 11-20 ('Only man
... pickled Leviathan'), CP(M), 533.]

The house abounds in remembrances of human prehistory: the
cellar 'Reminds our warm and windowed quarters upstairs
that / Caves water-scooped from limestone were our first
dwellings'; the archetype of the poet's workroom is
'Weland's Stithy'; like the 'prehistoric hearthstone, /
round as a birthday-button / and scared to Granny,' the
modern kitchen is the center of the dwelling; and, in
conclusion, 'every home should be a fortress, / equipped
with all the very latest engines / for keeping Nature at
bay, / versed in all ancient magic, the arts of quelling /
the Dark Lord and his hungry / animivorous chimeras.'
Nor is history forgotten: the bathroom is seen as a
shrunken tepidarium; the dining table is compared with
'Christ's cenacle' and 'King Arthur's rundle'; and
the peace of the living-room is felt against 'History's
criminal noise.' The function of each chamber is searched
in such depth that a psychological portrait of man is
achieved. Auden finds in defecation the prime Art, an
'ur-act of making'; in swallowing 'a sign act of reverence';
in sleeping a 'switch from personage, / with a state number,
a first and family name, / to the naked Adam or Eve.'
His psychological portrait is controlled, at times play-
fully, by religious conceptions:

     then surely those in whose creed
  God is edible may call a fine
    omelette a Christian deed.   [CP(M), 531]

Biology tends toward theology; our personal and animal
particulars are grounded in the divine ontology. Speech
is 'a work of re-presenting / the true olamic silence.'
This sequence of poems, entitled 'Thanksgiving for a
habitat,' is an essay in architecture, which is to say
the creation of a structure enabling the human organism
to perform its supernaturally determined functions of
praise and service. In a faithless age, there are

     no architects, any more
  than there are heretics or bounders: to take
    umbrage at death, to construct

> a second nature of tomb and temple, lives
>   must know the meaning of *if*.   [CP(M), 518]

While one regrets that Auden's Christian faith is so iffy,
its presence has enabled him to organize his centrifugal
variety of perceptions into a credible humanism.
The second half, 'In and Out' (a habitat has been previously defined as ' a place / I may go both in and out of'),
consists of poems, often about traveling, that are casual
in tone and middling in quality. The best is the last,
'Whitsunday in Kirchstetten,' a kind of annex to the house
poems, wherein the poet is discovered temporarily domiciled
in church. In the author's best new style, the long lines,
exotic vocabulary, and discursive sequiturs limn what was
rather conspicuously absent from the house sequence – a
sense of the 'public space,' the enveloping condition of
the world:

>   from Loipersbach
> to the Bering Sea not a living stockbroker,
>   and church attendance is frowned upon
> like visiting brothels (but the chess and physics
>   are still the same)....
>   Down a Gothic nave
> comes our Pfarrer now, blessing the West with water:
>   we may go.

Again 'Hammerfest,' a description of Auden's visit to
Norway's northernmost township, frames within his baroque
sense of lapsed time – 'the glum Reptilian Empire / Or the
epic journey of the Horse' – the geological innocence of a
region whose 'only communities.../ Were cenobite, mosses
and lichen, sworn to / Station and reticence.' And of
the many (too many) poems in haiku-stanzas, I liked best
'Et in Arcadia Ego,' a rephrasing of his habitual accus-
atory apostrophe to 'Dame Kind' – who 'Can imagine the
screeching / Virago, the Amazon, / Earth Mother was?' The
poem uses the exigencies of this Japanese form to generate
lines of great energy, both polysyllabic ('Her exorbitant
monsters abashed') and monosyllabic ('Geese podge home').
Auden is the supreme metrical tinkerer. Haiku, canzoni,
ballades, limericks, clerihews, alliterative verse (a
whole eclogue's worth) – there is nothing he will not
attempt and make, to some extent, work. His ability, as in
'Tonight at Seven-Thirty,' to coin an elaborate stanza-
form and to effortlessly repeat it over and over, evokes
the seventeenth-century metaphysicals and Tennyson: the
latter more than the former. His technical ingenuity
casts doubt upon the urgency of his inspiration. It is
one thing to sing in a form, whether it be Homeric
hexameters or Popian couplets, until it becomes a natural

voice; it is another to challenge your own verbal resources with insatiable experimentation. In any collection by Auden there are hardly two successive poems in the same form, which gives even his most integral sequences, such as the Horae Canonicae of 'The Shield of Achilles,' a restless and jagged virtuosity. As a poet, his vocation begins in the joy of fabrication rather than in an impulse of cele- bration: in ways it is strength, enabling him to outlive his youth, to explore, to grow, to continue to think, even - blasphemous suggestion! - to believe, in order to feed the verse-making machine. He is that anachronism, the poet as maker; but he makes expressions rather than, by mimesis, men and deeds. Compared to Eliot, he has no dramatic imagination. Despite an almost desperate metrical juggling, his plays and dialogues are the monologues of one very intellectually imaginative voice. He dramatizes all sides of an issue, but lacks the modesty, the impish and casual self-forgetfulness, that tossed off Prufrock, Cousin Harriet, Sweeney, and the curiously vigorous phantoms of 'The Waste Land.' If Eliot was a dramatist, Auden is an essayist, in the root sense: he will try any- thing, but his adventures never take him beyond the terri- tory of the first person singular. He is one of the few modern poets whose genius is for the long discursive poem; for all his formal invention, he has written best in two rather accommodating meters - a long, elegaic, unrhymed or loosely rhymed line less regular than pentameter, and the tetrameter quatrains or couplets associated with music hall lyrics and with light verse.

His light vein is very rich. What could be better than, say, this stanza from 'On the Circuit'? -

Since Merit but a dunghill is,
I mount the rostrum unafraid:
Indeed, 'twere damnable to ask
If I am overpaid.

or this, from 'After Reading a Child's Guide to Modern Physics'? -

Marriage is rarely bliss
But, surely, it would be worse
As particles to pelt
At thousands of miles per sec
About a universe
In which a lover's kiss
Would either not be felt
Or break the loved one's neck.

In his present pleasant house, to which his dream of

the City has congenially dwindled, Auden portrays his
workroom, 'The Cave of Making,' with 'windows averted
from plausible / videnda but admitting a light one /
could mend a watch by.' By such dry clear light, a dictionary at hand, he is best read - not, as he hopes, as 'a
minor atlantic Goethe' (the difference in generosity may
be less between Goethe and himself than between Goethe's
Europe and our America), but as a man who, with a childlike
curiosity and a feminine fineness of perception, treats
poetry as the exercise of wit. For almost always, in his
verse, the oracular and ecstatic flights fail; what we
keep are the fractional phrases that could be expressed in
prose, but less pointedly. In his own anthology of light
verse, he defines it as poetry written in the common
language of men. Powerfully attracted by the aristocratic
and the arcane, he has struggled to preserve his democratic
loyalties, his sense of poetry as a mode of discourse between civilized men. 'About the House,' though it contains
no single poem as fine as 'Ode to Gaea' from 'The Shield of
Achilles,' has nothing in it as tedious as the infatuated
concept-chopping of the 'Dichtung and Wahrheit' interlude
of 'Homage to Clio'; and on the whole marks a new frankness
and a new relaxation in tone. Auden remains, in the Spirit
as well as by the Letter, alive.

119. C.B. COX, AT HOME WITH AUDEN, 'SPECTATOR'

ccxvi, 4 February 1966, 141-2

C.B. Cox (b. 1928) is John Edward Taylor Professor of
English Literature at the University of Manchester, and
has co-edited 'Critical Quarterly' since 1959. His books
include 'Joseph Conrad: The Modern Imagination' (1974),
as well as studies in the practical criticism of poetry.

Auden's new book begins with a sequence of twelve poems
about the various rooms in his Austrian house, from the
most public to the most private. In the 'white-tiled
cabin Arabs call the House where Everybody goes,' he
meditates lightheartedly on the analogies between art
and daily evacuation. The maker strives in his chosen
medium 'to produce a De-narcissus-ised enduring excrement.'
   With much gusto and wit Auden deliberately shocks
readers who want poetry to be a substitute religion, a
form of magic offering panaceas for the times. In recent
years he has insisted with growing emphasis that poetry is

comparatively unimportant, only a game of knowledge. 'About the House' also includes his elegy for Louis MacNeice, in which he reflects sadly on the small influence his 'unpopular art' can have in our affluent society. Auden does not agree with Shelley that the poet is an unacknowledged legislator; this description is more appropriate to the secret police. In his selection of prose essays, 'The Dyer's Hand,' he argues that in modern society the poet is 'singularly ill-equipped to understand politics or economics'; his interest is in unique individuals and personal relations, while politics and economics are concerned with the average man (with whom the poet is bored to death). He is no prophet, for as soon as he raises his voice he sounds phoney. The man of action today is a scientist: 'When I find myself in the company of scientists, I feel like a shabby curate who has strayed by mistake into a drawing-room full of dukes.'

'About the House' has much in common with Auden's three previous books of verse, 'Nones' (1951), 'The Shield of Achilles' (1955) and 'Homage to Clio' (1960). There is the usual technical brilliance, the mixture of styles from a jolly toast for an Oxford feast to the quiet reflective tone of 'Hammerfest,' a poem describing ' the northernmost township on earth.' There are the usual surprising words ('olamic,' 'galimatia') to send us scuttling for our dictionaries; and even a poem from 'Homage to Clio,' 'On Installing an American Kitchen in Lower Austria,' under a new title, including the usual slight alterations, 'I' changed to 'we' so that the poem becomes less personal.

All this, together with the increased amount of light verse, might appear only further confirmation of some readers' belief that Auden's best work lies in the past. According to their view, Auden's insistence on poetry as a game of knowledge is only a rational justification for his withdrawal from active engagement in post-1945 society. Most of his best poems were written between 1933 and 1939, when he identified his own personal crises, the conflict between adolescent romantic heroism and fear of catastrophe, freedom and necessity, with the tensions driving Europe towards war. Such conflicts give a disturbing vitality to his verse which, after his emigration to America in 1939, he never recovered. For readers who prefer the early verse, 'Another Time,' published in 1940, already marks the replacement of neurotic strain and sinister landscape by a tone of leisured, almost academic, detachment.

These views seemed justified by the excessively literary poems that Auden produced in the 1940s, and although 'The Sea and the Mirror' (1944) and 'The Age of Anxiety' (1947)

had their admirers there was a general feeling that
Auden's pilgrimage from Freud and Marx to Kierkegaard and
Niebuhr might have solved his personal problems, but had
made him a lesser poet. The three books of short poems
published in the 1950s, however, showed that although he
was not producing so abundantly as in the mid 1930s, he
could still write poems as successful as 'In Praise of
Limestone,' 'Fleet Visit,' or 'Reflections in a Forest.'
In 1962 the publication of 'The Dyer's Hand' brought
increased understanding of his new techniques, and these
essays throw light on the themes and language of 'About
the House.' Perhaps the middle-aged Auden, reflective,
domestic, happy to write frivolous graffiti and much
occasional verse, will never achieve the greatness that
once was hoped for him; some of the poems in 'About the
House' seem too diffuse, not sharp enough in their wit.
But there is much gaiety and exuberance here, and Auden
is proving that among his many voices this latest modest,
wry tone is capable of many fine poems.

In a postscript to the elegy for Louis MacNeice, Auden
explains the serious philosophic and religious ideas that
underlie his light verse:

> At lucky moment we seem on the brink
> Of really saying what we think we think:
> But, even then, an honest eye should wink. [CP(M), 524]

Because modern science has destroyed our faith in the
naive observations of our senses, telling us that we cannot know what the physical universe is *really* like, art
can no longer be accepted in the traditional way as
'mimesis,' an imitation of nature. Poetry is a series of
analogies that can never be a completely adequate representation of either religious truth or 'the baffle of
life.' The poet, therefore, must 'wink,' must keep his
readers conscious that his words are part of a game.

This explains Auden's joke about art being
'de-narcissus-ised enduring excrement.' In 'The Dyer's
Hand' he says that 'the sterility of the substitution of
identity for analogy is expressed in the myth of Narcissus.'
The poet must not believe that the order and beauty of his
work accurately reflect himself or his world. This sense
of the inadequacy of poetry takes Auden further than Eliot
in his use of irony. Eliot's Prufrock describes his own
inadequacy - 'No! I am not Prince Hamlet, nor was meant
to be' - and his futility shows itself as typical of the
times; but the irony never turns on the poetry itself.
The incantatory rhythms impress on us that this view of
society is truth: similarly in 'The Waste Land' Eliot

imposed his own myth of reality on generations of readers. Auden refuses to persuade in this way. The conversational tones remind us that he is just another man talking at his ease.

It's difficult to illustrate this irony, for Auden's success depends on nuances of tone that move with technical virtuosity through each poem. 'Thanksgiving for a Habitat' begins:

> Nobody I know would like to be buried
>   with a silver cocktail shaker,
> a transistor radio and a strangled
>   daily help, or keep his word because
>
> of a great-great-grandmother who got laid
>   by a sacred beast.

The conversational opening places poet and reader at ease with each other; and there is no pretence that the poet is conveying oracular wisdom. With apparent casualness, he laughs at the heroic pretensions of the past. The exuberant fancy makes us conscious that he is playing with ideas, himself a part of the mundane world he describes. At the same time his words exist in a pattern, with four stresses in each line and a delicate play of internal rhyme, alliteration and assonance (nobody, know, radio etc.). This formal quality points to a possible meaning behind our experiences, though it does not insist too much. The poem, the game, exist between the ideal harmonies of 'that Paradisal state for which we all long' and the absurdities of this poor, bare, forked animal, man. In 'The Common Life,' a more gentle poem about friendship, Auden talks of:

> A living room the catholic area you
>   (Thou, rather) and I may enter
> without knocking, leave without a bow, confronts
>   each visitor with a style ...

'Thou, rather' recalls the I/Thou distinctions of Martin Buber, but the parenthesis makes such high-falutin statements about love slightly comic. It suggests an easy intimacy between the friends, the uniqueness of their relationship which no formulation of words can ever properly express.

The conversational ironic poems are the best in 'About the House,' but there are also moments of lyric spendour, when Auden's delight in the magic of words cannot be repressed. In 'Up There,' a poem on his attic, children transform the room into images of romance:

> Now a schooner on which a lonely only
> Boy sails north or approaches coral islands.

These lines remind us that Auden is one of the greatest
lyric writers of the twentieth century: they recall the
joyful alliteration of 'Look, stranger, on this island now
The leaping light for your delight discovers,' or Miranda's
villanelle in 'The Sea and the Mirror' - 'My Dear One is
mine as mirrors are lonely.' 'About the House' includes
one short beautiful lyric, 'Lost':

> Lost on a fogbound spit of sand
> In shoes that pinched me, close at hand
> I heard the plash of Charon's oar,
> Who ferries no one to a happy shore.

'About the House' is continually delightful to read
because Auden can manage such a variety of voices. On
several occasions he made me laugh out loud. 'On the
Circuit' captures the bewilderment of the visiting
American lecturer, swooping out of the skies to deliver
the same old talk:

> Then, worst of all the anxious thought,
> Each time my plane begins to sink
> And the No Smoking sign comes on:
> *What will there be to drink?*
>
> *Is this a milieu where I must*
> How grahamgreeneish! How infra dig!
> *Snatch from the bottle in my bag*
> *An analeptic swig?*

Auden has said that 'among the half-dozen or so things
for which a man of honour should be prepared, if necessary, to die, the right to play, the right to frivolity,
is not the least.' 'About the House' satisfies his own
desire for poetry that is 'subtle, various, ornamental,
clever,' unsuited to critics whose 'crude, provincial
gullets crave in books Plain cooking made still plainer
by plain cooks.' Are these recent poems as good as the
ones he wrote in the 1930s? Perhaps not, but does it
matter? After such gaiety and wit, such quiet friendly
conversation, to bother too much about this problem seems
as irrelevant as to compare the relative merits of a good
whisky and a pleasant wine.

120. CHRISTOPHER RICKS, WINKING, 'NEW STATESMAN'

lxxi, 4 February 1966, 166

Ricks (b. 1933) has been Professor of English at the University of Cambridge since 1975. His books include 'Milton's Grand Style' (1963), 'The Poems of Tennyson' (ed., 1969), 'Tennyson' (1972), and 'Keats and Embarrassment' (1974).

Disarming is the word for 'About the House'. What is harder to pinpoint is the moment at which such a word has to be said accusingly rather than thankfully. Thankfully, in the case of the four 'transliterations' (from Mickiewicz and others), 'Hammerfest', 'At the Party' and 'Time has taught you'. But mostly are we disarmed by the expertise of an old maestro, who can flick from us our bristling suspicion and glumness? Or is it that he drops his guard and his weapon so frankly, so engagingly, that nobody but a cad could possibly take advantage? Auden's old self-depreciation is still there, and still focused on the question of silliness ('I wish I weren't so silly'). Those who obey his injuction to honour Dame Philology may remind us that 'silly' has come down in the world - to be silly was once to be blessed and innocent. Auden probably hopes as much when he praises the bath as a place where 'a sage' may 'be silly without shame'. But how much of Auden's praise of Yeats may we carry over? 'You were silly like us' - but 'your gift survived it all'?
    One of the relevant sages is Goethe:

> I should like to become, if possible,
>   a minor atlantic Goethe,
> with his passion for weather and stones but
>   without his silliness
>   re the Cross.   [The Cave of Making, CP(M), 522]

'Re'? There is a certain pluck in that refusal to worry about a word's social origins or stylistic hypergamy - but why isn't the pluck mere foolhardiness? In any case Auden's hopeful resolution doesn't last long: soon we find:

> surely those in whose creed
> God is edible may call a fine
>   omelette a Christian deed.   [CP(M), 531]

Why isn't that a silliness about the Cross? The obvious counter-cry is of priggishness and puritanism, and Auden offers an epigram:

> At lucky moment [moments?] we seem on the brink
> Of really saying what we think we think:
> But, even then, an honest eye should wink. [CP(M),524]

But there are winks and winks, and too often the Auden one is obsessed with inviolability, and too much resembles the nervous tic of 'I know you know I know you know I know'.

Agreed, the point is often that he, you and I all know that the jokes are in a sense bad ones. But there are jokes too bad to be saved even by an avuncular phiz. Take the poem about the lavatory (dedicated, naturally, to the author of 'A Single Man') [Christopher Isherwood]:

> Banks have letter boxes
> Built in their façade,
> Marked For Night Deposits,
> Stocks are firm or liquid,
> Currencies of nations
> Either soft or hard.
>
> Global Mother, keep our
> Bowels of compassion
> Open through our lifetime...   [CP(M), 527]

The odd and clever thing, though, is the juxtaposition of such humour with a running commentary about good taste, rather as if to trick us into recalling just those U and non-U rules about language which the poems pretend to deplore. He begins 'Iceland Revisited' with 'Unwashed, unshat'. Ah, but don't forget that the well-bred do speak more bluntly, just as they eructate without embarrassment. 'Perfect taste', 'shows a lack of taste', 'a mark of ill-breeding', 'in the worst of taste', 'not vulgar - not yet': these are the recurring rumbles that warn us off any idea that we might accuse the omelette/ eucharist comparison of being in bad taste.

In what way does Auden's capitalising ('a Major Prophet taken short', 'a Perfect social Number') differ from A.A. Milne's ('a Good Hum, such as is Hummed Hopefully to Others')? Mainly in that Auden knows that we suspect it of being elephantine, and dares us - go on - into accusing him of not suspecting it too. How many tacit inverted commas are there in the following, which may mock the ad-man but does so with a watery grin?

                             for the funniest
          mortals and the kindest are those who are most aware
          of the baffle of being, don't kid themselves our care
          is consolable, but believe a laugh is less
               heartless than tears, that a hostess
          prefers it.   [CP(M), 534]

It may be said for such a Wayside Pulpit that it is democratic about language. In these poems, 'is a must' is
allowed to associate with clone, dowly, banausics,
depatical, olamic, demes and metic. Looking up the
words is less fun than it might be because of the sprink-
ling of misprints. An errata-slip catches three. There
is also 'In Memorium Louis MacNeice' and 'bone fide
architects'; the poem for Elizabeth Mayer ('that sound to
which you have answered for 80 years') is headed: 'on the
occasion of her 18th birthday'. Unless all these too are
ways in which the honest eye winks.

121. UNSIGNED REVIEW, WELL BRED, 'TIMES LITERARY SUPPLE-
MENT'

17 March 1966, 224

'We do poetry a profound disservice if we confine it to
the major experiences of life' is a notion that might
well have served as W.H. Auden's epigraph to this new
volume of verse; not only does he take his customary pains
to avoid the dreaded sin of seeming 'solemn', he also in
this book comes dangerously near to elevating a benign
insignificance of subject and response into some kind of
sine qua non for the really civilized poet. Being
civilized is still for Mr. Auden a matter of fixing a
reproving, saddened, faintly scoffing eye upon the apes,
on history, on other peoples' funny ways – and at this
level his touch is as certain and surprising of old – but
most of all it here requires civility; that is to say,
Mr. Auden celebrates the dispassionate, hospitable virtues,
keeps up discreet appearances, and aims above all to be
thought not pushing, not too personal. The book's
rhetorical assumptions are those of the dinner table
conversation, in mixed company ('a foul mouth gets the
cold shoulder'), and the skills it flourishes are anec-
dotal, learned, quaintly self-effacing.
    Mr. Auden's hostly poise is rarely worried or hastened:

emotion can approach the hearth if it is dressed for
dinner - uninvited it is spurned. 'Which of us', the poet
asks, 'Wants to be touched inadvertently?' Now and then
there are hints of a more fertile self-awareness; hints,
mainly, of despair - at aging, being out of touch or
lonely, not responding any longer to the old, icy monsters
- but it is a measure of the book's intentions that these
get neutralized into bland irony before they have a
moment to catch hold. Typical of this sort of defensive-
ness are the lines addressed to Louis MacNeice, in which
at one level Mr. Auden clearly means to scold MacNeice
for not having been more virtuous, but at the same time
will not let himself be caught in such a schoolmasterly
role; a roguish, collaborative note is kept alive as a
kind of insurance against being thought thin-blooded:

> God may reduce you
> on Judgment Day
>   to tears of shame,
>   reciting by heart
>   the poems you would
>   have written, had
>   your life been good.   [CP(M), 525]

However amiable the pervading sigh, it is difficult to say
this - as Mr. Auden typically would like to - 'without in
any way / seeming to blame'.

Mr. Auden's best obituaries have been of public figures
(though President Kennedy gets a few astonishingly arid
lines) rather than of private friends. Friendship, though,
is much invoked throughout the very mannered, sometimes
witty sequence of domestic-ceremonial verses that form the
bulk of 'About the House' - a large number of the poems
are in fact addressed to specific acquaintances - but is
never more than bleakly cordial when it actually appears;
for instance when Mr. Auden writes - in 'For Friends Only'
- of the sanctity of the visitors' room and offers to his
friends what seems intended as a heart-felt pledge, the
upshot is more a flourish of good breeding ('to "borrow"
stamps is a mark of ill breeding') than an effort of fine
feeling:

> Should you have troubles (pets will die,
> Lovers are always behaving badly)
> And confession helps, we will hear it,
> Examine and give our counsel;
> If to mention them hurts too much,
> We shall not be nosey.

The underplaying ('pets will die'), the priestly formality ('confession', 'counsel') are of course deliberate, but to what end? To protect the friendship or to shield the poet from its full consequences? The feeling lingers that untrivial troubles would be thought improper and not being nosey is a virtue that gets it both ways too neatly. Mr. Auden believes elsewhere that 'a laugh is less heartless than tears'. One can see what he is getting at, but there is little in this disappointing, trivial volume to command assent.

'Collected Shorter Poems 1927-1957'

London, November 1966; New York, October 1967

122. JOHN CAREY ON A SAVOUR OF DERELICTION, 'NEW STATESMAN'

lxxii, 23 December 1966, 941-2

Carey (b. 1934) is Merton Professor of English Literature
at the University of Oxford. His books include 'The
Violent Effigy: A Study of Dickens' Imagination' (1973),
and 'Thackeray: Prodigal Genius' (1977).

This extract is taken from Unpolitical Auden, a review
which includes comment on volumes by Betjeman, Thom Gunn,
Stevie Smith, and Peter Levi.

To deter trend-spotters Mr. Auden's 'Collected Shorter
Poems 1930-44' were printed in alphabetical order. His
new book appends most of the contents of 'Nones', 'The
Shield of Achilles' and 'Homage to Clio,' rewrites here
and there, and regroups the whole chronologically. The
added material spans a period which no one would advance
as Mr. Auden's most gripping or purposeful. The nervous
energy of his Marxist-Freudian days has drained into
Anglo-Catholicism. The celebrity leans back on his laurels
expatiating. wisecracking, fonder of first-person-plurals
('our future' replacing 'the future of the poor'),
touching up pathetic bits ('large sad eyes' for 'sad eyes',
'small birds' for plain 'birds'). The childlike excitement dims. A boy at heart becomes one of the boys. Yet
to number fallings-off would be altogether to misplace the
emphasis. Cooler this crater may be, but still hugely
active. Virtuosity boils and bubbles. Mr. Auden teeters
along the dictionary's edge - 'sottering', 'faffling',
'soodling' - and flings himself around the verse forms,
fighting for a voice that has not been 'pawed at and

gossiped over'. Perspectives shuffle and switch:
airliner-view of a forest - miles of leaves hiding 'tons
of pied pebbles that will soon be birds'; animal-view of
Mr. Auden - 'an inedible patch of unsatisfactory smell'.
Dryness and brilliance still cooperate:

> Herds of reindeer move across
> Miles and miles of golden moss
> Silently and very fast.   [The Fall of Rome, CP(M), 258]

All the same a savour of dereliction hangs about this
later, so-firmly-unpolitical Auden. 'All I have is a
voice,' he wrote in '1st September 1939', 'to undo the
folded lie' of authority. That stanza, symptomatically,
disappeared in 1950. Now the whole poem has gone.

123. JOHN WHITEHEAD, VIN AUDENAIRE, 'ESSAYS IN CRITICISM'

xviii, October 1967, 487-95

Whitehead (b. 1924) served with the Indian Army in Burma,
became a solicitor in 1952, and is now legal adviser to,
and director of, a major oil company. He has published
three books of poetry (1945, 1946, 1951) and contributed
essays and articles on literary and Eastern topics to
various periodicals.
    The title of the essay is borrowed from Messrs Faber's
advertisement in the Auden Double Number of 'New Verse'
(nos 26-7, November 1937)

An earlier collection of Auden's shorter poems covering
the period 1930-1944 was published in England in 1950.
Excluding the long poems, it followed, with only a few
additions and omissions, the text of 'The Collected Poetry'
(New York, 1945). These collections were subjected to a
book-length attack by the late J.W. Beach, who argued that,
by the arbitrary system on which the poems were arranged,
and the suppression of some poems and the revision of
others 'for ideological reasons', Auden with a deliberate
intention to mislead gave to his earlier work a Christian
flavour it had formerly lacked. Although mildly
challenged by M.K. Spears, and by Auden himself in the
Foreword to the present volume, Beach's main argument has
never been effectively refuted; and it is significant that

the poems are now arranged in chronological order, and
that many of those upon which Beach founded his thesis
have been either revised or discarded altogether. Indeed,
so ruthless has been Auden's renewed censorship of his
earlier work that the critic is once more presented with
the essential preliminary task of establishing the
relationship between the poems in the collection and the
work as it originally appeared. For this purpose it is
convenient to examine individually the four sections into
which the book is divided.

Part One (1927-1932). All the juvenilia (1922-1926)
have been excluded. Many schoolboy and early Oxford
poems, written under the influence of Hardy and Edward
Thomas, exist in manuscript and, although Auden has forbidden their publication, enough of them are accessible
elsewhere (for example, in Isherwood) to make their
exclusion a cause for regret. Of the privately printed
'Poems' (1928), containing twenty-seven poems, five,
having survived into the second, 1933 edition of the Faber
'Poems' (1930), are included. Seven more form part of
'Paid on Both Sides', which properly belongs in a collection of long poems or dramatic pieces, and for that reason
may have been reserved for a later volume. The seven
poems - including five others from 'Poems' (1928) -
which, having appeared in 'Poems' (1930), were replaced in
the second edition, have not been resurrected; but the
collection omits only five of the thirty poems comprised
in the latter edition: IX. 'It's no use raising a shout';
XIV. 'Sentries against inner and outer'; XXII. 'Get there
if you can'; XXVIII. 'Under boughs'; and XXX. 'Sir, no
man's enemy'. Except for XXVIII, which 'with flushing
pleasure' anticipated war, these were probably omitted
for other than 'ideological reasons' - XIV on the ground
of triviality; IX and XXII for their hearty didacticism;
and XXX because, according to the Foreword, preferring
old styles of architecture it was 'dishonest' to have
expressed a desire for new. As will be confirmed later,
the reasons Auden gives for suppressing poems should be
treated with reserve.

Since the poems from 'The Orators' properly belong in
their original context, the omission of twelve out of the
twenty included in the first, 1932 edition can be justified; but it is legitimate to object when, as the book
goes into successive editions, more and more poems are
jettisoned: two in 1934, five more in 1966. Whatever
aesthetic grounds may exist for excluding these often
trivial or undisciplined poems from the collection, 'The
Orators' is by its nature a magpie's nest, the
miscellaneous bits of verse forming part and parcel of its

fabric; and it is surely desirable to leave in its original state a book which is now so remote from its author
that his 'name on the title-page seems a pseudonym for
someone else'.

The amendments in this section consist of small verbal
corrections and the deletion of lines or whole stanzas,
designed to eliminate obscurities or to tighten loosely
constructed poems. Auden's early poems have so often been
criticised for their obscurity that it is ironical that
one's chief regret is the removal of the private references. Whoever Captain Ferguson may have been, one is
sorry to have heard the last of him. Several poems in
this section - the ten 'Shorts' (three of which appeared
in earlier volumes), 'Half Way' (a version of which
entitled 'Interview' was printed in 'Cambridge Left' in
1935) and 'Uncle Henry' - have been salvaged from an unpublished notebook. (See my article in the 'London
Magazine,' May 1965.) 'Half Way' provides an interesting
example of Auden's methods of amendment. The re-ordering
of words in the first stanza has introduced a *non sequitur*
with intentionally comic effect, and the deletion of the
third stanza with its references to Stinker and Bog-eyes
has resulted in the creation of a quite different type of
poem: originally belonging to the scoutmaster / conspirator
cycle, it has been transformed into a somewhat bizarre
Quest poem, a metamorphosis perhaps obliquely acknowledged
in the new title.

Part Two (1933-1938). For Auden now, his considerable
output of the mid-'Thirties represents an era of particular
sensitivity, as evidenced by his drastic treatment of the
poems which belong to this section. The omission of
poetry included in the plays written in collaboration with
Isherwood can be justified for the same reason as applies
to 'The Orators', but (since a few are included) two
lyrics in particular - 'You were a great Cunarder, I /
Was only a fishing smack' from 'The Dance of Death' (1933)
and 'Now through night's caressing grip' from 'The Dog
Beneath the Skin (1935) - might well have found a place in
the collection; and the 'Letter to Lord Byron', which
has recently been reprinted (in David Wright's Penguin,
'Longer Contemporary Poems') in sadly truncated form, falls
outside the category of Shorter Poems; but the omission
of many other poems of this period is less easily excused.
Of the thirty-one Poems in 'Look Stranger!' (1936), ten
have been discarded, amongst them 'August for the people',
'Here on the cropped grass' and 'The Chimneys are smoking'.
Since these three poems, having been excluded from 'The
Collected Poetry' (1945), were restored in the 1950 col-
lection, it is possible that Auden used the former as the

basis for the present collection, and that they were overlooked. However, the omission of others of a similar type
(for example, the Prologue and Epilogue, and 'Brothers,
who when sirens roar') suggests deliberate suppression.
Only eight of the fifty poems in 'Another Time' (1940)
have been excluded, but two of them are among Auden's
most famous - 'Spain' and 'September 1, 1939' - for both
of which omissions he has given an inadequate explanation.
In the Foreword he condemns 'Spain', a poem of twenty-six
(reduced to twenty-three in the earlier collections) four-
line stanzas, on the ground that its last two lines
('History to the defeated / May say Alas but cannot help
nor pardon') embody the 'wicked doctrine' that equates
goodness with success. Admittedly this last stanza, with
its clumsy syntax and direct borrowing from Wilfred Owen,
is a piece of rather contrived rhetoric, insecurely
tacked on to the poem to round it off, but the last two
lines have generally been taken as meaning that History
cannot help [the victim] nor pardon [the aggressor]: an
unexceptionable doctrine. His explanation for discarding
'September 1, 1939' appears in the Foreword to B.C.
Bloomfield's bibliography and concerns the much-quoted
line 'We must love one another or die'. When he came to
reprint the poem, Auden said to himself: 'That's a damned
lie. We must die anyway'; and so it was altered to 'We
must love one another *and* die' (which, understandably,
Beach took to be a 'deplorable misprint'). 'This didn't
seem to do either, so I cut the stanza. Still no good.
The whole poem, I realised, was infected with an incurable
dishonesty and must be scrapped.' And yet the meaning of
the line in its original form has generally been understood to be that the human species, unless it learns to
live at peace, will destroy itself in war - a view with
which we are now even less likely to disagree than in 1939.
It can be inferred perhaps that the real reason for the
suppression of these and many other poems of the same
period is that Auden no longer approves of the poet in
the role of political commentator. In the Foreword he
says he has no objection if anyone wants to look at his
writings from an historical perspective, but this is
precisely what these exclusions prevent. Until shortly
after his withdrawal to America in 1939, much of his work
was firmly rooted in its time and forms a commentary on
the progress of the international events that culminated
in Hitler's War. So influential was he among the Left-
wing English intelligentsia that he became - in the phrase
he applied to Freud - a whole climate of opinion, and
without these most characteristic poems the reader can
form no true judgment of his work of the period. A few

other omissions may be noted: 'Pascal'; 'Where do they come from?'; 'James Honeyman' (one of the three *Grand Guignol* ballads); and 'Epithalamion'. And curiously, whereas the earlier collections omitted the sonnet on A.E. Housman and included the one on Matthew Arnold, the position is now reversed. On the credit side, 'Night Mail', which was written as a commentary for a documentary film, and 'Detective Story' (a poem overlooked by Bloomfield) from 'Letters from Iceland' have been rescued.

Many of the retained poems in this section have been subjected to considerable revision, mainly to eliminate mannerisms of style ('slovenly verbal habits') which Auden now considers distasteful. For me, 'May with its light behaving' has been spoiled by this process, and 'Now the leaves are falling fast' turned into a quite different poem. Extensive revision has been carried out to the sonnet-sequence now called 'Sonnets from China', which appeared originally with a long verse Commentary (now discarded) in the travel-book, 'Journey to a War' (1939), written in collaboration with Isherwood. Of the original sequence of twenty-seven sonnets (which were reprinted without amendment in the two earlier collections), one, newly entitled 'A Major Port', has been moved to another group of poems, 'A Voyage', also derived from the travel-book; six have been discarded altogether; and the travel-book's dedicatory sonnet to E.M. Forster has been added as the last poem of the sequence. The remaining sonnets have been revised in accordance with three main principles. (1) The elimination of the once characteristic over-use of the definite article - for example, 'He was the Rich, the Bountiful, the Fearless' has become 'A conquering hero, bountiful and brave' (V, new numbering). The result is not always successful. The journalese of 'Our global story' (XVI) is not to be preferred to 'The life of man', nor 'teen-agers' (V) to 'the young'. (2) The extinguishment of excessive sibilants - for example, 'Fish swam as fish' has become 'Trout finned as trout' (I). (The same principle underlies the only new amendment to 'Lay your sleeping head', in which 'sensual' has been changed to 'carnal'.) (3) The correction of imperfect rhymes, as in Sonnet XIII in which 'he closed his eyes' has become, unhappily, 'he turned to ice', in order to chime with 'lice'; and, less happily still, 'He will not be introduced', so as to make a true rhyme with 'used', has become 'He will never be perused'. The reasons for other changes are less clear. To replace 'a thousand faces' by a myriad faces' (XII) introduces an incongruously Tennysonian note; and the change from 'The call of the forbidden cities' to 'Love for some far forbidden country' (XVI) inappropriately

shifts the reference from Mr. Norris's Berlin to Housman's
Shropshire. Again, it seems pedantic to change the
dragon's 'spoor' to the more technical 'slot' (X), a word
usually referable only to deer. The revision of the last
two lines of the Rilke sonnet (XIX) is also unfortunate,
because, intended to be a paraphrase of a passage from a
letter ('I went out in the cold moonlight and stroked
little Muzot as if it were a great animal'), it is now
further removed from what Rilke actually wrote. Only
Sonnet XX seems to me to have been markedly improved. In
this single case the meaning, imperfectly realised in the
original version, has now been fully projected and fixed.

Part Three (1939-1947). The principal works of these
years of War and Auden's commitment to Christianity are
the four long poems. Much of this section is therefore in
the nature of shavings from the carpenter's bench, in
particular the twenty-six pieces (out of a total of forty-
four) which originally appeared in the Notes to 'New Year
Letter' (1941). The Quest sonnets from the same volume
are included, as well as the 'Epilogue' (under the title
'The Dark Years'), but not the 'Prologue'. Among Twelve
Songs are included 'Sing, Ariel' from 'The Sea and the
Mirror' and 'When the Sex War ended' from 'For the Time
Being', the two long poems published together under the
latter title (1944/1945); and three pieces from 'The Age
of Anxiety' (1947/1948) appear as Three Dreams. None of
these is of much significance out of context. In the 1945
collection twenty-five poems appeared for the first time
in book form (they were reprinted in the 1950 collection),
of which five have been omitted from the present collection, among them, regrettably, 'Gold in the North', which
was written for 'Paul Bunyan'. This unpublished operatta
for Britten's score is now represented only by 'Carry
her over the water' and 'The single creature'. Perhaps
Auden has forgotten the excellent parody 'The Glamour
Boys and Girls Have Grievances Too' which appeared in
the 'New Yorker' in 1940 and deserves to be reprinted.
Indeed, it is a matter for regret that the full libretto
remains unpublished. Three stanzas have been deleted from
'In Memory of W.B. Yeats', and 'At the Grave of Henry
James' has now shrunk from twenty-eight to only ten
stanzas.

Part Four (1948-1957). The poems of these years of
Ischian summers, the early opera libretti written in collaboration with Chester Kallman, and Auden's appointment
as Professor of Poetry at Oxford are given virtually
complete and without amendment, and this section alone
deserves the title Collected Shorter Poems. In the
Preface to the earlier collections Auden divided his past

work into four classes: rubbish he regretted ever having conceived; good ideas which did not come to much; pieces he had nothing against except their lack of importance; and the few poems for which he was honestly grateful. In the 1966 Foreword he describes the three types of poem he has thrown out as the dishonest, the bad-mannered and the boring. It may be surmised that, if a decade hence he were to apply equally ruthless standards of selection to the poems in this section, the categories of condemnation would be enlarged so as to include the garrulous, the donnish and the cosy, and its bulk be considerably reduced. But it is to be hoped that by that time he will have come round to the view that a collection should comprise the bulk of his published work in its original form.

This part alone provides a complete enough text to permit a generalised discussion of the work. The War years can be seen to form a watershed, when the poet who had worn the doctrines of the fashionable medicine men like a succession of old school ties disappeared, to be replaced, after the spiritual struggle recorded in the long poems, by the reconciled man of the world, concerned rather with domestic virtues than the international wrong. The earliest post-War poems, published in 'Nones' (1952) - arguably his best book of shorter poems - communicate a sense of liberation and civilised enjoyment. To this period belong 'Under Which Lyre' (1946), his most assured occasional poem; 'Under Sirius' and the mock-Horatian 'Ischia', both warmed by the Mediterranean sun; the fine lyric 'Deftly, admiral'; and 'In Praise of Limestone', the first of a new *genre* which later degenerated into the laxer, more whimsical 'Bucolics' series. The group of poems on the theme of History, published in 'The Old Man's Road' (New York, 1956) and later included in 'Homage to Clio' (1960), are the products of a bad patch ('a misfortune that can befall any poet and often does' - Auden on MacNeice in 1964), but the collection concludes in a major key with the Horae Canonicae, and 'Good-bye to the Mezzogiorno' which ranks among his best poems of place.

The Index of First Lines (which, as a reviewer has pointed out, reads like a dictionary of quotations) is defective. Four poems have been left out: 'All had been ordered', 'Be patient, solemn nose', 'Once for candy', and 'With what conviction'. The single creature' is wrongly listed under 'Dog', and 'The Unknown Citizen' under 'He was found': these poems were correctly placed in the earlier collections. It is inconsistent to list individually the Sonnets from China but not The Quest Sonnets.

The collection is far from definitive. The student of
Auden's work still requires all the earlier volumes and,
unless he has ready access to an adequate library, a bulg-
ing file of photostats as well. No rules of general
application can be laid down for the compiling of collected poems, but two general principles in the matters of
suppression and revision should not lightly be
transgressed. 1. Once a poem has been published, it takes
on a life of its own in the consciousness of its readers;
as Auden wrote on the death of Yeats (another poet given
to compulsive tinkering), 'he became his admirers'. If
'manners' are a valid criterion, it is surely dis-
courteous for a poet to deprive his admirers of poems in
which they have already acquired a vested interest. 2.
Valéry's dictum which Auden is fond of quoting, 'A poem
is never finished; it is only abandoned', cannot be called
upon to justify every type of revision. The question of
'dishonesty' must inevitably arise when, for example, a
poem which contains the words 'Tonight in China' is
amended so as to reflect, not what he actually wrote
during his visit there in 1938, but what, thirty years
later in Kirchstetten, he wishes he had.
    And it is curmudgeonly in a poet possessing such an
abundant sense of humour to suppress all those poems which
have provided the pleasant occasion for parody: '"Yesterday", said Jones Minor eagerly, "for astringency and cold
baths at all hours; but today the quiet time. Yesterday
the case-book and the hairy heel, but today -"'.

'Collected Longer Poems'

London, October 1968; New York, April 1969

124. RICHARD MAYNE, CHORIC ORACULAR UNCLE, 'NEW STATESMAN'

lxxvi, 13 December 1968, 838

Richard Mayne (b. 1926) is a writer, and has been Special
Adviser to the President of the European Communities since
1979. His publications include 'The Recovery of Europe', and
a translation of Jean Monnet's 'Memoirs', for which he received the Scott Moncrieff Prize.
    This is taken from a review which also considers Auden's
T.S. Eliot Memorial Lectures, 'Secondary Worlds'.

Time confirms and winnows: Auden remains a master. His
first lines alone are a hyponotist's anthology:

August for the people and their favourite islands.

From scars where kestrels hover.

Happy the hare at morning for she cannot read.

Look, stranger, on this island now.

Sir, no man's enemy, forgiving all.

The Summer holds: upon its glittering lake.

    All these, designedly, are taken from prewar poems.
They spoke in challenges, often imperative: *Hark!* was the
form of their address. All Auden's critics have remarked
it. His voice was 'striking', 'compelled attention',
made 'impact', was 'an incantation'. 'He dramatises every-

thing he touches,' wrote Louise Bogan. Even his detractors
repeatedly called him 'arresting'; however finally dismissive, they responded to his rhetoric. His technique,
they saw, was traditional, more crudely strict than T.S.
Eliot's: he was less a rebel than an apprentice. What
was new was his swagger.

Today it jars, not least on Auden. But, despite it, the
spell of his opening words was seldom broken. Lines and
lyrics live that he wrote before 30 - 'Lullaby' ('Lay your
sleeping head, my love'):'The Watershed'; 'A Free One'
('Watch any day his nonchalant pauses, see'); 'The
Wanderer' ('Doom is dark and deeper than any sea-dingle');
'Our Hunting Fathers'; 'Through the Looking Glass'; 'May'
('...with its light behaving'); 'Dover'; 'Brussels in
Winter';'Musée des Beaux Arts'. If, at times, they
complexified simplicity, the best matched weight with apt-
ness, crisp new notes in a hard currency.

Mistakes were frequent. Those inattentive to tone
missed occasional falsities: it took Auden himself to
admit, after 36 years, that he'd never liked 'new styles
of architecture', much as he'd always wanted 'a change of
heart'. Solemn nonsense was talked, and solemnly contested,
about a 'Poetic Renaissance'. Some Marxist jingles made
many think Auden political. But his real role then was
choric, a chiding stance. Finger raised, icily foreboding, he plotted the bleak future like a satisfying
chess problem, all passion frozen into stylised royal
moves.

Auden's transition from Greek chorus, echoed above, to
Christian oracle might have seemed less remarkable had it
not followed a more spectacular removal - from Europe,
threatened by war, to the United States, a refuge whose
remoteness from world conflict, however impermanent,
appeared to some an apt setting for the bookish retreat
into piety of which, in their disappointed and now un-
friendly eyes, he was inexplicably but undeniably guilty.
Did such labyrinthine Jamesian periods as Caliban's in
'The Sea and the Mirror' reflect uneasiness masked by
the pat couplets of 'New Year Letter' and the ranging but
doctrinally tethered experiments of 'For the Time Being',
with Auden's newly rediscovered and still precarious faith?
To those who wondered how an eclectic and restlessly
'modern' mind could embrace a creed so positive about the
rationally unprovable, the hypothesis was, perhaps
diabolically, tempting. Was Christanity, for Auden, a
needed creative myth like those of Marx, Groddeck, Freud,
and fairy tales with which he had fruitfully flirted,
but one which, this time, demanded the security of lifelong marriage?

Evidence of struggle was there, if manfully mastered.
The ceaseless revision of early poems, a boon to the
scholar however hard for the critic, most often embodied
improvements, but also involved such apparent subterfuge
as rehabilitating a sermon once mainly derisive, and it
threw away, with the bathwater of 'We must love one another
or die', at least one surely healthy baby,' All I have is
a voice / To undo the folded lie.' The agnostic's
perpetual indecision was now stigmatised as 'a madness
of which you can only be cured by some shock'. Had
such a shock - his exile? his mother's death or his
reaction to it? - torn Auden from the roots of his
dazzling promise? Was his ever more manifold technical
mastery, like his use of the Gospels, of Shakespeare and,
in 'The Age of Anxiety', of alliterative Langland, a
disguise for deficiencies due to disorientation? What
place had poetry, once his whole craft and purpose, in
the larger life of a believer? What place had Auden,
always awkward with audiences, in a broad alien land far
from the fells and abandoned mineworks, the flattened
Pennine grasses, and the understanding of old friends?
    It took time to assimilate new modes of feeling, a
more open manner, and an easier, polite familiarity. Fear
of pomposity or self-parody led him into oddities and
lapses - 'awfully long', 'ever so comfy' - but he could
still command the view:

    Altogether elsewhere, vast
    Herds of reindeer move across
    Miles and miles of golden moss,
    Silently and very fast.   [CP(M), 258]

    At length a new style emerged, skilfully conversational,
deprecated unduly as 'the wry, the sotto-voce, / Ironic
and monochrome'. Slippered and unbuttoned, in 'About the
House' the once choric oracle became the uncle - learned,
witty, tender, hospitable, and wise.

in the life surrounding him rather than in his reading
(perhaps 'The Age of Anxiety' was a first struggling
attempt to do this), then a new Auden might result, a
'New Yorker' Walt Whitman viewing the American scene
through lenses coated with a European irony.

Ten years and three books later, one has to admit
that this hope was over-optimistic. True, with 'Nones'
(1952), 'The Shield of Achilles' (1955) and now 'Homage
to Clio' Auden has returned to the shorter poem as his
medium: the Supreme Old Masters have retreated (though they
have been replaced to some extent by the stale personages
of classical mythology), and his themes have become more
personal and have a greater chance of interesting. He has
begun to produce a kind of long reflective poem in a
stabilised tone in which every facet of his subject is
exhibited at leisure, The Bucolics in 'The Shield of
Achilles', 'Ode to Gaea,' 'In Praise of Limestone,' and
now 'Homage to Clio' and 'Goodbye to the Mezzogiorno':

[Like Donald Hall (see No. 114 above), Larkin quotes
first 10 lines of 'Goodbye to the Mezzogiorno', CP(M),
486.]

These poems are agreeable and ingenious essays, more
closely directed than his earlier excursions such as
'August for the people' or 'Here on the cropped grass,'
but their poetic pressure is not high - nor, indeed, is it
intended to be. They read like the reflections of a
practised and celebrated writer with no particular
worries who is free to indulge his tastes in reading and
travel, and as such we can accept them. Auden has not,
in fact, gone in the direction one hoped: he has not
adopted America or taken root, but has pursued an individual and cosmopolitan path which has precluded the kind of
identification that seemed so much a part of his previous
successes.

There would be no point in mentioning this if it did
not seem to have had regrettable poetic consequences.
Firstly, although he has by now recovered a dialect it is
all too often an extraordinarily jarring one, a wilful
jumble of Age-of-Plastic nursery rhyme, ballet folk-lore,
and Hollywood Lemprière served up with a lisping archness
that sets the teeth on edge.

Great masters who have shown mankind
An order it has yet to find ...
Now large, magnificent, and calm
Your changeless presences disarm
The sullen generations, still
The fright and fidget of the will,
And to the growing and the weak
Your final transformations speak, &c., &c.

Auden no longer parries the question 'Who are the great?'
with the poet's qualification

you must ask me who
Have written just as I'd have liked to do.

He has become a reader rather than a writer, and the Notes –
eighty-one pages of James, Kierkegaard, Chekhov, Rilke,
Nietzsche, Goethe, Milton, Spinoza and so on against fifty-
eight pages of text – gave warning how far literature was
replacing experience as material for his verse.
    Some critics might think this legitimate. The likely
consequences, however – loss of vividness, a tendency to
rehearse themes already existing as literature, a certain
abstract windiness – were very much the criticisms Auden
now invited. His first three American books were long,
ambitious, and stylistically variegated, yet held the
reader's attention only sporadically if at all. The
rambling intellectual stew of 'New Year Letter' was hardly
more than a vamp-till-ready; 'The Sea and the Mirror,'
which appeared in 1945, was an unsuccessful piece of
literary inbreeding; while although in 'For the Time being,'
also 1945, Auden works hard to reinvigorate the Christian
myth as a poetic subject, he is too often chilly ('weave
in us the freedom of The actually deficient on The justly
actual') or silly ('It was visiting day at the vinegar
works'). As for 'The Age of Anxiety' in 1948, I never
finished it, and have never met anyone who has.
    Now, contrary to what has sometimes been suggested, it
is no crime to write dull or even bad poetry. Even if it
were, Auden has earned a reprieve many times over.
Despite the bitter disappointment of the Forties for his
admirers, it was really no more than they could have
expected of a poet who had elected to remake his entire
poetic equipment. The question was how soon he would
get reorganised. His continued productivity, intermittent
successes such as the speeches of Caliban and Herod (Auden
has always been brilliant at prose parody – did he write
'Hetty to Nancy'?) and the sonnets in The Quest gave
grounds for hope. If his poetry could once take root again

125. JEREMY ROBSON, AUDEN'S LONGER POEMS, 'ENCOUNTER'

xxxiv, January 1970, 73-4

Robson (b. 1939), poetry critic of 'Tribune', 1962-72, has
been Managing Editor of Robson Books, London, since 1974.
Author of two books of poems, 'Thirty Three Poems' (1964)
and 'In Focus' (1970), he has also edited several anthologies including 'The Young British Poets' (1971) and
'Corgi Modern Poets in Focus', nos 2 and 4 (1971).

One begins to wonder whether long poems are called for more
often by critics than by poetry readers generally.
Certainly lament for the death of the long poem has become
a favourite critical theme. But while the old adage that
long poems are written by poets who cannot write short
ones remains largely true, it may be argued that the most
influential poems of this century have in fact been long.
'The Waste Land' and the 'Four Quartets' have been as
influential as any shorter work; and Pound's 'Cantos,'
Carlos Williams' 'Paterson,' and Ginsberg's 'Howl' have
all had - for better or for worse, and often for disaster -
their varying degrees of influence. Ask any young poet
from Greenwich Village or Liverpool to name the most
important poem in his life and it is likely that he will
point to 'Howl.' A young poet from Oxford might well pick
one of the others, or turn elsewhere, but I would be
surprised if the choice fell on any of the six works in
W.H. Auden's 'Collected Longer Poems.'
     Yet, Leavis apart, the majority of critics would seem
to grant Auden his just place as the most accomplished
and versatile of living poets, and one who has been, and
who remains, exceptionally influential. Clearly, he
dominated the generation of the 1930s with a power and
range that few could approach. Master of an impressive
number of forms, from the Ballad to the Blues, he was
all the more able to contain the see-sawing beliefs and
passions of the time. Committed, yet distanced, his
poetry was remarkable for its surface calm, the pincers
moving obliquely but firmly over their subject. The
tension could be riveting, especially where the aural
matrix was based on popular tradition, as in 'Refugee
Blues':

> Went to a committee; they offered me a chair;
> Asked me politely to return next year:
> But where shall we go to-day, my dear, but where
>   shall we go to-day?
>
> Came to a public meeting; the speaker got up and said:
> 'If we let them in, they will steal our daily bread';
> He was talking of you and me, my dear, he was talking
>   of you and me....

The influence of music on Auden's verse, apparent in this
poem and throughout the longer works, has always been
salient; even his worst lines often 'sound' impressive.
Indeed the poems on which his reputation will finally come
to rest may well be the magnificent early lyrics - far away
from the world of Spain and Fascism against which he cried
out so forcefully in much-quoted poems he no longer favours.

With his move to America in 1938, Auden's area of
interest and commitment changed visibly. By 1940 the
Auden conception of love had moved away from an ideal union
of man and woman, or of a brotherhood of man ('we must love
one another or die') to a Christian ideal, making one
aware of what Spender has called 'the odd impersonality'
of Auden. Coated more with the philosopher's semantics,
the four long poems of this later period ('New Year Letter',
'For the Time Being', 'The Sea and the Mirror', 'The Age
of Anxiety') are in the main colder, more distant, more
cerebral than any of Auden's previous work; they contrast
strikingly with the earliest of the longer poems included
in this Collection 'Paid on Both Sides' (published 1930)
and 'Letter to Lord Byron' (published 1937) - the first a
rather earnest, at times muddled verse play concerning a
blood feud (or is it school-gang rivalry, or both?), the
second a rollicking, deliberately chatty 'long' poem full
of the dry self-aware wit of which Auden is master.
   'Letter to Lord Byron' is an inventive, technically
dazzling piece of writing, a triumph of taste. It sets
a tone and, for all its length, rarely slips from it. As
befits its subject the poem is self-mocking, but it mocks
also many sacred establishment shrines. To read it is to
eavesdrop on witty gossip about the age and its values and
to learn something also about the author's own life and
tastes, for it contains a vivid section of autobiography.
The poem is a lap of honour taken at high speed. 'I like
your verse because she's gay and witty' writes Auden to
Byron, and here one might pay the same compliment to Auden.
   The outward setting of Auden's 'New Year Letter'
(January 1, 1940) is his newly-adopted America. Already the

change in tone from the only slightly earlier 'September 1, 1939' is dramatic. The personal anguish that reached its climax in the (now discarded) lines, 'All I have is a voice / to undo the folded lie,' has distanced to, 'Art is not life and cannot be / a midwife to society.' The attempt in 'New Year Letter' to relate art, religion, and society within an agreed Kierkegaardian design seems far removed from the ragings of Europe which remain the poem's inevitable backcloth and its point of departure. The guns are distant:

> The cities we abandon fall
> To nothing primitive at all;
> This lust in action to destroy
> Is not the pure instinctive joy
> Of animals, but the refined
> Creation of machines and mind....

Such questions of How, Why, and What, indeed the whole gamut of Existentialist Choice which 'New Year Letter' raises, are as relevant to Western society now as they were to Auden then. Whether or not they are organic to the poetry as a whole is another matter. For all the range and muscle of the verse, the refined hypnotic couplets falling just so, the ideas appear to be somehow removed from the poetry in a way they rarely are in either the earlier or later short poems. There are marvellous sections, to be sure, whole passages (short poems almost) where the verse opens out suddenly from close arguing into poetry of great dignity; but these are often linked to memories, or are lyrical asides touching the 'real' world, and as such are only incidentally related to the poem's high theme and dialectics:

> Delighted with their takings, bars
> are closing under fading stars;
> The revellers go home to change
> Back into something far more strange,
> The tightened self in which they may
> Walk safely through their bothered day....

In the two long poems published in 1944, 'For the Time Being' (a Christmas Oratorio) and 'The Sea and the Mirror' (a 'commentary' on 'The Tempest'), Auden's apparent ability to command almost any verse form is given full rein. The former is often deemed a high-water mark in the poet's achievement. It seems to me, however, an unhappy amalgam of two styles - the rhetorical / pontifical, and the colloquial. On the deeper level, Auden has edged here into

Eliot territory without ever really inhabiting it; even
some of the familiar symbolism appears (the garden, the
rose). The lighter, colloquial interpolations, superb in
themselves, only serve to highlight the surrounding
rhetoric. Admittedly, as Richard M. Ohmann maintains in
'Auden's Sacred Awe' (1963) 'the real world is for Auden
an allegorical text, and the intellectual contrasts that
can be placed upon it are paramount....' Nevertheless, a
great deal of the 'real' *is* present, many wholly-realised
passages touching the lives of ordinary people (The Wise
Men, The Shepherds) sitting unhappily beside the more
abstract, clinical versifying.

Stylistically, 'The Sea and the Mirror' is altogether
surer; nowhere are form and metre more tactfully used to
match character. Strangely, despite its necessary
literary overtone, the world created in this poem is a
tangible one. Prospero's opening speech, for instance, is
that of a man of flesh and blood. His words to Ariel, as
he leaves the island, are convincing:

> Over there, maybe, it won't seem quite so dreadful
> Not to be interesting any more, but an old man
>   Just like other old men, with eyes that water
> Easily in the wind, and a head that nods in the
>   sunshine....

The Master and Boatswain's rumbustious song, Miranda's
beautiful villanelle, are Auden at his sophisticated best.
Less happy is the closing piece of Jamesian pastiche
(Caliban to the Audience) which, for all its virtuoso
appeal, stands aloof from the poetry in a way that under-
scores Thomas Blackburn's contention (in 'The Price of an
Eye') that too often in Auden 'the voice of the poet is
drowned by the chatter of the don.'

Perhaps that remark is more properly true of 'The Age
of Anxiety' (published 1947) which soon leaps, after its
direct opening, into an area of metaphysical speculation.
As in 'For the Time Being,' Auden seems only too aware of
the dramatic problems, introducing colloquialisms, echoes
of popular songs, parody - all the tricks from his fertile
hat - to modernise the tone and keep the action within
the realm of theatricality. Repeatedly though, these
props, which work so stunningly on their own terms in the
shorter poems, remain contrivances here: the poetry and
the subtle intellectualising, the man and the complicating
mind, moving in a parallel direction, fusing only occasionally.

So, as elsewhere in the 'Longer Poems,' there is the
magician's display rather than the ignition, and one is

left with memories of individual short poems - complex,
dazzling, distinct, yet never forming quite the organic
whole which makes, say, 'The Waste Land,' not so much a
long poem, but a poem which had to be its length.

'City Without Walls'

London, September 1969; New York, January 1970

126. JOHN BAYLEY, HALCYON STRUCTURES, 'LISTENER'

lxxxii, 25 September 1969, 413-14

Bayley (b. 1925) is Warton Professor of English Literature, and a Fellow of St Catherine's College, the
University of Oxford. His books include 'Tolstoy and the
Novel' (1966), 'The Uses of Division: Unity and Disharmony
in Literature' (1976), 'An Essay on Hardy' (1978), and
'The Romantic Survival: A Study in Poetic Evolution'
(1957), which puts forward a most persuasive case for
appreciating the essential romanticism of Auden, a writer
for whom poetry as 'escape art', contraption or 'robust
game', is essentially disconnected from the phenomenology
of real life or poetry as 'Parable art'.

W.H. Auden is the rarest kind of poet in a post-romantic
age: interested not in himself but in the plural aspects
and manifestations of the world which he turns into his
art; interested in people and animals as in ideas and
landscapes, rivers, buildings, metres, histories, coigns
and quirks. In his poetry, as in Renaissance rhetoric and
the diagrams of Vitruvian man, the human being can take on
the impersonal contours of nature or art without ceasing to
be human: one poem in this book is called 'Profile',
another, 'River Profile'. All this is rare in an age in
which even reportage can become a sort of self-caress
(witness Norman Mailer's pieces on the Moonshot) and in
which most good poetry embodies My Sense of Myself, cast
as Aged Endymion (Robert Graves), The Child who Died
(Robert Lowell), The Child about to Die (Sylvia Plath) -
an age in which the Poet as Poem seems not so much the

answer to, as the only possible formulation of, the increasingly baffled and plaintive question: how can language accommodate me?

Whatever its virtues and powers, such poetry is claustrophobic; beside it, even the world of the Symbolists, in which towers, swans, lakes or schoolchildren are properties of the poetic mind, seems to give us some elbow-room on life in common. Much poetry today gets more and more trapped in its box, like television, and by comparison the 'halcyon structures' which Auden continues to erect appear like the Baroque theatre or the old-fashioned cinema.

The converse of claustrophobia in modern poetry (and not only poetry) is what reviewers call 'profound seriousness'. The phrase has been applied with proper respect both to Auden's poems and essays, but however well-intentioned an obeisance to a large figure in literature, it has not the smallest relevance. Profoundly serious writers today are those who for various reasons - they may be urgent and worthy ones - distrust the power of art to say things for them, and suppose that the artificial, the carefully fashioned and ingeniously crafted, is capable only of being itself.

It is true that Auden has drawn a distinction between the poetry of Ariel, the poetry of delight, and that of Prospero, the poetry of wisdom, but it works only as a helpful and commonsensical diagram. The two cannot be separated: but delight calls for more experience in the reader - something corresponding to the craft that has brought it into being - in order to reveal its wisdom. Shakespeare in 'Venus and Adonis' is as *wise* as Fulke Greville (whom it would be meaningful to call a 'profoundly serious' poet) once we have learnt to understand and participate in the rich idioms of the art that does not conceal art but revels in it. The poetry that begins in 'contraption' (to use another Auden term) may none the less end in revelation, but it will not get there by way of seriousness, profound or otherwise.

Auden's early poetry often employed portentousness as an engaging device of rhetoric and artificiality, but never seriousness (insofar as 'Spain' was a 'serious' poem it was a bad one). 'Consider this, and in our time' ('Poems', 1930) was a superb bit of rhetoric that used several devices Auden has since discarded - for example, a threateningly ellipsed and telegraphic syntax dotted with anacolutha - to create a mood that was commonplace in intellectual circles at the time but was never so successfully caught in poetic language.

In 'City Without Walls' he meditates on equally commonplace topics of our time - the vistas of boredom and

neurosis, compulsory leisure and compelled privacy; the
cult of sport and violence instead of work and war, the
possibility of the Bomb and its aftermath - and in the
hands of his idiom and metre (a cunning fusion of rhyme-
less classical measures with the stressed alliterations of
Old English poetry) these ordinary fears and foretellings
become a sort of magic compound delighting the eye and yet
engaging the mind. Rhetoric and meditation combine -
Ulysses summoning up the terrors of time and anarchy in
'Troilus and Cressida,' on the one hand, and on the other
Tennyson's honey-tongued flirtation in 'In Memoriam' with
the gropings of Victorian science.

[Quotes stanzas 9-14 of 'City Without Walls', CP(M), 563
563-4.]

Yet another rhetorician, Langland, is played on as a mute
variable in the withdrawal sequence.

> Thus I was thinking at three a.m.
> In Mid-Manhattan till interrupted,
> cut short by a sharp voice.

It tells the poet not to play 'Jeremiah-cum-Juvenal', and
he retorts: 'So what, if my words are true.'

> Thereupon, bored, a third voice:
> 'Go to sleep now for God's sake!
> You both will feel better by breakfast time.'

Evading without deprecation ' the preacher's loose
immodest tone', Auden secures for himself the last reward
of the picking and unpicking scald - to be most simply
himself when his verse is at its most entrancingly
mannered. Accuracy and affection, the proper way to
observe both animals and men, is present in his 'Mosaic
for Marianne Moore', in which the animals she describes
get a voice for their acknowledgments:

> For poems, dolphin-graceful as carts from Sweden,
> our thank-you should be a right
> good salvo of barks...

And in the 'Eulogy' for Professor Nevill Coghill:

> you countenanced all species,
> the alphas, the bone-
> idle, the obstreperous
> and the really rum...

A penetrating familiarity comprehends in its glance the
animal in us all that yawns and scratches and lusts as a
part of our angelic faculty and our god-like apprehension.
Auden is singularly and excellently lacking in the modern
dualism that is obsessed with the flesh and its mechanic
achievements ('Run smoothly by Jaguar farmers') and yet
cannot see itself performing the act. For him the flesh is
spiritual because comic, more accurately and lyrically
mimed in the copulations of the zoo than in those of the
modern screen, and a *gestalt* for ever out of reach of the
ludicrous *selbstlichkeit* of a Henry Miller, whose pudenda
tick like parts of his typewriter.

> For a while
> we talked by the fire,
> then, carrying candles, climbed
> steep stairs. Love was made
> then and there: so halcyoned,
> soon we fell asleep
> to the sound of a river
> swabbling through a gorge.   [Since, CP(M), 584]

'Love was made' - the casual passive tells us much about
the poet's ability not to be himself when doing what
everyone else does, and 'Song of the Devil' shows him
still retaining (as in 'City Without Walls') an affection
for Groddeck's theories, which have stood the test of
time better than most others of their epoch.

[Quotes stanzas 1 and 3 of 'Song of the Devil', CP(M),
587.]

The most remarkable *tour de force* in this collection
are the eight songs from 'Mother Courage', metrically the
most subtle ballads Auden has given us. Their air of
simplicity conceals a degree of technical experience and
sophistication that makes the point a great deal better
than does the 'war equals capitalism' insistence of
their originals. 'Song of Fraternisation' -

> That May the days were bright,
> And starry every night.
> The regiment stood on parade:
> They gave their drums the usual thwack,
> They led us then behind a stack,
> Where they fraternised with us

- 'Song of Unconditional Surrender', and 'Song of the
Soldier before the Inn' -

No sermon, now, Rev! It's a crime.
The cavalry have no time,
Dying for King and Country

- seem to me as superior to Brecht as the songs in
Pushkin's 'Feast in Time of Plague' are superior to their
prototypes in John Wilson's 'City of the Plague'. But then
Brecht, unlike Auden or Pushkin, is undoubtedly a 'profoundly serious' writer.

127. JOHN FLETCHER ON CLASSICAL SIMPLICITY AND DIRECTNESS, 'SPECTATOR'

ccxxiii, 13 December 1969, 827-8

John Fletcher (b. 1937) is Professor of Comparative
Literature at the University of East Anglia. His
publications include 'The Novels of Samuel Beckett' (1964),
'Samuel Beckett's Art' (1969), 'A Critical Commentary on
Flaubert's Trois Contes' (1968), and 'Claude Simon and
Fiction Now' (1975).
   Our Man in New York, from which this is taken, includes
notice of 'Auden's Poetry', by Justin Replogle, and of
'The Elder Edda', translated by Auden and Paul B. Taylor.

Auden, who has known vogue in the past, seems to be a rather
unfashionable poet these days. The earnest young don't
appear to have much time for his wry kind of introspection,
and the earnest middle-aged probably feel that he has let
them down by turning Christian and American. And even
the connoisseur of contemporary verse, who might be
expected to react favourably to Auden's virtuosity and
knowing allusiveness, may well find some of the pieces
in his latest collection embarrassingly direct:

   Who am I now?
An American? No, a New Yorker,
who opens his *Times* at the obit page,
whose dream images date him already,
awake among lasers, electric brains,
do-it-yourself sex manuals,
bugged phones, sophisticated
weapon-systems and sick jokes.   [CP(M), 623-4]

But in lines like these the old familiar Auden is all
there in strength: the prosody, the idiom and the tone
are inimitably characteristic. What is new, as Justin
Replogle points out in his enlightening and helpful essay,
is the nostalgia, and a certain engaging kindliness which
marks a mellowed Auden. The shift is not without its
dangers though, as this collection sometimes reveals, and
sentimentality is the most obvious of these. The 'Elegy
in Memoriam Emma Eiermann' may well be offered as an
'occasional poem', but that doesn't excuse the coyness of
'a housekeeper is harder / to replace than a lover',
nor the embarrassing last line which the poet tries to pull
off by couching it in German ('Du gute, schlaf in Ruhe').
It's unfortunately only too easy to pillory the lines that
make you squirm uncomfortably (how about 'Love was made /
then and there'?) Happily, the old Auden self-mockery comes
to the rescue just in time in the realisation that he 'at
least can learn / to live with obesity / and a little
fame.'
    In fact, as Replogle domonstrates, Auden has always
relied heavily and fruitfully on conflicting voices in his
poetry. The title piece, 'City Without Walls' itself,
has three: two that Replogle would call Poet and Antipoet, and a third, 'bored' voice, which pricks the others'
balloons: '"Go to sleep now for God's sake! / You both will
feel better by breakfast time."' And, most important of
all, there is the fortunate fact that Auden is a comic
poet, who has managed to marry the comic style of the
'thirties with a comic vision that distinguishes the poet
of the 'fifties and 'sixties. The resulting wit in some
of the new pieces is little short of magnificent; it works
best in the epigrams, like this one:

> The Queen fled, leaving
> books behind her
> that shocked the pious usurper.

Or in this charming limerick:

> The Marquis de Sade and Genet
> Are highly thought of to-day,
>   But torture and treachery
>   Are not his kinds of lechery,
> So he's given his copies away.   [Marginalia]

Amateurs of porn (as Auden might put it), this is meant
to warn.
    But it's not all donnish fun positively inviting loving
pastiche by intrigued habitués of the SCR, who will revel

in such visions as that of the 'cheerful . . . unoccu-
pied bar-stools . . . free for some hours from the weight
/ of drab defeated bottoms'. Some of it, if ostensibly
self-directed, strikes uncomfortably home: 'He likes
giving presents, / but finds it hard to forget / what
each one cost.' Perhaps (*pace* Replogle, who maintains that
the mature Auden celebrates life's 'blessedness'), the poet
has found his true vocation - as the antipoet characteristically puts it - in the *Schadenfreude* of a 'Jeremiah-
cum-Juvenal'. In 'City Without Walls' it seems to me that
Roman satirist and Jewish prophet meet to celebrate
through Auden something rather different from the blessed
nature of existence. That something lies somewhere between
the Devil's denunciation ('I'm so bored with the whole
fucking crowd of you / I could *scream*!') and a kind of
low-Tory disillusionment:

> The class whose vices
> he pilloried was his own,
> now extinct, except
> for lone survivors like him
> who remember its virtues.   [Marginalia]

This kind of utterance is not, as I said before, very
fashionable now. But this does not necessarily mean that
Auden is not, for all his weaknesses, one of our major
poets most likely to survive provided the planet does too.
About this Professor Replogle is none too confident. He
fears that Auden's heavy reliance on 'usage specialities'
will date him rapidly. This may well be true of some of
his more playful verse, and probably no one will be sorry.
But there's nothing modish about the language of the lines
I've just quoted (unlike the excruciating 'Non-U' - yes
indeed - on p. 48).

This latest collection reveals an Auden of classical
simplicity and directness. If it sinks without trace,
this probably won't be because of the occasional voguish-
ness, but because (and isn't that just what Auden is
talking about?) a master-poet's simplicity and directness
may no longer be able to get through to posterity's
punch-drunk sensibilities.

128. MONROE K. SPEARS, A SABINE FARM NEAR KIRCHSTETTEN,
'YALE REVIEW'

lx, Autumn 1970, 90-6

Spears (b. 1916), who is an Executor of the Estate of
W.H. Auden, edited 'Sewanee Review', 1952-61, and has
been Libbie Shearn Moody Professor of English at Rice
University since 1964. His books include 'Dionysus
and the City: Modernism in Twentieth Century Poetry'
(1970), 'Space against Time in Modern American Poetry'
(1972), and 'The Poetry of W.H. Auden: The Disenchanted
Island' (1963), an invaluable critical companion.

Four books by Auden - 'City Without Walls', 'Secondary
Worlds', 'Collected Longer Poems', 'A Certain World',
and 'Auden's Poetry', by Justin Replogle - are discussed
in this review.

See also The Divine Comedy of W.H. Auden, 'Sewanee
Review', xc, 1, Winter 1982, pp. 31-52.

For some time Auden has been suggesting occasionally a
parallel between himself and Horace - a parallel that he
seems to find both amusing and significant. When he began
working with syllabic meters, Horace was one of the models
Auden had in mind, and this has remained a central point
of contact: the greatest modern virtuoso of metrics has
learned much from the ancient master. A more obvious
similarity, however, is that the mode of life and the poetic
themes Auden has cultivated of late resemble strikingly
those pursued by Horace in retirement on his Sabine farm.
True, Auden's farm near Kirchstetten (humanized and
mythologized in his last volume, 'About the House') was
given him by no Maecenas but earned by hard professional
toil, and he lives there only half the year (returning for
the other half to the New York that Robert Lowell and
others have been ever more explicitly paralleling with
Rome). But the farm represents a kind of unexpected
security and rootedness in his latter days, a place out of
but not remote from the world of affairs; and the Horatian
role of rural urbanity, retired but worldly satirist and
sage, is one that Auden plays with gusto. 'The Horatians,'
in 'City Without Walls,' puts it realistically and
absolutely minimally: Horatians are inappropriate to
either grand or comic opera; their most credible fictive
world is that of the Whodunit. They share a love for
some particular place, having no ambitions to get into

society or other temptations of the capital. Their tastes
'run to / small dinner parties, small rooms, / and the
tone of voice that suits them, ' wishing for at most 'a
genteel sufficiency of / land or lolly.' Zoos, museums,
botanical gardens play Maecenas to them, as has the
Anglican Church for the 'British branch of the family.'
Compared to Pindar or other 'great foudroyant masters who
don't ever amend,' they are, for all their polish, 'of
little stature,' and compared to authentic martyrs, they
are of no account. All they can do is what it seems to
them they 'were made for, look at / this world with a
happy eye / but from a sober perspective.'

The case for Horace, and for the Horatian side of
Auden, is put more positively in 'Ode to Terminus.'
Celebrating the virtues of the city, of humanity, and of
moderation, this poem occupies a central position in the
volume. Auden here contrasts the worlds of the immensely
large and extremely small revealed to us by the scientists
to the human world of everyday life and the senses. Whatever 'microbiology may think,' this 'is the world we /
really live in and that saves our sanity, / who know all
too well how the most erudite / mind behaves in the dark
without a / surround it is called on to interpret,' for
under such circumstances it discards 'rhythm, punctuation,
metaphor' and 'sinks into a driveling monologue, / too
literal to see a joke or / distinguish a penis from a
pencil.' Hence he invokes Terminus the Mentor, 'God of
walls, doors, and reticence,' who gives to the city games
and grammar and meters, who enables translation, and who
opposes the colossal immodesty that has led us to plunder
and poison our world and that inspires 'self-proclaimed
poets who, to wow an /audience, utter some resonant lie.'

Auden is in many respects a larger figure than Horace.
To begin with the superficial, his works are larger in
bulk and variety, and his range of knowledge and awareness
- scientific, historical, religious; e.g., all the complex
interplay between Roman and Gothic that makes up Austrian
Baroque - vastly greater. More importantly, he is a
better moralist. Instead of the somewhat prudential,
calculating, mildly selfish worldliness that appears in
Horace (where the least credulous thing is to seize the
day), Auden reveals a profoundly though unobtrusively
religious attitude, based on certain absolutes. Like
Horace, he knows and accepts himself with all his
frailties and limitations, and all humanity with himself;
but he has an enormously greater awareness of what it
means to be human, of the nature and interactions of man's
soul, mind, and body, and of the relation of the human
to other forms of life.

Aside from such generalities (which may conjure up ghostly legions to fight once more for the Ancients against the Moderns), there is one way in which Auden literally and unquestionably advances beyond Horace in this volume. Horace died at the age of fifty-seven; now six years beyond that, Auden is approaching the threshold of old age, and his confrontation of this fact and of the changes in the external world and in himself is the central theme of 'City Without Walls.'

Old age, anticipated and real, has been the great modern subject for poetry. Why this should be so cannot be discussed here; perhaps the accelerating rate of change and the increasingly problematical relation to the past give the theme a special urgent poignancy in our time, though the essential situation - the facing of the fact of death - does not change. At any rate, our major poets have dealt with it almost obsessively, often beginning (like Yeats and Eliot) while they themselves were still young, and continuing until they enter the condition so long anticipated. Yeats (most obviously in 'Nineteen Hundred and Nineteen,' 'Among School Children,' and the Byzantium poems), Eliot ('Gerontion,' 'A Song for Simeon,' 'Little Gidding'), Stevens ('Notes Toward a Supreme Fiction'), and Williams ('Asphodel, That Greeny Flower') were inspired by it to some of their greatest poetry. Auden sails to no Byzantium in defiance or despair, nor is his attitude like that of Eliot's personae, either the gloomy ones with a strictly minimal faith or the incredulously happy ones who receive grace in extreme old age, from 'Marina' to 'The Elder Statesman.' Instead, Auden remains steady on an even keel, trying to be rational and truthful; he accepts both himself (without self-indulgence, but rather with an increasingly clear realization of what he is really like) and the age, with all its rapid and drastic changes. The title poem, 'City Without Walls,' is a good example: the speaker turns from a marvelously funny and incisive denunciation of Megalopolis and its probable future to denounce himself for his *Schadenfreude* in playing 'Jeremiah-cum-Juvenal' and then to ridicule both previous voices in his interior household for taking themselves so seriously: 'Thereupon, bored, a third voice: / "Go to sleep now for God's sake! / You both will feel better by breakfast time."' For this cheerfulness Auden takes no credit, ascribing it candidly to inheritance and a fortunate childhood; it is temperament, not faith, that is responsible.

'Profile' is a good example of this very personal and yet objective kind of poem about aging, without self-pity or Jeremiad, accepting both himself and the changing times.

It is in the *haiku* form (seventeen syllables in three
lines, with the number per line optional, as Auden writes
it); no depths are revealed, as the title indicates, but
limited observations are made, with candor and detachment.
There is neither apology nor boasting. Thus Auden begins
by observing that he thanks God daily for being born and
bred 'a British Pharisee': 'A childhood full of love / and
good things to eat: / why should he not hate change?' As to
sins, 'Gluttony and Sloth / have often protected him / from
Lust and Anger.' His personal habits are discussed, with
their psychological bases: 'The way he dresses / reveals
an angry baby, /howling to be dressed.' Faults and virtues,
trivial or important, take their places in a revealing
portrait: 'He has often stamped his feet, / wept on occasion, / but never been bored.' 'Vain? Not very, except /
about his knowledge of metre / and his friends.' 'He likes
giving presents, / but finds it hard to forget / what each
one cost.' 'Without a watch / he would never know when / to
feel hungry or horny.' Realizing his good luck, 'he
wonders why so few / people kill themselves'; in the sub-
way he asks, 'Can I really be / the only one in this car /
who is glad to be alive?' And the ending maintains the
balance nicely: 'On waking, he thinks: "Precious,
Precious Me! / A fig for your detractors!" / On going to
bed: / "What am I to do? / Again You have let Us down."'
    In the next poem, 'Since,' he remembers an episode of
happy love thirty years before, rejoices in it, and
refuses to complain: 'Solitude? Rubbish! / It's social
enough with real / faces and landscapes / for whose
friendly countenance / I at least can learn / to live
with obesity / and a little fame.' If this one seems a
little flat and low-keyed, 'Forty Years On' produces a
livelier Shakespearean flavor, employing the persona of
Autolycus once more: the rogue-poet, aging, affluent,
and almost respectable, refuses to be solemn though he
dreams of death. Auden provides him with a song suitable
for tastes that no longer like ballads.
    The fifth and last section of the long poem called
'Marginalia' again deals explicitly with Auden himself.
(Except for one limerick about de Sade and Genet, the form
is either the *haiku* or the *tanka* of thirty-one syllables
in five lines.) Most of this is very low-keyed indeed:
'His thoughts pottered / from verses to sex to God / without punctuation.' He thinks of the new generation 'who
never walk, drink no wine, / carry transistors.' He
comments sensibly on sex and age: 'The shame in ageing /
is not that Desire should fail / (Who mourns for something /
he no longer needs?): it is / that someone else must be
told.' Then there are 'Thoughts of his own death, / like
the distant roll / of thunder at a picnic.' And then the

two are fused together cheerfully and without fuss:
'Pulling on his socks, / he recalls that his grand-pa /
went pop in the act.' Thinking of his early poetry, he
remarks in the final stanza: 'The class whose vices / he
pilloried was his own, / now extinct, except / for lone
survivors like him / who remember its virtues.'
    After 'Fairground,' a fine poem about youth and age,
comes ' In Due Season,' about the seasons and their
meanings to human beings as contrasted to birds, beasts,
and plants. It is chiefly a poem in praise of winter,
time ' for reading of thoughts, time for the trying out /
Of new metres and recipes ...': in this season 'Nature's
mask is relaxed into a mobile grin, / Stones, old shoes,
come alive, born sacramental signs, / Nod to us in the First
Person of mysteries / They know nothing about, bearing a
message from / The invisible sole Source of specific
things.' The analogy with the seasons of human life needs
no pointing up.
    The last poem, 'Prologue at Sixty,' recapitulates the
theme of the personal confrontation of old age. Typically,
it begins by praising trees, as contrasted to the 'anxious
species.' From the Kirchstetten landscape, with its
reminders of the Holy Roman Empire, he meditates his non-
Roman ancestry, 'a Son of the North, outside the *limes*';
but his ancestors, he says, if 'crude and cruel,' were
'not calculating.' In a brief and suggestive epitome,
he translates the Gospel that 'onion-towers / of five
parish churches preach in Baroque':

>   to make One, there must be Two,
>   Love is substantial, all Luck is good,
>
>   Flesh must fall through fated time
>   From birth to death, both unwilled,
>   But Spirit may climb counterwise
>   from a death, in faith freely chosen,
>   to resurrection, a re-beginning.

After ten years of residence, his Kirchstetten landscape
has 'added its names to my numinous map,' which he briefly
sketches from the '*Solihull* gas-works' and mines of his
boyhood to '*Carnegie Hall* and the *Con-Ed* stacks / on *First
Avenue*' of contemporary New York. Asking ' Who am I now?'
he decides that he is not an American but a New Yorker
'who opens his *Times* at the obit page' and 'whose dream
images date him already.' He asks, finally, 'Can Sixty
make sense to Sixteen-Plus?' and answers hopefully,
invoking (as often in his later verse) the analogy of
Pentecost. The conclusion is a prayer: 'Giver-of-Life,

translate for me / till I accomplish my corpse at last.'
    'City Without Walls' contains no sequences or cycles,
no groups of poems related by any sort of common framework; aside from the recurrent themes already discussed,
its emphasis is upon variety. The keynote of the volume
might be described as a kind of Drydenian professionalism,
shown in the large number of poems commissioned or
occasional, all produced with integrity and self-respect,
impeccable in technique, and with a very high entertainment level. Thus the 'Four Commissioned Texts' are,
even without the music, film, or sound and light they are
intended to complement, extraordinarily interesting; among
them are the film commentary 'Runner,' a modern equivalent
of Pindar's odes praising athletes; 'The Twelve,' words
for an anthem about the Apostles; and 'Moralities,'
written for musical setting and based on Aesop, but put
into thoroughly modern and amusing verse: the frogs and
their king, the crows who want to sound like horses (they
say, 'Away with Dominant and tonic! / Let's be chic and
electronic. / Down with the Establishment! / Up with non-
music, the Sound-Event!'), and the voyagers who pray only
when threatened with disaster. In these, as in the
versions of Brecht songs from 'Mother Courage' and
especially the 'Song of Ogres' and 'Song of the Devil,'
Auden is writing in his very best vein of light verse, his
ear, better than ever, catching the precise tone of
colloquial speech and cliché and his technical facility
dazzling. I wish he had included the text he wrote for the
film 'US,' shown at the San Antonio HemisFair and elsewhere; in these eloquent couplets Auden showed his pres-
cient concern about man's pollution of his environment
long before this became fashionable. But he has expressed
this concern powerfully in many other poems and in prose;
man's rape of his physical world and his tyranny over
other forms of life are forms of *hubris*, he seems to feel,
and likely to be followed by *nemesis*.
    Finally, there are the occasional poems, an extra-
ordinarily varied group. There is an elegy to Joseph
Weinheber, the Austrian poet who lived in the house next
door to Auden's until his death in 1945: this is a grave
and tender meditation on providence, poetry, war, and
the relation of all these to the love of this particular
place ('Amor Loci' is the title of another poem in the
volume, and a recurrent theme). After a respectable
'Epithalamium' for a relative, there is a 'Eulogy' on
the retirement of his Oxford tutor, Nevill Coghill -
nostalgic, affectionate, and a fine tribute to a teacher
who ' was not a *Heldentenor* / of the lecture hall, / not
a disciple-hunting / Socratic bully, / not a celibate

glutton / averse to pupils / as to mal-edited texts,' but
one who 'countenanced all species' and managed never to
look 'cross or sleepy.' Next there is an elegy for his
Austrian housekeeper; it is neither condescending nor
sentimental, and full of a vivid sense of her as a person.
A 'housekeeper is harder / to replace than a lover,' he
observes, celebrating the peculiarities of this 'dear
oddling' with her 'loyal but critical eyes.' There is
lastly a 'Mosaic' for Marianne Moore's eightieth birthday,
which seems to me rather to miss fire. But the elegies
for Weinheber and the housekeeper and the eulogy for
Coghill are, I think, among Auden's best such poems, full
of a strong sense of the unique personality and relation
to the poet of the subject, with meditations and reflections suggested by his occupation and career. The volume
is dedicated to Peter Heyworth, the London music critic,
with the moving comment: 'At Twenty we find friends for
ourselves, but it takes Heaven / To find us one when we
are Fifty-Seven.'

'Epistle to a Godson'

London, October 1972; New York, September 1972

129. FRANK KERMODE, FAITHING AND BLITHING, 'LISTENER'

26 October 1972, 551-2

Kermode (b. 1919) has been King Edward VII Professor of
English Literature, and a Fellow of King's College,
Cambridge University, since 1974. His books include
'Romantic Image' (1957), 'The Sense of an Ending' (1967),
'The Classic' (1975), and 'The Genesis of Secrecy' (1979).

> At Twenty I tried to
> vex my elders, past Sixty it's the young whom
> I hope to bother.

Auden's new collection will hardly vex or bother anybody:
it will give pleasure to all who have learned to take
pleasure from his games, and bore or disappoint those who
either haven't, or who gave him up when he grew quieter,
more explicit, more conversational. It is true that from
behind his new mask of reasonably patient old age he
scolds, in his civil way, the young - for their abuse of
language, their amorous habits, even, it sometimes
seems, for their not having had nannies instead of cars
and television sets. It may be that he intends his skills
at 'verbal games' - the metrical and lexical range and
accuracy he must certainly find wanting in a lot of *their*
poetry - to stand as a permanent and deeper reproach to
them: but they might reasonably suspect that he is more
interested in himself than in them.

> Blessed be all metrical rules that forbid automatic
> responses,
> force us to have second thoughts, free from the fetters
> of Self, [CP(M), 642]

he remarks: and though it is true that this collection is
surprisingly autobiographical when you consider that its
author often expresses his belief that a poet's life is
nobody's business but his own, it is also true that all
his revelations are carefully filtered, and that the
pleasure he takes in overcoming technical difficulties is
partly a delight in the reticence they impose on his
verses.

For example, Auden not only delights in strange words,
but provides contexts for them, and this practice is
unlikely to bring on anything very confessional. More and
more, in recent years, it has become advisable to have the
'OED' - and possibly also 'Webster's - at hand when reading him, and this book contains one poem called 'A Bad
Night: A Lexical Exercise' which can only, one supposes,
have been written in order to accommodate a list of words
copied out from the dictionary: odded, blouts, pirries,
stolchy, glunch, sloomy, snudge, snoachy, scaddle, cag-
mag, hoasting, drumbles. All, as it happens, are in
'OED'. Sometimes you find two learned freaks together,
in such a way that it looks as if the poet has only that
morning been browsing: eutrophied, eucatastrophe; obtemper,
obumbrate. If you think he was the first to make sparrows
phip, look again at 'OED'. On the other hand, there is
a growing tendency to make verbs of nouns: to faith, to
monster, to violent, to blithe, to decent - a whim with
less lexicographical support. Such words occur, very
often, in conversational passages, whose syntax offers no
resistance to the cursory reading, and have an effect
that is rather hard to define. They constitute an assertion of some kind, an extension of the claims he has often
made concerning the inexhaustibility of human langauge,
and the duty of poets to know and use as much of it as
possible. He is as sharp as Chomsky on the uniqueness
of language: birds have no language, though they sing;
their difference from poets is that birds always repeat
themselves, and are therefore incapable of lying, unconscious of past and future, death and time. 'Let them
leave language to their lonely betters,' said one earlier
poem: the notion is repeated here.

Given that the poet's game is a social one and of
limited importance to the Christian, he has nevertheless a
duty to be orderly, harmonious, and aware of his human
place in a largely inhuman world:

              to give a stunning
    display of concinnity and elegance
    is the least we can do, and its dominant
        mood should be that of Carnival.
    Let us hymn the small but journal wonders

    of Nature...   [CP(M), 626]

Again and again he recurs to the rest of creation, the
other inmates, from the mammals down to yeasts,
aerobics and anaerobics, the teeming life he slaughters
whenever he undresses or takes a bath. The best poem
in this book, I think, is 'The Aliens', which first
examines our friendly relationship with the plants, then
acknowledges our kinship with the hot-blooded beasts, and
finally considers the aliens, the insects:

    But between us and the Insects,
    namely, nine-tenths of the living, there grins
                       a prohibitive fracture
    empathy cannot transgress. (What Saint
                    made a friend of a roach or
    preached to an ant-hill?)

And so on, in these gabby hexameters, till the whole
thing is worked out in an elegant theological-evolutionary
conceit. They are the comments of a man concerned with a
purely human and un-tragic situation: moving towards death,
owning a past, possessing 'a sense of real occasion, of
beginnings and endings', aware of his moment in history.
   This moment is the subject of the pleasing title
poem, 'Epistle to a Godson', which turns on the notion
that there is no longer any relevant wisdom the old can
offer the young: there is a moment of kindly nostalgia
in which Auden, characterising the lost futures of his own
youth, remembers his early exercises in the sinister-
grotesque. Then, he says, we knew the future 'as a named
and settled landscape'; and the evil was easily recognis-
able - 'evil Count ffoulkes in his tall donjon'. Yet
this relaxed refusal to deal in phoney wisdom is cunningly
presented as wise, or anyway knowing: and when the poem
closes with 'worldly maxims', they tend to be more obscure
than the refusal to go in for such things.
   What seems to be the settled pose of the latest Auden
is less that of the defender of wisdom than that of the
lover of order. Led, and not for the first time, to
consider the political implications of his desire for
order in poems, he denies, as usual, that there are any.
Any state as well-ordered as a good poem, he has said,
would be barbarously authoritarian: great artists may be
politically intolerable and Wagner, he now adds, was a
crook and an anti-semite. Even his own dreams are

condemned because they conform to no prosodic discipline, and do not mean what they say. The Aging Poet is well aware of his limited responsibilities: he is defender and exponent of an order which has very little to do with all the fertile dissoluteness of his own distant youth, and none with that of the youth with which he shares the world now. This is the theme of 'Doggerel by a Senior Citizen':

> When couples played or sang duets,
> It was immoral to have debts:
> I shall continue till I die
> To pay in cash for what I buy...
>
> Though I suspect the term is crap,
> If there *is* a Generation Gap,
> Who is to blame? Those, old or young,
> Who will not learn their Mother-Tongue.

So he respresents himself: out of period sometimes lonely, often glum; supported by friendship and by an unexcitable Christian faith. But what is perfectly clear is that knowing things, handling words, exercising unimpaired intelligence in those long elaborately prosodic, conceited sentences are also reasons for survival. This book has not quite the strength and wit of the last two, but there is no hint that the decline is more than a temporary dip.

130. CLIVE JAMES, UNSIGNED REVIEW, A TESTAMENT TO SELF-CONTROL, 'TIMES LITERARY SUPPLEMENT'

12 January 1973, 25-6

Clive James (b. 1939) is a writer and broadcaster (and for several years television critic for the 'Observer'); his publications include 'Unreliable Memoirs' (1980) and 'The Crystal Bucket' (1981). This review is reprinted in his collection of essays 'At the Pillars of Hercules' (1979).

'You don't need me to tell you what's going on:' writes W.H. Auden in his latest book's first piece, 'the ochlo-cratic media, joint with under-the-dryer gossip, process and vent without intermission all to-day's ugly secrets. Imageable no longer, a featureless anonymous threat from behind, to-morrow has us gallowed shitless: if what is to happen occurs according to what Thucydides defined as "human", we've had it, are in for a disaster that no four-letter words will tardy.'

This passage is highly interesting prose, detectable only in its lexical intensity as the work of a poet: Hazlitt, right on this point as on so many others, long ago laid down the word about the giveaway proneness to local effect. An ochlocracy is mob rule; the 'OED' last noticed 'joint' being used that way in 1727; to gallow is an obsolete form of to gally, which is itself a way of saying to frighten that hasn't been heard for a long time anywhere except in a whaling station; 'tardy' as a verb staggered on a few years past its moment of glory in 'A Winter's Tale' to disappear in 1623. But let's start again.

In the title poem of his latest book, W.H. Auden writes:

... You don't need me to tell you what's
going on: the ochlocratic media,
   joint with under-the-dryer gossip,
   process and vent without intermission

all to-day's ugly secrets. Imageable
no longer, a featureless anonymous
   threat from behind, tomorrow has us
   gallowed shitless: if what is to happen

occurs according to what Thucydides
defined as 'human', we've had it, are in for
   a disaster that no four-letter
   words will tardy.

This passage is highly interesting poetry, but only within the confines of Auden's strictly prosaic later manner. Sentences wriggle intricately and at length down the syllabic grid.

Blessed be all metrical rules that
   forbid automatic responses,
force us to have second thoughts,
   free from the fetters of Self,   [CP(M), 642]

The greatest modern verse technician, Auden long ago ran out of metrical rules needing more than a moment's effort to conform to. Technically, his later manner - which involves setting up a felt rhythmic progress inside an arbitrary syllabic convention - is really a way of restoring to the medium some of the resistance his virtuosity earlier wiped out. This technical mortification is closely allied with the ethical stand forbidding any irrationali- ties, all happy accidents. No automatic responses, no first thoughts. Helping to explain the omission of certain poems from his 'Collected Shorter Poems 1927 - 1957', Auden wrote in 1966:

> A dishonest poem is one which expresses, no matter how well, feelings or beliefs which its author never felt or entertained. For example, I once expressed a desire for 'New styles of architecture'; but I have never liked modern architecture. I prefer *old* styles, and one must be honest even about one's prejudices. Again, and much more shamefully, I once wrote:
>
> > History to the defeated
> > may say alas but cannot help nor pardon.   [EA, 212]
>
> To say this is to equate goodness with success. It would have been bad enough if I had ever held this wicked doctrine, but that I should have stated it simply because it sounded to me rhetorically effective is quite inexcusable.

Glumly reconciling themselves to the loss of 'September 1, 1939' in its entirety and favourite fragments from other poems engraved in the consciousness of a generation, critics respectfully conceded Auden's right to take back what he had so freely given. It was interesting, though, that no strong movement arose to challenge Auden's assumption that these youthful poetic crimes were committed by the same self being dishonest, rather than a different self being honest. Auden was denying the pluralism of his own personality. It was his privilege to do so if he wanted to, but it was remarkable how tamely this crankily simplistic reinterpretation of his own creative selfhood was accepted.

More remarkable still, however, was the virtual silence which greeted the spectacle of a great modern talent disallowing the automatic response, proclaiming the virtues of knowing exactly what you mean against the vices of letting the poem find out what *it* wants to mean. Auden had apparently worked his way through to the last sentence of the 'Tractatus Logico-Philosophicus'. 'Wovon man nicht sprechen kann', Wittgenstein had written, 'darüber muss man schweigen.' What we cannot speak about we must pass over in silence. It was piquant to find the poet who above all others seemed to command the secret of modern magic occupying this position so very long after the philosopher who thought of it had moved out. Here was a man attacking the validity of his own serendipity, discrediting his own trick of setting up a bewitching resonance. Long before, combining with Louis MacNeice in preparing that seductive lash-up of a book 'Letters from Iceland', Auden had written:

> And the traveller hopes: 'Let me be far from any
> Physician'; And the poets have names for the sea;

But on the way to press·this was accidentally transformed into

> And the traveller hopes: 'Let me be far from any
> Physician'; And the ports have names for the sea;

Noting straight away that 'ports' suggested more than 'poets', Auden let the slip stand. The names that ports have for the sea are likely to be functional as well as mythical, mistrustful as well as admiring, many-rooted rather than casually appropriate - in a word, serious. Or so we guess. Or so the unexpected ring of the word, its unpredictability in that context, leads us to conjecture - gives us *room* to conjecture. And this thinking-space, the parkland of imagination that existed in Auden's earlier manner, was what marked it out - and what he annihilated in forming his later manner. There have been artists who possessed some of Auden's magic and who went on to lose it, but it is hard to think of anyone who deliberately suppressed it. All conscious artists feel the urge to refine what is unique in their work, but few interpret this call to refine as a command to eliminate. Unless we are dealing with a self-destructive enthusiast - and Auden on the face of it can scarcely be categorized as one of those - then we are up against that most disciplined of all artistic adventurers, the man who gets sick of his own winning streak.

Pick up a Photostat of the 1928 'Poems' and read it through (it takes about twenty minutes): was there ever a more capacious young talent? It goes beyond precocity.

> We saw in Spring
> The frozen buzzard
> Flipped down the weir and carried out to sea.
> Before the trees threw shadows down in challenge
> To snoring midges.
> Before the autumn came
> To focus stars more sharply in the sky
> In Spring we saw
> The bulb pillow
> Raising the skull,
> Thrusting a crocus through clenched teeth.   [EA, 437]

Hindsight lends us prescience, but it is permissible to claim that merely on the basis of this passage's first three lines we would have pronounced the writer capable of virtually anything. The way the turn from the second line into the third kinetically matches the whole stated action is perfect and obviously instinctive - what other men occasionally achieve was all there as a gift.

> The sprinkler on the lawn
> Weaves a cool vertigo, and stumps are drawn;...[EA, 437]

Elated by the effortless lyricism of a coup like this, we need to remember not just Auden's age, but the time. Yeats had not yet finished forming the compact musicality of his last phase, and the authoritative clarities of the first of Eliot's Quartets were still years away. Auden got this sonic drive absolutely from out of the blue. The plainest statement he could make seemed to come out as poetry:

> Nor was that final, for about that time
> Gannets blown over northward, going home...   [EA, 24]

It was a Shakespearean gift, not just in magnitude but in its unsettling - and unsettling especially to its possessor - characteristic of making anything said sound truer than true. In all of English poetry it is difficult to think of any other poet who turned out permanent work so early - and whose work seemed so tense with the obligation to be permanent. In his distinguished essay on Auden, John Bayley penetratingly pointed out that it was not in Auden's creative stance ever to admit to being young. What has not yet sufficiently been noticed is that it was not in the nature of Auden's talent to win sympathy by fumbling towards an effect - to claim the privileges of the not yet weathered, or traffic in the pathos of an art in search of its object. Instant accomplishment denied him a creative adolescence.

As always in Auden, ethics and techniques were bound up together. Barely out of his teens, he was already trying to discipline, rather than exploit, the artistic equivalent of a Midas touch. It is for this reason that the 'Scrutiny' group's later limiting judgments and dismissals of Auden were wrong-headed as well as insensitive: they were branding as permanently undergraduate the one major modern gift which had never been content with its own cleverness for a moment. They missed the drama of Auden's career in the 1930s and 1940s, never realizing that the early obscurity and the later bookishness were

both ways of distancing, rather than striving after,
effect. The moral struggle in Auden was fought out
between what was possible to his gift and what he thought
allowable to it: the moralists, looking for struggles of
a different kind, saw in his work nothing but its declarative self-assurance. The more he worked for ironic poise,
the more they detected incorrigible playfulness. Subsequent critical systems, had they been applied, would not
have fared much better. Suppose, for example, that our
standards of the desirable in poetry are based on the
accurate registration of worldly things. We would think,
in that case, that a man who had come from the frozen
buzzards of 1928 to the etymological fossicking of 1972
had moved from the apex of an art to the base. But
suppose the ability to send frozen birds flipping over
the mind's weir came too easily to be gone on with? What
then?

[Quotes 1-13 of 'Doom is dark and deeper than any sea-
dingle...' ('The Wanderer'), CP(M), 62.]

Quoted from the first public edition of 'Poems', this
stanza was the kind of thing which made Auden the hero of
the young intelligentsia. Noteworthy, though, is the way
in which the enchanting declarative evocation discussed
above is painstakingly avoided. The stanza's rhythmic
progress is as dazzlingly erratic as a skyrocket toppled
from its bottle. The switchback syntax, the Hardyesque
hyphenated compounds - they pack things tight, and the
reader is never once allowed to draw an inattentive
breath. One of the many triumphs of Auden's first public
volume was that this difficult verse came to be regarded
as equally characteristic with the simpler felicities
that were everywhere apparent.

Beams from your car may cross a bedroom wall,
They wake no sleeper; you may hear the wind
Arriving driven from the ignorant sea
To hurt itself on pane, on bark of elm
Where sap unbaffled rises, being spring;..   [EA, 22]

Merely to mention the headlight beams crossing the wall
was enough to create them for the reader's dazzled eye.
But Auden's maturity had already arrived: he was well
aware that such moments were not to be thought of as the
high points of poetry - rather as the rest points. Take,
for example, these lines from 'Prologue', the opening
poem of his 1936 collection 'Look, Stranger!'

> And make us as Newton was, who in his garden watching
> The apple falling towards England, became aware
> Between himself and her of an eternal tie.   [EA, 119]

The apple falling towards England is superb, but poetry
which had such effects as a *raison d'être* would be a
menace. This very instance has in fact come under critical
attack - an accusation of decadence has been levelled.
But it should be obvious that Auden had no intention of
allowing such facility to become fatal. Set against it
were the inhibitors; syntactical, grammatical, lexical.
And with them they brought ambiguity, resonance, areas of
doubt and discovery - all the things his later poetry was
to lose. The suggestiveness of Auden's poetry lay in the
tension between his primal lyricism and the means employed
to discipline it. The suggestiveness couldn't survive
if either term went missing. And eventually it was the
lyricism that went.
  Looking through the individual collections of Auden's
poems, each in succession strikes us as transitional. On
each occasion there seems to be a further move towards
paraphrasable clarity. Even at the height of his
bookish phase (in, say, 'New Year Letter') Auden is still
being more narrowly clear than he was before. Gradually,
as we read on to the end, we see what kind of progress
this has been. It has been a movement away from excitement
and towards satisfaction.
  'Epistle to a Godson' is like 'About the House' and
'City Without Walls' in being utterly without the excitement
we recognize as Audenesque. And yet it, like them, gives
a peculiar satisfaction: the patriarch grunts, having seen
much and come a long way. The book is flat champagne, but
it's still champagne. Part of Auden's genius was to know
the necessity of chastening his talent, ensuring that his
poetry would be something more enduring than mere magic.
The resource and energy he devoted to containing and
condensing his natural lyricism provide one of the great
dramas in modern literary history. Pick up 'Look, Stranger!'
or 'Another Time' - they read like thrillers. Every poem
instantly establishes its formal separateness from all the
others. Through Auden's work we trace not just themes but
different ways of getting something unforgettably said:
the poem's workings are in the forefront of attention.
Finally the contrast between the early and the late
manners is itself part of the drama. To understand Auden
fully, we need to understand how a man with the capacity
to say anything should want to escape from the oppression
of meaning too much. Late Auden is the completion of a
technical evolution in which technique has always been

thought of as an instrument of self-denial. What Auden
means by the fetters of Self is the tyranny of an
ungoverned talent, and his late poetry is a completed
testament to the self-control which he saw the necessity
for from the very start - the most commendable precocity
of all.

131. DENIS DONOGHUE, GOOD GRIEF, 'NEW YORK REVIEW OF BOOKS'

19 July 1973, 17-18

Donoghue (b. 1928) holds the Henry James Chair of Letters
at New York University. His works include 'Connoisseurs
of Chaos: Ideas of Order in Modern American Literature'
(1966), 'The Ordinary Universe: Soundings in Modern
Literature' (1968), 'Thieves of Fire' (1973), and 'The
Sovereign Ghost: Studies in Imagination' (1976).
    This review also considers Auden's 'Forewords and After-
words', selected by Edward Mendelson, 'Man's Place: An
Essay on Auden', by Richard Johnson, and 'W.H. Auden as a
Social Poet', by Frederick Buell.

'For Valéry,' W.H. Auden has remarked, 'a poem ought to be
a festival of the intellect, that is, a game, but a solemn,
ordered, and significant game, and a poet is someone to
whom arbitrary difficulties suggest ideas.'* For Valéry,
and now for Mr. Auden, especially in 'About the House,'
'City Without Walls,' and 'Epistle to a Godson,' books
written according to the principle that, whatever life is,
poetry is a carnival. The poet begins with language,
delighting in the exercise of its possibilities, and he
stops short of Mardi gras only by requiring his language
to recognize the existence of the primary world in which
we live.
    The poem makes a secondary world, according to pres-
criptions as congenial as they are ingenious. In 'Epistle
to a Godson' the primary world contains for the most part
certain grand maladies of the quotidian: age, loss, grief,
loneliness, violence, nuances of damage, bloody-minded
monsters at large. The secondary world is still managed
with the most charming intention, and a prosody of good
humour, good taste, good luck. The dominant tone implies
that the quest is now too perilous to be undertaken

* [Un Homme d'Esprit, in 'Forewords and Afterwords',
   London: Faber & Faber, 1973, 363.]

directly, better wait till morning and the possibility of
'cleansed occasions.' Meanwhile the poet writes short,
brisk poems, a few smacks administered to the world's
bottom, for its good. There is a lot of grousing, but
no harm is meant, the poet is merely telling young people
to mind their manners, speak decent English, and wash
occasionally.

Mr. Auden has become a crusty old fellow somewhat before
his time; by my reckoning he is only sixty-six but he
talks, in this book, like something carved on Mount
Rushmore. The familiar ghost of T.S. Eliot's 'Little
Gidding' disclosed three gifts reserved for age: first,
'the cold friction of expiring sense / Without enchantment';
second, 'the conscious impotence of rage / At human folly';
and finally, 'the rending pain of re-enactment / Of all
that you have done, and been.'

'Epistle to a Godson' takes a milder view of its gifts.
There is still a touch of enchantment, there are good
friends, there is music. Human folly is inescapable, but
Mr. Auden does whatever poetry can to turn the impotence
of rage into irony, keeping his temper as sweet as
possible. 'Our world rapidly worsens': well, perhaps it
does, but I don't propose to worry too much if the only
evidence produced in the poem is the fact that Mr. Auden
at Schwechat Flughafen was frisked by a cop for weapons.
Methinks he protests too much. As for Eliot's last gift
to the aged, Mr. Auden does not trouble himself too
much or spend his spirit fruitlessly re-enacting what he
has done or been. He takes Yeats's line on that, forgives
himself a lot, casts out remorse. And rightly so.

Leaving the blues aside, Mr. Auden tells us something
of the world as it would be if God had consulted the poet
before making it. It would be a sweet world ruled by
the laws of prosody, a lot of rhymes, 'a stunning display
of concinnity and elegance,' a lot of freedom, short of
anarchy. From an earlier poem: 'A sentence uttered makes
a world appear / Where all things happen as it says they
do.' Such a world would be a gentle place, 'nothing obscene
or unpleasant,' since 'only the unscarred overfed enjoy
Calvary / as a verbal event.' Things would be easy on the
senses, there would be plenty of time for love and wit.
No excess though: against Blake, Mr. Auden says that the
road of excess leads, more often than not, to the Slough
of Despond.

Sometimes, in such a mood, Mr. Auden is inclined to
say to his juniors; listen, kiddos, I've had my life, why
should you whine about yours? Or words to that effect.
In one poem he tells those who may be curious about Circe's

charms that they can take his word for them, they're over-
rated. Free love is discouraged, like free verse, and
for similar reasons, apparently. In 'Moon Landing,'
reversing Johnson's famous remark to Boswell about the
Giant's Causeway, Mr. Auden says of the moon that it was
probably worth going to see, but not worth seeing. The
gist of the rhetoric is that the primary world should be
modeled on the best of the available secondary worlds: our
institutions like our symphonies. State occasions would
be featured like proper names, which are *'an-sich* poetic,'
as amenable as limestone.

Mr. Auden's images of value are those now familiar to us
from his poems of the last decade. He praises 'a watered /
lively garden' and remains uncharmed by deserts. He much
prefers nature when she's courteous than when she's
throwing a tantrum: 'earth-quakes, floods, eruptions, /
seem a bit vulgar.' It is my impression that animals get
a better press in 'Epistle to a Godson' than in earlier
books, mainly because their inability to listen to a story
is now felt as a minor defect in view of their instinctual
certainties, lucidities apparently superior to those of
men, officially 'their lonely betters.'

Insects are still separated from our affections by 'a
prohibitive fracture empathy cannot transgress.' Mice are
addressed with a certain fellow-feeling I cannot share. I
could not love even a white one. Mr. Auden is tender to
dogs, bacteria, and many other instances of life, though
he reserves the right to be selective and to play
favorites. He thinks well of plants, mainly because their
response to a gardener's handling shows that they 'like
to be given the chance to get more than a self-education.'
Of minerals in this book he has little to say, having said
so much and so warmly in earlier poems of great celebrity;
but he has a wonderful line about the regime of minerals
'where what is not forbidden is compulsory.' Naturally,
most of the grousing poems are about man, presented as a
nuisance, with rare exceptions. Still, He's all we have
besides, He's a miracle, God knows, 'for who is not
certain that he was meant to be?"

But the trouble is that man, this miraculous fellow, is
a bore and, increasingly nowadays, a dangerous clown. He
ought to live with joy and laughter, good food, good music.
His books ought to be delightful, not 'plain cooking made
still plainer by plain cooks,' to recite an earlier version
of the poet's plaint. If 'the truest poetry is the most
feigning,' poets should feign like mad, but take care not to
go crazy. So Mr. Auden, it is well known and in part approved, has been making merry with the dictionaries in recent
years. I suppose he thinks of them as pure poetry, containing

thousands of words virtually untouched by human hands;
marvelous words now archaic, obsolete, and for that very
reason waiting to be resuscitated by a poet addicted to
that pleasure.

In this book he uses 'faith' as a verb, its object
someone you trust. 'Conster' is used instead of its
current form 'construe.' 'Annoy' is a noun, 'odd' a verb,
'decent,' 'false' are verbs. 'In tift' is Anglo-Saxon for
'in good order.' 'Blithe' is used as a transitive verb;
'librate' instead of 'oscillate,' so to librate between
a glum and a frolic, in the poem 'Talking to Myself,' is
presumably to give the movement a moony touch, the
libration of the moon being the only sense in which the
word is still recalled.

Again, Mr. Auden runs to the dialect dictionaries.
Instead of asking what the moon landing means or portends,
he asks 'What does it osse?' a Cumberland verb recently
deceased and therefore desperately in need of Mr. Auden's
attention. In 'Talking to Mice' the sight of a dead mouse
'obumbated a week.' At first I suspected a misprint
for 'obumbrated,' a word well represented in the great
'OED', meaning 'overshadowed.' Perhaps it is a misprint,
like Yeats's 'soldier' for 'solider'; unless Mr. Auden
wanted to touch the word with 'abate' as an even darker
shadow falling upon the first. In any case, the verb
stands for the formal acknowledgement of grief, and
its archaic air takes some of the harm out of the occasion
by observing the decencies with a particular mark of
attention, a Latin mark more plangent than the Saxon version
which has survived.

The only point I want to make is that Mr. Auden, who
likes a lark as well as anybody, is not merely larking
with the dictionary: in nearly every novelty he has a sound
reason, but also a sense reason. 'O Happy Grief!' is all
sad verse can say': a motto from an earlier book, practiced
in this one so that the grief, redeemed by the poet's
language, becomes good without losing its other attributes.
A grudging reader, faced with Mr. Auden's novelties, might
refuse to acknowledge a serious purpose being pursued,
might declare in anger that he writes thus not because it
is necessary but because it is possible. Such people remind
me of a passage in Henry Adams's 'Democracy' where envy is
the topic and Madeleine the occasion: 'People who envied
her smile said that she cultivated a sense of humour in
order to show her teeth.' My own view is that for such a
cause any reason is good enough. If Mr. Auden starts with
language rather than with big thoughts, good luck to him;
one judges by results.

'Epistle to a Godson' is Mr. Auden's first collection
of new poems since 'City Without Walls' (1969). It begins
with a godfather's advice, not Marlon Brando's 'Make him
an offer he can't refuse' but the Red Knight's admonition,
somewhat modified to take account of the fact that its
object is Philip Spender not Alice: 'Turn out your toes
when you walk - and remember who you are.' The book ends
with a soul's address to its body, pleading for the boon
of a quick death when the time comes:

Remember: when *Le Bon Dieu* says to You *Leave him!*,
please, please, for His sake and mine, pay no attention
to my piteous *Dont's,* but bugger off quickly.[CP(M), 654]

Between these good counsels there are poems about
doctors, illness, 'my sad flesh,' the distinction between
persons and animals, the superiority of sight to hearing
(all sensory things considered), photography, music
(notably that of the first cuckoo in spring), the weather,
William Empson (in praise), and 'eucatastrophe,' 'regeneration beyond waters.' Mr. Auden welcomes a theme only
when it has given him some sign, however demurely, that if
properly appreciated it will respond with affection.
Courtship, thereafter, is a matter of style, and if it
seems easy the appearance is deceptive: it takes a rich
mixture of grace and luck to win, even with a smiling
theme. If the theme keeps its distance, refuses to meet
the poet's eye, then Mr. Auden leaves it alone: why should
the aging eagle stretch his wings, he is not trying to
write 'Paradise Lost'. He has certainly done enough, in
'Epistle to a Godson', to please me. Our world can't be
worsening intolerably if it is still possible for a poet
to write about its manifestations so charmingly.

'Thank You, Fog'

London, September 1974; New York, November 1974

'Thank You, Fog' is a posthumous collection edited by
Edward Mendelson.

132. PHILIP TOYNBEE, GOODBYE TO AUDEN, 'OBSERVER'

29 September 1974

Toynbee (1916-81), a novelist, poet, and writer of non-
fiction, joined the editorial staff of the 'Observer' in
1950. His books include 'The Savage Days' (1937), 'A School
in Private' (1941), 'Friends Apart: A Memoir of Esmond
Romilly and Jasper Ridley in the Thirties' (1954), 'Views
from a Lake' (1968), and 'Towards the Holy Spirit' (1973).
   See also a warm memoir by Peter Vansittart, A Capacity
for Friendship, 'London Magazine', 21, 8, November 1981,
pp. 22-9.

The last lines of verse that Auden wrote before his death
exactly a year ago today do not appear in the text of this,
his final and slenderest volume; but Mr Edward Mendelson,
who has edited these leavings, provides them for us in his
introductory note. Here they are:-

   He still loves life
   but O O O O how he wishes
   the good Lord would take him.

The first of these three lines sounds all too like a

piece of perfunctory bravado; or perhaps like the tribute
to a zest which had departed. The sad truth seems to be that
Auden's life grew grimmer and grimmer towards its close,
and that his final 18 months in England - after 33 years
of expatriation, mostly in America - were often a hell of
alcoholic and sexual indignity. One of the few times I met
him was in the late sixties, and I have never been in the
company of anyone so infectiously distracted, so frenziedly
restless and uneasy.

This makes it all the odder that the poems of Auden's
last decade should have been such a continuous celebration,
if the word is not too jolly, of all those virtues and
tastes which have been the traditional accompaniment of
successful ageing. In verse after verse he extolled the
seemly, the decorous, the domestic; deprecated all extreme
emotions or attitudes; adopted the posture of some wisely
tamed old master whose oats had long ago been sown and who
had at last achieved that mildly ironical tranquillity which
sits so well on a wrinkled brow.

The epigraph to this final volume is entirely typical of
the public person whom Auden had been presenting for so
many years:-

None of us are as young
as we were. So what?
Friendship never ages.

This is typical, alas, not only in the commonplace
nature of the sentiment; but also in the feebleness of its
expression. (Needless to repeat that the more Eternal a
Verity the newer and sharper the words which must be found
to revivify it.) This is not to say that Auden wrote no
good and truthful poetry during the last decade. His wit
never entirely deserted him; his ear never lost its ability
to discover subtle new sounds and rhythms; at his best he
could achieve a melancholy eloquence. Indeed, his last
volume, 'Epistle to a Godson' (1972), seemed to me the best
he had produced for many years. Nor is the present volume
withouts its mild felicities, its occasional joyous reminders of the great poet who was crumbling so painfully
away - and evidently looking forward so urgently to his
release. This is from the poem which gives the volume its
title:

[Quotes 11. 19-30 of 'Thank You, Fog', CP(M), 657.]

There seem to be even more neologisms than there used
to be, and one old trick has become a persistent tic. In
an epigrammatic tribute to the English language Auden

remarks that 'we can very easily turn Nouns, if we wish,
into Verbs.' And this he domonstrates over and over again:
'Cannot conceit' for the obvious 'conceive'; 'the tortoise
aspected the vagrant moods of the Weather.'... The arch
and whimsical remained to the end the worst pitfalls into
which the elderly Auden was liable to tumble: though he
tumbled, it must be admitted, with a fairly obvious defiance, as if this, too, were some sort of mild joke
against the reader as well as against himself.

How can I lighten the gloom of this valediction? Well,
some of the short epigrams are good; and look better when
we look at them longer:-

> When truly brothers,
> men don't sing in unison
> but in harmony.

or

> Whatever their personal faith,
> all poets, as such,
> are polytheists.

There are beautiful lines in several of these poems; and it
is just possible that the haunting 'Lullaby' might creep
into the canon of authentic Auden successes. The future
biographer will be grateful for 'A Thanksgiving,' in which
Auden gives us a succinct résumé of his intellectual and
spiritual history. He pays a kindly tribute to all his
mentors:-

> Fondly I ponder You all:
> without You I couldn't have managed
> even my weakest of lines.

But his final guardians are Horace and Goethe; Horace for
being the 'adroitest of makers' and Goethe because he saw
more in stones than Newton ever managed to see in them.

But I am not that biographer and I daresay it would not
be *comely* in me - a typical late-Auden word - to speculate
here on the strange final conglomeration of Auden's beliefs,
his daily life and the person he presented to us in his
later verse. All I can say now is that cruel od Dissoci-
ation seems to have been at work here in a particularly
virulent form. Would it have been if the frenzied figure I
talked to in Austria six years ago had allowed his frenzy
to get into his beliefs and thence into his verse? Or could
he keep his head above water only by adopting a public

stance which corresponded so little to the tormented private reality?

I doubt whether compensatory verse is ever very good
poetry; and if it is true, as I cannot help suspecting,
that in too many of Auden's later volumes he was clinging
to a part rather than expressing the truth of his distress, then this may well account for the dismay so many of
the oldest admirers of this marvellous poet have felt at
the note of unreality which had crept into too much of his
later verse.

133. JOHN FULLER, FOOTNOTES, 'NEW REVIEW'

i, 7, October 1974, 76-8

Poet, playwright, and literary critic, Fuller (b. 1937) has
been a Fellow of Magdalen College, Oxford, since 1966. His
books include 'Fairground Music' (1961), 'Cannibals and
Missionaries' (1972), 'Epistles to Several Persons' (1973),
'The Illusionists - A Tale' (1980), and a conscientious
commentary on Auden, 'A Reader's Guide to W.H. Auden' (1970).

The latest Auden (not only this posthumous collection, but
its final revelation of what we already give the normative
label of 'late Auden') is largely a footnote to 'Epistle
to a Godson', a wry attention to the poet's habitat divided
between thanksgiving and grouching. In many of the 18 poems,
20 shorts and ten-page masque which comprise 'Thank You,
Fog', the golden age is lamented, friends are celebrated
and the modern world reviled. If we can get to the moon,
why can't we also get beyond the internal combustion
engine? Why can't they invent 'an odorless and noiseless /
staid little electric brougham'? There is a looming reality behind this charming notion, I understand, as there
is real substance in late Auden. Like late Auden it is
couched in fey terms, though, and we come to believe in his
curses only through the decorated mirrors of mild jokes. In
the past this has worked brilliantly, with enormous sur-
realistic spite or (rather later) with wit borrowed from
idols like Sydney Smith, but in this late late Auden the
attitudes have fallen back upon their own resources,
strained, repetitive, openly resentful or soggily epicurean - the brougham without the electricity.

The grouching comes off worst. In the masque 'The

Entertainment of the Senses' (written with Chester Kallman)
he prods the debasement, particularly the erotic debasement, of modern life. The five senses enter as prancing
apes and in turn remind the audience of the equality of
their sensual enjoyments: genuine simulated sealskin
briefs, vaginal deodorants, tasteless food, ubiquitous
cameras and transistor radios, and so on. Hardly in the
vanguard of satire, the attack is dissipated by the ragged
prosody possibly felt to be associated with this genre.
Taste, for instance, might have been funny if the effect
of using doggerel anapaests in the manner of the acolytes'
masque in 'Volpone' had been more finely judged:

> And if I had intentions more directly
>   erotic,
> I'd remember that Cupid's gone
>   macrobiotic;
> Though his too-divine packaging rouse
>   appetite,
> It won't show that his palate has gone
>   with his sight.   ['The Entertainment of the Senses']

The metrically fudged 'rouse appetite', the repetition of
'gone' and resulting ambiguity, the uncertainty about what
'it' refers to and whether it does the showing before or
after you've eaten this glamorous but tasteless food, all
these serve to complicate an already slightly involved and
delicate poetic aperçu. Unnecessarily, one would have
thought. The point of the masque is that it is hardly even
worth it to be an *honest* sensualist, since death awaits
everyone, but again, this is obscured by a double negative
in the refrain which creates a self-contradiction I found
impossible to unravel. And finally damaged by an irrelevant
joke against critics of Auden the Reviser ('When you get a
little older / You'll discover like Isolde: / "We must love
one another *and* die!"'). Dreadful to think that this was
his last word on that particular crux.
   Remembering 'About the House', a finer collection than
many reviewers supposed, one would expect to find Auden
better at praising than complaining. And yes, there are
some successes here, on Gilbert White, for instance, or on
his own body ('Sing, Big Baby, sing lullay'). Death is at
hand, and the stoical attitude in poems like 'No, Plato,
No' is wholly admirable and moving. But often the mood of
thanksgiving strikes the wrong kind of private note, and
the peculiarities of style so freely encouraged by the late
Auden work over-vigorously for effects they hardly need to
achieve.
   The title poem, for instance, is grateful for a dismal

feature of the English weather which has for one week at
Christmas kept strangers out of the charmed circle:

> Indoors specific spaces,
> cosy, accommodate to
> reminiscence and reading,
> crosswords, affinities, fun:
> refected by a sapid
> supper and regaled by wine,
> we sit in a glad circle

There is little time or inclination in the poem for speculation about the 'four Selves, joined in friendship' or
the nature of the feelings which bind them. After all, one
may say, that ground has been covered in such poems as 'A
Summer's Night', not so far in spirit from this one with
its 'metaphysical distress, / Our kindness to ten persons'.
But the dimensions of the earlier poem, once invoked, im-
measurably reduce the reader's response to 'Thank You, Fog'.
There is no irony here, no social perspective, not even a
perfectly communicated sense of occasion. When Auden wants
to say that the fog has stopped the birds singing, he
writes:

> ...even those birds whose blood
> is brisk enough to bid them
> abide here all the year round,
> like the merle and the mavis,
> at Your cajoling refrain
> their jocund interjections,
> no cock considers a scream...

A pretty passage and no one could really object to these
poetic words for the blackbird and the thrush (unless the
popularity of the girls' names hinders such a harking back
to Drayton *et al.*) but the sound of the lines is irresis-
tibly suggesting that the birds are in fact singing. Why
choose such musical and percussive words to describe them
not singing? Or allow the syntax to encourage a momentary
ambiguity in the word 'refrain'? Late Auden is verbally
astonishing, but occasionally inappropriate to my ear: it
is a matter of lexical verification that the 'sapid' supper
quoted above should have been very good to eat, but verbal
associations continue to tell one that it couldn't have
been. Incidentally, what is to be said about his grammatical caprice of substitution (habitual at the end, and frequently perplexing to readers)? It's not easy to deny the
validity of turning nouns into verbs, or passive verbs into
active ones. It all depends on how often you do it, and

whether (say) unfortunate echoes of uncouth speech-habits
are ever accidentally the result (as in the atrocious
lines 'He has never learned you, it seems, about fig-leaves'
and 'Poets have learned us their myths', where in addition
one might imagine that to contrive this example twice in
one book suggests that the poet might have begun to say it
in real life.)

The collection is not, of course, as occasional as perhaps I have suggested. There are numerous poems of ratiocination, full of fascinating notions. The author of 'Unpredictable but Providential', for instance, is still the
late Auden we like. But is there anything in the book
which has not been done before, and done better? I think
not. Often, of course, one is reminded not only of more
substantial disquisitions on the absurdities of science or
the horrors of modern urban life in other recent collections, but of early, now classic treatment of fundamental
Auden subjects. Any comparison is not heartening. Take one
example, that of the difference between men and animals.
'Address to the Beasts' in the present collection ends:

Distinct now,
in the end we shall join you
(how soon all corpses look alike)

but you exhibit no signs
of knowing that you are sentenced.
Now, could that be why

we upstarts are often
jealous of your innocence,
but never envious?

The central point is anticipated in the chorus, 'Happy the
hare at morning' from 'The Dog Beneath the Skin'. There,
man is shown to be at the mercy of his culture, which is a
desperate effort to forget the anticipated fact of death.
The liturgical tone has moral grandeur and there are intellectual short-cuts: plenty, in fact, for any old Leavi-
site to hate. But it is a colourful and sure-paced poem
in which simple language and observation at the right moments carry a genuine weight of feeling:-

But what shall man do, who can whistle tunes by heart,
Know to the bar when death shall cut him short, like
                              the cry of the shearwater?

The later poem substitutes the appearance of argument
(the 'but' and 'now' in the extract quoted above are
surely the weakest of rhetorical links when you examine
them) and a much more detached and playful sense of cate-
gorising. 'Often jealous' / 'never envious' is an illuminating distinction only if one is in a mood for aphorism:
there are many such pleasing devices in 'The Dyer's Hand',
more positively engineered.

It is thus that one reads late Auden for pleasure in
the quizzical asides of a critical consciousness, rarely
for sheer poetic pleasure. And (dare one say it?) his
truths became almost *too* central. When he was not at the
last simply indulging in local grumbling or praising, he
reached too easily for anthropological or metaphysical
ideas that, while sometimes astounding, were frequently
merely truisms or even *remarks* couched in his particular
brand of relaxed but lexically quaint discourse. It is a
comfortable poetry, even (perhaps mostly) when enquiring
where Christ got that extra chromosome from, or preferring
a painted wizard to bewigged Descartes. These worlds co-
existed in his head, all battles done, no new sparks
struck. We came in the end to miss the arguable truth, the
partial view, the social engagement - all those kinds of
special pleading that required dazzling metaphorical and
musical performances from the poet.

'Collected Poems'

London, September 1976; New York, October 1976

134. SEAMUS HEANEY, SHORTS FOR AUDEN, 'HIBERNIA'

8 October 1976, 21

Widely regarded as Ireland's most distinguished contemporary
poet, Heaney (b.1939) is author of 'Death of a Naturalist'
(1966), 'Door into the Dark' (1969), 'Wintering Out' (1972),
'North' (1975), 'Field Work' (1979), and 'Preoccupations:
Selected Prose 1968-1978' (1980).

For almost fifty years W.H. Auden wrote what he called
'shorts', quick chasers for the longer work, the clippings
and shavings of the poetic workshop: epigram, haiku, cleri-
hew, ballyhoo. They were an indication of the fecundity of
his 'intellectual baggage', as Maritain put it, the equivalent in the literary sphere of his frugality and economy in
the domestic. They were also a demonstration of what has
been called 'the good crack principle' which insists that
poetry should often aspire to the status of entertainment.
e.g. 'Thomas Moore / Caused a furore/Every time he bellowed
his/Irish Melodies', or 'Let us honour if we can / The vertical man/Though we value none/But the horizontal one'.
    Auden was also inclined to write prose in short bursts,
so that the thing worked like a crazy paving or a set of
stepping stones for the intelligence. When he faced the
bull of reality, he was more a bandillero than a picador or
matador: he made nimble dashes at the neck muscles, conspicuously rapid and skilful forays that were closer to the
choreographer's than to the killer's art, closer to comedy
than tragedy.
    Yet in the beginning, this metaphor invoking the panache
of the *corrida* would not have served. Then we would have

been forced to think of the *Holmgang* (holmgang, Old Norse:
'going to the holm' or islet on which a duel was fought,
hence a duel to the death). The barbarism of Northern
Europe, ancient and modern, blew like a cold wind through
the verse. A few lines are enough to remind us that the
civility of the later verse sells the auditory imagination
short: 'Doom is dark and deeper than any sea-dingle...'
'Who stands, the crux left of the watershed, / On the wet
road between the chafing grass...' 'Who will endure / Heat
of day and winter danger...'
     Auden is a Norse name. His lifeline stretched into the
Anglo-Saxon landscape and deposits where 'the dead howl /
Under headlands in their windy dwellings'. When he was commissioned to write a travel book, he went to Iceland, sea-
faring north, a wanderer in saga-land, Grendel country.
That was in 1936. In 1965, in a poem called 'Amor Loci',
he was still committing himself to a desolate landscape,
still envisaging the desert places as the guarantee of his
imagination:

> How, but with some real focus
> of desolation
> could I, by analogy,
> imagine a love
> that, however often smeared,
> shrugged at, abandoned
> by a frivolous worldling,
> does not abandon?   [CP(M), 586]

     'A frivolous worldling' - at times he certainly was.
The mighty fluency that gave us 'Letter to Lord Byron',
surely the twentieth century poem that is the apotheosis
of the good crack principle, more and more settled for a
kind of high-table garrulousness. That original clipped
and speedy utterance which was the perfect technique for
flushing and bagging 'the lion griefs' in sonnet sequences,
or formal lyrics, or hypnotic ballads, finally slipped
into a tone somewhere between camp and costive. When public
terror and private passion haunted the roots of the poems,
the detachment and definition in the voice maintained the
lines in high tension. When he settled into an imperious
and impatient domesticity, holding the fort of a menaced
bourgeois culture, the detachment occasionally mutated towards indifference and a kind of educated in-talk.
     There is a story about a Ballymena listener calling the
BBC one morning in 1969, after the Northern Ireland news
had given a lot of coverage to speeches by civil rights
leaders the previous evening. 'Tell us this,' he said,
'are yez Unionists are are yez not?' At the centre of
Auden's work, an equally categorical question is implicit:

'Tell us this, are yez civilised or are yez not?' For
while it is true that his feelings quickened in the
presence of the desolate and worn-out and primitive, the
counter-truth holds also: the human achievements of art,
manners, social intercourse, just government, are all that
are worth living for.

Hence the political Auden, and those poems like 'Spain'
and 'September 1, 1939' which he suppressed because they
stated the counter-truth too shrilly, rhetorically, 'dis-
honestly'. They do not appear in this edition that has
been prepared by his literary executor and includes all
the poems that he wished to preserve, in a text that represents his final revisions. They will be reprinted, however, in a volume due next year, to be called 'The English
Auden'. That book will also include a selection of other
suppressed and unpublished prose and verse from the early
period.

The title of the forthcoming volume is an allusion to
Auden's two careers, one in England in the twenties and
thirties, and the other in America after that. I think it
was unfortunate for England and the native English sensibility, if perhaps fortunate for Auden himself, that he
emigrated. He was the one English writer who was the heir
to Lawrence as prophet and diagnostician of the country's
spiritual and social ennui. By 1940 he was buoyant on the
gratitude and excitement of an audience which he had created, and he chose to distance himself from them. There was
nothing Joycean about the exile, distance did not lend intensity to the view. Instead it bred an eccentric gen-
tility. Auden's later poems constitute a flourish of personality and intelligence, a prodigal play of ideas about
the good life to which one's response must be delighted
Deo Gratias. But it is work in which the self is forced to
make all the running, and for the highest art, the self is
best melded with the intensities and occasions of the
world which produced it and surrounds it. There is something parabolic in the picture of Auden in the final year of
his life, returned home to Oxford, sitting there in a
coffee shop not so much unapproachable as unapproached,
isolated at last in the very world where he had first discovered community.

Is it bad manners (an Auden taboo) to wonder about the
relationship between the way he held experience at arm's
length and his homosexuality? The climax of one of the late
nostalgic love poems occurs in the phrase 'love was made'.
The passive voice enters at the most active moment, grammar
contrives to make passion hygienic. Had his virtuosity, his
assiduous cultivation of finish, of verbal surface, anything to do with the fact that society forced him to regard

his intimate nature as Vicious? Certainly, in 'Three Posthumous Poems', published for the first time in this volume,
the bare cry of release, the bleak satisfactions of self-
knowledge suggest a mode that might have cut a deeper
groove than the ones we know:

>   To-night, for instance, now that
>   Bert has been here, I
>   listen to the piercing screams
>   of palliardising cats
>   without self-pity.   [Minnelied, CP(M), 562]

Auden was an epoch-making poet on public themes, the
register of a new sensibility, a great sonneteer, a writer
of perfect light verse, a prospector of language at its
most illiterate roots and a dandy of lexicography at its
most extravagant reaches. There is a Victorian bulk to
this book that contains his confident, abundant, peremp-
tory, insouciant opus. A hundred years from now Auden's
work will certainly be in permanent and outstanding profile, and for all one's niggardly withholdings, in the end
one assents with a 'yes' as pleasured and whole-hearted as
Molly Bloom's.

135. IRVIN EHRENPREIS, INSIDE AUDEN'S LANDSCAPE, 'NEW YORK
REVIEW OF BOOKS'

xxiv, 1, 3 February 1977, 10-12

Ehrenpreis (b.1920) is Linden Kent Professor of English at
the University of Virginia. His books include 'The Types
Approach to Literature' (1945), 'The Personality of Jonathan Swift' (1958), and 'Literary Meaning and Augustan
Values' (1974).

The fat new volume of Auden's 'Collected Poems,' superbly
edited by Edward Mendelson (and hideously produced by the
publisher), gives us extraordinary opportunities to notice
the persistence of the poet's themes and devices. Even in
the dark, portentous poems of Auden's early career, there
were clear designs, the language of common speech, and an
unpremeditated, dramatic manner. It was, in fact, the
balance of these elements against the enigma that drew us in.
If the poems sounded at times like riddles, if the syntax

was often knotty, yet the words remained natural and the
meaning seemed important. Though we might be unsure of his
sense, the author was evidently speaking straight to us,
and on timely, even urgent matters. He seemed to assume
that we understood, that we belonged to his tribe; and as
we groped to trace the way, we felt we were just not sharp
enough to follow him.

> The latest ferrule now has tapped the curb,
> And the night's tiny noises everywhere
> Beat vivid on the owl's developed ear,
> Vague on the watchman's, and in wards disturb
> The nervous counting sheep.
>   (1933, in the periodical 'New Verse' [EA, 147])

This is the opening of a sonnet about the poet's missing
his beloved. But how much more it seemed to imply!
    When the meaning of such poems emerged, it often dealt
with the separation or opposition of mysterious persons or
groups; with a distinction between two psychic conditions
and the yearning for a change from one to the other; with
movements between vague regions that seemed oddly cut off
and yet neighboring. Slowly, we realized that change of
place meant change of condition, that the outer landscape
reflected inner moods, and the transformations desired were
moral or emotional.
    In Auden's best work the blend of openness with reserve,
of well-defined form and riddling tone, of lucid and yet
veiled speech, makes in general two subtle impressions:
either that valuable truths are being conveyed, or that a
distinguished person is showing us, his fellow tribesmen,
a self he hides from strangers:

> I see it often since you've been away:
> The island, the veranda, and the fruit;
> The tiny steamer breaking from the bay;
> The literary mornings with its hoot;
> Our ugly comic servant; and then you,
> Lovely and willing every afternoon.   [EA, 423]

So begins another poem, of the same vintage, reduced in a
later version to a little song ('Collected Poems,' p. 60).
How discreet or perhaps evasive the revelation was may be
judged from a poem written more than thirty years later,
when the poet's boundary between private and public terri-
tories had been moved pretty far:

[Quotes stanzas 1-2, and 7, of 'Glad' (from Three Posthumous Songs), CP(M), 561.]

Auden's later work preserved the element of enigma, in a tangential approach to surprising topics and with exotic words dropped casually into ordinary speech. But the tone remained the sort that members of a harmonious family take toward one another. So Auden holds us with agreeable modulations of language - from slang to eloquence, from the colloquial to the technical - implying a privileged relation between him and ourselves. We respond to his candour, intimacy, faith in our sympathy. We stand with him against the Others.

Poems like 'In Praise of Limestone' and 'The Horatians' mix casual endearments or in-group signals with thoughts on aesthetics. In such poems Auden exposes his tastes and prejudices. He celebrates his landscapes, rises to sublimity, then stoops to the humble talk one uses with close friends or relations - and with oneself. But he stops consciously short of exhibitionism, perhaps just short: he veers away from scandal and indecency.

The efficiency with which Auden traveled about his poetic universe depended on a knack of dividing it up into classes or gradations between which traffic was convenient. It's not for nothing that he wrote an ode to Terminus, the god of boundaries. From his early poems to his latest Auden approached his materials as a cataloguer.

He was eager to put things - morals, detective stories, mining machinery, God - in their proper places. Art, he wrote in 'The Sea and the Mirror,' presents us with 'the perfectly tidiable case of disorder.' So he tidied up the world like an affectionate housekeeper arranging a playroom for children: 'To set in order - that's the task / Both Eros and Apollo ask' ('New Year Letter,' 11. 56-57).

By a reflex action he seemed to arrange his important experiences as a collector of specimens would arrange rocks and minerals. He analyzed people and incidents into types that lent themselves to abstraction, illustrating principles of ethics or psychology. Sometimes he merely personified the categories, as in an attack on English society during the mid-Thirties:

> Greed showing shamelessly her naked money,
> And all Love's wondering eloquence debased
> To a collector's slang, Smartness in furs,
> And Beauty scratching miserably for food...
> ('Birthday Poem'   [EA, 157])

This echoes Book IV of Pope's 'Dunciad' (11. 21-30). But Auden at his best did not stop at personification; he embodied the abstractions in curious or supreme examples. So when he wished to celebrate The Poet, he wrote magnifi-

cently about Yeats. When he wished to celebrate The Healer,
he wrote almost as well about Freud. When he wished to
celebrate a way of life, he identified with the limestone
landscapes he loved, and described some typical inhabitants of southern Italy (probably Ischia):

> Watch, then, the band of rivals as they climb up
>   and down
>   Their steep stone gennels in twos and threes,
>   at times
> Arm in arm, but never, thank God, in step; or
>   engaged
>   On the shady side of a square at midday in
> Voluble discourse, knowing each other too well
>   to think
>   There are any important secrets....
>   ('In Praise of Limestone')

Auden's best poems breathe, like this one, an air of
self-confident control but a lack of self-importance. Like
Dr. Johnson, the poet felt cheerfully communicative about
matters which interested him: biology and morals, religion
and ritual, geology, music, and Icelandic sagas. By fitting
them into one of his schemes, the poet brought them into
his family, even as he brought in the reader.

Auden's father was a doctor, fond of archaeology and the
sagas. His mother had been a hospital nurse, and was highly
cultivated, religious, and musical. She would sing the part
of Wagner's Tristan, in the love-potion scene, to young
Wystan's Isolde. Auden's elder brother John became a distinguished geologist. So the culture the poet disseminated
in verse belonged to him by right of inheritance.

The impulse to classify may have sprung from Auden's
background too, but the poet's use of the impulse was his
own. Many of the poems entertain us through his habit of
playing solemn games with his categories, especially with
certain divisions between opposed sides. Auden liked to
separate people - or creatures, or ideas, etc. - into mutually exclusive groups, each with its own rules; and he
liked telling why they must remain apart. He would go on to
treat the consequences of their separation, sometimes explicitly and sometimes cryptically.

But then he would also turn on himself by arranging a
passage between the groups. Or he would call for a linkage,
produced by means that happily transcended the principle of
separation. As the reader takes in the game, he first enjoys discovering the scheme of oppositions and its rules;
then he enjoys the benevolent dissolution or transcendence
of both.

In the political poetry that Auden wrote during the
Thirties, he used to divide the ranks of the oppressors
from those of the oppressed and to invoke portents of revolution. But he naturally hinted that his own roots belonged
to the former, that by a leap of sympathy he could still
identify himself with the latter, and that in some sense
love (charity, brotherhood, etc.) might make a bridge.

A wholly attractive instance is 'A Summer Night,' in
which the poet reflects on his good fortune as a member
of a privileged circle and (in stanzas ultimately deleted)
thinks of the 'gathering multitudes outside / Whose glances
hunger worsens' - those from whom he looks for a revolutionary explosion. Yet he still hopes that, as an ideal,
the affectionate harmony of the old culture will survive
the change and be a calming example for the new.

When the process of dividing and rejoining turns inward,
we meet a poem like 'Through the Looking-Glass.' Here the
poet, celebrating Christmas with his family, longs for the
presence of his secret lover, excluded from the domestic
circle. So he dreams of a world naturalized to the forbidden love, in which the father, the mother, the poet, and
the lover could all exist in harmony.

Thus Auden's drive to establish and cross boundaries
went beyond political and social classifications. It
started from deeply moral concerns and easily took the form
of psychological and religious distinctions: neurosis and
health, faith and doubt. Regularly, the poet brought the
distinctions to life by relating them to conflicts within
the self and by inventing fresh images of transcendence.
Even as he noticed the difficulty of crossing a frontier
or of bridging a gap, he would insist the change had to be
made.

This turn of mind led to another. Auden was struck by
the way the commonplace hides the extraordinary, and the
outside of things grows from and yet misrepresents their
inside: 'our selves, like Adam's / still don't fit us exactly' ('Moon Landing'). Even a world that looks benign
makes no response to human misery ('Musée des Beaux Arts');
and utter transformations of character may produce no
visible change in one's aspect or manner ('A Change of
Air'). In 'The Model' Auden deals with the rare instance of
an octogenarian who looks as good as she is.

But the opposite case bothered him chronically: color-
less lives whose essence is evil. In 'Paid on Both Sides'
ordinary people who buy Christmas turkeys wilfully involve
themselves in an insanely murderous feud: 'these faces
are ours,' says the chorus. Similarly, 'Gare Du Midi' shows
us a secret agent, come to destroy a city, who looks as
nondescript as the train in which he arrived.

The persistence of the motif suggests that the poet was
reflecting his own moral ambiguity. In 'James Honeyman,'
written when Auden was thirty, he described an ordinary man
with a genius for chemistry, who hopes to invent a
poisonous gas. As Honeyman walks out on Sunday, helping his
wife to push the baby carriage, he says 'I'm looking for a
gas, dear, / A whiff will kill a man.' Thirty years later,
in 'Josef Weinheber,' Auden writes about 'good family men'
who keep watch, 'devoted as monks, / on apparatus / inside
which harmless matter / turns homicidal.' Ultimately, the
problem of conversion, or of bowing to what is best in
one's nature, becomes the task of making the person be himself, closing the gap between inner and outer worlds.

I suppose there is a biographical explanation for such
patterns; and it may also account for another feature of
Auden's work: the rendering of psychic states in terms of
landscape. His imagery easily translated time into space,
or changes in personality into changes of location. But
the plain unfolding of the self in time seemed more of a
challenge to him. At least, Auden handled it with effort,
often framing it in the enormous map of phylogeny, or of
the evolution of the universe. In a late poem, 'The Aliens,'
he surprisingly finds the metamorphosis of insects an
utterly unhuman idea, although he well knew how commonly it
has served as a metaphor of man's spiritual history.

Movement in space, whether symbolic or 'real,' seemed
effortless for his imagination. He found it convenient to
describe maturing as growing 'taller' in his early poems.
Later, he could talk about the shift from a worldly to a
religious frame of mind as 'A Change of Air'; or he could
describe the aspiration to grace as 'The Quest' of a hero
in mythical regions.

A remarkable feature of Auden's symbolic landscapes is
the recurrence of certain elements: bleak, north of England
scenery, with mines or mining equipment, often abandoned.
The poet tells us that when he was a child, between the
ages of six and twelve, he enjoyed elaborate daydreams of
lead mining in a northern setting.

It is not hard to see, in the way Auden grew up, the
origins of his fondness for landscapes in general and for
certain scenes in particular. Even when he was little, he
went on hikes and climbs in hilly places with his father
and elder brothers. One summer in Wales the boys found a
tannery, a ginger ale factory, and three river dams to
occupy them.

The next year, the First World War broke out. Auden's
father joined the medical corps, Mrs. Auden gave up their
house near Birmingham, and sent her three boys to boarding
school. Auden was seven; the fantasies had begun. When he

was twelve, his father returned and the fantasies faded.

During the school vacations, while her husband was away,
Mrs. Auden used to rent furnished rooms for the fatherless
family in different parts of the country that had objects
of interest to her children. They would all go on long
walks together, observing the local scenery, architecture,
and ancient industries. As Auden's brother John put it,
'We studied menhirs and stone circles, gold and lead mines,
blue-john caverns, pre-Norman crosses and churches.'

I suppose the landscape of the boy's daydreams was
carried over from the rooted, united family of his pre-
school period; so it would have joined the wartime present
to the harmonious past, and therefore would have comforted
the quasi-orphan. The bleakness of the imaginary places
and the depth of the mines suggest 'objective correlatives'
for the child's loneliness, the father's absence, the need
to dig beneath the surface of the mother's and the schoolmaster's discretion.

Auden's first published poem was about lead miners who
toiled so that cathedrals might have roofs, and that the
wealth gained might provide ornaments for a lady whose
knights errant were seeking adventure in remote lands
('Lead's the Best,' 'Oxford Outlook,' 1926). Almost a
quarter-century later, in a superb poem 'Not in Baedeker,'
Auden returned to the theme. Again the lead gave roofs to
cathedrals; but no longer did it subsidize ornaments for
ladies; instead, it became the linings of coffins, perhaps
because Auden's mother had died in 1941. The theme of the
hero finding adventure abroad, while the beloved follows
the usual routines at home, turns up in several forms,
notably in 'Who's Who,' a neat, incisive comment on the
blindness of love.

We do know that Auden tied his own character to that of
his mother. There are verses and anecdotes to illuminate
the sympathy between them:

> Father at the wars,
> Mother, tongue-tied with shyness,
> struggling to tell him
> the Facts of Life he dared not
> tell her he knew already.
>
> ('Collected Poems', p.602)

When Mrs. Auden went for long walks with her children, she
sometimes accommodated herself behind a stone wall, invariably warning the boys not to watch. Young Wystan once
asked, across the wall, what would happen if they did
watch, and was told not to be cheeky. He went no further.

Auden described his mother's family as quick, short-

tempered, generous, and inclined to neurosis. She herself
stood for eccentricity and fantasy; his father, for stability and reality. Dr. Auden was not conspicuously religious, and let his wife have her way in many things. Like
both parents, the poet wanted to help and look after people;
but he had a bossiness that does not seem paternal. His
elder brother John reports that when Auden disapproved of
someone's behavior, he used to say, 'Mother would never
have allowed that.'

Didacticism and the impulse to set things in order are
traits that encourage categorizing. To strengthen them,
there were primitive dichotomies: the split in the self
between the child who obeys his parents and the one who
resists or ridicules them; or between the adult who labors
openly at respectable tasks and the one who enjoys illicit
pleasures in secret. Auden's early work 'The Orators' is
built on such polarities.

They melt into others. Auden drew a line between the
fortunate members of his privileged family and those excluded from it; and he dwelt on the distinction between
the youngest (worst off, best off) son and his senior sib-
lings. At school and in the constantly new homes of his
vacations, I suppose the uprooted child would have elaborated such divisions; he would have translated them into
maternal categories and used them to make his strange
surroundings manageable and 'familiar.'

Processes like these may have started Auden in his creative patterns, but his adaptations of them were the accomplishment of his genius. It was by a profound act of imagination that he brought the terrible events of four decades
into his moral and psychological schemes. It was through
high art that he mastered verse forms of pyrotechnic
variety and matched them to his meanings. In his finest
poems the housewifely, didactic impulse becomes merely
the ground on which the inner self joins the outer, har-
monized by the metrical design. 'The Horatians' identifies
the modern Anglo-American poet with the ancient Roman and
uses a Horatian stanza. 'In Praise of Limestone' mingles
the character of the author with the rural landscapes he
loved; and its elegiac distichs recall poets like Tibullus,
who praised the country life in Italy.

As for Edward Mendelson's edition of Auden's 'Collected
Poems,' it is a triumph of exact scholarship. In general,
the choice of poems and the texts exhibit Auden's final
judgments and revisions. Mendelson has allowed almost no
misprints to disfigure this huge body of work, and he has
painstakingly supplied dates of composition wherever
possible.

Many readers will regret that Auden omitted or altered
lines, stanzas, and whole poems that they remember with
pleasure. (Several of those-I have drawn on do not appear
in the 'Collected Poems.') Since Mendelson worked under
Auden's instructions, he could hardly avoid an editorial
policy that would have pleased the poet more than anyone
else.

But most of the revisions could easily be defended; and
those few poems which are here added to the canon must be
called fascinating. In any case, the editor promises a
further collection that will supply many of the present
volume's omissions. Meanwhile, only those who have tried
their hand at textual scholarship will appreciate the intelligence, imagination, and energy that went into the pre-
paration of the book.

Select Bibliography

A. BIBLIOGRAPHIES

BLOOMFIELD, B.C., 'W.H. Auden: A Bibliography: The Early
Years through 1955'. Charlottesville: University Press of
Virginia, 1964.
Foreword by W.H. Auden.
BLOOMFIELD, B.C., and MENDELSON, EDWARD, 'W.H. Auden: A
Bibliography 1924-1969'. Charlottesville: University Press
of Virginia, 1972.
The standard bibliography, supplemented by Addenda to
Bloomfield and Mendelson, 'W.H. Auden: A Bibliography',
'The Library', Sixth Series, 4, 1, March 1982, pp. 75-9.
CLANCY, JOSEPH P., A W. H. Auden Bibliography 1924-1955,
'Thought' (Fordham University), xxx, Summer 1955, pp. 260-70.

B. REFERENCE GUIDE

GINGERICH, MARTIN E., 'W.H. Auden: A Reference Guide'.
Boston, Mass.: G.K. Hall; London: Prior, 1977.
A selective guide to secondary sources (books and articles)
on Auden, with a brief description of each entry.

C. BIOGRAPHIES

CARPENTER, HUMPHREY, 'W.H. Auden: A Biography'. London:
Allen & Unwin, 1981.
OSBORNE, CHARLES, 'W.H. Auden: The Life of a Poet'. London:
Methuen, 1980.

D. OTHER BOOKS

ALVAREZ, A., W.H. Auden: Poetry and Journalism, in 'The
Shaping Spirit'. London: Chatto & Windus; American edn,
'Stewards of Excellence', New York: Scribner's, 1958.
BAHLKE, GEORGE W., 'The Later Auden: From "New Year Letter"
to "About the House"'. New Brunswick: Rutgers University
Press, 1970.
BAYLEY, JOHN, W.H. Auden, in 'The Romantic Survival'.
London: Constable, 1957.
BEACH, JOSEPH WARREN, 'The Making of the Auden Canon'.
Minneapolis: University of Minnesota Press, 1957.
BERGONZI, BERNARD, 'Reading the Thirties'. London:
Macmillan, 1978.
BLAIR, JOHN G., 'The Poetic Art of W.H. Auden'. Princeton,
N.J.: Princeton University Press, 1965.
BROOKS, CLEANTH, Frost, MacLeish and Auden, in 'Modern
Poetry and The Tradition'. Chapel Hill: University of North
Carolina Press, 1939.
BUELL, FREDERICK, 'W.H. Auden as a Social Poet'. Ithaca,
N.Y.: Cornell University Press, 1973.
CARTER, RONALD, 'W.H. Auden'. Milton Keynes: Open Univer-
sity Press, 1975.
DAVISON, DENNIS, 'W.H. Auden'. London: Evans Brothers,
1970.
DAY-LEWIS, C., 'A Hope for Poetry'. Oxford: Basil
Blackwell, 1934.
DUCHÊNE, FRANÇOIS, 'The Case of the Helmeted Airman, A
Study of Auden's Poetry'. London: Chatto & Windus, 1972.
EVERETT, BARBARA, 'Auden'. Edinburgh: Oliver & Boyd, 1964.
FINNEY, BRIAN, 'Christopher Isherwood: A Critical Bio-
graphy'. London: Faber & Faber, 1979.
FRASER, G.S., 'Vision and Rhetoric'. London: Faber &
Faber, 1959.
FULLER, JOHN, 'A Reader's Guide to W.H. Auden'. London:
Thames & Hudson; New York: Farrar, Straus & Giroux, 1970.
GILLIE, CHRISTOPHER, The Critical Decade 1930-1940, in
'Movements in English Literature 1900-1940'. Cambridge
University Press, 1975.
HARDY, BARBARA, The Reticence of W.H. Auden, in 'The
Advantage of Lyric'. London: Athlone Press, 1977.
HENDERSON, PHILIP, The Age of Auden, in 'The Poet and
Society'. London: Secker & Warburg, 1939.
HOGGART, RICHARD, 'Auden: An Introductory Essay'. London:
Chatto & Windus; New Haven: Yale University Press, 1951.
HOGGART, RICHARD, 'Speaking to Each Other' (vol. 2),
'About Literature'. London: Chatto & Windus, 1970.
HOGGART, RICHARD, 'W.H. Auden'. London: Longmans for the
British Council, 1957.

HYNES, SAMUEL, 'The Auden Generation: Literature and Politics in the 1930s'. London: Bodley Head, 1976; rpt London: Faber & Faber, 1979.
ISHERWOOD, CHRISTOPHER, 'Christopher and His Kind: 1929–1939'. London: Eyre Methuen, 1977.
ISHERWOOD, CHRISTOPHER, 'Lions and Shadows: An Education in the Twenties'. London: Hogarth Press, 1938.
JARRELL, RANDALL, 'Kipling, Auden & Co.: Essays and Reviews 1935-1964'. New York: Farrar, Straus & Giroux, 1980; Manchester: Carcanet Press, 1981.
Reprints of all of Jarrell's uncollected reviews of Auden.
JARRELL, RANDALL, 'The Third Book of Criticism'. New York: Farrar, Straus & Giroux, 1969.
Includes both Changes of Attitude and Rhetoric in Auden's Poetry, reprinted from 'Southern Review', vii, Autumn 1941, and Freud to Paul: The Stages of Auden's Ideology, reprinted from 'Partisan Review', xii, Fall 1945.
JOHNSON, RICHARD, 'Man's Place: An Essay on Auden'. Ithaca: Cornell University Press, 1973.
LEAVIS, F.R., 'New Bearings in English Poetry' (1932). 2nd edn, London: Chatto & Windus, 1950.
Includes Retrospect 1950, which rehearses Leavis's response to Auden.
LUCAS, JOHN (ed.), 'The 1930s: A Challenge to Orthodoxy'. Hassocks, Sussex: Harvester Press, 1978.
Includes Arnold Rattenbury's article (see Introduction, p. 54 above), and a notable essay by Tom Paulin, 'Letters from Iceland': Going North.
MACNEICE, LOUIS, 'Modern Poetry: A Personal Essay'. London: Oxford University Press, 1938.
MAXWELL, D.E.S., 'Poets of the Thirties'. London: Routledge & Kegan Paul, 1969.
MENDELSON, EDWARD, 'Early Auden'. London: Faber & Faber, 1981.
MITCHELL, DONALD, 'Britten and Auden in the Thirties: The Year 1936'. London: Faber & Faber, 1981.
NELSON, GERALD, 'Changes of Heart: A Study of the Poetry of W.H. Auden'. Berkeley and Los Angeles: University of California Press, 1969.
ORWELL, GEORGE, 'Inside the Whale'. London: Gollancz, 1940.
OSTROFF, ANTHONY (ed.), 'The Contemporary Poet as Artist and Critic'. Boston: Little, Brown, 1964.
Includes a Symposium on W.H. Auden's 'A Change of Air', essays by George P. Elliott, Karl Shapiro, and Stephen Spender, with a reply by Auden; reprinted from 'Kenyon Review', xxvi, Winter 1964.
POWELL, DILYS, 'Descent from Parnassus'. London: Cresset Press, 1934.
PRITCHARD, WILLIAM H., 'Seeing Through Everything: English Writers 1918-1940'. London Faber & Faber, 1977.

REPLOGLE, JUSTIN, 'Auden's Poetry'. Seattle: University of
Washington Press, 1969.
REEVES, JAMES, 'The Poets and their Critics', vol. 3: 'From
Arnold to Auden'. London: Hutchinson, 1969.
Critical extracts by Auden and other writers including
C. Day-Lewis, Christopher Isherwood, Cleanth Brooks,
Francis Scarfe, F.R. Leavis, Righard Hoggart, John Bayley,
Stephen Spender, and J.G. Blair.
SAVAGE D.S., The Strange Case of W.H. Auden, in 'The Per-
sonal Principle'. London: Routledge, 1944.
SCARFE, FRANCIS, 'Auden and After: The Liberation of Poetry
1930-1941'. London: Routledge, 1942.
'Shenandoah', xviii, 2, Winter 1967.
Contains memoirs and critical articles by writers including
E.R. Dodds, Naomi Mitchison, and Bonamy Dobrée.
SKELTON, ROBIN (ed.), 'Poetry of the Thirties'. Harmonds-
worth, Middlesex: Penguin, 1964.
SPEARS, MONROE, K., 'Auden: A Collection of Critical
Essays'. Englewood Cliffs, N.J.: Prentice-Hall, 1964
(Twentieth Century Views).
An important collection, including essays by Cleanth
Brooks, Stephen Spender, Marianne Moore, John Bayley, and
G.S. Fraser, with a good Introduction.
SPEARS, MONROE K., 'The Poetry of W.H. Auden: The Dis-
enchanted Island'. New York: Oxford University Press, 1963.
SPENDER, STEPHEN, The Airman, Politics and Psychoanalysis,
in 'The Destructive Element'. London: Jonathan Cape, 1935.
SPENDER, STEPHEN, 'Letters to Christopher' (ed. Lee
Bartlett). Santa Barbara, California: Black Sparrow Press,
1980.
SPENDER, STEPHEN (ed.), 'W.H. Auden: A Tribute'.
London: Weidenfeld & Nicolson, 1975.
SPENDER, STEPHEN, 'World Within World'. London: Hamish
Hamilton, 1951.
SYMONS, JULIAN, 'The Thirties: A Dream Revolved'. London:
Cresset Press, 1960; rev. edn., London: Faber & Faber, 1975.
TOLLEY, A.T., 'The Poetry of the Thirties'. London:
Gollancz, 1975.
WAIN, JOHN, 'Professing Poetry'. London: Macmillan, 1977.
WEATHERHEAD, A. KINGSLEY, 'Stephen Spender and the
Thirties'. London: Bucknell University Press/Associated
University Presses, 1975.
WOOLF, VIRGINIA, 'Collected Essays' (vol. 2). London:
Hogarth Press, 1966.
WRIGHT, GEORGE T., 'W.H. Auden'. New York: Twayne, 1969.

E. MEMORIAL ESSAYS AND TRIBUTES

ELLMANN, RICHARD, W.H. Auden 1907-1973, 'New York Review of Books', 12 December 1974, 26-7.
FOOTE, TIMOTHY, Auden: The Age of Anxiety, 'Time', 8 October 1973, 113-14.
FRASER, G.S., Glimpses of the Poet, 'Adam International Review', 379-84, 1973-4, 23-6.
FULLER, ROY, W.H. Auden, 1907 to 1973, 'Listener', 90, 1973, 439.
GOWDA, H.H. ANNIAH, W.H. Auden: A Tribute, 'Literary Half-Yearly', 15:1, 1974, 16-21.
HOLTHUSEN, HANS EGON, W.H. Auden in Memoriam, 'Merkur', 27:12, 1973, 1193-5.
JAMES, CLIVE, Auden's Achievement, 'Commentary', 56:6, December 1973, 53-8; reprinted (Farewelling Auden: (iii) On his Death) in 'At the Pillars of Hercules', London: Faber & Faber, 1979.
JARDINE, RUPERT, Auden: The Compelling Years, 'Adam International Review', 379-84, 1973-4, 34-8.
LAW, PAM, A Ritual of Homage for W.H. Auden, 'Poetry Australia', 10, 1974, 83-8.
MENDELSON, EDWARD, W.H. Auden, 'Times Literary Supplement', 7 December 1973, 1508.
NÄNNY, MAX, W.H. Auden, 'Neue Zürcher Zeitung', 14 December 1973, 53.
PASCU, A., W.H. Auden - Poetul, 'Cronica', 8:47, November 1973, 12.
PASINETTI, P.M., Pensieri su Auden, 'Corriere della sera', 6 November 1973, 3.
PESCHMANN, HERMANN, W.H. Auden (1907-1973), 'English', 23, Spring 1974, 3-4.
REES, SAMUEL, 'What Instruments We Have': An Appreciation of W.H. Auden, 'Anglo Welsh Review', 24:3, 1974, 9-18.
SISSMAN, L.E., W.H. Auden, 'Atlantic Monthly', 233:1, 1974, 18-19.
SOLOMON, PETRE, W.H. Auden, 'Luceafărul' (Bucharest), 17 November 1973, 10.
SPEARS, MONROE K., In Memoriam W.H. Auden, 'Sewanee Review', 82, Fall 1974, 672-81.
SPENDER, STEPHEN, et al., W.H. Auden (1907-1973), 'New Statesman', 86, 5 October 1973, 478-80 (personal tributes by Spender, Philip Larkin, Charles Monteith, John Betjeman, Frank Kermode, and William Coldstream).
STANCIU, VIRGIL, Wystan Hugh Auden, 'Steaua', n.s. 24:22, November 1973, 12.
STANFORD, DONALD E., W.H. Auden (1907-73), 'Southern Review', 9:4, 1973, xix-xx.
THWAITE, ANTHONY, On Auden's Death, 'Encounter', 41, December 1973, 52-3.

THWAITE, ANTHONY, W.H. Auden: 1907-1973, 'Literary Half
Yearly', 15:1, 1974, 1-11.
UPWARD, EDWARD, Remembering the Earlier Auden, 'Adam
International Review', 379-84, 1973-4, 17-22.

F. SUPPLEMENTARY REVIEWS: A SELECTION

'W.H. Auden: A Bibliography 1924-1969', by B.C. Bloomfield
and Edward Mendelson (see above), takes the year 1969 as a
terminus ad quem, and includes a partial listing of British
reviews of 'City Without Walls' which was issued in September that year. The list below is an attempt to supplement 'W.H. Auden: A Bibliography' with a selection of the
periodical reviews of 'Epistle to a Godson' (1972), 'Thank
You, Fog' (1974), 'Collected Poems' (1976), and 'The
English Auden' (1977). The purpose is to provide a record
of many of the shorter first reviews, some of which (but
by no means all) are inevitably of ephemeral value; longer
essay-articles may be located in standard bibliographies
such as 'Annual Bibliography of English Language and
Literature'. My principal source has been the press-cutting
files of Faber & Faber, London, so that this checklist is
for the most part confined to the first reviews of British
editions. This section does not significantly overlap with
Martin E. Gingerich's 'W.H. Auden: A Reference Guide'
(1977), which has a terminus date of 1976 and understandably (since a brief description accompanies each item
therein) omits many initial reviews in favour of essay-
articles. By the same token, what follows does not include
items reprinted in the present volume, nor the periodical
reviews and essays discussed or mentioned in the Introduction and notes above. This list is therefore complementary
to Gingerich's reference guide, and both together represent
no more than an incomplete supplement to 'W.H. Auden: A
Bibliography'. Edward Mendelson proposes in due course to
bring out a third edition of that excellent standard bibliography.
   The word '(from)' indicates a review which includes
comment on a book or books other than that by Auden.

'Epistle to a Godson' (1972)

ABSE, DANNIE, Auden on Form, 'Sunday Times', 8 October 1972.
AMIS, MARTIN, (from) Formidable Wit, 'Times Educational
Supplement', 6 April 1973.
ANON, (from) Quick Flips, 'Daily Express', 12 October 1972.
BAYLEY, JOHN, Godfather Poet, 'Books and Bookmen', Febru-
ary 1973.

BERGONZI, BERNARD, Arch Angle, 'Financial Times', 12 October 1972.
BRACE, KEITH, Auden Dips into the Rag-Bag, 'Birmingham Post', 14 October 1972.
CORNWELL, JOHN, (from) Graves and Auden, 'Oxford Mail', 26 October 1972.
COX, C.B., (from) Pick of the Poets, 'Sunday Telegraph', 31 December 1973.
CURTIS, ANTHONY, Auden Alive, 'Financial Times', 12 October 1972.
DODSWORTH, MARTIN, Dictionary Drunk, 'Guardian', 12 October 1972.
E.E., Poetry and Poets, 'Oxford Times', 5 January 1973.
EAGLETON, TERRY, (from) Humble Myths, 'Tablet', 1 December 1972.
FULLER, ROY, (from) Love, Wit and Wisdom, 'Daily Telegraph', 2 November 1972.
HOPKINS, KENNETH, (from) Poetry: The Old and the New from Shelley to Milligan, 'Eastern Evening News', 18 December 1972.
JENNINGS, ELIZABETH, (from) Auden's Approach 'Scotsman', 28 October 1972.
LONGLEY, EDNA, (from) The Ant and the Grasshopper, 'Irish Times', 4 November 1972.
NICHOLSON, NORMAN, Grow Old Along with Auden, 'Church Times', 22 December 1972.
NYE, ROBERT, Bothering the Young, 'The Times', 12 October 1972.
RICKS, CHRISTOPHER, Natural Linguistics, 'Parnassus', 1:2, 1973.
SMITH, IAIN CRICHTON, (from) Two Poets Looking Backwards, 'Glasgow Herald', 2 December 1972.
TILLER, TERENCE, Dispassionate, Low-Keyed Auden, 'Tribune', 23 February 1973.
TOYNBEE, PHILIP, Mellow Fruitfulness, 'Observer', 8 October 1972.

'Thank You, Fog' (1974)

ABRAHAMS, LIONEL, Last Poems by Auden, 'Rand Daily Mail', 4 December 1974.
ANDREWS, LYMAN, (from) Images of Home, 'Sunday Times', 6 October 1974.
ATLAS, JAMES, Earth, Receive an Honored Guest, 'Poetry', 126, June 1975.
BATESON, F.W., Auden's Last Poems, 'Essays in Criticism', 25:iii, 1975.
BAYLEY, JOHN, The Ultimate Contraptions of the Guy, 'Times

Literary Supplement', 4 October 1974.
BEER, PATRICIA, Northerner's Conclusion, 'Listener', 3 October 1974.
BRACE, KEITH, A Touch of the Old Auden in His Last Volume, 'Birmingham Post', 5 October 1974.
CURTIS, ANTHONY, Memorial to Auden, 'Financial Times', 4 October 1974.
DENNIS, NIGEL, Thank You, Auden, 'Sunday Telegraph', 13 October 1974.
EAGLETON, TERRY, (from) Sociable and Sensible, 'Tablet', 23 November 1973.
FENTON, JAMES, Auden's Last Bow, 'New Statesman', 27 September 1974.
FULLER, ROY, All Auden's Last Poems?, 'Daily Telegraph', 3 October 1974.
GRIGSON, GEOFFREY, (from) Last Words from a Master, 'Country Life', 31 October 1974.
GRUBB, FREDERICK, A Liberal Oldie, 'Tribune', 17 January 1975.
JACKSON, BRIAN, (from) Davie's Home Thoughts, 'Guardian', 3 October 1974.
LONGLEY, EDNA, (from) Recent Poetry, 'Irish Times', 30 November 1974.
MURRAY, LES, Closing of Accounts, 'Morning Herald' (Sydney), 5 February 1975.
NICHOLSON, NORMAN, Thank You, Auden, 'Church Times', 22 November 1974.
NYE, ROBERT, (from) Poetry, 'The Times', 10 October 1974.
RAINE, CRAIG, Writing at Half-Mast, 'Times Educational Supplement', 3 January 1975.

'Collected Poems' (1976)

ACKROYD, PETER, Poetic Licence, 'Spectator', 18 September 1976.
AUSTIN, RICHARD, untitled review, 'The Month', January 1977.
BOLAND, EAVAN, review, 'Irish Times', 18 September 1976.
BROMWICH, DAVID, An Oracle Turned Joker, 'Times Literary Supplement', 17 September 1976.
EAGLETON, TERRY, First-Class Fellow-Travelling: The Poetry of W.H. Auden, 'New Blackfriars', 57, December 1976.
EWART, GAVIN, untitled review, 'British Book News', December 1976.
GRIGSON, GEOFFREY, (from) Imitators and Abbreviators, 'Country Life', 30 September 1976.
HEATH-STUBBS, JOHN, Flowers Duel Incessantly, 'Tablet', 23 October 1976.

HOGGART, RICHARD, Master's Choice, 'New Society', 16 September 1976 (see also Edward Mendelson's letter in response, 'New Society', 7 October 1976).
LINDSAY, JAMES, (from) Auden: A Minor Atlantic Goethe?, 'Oxford Literary Review', 2:1, 1977.
McGILCHRIST, IAIN, Mighty Hot Magic, 'Listener', 25 November 1976.
MITCHISON, NAOMI, The Political Muse, 'Books and Bookmen', November 1976.
NICHOLSON, NORMAN, Compleat Auden, 'Church Times', 26 November 1976.
NYE, ROBERT, (from) Poetry, 'The Times', 28 October 1976.
SEYMOUR-SMITH, MARTIN, (from) Poetry Now, 'Financial Times', 30 December 1976.
TOYNBEE, PHILIP, Auden's Authorised Version, 'Observer', 17 October 1976.
WRIGHT, DAVID, The Fading of the Fires, 'Times Educational Supplement', 17 September 1976.

'The English Auden' (1977)

BERGONZI, BERNARD, A Sense of Geography, 'Times Literary Supplement', 11 November 1977.
BOLAND, EAVAN, An Art of Omission, 'Hibernia', 9 October 1977.
FENTON, JAMES, (from) Under the Influence, 'New Review', 4:45/6, December-January 1977-8.
FULLER, JOHN, In a Mad Family, 'New Statesman', 11 November 1977.
GRIGSON, GEOFFREY, Auden at First, 'Guardian', 10 November 1977.
HAFFENDEN, JOHN, Early Auden, 'PN Review', 5:4, 1978.
NYE, ROBERT, 'In terms of his own best verse', 'The Times', 1 December 1977.
PESCHMANN, HERMANN, New Styles of Architecture, 'Times Educational Supplement', 6 January 1978.
PORTER, PETER, Auden's Cornucopia, 'Encounter', February 1978.
SPENDER, STEPHEN, Seeing Auden Plain, 'Sunday Telegraph', 6 November 1977.
SYMONS, JULIAN, Auden: A Prophet Honoured, 'Sunday Times', 20 November 1977.
TOYNBEE, PHILIP, Return of the Native, 'Observer', 13 November 1977.

G. A MISCELLANY, 1970-6

This section is intended to provide some addenda to 'W.H.
Auden: A Reference Guide' (1977), by Martin E.
Gingerich (see above), which offers selective and informative coverage of writings about Auden in the period from 1931 to
1976, and usefully complements the more comprehensive lists
in 'W.H. Auden: A Bibliography', by Bloomfield and Mendelson. The checklist below is almost certainly incomplete as
a supplement covering the last period in Gingerich, and
readers are advised to consult this section only alongside
'W.H. Auden: A Reference Guide'.

BOHRINGER, SUE BARNETT, '"In So Far as We Have to Look For-
ward to Death as a Fact": A Study of W.H. Auden's Attitude
Toward Time'. Unpublished doctoral dissertation, University
of Tennessee, 1976.
BRADSHAW, JON, Holding to Schedule with W.H. Auden,
'Esquire', 73, January 1970, 137-9.
CARRUTH, HAYDEN, W.H. Auden, Poet of Civility, 'Southern
Review', 6, January 1970, 245-9.
COHEN, MARVIN, An Interview with W.H. Auden, 'Arts in
Society', 12, 1975, 365-7.
DZENITIS, SIGURDS, 'Die Rezeption deutscher Literatur in
England durch Wystan Hugh Auden, Stephen Spender und
Christopher Isherwood'. Hamburg, Lüdcke, 1972.
FRY, PHILLIP, and JAMES W. LEE, An Interview in Austin
with John Lehmann, 'Studies in the Novel', 3:1, Spring
1971, 80-96 (comments on the influence of Auden and
others).
GANIM, CAROLE, The Divided Self: Caliban from Shakespeare
to Auden, 'Kentucky Philological Association Bulletin',
1975, 9-15.
GUILLOT, CLAUDE, Auden trois ans après: une image du
poète à travers ses Selected Poems, 'Études anglaises', 29,
1976, 545-55.
GUILLOT, CLAUDE, W.H. Auden et la guerre d'Espagne,
'Caliban', 13, 1976, 95-111.
HAZARD, FORREST E., The Ascent of F6: A New Interpretation,
'Tennessee Studies in Literature', No. 15, 1970, 165-75.
HENNESSY, MICHAEL, 'The Country of Consideration': Auden's
Search for Place, 'Thoth' (Dept of English, Syracuse Uni-
versity), 15:3, 1975, 15-25.
HYNES, SAMUEL, Auden and MacNeice, 'Contemporary Litera-
ture', 14, 1973, 378-83.
JACKSON, LAURA (RIDING), Some Autobiographical Corrections
of Literary History, 'Denver Quarterly', 18:4, 1974, 1-33.
KENEDY, R.C., The Longer Poems of W.H. Auden, 'Art Inter-
national', 16:3, 1972, 49, 67-72.

KINGSLEY, LAWRENCE WILSON, 'The Modern Elegy: The Epistem-
ology of Loss'. Unpublished doctoral dissertation, Univer-
sity of Wisconsin, 1973.
LUCIE-SMITH, EDWARD, A Foreign School?, 'New Statesman',
30 April 1971, 598-99 (on 'The Ascent of F6' and 'The Dog
Beneath the Skin').
MENDELSON, EDWARD, The Auden-Isherwood Collaboration,
'Twentieth Century Literature', 22, 1976, 276-85.
MILLARD, G.C., The Political and the Poetic: A Considera-
tion of Auden's 'Spain', 'English Studies in Africa'
(Johannesburg), No. 18, 1975, 17-22.
NEMEROV, HOWARD, A Word from the Devil's Advocate, 'Parnas-
sus', 4:1, 1975, 131-6.
O'DONNELL, AGNES BOYLE, 'From Myth to Drama: A Study of the
Verse Plays of W.H. Auden'. Unpublished doctoral disserta-
tion, University of Pennsylvania, 1976.
RAICHURA, SURESH, and AMRITJIT SINGH, A Conversation with
W.H. Auden, 'Southwest Review', 60, 1975, 27-36.
REBELO, LUÍS DE SOUSA, A Poesia de W.H. Auden, 'Colóquio
Letras', 14, 1973, 73-6.
STARKMAN, MIRIAM K., The 'Grace of the Absurd': Form and
Concept in W.H. Auden's 'For the Time Being', 'Harvard
Theological Bulletin', No. 72, 1974, 275-88.
STEBNER, GERHARD, Wystan H. Auden und Christopher Isher-
wood: 'The Ascent of F6', in HORST OPPEL (ed.), 'Das
moderne englische Drama: Interpretationen', 3rd edn,
revised. Berlin: Schmidt, 1976.
THAIRS, S.M., 'W.H. Auden: The Relationship Between a
Writer and His Socio-Political Environment'. Unpublished
MA dissertation, University of Liverpool, 1974.
TOYNBEE, PHILIP, Five Young Writers Who Changed My World,
'Observer Colour Magazine', 20 June 1976, 17-19.
WAHL, WILLIAM B., 'Poetic Drama Interviews: Robert
Speaight, E. Martin Browne and W.H. Auden'. Salzburg:
Institut für englische Sprache und Literatur, Universität
Salzburg, 1976.
WEBB, EUGENE, The Religious Thought of W.H. Auden: The
Ambiguity of the Sacred, 'Soundings', 57, 1974, 439-57.

Index

The index is divided into two parts: I Works by Auden; II General Index.

I WORKS BY AUDEN

Individual poems which originally appeared without titles in first editions of the 1930s are indexed by first lines (keyed to initial words). In an effort to minimize the inevitable confusion created by Auden's later revisions, and more especially by his introduction and alterations of titles, many first-line titles are also entered under their separate titles. Readers are in any event referred to Appendix II of 'Collected Poems' (ed. Mendelson, 1976) for an authoritative checklist of variant titles.

A title in quotation marks (e.g. 'Homage to Clio') indicates the volume of that title, whilst the same title placed next in order (without quotation marks) indicates the title-poem of that volume.

Long sections or sequences within volumes, such as Journal of an Airman (in 'The Orators') and Horae Canonicae (in 'Shield of Achilles'), are given separate index entries in addition to the individual poems of such sections or sequences.

II GENERAL INDEX

THE CRITICAL HERITAGE SERIES

GENERAL EDITOR: B. C. SOUTHAM

Volumes published and forthcoming